HISTORY IN DISPUTE

ADVISORY BOARD

Edited by **Char Miller, Mark Cioc, and Kate Showers**

A MANLY, INC. BOOK

ST. JAMES PRESS

AN IMPRINT OF THE GALE GROUP

DETROIT • SAN FRANCISCO • LONDON
BOSTON • WOODBRIDGE, CT

HISTORY IN DISPUTE

Volume 7 ▪ Water and the Environment Since 1945: Global Perspectives

Matthew J. Bruccoli and Richard Layman, *Editorial directors.*

Karen L. Rood, *Senior editor.*

Anthony J. Scotti Jr., *Series editor.*

James F. Tidd Jr., *In-house editor.*

Philip B. Dematteis, *Production manager.*

Kathy Lawler Merlette, *Office manager.* Ann M. Cheschi, Amber L. Coker, and Angi Pleasant, *Administrative support.* Ann-Marie Holland, *Accounting.*

Phyllis A. Avant, *Copyediting supervisor.* Brenda Carol Blanton, Allen E. Friend Jr., Melissa D. Hinton, William Tobias Mathes, Nancy E. Smith, Elizabeth Jo Ann Sumner, *Copyediting staff.*

Janet E. Hill, *Layout and graphics supervisor.* Zoe R. Cook, *Lead layout and graphics.* Karla Corley Brown, *Layout and graphics.*

Charles Mims, Scott Nemzek, Paul Talbot, *Photography editors.* Jeff Miller, *Photo permissions.* Joseph M. Bruccoli and Zoe R. Cook, *Digital photographic copy work.*

Cory McNair, *SGML supervisor.* Frank Graham, Linda Dalton Mullinax, Jason Paddox, and Alex Snead, *SGML staff.*

Marie L. Parker, *Systems manager.*

Kathleen M. Flanagan, *Typesetting supervisor.* Mark J. McEwan, Patricia Flanagan Salisbury, and Alison Smith, *Typesetting staff.*

Walter W. Ross, *Library researcher.* Steven Gross, *Assistant library researcher.* Tucker Taylor, *Circulation department head, Thomas Cooper Library, University of South Carolina.* John Brunswick, *Interlibrary-loan department head.* Virginia W. Weathers, *Reference department head.* Brette Barclay, Marilee Birchfield, Paul Cammarata, Gary Geer, Michael Macan, Tom Marcil, and Sharon Verba, *Reference librarians.*

St. James Press
27500 Drake Road
Farmington Hills, MI 48331

ISBN 1-55862-413-9

St. James Press is an imprint of The Gale Group.

Printed in the United States of America

10 9 8 7 6 5 4 3 2 1

CONTENTS

ABOUT THE SERIES

History in Dispute is an ongoing series designed to present, in an informative and lively pro-con format, different perspectives on major historical events drawn from all time periods and from all parts of the globe. The series was developed in response to requests from librarians and educators for a history-reference source that will help students hone essential critical-thinking skills while serving as a valuable research tool for class assignments.

Individual volumes in the series concentrate on specific themes, eras, or subjects intended to correspond to the way history is studied at the academic level. For example, early volumes cover such topics as the Cold War, American Social and Political Movements, and World War II. Volume subtitles make it easy for users to identify contents at a glance and facilitate searching for specific subjects in library catalogues.

Each volume of *History in Dispute* includes up to fifty entries, centered on the overall theme of that volume and chosen by an advisory board of historians for their relevance to the curriculum. Entries are arranged alphabetically by the name of the event or issue in its most common form. (Thus, in Volume 1, the issue "Was detente a success?" is presented under the chapter heading "Detente.")

Each entry begins with a brief statement of the opposing points of view on the topic, followed by a short essay summarizing the issue and outlining the controversy. At the heart of the entry, designed to engage students' interest while providing essential information, are the two or more lengthy essays, written specifically for this publication by experts in the field, each presenting one side of the dispute.

In addition to this substantial prose explication, entries also include excerpts from primary-source documents, other useful information typeset in easy-to-locate shaded boxes, detailed entry bibliographies, and photographs or illustrations appropriate to the issue.

Other features of *History in Dispute* volumes include: individual volume introductions by academic experts, tables of contents that identify both the issues and the controversies, chronologies of events, names and credentials of advisers, brief biographies of contributors, thorough volume bibliographies for more information on the topic, and a comprehensive subject index.

PREFACE

"If there is magic on this planet," Loren Eiseley has written, "it is in water." Part of its magical quality lies in its profound, elemental influence on the physical world. Seen from the depths of outer space, it defines the contours of what we have come to call the Blue Planet. Whether visible on the surface or locked underground, whether channeled between riverbanks, bounded by lakefront or beach, or stored in icecaps or aquifers, water gives shape to continental landmasses as well as to local bioregions.

Water is just as essential to life on Earth. That reason is why human beings have always expended so much energy in locating and consuming this most precious and wet resource. It also helps explain why we have battled over who would control its varied sources, struggles that occasionally have exploded into open warfare. We may be more conscious than other earthly biota of how critical it is to maintain consistent access to this life-sustaining fluid, but all existence is organized around its presence and absence.

A renewable resource, water would seem to be in infinite supply. This planet's hydraulic cycle is complex but sustained—the sun's heat evaporates groundwater into the atmosphere, where it cools and returns to the earth's surface in the form of rain or snow. This water-exchange loop, in the words of the Population Report of the Johns Hopkins School of Public Health, "acts like a giant water pump that continually transfers freshwater from the oceans to the land and back again." Just how efficient this process can be is reflected in the astonishing number of gallons of water daily carried in the atmosphere above the United States—an estimated forty trillion.

However, there are qualifications to this system that challenge our assumptions about its capacity to forever serve unlimited human consumption. Although approximately 70 percent of the Earth's surface is water, most of it is in the form of saltwater oceans. Potable supplies are not, therefore, unlimited. According to data that the Johns Hopkins School of Public Health has gathered, by "volume, only 3% of all water on earth is fresh-water, and most of that is unavailable." It is so because it is frozen, "locked away in the form of ice caps and glaciers far removed from most human habitation"; other potential supplies are located in deep aquifers, currently inaccessible due to pumping costs. Readily available freshwater that can be tapped from lakes, rivers, and low-level underground sources amounts to a paltry 1 percent of the earth's water. "Only this amount is regularly renewed by rain and snowfall and thus available on a sustainable basis," the Johns Hopkins University Population Information Program concludes. "In all, only one-hundredth of one percent of the world's total supply of water is considered easily accessible for human use."

That amount is still a lot of water. The best guesses are that annually humans have access to between twelve and fourteen billion cubic meters of water—approximately nine thousand cubic meters per person, an estimate based on 1989 population figures. However, as the earth's human population swells, the amount of water available has and will continue to decline. If, as projected, the population increases by two billion in 2025, then annual per capita water supplies will drop to 5,100 cubic meters, about half of what had been available a mere thirty-five years earlier.

The link between size of population and available water supplies is further complicated by the fact that the planet's hydrological system does not evenly distribute water—either by place or season or year. For example, Iceland has available an estimated six hundred thousand cubic meters per capita each year while arid Kuwait has but seventy-five cubic meters. China is its own extreme: "The essence of [its] water problem is that the nation possesses 21 percent of the earth's population," Jacques Leslie observes in *Harper's* (July 2000), "but only 7 percent of its freshwater."

Other countries and regions face similarly striking disparities. The vast Amazon watershed accounts for 20 percent of average global runoff, but only ten million people live within that river basin. Another of the world's major river systems, the Congo, which carries 30 percent of Africa's annual runoff, holds roughly 10 percent of its population. Of the continents, North America has considerably more water per person (19,000 cubic meters) than Asia (4,700 cubic meters), even though Asia accounts for more than 30 percent of the earth's total runoff. Much of the Asian runoff, though, is seasonal. The pounding monsoonal rains that sweep over the densely populated Indian subcontinent during the summer months, for example, produce 90 percent of the annual rainfall; little precipitation occurs during the succeeding three seasons, challenging the capacity of south Asian nations to capture but 20 percent of potential water resources. The global ramifications of this data, concludes the Johns Hopkins University Public Health study, are troubling: "About three-quarters of annual rainfall comes down in areas containing less than one-third of the world's populations. Put the other way around, two-thirds of the world's population live in areas receiving only one-quarter of the world's annual rainfall."

This uneven pattern of distribution, when combined with rapid population growth, international economic development, and increased urbanization, is intensifying pressures on available water supplies. Already, more than thirty nations in Africa and the Near East suffer from various degrees of water scarcity. Their numbers will grow: by 2025, another fifteen or more countries will join those experiencing water shortages, and another wave of states with huge populations, such as China and Pakistan, will soon follow.

Add to this list of problems the expanding threat of unclean water. The sources of groundwater pollution are many and widespread. In developing and underdeveloped regions, sewage and other effluent befoul the local rivers and lakes that are also used for domestic consumption. In industrialized countries, the contamination of underground and surface supplies continues despite sophisticated treatment plants, due to historic neglect, contemporary chemical spills, agricultural fertilizer runoff, and an evolving array of industrial pollutants. These dangers have a collective and serious impact on public health. Many experts believe that one billion people–a sixth of the world's population–do not have access to safe drinking water, a deprivation heavily concentrated among the poorest and least healthy human communities.

Along the Mexico–United States border, for instance, a region that contains some of the fastest-growing cities and some of the most health-compromised neighborhoods in both countries, potable water is in short supply. Supplies will only get tighter because booming populations have had a deleterious impact on water quality. As the *Washington Post* reported in November 2000, "U.S. health officials say the rates of two waterborne diseases, hepatitis A and shigellosis, along the U.S. side are three times the national average." Yet, the rates of disease "are far worse in Mexico. Ciudad Juárez reports about 650 cases of hepatitis A a year, almost 10 times the rate of El Paso [Texas]," which is sited directly across the Rio Grande. Nevertheless, the national boundary offers no protection. "We share everything," a local health official in El Paso acknowledges: "air, water, hazardous waste, pollution, infectious diseases. What affects one side of the border affects the other. Transportation being what is, if there is a large outbreak of hepatitis A in Reynosa [Mexico], it can travel with the trucks up to Houston, to Chicago, to New York."

It is precisely the prospects and perils endemic to this interconnectedness that led *Civilization,* the magazine of the Library of Congress, to devote a special section of its October/November 2000 issue to "Water: The Globe's Most Precious Resource, The World's Most Pressing Problem." Guest editor Mikhail Gorbachev, former head of the Soviet Union, argues that "clean water is a universal human right" and that therefore "we have a corresponding responsibility to ensure that the forecast of a world where, in 25 years time, two out of every three people face water stress is proven wrong." Only a renewed commitment to "human solidarity" will enable human society to face "a task of this magnitude," writes Gorbachev, who now directs Green Cross International, an organization he founded in 1993 to "create the conditions for a sustainable future by cultivating a more harmonious relationship between humans and the environment." An urgent sense of collaboration must exist within and between international and regional governments, "economic actors and stakeholders," and, given the complexity of the global dimensions of the problem, must shape "the political will among governments to work in good faith both with their neighbors and their own people."

Gorbachev's ambitious hopes are nonetheless laced with this fear, that if "water security" cannot be achieved for all people, then "social, economic, and national stability are imperiled." How can society achieve this security? What is the best way to avoid potentially devastating (and international) conflict?

For Kofi Annan, Secretary General of the United Nations, an answer lies in U.N.-brokered mediations that "can help humanity confront the threat posed by the unsustainable exploitation of water resources and the broader danger of living on a planet irredeemably spoiled by careless human activity." Technology many resolve "some of the environmental challenges we face," he notes in the *Civilization* forum, but "we would be foolish to count on them and to continue with business as usual." More productive would be the adoption of a global commitment to a "new ethic of conservation and stewardship of Earth's water."

As part of that ethic, Madeleine K. Albright, U.S. Secretary of State, released on Earth Day 2000 an initiative she called "An Alliance for Global Water Security in the 21st Century." Its collaborative rhetoric, like that of Gorbachev and Annan, envisions the creation of transnational water management policies that adhere to "a basin-wide or watershed basis"; only in this way will countries that share resources, such as rivers and lakes, "cooperate in using them wisely." Diplomatic energies should be focused on bringing local rivals to the negotiating table, securing financial support and relevant technological transfers, and encouraging broad public participation in determining future courses of action. Although in her contribution to *Civilization* Albright did not identify specific places where such ideas might be most effective, there are many controversial environments in which they might be tested; none more so than the Jordan River Valley, a watershed whose small flow is bound up with the fate of Israel, Jordan, Syria, and Lebanon.

In the past, especially in the aftermath of World War II, international efforts to resolve water crises usually resulted in the construction of massive water projects along major river systems in industrial and nonindustrial states. The great dam-building era, funded by central governments and private sources, led to the creation of more than 45,000 major dams. In the United States, Canada, Mexico, Turkey, Egypt, southern Africa, China, and India huge barriers arose to control floodwaters and fill reservoirs, providing water for irrigated agriculture, hydroelectricity, and human consumption. The impact of these extraordinarily expensive initiatives in some cases was startling. The economy of the Pacific Northwest of the United States was thoroughly modernized with the advent of a concrete network of dams that transformed the Columbia River and its tributaries into what historian Richard White has tagged an "organic machine." Farmers and urbanites have taken full advantage of its cheap water and power.

The disadvantages of dams are many, and their construction–regardless of site–has come with countless financial, environmental, and social consequences. Many nations often stagger under the cost overruns and debt burdens that large dams impose on their economies. When, as they are designed to do, these structures fundamentally alter stream flow, they destroy habitat for fish and wildlife and thus undercut the lives and livelihoods of people who depend on each. As waters back up behind the dams, they inundate once-valued communities and landscapes; over the past fifty years, an estimated forty to eighty million people worldwide have been displaced. These losses have been particularly heavy in the former Soviet Union, which contains eleven of the world's twenty-five largest reservoirs. In Gorbachev's retrospective analysis, a "thoughtless tampering with nature has left a terrible legacy–not least in my own region, where untold thousands of acres of fertile land have been lost, and where man-made catastrophes such as the dessication of the Aral Sea have caused immeasurable suffering."

Such losses and the controversies they engendered have forced a rethinking of the long-standing purposes and place of dams in the environment. To resolve some of the nagging issues surrounding the continued reliance on dams, in April 1997 the World Commission on Dams (WCD) was established, with twelve members drawn from a wide spectrum of social, political, and economic interests. In its first, formal report released in mid-November 2000, the WCD acknowledged that dams have "made an important and significant contribution to human development" but qualified its praise by asserting that in "too many cases an unacceptable and often unnecessary price has been paid to secure those benefits, especially in social and environmental terms, by people displaced, by communities downstream, by taxpayers and by the natural environment." Future dam development must address five core values hitherto observed more often in the breach–equity, efficiency, participatory decision making, sustainability, and accountability.

Yet, even the most implacable of critics–including Sandra Postel, whose *Pillar of Sand: Can the Irrigation Miracle Last?* (1999) chronicles the manifold failures of the great dam-building era–recognize their centrality to modern life. "I think there is no way we could be supporting a population of 6 billion today without dams," she confided to Jacques Leslie in *Harper's*. "Water comes at uneven times of the year, and we have got to have a way to store it. The question is how."

That question comes paired with others concerning the mechanisms by which water is distributed, and on what basis; who gets what, and why? "At the heart of the matter is the value we assign to different uses of water," Gorbachev asserts. For orthodox economics, that value is determined by the price individual consumers, institutions, or governmental entities are willing to pay; like any other commodity, water's pricing structure is set by demand and flows to those who can afford it. Others dispute the "commoditization" of water—if access to it is a human right, then provisions must be made to insure its equitable and cheap distribution to the poor and marginalized. Gorbachev tries to strike a balance between these two positions: There "is no universal blueprint, but it is clear that neither of the two extreme stances—one advocating that water should be free for all and the other promoting full-cost pricing for all water supplies is desirable. We must remember that the value and the price of water are two very different things; water must be used efficiently, but it also must be available for all—including for natural ecosystems."

The proposal is fair enough, but negotiating this conundrum has been, and will remain, tricky. As the many essays in this volume reveal, since 1945 some of the most intense and bruising social struggles have revolved around water; no place or people has been immune. These battles will only intensify as Earth's population soars in the twenty-first century. Perhaps this demographic pressure will finally force us to be better stewards of this Blue Planet, and thereby to acknowledge, in Jacques Leslie's words, "that our relationship to water is intimate, complex, and primal." He might have also said, final, for it is in its inescapable finality that makes this essential, life-giving fluid so magical.

The act of making a book is no less miraculous. I am grateful to the many authors who leapt at the opportunity to participate in this project, including some who did so at the last moment. I also owe a great debt of thanks to the volume's associate editors, Mark Cioc of the University of California at Santa Cruz and Kate Showers of Boston University, who secured contributions from Europe and Africa respectively; Kate Showers would like to acknowledge the further aid of Lyla Mehta of the University of Sussex. Finally, it is important to note that many of the authors were willing to write from a perspective with which they disagreed, a mark of their remarkable commitment to the contest of ideas, to their principled assumption that history is always in dispute.

—CHAR MILLER, TRINITY UNIVERSITY,
SAN ANTONIO, TEXAS

CHRONOLOGY

Boldface type refers to a chapter title.

1946

Turkey and Iraq sign the Protocol on Flow Regulation of the Tigris and the Euphrates Rivers and Their Tributaries. (*See* **Euphrates-Tigris Basin**)

1948

30 JUNE: The U.S. Congress passes the Federal Water Pollution Control Act with a goal of eliminating or reducing the pollution of interstate waters and tributaries and improving the sanitary condition of surface and underground waters. (*See* **U.S. Water Pollution**)

1949

MAY: President Harry S Truman signs into law the Arkansas River Compact between Kansas and Colorado. (*See* **Arkansas River Valley**)

1950

19 JANUARY: Uganda (on behalf of Egypt) and the United Kingdom sign an agreement regarding cooperation in meteorological and hydrological surveys in certain areas of the Nile Basin.

2 FEBRUARY: Canada and the United States sign the treaty Concerning the Diversion of the Niagara River, which aims at regulating the flow of water over Niagara Falls, mainly for scenic purposes, by limiting the diversion of designated waters. (*See* **Great Lakes**)

8 APRIL: Protocol to establish a tripartite standing committee on polluted waters is signed at Brussels by Belgium, **France,** and Luxembourg.

9 AUGUST: Signing of the U.S. Federal Aid in Fish Restoration Act (also known as Dingell-Johnson Sport Fish Restoration Act) authorizes the federal government to cooperate with state fish and game departments in fish restoration and management projects. (*See* **Chesapeake, Pacific Salmon, and Salmon Populations**)

1951

Syria begins to develop the Al-Ghab Project, a 46,000-hectare agricultural irrigation project that draws water from the Orontes River Basin. (*See* **Euphrates-Tigris Basin**)

1952

10 JULY: The U.S. Congress passes the McCarran Amendment, which waives the sovereign immunity of the United States where there is a suit designed to establish the rights to a river or other source of water, or the administration of such rights, where the United States appears to own or be in the process of acquiring rights to any such water.

1954

4 AUGUST: The U.S. Congress passes the Watershed Protection and Flood Prevention Act, which states that erosion, flooding, and sediment damages in the watersheds of rivers and streams constitutes a menace to national welfare because of damage to property and loss of life. The federal government is thus mandated to cooperate with states and their political subdivisions for the purpose of preserving, protecting, and improving the land and water resources of the nation and the quality of the environment. (*See* **U.S. Wetlands**)

1955

Completion of the Kakhovka Dam in Ukraine creates the largest human-made reservoir (182,000 m^3 x 106) in the world.

5 AUGUST: The Federal People's Republic of Yugoslavia and Hungarian People's Republic enter into an agreement creating the

Yugoslav-Hungarian Water Economy Commission. (*See* **Tisza Chemical Spill**)

1956

11 APRIL: The U.S. Colorado River Basin Water Project Act authorizes the secretary of the interior to construct a variety of dams, power plants, reservoirs, and related works. The act also authorizes and directs the secretary, in connection with the development of the Colorado River Storage Project and participating projects, to investigate, plan, construct, and operate facilities to mitigate losses of and improve conditions for fish and wildlife, as well as construct public recreational facilities. (*See* **Big Dams, Grand Canyon,** and **Mexican Water Treaty**)

18 AUGUST: The Union of Soviet Socialist Republics (U.S.S.R.) and the People's Republic of China meet in Peking to sign an Agreement to Determine the Natural Resources of the Amur River Basin and the Prospects for Development of its Productive Potentialities and on Planning and Survey Operations to Prepare a Scheme for the Multipurpose Exploitation of the Argun River and the Upper Amur River.

1958

23 JANUARY: The Argentine Republic and Paraguay sign an Agreement Concerning a Study of the Utilization of the Water Power of the Apipé Falls.

29 JANUARY: The U.S.S.R., Yugoslavia, Bulgaria, and Romania sign a Convention Concerning Fishing in the Waters of the Danube.

12 MARCH: The Czechoslovak Socialist Republic and Polish People's Republic sign an Agreement Concerning the Use of Water Resources in Frontier Waters. (*See* **The Baltic**)

1959

29 APRIL: Norway, Finland, and the U.S.S.R. sign an Agreement Concerning the Regulations of Lake Inari by means of the Kaitakoski Hydroelectric Power Station and Dam. (*See* **Finland**)

8 NOVEMBER: Sudan and the United Arab Republic sign an Agreement (with Annexes) for the Full Utilization of the Nile Waters.

1960

Completion of the Sanmenxia Dam on the Huang He (Yellow) River, China, floods 66,000 hectares of some of the most fertile agricultural land in the world and displaces 410,000 people.

1961

17 JANUARY: Canada and the United States sign the Columbia River Treaty, which aims at achieving the development of water resources of the **Columbia River** Basin in a manner that will make the largest contribution to economic progress and human welfare for both countries. The treaty specifically addresses cooperative measures for hydroelectric power generation and flood control. The treaty was ratified by the United States on 16 March 1961 and by Canada on 16 September 1964. (*See* **Pacific Salmon**)

4 OCTOBER: The Wetlands Loan Act authorizes an advance of funds against future revenues from sale of "duck stamps" as a means of accelerating the acquisition of migratory waterfowl habitat. (*See* **U.S. Wetlands**)

20 DECEMBER: **France,** Luxembourg, and the Federal Republic of Germany sign Protocol Concerning the Establishment of an International Commission to Protect the Moselle against Pollution.

1962

Completion of the Kaptai hydropower dam in Bangladesh displaces more than one hundred thousand people from the Chakma ethnic minority and floods approximately two-fifths of their cultivable land. This inundation helps to spark a bloody conflict between the Buddhist Chakma and Muslim Bengali settlers. (*See* **Indian Dams**)

16 JUNE: Sections of Rachel Carson's *Silent Spring* first appear in *The New Yorker,* sparking an outcry in concern over the impact of human-released chemicals on the environment. (*See* **Mississippi River** and **U.S. Wetlands**)

1963

The Grangeville Dam is dynamited to restore salmon runs on the Clearwater River in Idaho. (*See* **Columbia River**)

29 APRIL: Switzerland, the Federal Republic of Germany, France, Luxembourg, and the Netherlands sign an Agreement on the International Commission for the Protection of the Rhine Against Pollution. (*See* **Rhine Canal** and **Salmon 2000 Project**)

26 OCTOBER: Cameroon, Ivory Coast, Dahomey, Upper Volta, Mali, Niger, Nigeria, and Chad sign an Act Regarding Navigation and Economic Co-operation between the States of the Niger Basin at Niamey by Cameroon.

1964

3 SEPTEMBER: The signing of the Land and Water Conservation Fund Act authorizes the chief of engineers, under the U.S. secretary of the army, to develop and maintain water-development projects and outdoor recreation facilities. (*See* **U.S. Water Pollution**)

25 NOVEMBER: Cameroon, the Ivory Coast, Dahomey, Guinea, Upper Volta, Mali, Niger, and Chad sign an Agreement Concerning the Niger River Commission and the Navigation and Transport on the River Niger at Niamey.

1965

9 JULY: The U.S. Congress passes the Federal Water Project Recreation Act, which declares that recreation, as well as fish and wildlife enhancement, be given full consideration as purposes of water-development projects under certain situations. Additionally, it authorizes the use of federal water-project funds for land acquisition in order to establish refuges for migratory waterfowl and authorizes provision of facilities for outdoor recreation, and fish and wildlife, at all reservoirs. (*See* **U.S. Water Pollution** and **Riparian Ecosystems**)

22 JULY: The Water Resources Planning Act establishes the Water Resources Council to be composed of cabinet representatives, including the U.S. secretary of the interior. Title II establishes the River Basin Commissions and stipulates their duties and authorities.(*See* **U.S. Water Pollution**)

30 OCTOBER: Passage of the Anadromous Fish Conservation Act directs the U.S. secretary of the interior to make studies and recommendations for the conservation and enhancement of anadromous fisheries resources. (*See* **Pacific Salmon** and **Salmon Populations**)

1966

The Helsinki Rules on the Uses of the Waters of International Rivers is passed.

Syria begins to develop the Euphrates River with the Euphrates Valley Project. (*See* **Euphrates-Tigris Basin**)

30 APRIL: Austria, Switzerland, and the Federal Republic of Germany sign an Agreement Regulating the Withdrawal of Water from Lake Constance. (*See* **Salmon 2000**)

15 OCTOBER: The U.S. Congress passes the National Wildlife Refuge System Administration Act, creating the National Wildlife Refuge System to consolidate the efforts of the federal government for conservation of fish and wildlife. It also passes the National Sea Grant College and Program Act. (*See* **U.S. Wetlands**)

2 NOVEMBER: The U.S. Fur Seal Act of 1966 prohibits the taking, including transportation, importing, or possession, of northern fur seals and sea otters. Exceptions are authorized for Native Americans, Aleuts, and Eskimos who dwell on the coasts of the North Pacific Ocean, who are permitted to take fur seals and dispose of their skins.

19 DECEMBER: Denmark, Norway, and Sweden sign the Agreement on Reciprocal Access to Fishing in the Skagerrak and the Kattegat.

1967

U.S. military forces begin to spray approximately 19 million gallons of the herbicide Agent Orange to reduce foliage in Southeast Asia. Agent Orange is later determined to contain the dioxin TCDD, which is harmful to humans.

22 SEPTEMBER: The Agreement Concerning a Study on the Navigability of the Central Portion of the Niger River is signed at Niamey.

1968

2 OCTOBER: The U.S. Congress passes the Wild and Scenic Rivers Act, in which "certain selected rivers of the Nation which, with their immediate environments, possess outstandingly remarkable scenic, recreational, geologic, fish and wildlife, historic, cultural or other similar values, shall be preserved in free-flowing condition, and that they and their immediate environments shall be protected for the benefit and enjoyment of present and future generations." (*See* **Riparian Ecosystems**)

23 OCTOBER: Bulgaria and Turkey sign an Agreement Concerning Co-operation in the Use of the Waters of Rivers Flowing through the Territory of Both Countries, including the Maritsa, Tundzha, Veleka, and Rezovska Rivers.

1969

1 JANUARY: The National Environmental Policy Act is passed, outlining a policy to prevent or minimize damage to the U.S. environment. This act authorizes the creation of the Counsel on Environmental Policy to advise the president on environmental issues and triggers the creation of the Environmental Protection Agency (EPA). (*See* **Great Lakes, Nuclear Power Plants, Salmon Populations,** and **U.S. Water Pollution**)

23 APRIL: The Treaty of the River Plate Basin (*Traité du Bassin du Rio de la Plata–Tratado de la Cuenca de la Plata*) is signed by Brazil, Argentina, Bolivia, Paraguay, and Uruguay.

22 JUNE: The Cuyahoga River in Ohio catches fire–fueled by flammable pollutants from steel mills, paint factories, chemical plants, and sewage–galvanizing the U.S. environmental movement. (*See* **Great Lakes** and **U.S. Water Pollution**)

29 NOVEMBER: The International Convention on Civil Liability for Oil Pollution Damage prescribes uniform international rules and procedures for determining questions of liability and providing adequate compensation where damage is caused by pollution resulting from the escape or discharge of oil from ships. (*See* **Med Plan**)

1970

Iraq develops the General Scheme for Planning and Land Resources of Iraq with the help of the Soviet Union.

The San Juan–Chama Project, an eleven-feet diameter, twenty-seven-mile-long system of water diversion tunnels, is completed in the United States. Each year this system moves 110,000 acre-feet of water from the San Juan watershed in Colorado, under the Continental Divide, and into the Rio Grande watershed in New Mexico. (*See* **Mexican Water Treaty**)

The U.S. National Oceanic and Atmospheric Administration (NOAA) is established.

2 JANUARY: The Water Bank Act of 1970 creates contracts with landowners to preserve wetlands and retire adjoining agricultural lands and clarifies that wetlands include artificially created inland freshwater areas. (*See* **U.S. Wetlands**)

22 APRIL: The first Earth Day of the United States, organized by Senator Gaylord Nelson (D-Wisconsin), calls for a national teach-in on the environment. (*See* **Great Lakes** and **U.S. Water Pollution**)

30 SEPTEMBER: The Canada Water Act is proclaimed. (*See* **Great Lakes**)

1971

2 FEBRUARY: Ramsar Convention on Wetlands of International Importance, Especially as Waterfowl Habitat is signed in Ramsar, Iran.

13 AUGUST: The first Canada-Ontario Agreement Respecting the Great Lakes Basin Ecosystem is signed, facilitating the conclusion of the first Great Lakes Water Quality Agreement (1972) between Canada and the United States. (*See* **Great Lakes**)

29 DECEMBER: The Convention on the Prevention of Marine Pollution by Dumping of Wastes and Other Matter seeks to control and prevent marine pollution caused by the dumping at sea of wastes and other matter from vessels, aircraft, platforms, and other man-made structures.

1972

22 MARCH: The U.S. Congress passes the Coastal Zone Management Act (Healthy Coasts Act), encouraging states to preserve, protect, develop, and, where possible, restore or enhance valuable natural coastal resources such as wetlands, floodplains, estuaries, beaches, dunes, barrier islands, and coral reefs, as well as the fish and wildlife using those habitats. (*See* **U.S. Wetlands**)

5–16 JUNE: The U.N. Stockholm Conference on the Human Environment convenes with the objectives of using international cooperation to safeguard and conserve natural resources, maintain renewable resources, share nonrenewable resources, establish standards of environmental management with international cooperation, regulate pollution, promote environmental management, link environmental concern and development, and give less-developed countries incentives to promote rational management.

21 SEPTEMBER: Canada and the United States sign an Agreement Relating to the Establishment of a Canada–United States Committee on Water Quality in the St. John River and its Tributary Rivers and Streams Which Cross the Canada–United States Boundary. (*See* **Great Lakes**)

18 OCTOBER: The Federal Water Pollution Control Act Amendments of 1972 (Clean Water Act), is passed by the U.S. Congress, establishing the federal government as the primary water-control regulation enforcer. (*See* **Salmon Populations, U.S. Water Population,** and **U.S. Wetlands**)

21 OCTOBER: The U.S. Congress passes the Marine Mammal Protection Act, authorizing regulation and permit programs for the taking and import of marine mammals. Alaskan Aleuts, Indians, and Eskimos who reside in Alaska are given some exceptions.

23 OCTOBER: The U.S. Marine Protection, Research, and Sanctuaries Act of 1972 creates a permit program that is to "prevent or strictly limit the dumping into ocean waters of any material that would adversely affect

human health, welfare, or amenities, or the marine environment, ecological systems, or economic potentialities."

22 NOVEMBER: The Great Lakes Water Quality Agreement, signed by Canada and the United States, expresses a cooperative commitment to restore and maintain the chemical, physical, and biological integrity of the Great Lakes Basin ecosystem. (*See* **Great Lakes**)

1973

10 AUGUST: Passage of the Agriculture and Consumer Protection Act authorizes the U.S. government to contract with landowners for conservation of soil and water resources.

30 AUGUST: Mexico and the United States sign an Agreement on the Permanent and Definitive Solution to the International Problem of the Salinity of the Colorado River. Although they had agreed in 1944 to share the waters equally, they had not planned for growth and the diversion of an upriver tributary (the Wellton-Mohawk Irrigation Project) that dumped minerals into the river. (*See* **Mexican Water Treaty**)

1 NOVEMBER: Benin, Ghana, the Ivory Coast, Mali, Niger, Togo, Upper Volta, and the World Health Organization (WHO) sign an agreement governing the operations of the Onchocerciasis Control Programme in the Volta River Basin Area.

2 NOVEMBER: The International Convention for the Prevention of Pollution from Ships (MARPOL) is adopted in London. (*See* **Med Plan**)

25 NOVEMBER: Niger, Benin, Chad, Guinea, Ivory Coast, Mali, Nigeria, Cameroon, and Upper Volta sign the Agreement Revising the Agreement Concerning the Niger River Commission and the Navigation and Transport on the River Niger.

28 DECEMBER: The U.S. Congress passes the Endangered Species Act, providing a legal protocol for the conservation of endangered species and the ecosystems upon which they depend. (*See* **Big Dams, Pacific Salmon, Salmon Populations,** and **Riparian Ecosystems**)

1974

5 FEBRUARY: The Intervention on the High Seas Act authorizes measures to prevent and mitigate oil pollution and other noxious damage on the high seas that affect U.S. coastlines and related interests. The act implements the International Convention Relating to Intervention on the High Seas in Cases of Oil Pollution Casualties and the Protocol Relating to Intervention on the High Seas in Cases of Marine Pollution by Substances Other Than Oil. (*See* **Med Plan**)

16 DECEMBER: The U.S. Congress passes the Safe Drinking Water Act of 1974, which aims to protect the quality of drinking water in the United States. This law focuses on all waters actually or potentially designed for drinking use, whether from surface or underground sources. (*See* **Community Water Supply, Edwards Aquifer, Ogallala Aquifer, U.S. Water Pollution,** and **Water: Commodity**)

1975

7 AUGUST: A typhoon in the Henan Province, China, results in the worst dam disaster in the world. The Banqiao Dam overflows and bursts, setting off a chain reaction of as many as sixty-two additional dam bursts downstream and creating a lake covering several thousand square kilometers. Flooding kills 85,000 people and traps two million. In the weeks following the flood an additional 145,000 people die as a result of starvation, disease, and injuries.

1976

13 APRIL: The U.S. Congress passes the Fishery Conservation and Management Act of 1976 (FCMA), also known as Magnuson Fishery Conservation and Management Act; establishes a two-hundred-mile fishery conservation zone, effective 1 March 1977, along the borders of U.S. territory; and sets up Regional Fishery Management councils comprised of federal and state officials, including members from the Fish and Wildlife Service. This act extends federal management to marine fisheries and initiates U.S. control over foreign boats fishing in these waters. (*See* **Columbia River**)

5 JUNE: The Teton Dam in Idaho collapses as it is being filled, killing fourteen people and causing more than $1 billion in damages.

22 OCTOBER: The Water Resources Development Act of 1976 authorizes additional water projects for development by the U.S. Army Corps of Engineers, modifies previously authorized projects, and includes specific conservation measures for some of the projects including but not limited to: (1) the Lower Snake River Fish and Wildlife Compensation Plan, (2) the White River Basin, Beaver Dam trout production measures (fish hatchery), and (3) the Mississippi River "Great River Study."

1977

Bangladesh and India sign an Agreement on Sharing the Ganges Waters.

Turkey subsumes the development of the Tigris and Euphrates Rivers under the title Southeastern Anatolia Project (*Güneydogu Anadolu Projesi,* or GAP). (*See* **Euphrates-Tigris Basin**)

14–25 MARCH: U.N.-sponsored Conference on Water at Mar del Plata convenes in Argentina.

1978

3 JULY: Bolivia, Brazil, Colombia, Ecuador, Guyana, Peru, Suriname, and Venezuela sign the Treaty for Amazonian Cooperation for the purpose of pooling regional efforts and to promote the harmonious development of the Amazon region. Additionally, this treaty promotes an equitable distribution of the benefits of development among the contracting parties so as to raise the standard of living of their peoples and achieve total incorporation of their Amazonian territories into their respective national economies.

24 AUGUST: Rwanda, Burundi, and Tanzania sign an agreement for the establishment of the Organization for the Management and Development of the Kagera River Basin.

21 OCTOBER: The Locks and Dam 26 Replacement Act authorizes the U.S. Army Corps of Engineers to replace Locks and Dam 26 on the Mississippi River at Alton, Illinois, and to replace terrestrial wildlife habitat inundated by the construction on an acre-for-acre basis in Illinois and Missouri.

22 NOVEMBER: Canada and the United States agree on a revision of the Great Lakes Water Quality Agreement with a toxic pollutant focus. (*See* **Great Lakes**)

1979

3 DECEMBER: Agreement for the Protection of the Rhine against Chemical Pollution is signed at Bonn by Switzerland, the European Economic Community (EEC), Federal Republic of Germany, France, Luxembourg, and the Netherlands. (*See* **Rhine Canal**)

1980

Turkey and Iraq establish the Joint Technical Committee on Regional Waters. (*See* **Euphrates-Tigris Basin**)

The three-hundred-meter earth-fill Nurek Dam, the highest dam in the world, is completed in Tajikistan.

Over the course of planning and construction of the Chixoy Dam in Guatemala (1980–1982), 378 Maya Achí Indians who opposed forced relocations are murdered in Río Negro, a town in the submergence zone.

26 JUNE: The U.S. Congress passes the Acid Precipitation Act of 1980 to coordinate acid-rain research.

21 OCTOBER: The Act to Prevent Pollution from Ships requires ships in U.S. waters, and U.S. ships, wherever located, to comply with the International Convention for the Prevention of Pollution from Ships (1972). (*See* **Med Plan**)

21 NOVEMBER: Convention creating the Niger Basin Authority (with protocol relating to the development fund of the Niger Basin) is signed by Niger, Benin, Chad, Guinea, Ivory Coast, Mali, Nigeria, the United Republic of Cameroon, and Upper Volta.

5 DECEMBER: The U.S. Congress passes the Pacific Northwest Power Planning and Conservation Act of 1980, which mandates that fish and wildlife receive "equitable treatment" with the other objectives of hydroelectric projects. One goal of this act is to protect, mitigate damage against, and enhance the numbers of Pacific salmon and steelhead trout. (*See* **Columbia River, Pacific Northwest, Pacific Salmon,** and **Salmon Populations**)

15 JULY: The EEC passes the Council Directive Relating to the Quality of Water Intended for Human Consumption, which is later amended by Directive 81/858, consequent upon the Accession of Greece, and the Act of Accession of Spain and Portugal of 12 June 1985. (*See* **Water: Commodity**)

1981–1990

The United Nations declares the 1980s to be the International Drinking Water and Sanitation Decade.

1982

10 DECEMBER: The United Nations Convention on the Law of the Sea (UNCLOS III) is signed at Montego Bay, Jamaica, although it is not ratified by the United States until 1994.

1983

Syria joins the meetings of the Joint Technical Committee on Regional Waters. (*See* **Euphrates-Tigris Basin**)

17 FEBRUARY: The California Supreme Court, in a 1983 precedent-setting decision, rules that the state has an obligation to protect places such as Mono Lake "as far

as feasible," even if past water-allocation decisions must be reconsidered.

26 AUGUST: Canada and Denmark sign the Agreement for Cooperation Relating to the Marine Environment that aims at developing further bilateral cooperation in respect of the protection of the marine environment of the waters lying between Canada and Greenland and of its living resources, particularly with respect to preparedness, measures as a contingency against pollution incidents resulting from offshore hydrocarbon exploration or exploitation and from shipping activities that may affect the marine environment of these waters.

1984

26 MARCH: The U.S. Congress passes the National Fish and Wildlife Foundation Establishment Act of 1984, establishing the National Fish and Wildlife Foundation, a federally chartered charitable, nonprofit corporation to administer donations of real or personal property, or interests therein, in connection with Fish and Wildlife Service programs and conservation activities in the United States. (*See* **Columbia River, Nuclear Power Plants, Riparian Ecosystems,** and **U.S. Wetlands**)

2 APRIL: Canada and the United States sign the Skagit River Treaty, which sets out Canadian obligations relating to the agreement concluded between British Columbia and Seattle by which the latter consents not to construct the High Ross Dam, a structure that would have the effect of raising the level of Ross Lake and the Skagit River at the international boundary, provided that British Columbia supply the city with the electricity approximately anticipated from the construction of the dam. (*See* **Columbia River** and **Pacific Northwest**)

31 OCTOBER: The U.S. Congress passes the Atlantic Striped Bass Conservation Act, which recognizes the commercial and recreational importance, as well as the interjurisdictional nature, of striped bass; it establishes a state-based, federally backed management scheme.

1985

15 MARCH: The Pacific Salmon Treaty Act implements the Pacific Salmon Treaty between the United States and Canada (28 January 1985); establishes the requirements for commissioners and the subsidiary Northern, Southern, and Fraser River panels; and authorizes federal regulatory preemption by the secretary of commerce to meet treaty obligations. (*See* **Columbia River, Pacific Salmon,** and **Salmon Populations**)

DECEMBER: Kansas files suit against Colorado for "materially" depleting the river flow into John Martin Reservoir and for noncompliance with the provisions of the Arkansas River Compact. (*See* **Arkansas River Valley**)

1986

The Seoul Rules on International Groundwaters, which expand the Helsinki Rules, are accepted by the International Law Association.

8 OCTOBER: The U.S. Congress passes the Colorado River Floodway Protection Act, which prohibits all new federal funding or financial assistance for any purpose, federal flood insurance for new construction or substantial improvements begun six months after enactment on existing structures, and the granting of new federal leases in the area. (*See* **Big Dams** and **Grand Canyon**)

14 NOVEMBER: The Interjurisdictional Fisheries Act of 1986 repeals and replaces the Commercial Fisheries Research and Development Act and provides for grants by the U.S. secretary of commerce to states for management of interjurisdictional commercial fishery resources. (*See* **Columbia River, Salmon Populations,** and **Chesapeake**)

1987

Turkish prime minister Turgut Özal proposes the Peace Water Pipeline Project to transport water from the Seyhan and Ceyhan Rivers to various countries in the Middle East. (*See* **Euphrates-Tigris Basin** and **Jordan River**)

The Organization for the Development of the Senegal River Convention Relating to the Status of the Senegal River is established.

17 JULY: The Protocol of Economic Cooperation Between Syria and Turkey is signed. (*See* **Euphrates-Tigris River**)

3 SEPTEMBER: Agreement Between the Hashemite Kingdom of Jordan and the Syrian Republic for the Utilization of the Waters of the Yarmuk River is signed in Amman. (*See* **Jordan River**)

18 NOVEMBER: Protocol to Great Lakes Water Quality Agreement establishes special programs for forty-three Areas of Concern, pollution "hot spots" throughout the Great Lakes Basin. (*See* **Great Lakes**)

19 DECEMBER: The U.S. Congress passes the Marine Plastic Pollution Research and Con-

trol Act of 1987, amending the Act to Prevent Pollution from Ships, which prohibits the dumping of plastics into U.S. waters or by U.S. ships, wherever located.

19 DECEMBER: The Driftnet Impact Monitoring, Assessment, and Control Act of 1987 amends section 206 of the Magnuson Fishery Conservation and Management Act to incorporate and expand upon the provisions of the Driftnet Act, which directs the U.S. secretary of the interior, in cooperation with the secretary of commerce and secretary of state, to provide information on the impacts of large-scale driftnet fisheries on seabirds in the North Pacific Ocean.

29 DECEMBER: The U.S.-Japan Fishery Agreement Approval Act of 1987 approves an agreement between the two countries on management measures for fisheries off the coast of the United States.

1988

16 JUNE: The Environmental Protection (Organotin Antifouling Paint Control) Regulations prohibit the use of antifouling paints containing organotin (TBT) on vessels that are twenty-five meters or less in length, unless the hull is aluminum.

1 NOVEMBER: The Lead Contamination Control Act of 1988 requires U.S. schools to make available to the public, teachers, other school personnel, and parents the results of any testing for lead contamination and to notify parent, teacher, and employee organizations of the availability of these results.

1989

Sacramento River Chinook salmon are listed as endangered under the U.S. Endangered Species Act. (See **Columbia River, Pacific Salmon,** and **Salmon Populations**)

24 MARCH: The oil tanker *Exxon Valdez* runs aground in Prince William Sound on the southern coast of Alaska, spilling eleven million gallons of oil. More than 5,000 sea otters, 300 harbor seals, 22 killer whales, 150 bald eagles, and an estimated 250,000 waterfowl are killed.

26 OCTOBER: The Canada–United States Agreement on the Souris River Basin provides for the construction, maintenance, and operation of the Rafferty and Alameda Dams and other works by Canada in the Souris River Basin in Saskatchewan for the purposes of water supply in Canada and flood control in the United States.

13 DECEMBER: The North American Wetlands Conservation Act provides funding and administrative direction for implementation of the North American Waterfowl Management Plan and the Tripartite Agreement on wetlands among Canada, United States, and Mexico. (*See* **U.S. Wetlands**)

1990

The Water Supply and Sanitation Collaborative Council (WSSCC) is formed to maintain momentum of the Drinking Water and Sanitation Decade. (*See* **Community Water Supply** and **Water: Commodity**)

The Coastal Nonpoint Source Pollution Control Program (Section 6217 of the Coastal Zone Act Reauthorization Amendments of 1990) is passed, requiring twenty-nine states and territories to develop Coastal Nonpoint Pollution Control Programs to address nonpoint pollution problems in coastal waters. (*See* **Chesapeake**)

Turkey proposes the Three-Staged Plan for Optimum, Equitable and Reasonable Utilization of the Transboundary Watercourses of the Tigris-Euphrates Basin to Syria and Iraq for more effective utilization of those rivers. (*See* **Euphrates-Tigris Basin**)

At the urging of community members, the International Joint Commission recommends that Lake Superior be a demonstration area where no discharges of persistent toxic chemicals would be allowed. (*See* **Great Lakes**)

APRIL: The Syrian–Iraqi Agreement on the Utilization of the Euphrates Waters is signed. (*See* **Euphrates-Tigris Basin**)

JUNE–AUGUST: Record monsoon rains in Burma, Bangladesh, and India cause severe flooding and affect more than three million people. (*See* **Indian Dams**)

18 AUGUST: The Oil Pollution Act of 1990 establishes new requirements and extensively amends the Federal Water Pollution Control Act (1972) to provide enhanced capabilities for oil-spill response and natural resource damage assessment by the U.S. Environmental Protection Agency (EPA). (*See* **U.S. Water Pollution**)

8 OCTOBER: The Convention on the International Commission for the Protection of the Elbe is signed by the Federal Republic of Germany, Czech and Slovak Federal Republic, and the European Economic Community. (*See* **Gabcikovo Dam**)

16 NOVEMBER: The U.S. Congress passes the Great Lakes Critical Programs Act of 1990, which contains several titles relating to the Great Lakes, Lake Champlain, Long Island Sound, and Lake Onondaga. The Environmental Education Act of 1990 establishes the Office of Environmental Education

within the EPA to develop and administer a federal environmental-education program. (*See* **Great Lakes** and **U.S. Water Pollution**)

28 NOVEMBER: The Dolphin Protection Consumer Information Act establishes conditions for protection of dolphins by ocean vessels when harvesting tuna with purse seine nets. It provides labeling standards for tuna products that are exported from or offered for sale in the United States, and it sets the penalty for noncompliance at a maximum of $100,000 for any single action.

29 NOVEMBER: The Coastal Wetlands Planning, Protection and Restoration Act engages the U.S. Fish and Wildlife Service in interagency wetlands restoration and conservation planning in Louisiana. It also expands the administration of federal grants to acquire, restore, and enhance wetlands of coastal states and the territories. (*See* **U.S. Wetlands**)

29 NOVEMBER: The Nonindigenous Aquatic Nuisance Prevention and Control establishes a broad new federal program to prevent introduction of, and control the spread of, nonnative aquatic nuisance species and the brown tree snake into the United States. (*See* **Riparian Ecosystems**)

1991

The U.S. Congress appropriates $1 million to establish the Great Lakes Basin Program for Soil Erosion and Sediment Control. (*See* **Great Lakes**)

FEBRUARY: The worst flooding this century hits southern Iran.

JUNE: One hundred thousand people are left homeless in Bombay after the worst monsoonal floods in recorded history. (*See* **Indian Dams**)

JUNE: A freak storm brings snow, rain, and hurricane-force winds to the desert region of Chile and turns some of the driest areas in the world into floodplains.

Floods leave ten million people homeless along the Yangtze River in China.

AUGUST: The worst flooding in fifty years hits Burma.

AUGUST: The Danube River reaches record levels in Vienna, Austria.

SEPTEMBER: The southeast Asian monsoonal floods are the worst on record. Cambodia suffers the most serious inundation in recent history.

20 NOVEMBER: The Snake River sockeye salmon is listed as endangered under the Endangered Species Act. (*See* **Columbia River, Pacific Salmon,** and **Salmon Populations**)

DECEMBER: The longest sustained rainfall in forty years causes massive flooding in Egypt and Israel. (*See* **Jordan River**)

1992

JANUARY: International Conference on Water and the Environment (ICWE), held in Ireland, issues the Dublin Statement on Water and Sustainable Development.

JULY: The worst flood in fifty years occurs in the Fujian province of China and affects more than nine million people.

14 SEPTEMBER: The Agreement between the Government of the Republic of Namibia and the Government of the Republic of South Africa on the establishment of a permanent water commission is signed at Noordoewer. (*See* **African Dams** amd **Southern Africa**)

23 OCTOBER: The Wild Bird Conservation Act establishes a new federal system to limit or prohibit imports of exotic bird species into the United States. (*See* **Riparian Ecosystems**)

4 NOVEMBER: The Clean Vessel Act of 1992 amends the Federal Aid in Sport Fish Restoration Act, allowing the secretary of the interior to issue grants to coastal and inland states for pump-out stations and waste-reception facilities to dispose of recreational boater sewage.

1993

The North American Agreement on Environmental Cooperation between the Government of Canada, the Government of the United Mexican States, and the Government of the United States of America is signed. (*See* **Great Lakes**)

11 FEBRUARY: A paraffin oil spill off the coast of the Netherlands kills more than thirty thousand waterfowl.

MAY–SEPTEMBER: Flooding in the U.S. Midwest spreads across nine states and four hundred thousand square miles. Fifty people die as a result of the flood, which lasts for more than two hundred days in some locations. Damages approach $15 billion.

SEPTEMBER: Massive flooding in the Swiss, French, and Italian Alps triggers severe mudslides and submerges towns.

NOVEMBER: More floods strike in the Swiss Alps as Lake Maggiore reaches its second-highest level this century.

DECEMBER: A state of emergency is declared in Kaikoura, as large parts of southern New Zealand are flooded.

DECEMBER: The worst flooding in sixty to one hundred years hits northern Europe; scores of towns in Germany, France, and Belgium are evacuated; and a state of emergency is declared in the Netherlands. (*See* **France** and **Rhine Canal**)

1994

The U.S. Congress approves reparations payment to the Colville Confederated Tribes of a $54 million lump sum and annual payments of $15.25 million to continue for as long as the Grand Coulee Dam produces power. It is one of the largest sums ever granted a Native American tribe. These reparations are awarded for the loss of villages, land, salmon runs, and burial sites as a result of the damming of the Columbia River in Washington. (*See* **Columbia River, Native American Reservations,** and **Pacific Salmon**)

SEPTEMBER: Manibeli Declaration Calling for a Moratorium on World Bank Funding of Large Dams is endorsed by 326 groups and coalitions in 44 nations. (*See* **African Dams, Gabcikovo Dam,** and **Indian Dams**)

1995

The Columbia River in the Pacific Northwest produces 533 tons of salmon, down from 20,000 tons annually a century earlier. Projected population numbers for the twenty-first century predict a loss of nearly two billion tons of salmon from the local economy and world food supply. (*See* **Columbia River, Pacific Salmon,** and **Salmon Populations**)

Floods in Argentina and Paraguay cost $2.5 billion.

At one location on the German/French border, the Rhine floodwaters rise 7.62 meters above flood level, which occurred only four times from 1900 to 1977, an average of once every twenty years. Since then, that level has been breached ten times, an average of once every other year. (*See* **France** and **Rhine Canal**)

JANUARY: A two-thousand-kilometer-square area of the Antarctic Peninsula ice shelf disintegrates into the ocean, likely a consequence of weakening caused by several consecutive warm summer seasons in the 1990s.

5 APRIL: The Agreement on the Cooperation for the Sustainable Development of the Mekong River Basin is signed by Cambodia, Laos, Thailand, and Vietnam.

MAY: The U.S. Supreme Court rules for Kansas in its suit against Colorado over the administration of the Arkansas River Compact. (*See* **Arkansas River Valley**)

16 MAY: The Protocol on Shared Watercourse Systems in the Southern African Development Community (SADC) Region is signed at Maseru, Lesotho. (*See* **African Dams** and **Southern Africa**)

JUNE: Floods in Turkey cause $2 billion in damages.

A cyclone kills ten thousand people in India.

21 JUNE: A wastewater lagoon on a North Carolina hog farm bursts and spills twenty-two million gallons of raw manure and urine, which causes a massive fishkill on the New River. Red tide outbreaks follow along the Atlantic coast.

1996

The Federal Agriculture Improvement and Reform Act of 1996 authorizes more than $2.2 billion in additional federal funding for conservation programs, extends the Conservation Reserve Program and Wetland Reserve Program, and creates new initiatives to improve natural resources on private lands in the United States. (*See* **U.S. Wetlands**)

SPRING: The World Water Council–established as a nonprofit, nongovernmental umbrella organization located in the city of Marseilles in southern France–is devoted to the critical issues of long-term global water policy and to advocating solutions to problems of water-resource management. (*See* **Community Water Supply** and **Water: Commodity**)

22 MARCH: Flood-level waters are released from Glen Canyon Dam in an experimental attempt to re-create the dynamics of the natural flow of the Colorado River through the Grand Canyon. The experiment is deemed a success for rebuilding sandbars, beaches, and fish habitat; however, this flooding falls short of mimicking the historic dynamics of the river.

11 OCTOBER: President Bill Clinton signs the Sustainable Fisheries Act Amendments to the FCMA, which was overwhelmingly approved by Congress. The law directs federal agencies to plan actions that protect marine resources for the long term. (*See* **Pacific Salmon** and **Salmon Populations**)

1997

The United Nations opens the Convention on the Non-Navigational Uses of International Watercourses to the ratification of the member states.

18 AUGUST: The steelhead trout is listed as endangered, including all naturally spawned populations (and their progeny) in streams in the Columbia River Basin upstream from the Yakima River, Washington, to the U.S.-Canadian border. (*See* **Columbia River** and **Salmon Populations**)

1998

The National Aeronautics and Space Administration (NASA) Mars Global Surveyor records images of canyons and spiraling troughs, what many scientists believe to be evidence of water outside of the ice caps on the planet. This discovery is further encouragement that there may once have been or still is life on Mars.

Turkey and Syria come to the brink of war because of Syrian support to Kurdistan Workers Party (PKK) terrorism. Syria agrees to cut her support to PKK in the Adana Declaration of the same year. (*See* **Euphrates-Tigris Basin**)

Hurricane Mitch, the deadliest Atlantic storm in two hundred years, causes an estimated eleven thousand deaths in Honduras, Nicaragua, Guatemala, and El Salvador. Damage estimates are $4 billion in Honduras (equal to one-third of its GDP) and $1 billion in Nicaragua. About half of the population of Honduras is evacuated; 70 percent are without clean water; and the risk of disease is significant.

Bangladesh suffers its most extensive flood of the century in the summer. Two-thirds of this low-lying nation at the mouth of the Ganges and Brahmaputra Rivers is inundated for months: thirty million people are left temporarily homeless; ten thousand miles of roads are heavily damaged; and the rice harvest is reduced by two million tons. Damage estimates exceed $3.4 billion.

Floods in Argentina and Paraguay cost $2.5 billion.

JANUARY: An ice storm in Canada and New England costs $2.5 billion, brings down thousands of miles of power lines, and wipes out the sugar-maple industry in some areas.

JUNE: Floods in Turkey cause $2 billion in damages.

A cyclone kills ten thousand people in India.

JUNE–AUGUST: Nearly record flooding in the Yangtze River Basin does $30 billion dollars in damage, displaces 223 million people, and kills another 3,000 people. Premier Zhu Rongji personally orders a halt to tree cutting, shifting state harvesting systems into planting systems, stating that the water-storage and flood-control capacity of the trees make them three times more valuable standing than fallen.

1999

Abdullah Öcalan, leader of PKK, is caught in Kenya and imprisoned on Imrali Island of Turkey. (*See* **Euphrates-Tigris Basin**)

The Indus River in northern India reaches record high levels because of increased glacial melt in the Himalayas. Concern arises over the future of the glacial-fed rivers with predictions that with current rates of shrinkage up to a quarter of the global mountain-glacier mass could disappear by the year 2050. (*See* **Indian Dams**)

FEBRUARY: The Nile Basin Initiative launches in Dar Es Salaam, Tanzania. Member countries include Burundi, Congo, Egypt, Ethiopia, Kenya, Rwanda, Sudan, Tanzania, and Uganda.

1 JULY: The 167-year-old Edwards Dam on the Kennebec River, Maine, is breached, with an intent of opening spawning habitat to several species of fish. In 1997 the Federal Energy Regulatory Commission determined that the ecological gain from its removal outweighed the gain from its continued operation. (*See* **Big Dams**)

12 DECEMBER: A Maltese-registered oil tanker breaks up off France, spilling three million gallons of oil, devastating the beaches along the Brittany coast.

2000

30 JANUARY: A dam of a tailing lagoon at a gold mine near Baia Mare, in northwestern Romania, breaks, washing one hundred thousand cubic meters of stored wastewater down the Someş River. Contaminants reach the Tisza River in Hungary with a concentration eight hundred times greater than the acceptable maximum level, leaving in its wake tons of dead fish and other aquatic life. (*See* **Tisza Chemical Spill**)

26 SEPTEMBER: British foreign secretary Robin Cook states that his government may refuse to underwrite a British firm involved in a controversial Turkish dam project because of environmental and human-rights concerns. (*See* **Euphrates-Tigris Basin**)

27 SEPTEMBER: Iceberg B–20, ten times the size of Manhattan Island, is reported having broken free from the Ross Ice Shelf in the Antarctic.

JUNE: Flooding in Nepal spreads over seventy-two out of seventy-five districts, except for Manang, Mustang, and Terathum. As of 14 August 2000, 110 people have been killed, 11 are missing, 70 injured, and a total of 8,630 families have been affected while 2,766 houses have been destroyed. The total property loss to date is estimated at more than $6.3 million.

16 NOVEMBER: The Report of the World Commission on Dams is released. This document is "the first comprehensive global and independent review of the performance and impacts of large dams," and recommends "options available for water and energy development."

AFRICAN DAMS

Did large dams contribute to the development of African nations?

Viewpoint: The construction of large dams in Africa had more positive than negative impacts on local, national, and regional economies, agriculture, industry, and the health and well-being of millions of people on the continent.

Viewpoint: Large dams harmed the environment and often hurt low-income people, while the dam-related water supply and hydroelectricity overwhelmingly benefited large corporations and wealthy households.

The construction of a hydroelectric dam at Kariba Gorge on the Zambezi River in the mid 1950s ushered in an era of major dam building on the African continent. Although the Kariba Dam was built expressly to supply electricity to the copper mines of Zambia (then Northern Rhodesia) and the growing industry and cities in Zimbabwe (then Southern Rhodesia), most large dams in Africa were built as part of integrated river-basin planning schemes.

The idea of Integrated River Basin Development was first proposed by the U.S. Army Corps of Engineers in 1914 and was first fully expressed in the Tennessee Valley Authority (TVA, created in 1933). With its dams and hydroelectric-power generation, the TVA was proclaimed a successful demonstration of a scientifically based rational approach to resource conservation. A United Nations (U.N.) panel of experts adopted "the TVA model" in 1958. The Kariba Dam proved that massive infrastructure could be built in remote locations, and the era of river-basin planning—with dams as major components—began in Africa.

Although integrated river-basin development projects were expensive and required nations to incur large debts, they were described as having multiple purposes and, therefore, many benefits. Dams were used for flood control, created lake fisheries, extended agricultural land through the provision of irrigation, and generated electricity. Each of these elements, in turn, had economic benefits. Flood control prevented downstream damage, lakes provided the opportunity for commercial fisheries, irrigated land developed larger and more-reliable harvests, and electricity generated industrial growth. The construction of at least twenty-six of these large dams, however, resulted in the forced displacement of thousands of people when their villages and grazing, agricultural, and hunting lands were inundated. Disruption of these lives was justified by the economic benefits that the nation as a whole accrued.

A major criticism of dam-based projects was this destruction of rural lives and cultures. Though never part of an integrated river-basin project, the five planned dams of the Lesotho Highlands Water Project (LHWP) have been cited as an example of a good, nondestructive dam project. Only thousands, rather than tens of thousands, of people will have been displaced, and relatively small amounts of grazing and agricultural area will have been inundated, when all the dams have been constructed. The reversal of flow of the Malibamatso River (headwaters of the Orange River) to transfer water from the mountains of Lesotho to the Gauteng Province, industrial and population centers of South Africa, will provide water to the historically underserved Johannesburg townships and a regional benefit through economic growth.

Viewpoint: The construction of large dams in Africa had more positive than negative impacts on local, national, and regional economies, agriculture, industry, and the health and well-being of millions of people on the continent.

In the 1970s an estimated 90 to 95 percent of the people in the north, the so-called industrialized countries, had access to clean drinking-water supplies. In the south, or the developing world, the percentage of people with access to clean drinking-water supplies stood at around 33 percent. In Africa, the percentage was even lower, around 28 percent. A major goal of states and peoples in Africa, therefore, has been to expand water availability through various means, including the construction of dams and interbasin water-transfer projects.

Water, which generally had been considered an unlimited resource that could be exploited as needed by local people, increasingly was seen as a scarce and valuable commodity. While the African continent has only 11 percent of the runoff in the world, it has 13 percent of the population—some 780 million people live in fifty-three countries. At the end of the twentieth century, around 300 million people lived in water-stressed countries; that is, they lacked sufficient water to meet the basic needs of their populations. According to United Nations (U.N.) projections, by the year 2025 a fairly sizable proportion of the populations of African countries will not have sufficient water to meet basic needs. Projections indicate that this number will increase to 1.1 billion, three quarters of the population on the continent at that time. As a consequence, the governments of African states, development organizations, and donor agencies employed a variety of strategies to expand water availability, promote water conservation, reduce wastage, and bring about more sustainable use of water.

Sixty international river basins in Africa make up 62 percent of the surface area, the highest percentage on any continent. International river basins are defined to mean those that are shared by two or more countries. Most African nations have access only to a single river basin. Some countries, however, have as many as nine international river basins, one example being the Democratic Republic of the Congo (DRC).

African riparian ecosystems are generally highly productive from the standpoint of the diversity of species, as well as the quality and quantity of soils and other resources upon which millions of people depend. Rivers in Africa were often dammed, and in some cases large-scale water-transfer schemes were created. The goals and objectives of those who planned these projects varied. They included flood control; provision of water for agricultural, industrial, and domestic usages; energy creation (especially hydroelectric power); facilitation of transport; promotion of tourism and recreation; development of fisheries; and expansion of employment, incomes, and business opportunities. Attention was also paid to maintaining the ecological integrity of rivers and promoting conservation in river basins.

Hydroelectric power constituted a small but important end-use of water in Africa. Several major development projects were tied to hydroelectric dams, including ones in the Kafue, Nile, Orange, Volta, and Zambezi river basins. Hydropower was seen as a clean, dependable, and renewable energy source. While some have argued that the era of "big dam" projects in Africa is over, this contention does not mean that there were no large dams under construction at the turn of the century. In fact, there were many large-scale water projects being implemented in Africa, including the Lesotho Highlands Water Project (LHWP)—at $4 billion, the largest development project on the continent at the end of the twentieth century. There were plans for even bigger projects, notably the Western Desert Project of Egypt and transfer schemes that would take water out of the Nile and under the Suez Canal into the Sinai peninsula.

Dams were seen by some as "useful pyramids"—monumental engineering projects that underscored the ability of humans to "control nature." The primary purpose of many early large dams (those fifteen meters in height or greater) was to regularize the flow of rivers and make water accessible during periods when it was not normally available (for example, during the dry season). Some large African dams are multipurpose in nature, combining the generation of hydropower with provision of water for irrigation and domestic supplies. Others were built specifically for generating electricity. Besides producing power for urban and rural areas, dams could be sold to other countries,

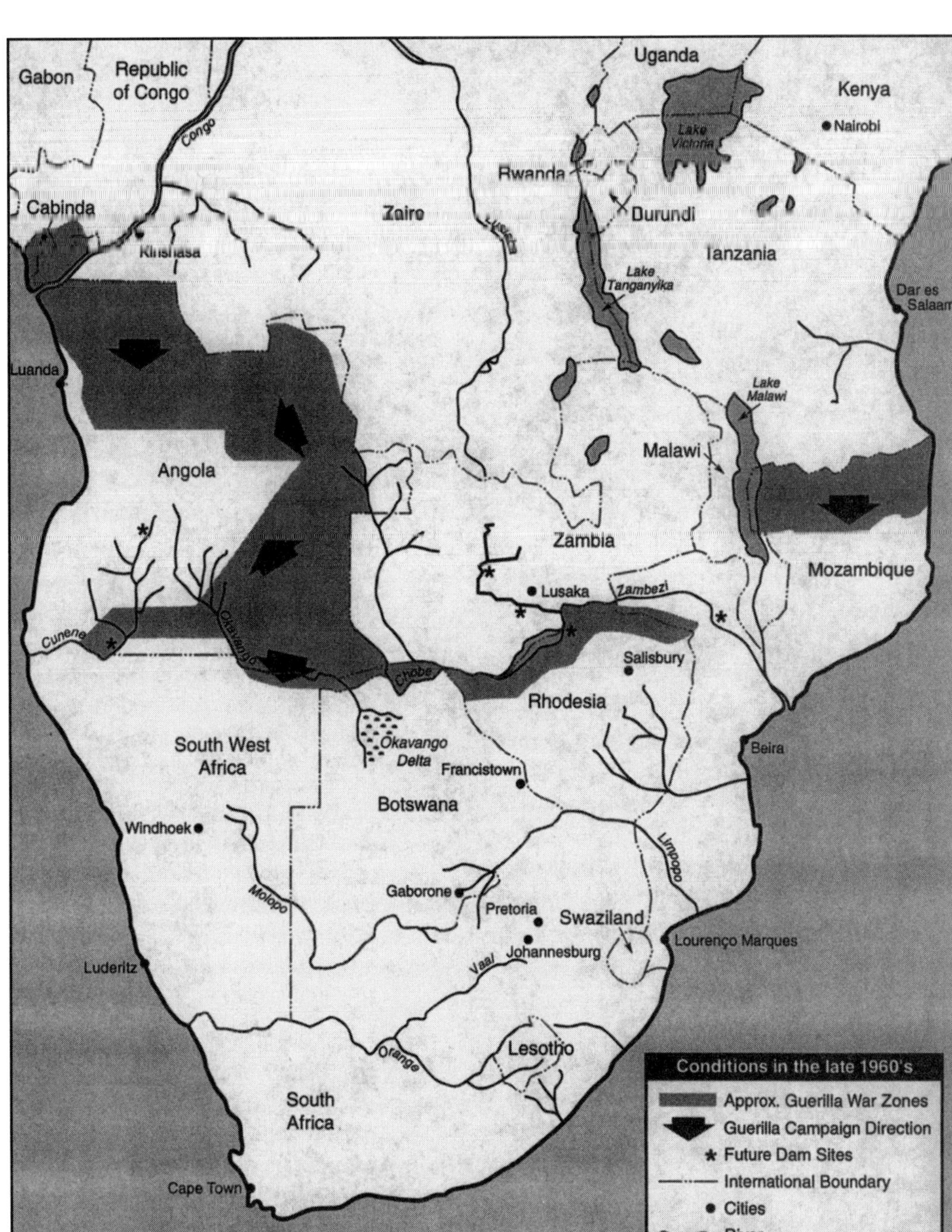

A map of Southern Africa in the late 1960s

(Manuel King)

thus providing income for the state or companies involved.

An important feature of several African dam projects was the construction of reservoirs for water storage. One of the oldest reservoirs in Africa was constructed in 1800 B.C.–a large facility in the Fayum Depression of western Egypt. Another large reservoir was built by the kingdom of Meroë, in what is now northern Sudan, in 275 B.C. Efforts were made many times to construct dams or barrages on the Nile River, some of which failed during construction, as was the case, for example, with the Kafara Dam of Egypt, built in around 2500 B.C.

Dam projects frequently require a tremendous amount of capital expenditure on the part of a nation-state, and in some cases they are the single largest development expenditure of a government. In Africa some of the most ambitious dam projects required outside inputs of both capital and technical expertise, as was the case with the Aswan High Dam of Egypt, completed in 1970. The president of Egypt, Gamal Abdel Nasser, saw the dam as both the preeminent symbol of Egyptian power and as a means of promoting industrialization, agricultural development, and economic self-sufficiency in his country.

The construction of the Kariba Dam on the Zambezi River, between what is now Zambia and Zimbabwe, in the 1950s had several benefits, according to advisers, planners, and consulting firms involved in its construction. A major gain was the generation of hydroelectric power. The construction of Kariba, which is an arch dam 128 meters in height, resulted in the creation of Lake Kariba, the first reservoir in the world to have more than 100 million acre-feet of storage capacity. This reservoir, which was 5,100 square kilometers in size, provided opportunities for the commercialization of fisheries and the expansion of tourism and recreation. Construction of the dam provided employment opportunities and higher incomes for some local people.

While 57,000 people, many of whom were Tonga-speakers, were relocated as a result of the construction of Kariba Dam, some were subsequently able to reestablish themselves economically, and education levels of the Tonga population rose significantly. From the standpoint of the government of Zambia, the local population, which up to that time had been relatively isolated, was integrated more closely into the national economy.

The Akosombo Dam on the Volta River in Ghana, completed in 1965, is an embankment dam 134 meters high and is aimed primarily at power generation. It was the centerpiece of the Volta River Project—at the time the largest single project undertaken in West Africa. The project helped Ghana diversify its economy and had many spin-off effects, including an expansion in physical and social infrastructure, as well as agricultural and business opportunities for many people who had lived in and adjacent to the Volta Basin.

At the end of the twentieth century, greater involvement of local people in project planning, implementation, management, and evaluation has been emphasized. One area in which progress has been made in planning and implementing river-basin-development projects was the degree to which local populations were consulted and had the opportunity to take part in the decision-making process. Compensation programs were put in place for people who were forced to relocate and included high quality replacement housing, fodder for their animals, and, in some cases, annuities that allow them to invest in the future. Many of the people in Lesotho affected by the LHWP, for example, will be better off once they have relocated into more-productive agricultural areas in the foothills and to urban areas, where they can generate income more easily.

The river basins of Africa at the turn of the century are in many ways development heartlands where tens of millions of people have been able to expand agricultural yields and raise living standards. In some countries in Africa, such as Egypt, irrigation underpins the agricultural economy. Nations such as Lesotho generate substantial royalties through the sale of water to other states, funds that are reinvested in local-level development. Access to clean water has increased in several parts of Africa, contributing to an improvement in nutrition and health.

As a district government official stated at a conference on transboundary water resources management in southern Africa, "Dams are crucial to our survival. What we need to ensure is that the benefits from these dams outweigh the social, environmental, economic, and political costs." A way to accomplish this goal, he suggested, is not to stop building dams but rather to construct facilities that maximize the ecological benefits of flooding and minimize the risks. Given the growth of population and the expanding requirements for water, food, and energy in Africa, dams and river-basin-development projects represent some of the most important means by which the twin goals of economic development and conservation can be met.

—ROBERT K. HITCHCOCK, UNIVERSITY OF NEBRASKA

Viewpoint: Large dams harmed the environment and often hurt low-income people, while the dam-related water supply and hydroelectricity overwhelmingly benefited large corporations and wealthy households.

One debate over the merits of large dams, which has been extremely important in practical terms, concerns distributional benefits and costs. Who wins and loses when large dams are built? Disturbing answers emerged from the two largest dams in the most socioeconomically unequal region of the world, Southern Africa: the Kariba Dam on the Zambezi River and the Lesotho Highlands Water Project (LHWP). These structures were constructed to serve, respectively, the main mining and manufacturing region in Zambia and Zimbabwe during the late 1950s when the two countries were both British colonies and the main industrial/population conglomeration in the region (Johannesburg, South Africa) from the mid 1980s–at the peak of apartheid–through the end of the twentieth century.

The following distributional concerns emerged from debates over the Kariba and Lesotho dams:

• too much money was (and still is) spent on these large dams in relation to other uses of funds that are a more urgent priority to the majority of citizens, uses that would save water, prevent environmental damage, and minimize displacement of local peoples and would result in fairer distributions of water in a region had one of the most unequal systems in the world;

• too high a proportion of the costs of large dams were (and still are) passed to low-income people, who therefore paid for electricity and water that was (and is) predominantly wasted by inefficient, hedonistic users;

• too much emphasis was (and still is) placed upon enhancing the short-term profits of major corporate electricity or water customers as justification for dam construction, without considering either the long-term costs borne by government or the equally vital short-term water and electricity requirements of low-income people who were too often denied access because of affordability;

• too much of the money borrowed for large dams originates from "hard-currency" sources–which in turn benefit foreign lenders (especially the World Bank) and transnational corporate suppliers–when in fact local sources of cement, steel, and labor comprised the main cost inputs and should be obtained from local financial markets;

• too often, dam construction was (and still is) motivated by geopolitical and multinational corporate interests, which were ultimately hostile to both democracy and the material interests of the majority of the citizenry of a given country or region.

To briefly summarize evidence that supports this multiple critique, one can first consider how the design of the Kariba Dam was based upon financial calculations reflective of distorted colonial-era priorities. Hydroelectricity needs of multinational corporations were met first, because cost-benefit calculations did not incorporate the developmental needs of low-income, black people (including those displaced by rising water) with shorter timeframes. In addition, hydroelectricity generated at Kariba was (and still is) priced inappropriately high to consumers, initially when few black people had access to the colonial-era electricity grid.

Second, the contemporary case of water drawn from the LHWP for Johannesburg-area consumption sparked several controversies (aside from environmental concerns about the largest cross-watershed transfer in Africa): financial-sanctions busting, hard-currency loans, corruption, World Bank "conditionalities" and pricing advice, and the distributional consequences of resulting tariffs.

These case studies cover most of the distributional issues associated with dams in Southern Africa. They are also not "bad" examples, as conventionally understood in the mainstream development industry. Kariba is a long-standing success, not least because a large, vibrant tourist resort (mainly enjoyed by the white, wealthy minority of the region) was created at the dam site. Likewise, the Lesotho case allowed the World Bank to claim that further loans would help to "prove that not all big dams are bad," as a 1998 briefing document argued. The cases, therefore, are the largest, most important, inter-regional, and conventionally applauded dam projects in at least one key region of the world. The dams also contributed to the inequality and oppression that led to civil war in the first case and to severe urban social movement protest and geopolitical conflict in the second.

The Kariba Dam is located on the border of Zimbabwe and Zambia. The World Bank granted its largest single loan up to that point (£28.6 million) to help finance the £74 million structure. Hard-currency financing from the bank was used, inexplicably, even though most inputs associated with construction, aside from turbines, were drawn from local sources. When filled in 1959, Kariba Lake was the largest artificial body of water in the world (with a volume four times greater than the then-second biggest dam reservoir on earth).

The main point behind building the Kariba Dam was to supply energy over nine hundred kilometers of transmission lines to colonial Zambian copper mines and smelters owned by just two firms: Anglo American Corporation (based in apartheid South Africa) and Roan Selection Trust (whose ownership was ultimately American). On the south bank of the Zambezi, in colonial Rhodesia (now known as Zimbabwe), the World Bank in 1952 had ensured a steady increase in demand for hydropower through a $28 million loan for the urban electrification of white businesses and suburban areas, leaving most of the country in the dark.

The dam filled a gorge that had been occupied by 57,000 Tonga (Batonka) people. Displacement affected nearly twice as many people as had been estimated in the original studies. As an alternative to Kariba, a much smaller run-of-the-river dam on the Kafue River tributary of the Zambezi was also considered and would have had the advantage of virtually no human displacement. This relocation, however, was not factored in as a social cost; instead, atten-

THE LESOTHO HIGHLANDS WATER PROJECT: THE ALEXANDRA RESIDENTS' CLAIM

DATE: 23 April 1998

TO: The World Bank Inspection Panel, 1818 H Street, N.W., Washington, D.C. 20433

FROM: Three anonymous Alexandra Township residents

Relative water access by low-income consumers. Gauteng consumers bear the bulk of the LHWP costs, both for capital and recurrent expenditures. But millions of the province's low-income citizens are already beset by severe problems of poverty, disease, environmental decay, geographical segregation and women's oppression due to the inadequate levels and high costs of water and sanitation services. South Africa's inequality in access to water is striking. According to a recent Central Statistical Services Household Survey, only 27% of African households have running tap water inside their residences and only 34% have access to flush toilets. By consuming less than 2% of all South Africa's water, the country's black township residents together use less than a third of the amount used in middle- and upper-income swimming pools and gardens, not to mention white domestic (in-house) consumption or massive water wastage by white farmers who have had enormous irrigation subsidies over the years and who use 50% of South Africa's water. Moreover, out of every 100 drops that flow through Gauteng pipes, 24 quickly leak into the ground through faulty bulk infrastructure. Still more waste occurs in leaky communal, yard and house taps. In the higher elevations of Alexandra township, these problems are witnessed in the perpetual lack of water pressure. Hundreds of thousands of low-income people in Alexandra and other townships have no immediate house or yard access to reticulated water supplied by our Johannesburg municipality, and instead receive at best only communal access, with all the public health problems that this implies. Indeed, the lack of available water on a universal basis means that public health conditions are worse; geographical segregation of low-income Gauteng residents (from wealthier residents) is more extreme; women are particularly inconvenienced, and their income-generation and caregiving capacities are reduced; and the environment is threatened (in part because of the shortage of water-borne sanitation). For reasons established below, we believe that the LHWP expansion will exacerbate rather than ameliorate our access, equity and quality problems. This could not come at a worse time, as Gauteng municipalities—including Johannesburg—are suffering extremely serious financial difficulties that are forcing them to dramatically increase the pace of water cut-offs to low-income consumers, as well as the retail price of water.

Alternatives not explored sufficiently. Are there alternatives to Phase 1B? Bank staff do not know, for as far as we can determine, the desire by communities to address our townships' own water-infrastructure shortcomings—especially leaky connector pipes, but also leaky water taps that together cost Sowetans approximately 40% of our water—has never been fully explored or supported by Bank staff. The possibility for changing water usage patterns through progressive block tariffs has not been factored in (in part because Bank staff explicitly oppose differential pricing of water). The impact of water conservation education has not been considered. The possibilities for regulations prohibiting excessive watering of suburban gardens has not been addressed by Bank staff. The potential for saving water through clearing invasive alien trees has not been calculated. The physical replacement or installation of low-flow showerheads, dual-flush toilets, and similar mechanical interventions have not been addressed. These are crucial alternatives which could ameliorate the need for the remaining phases of the Lesotho project. These alternative options have not been taken seriously, as far as we can tell from analysing Bank-supplied information. . . .

tion was focused far more on the Rhodesian colonialists' "Noah's Ark" rescue of wild animals trapped on islands by the rising water.

For economists of the period, a core problem was the temporal character of investment valuation, in light of the time-related rate of interest and repayment burden. Evidence assembled by D. S. Pearson and W. L. Taylor, in *Break-Up: Some Economic Consequences for the Rhodesias and Nyasaland* (1963), suggests that the huge Kariba investment systematically crowded out basic-needs alternative investments that would have been favored by low-income people. The project paid off for multinational mining firms quickly, but it took many decades for government to realize sufficient broader benefits so as to cover the costs.

Thus, Kariba supported corporate interests through the provision of hydroelectricity and colonial rule through hard currency. From the standpoint of the impoverished majority in Zimbabwe, hydroelectricity generation of Kariba—responsible at independence in 1980 for nearly 30 percent of the national grid supply—potentially was an offsetting factor. During the Rhodesian era, white rulers denied electricity connections to 86 percent of all black households, even as late as 1979.

After independence, pricing of Kariba hydroelectricity was micromanaged by the World Bank. A joint study with the United Nations Development Programme (UNDP) in 1982 led to an energy-sector loan in 1984. The Bank and UNDP argued that Zimbabweans' "income levels will not rise sufficiently to encourage fuel substitution by the African population." Instead of charging wealthy consumers more (through cross subsidies) in order to allow the poor access to grid electricity, "an extensive reforestation program is urgently needed" because the Bank/UNDP assumed people would continue chopping down local wood sources for energy. These conclusions were based on the assumption of "rational energy pricing policies": for example, phasing out even the slightly subsidized electricity that then applied.

By 1987 still only 20 percent of households (a meager 6 percent increase from 1980) were electrified, and there was no subsequent progress because of declining subsidies. That year the Bank granted a $44.4 million loan for refurbishing the Kariba facilities, again conditional on "economic pricing for energy products" (for example, no subsidy for poor people). By 1996 the Zimbabwe Electricity Supply Authority (ZESA) still only provided electricity to 21 percent of the population.

Similar distributional issues were associated with the construction of the biggest dam project in Africa, the LHWP, although, instead of electricity pricing, the central problems related to economic calculations and financing policy associated with retail-water consumption by residents of Johannesburg. Water from the Maluti Mountains of tiny, landlocked Lesotho ordinarily tumbles down to the Orange River in South Africa, across a vast stretch of extremely fertile and then arid South African land, becomes the border with Namibia, and makes its way into the Atlantic Ocean. In 1998 the LHWP began diverting to the Johannesburg area what will amount to a billion cubic meters of water annually—in Phases 1A (complete) and 1B (under construction from 1998), at a cost of more than $2 billion—through dams and cross-catchment tunnels. LHWP water travels to the Vaal River and, hence, into an industrial complex ranging from the steel industry cities along the river, through Johannesburg (the largest manufacturing and mining complex in Africa), to Pretoria (the capital city of South Africa).

Fundraising for the LHWP initially occurred under conditions of financial sanctions against the apartheid government of South Africa (which was accomplished surreptitiously, through a London account established by the World Bank). South Africa has always had enormous influence over Lesotho politics, not just during apartheid, but as recently as 1998, when the South African National Defense Force invaded Lesotho to defend the LHWP Katse Dam in the wake of a coup. Another factor was blatant corruption by some of the largest multinational dam-building companies in the world, which from 1988 to 1998 paid at least $2 million into the Swiss bank accounts of the head of the LHWP authority of the Lesotho government, who in turn was vigorously defended by the World Bank when Lesotho officials notified him of impending dismissal in 1994.

The Lesotho case occurred in a context of geopolitical manipulation and classical development mismanagement. In addition, the LHWP also teaches about distributional aspects of water supply (hydroelectric power is only a small component of the project) and the possibility of substituting conservation (demand-side management) measures for costly new dam construction.

The distributional critique of the LHWP emerged in 1998 from residents of Soweto and Alexandra townships in metropolitan Johannesburg. During the late 1990s more than 1.5 million urban residents of Gauteng Province (in which Johannesburg is located) did not have direct access to water. To provide a supply of fifty liters per person per day would have required only twenty-two million cubic meters of additional supply annually, representing a small fraction of the water that middle- and upper-income Gauteng consumers use to water their gardens and fill swimming pools. At full capacity the first two dams (Phases 1A and 1B) of the LHWP will together provide about a billion extra cubic meters of relatively clean mountain water per year to Gauteng. (Of that, nearly 60 percent is likely to be used in irrigation for white-owned farms, another important distributional factor).

Who pays for the dam, however? Communities in the black townships of Soweto and Alexandra claimed that the LHWP makes it harder for Gauteng municipalities, especially Johannesburg, to keep water prices down, desist from water cutoffs, and repair leaking pipes in the townships. In April 1998 three Alexandra civic leaders argued (unsuccessfully) to the World Bank Inspection Panel—an internal oversight unit with a mixed record—that by delaying Phase 1B for an estimated seventeen years, resources could be spent on conservation and maintenance, as well as on redistributing water to township households.

The legacy of apartheid water maldistribution was exacerbated, the Alexandra residents alleged, by the dramatic cost increase associated with Lesotho water (five times the cost of existing Vaal River sources), which, when passed on through several government bureaucracies to municipalities and retail consumers, was disproportionately charged to those who had been historically oppressed by lack of access to water. While bulk water charges to municipalities rose by 35 percent, in large part caused by the LHWP between 1995 and 1998, the bills for the first (lowest) segment of the Johannesburg block tariff increased by 55 percent, indicating that—relatively speaking—first-block consumers paid a higher proportion of the increase than did consumers who used more water.

In addition, the pricing mechanism for the incoming Lesotho water also prevented municipalities from using water accounts as a means of cross-subsidising other local government activities. The two dozen Gauteng municipalities dependent upon Lesotho water ran a deficit of $10 million in 1997 (on $200 million revenues), in contrast to the rest of South African municipalities, which ran a $5 million surplus (on $500 billion in revenues). Under financial stress, Gauteng municipalities, including Johannesburg, began cutting water supplies to low-income people who were not paying bills; of several thousand in 1997 alone (the last date records exist), only 20 percent could afford to pay arrears and be reconnected.

Was (and is) there an alternative to the five dams planned in the entire LHWP? The alternative strategy of "demand-side management" was not opposed by any of the interested parties, although the Bank would not accept claims (for example, by the director of the South African "Working for Water" program) that 30 to 40 percent water savings could be achieved through conservation strategies. The Alexandra residents listed a variety of reforms consistent with demand-side management, but alleged that because of the LHWP, these would not be implemented.

The reason that construction of huge dams crowds out alternative strategies is that the enormous cost of construction requires high volume water consumption to pay for it. The incentive structure for government authorities, therefore, is to delay water-saving strategies, since the first priority is to sell the maximum amount of LHWP water to pay the interest on loans associated with construction costs. Conservation makes full cost-recovery that much harder.

Two obvious conclusions, therefore, are that:

• given the bias of access—and wastefulness—in water use toward wealthier, predominantly white, consumers, redistributive measures should become a much higher priority, and;

• given the perennial shortages of water in South Africa and the threat of drought, demand-side management should be given much higher priority by authorities—both on redistributive and conservation grounds.

Are large dams a fair way to enhance energy and water-related resources for development, or do their size, prestige, and financing techniques invariably subject megadams to political pressure and economic power that ultimately favor large corporations and the rich? Large dams unnecessarily enhance inequality, as seen in these two case studies, because white-owned/controlled corporations and wealthy white (and subsequently also black) households in southern Africa benefited disproportionately.

If this argument has merit, how should the distributional inequity associated with large dams be contested? The building of Kariba contributed to anger throughout black Zimbabwe, first that many people were evicted from their traditional homelands, and second that the power and wealth of white colonialism and allied corporate interests were amplified enormously, thanks to the new source of electricity, at the expense of the entire society that was required to repay the World Bank and Commonwealth loans. Similar passions emerged in Soweto and Alexandra townships in South Africa over the extent to which poor people with inadequate water paid higher bills to support extremely expensive dams that mainly benefited the wealthy.

Common to both case studies, however, was the fact that low-income people did not successfully resist the dams and have not yet found a way to shift the distribution of benefits in their favor. The Zimbabwean black nationalist movement turned to guerrilla war during the 1960s–1970s, but after their victory in 1979, no substantive difference was made in the 1980s–1990s from the standpoint of electricity redistribution. Nor did the appeal by Alexandra residents to the World Bank Inspection Panel have "any effect," except perhaps to slow Phase 2 discussions.

In contrast, dams such as the Sardar Sarovar projects on the Narmada River in India and the proposed Arun Dam in Nepal encountered intense opposition by grassroots activists and their international allies, leading to World Bank funding withdrawals in both cases during the mid 1990s. By the late 1990s the World Bank was sufficiently embarrassed by protests against dams, especially from affected people's movements (working in close alliance with environmentalists such as the International Rivers Network and Center for International Environmental Law), that it took recourse in the establishment of a World Commission on Dams. The commission was chaired, from 1998–2000, by South African water minister Kader Asmal, who in November 2000 achieved the surprising accomplishment of a consensus report, signed by both dam builders and dam opponents.

Not many of the concerns associated with distributional issues—aside from displacement of people living in submerged areas—were successfully raised by dam opponents within the commission. Nevertheless, across the world at the dawn of the twenty-first century, new militancy was emerging precisely around the way in which globalization generated the worst-ever social inequality in the world. Many leading international organizations and governments finally began to fret that the excessive power and prerogative enjoyed by transnational corporations and international financial institutions during the late twentieth century was generating a vicious backlash. It would be up to the people affected in Southern Africa to join the new global movement for social justice and add their demand that large dams, whose benefits are disproportionately controlled by corporations and rich households, to finally redress, through cross-subsidized, gender-sensitive and environmentally conscious systems that charge the rich more, and provide a lifeline supply of water and energy to all.

—PATRICK BOND, WITS UNIVERSITY GRADUATE SCHOOL OF PUBLIC AND DEVELOPMENT MANAGEMENT

References

W. M. Adams, *Wasting the Rain: Rivers, People, and Planning in Africa* (Minneapolis: University of Minnesota Press, 1992).

Patrick Bond, "Lesotho Dammed," *Multinational Monitor* (January/February 1997).

Bond, "The Political Economy of Dam Building and Water Supply in South Africa: Contesting the Impact of the Lesotho Highlands Water Project on Johannesburg," in *Environmental Justice in South Africa,* edited by D. McDonald (London: James Currey Press, forthcoming).

Bond, *Uneven Zimbabwe: A Study of Finance, Development and Underdevelopment* (Trenton, N.J.: Africa World Press, 1998).

James Ferguson, *The Anti-Politics Machine: "Development," Depoliticization and Bureaucratic Power in Lesotho* (Cambridge & New York: Cambridge University Press, 1990).

Korinna Horta, "Making the Earth Rumble: The Lesotho-South Africa Water Connection," *Multinational Monitor,* 17 (May 1996).

Horta, "The Mountain Kingdom's White Oil: The Lesotho Highlands Water Project," *The Ecologist,* 25 (1995): 227–231.

D. Letsie and Bond, "Debating Supply and Demand Aspects of Bulk Infrastructure: Lesotho-Johannesburg Water Transfer," in *Empowerment through Service Delivery,* edited by Meshack Khosa (Pretoria, South Africa: Human Sciences Research Council, 2000).

Patrick McCully, *Silenced Rivers: The Ecology and Politics of Large Dams* (London & Atlantic Highlands, N.J.: Zed Press, 1996).

Cheryl Payer, *The World Bank: A Critical Analysis* (New York: Monthly Review, 1982).

D. S. Pearson and W. L. Taylor, *Break-Up: Some Economic Consequences for the Rhodesias and Nyasaland* (Salisbury, South Rhodesia: Phoenix Group, 1963).

R. Southall, "Is Lesotho South Africa's Tenth Province?" *Indicator SA,* 15 (1998): 4.

Elaine Windrich, *Britain and the Politics of Rhodesian Independence* (London: Croom Helm, 1978; New York: Africana, 1978).

ARKANSAS RIVER VALLEY

Why did the Arkansas River Valley, once a rich center of irrigated agricultural production, go into sharp decline in the second half of the twentieth century?

Viewpoint: The decline of agriculture in the Arkansas River Valley was predictable due to the limitations of irrigation.

Viewpoint: The economic success of irrigation agriculture in the Arkansas River Valley was primarily dependent on national and international commodity prices over which the local farmers and water managers had little control.

The lure of turning arid lands into greenbelts has been consistent across time and place. Development of irrigation systems to extend the reach of a river, or to supplement low rainfall in a region, has persisted from the ancient world to the present, and in terrain as diverse as the Anatolian Plain, the American Southwest, and China. Human ambitions to make the Arkansas River Valley in the United States into an irrigated Eden thus were not unique, but then neither was the collapse of those ambitions an unusual occurrence.

Beginning in the late nineteenth century, farmers, politicians, corporate enterprises, and governmental agencies schemed to bring water to the American West, and to make this so-called desert bloom. Progressive Era convictions that the application of technology to nature would enhance productivity in this dry region, and the creation of the Bureau of Reclamation in the U.S. Department of Interior to expend federal dollars to reinforce this faith, ushered in an unprecedented period of construction. Ditches, dams, tunnels, and pipelines, among other related conduits of captured water, received considerable funding. Local monies were also invested up and down the major watersheds, all with the hope of replicating other, more-humid climates, and the agricultural economies they sustained.

As with these other efforts, the extensive labor and capital expended along the Arkansas River, from its headwaters in Colorado through the western Kansas plains down through Oklahoma, bore fruit. At least for a time, irrigated farming flourished, first among sugar-beet producers and later among those who grew cantaloupes and onions. It did not hurt that during some of the period, the area benefited from good rains. Success brought greater demands on the often low flow of the river, however, as well as legal challenges from downstream users who were angered about upstream diversions. To resolve the social tensions, impound larger amounts of water, and draw on other distant supplies, the federal government built dams and reservoirs along the river and in the 1980s completed the Fryingpan/Arkansas Transmountain Water Project.

These massive investments ultimately could not forestall the collapse of the regional economy. For some, the responsibility for this failure lies with the flaws imbedded within the concept of irrigation agriculture, which they argue is (and has long been) a formula for disaster. Manipulating water resources is expensive and environmentally unsound. In seeking to control the hydrology of the Arkansas River, water managers created new, unanticipated problems and then resorted to technological fixes that simply compounded their original errors. The crash of Arkansas River Valley agriculture was sadly predictable.

By contrast, others suggest that for all the problems associated with irrigation, it alone was not the key to the downturn in farming in this arid region. These analysts instead focus on the critical role that the marketplace played in determining the rise and fall of the regional economy. Depressed commodity prices around the world, rising costs of transportation of crops to market, and the utilization of evermore-expensive farm technologies are among the many factors that have bedeviled the capacity of valley farmers to reap a profit from their labors. Even with plentiful water and a bounteous harvest, Arkansas River Valley producers have not been able to finesse the economic forces that determine international, national, and regional development.

Viewpoint: The decline of agriculture in the Arkansas River Valley was predictable due to the limitations of irrigation.

Societies based upon irrigation have experienced great difficulties in maintaining themselves over any long expanse of time. The great ancient irrigation works of the Fertile Crescent (Mesopotamia; present-day Iraq) now lie buried in sand. The once-extensive Hohokam and Chacoan ditches are dusty, bare ruins of Native American ingenuity in the present-day American Southwest. Similarly, try as they might to make it work, creating a flourishing irrigation society overwhelmed the good intentions of the people in the Arkansas River Valley.

Promoters and irrigators dreamed of turning the valley into a cornucopia filled with prosperous farms and cities. Their aspirations, however, met head-on with severe adaptation problems to the ecology of the valley. The dreams of devising a cooperative society, moreover, repeatedly were undercut by the reality of confrontation and conflict. Irrigators' efforts to resolve mounting social and ecological problems often led to greater concentrations of authority in the hands of a few to guide the irrigation work of the many. As if these difficulties were not enough, the economics of irrigation seldom produced consistent abundance for its practitioners. From the 1870s all of these problems combined to precipitate a severe decline in the practice of irrigation throughout the entire valley in the final decades of the twentieth century.

Irrigation promoters and advocates throughout the Arkansas River Valley were a cross of social, economic, and moral visionaries. Theodore C. Henry was one of the most important irrigation promoters to ever toil in the valley. At the core of his social vision lay the belief in the common, or cooperative, ownership of ditch systems. His dreams of economic prosperity embraced the belief that "a family of five persons, during a decade, can more safely rely upon the production of ten acres of irrigated land in Colorado for a livelihood than upon one hundred and sixty acres of nonirrigated land in Kansas." The moral improvement came in transforming a land that was "wanting," as one editorialist saw the valley, "till the resources of the river" were employed in irrigation. While "want" carries with it economic and material undertones, it also harbors the notion of a character deficiency that can be corrected through proper behavior. Early promoters were so taken with these ideals of social, economic, and moral well-being through irrigation that they dubbed the Arkansas Basin the "Valley of Content."

Henry's views encapsulated the labors and thoughts of people working in the valley for decades to come. In 1927 Michael Creed Hinderlider, state engineer of Colorado, predicted a grandiose future for the region. This powerful water bureaucrat foresaw the creation of a continuous "urban community" from Canon City to the Kansas-Colorado line, more than 250 miles of valley, in which people would thrive in "stately homes and magnificent parks." He thought "mutual organizations," or cooperative endeavors, would prosper within a "common community of interest inter-related and interdependent, and all finally dependent upon that absolute necessity—water." Given such optimism, why did irrigators start abandoning the valley over the last fifty years of the twentieth century?

One answer, applicable regardless of place or time, is that irrigation has inherent ecological liabilities. Under the best of circumstances, irrigation is a difficult form of agriculture to maintain for any length of time. The Arkansas River Valley, from Pueblo, Colorado, downstream to Dodge City, Kansas, has consistently presented irrigators with wearisome conditions for the employment of technology. One impediment is the erratic stream flow in the river—the Arkansas was never a perennial flowing stream; historically, it has been an intermittent water-

John Martin Dam and Reservoir

way. Even before the practice of irrigation, certain low rainfall patterns produced a dry riverbed. The majority of irrigation works went up in the 1880s, a period of abundant rainfall for crop production throughout the Great Plains. Builders and settlers thought this condition was normal, but once all of the canals began operating at full capacity it became painfully obvious that too many companies were placing great demands on limited river flow.

While often scant currents coursed through the valley and left most demands upon it unsatisfied, at other times too much water inundated the area–destroying ditches, fields, and crops. The flood of June 1921, for instance, wreaked particular havoc throughout the valley. Huge torrents lifted control gates out of their settings, completely buried diversion works in silt, eroded ditches, and washed away crops in a wide swath stretching from Pueblo to Garden City, Kansas.

An added worrisome ecological nightmare came with the compounding buildup of salinity in the river flows. Soils contain salts, which irrigating dislodges and adds to the return flows reentering the river after evaporation and plants have their take. Salinity levels continue to accrue with each reuse of return flows, and if not checked, they will ultimately render crop growth mute. Historically, this problem has been the ruination of countless irrigation societies across the planet, and irrigators in the Arkansas River Valley have not escaped the deleterious effects of salinity.

Salinity levels continued to climb despite efforts to improve soil drainage and quality. In some places the Arkansas River contains more salts in its flows than any other U.S. river. This condition has always meant two things to farmers: decreasing crop yields and increasing costs of production. These problems, coupled with falling crop prices because of overproduction throughout the nation, put a hard squeeze on the profitability of irrigated farming in the valley. In the last fifty years of the twentieth century, these impediments alone discouraged hundreds of farmers from continuing their operations.

Rising levels of salinity contributed to, and compounded the problems with, phreatophytes–plants that draw copious amounts of water for their livelihood. Trees, such as cottonwoods and salt cedars, have flourished throughout the valley to the detriment of crop production. Cedars have especially done well as they thrive in salt-impregnated stream flows.

While in some respects farmers achieved elements of a cooperative society through the mutual ownership of their respective ditch companies, they also fell prey to unrelenting social conflict. The massive extent of some ditch systems created problems with the equal distribution of water throughout their canals, and this situation often led to serious acrimony among users. Farmers' demands for more water than the river could provide created the need for an elaborate state apparatus to regulate water usage.

Colorado law and water-use customs encouraged farmers to maximize the employment of the river flow. Consequently, irrigators downstream in Kansas often left their diversion gates open only to receive mere trickles that were unconsumed by their neighbors upstream. Of course, Kansans took righteous umbrage at Coloradans' water uses, and they pleaded their case to the United States Supreme Court three times in the twentieth century. The Court in 1907 gave little relief to Kansans; a 1943 judgment encouraged the creation of an interstate river compact and commission to deal with the problems between the two states; and a May 1995 ruling granted Kansans considerable relief in terms of increasing the river flow reaching systems around Garden City, and in terms of remuneration for their economic losses.

In an attempt to mitigate this conflict, irrigators attempted to employ greater levels of technological domination over the hydrology of the valley. The federal government played a crucial role in providing this technology through the work of the Army Corps of Engineers, which built the John Martin Dam and Reservoir in the 1930s and 1940s. The Bureau of Reclamation constructed the Fryingpan/Arkansas Transmountain Water Project, which was finished in the 1980s.

These structures also concentrated greater social and economic control over the water flows of the valley into the hands of federal bureaucrats and judges, along with a growing cadre of consulting engineers and lawyers. Moreover, the extensive work of resolving litigation, devising social arrangements for administrating water flows, and building and maintaining these highly sophisticated water-control systems, were enormously costly for taxpayers, especially those in Kansas and Colorado, as well as the farmers of the Arkansas River Valley.

The historical difficulties in finding marketable crops contributed to the ecological and social problems associated with irrigation. High-value truck crops such as onions and cantaloupes proved profitable in the valley. Between 1890 and 1950 sugar-beet production flourished until international tariffs and cane production made it completely unprofitable. By the mid 1950s sugar-beet-processing plants began shutting down throughout the valley. Alfalfa served the cattle industry clustered near the small cities of western Kansas, but ditch irrigators were placed at a distinct disadvantage with those who could produce lower-cost yields through the vast proliferation of pump irrigation across the High Plains.

Farmers left the valley even where irrigation worked best. In 1999 irrigators of the Rocky Ford Ditch Company sold their water rights to Aurora, a city whose name means "golden" in Spanish. These farmers and their predecessors had enjoyed ample water supplies, tilled fertile soils, and raised highly specialized and profitable crops. Still, even they could not contend with the mounting ecological, social, and economic problems associated with irrigation farming. Metaphorically, and actually, this transference symbolized the movement of water uphill to money—out of the Arkansas River Valley to the City of Gold along the Front Range.

These farmers were not the first, nor will likely be the last, to liquidate their holdings. The entire valley is dotted by abandoned canals and diversion works; deserted, salt-saturated fields now produce little more than Russian thistles. In the last 130 years, the effort to escape the historical liabilities and limitations of irrigation has only reproduced these obstacles in the Arkansas River Valley.

—JAMES E. SHEROW,
KANSAS STATE UNIVERSITY

Viewpoint: The economic success of irrigation agriculture in the Arkansas River Valley was primarily dependent on national and international commodity prices over which the local farmers and water managers had little control.

The expectations, goals, and dreams of those individuals who developed irrigation agriculture along the Arkansas River in Colorado and Kansas in the 1870s and 1880s must be set in the context of their times. This period was one of booming growth and high expectations throughout the Great Plains. The Civil War (1861–1865) had recently ended, shifting the national focus from war and destruction to economic expansion and migration. Railroad companies raced to lay tracks to the Pacific Coast and, in the Great Plains, to control the hinterland and its expected agricultural bonanza. Settlers were necessary to open the region to

THE UNREALIZED VISION FOR THE ARKANSAS RIVER VALLEY

In an address to the Rocky Ford Chamber of Commerce on 8 November 1927, Michael Creed Hinderlider, the State Engineer of Colorado, asserted that:

Picture if you will, the possibilities of this Valley, yes the probabilities within the next twenty-five to fifty years—a teeming population forming a continuous urban community extending from above Canon City to the State Line; wide avenues of traffic and intermingling line of electric communication and transportation: stately homes and magnificent parks replacing the unsightly alkalied and ravaged river bottoms; efficiently managed and carefully maintained systems of canals and reservoir; thoroughly tilled farm-steads and gardens; great elevators, sugar mills and factories; mutual organizations for the harvesting and marketing of crops; motorized industries yet unknown; and a great city; with flourishing towns with their myriad of human beings which must be fed, all forming a common community of interest inter-related and inter-dependent, and all finally dependent upon that absolute necessity—water.

The picture just drawn is not chimerical but one of reality of this same valley of yours, but a few years removed.

Source: *"Discussion of Supplemental Water Supply Possibilites for the Arkansas Valley," November 8, 1927, Michael Creed Hinderlider Collection, Colorado Historical Society, Denver.*

agricultural production, and many areas across this region were shamelessly "boomed" (promoted through great exaggeration) by railroads and land developers to national and international audiences. Land was available at little or no cost; thousands of Americans and Europeans sought to be a part of this boom; and extensive areas of the Plains were broken to agriculture–both irrigated and dryland. The development of irrigation agriculture in the Arkansas River Valley was just one small facet of this much-larger pattern of expansion and optimism that characterized the region and historical period.

A century and a quarter later a local economy based on irrigation agriculture faltered, economic stagnation or decline long characterized much of this area, and out-migration extending back for at least fifty years was the predominant demographic characteristic for most Arkansas River Valley (and Great Plains) counties. What happened? Why have the visions of the early developers and settlers not been achieved? What caused the economic and historic trajectory of this area to differ so fundamentally from that initially foreseen? The answers to these questions are found in a complex interplay of environment, economy, and technology set in a changing local, regional, and international context.

The enthusiasm associated with the development and promotion of irrigation agriculture in the Arkansas River Valley was not grounded in an understanding of local environmental conditions. Indeed, folk wisdom of the period suggested that "rain follows the plow"–that by breaking the sod and introducing agriculture, the area would thereby receive increased amounts of precipitation. Moreover, developers did not have long-term data to determine basic river-flow characteristics such as volume, seasonality, or annual variability. Without this knowledge, the developers typically brought more land under ditch than the river could support. Under a prior appropriations scheme, the ditch with the earliest appropriation date got its allocation of water before one with a later date, which in turn, got its allocation before the third ditch, and so forth. During the relatively dry years, ditches with later appropriation dates might well get too little water delivered at the wrong time to make a crop. For the irrigated lands in the Otero County, Colorado, area, this situation meant that the availability and predictability of water was increasingly problematic for ditches with fifth through eighth priorities. In an attempt to counteract the linked problems of inadequate and untimely supplies of water, the history of local irrigation development has been marked by the creation of many off-channel reservoirs, transmountain water diversions, and the construction of the John Martin and Pueblo dams. While adequate and timely water supplies are necessary for agricultural production, they have not been sufficient. Agricultural success requires good markets.

The agricultural history of the Arkansas River Valley may be characterized as the quest for a reliable and financially rewarding cash crop. While much of the production of food and fodder from the early farms was for home consumption, some production for market has always been required. Alfalfa was one of the first crops under extensive cultivation: it was not long before production exceeded local demand. Distance, a largely undeveloped transportation system, and the relatively low value of this crop prevented significant export to regional markets. As one consequence, local agriculture languished. Shortly thereafter, a variety of cantaloupe was developed in Rocky Ford, and soon train carloads were being shipped from the area. Ripe melons, however, have a relatively short shelf life; transportation was both slow and lacking refrigeration, and farmers got paid only when the melons were sold at market. When more than one hundred carloads spoiled in a hot St. Louis railyard, farmers suffered substantial losses and cantaloupe production fell. Interest then shifted to sugar beets as a primary cash crop. Sugar beets appeared to be an ideal crop as they grew well in the area, were a high-value crop, and their processing provided wage labor opportunities for farmers during the previously slack fall and winter seasons. Building beet-sugar-processing plants ("sugar-beet factories") caused significant local booms. These factories were the largest single-building industrial facilities in the area and their construction, often with locally manufactured bricks, together with the transport and assembling of the equipment, brought about significant demand for labor and in the supporting service sector. Cultivation of the crop itself also had high labor demands and caused local economies to expand. Almost every town in the valley wanted to get in on the sugar boom and five factories were built between Rocky Ford and Garden City. Yet, the factories at Las Animas and Lamar soon closed, and existing plants had low capacity and economically marginal facilities. To keep the remaining factories profitable required increasing their production output, but the local supply of beets was generally inadequate to match expanding production capabilities. Perhaps the most limiting factor was that beet sugar was a "political" commodity–its price and acreage allotments vacillated with congressional actions, tariffs, and foreign relations. Local factories struggled on until the 1950s, when beet sugar lost much of the market to corn-derived and artificial sweeteners, and the aging plants were closed as a result.

National agricultural trends also had an impact on the Arkansas River Valley. As the amount of irrigable land in the valley was fixed, increased farm mechanization led to fewer–but larger–farms and reduced rural populations. Fewer people, together with better vehicles and improved roads, led to the decline of local service centers in favor of county-seat communities and regional commercial centers. Mechanization also required increased economic returns from cash crops to finance the ever-growing cash outlays.

Much of the latter years of the century witnessed a general decline in agricultural commodity prices combined with increased input costs. This disparity resulted in a general economic decline which, in turn, lessened the farmers' ability to maintain the irrigation infrastructure–headgates, canals, laterals, and drainage ditches. Boggy soils and increasing salinity were partial effects of this inadequate maintenance. Although the application of current technology and improved techniques had the potential to mitigate or forestall the well-known, longer-term consequences of irrigation, the declining agricultural economy generally could not support the costs of these improvements.

Successful agricultural economies, and the health of communities reliant upon them, require both appropriate environmental conditions and a good market for their products. Although inadequate watering may cause crop failure, plenty of water and excellent yields do not guarantee an economic return on investment because of a dependence on markets and commodity prices. Simply stated, water is a necessary input but is not sufficient for economic success. Markets are national and international in scope, and local farmers exert little influence on prices. The alfalfa, cantaloupe, and sugar-beet examples cited above illustrate the long term dependence of local farmers on nonlocal markets that are well beyond their ability to control. As price-takers–not price-setters–farmers, individually, are vulnerable bit players in an economy that changed fundamentally over the past century from one based on agriculture to one where agriculture itself is of secondary importance. The economic, demographic, and environmental conditions of the agricultural communities in the Arkansas Valley, as well as sales and out-of-basin water transfers, may be best understood through an analysis of declining position of its agricultural produce in a greatly changed local, regional, and international context.

–KENNETH R. WEBER, NATIONAL PARK SERVICE

References

Mark Fiege, *Irrigated Eden: The Making of an Agricultural Landscape in the American West* (Seattle: University of Washington Press, 1999).

Lawrence J. MacDonnell, *From Reclamation to Sustainability: Water, Agriculture, and the Environment in the American West* (Niwot: University of Colorado Press, 1999).

Dena S. Markoff, "A Bittersweet Saga: The Arkansas Valley Beet Sugar Industry, 1900–1979," *Colorado Magazine,* 56 (Summer/Fall 1979): 161–178.

Anne M. Marvin, "Irrigation and Boosterism in Southwest Kansas, 1880–1890," *Kansas History,* 19 (Spring 1996): 36–51.

James Earl Sherow, "The Chimerical Vision: Michael Creed Hinderlider and Progressive Engineering in Colorado," *Essays and Monographs in Colorado History,* 9 (1989), pp. 37–59.

Sherow, "Marketplace Agricultural Reform: T. C. Henry and the Irrigation Crusade in Colorado, 1883–1914," *Journal of the West,* 31 (October 1992): 51–58.

Sherow, *Watering the Valley: Development along the High Plains Arkansas River, 1870–1950* (Lawrence: University of Kansas Press, 1990).

Alvin T. Steinel, *History of Agriculture in Colorado: A Chronological Record of Progress in the Development of General Farming, Livestock Production and Agricultural Education and Investigation, on the Western Border of the Great Plains and in the Mountains of Colorado, 1858 to 1926* (Fort Collins, Colo.: State Agricultural College, 1926).

Mark J. Wagner, "The Parting of the Waters—The Dispute between Colorado and Kansas over the Arkansas River," *Washburn Law Journal,* 24 (Fall 1984): 99–120.

Kenneth R. Weber, "Great Plains, Small Towns: Population Change in a Region's Town's and Cities," *Forum of the Association for Arid Lands Studies,* 10 (1994): 21–28.

Weber, "Otero County: A Demographic History of a Colorado High Plains County, 1889–1987," *Social Science Journal,* 26 (1989): 265–275.

Weber, "What Becomes of Farmers Who Sell Their Irrigation Water? The Case of Water Sales in Crowley County, Colorado," report prepared for The Ford Foundation, Environment and Behavior Program, Institute of Behavioral Science, University of Colorado, Boulder, 1989.

Michael E. Welsh, *U.S. Army Corps of Engineers: Albuquerque District, 1935–1985* (Albuquerque: University of New Mexico Press, 1987).

THE BALTIC

What role did water-related environmental problems play in the collapse of communism in the Soviet bloc?

Viewpoint: Environmental activism enjoyed widespread popular support in Poland in the 1980s, at a time when the Solidarity movement was suppressed. Once the Soviet bloc collapsed, however, environmentalism became less important than democratic reform and economic liberalization.

Viewpoint: Glasnost-era environmental activism in Estonia was not an opportunistic surrogate for anti-Soviet rhetoric, but a genuine movement to preserve and protect the water and land resources of the Baltic republic from the threatened expansion of Soviet-mandated phosphate and oil-shale mining operations.

The collapse of the Soviet Union and the Soviet bloc occurred amid a growing environmental crisis in Eastern Europe. To compete with the Western world, Soviet-style industrial development took place without much attention being paid to environmental matters. When the worldwide environmental movement began to gain momentum in the 1960s and 1970s, the western democratic countries responded by passing stringent laws designed to clean up their streams, skies, and land. Yet, in the Soviet bloc—which seemed immune to popular discontent—the water, air, and soil in urban industrial regions continued to worsen with every passing year. By the 1980s the environment had deteriorated to such an extent that, as Murray Feshbach and Alfred Friendly Jr. have suggested in *Ecocide in the USSR: Health and Nature under Siege* (1992), "when historians finally conduct an autopsy on the Soviet Union and Soviet Communism, they may reach the verdict of death by ecocide."

Both of the following authors agree that the political and ecological collapse of the Soviet bloc occurred simultaneously and that these two issues were linked. They disagree as to how much environmental issues (chief among them, water-related ones) shaped the transition from communist to postcommunist societies in Eastern Europe. Drawing on the experience in Poland, Mark Cioc contends that the environmental movement functioned as a surrogate for the Solidarity movement when it was suppressed in the 1980s and that environmental issues took a backseat once political reform came in the 1990s. Using Estonia as an example, Robert W. Smurr argues that environmental issues were central to all aspects of the political revival and independence of this Baltic nation.

Viewpoint: Environmental activism enjoyed widespread popular support in Poland in the 1980s, at a time when the Solidarity movement was suppressed. Once the Soviet bloc collapsed, however, environmentalism became less important than democratic reform and economic liberalization.

Soviet-style industrial development destroyed the environment in Poland as much as it did elsewhere in Eastern Europe. In 1985 the Polish parliament declared that four regions were environmental "disaster areas": Gdansk (formerly Danzig), where the Vistula River reaches the Baltic Sea; the coal-mining district of Upper Silesia; the industrial region around the ancient capital of Kraków; and the copper production region of Legnica/Glogów. Worst affected were the water supplies of the eleven million people who lived in these regions—nearly one-third of the entire population of Poland.

It is worth mentioning some of the main problems that characterized these four regions in the twilight years of communist rule. The Vistula River flows from south to north through the heart of Poland on its way to the Baltic Sea. As late as 1980 half of the eight hundred towns and villages on its banks still lacked sewage-treatment facilities and thus dumped their raw sewage into it. By the time the river reached the Gulf of Gdansk and the Baltic Sea, it was so polluted with nitrogen, phosphorus, mercury, cadmium, zinc, lead, copper, phenol, chlorinated hydrocarbons, and human sewage that its waters were unfit for industrial or urban use. Vacationers were advised not to bathe along the Baltic coast in the vicinity of Gdansk. Most of the water pollution in Upper Silesia (the major coal-producing region) stemmed from the fact that mine water, coal dust, and phenol (from coal processing) were being dumped into the nearby streams or allowed to seep into the groundwater. These pollutants not only poisoned water supplies but also made river water unsafe for use in crop irrigation. Kraków, the grand old medieval capital of Poland, lies in a low valley, making it poorly situated for heavy industry. A cloud of bad air, caused by smoke emitted from the surrounding smokestacks, hung over the city almost continually. When it rained, airborne particles dissolved to become "acid rain," which ate away the famous stone buildings and historic statues in the city. The rain was so acidic that it even dissolved the gold roof of the Sigismund Chapel of Wawel Cathedral, requiring extensive restoration work. In the Legnica/Glogów copper region the water and air were so polluted that locally grown vegetables contained more than one hundred times the maximum acceptable limit for cadmium, zinc, and lead.

By the 1980s matters were so bad in these four "disaster areas" and the prospects for improvement so grim that the Polish government admitted that the only safe thing to do would be to evacuate the entire population. Since removing eleven million people was not a feasible solution, the citizenry had little choice but to inhale bad air, drink polluted water, and consume contaminated food. In any case, the environment elsewhere in Poland was only marginally better. Polish officials privately confided in 1988 that two-thirds of all its rivers were polluted beyond use; that only 1 percent of the surface water was fit to drink; and that most crops were tainted to one degree or another with toxins, either from airborne pollutants that fell as rain or waterborne pollutants that came from irrigation. Uncontrolled industrial and agricultural production (including excessive fertilizer use), coupled with the absence of adequate treatment plants, had all but destroyed the naturally abundant supply of fresh water in Poland. The absence of laws was not the problem. The National Water Act of 1974 spelled out in detail the rules that were supposed to govern surface, ground, and coastal waters. The government, however, did not enforce the law out of fear that it would undermine the already fragile economy.

Despite a climate of political repression in Eastern Europe during the 1970s, grassroots groups began to mushroom and express their outrage at the environmental damage taking place in their country. In 1981 many of these groups joined together to become the Polish Ecological Club (*Polski Klub Ekologiczny,* or PKE), headquartered in Kraków. In a PKE publication the group called itself "a social movement of people conscious of the dangers associated with the unsettling of biological balance by technical civilization and by the consumptionist model of life, acting for the good of the nation in the fields of nature protection and protection of the environment in which man lives." What it sought was nothing less than a total transformation of Poland into a green society. The PKE enjoyed a modicum of success in its early years. In 1981, for instance, it successfully lobbied for the closure of the Skawina Aluminum Works on the grounds that its high fluorine emissions were destroying the landscape south of Kraków. The PKE also had some success halting plans to construct new nuclear-power plants, especially in the wake of the 1986 Chernobyl accident in Ukraine (Poland received more of the radioactive fallout than any other Eastern European state). At the end of the 1990s

Marshland in the Lahemaa National Park, Estonia

(F Jussi)

the PKE remained the most important nongovernmental organization (NGO) in the field of Polish environmental policy.

The PKE, however, did not operate in a political vacuum. That it was able to establish itself as an independent organization and exert some influence over national economic affairs was owed almost entirely to the establishment of Solidarity, the independent trade-union movement that emerged during the steel strikes of 1980. Solidarity changed Polish politics and society forever, creating the atmosphere in which NGOs could come into existence. As PKE officials themselves readily admitted, the club would never have come into being had it not been for Solidarity. The government had censored all information about the health hazards caused by pollution and kept all scientific reports under lock and key throughout the 1960s and 1970s. This censorship only came to an end when Solidarity burst onto the scene in spectacular fashion. The various local and regional environmental movements of the 1970s had been completely stymied in their efforts to bring environmental issues to the public's attention: the spark they needed to ignite a debate came from the Solidarity movement.

The early Solidarity leaders rarely ventured into environmental politics, preoccupied as they were with the task of establishing themselves as an institution and promoting their own political agenda. The labor movement, however, allied itself with the PKE, both in terms of personnel and ideas. Solidarity, for instance, joined forces with the PKE to force the closure of the Skawina Aluminum Works, even though it meant unemployment for many of their rank-and-file members (in fact, it is still unclear whether primary credit for the closure should go to the PKE or to Solidarity).

Yet, if trade unionism overshadowed the environmental movement in the early days, the situation began to reverse itself rapidly when the Polish government declared martial law in December 1981 and clamped down on Solidarity, forcing it to go underground. Under martial law all forms of public political dissent were banned. By a quirk of fate the government took the view that pollution was a nonpolitical issue and therefore one that did not endanger the regime. That decision provided environmentalists with a golden opportunity to get their message across (while offering a clandestine method for political activists to channel their anticommunist sentiments and desires for democratic reform through environmental issues). Like most other NGOs in Poland, the PKE was forced to go underground when martial law was declared, but it reemerged in 1983 as a quasi-tolerated opposition group after it clearly enunciated that it was a club of "experts" and not a social movement. Its numbers swelled to more than six thousand in the wake of the Chernobyl disaster, which the PKE skillfully exploited as part of its environmental rhetoric. The PKE, in fact, was so successful that the Polish government felt compelled to create its own counter-club of "experts"—known as the "Social Ecological Movement." This move had the effect of fueling the public discussion by providing a new avenue for discourse and by generating new disputes regarding facts and figures. Recognizing that the environment was a hot-button issue, Polish United Workers Party First Secretary Wojciech Jaruzelski, in his June 1986 speech to the Tenth Congress of the Polish Communist Party, even included it as one of the most pressing problems faced by the nation—thus, further legitimating pollution as a political concern.

In the late 1980s things began to change as Soviet leader Mikhail Gorbachev's ideas of perestroika and glasnost began to percolate into Polish politics. By September 1989 Solidarity leaders had taken over the reins of government, and once again democratization and market reform emerged as the top priorities. Membership in Solidarity rose to ten million and its leader, Lech Walesa, was elected the new president of Poland. By contrast, environmental issues began to take a backseat. The PKE itself stayed out of the political fray, preferring to remain true to its chosen course as an NGO composed of experts. Individual members, nevertheless, played key roles in the creation of two new political parties—the Polish Ecological Party and the Polish Green Party—neither of which found much resonance among voters in the 1990s.

As elsewhere in Eastern Europe, voter apathy on environmental issues was largely the result of forces beyond the control of the PKE and its members. The overriding concern of the governments and peoples in the postcommunist world was rapid economic transformation along neoliberal economic lines. The environment was thus largely viewed as an "externality" that could be sacrificed in the interest of rapid economic growth. Fortunately this emphasis did not mean that the Polish environment continued to deteriorate: the mere act of jettisoning Communist-era production practices was itself a pro-environmental act. The surface, ground, and coastal waters steadily improved as new and cleaner technologies replaced old ones. The Baltic coastline became significantly cleaner during the 1990s, not least because the Swedish government offered financial and technical assistance in the cleanup of the Vistula and other Polish rivers. Acid rain was also less of a problem; people living in mining regions experienced fewer health risks. The triumph of Solidarity's priorities over those of the PKE, however, meant that the chief goal of the environmental movement—to make Poland "green"—was never achieved. On the contrary, Poland was well on its way to becoming a Western-style consumer society.

It seems paradoxical that public awareness of the Polish environmental crisis peaked in the 1980s at the very moment that public discourse in general was being suppressed by the Jaruzelski regime. In fact, the temporary banning of Solidarity proved to be a boon for environmentalists and the government alike: it gave the PKE a national forum for the first time and provided the government, which feared Solidarity far more than the PKE, an escape valve for social discontent.

—MARK CIOC, UNIVERSITY OF CALIFORNIA, SANTA CRUZ

Viewpoint: Glasnost-era environmental activism in Estonia was not an opportunistic surrogate for anti-Soviet rhetoric, but a genuine movement to preserve and protect the water and land resources of the Baltic republic from the threatened expansion of Soviet-mandated phosphate and oil-shale mining operations.

Cultural and environmental historians have noted that nations and cultures pass through phases in which their local landscapes and perceptions of nature become, for various reasons, elevated above that of the daily norm. As a result of both the liberalizing policies of Soviet leader Mikhail Gorbachev's glasnost campaign and, ironically, continued Soviet-mandated environmental degradation, the late 1980s indisputably became a period of greater enthusiasm for environmental protection in Estonia. It was a period in which conservation-based civic organizations played a central role in emphasizing and elevating the place of the natural world in the mind of most Estonians. Although many of those individuals who protested Soviet environmental policies also desired greater political, economic, and cultural autonomy for Estonia, environmental concerns remained a central grievance of the tiny Soviet republic. Because the virulence of this complaint stemmed from a remarkable indigenous tradition of nature conservation and preservation, it is a mistake to dismiss the movement as a mere Trojan horse used by opportunistic nationalists.

POLLUTION IN THE SOVIET BLOC

For the last two decades, people in this historic city [Kraków], a former seat of the Polish kings, have watched as corrosive soot from a steel mill slowly destroyed its treasured monuments, blackening the ancient red brick of the Jagiellonian University and rendering medieval carvings at the Wawel Castle into shapeless stumps of stone.

A decade ago, Poland's Communist government did not even allow scientists and journalists in Krakow to mention the pollution in public. Not until 1981 were they allowed to establish an environmental club to study the threat. And until recently, anyone seeking to stage a peaceful demonstration calling attention to the problem was likely to be handed a two-year prison sentence. . . .

In Poland, regions covering 13,500 square miles—11 percent of the country's land area—and including one-third of the national population were declared environmentally endangered by a comprehensive study by the National Academy of Science last year. Six million people were said to be living in "environmental disaster areas." More than 125,000 acres of Polish forest already have been destroyed, and half of the country's total forest area is threatened by air pollution.

Ninety-five percent of the river water in Poland is now unfit for drinking, half of the lakes have been irreversibly contaminated, and more than three-quarters of drinking water sources do not meet official standards of purity, according to Polish scientists. Warsaw and Triana, Albania are the only capital cities in Europe that do not treat their sewage. Much of the food Poles consume also is contaminated with toxic metals, and milk in some areas of the country has been declared unfit for children under the age of 6.

The environmental problems are particularly severe in the southern industrial region of Silesia, which forms the eastern edge of a vast zone of environmental devastation stretching south into Bohemia in Czechoslovakia and east into East Germany. Lead concentrations in the Silesian soil exceed standards by 150 to 1,900 percent. Concentrations of soot in the air are up to 35 times greater than that judged dangerous to health. Life expectancy in the region is lower than in the rest of Poland and has fallen in recent years, while complications with pregnancies are far above national levels. A report issued last year by the Polish Chemical Society said that air pollution and other kinds of environmental damage appear to have caused substandard health in 30 to 45 percent of schoolchildren.

Although Hungary's environmental problems are not as severe as those of Poland, Czechoslovakia, and East Germany, the country still faces severe threats from air and water pollution. Air pollution in Budapest, whose streets are clogged with thousands of cheap East Bloc cars and buses, is so severe in the winter that one study estimated a one-hour walk outdoors causes the same harm to one's lungs as smoking a pack of cigarettes. Hungary's Environmental Ministry says one in 17 deaths in the country is related to air pollution. Rivers flowing from the Soviet Union are contaminated even before they reach Hungary.

The catastrophic effect of the socialist economic system on the environment has been a major factor in persuading the elites that change was essential. . . .

Source: *Jackson Diehl, "New Breeze in Soviet Union Is Fouled By Pollution," Washington Post, 18 April 1989, as printed in the* Congressional Record, *volume 135 (17 October 1989 to 26 October 1989), pp. 25981–25982.*

The few English-language articles that deal with issues of Estonian conservation and environmental efforts tend to conclude that environmental campaigns within Soviet Estonia were essentially ways of expressing politics by other means. For example, about environmental degradation in Estonia, Matthew R. Auer flatly—and incorrectly—stated in an *East European Quarterly* (1996) article that "the conflict was political rather than cultural." Western authors have placed the movement in the framework of a larger all-Soviet or pan–East European phenomenon and have thereby overlooked the unique and historical characteristics of the Estonian environmental movement altogether. This broad view has led scholars such as Auer to suggest incorrectly that similar to most East European countries, the efforts of Estonian environmentalists in the late 1980s amounted to little more than a clever ruse. In fact, Estonian activism must be understood on its own terms as the product of an existing tradition in which particular images of "nature" came to symbolize key components of national identity.

The fact that Estonia comprised only 0.2 percent of the territory and 0.6 percent of the population of the Soviet Union belies much of its enormous moral and political influence within the former empire. It was indisputably a nation whose impact on Soviet history was far out of proportion to its size, for the political ramifications of its drive for independence reverberated throughout the Soviet Union. Only one year after the nuclear accident at Chernobyl in Ukraine (1986), Moscow publicized its plans to expand the environmentally disastrous phosphate mines in the northeastern region of Estonia, an act that sparked the independence movement in that Baltic nation and fostered its "Second Awakening Age." Specialists told Estonians that the planned mining expansion could threaten up to one-third of the groundwater supply in the republic. Estonia immediately thereafter led other disgruntled republics not only by decrying the "ecological illiteracy" of leaders in Moscow, but also by seeking greater environmental, economic, and political concessions from the Kremlin.

The history and influence of the Estonian conservation ethic and related civic organizations was much older than that of the Soviet period alone. Indeed, if one is to properly understand the strength of Soviet-era environmental politics in Estonia, one must look not only to the history of its vibrant civil society in the pre-Soviet era, but to its citizens' perceptions of the physical landscape of their territory as well. Because, as Anthony Smith has noted in *The Ethnic Revival* (1981), "nationalism as an ideology and movement is very much concerned with the practical and symbolic uses of land," a nation that has honored and celebrated its native landscape for countless generations can be expected to persistently defend any threat to its perceived "homeland."

Symbolic uses and representations of Estonian nature and landscape emerged most conspicuously in the late nineteenth century during the so-called Awakening Age, that is, more than a half century before the Soviet Union annexed Estonia (1940). The themes Awakening Age intellectuals derived from Estonian country life coincided with an era in which Estonians were deliberately developing, defining, and imagining their cultural and political national consciousness. This powerful link between the nation and its environment was only strengthened during the first period of Estonian independence (1920–1940), for then preservation was increasingly tied to patriotism.

Marxist ideology and Soviet practice often pursued policies that directly assaulted central aspects of Estonian culture; therefore, it came as no surprise when the Soviet Union challenged the Estonian environmental tradition and its vibrant civil society upon the latter's forced annexation. The "Great Transformation of Nature" campaign of the Stalin era is a case in point: Soviet bureaucrats emphasized the imperative to "declare war against nature" during the same period when independent Estonia was searching for the proper location to establish its first national park. Thus, when the Soviet Union forcibly incorporated Estonia, the ideological positions about perceptions of the natural world were already clearly defined.

Collectivization and severe social restructuring followed Soviet annexation and curtailed all earlier conservation efforts. After only a few years of inactivity, however, Estonians soon re-employed several methods to preserve their threatened natural world and to protect their similarly menaced culture. The republic enacted a powerful nature-protection law in 1957, enthusiasts founded the enormously popular Estonian Nature Conservation Society in 1966, and conservationists established the first national park (Lahemaa) in the Soviet Union in 1971.

Despite its bucolic setting, one need not travel far from Lahemaa National Park to see evidence of Soviet-style utilitarianism; oil shale and phosphate mines that threatened Lahemaa and much of northeast Estonia lay just beyond the borders of the park itself. Here one encountered an enormous environmental and visual wasteland, often described by visitors as a "moonscape." In this relatively flat country where the highest natural feature is only 318 meters above sea level, and where the relative heights of more local landforms rarely exceed 20 meters, the visual and psychological impact of hundreds of cinder hills–some attaining heights of up to 115 meters–was staggering. Indeed, the Estonian mountain of greatest relative height (with respect to the surrounding ground) was made of ash. Nor were these scenes of visual devastation limited to the vertical: 160 million tons of the unwanted slough covered twenty square kilometers of ground near one of the industrial sites.

Oil shale and phosphate were at the core of this environmental devastation. Oil shale, so-called "brown gold," was transformed by inefficient and highly polluting Soviet technology into electrical power, oil, gas, and ash. Phosphate was crushed to make an ineffectual fertilizer. In the case of oil shale, an average of 25 metric tons of overburden must be removed per every ton of oil shale mined. In addition to the environmental and visual blight caused by oil-shale mining, the power plants that burned the mineral both spewed enormous quantities of gasses, dust, and ash into the atmosphere and left behind one-half of the mined resource as lye-lime ash. In general, oil-shale mining leaves in its wake five kinds of waste: ash of thermal power plants, dirt and residues of mining, wastes of related chemical industries; water pumped out of the mines; and radioactive materials. More than half of the annual thirty-one million metric tons of oil shale mined in Estonia ended up piled on the earth as inorganic residue, and an average of three hundred million cubic meters of water was pumped out as waste every year from the mines. The estimated two hundred thousand to five hundred thousand tons of dust the three major electrical plants churned out annually from their gargantuan chimneys included high levels of lead, arsenic, mercury, zinc, copper, uranium, and cadmium. Residents in neighboring towns had to beat the dust out of their overcoats daily.

Disturbed by gloomy visual images and suffering from cultural insecurities as Estonians may have been, Soviet policies posed the greatest immediate threat to the environment and the physical health of local residents. Several factors are thought to have contributed to the bleak state of northeast Estonia's environment. First, the ash that the power plants dumped in huge hills was particularly harmful since it contained both sulfuric acid and heavy metals; when it rained the acid dissolved the heavy metals, and the resulting toxic runoff contaminated rivers and groundwater supplies. Second, fires were responsible for releasing heavy metals into the ecosystem. Rather than making use of the low-grade shale overburden in local power plants, phosphate miners more frequently disposed of the mineral in huge piles. Their careless disposal methods led to the formation of sulfuric acid, which in turn caused self-ignition. The resultant fires—which often smoldered for years—also released heavy metals into the atmosphere and water; the enormous fires that began in the mid 1960s, for instance, took more than ten years to extinguish. Third, as a result of these fires, wells in the region were polluted with oil and high levels of phenols, and water that was used in attempts to extinguish the flames carried high levels of hydrocarbons back to surrounding rivers and lakes. Most disturbing of all, by 1982—that is, years after the waste had accumulated and fires smoldered—there still was not a single special storage facility in Estonia designed for removing harmful elements from industrial waste. Thus, harmful materials easily found their way from the slough into open-water sources and groundwater supplies.

It was not until the relative freedoms of glasnost in 1988 that scientists from an Estonian Research Institute could publish their findings which indicated that there were approximately eighty types of disease-inducing organic compounds in the air around the oil-shale plants. Local inhabitants were also found to have twice the amount of lead, cadmium, and mercury in their blood than a distant control group. Because of these reports, residents learned for the first time that in comparison to the Estonian average, the frequency of diseases in the oil-shale region was at least one-third higher.

The assault on northeast Estonian residents' visual and olfactory senses, to say nothing about their health, was ubiquitous and unavoidable. Even as bleak a scene as much of the region presented, Soviet officials did little to address the problem. Rather, it was the scientific elite in Estonia—inheritors of a vibrant prewar civic society—who persistently tried to steer Moscow-centered ministries to be more responsible in their exploitation of Estonian natural resources. Until the late 1980s, then, much of the impetus for change in Soviet environmental policies already stemmed from incessant Estonian demands.

These demands dramatically increased in 1987. On 25 February of that year, the popular nature program *Panda* informed its television audience that Moscow authorities were planning to expand an already huge phosphate-mining operation in the northeastern area of the republic. This broadcast, and the subsequent environmental protests it spawned, jump-started the drive for Estonian independence. The press, quickly following the example set by the *Panda* broadcast, exploded with articles examining environmental degradation in Estonia. Authors warned Estonians about the environmental hazards in no uncertain terms. "We are living on the border," wrote an Estonian journalist, "where the environment cannot deteriorate further."

The virulence of the emergent "Phosphate War" is best gauged by the response from Moscow. Shortly after the pivotal *Panda* broadcast, Gorbachev visited the republic, mingling with the people in a typical glasnost-style performance. After the head of the Estonian Writers' Union openly raised the mining issue with the General Secretary, a response came with uncharacteristic speed. In April 1987 TASS announced that planning work on the largest phosphate deposit in Europe had been halted. Students in Tartu, flushed with the sense of victory, substituted green ecological banners for the standard red ones during the annual May Day Parade in the university town.

Ultimately, the Estonians' continued identification throughout the Soviet era with the territory and landscape of their homeland, as well as their many civic organizations associated with its protection, resulted in a solid foundation from which the nation was prepared to challenge Soviet hegemony when Gorbachev introduced his glasnost campaign. Thus, when the head of the Estonian fertilizer ministry made public his plans to expand phosphate mining during the *Panda* broadcast, the nation was prepared to react. The protest movement–established as it was with the sole aim to protect and preserve the environment–gained its strength and nationalistic character from the Estonian tradition of civic activism. Its power also increased because no amount of rhetoric and no level of official obfuscation could hide the fact that the air stank, that children were becoming sick, that rivers and forests were dying, and that toxic dumps were growing in size. In short, the Soviet Union simply could not conceal the appalling toll that its ideology was wreaking on the environment of Estonia, and the relative freedoms of glasnost gave much more opportunity for Estonians to voice their concerns in this regard.

–ROBERT W. SMURR, UNIVERSITY OF WASHINGTON, SEATTLE

References

Matthew R. Auer, "The Historical Roots of Environmental Conflict in Estonia," *East European Quarterly,* 30 (Fall 1996): 353–380.

Samuel H. Barnes and János Simon, eds., *The Postcommunist Citizen* (Budapest: Erasmus Foundation, 1988).

Jane I. Dawson, *Eco-Nationalism: Anti-Nuclear Activism and National Identity in Russia, Lithuania, and Ukraine* (Durham, N.C.: Duke University Press, 1996).

Joan DeBardeleben, ed., *To Breathe Free: Eastern Europe's Environmental Crisis* (Washington, D.C.: Woodrow Wilson Center Press; Baltimore: Johns Hopkins University Press, 1991).

Murray Feshbach and Alfred Friendly Jr., *Ecocide in the USSR: Health and Nature Under Siege* (New York: BasicBooks, 1992).

Barbara Hicks, *Environmental Politics in Poland: A Social Movement Between Regime and Opposition* (New York: Columbia University Press, 1996).

Tõnis Kaasik, "Sustainable Development as a Common Security Instrument: The Ida-Virumaa Case," in *Ecological Security of the Baltic States, Nordic Countries and Northwest Russia,* edited by Kaasik (Tallin: Academy of Sciences, 1995), pp. 32–39.

John M. Kramer, "The Environmental Crisis in Eastern Europe: The Price of Progress," *Slavic Review,* 42 (Summer 1983): 204–220.

"Panel on Nationalism in the USSR: Environmental and Territorial Aspects," *Soviet Geography,* 30 (June 1989): 441–509.

Polski Klub Ekologiczny (PKE), *Deklaracja Ideowa i Tezy Programowe Polskiego Klubu Ekologicznego* (Kraków: Nakl. Uniwersytetu Jagiellonskiego, 1989).

Phillip R. Pryde, ed., *Environmental Resources and Constraints in the Former Soviet Republics* (Boulder, Colo.: Westview Press, 1995).

Toivo U. Raun, *Estonia and the Estonians* (Stanford, Cal.: Hoover Institution Press, Stanford University, 1987).

Antti Roose, *Põlevkivist Ehitatud Eesti,* translated by Erika Puusemp as *Estonia Built on Oil Shale* (Rakvere, Estonia: Virumaa Foundation, 1991).

Sabine Rosenbladt, "Is Poland Lost? Pollution and Politics in Eastern Europe," *Greenpeace* (November/December 1988): 14–22.

Anthony Smith, *The Ethnic Revival* (Cambridge, U.K.: Cambridge University Press, 1981).

Mare Taagepera, "The Ecological and Political Problems of Phosphorite Mining in Estonia," *Journal of Baltic Studies,* 20 (Summer 1989): 165–174.

Taagepera, "Pollution of the Environment and the Baltics," *Journal of Baltic Studies,* 12 (Fall 1981): 260–274.

Jon Thompson, "East Europe's Dark Dawn," *National Geographic,* 179 (June 1991): 36–69.

Lloyd Timberlake, "Poland–The Most Polluted Country in the World?" *New Scientist,* 92 (22 October 1981): 248–250.

Arthur H. Westing, "The Greening of Estonia," *Environmental Conservation,* 15 (Winter 1988): 299–302.

BIG DAMS

What was the effect of large dams in the American West?

Viewpoint: Over the past century, dams provided enormous benefits in the American West by converting it into a more-livable region.

Viewpoint: Big dams provided much-needed flood control, storage, irrigation, and power, but those who designed and built them overlooked impacts on communities and the environment.

The central problem confronting European Americans who pressed beyond the one-hundredth meridian in the United States after the Civil War ended in 1865, and those who wanted to establish agricultural communities, was the lack of water. This barrier to western settlement was unlike any that faced the first settlers in the East. There, water was generally abundant and available year-round. In the West, however, rivers that ran full and fast in the spring often dried up in the late summer and fall. It did not help matters that much precipitation in the region came during the winter months when it would be of little use to irrigators. To resolve this problem, many westerners argued for the development of storage reservoirs and works to capture winter rains and spring floods for release in the late summer and early fall.

The notion that reserved water would enable settlers to "reclaim" the arid western landscape land was first articulated in the late nineteenth century and gained considerable political support in the early twentieth century. In 1902 President Theodore Roosevelt signed the Newlands Reclamation Act, an initiative that Representative Francis Griffith Newlands (D–Nevada) had sponsored. Funding for projected irrigation projects would come through the sale of public lands in the West, and as dams and water ditches were constructed, additional acreage would be sold, expanding agricultural settlement patterns across a vast expanse.

Rarely challenged, the development of water-resource projects received even greater impetus during the Great Depression (1929–1941), when President Franklin D. Roosevelt extended his cousin's bold support for western irrigation. To create jobs, generate electricity, and provide flood control, the Roosevelt administration poured millions of dollars into several massive dam complexes along the Columbia and other river systems. Federal spending on such work continued into the 1960s, by which time many of the western watersheds were thoroughly bottled up, and their waters distributed to irrigators and urban areas through a complicated network of canals and pipes. This development was how the West was won.

There were losses, however, associated with the more than sixty years of dam building. Various aquatic species were threatened, or became extinct; Native American sacred sites and much-heralded geological formations disappeared beneath rising reservoirs. By the 1950s a nascent environmental movement began to protest individual dams and the philosophy that drove their development. Building public support for their cause, lobbying Congress, and filing lawsuits, environmentalists began to chip away at the hitherto uncritical acceptance of the necessity for an irrigated western landscape. In the 1970s the Big Dam era came to a halt, a result of legal confrontations, tight budgets, and new environmental regulations. It mattered, too, that there was an absence of additional good dam sites—reclamation was stopped by its own successes.

Viewpoint: Over the past century, dams provided enormous benefits in the American West by converting it into a more-livable region.

The evolution of large-scale water-resource development projects in the American West had its roots in the Jeffersonian ideal of the yeoman farmer and in the concept of Manifest Destiny. Early supporters of western settlement and development recognized the necessity of irrigation, a concept foreign to settlers from the water-rich East where abundant precipitation made such developments unnecessary. The cost of developing water storage and distribution facilities, however, was enormous, leading to the call for a federally supported "reclamation" program. What ensued over the next one hundred years brought benefits and consequences far beyond those envisioned by early irrigation supporters.

In the latter part of the nineteenth century, Congress passed several laws aimed at promoting settlement of the West through disposal of public lands and the development of irrigation. While partly successful, these efforts proved unsatisfactory. The cost of developing irrigation storage and distribution systems was high, and few private enterprises could afford such endeavors. During the 1890s the demand for federally sponsored irrigation development in the West grew, and meetings were held throughout the nation to garner support for a federal reclamation program.

As the twentieth century approached, the voice of the western irrigation movement grew. Led by Representative Francis Griffith Newlands (D–Nevada) and other activists, the movement gained momentum. In 1900 each of the major political parties inserted proirrigation planks in their platforms, taking the movement out of the West and making it a national issue. The first bills introduced in Congress to establish a federal reclamation program failed, but support continued to grow.

The "reclamation" movement received a significant boost when Theodore Roosevelt became president in 1901. A former resident of the arid western regions and a strong supporter of irrigation, Roosevelt had firsthand knowledge of conditions in the West. Moving swiftly to establish a federally supported reclamation program in the West, Newlands reintroduced his reclamation bill, which quickly moved through both houses of Congress and was signed into law by Roosevelt on 17 June 1902.

Under the terms of the Newlands Reclamation Act, the secretary of the interior was authorized to locate and construct irrigation works in the sixteen states and territories located in the western United States. Funds for construction of those projects were to come from the sale of public lands within those states and territories. Following completion of project facilities, land would be opened for settlement under provisions of various homestead laws and in tracts no larger than 160 acres. The acreage limitation was designed to prevent land speculation and to encourage homesteading by individuals and families–a major focus of western irrigation supporters.

Within weeks following passage of the act, the Reclamation Service was formed under the jurisdiction of the U.S. Geological Survey. Frederick H. Newell, chief of the Survey's Division of Hydrography, was appointed head of the new service and given the title of Chief Engineer. In forming the organization, Newell drew heavily from the ranks of his former division, appointing men who had been involved in western-resource surveys for nearly a decade. The first projects began to take shape in Nevada, Arizona, and other western territories and states. Soon, reclamation engineers began pushing the limits of dam-building technology, building larger and higher dams than had ever before been imagined, culminating with construction of the 350-foot-high Arrowrock Dam on the Boise River in Idaho. At the same time, the U.S. Army Corps of Engineers was expanding its role in water-resource development to include hydropower. Historically concerned with navigation and flood control, in the early twentieth century the Corps turned its attention to hydropower development with construction of Wilson Dam at Muscle Shoals on the Tennessee River, beginning a program of development that would see the Corps become the largest producer of hydropower in the United States.

The passage of the Boulder Canyon Project Act in 1928 signaled the beginning of the era of large, multipurpose water-resource development. The act authorized construction of Hoover Dam on the Colorado River, citing the primary benefits as flood control, navigation, hydropower, and irrigation. This legislation marked the first time that a major project had been approved citing multiple benefits, signaling the clear advance of the federal government into electrical-power production, and the beginning of basin-wide planning. Hoover Dam, at 725 feet high, was the largest dam in the world and held back two years of Colorado River flows, allowing the river to be turned on and off like a faucet.

The election of Franklin D. Roosevelt in 1932 provided a boost for western water-resource development, as new federally sponsored developments began to take shape on the Columbia and Missouri Rivers. In the East, the Tennessee Valley Authority (TVA) developed a series of dams and power plants that spanned seven states. The construction of Grand Coulee Dam on the Columbia River in Washington State during the latter part of the 1930s proved timely as the electricity it produced powered many wartime industries, contributing significantly to the defeat of the Axis powers.

Following World War II, large-scale water-resource development increased significantly as the Bureau of Reclamation and the Corps of Engineers combined in a coordinated program to develop the water resources of the Missouri River Basin. Development also intensified in California, and along the Colorado, Columbia, and Snake Rivers. In the early 1950s the Bureau of Reclamation proposed construction of a dam in Echo Park on the Green River in Dinosaur National Monument, Colorado. As part of a comprehensive plan to develop the Upper Colorado River Basin, Echo Park Dam was seen by many as unnecessary and an environmental disaster. An enormous campaign, led by the Sierra Club and other environmental groups, succeeded in defeating the proposed construction, signaling the beginning of the end of the era of large-scale water-resource projects.

In 1964 the Bureau of Reclamation completed construction of the controversial Glen Canyon Dam, the key feature of the Colorado River Storage Project. Towering more than seven hundred feet above the bed of the Colorado River, Glen Canyon Dam stands as a monument to the struggle between western-resource development and environmental protection. Project construction continued for two decades after Glen Canyon, but on a much-reduced scale: few new large-scale developments were authorized and several that had been previously authorized were never built or were canceled.

Glen Canyon Dam on the Colorado River in northern Arizona

(Michael Collier)

The increasing awareness of the environmental consequences of large-scale water-resource development contributed significantly to the growing opposition to such projects, and the Bureau of Reclamation and the Army Corps of Engineers, the two largest water-resource developers, received the bulk of the criticism. Also contributing to the opposition to water-resource development was a growing distrust of government and a lack of confidence in the necessity for such large-scale projects.

Much of the criticism that was leveled at the Bureau of Reclamation and the Corps of Engineers has significant merit. Large-scale water-resource developments are not without consequences. On many rivers, which once teemed with salmon and other migrating fish, fewer and fewer species returned each season, and some disappeared altogether. Entire species of aquatic life were replaced by nonnative species, which thrived in ecosystems altered by dam construction. Spectacular canyons were replaced with hundreds of square miles of flat-water reservoirs. Hundreds of communities, many of them Native American and Hispanic, were disrupted and displaced to make room for dams and reservoirs; often compensation has been minimal for lands that had been home to those communities for many generations.

While the negative consequences of dam construction were considerable, so too were the benefits. Dams and facilities constructed and operated by the Bureau of Reclamation, the largest single water supplier in the West, deliver water to more than thirty-one million municipal and industrial users, including irrigation and domestic water for fifteen Indian reservations; irrigate more than ten million acres of farmland that produce 60 percent of the vegetables, as well as 25 percent of the fruits and nuts, in the United States; and provide recreational opportunities for more than ninety million people each year. In addition, hydropower operations provide about one-third of the power generated in the West, and each year federally operated dams and reservoirs prevent $5 billion in damage caused by floods.

Although enormous, the benefits provided by large-scale water-resource projects cannot by themselves justify the environmental and cultural disruptions that they have caused. Without these projects, the West would not be what it is today, much to the delight of some. The reality of the situation is that large dams have become an integral part of the western landscape and will continue to be so well into the twenty-first century. Nothing can be done to restore the environment to its pre-dam condition, but the lessons learned during the past century can play an important role in reducing the negative effects of water-resource development.

At the beginning of the twenty-first century, significant research was under way aimed at mitigating the negative effects of dam construction. Federal agencies and environmental groups were investigating ways to recover fish and wildlife species and restore riparian and wetland habitats. Solutions under investigation included increased instream flows, reservoir-release temperature-control programs, river and stream channel restoration, and water-quality improvement programs. Studies looked at the removal of several dams that outlived their economic lives and no longer provided sufficient benefit to justify their continued operation. In addition, federal agencies involved in water-resources management were working to fulfill their trust obligations to Native American nations and tribes and provide those communities with a share of the benefits for which they so dearly paid.

A century of water-resource development in the American West helped turn it into one of the most livable regions in the United States, while at the same time threatening to undo much of the beauty and environmental diversity that attracted people to the region. Through close and thoughtful examination of past developments and the conscious application of the lessons learned from these past endeavors, dams, the ultimate expression of the built environment, and the diverse natural environment of the West can exist in balance, each providing significant and needed benefits to the people of the region.

—JOE SIMONDS, U.S. BUREAU OF RECLAMATION

Viewpoint: Big dams provided much-needed flood control, storage, irrigation, and power, but those who designed and built them overlooked impacts on communities and the environment.

The history of environmental change in the twentieth century includes alterations to the natural world, visible and invisible. Among the visible changes, air and water pollution, suburban sprawl, and structures for storing and conveying water were among the most prominent. Perhaps no single aspect of mankind's built environment has been as potent a symbol of environmental transformation as the large dams constructed in the American West during the Great Depression (1929–1941). President Franklin D. Roosevelt, determined to alleviate unemployment as part of the New Deal, made it a priority to build a series of dams and power plants along the seven-state course of the Tennessee River. The Tennessee Valley Authority (TVA), authorized by Congress in 1933, was aimed at water "development" for flood control, navigation, and power generation as well as counteracting the Depression across a major region in the South. The TVA, a federal agency possessing considerable authority, was a success story in terms of power generation and in spawning industrial growth, though it also proved costly to thousands of farmers whose land was inundated. The regional-development concept underlying the TVA was never implemented elsewhere, in part because private power companies stoutly opposed valley authorities on the Columbia and Missouri Rivers. Nonetheless, the Roosevelt administration spurred regional economic growth by authorizing Grand Coulee Dam on the Columbia and Fort Peck Dam on the upper Missouri in Montana, and completed Boulder Dam on the lower Colorado, which had been authorized during the Coolidge administration.

Each of these large-scale public-works projects in the South and West employed tens of thousands of people during the peak of the Depression, and became symbols of the New Deal response to economic catastrophe. Boulder Dam, like Grand Coulee, was multipurpose, designed to control damaging floods, supply municipal water to Los Angeles, generate power for the Southwest, and—almost as an afterthought—provide recreation in a desert region. All of these dams provided substantial unemployment relief, set in motion regional economic development, and captured the allegiance of a coalition of big dam supporters, including power cooperatives, farmers and ranchers, and banks and construction firms.

While the New Deal launched the big dam era, World War II (1941–1945) and the ensuing Cold War intensified and extended the dam-building program. Demands for power and flood control, coupled with lofty visions of urban and industrial boosters, produced record budgets for the U.S. Army Corps of Engineers and Bureau of Reclamation. The latter finished Shasta Dam on the Sacramento River in northern California and Friant Dam on the San Joaquin in 1945, two major dams of the Central Valley Project. Congress approved the Flood Control Act of 1944, authorizing the construction of several big dams along the Missouri River, including the Garrison and Oahe, constructed by the Corps of Engineers in North and South Dakota, respectively. Throughout the 1950s and 1960s, dams were built on the Missouri, Snake, Columbia, American, and Colorado Rivers, while in 1966 the Corps finished Kinzua Dam in Pennsylvania on the upper Allegheny River.

Marc Reisner, in *Cadillac Desert: The American West and Its Disappearing Water* (1986), called these the "go-go years" in big dam history, yet they produced more than simply an abundance of large dams. The period also gave rise to a set of assumptions about the benefits of dams that underlay a generation of thought about human mastery over watercourses in the nation. The first guiding principle held that technological design and engineering planning could at once control nature—"tame wild rivers," as bureau officials liked to say—while transforming water into a valued commodity. That notion wrapped itself around the visions of boosters, regional economic interests, and engineers who praised massive dams such as Hoover, Glen Canyon, and Grand Coulee. The very size of these dams was meant as a showcase of American engineering and national strength. Boosters fondly cited impressive statistics of the amount of concrete that it took to build the great dams, and likened them to the pyramids of Egypt and other feats of human labor to demonstrate U.S. determination and power over untamed rivers.

Another prevailing assumption during this period held that nature was imperfect and that dams would improve rivers. Whether the challenge was irrigating arid landscapes, supplying water to cities, or protecting valuable farmland from floods, engineers assumed that big dams offered the perfect solution. As for fish and other species that relied on rivers, they would thrive by the application of science and technology. Salmon would be saved from dams blocking rivers by fish ladders or by raising salmon in hatcheries and trucking them around dams to the sea. The big dams and their reservoirs would improve fishing, upstream and down. No sacrifice was needed.

A third assumption held that the economic benefits of dams transcended the costs to landowners and nearby communities. That notion made it possible to proceed with massive dams and reservoirs that flooded farmland in the Tennessee, Missouri, and Columbia basins and displaced many people from their homes and properties. Native American communities particularly suffered, sacrificing fishing spots, hunting and gathering lands, and burial grounds. Kinzua Dam on the Allegheny River inundated nine thousand acres of reservation land of the Seneca, including their Cornplanter burial ground and hunting lands. In so doing, one of the first Indian treaties, dating to President George Washington's administration in 1794, was broken. Garrison Dam on the Missouri flooded 152,000 acres of productive farm and garden lands in central North Dakota, home to the Three Affiliated Tribes; Bonneville and Grand Coulee Dams on the Columbia inundated Indian dip-net fisheries; and The Dalles Dam erased the revered fishing site at Celilo Falls, Oregon. Thus, functioning economies of the Native Americans and others were sacrificed to larger notions of economic and cultural "progress."

A final tenet was that the advantages of "improving" rivers by means of dams surpassed the benefits of maintaining river flows for fish and other wildlife and preserving scenic canyons and wild rivers. Yet, not all Americans agreed with that proposition. Beginning in the 1940s conservationists fought proposals for dams near Lake Solitude in the Bighorn Mountains, along the upper Selway and Clearwater Rivers in Idaho, and others that threatened wilderness areas and national parks and monuments. In the 1950s the bureau proposed dams on rivers flowing through Glacier and Grand Canyon National Parks as well as Dinosaur National Monument. Conservationists, fearful that the integrity of the park system was at stake, threw considerable effort into a national campaign against Echo Park Dam in Dinosaur, which they believed would set a dangerous precedent of permitting dams in the park system.

LARGE AND MAJOR DAMS BY COUNTRY

	LARGE DAMS (1986 DATA)		MAJOR DAMS (1994 DATA)	
1	China	18,820	USA	50
2	USA	5,459	CIS	34
3	CIS	c. 3,000*	Canada	26
4	Japan	2,228	Brazil	19
5	India	1,137	Japan	19
6	Spain	737	Turkey	11
7	South Korea	690	China	10
8	Canada	608	Germany	9
9	Great Britain	535	Italy	9
10	Brazil	516	Switzerland	9
11	Mexico	503	Argentina	8
12	France	468	India	7
13	South Africa	452	France	5
14	Italy	440	Mexico	5
15	Australia	409	Austria	4
16	Norway	245	Colombia	4
17	Germany	191	Iran	4
18	Czechoslovakia	146	Spain	4
19	Switzerland	144	Australia	3
20	Sweden	141	Pakistan	3

* The former USSR declared to ICOLD only the 132 large hydroelectric dams under the control of the Ministry of Energy and Electrification. If the dams built by the Ministry of Agriculture and local authorities were included, according to ICOLD, the number of large dams in the USSR (now CIS) should be 2,000–3,000. See text for explanation of ICOLD definitions.

Source: *Patrick McCully,* Silenced Rivers: The Ecology and Politics of Large Dams *(London & Atlantic Highlands, N.J.: Zed Books, 1996), p. 3.*

After a protracted battle, in 1956 groups such as the National Parks Association, Sierra Club, and Wilderness Society defeated the Echo Park Dam and ensured its removal from the Upper Colorado River Storage Project.

During construction of Glen Canyon Dam in northern Arizona in the late 1950s, conservationists and river runners became aware of the haunting beauties of the red rock country, prompting the publication of a lavishly illustrated volume, Eliot Porter's *The Place No One Knew: Glen Canyon on the Colorado,* by the Sierra Club in 1963. Meanwhile, conservationists campaigned unsuccessfully for a barrier dam to protect Rainbow Bridge from the rising waters of Lake Powell. Along with Echo Park and Glen Canyon, this battle provided the backdrop to the climactic confrontation over the proposed Marble and Bridge Canyons dams inside the Grand Canyon. The Sierra Club protest of those dams included full-page advertisements in *The Washington Post* and *The New York Times,* asking rhetorically, "Should We Also Flood the Sistine Chapel So Tourists Can Get Nearer to the Ceiling?" The resulting public outcry against the dams forced the Department of the Interior to abandon them in exchange for a coal fired power plant near Page, Arizona. The success of organized conservationists in stopping Echo Park and the Grand Canyon dams proved to be monumental triumphs at the dawn of the environmental movement in the 1950s and 1960s. The outcome of these celebrated campaigns that captured public attention reaffirmed the commitment to the national park system, while also contributing to the passage of the Wilderness Act of 1964 and Wild and Scenic Rivers Act of 1968.

While few could deny the significance of these triumphs, the fact remained that environmentalists lacked the power to stop most dams in the first part of the twentieth century. With little legal ground on which to stand, conservationists relied on economic, ecological, and moral arguments to combat the dams. In the early 1950s, for instance, the Oregon Fish Commission said that once the four dams on the lower Snake River were in place they would dramatically reduce the number of juvenile salmon reaching the sea. Although considerable scientific evidence bolstered its case, efforts to protect salmon were drowned out by the formidable clout of the business community, which championed the dams to make Lewiston, Idaho, into a seaport. Navigation and hydropower interests eventually carried the day and, beginning in 1961, the Ice Harbor, Lower Monumental, Little Goose, and Lower Granite dams were built. The Cold War also helped win approval of these dams, for it elevated the importance of hydropower availability to support the nuclear plant at Hanford. With no laws requiring public comment on the environmental effects of dams, builders had a free hand in conceiving of grand engineering and environmental manipulation of rivers and riparian habitat.

For this reason, passage of the National Environmental Policy Act of 1969 (NEPA) provided a legal weapon of signal importance to environmentalists. NEPA required the preparation of an environmental impact statement for all federal projects, and the lack of an adequate one could, and did, lead to litigation. In 1974 the Natural Resources Defense Council, Trout Unlimited, and the Uintah chapter of the Sierra Club filed a lawsuit in federal district court in Utah against the bureau for the inadequacy of its environmental impact statement on Upper Stillwater Dam and the Bonneville Unit of the Central Utah Project (CUP). The suit delayed the CUP for several years. The Audubon Society employed the same tactic to delay the Garrison Diversion Unit in North Dakota—a plan to transport Missouri River water to eastern North Dakota—which would mean inundation of thousands of acres of wetlands. Garrison too was delayed for years. Discovery of the snail darter in the Tennessee River, coupled with passage of the Endangered Species Act in 1973, held up the Tellico Dam.

Still, while NEPA and the Endangered Species Act empowered environmentalists against dams, these laws did not prevent the erection of thousands of the structures on American rivers. Taken as a whole, these dams instigated enormous ecological changes. Replacement of seasonally flooding rivers with huge fluctuating reservoirs dramatically altered the riparian habitats of birds and mammals and transformed riverine habitats of fish. On the Missouri River, the Garrison, Oahe, and Big Bend Dams and channelization of the riverbed greatly affected the habitat of birds, fish, and other wildlife and disrupted the streambeds and riverbanks. Glen Canyon Dam on the Colorado River created a clear and cold river downstream of the dam, giving rise to a prized trout fishery. Nonetheless, power demands make for fluctuating water levels downstream, eroding beaches in the Grand Canyon and eliminating fragile riparian habitats of plants and animals. Lake Powell traps phosphorous, a critical nutrient for sustaining fish in Lake Mead downstream. No rivers, however, reveal the damage caused by dams as starkly as the Columbia and Snake. These waterways provide transportation and hydroelectric power vital to the Northwest, but the dams and their turbines proved disastrous to salmon.

The emergence of these environmental problems contributed to the rapid demise of the big-dam era in the 1970s and 1980s. Environmental laws, along with important ecological research, left a residue of bitterness and regret about big dams. Furthermore, rising inflation and budget deficits crippled the dam-building agencies. There were furthermore few suitable dam sites left, while presidential administrations and Congress no longer backed the big projects with the energy that they had in the first two postwar decades.

The backlash against dams surged in the 1990s with a vigorous movement to knock down some of the most environmentally destructive dams. Environmentalists and others coalesced behind efforts to breach the lower Snake dams in Idaho, Savage Rapids Dam on the Rogue River in Oregon, two dams on the Elwha River in Washington, and even Glen Canyon Dam, which had become a symbol to many of the arrogance of mankind in manipulating the Colorado River. These efforts may not succeed, but the rapid emergence of the breaching movement within a few years in the early and middle 1990s, especially in the West, is perhaps the clearest sign that the once-treasured assumptions of the big dam era are largely gone. Most of the big dams remain, but the nearly universal acceptance of their social, economic, and environmental benefits that held sway in the early decades of the twentieth century no longer exists.

–MARK HARVEY, NORTH DAKOTA STATE UNIVERSITY

References

Stephen W. Carothers and Bryan T. Brown, *The Colorado River Through Grand Canyon: Natural History and Human Change* (Tucson: University of Arizona Press, 1991).

Philip L. Fradkin, *A River No More: The Colorado River and the West,* revised edition (Berkeley: University of California Press, 1996).

Mark W. T. Harvey, *A Symbol of Wilderness: Echo Park and the American Conservation Movement* (Albuquerque: University of New Mexico Press, 1994).

Beatrice Hort Holmes, *A History of Federal Water Resources Programs, 1800–1960* (Washington, D.C.: U.S. Department of Agriculture, Economic Research Service, 1972).

Holmes, *A History of Federal Water Resources Programs, 1961–1970* (Washington, D.C.: U.S. Department of Agriculture, Economics, Statistics, and Cooperatives Service, 1979).

Donald C. Jackson, *Building the Ultimate Dam: John S. Eastwood and the Control of Water in the West* (Lawrence: University Press of Kansas, 1995).

Michael L. Lawson, *Dammed Indians: The Pick-Sloan Plan and the Missouri River Sioux, 1944–1980* (Norman: University of Oklahoma Press, 1982).

Jaques Leslie, "Running Dry: What Happens When the World No Longer Has Enough Freshwater?" *Harper's Magazine,* 301 (July 2000): 37–52.

Keith C. Petersen, *River of Life, Channel of Death: Fish and Dams on the Lower Snake* (Lewiston, Idaho: Confluence Press, 1995).

Marc Reisner, *Cadillac Desert: The American West and Its Disappearing Water* (New York: Viking, 1986).

Martin Reuss and Charles Hendricks, *U.S. Army Corps of Engineers: Brief History,* 25 August 2000, Internet website.

Michael C. Robinson, *Water for the West: The Bureau of Reclamation, 1902–1977* (Chicago: Public Works Historical Society, 1979).

Robert Kelley Schneiders, *Unruly River: Two Centuries of Change Along the Missouri* (Lawrence: University Press of Kansas, 1999).

William Joe Simonds, "The Bureau of Reclamation and its Archaeology–A Brief History," *CRM,* 23 (2000): 5–8.

Jeffrey K. Stine, *Mixing the Waters: Environment, Politics, and the Building of the Tennessee-Tombigbee Waterway* (Akron, Ohio: University of Akron Press, 1993).

Joseph E. Taylor III, *Making Salmon: An Environmental History of the Northwest Fisheries Crisis* (Seattle: University of Washington Press, 1999).

U.S. Department of the Interior, *The Hoover Dam Documents,* prepared by Ray Lyman Wilbur and Northcut Ely (Washington, D.C.: U.S. Government Printing Office, 1948).

U.S. Department of the Interior, Bureau of Reclamation, *Investing in the Future: Fiscal Year 1998 Annual Report* (Washington, D.C.: U.S. Government Printing Office, 1999).

U.S. Western Water Policy Review Advisory Commission, *Water in the West: The Challenge for the Next Century: Report of the U.S. Western Water Policy Review Advisory Commission* (Arlington, Va.: The Commission, 1998).

William E. Warne, *The Bureau of Reclamation* (New York: Praeger, 1973).

William Bruce Wheeler and Michael J. McDonald, *TVA and the Tellico Dam, 1936–1979: A Bureaucratic Crisis in Post-Industrial America* (Knoxville: University of Tennessee Press, 1986).

Richard White, *The Organic Machine* (New York: Hill & Wang, 1995).

Charles F. Wilkinson, *Crossing the Next Meridian: Land, Water, and the Future of the West* (Washington, D.C.: Island Press, 1992).

BOTSWANA

Was a policy of fencing and borehole development wise for the management of the Kalahari Desert in Botswana?

Viewpoint: Fencing and boreholes promoted the expansion of the livestock industry that was essential for economic development in Botswana and consistent with the development objectives of the majority of its people.

Viewpoint: Fencing and boreholes promoted unsustainable exploitation of the Kalahari ecosystem at the expense of wildlife and wild foods upon which the livelihoods of rural people were based.

Much of the southern African nation of Botswana consists of the semiarid Kalahari (Kgalagadi) Desert. In the north are the swamplands of the Okavango Delta; to the east are the more-fertile and better-watered Shashe and Limpopo River watersheds. This 20 percent of the nation is home to more than 80 percent of the population.

The hunter-gatherer San people traditionally lived in the Kalahari Desert, subsisting on wildlife and wild plants. The more numerous (and urban) Tswana people predominated in the east, tending herds of cattle and small stock. Among the Tswana, wealth and power were traditionally derived from the possession of cattle, which were important for ceremonial and ritual purposes, cultivation of fields, and provision of meat, milk, and hides.

At independence in 1966, Botswana was one of the poorest countries in the world. Within five years conditions changed drastically: diamonds and beef became major export products. Substantial diamond mines were opened at Orapa (1971) and Letlhakane (1977) in the north and at Jwaneng (1978) in the southern Kalahari. Soon after independence the government established the Botswana Meat Commission (BMC), a parastatal with control over 90 percent of the purchase and slaughter of cattle, and nationalized the slaughterhouse at Lobatse. Then, in the early 1970s, the government negotiated favorable access to European markets for frozen Botswana beef.

As a signatory to the Lomé Convention (1975), Botswana secured a beef-export quota and 90 percent reduction in tariffs after Britain joined the European Economic Community (EEC, 1973). The Botswana livestock industry suddenly had a large market, but was unable to supply it. The lack of surface water in a semiarid landscape and frequent disease outbreaks limited the size of the national herd, while many farmers proved reluctant to thin their herds and sell to BMC, despite favorable prices. The government responded with a policy of commercialization and privatization of the livestock industry, through fencing and borehole development.

Unintended consequences have been a drastic reduction in wildlife populations and the loss of many important wild food resources in the Kalahari, with attendant constraints on the way of life of the indigenous San people, and a shift from renewable surface water to a dependence upon nonrenewable (fossil) water supplies.

Viewpoint: Fencing and boreholes promoted the expansion of the livestock industry that was essential for economic development in Botswana and consistent with the development objectives of the majority of its people.

The semiarid climate, periodic droughts, poor soils, and lack of perennial water supplies in Botswana, coupled with its "Protectorate" status of indirect colonial rule by the British, meant that at independence in 1966 it was one of the least-developed countries in the world. Rapid economic growth ensued, primarily caused by the exploitation of diamond reserves in the Kalahari, but also attributed to foreign aid and a generous European Union (EU) agreement on beef exports. The latter, termed the Beef Protocol, promoted livestock development in Botswana and led to the effective control of diseases through veterinary cordon fencing.

Wildlife and livestock populations in semiarid environments are not stable. Importantly, one should emphasize Kalahari wildlife populations were characterized by instability in the late twentieth century. That is, the population sizes of most large herbivores fluctuated dramatically by following the "boom" and "bust" cycles that coincide with "wet" and "dry" rainfall spells. Drought, disease, desiccation, and hunting pressures have therefore all been important in determining spatial and temporal variations in the size and nature of wildlife resources in the Kalahari.

In the severe drought of the 1980s the key large herbivore populations in the Kalahari, for example the wildebeest and hartebeest, experienced a drastic decline. Their numbers steadily increased in the following decade, although future recovery to their former levels seemed unlikely. Drought and veterinary cordon fences precipitated this decline, with the fences blocking the drought-related movements of wildlife to permanent water supplies. Subsequently, boreholes were drilled for wildlife in the protected areas of the Kalahari. The provision of these wells was funded by the EU in an attempt to establish a sustainable balance between wildlife and livestock sectors and to prevent the drought-related movements of wildebeest into areas that were dominated by livestock and people. It represented a costly, but effective, management tool that overcame the fact that development pressure had reduced the range of Kalahari wildlife.

During the colonial period, the desire to build up the national herd of the then-Bechuanaland Protectorate had been largely frustrated by repeated droughts and disease outbreaks. The rinderpest epidemic that swept through southern Africa in 1896–1897 had decimated the national herd. Drought and disease occurrences continued in independent Botswana, hindering efforts to establish the nation as a major supplier of beef to the world market.

Two developments were particularly critical in providing the means for a period of unprecedented growth in the livestock sector after independence: the introduction of deep-drilling borehole technology, which overcame the problem of a lack of surface water in the Kalahari, and the development of an extensive network of veterinary disease-control fencing, which overcame such crippling infections as foot-and-mouth disease.

As J. H. Cooke asserts in *Geography Journal* (1985), borehole technology, which was able to reach fossil aquifers several hundred meters below the sand, broke down the "age-old protection" that a permanent lack of surface water afforded to the Kalahari. Coupled with a lucrative tariff reduction on beef exports levied by the EU and increasingly privileged access to their markets since 1972, it provided for considerable expansion into sandveld pastures in the good rainfall years of the 1970s under the auspices of the Tribal Grazing Lands Policy (TGLP). The expansion took place into areas occupied by low-density hunter-gatherer populations, who moved to the boreholes and became incorporated into the livestock sector as herders.

Fencing to control livestock movements increasingly accompanied the drilling of boreholes in the Kalahari. Almost every livestock-related study conducted in the last thirty years of the twentieth century pointed to the ecological deterioration of the rangeland as a direct consequence of keeping excessive numbers of domestic stock. This contention received substantial support from environmental studies and observations, including the analysis of satellite imagery. Unfenced communal rangelands, in particular, were overstocked and overgrazed because of the absence of effective management that prevailed on fenced ranches with their own, effectively private, water supply.

Fencing the rangeland was therefore necessary to curb overgrazing and impose an effective system of management upon stocking rates in the livestock sector. Under a rotational grazing system using fenced paddocks, grazing land could be held in reserve and forage flows in the critical dry season more effectively managed. Moreover, fencing also enabled herd improvement through selective breeding, by separating bulls and weaners from the rest of the herd. One of the major

IMPACT OF THE NORTHERN BUFFALO FENCE

The Northern Buffalo Fence (NBF) to the north of the Okavango, was built in 1991 and completed in 1996 sealing off 7,200 square kilometres of wildlife habitat from the Moremi and Chobe National Parks and West Caprivi Game Reserve. The following report detailed some of the damage caused by the fence.

Editor's Note: *The inclusion of this sidebar in the chapter in no way reflects upon the views or work of Jeremy Perkins.*

One Bushman at Godikwa, an ex-DAHP worker who has worked on the fence for several years, said: "with my own eyes I have seen every kind of animal die along the fence, except for elephant. Many, many animals have been killed on the fence since 1991."

"It is very difficult to find the dead animals because they (vet. workers) take away the bones and bury the skins of the animals," says another Godikwa resident.

One man, who a few days prior to the interview, had witnessed veterinary workers remove the carcass of a zebra from the fence, said: "The veterinary workers will never talk to you about the dead animals because they are scared of losing their jobs."

Khwe of Godikwa, Shishikola, Dobega and Wosha, indicate substantial and ongoing deaths as a result of the NBF blocking natural wildlife movements. For the recently extended 45 km section (from beacon 566 northwards), the following deaths were reported by those interviewed:

•5 Giraffe — deaths reported for January to June

•2 Giraffe — deaths reported for July to September

•2 Buffalo — died in September

•2 Elephant (cow and calf) — died in September–not confirmed

•Roan (numbers unknown) — died in September

One old man at Dobecha described the death of one of the above elephants: "the front legs went into the fence between the cable and the wires and then the elephant fell forwards, over the fence on the other side. In that way it became trapped and died."

Informants say there are probably many other deaths they did not learn about as they rely on information from Bushmen moving through the area or from veterinary workers.

The people confirmed that wildlife to the west of the NBF was (at the time of interview) trying to go east towards the Kwando. "A lot of wildlife are trapped on this side (western). Many sable are also trapped and trying to get through," explained a resident.

Another resident of Godikwa said: "Animals now have no water on this side (western side) of the fence. . . . elephant and wildebeest are trying to get their water from leaves."

The headman of Shishikola also pointed out that: "The elephants have no water here and are trying to get to the Kwando River. They move mostly at night when it is cool and the big government trucks are gone."

Godikwa residents say predators have increased in their area because they are attracted by game that is now congregated against the western side of the NBF. They reported recent cases of deaths of dogs, horses and donkeys as a result of a concentration of lions in the area. . . .

Source: *Arthur Albertson, "Northern Botswana Veterinary Fences: Critical Ecological Impacts, January 1998,"* Okavango Wildlife Society, *Internet website.*

problems in the livestock sector was that about 70 percent of the cattle population and 90 percent of the goats were in the hands of communal producers. Since these rangelands were unfenced, overstocked, and poorly managed, a tragedy of the commons ensued, resulting in severe range degradation.

The direct link between communal land ownership and range degradation thus led to the privatization of rangeland and commercialization of the livestock industry. An improved contribution of the livestock sector to the GDP (gross domestic product), through increased off-take and export sales, and reduced range degradation through rationalization of access to and ownership of land, was expected to follow. Consequently, these twin pursuits formed the basis of official planning in the livestock sector in the early 1970s, a policy that was supported by a substantial amount of research, both locally and internationally. Moreover, animal production experiments showed that commercial ranches were twice as productive as traditional "cattleposts," such that the potentially detrimental economic effects of lower stocking rates on fenced ranches could be offset by higher animal productivity.

Fencing also controlled the spread of disease. Buffalo populations in northern Botswana were infected with SAT 1,2 1 and 3 FMD viruses that can be, albeit infrequently, transmitted to domestic cattle either directly or indirectly by antelope. There was also abundant evidence that buffalo/cattle transmission occurred on many occasions in Botswana between 1930 and 1980. Transmission was reduced only by the imposition of veterinary cordon fences for disease control that effectively separated livestock and buffalo populations and the use of more efficient vaccines. Fences were, therefore, a necessary prerequisite to the effective development of the livestock sector and growth of the economy through beef-export sales.

Other direct benefits of veterinary cordon fences included inhibition of wildlife and human trespass that provided protection against poaching; recognition by certain wild animals that fences separated safe and hostile territory; and reduction of the need for problem animal control in areas adjacent to game reserves. Indirect benefits included boundary reinforcement where fences were aligned, facilitating administration and law enforcement, as well as reducing land disputes; and allowing conflicting land uses in adjacent areas, although this practice was not necessarily desirable on ecological or economic grounds. Another benefit was that animals could be traced to their ranch of origin, a plan instituted by the EU so that individual animals could be returned to their owners. This "passport scheme" ensured that fencing would remain an integral part of livestock development in Botswana.

Fencing also promoted livestock development over wildlife-based tourism. While tourism represented the single-largest nonmineral income and employment industry in Africa, Botswana had not kept pace with the performance of its southern neighbors. The tendency in Botswana was for growth to be dominated by low yield, regional tourism, that of relatively short duration and little economic benefit to local rural people. A report by the Hotel and Tourism Association of Botswana (HATAB) stated that "the implementation of tourism policy has not been palatable to the private sector, particularly to the would-be local Batswana and resident businessmen." Consequently, tourism provided a poor rate of return to the local population, with the high-cost, low-volume market dominated by expatriate owners and operators. The livestock sector thus remained of primary importance to local people.

Indeed, as a representative of the Ministry of Local Government and Lands Permanent Secretary's Office put it, "The rearing of cattle in Botswana culture is basically the wish of every Motswana [person from Botswana]. I don't know if I can find something similar to that in Western culture. It is a given–and if you ever put any Motswana in a position where you are basically saying to them you may not have livestock you are interfering with their rights."

–JEREMY PERKINS, NATURAL RESOURCES AND PEOPLE, LTD.

Viewpoint: Fencing and boreholes promoted unsustainable exploitation of the Kalahari ecosystem at the expense of wildlife and wild foods upon which the livelihoods of rural people were based.

Semiarid ecosystems are primarily driven by variations in time and space of rainfall and nutrients, fire, and grazing. These factors interact and determine the structure, character, functioning, and dynamics of savannas. Plant growth is directly correlated with rainfall, as is the number of large herbivores. In the predominantly dry environment of the Kalahari in southern Africa, the dominant wild large herbivores have had to adapt to drought cycles and the pronounced variation in the distribution and occurrence of rainfall. The ecological constraints of low plant productivity and an absence of surface water has meant that the key to managing the animal populations is to keep the ecosystem open and flexible.

The earliest and most comprehensive study of Kalahari wildlife commissioned by the then-European Economic Community (EEC) stated that: "What is certain is that the two very large populations of hartebeest and wildebeest display one outstanding characteristic: mobility. . . . It must be assumed that this nomadism is one of the preconditions of their success which means that to curtail it is to risk what might well prove massive reductions in their populations."

Despite this fact, during the last thirty years of the twentieth century there was an unprecedented increase in fencing in the Kalahari, both for disease-control purposes and the "management" of both livestock and wildlife populations. Disease-control fencing was greatly boosted by the Beef Protocol, a lucrative subsidy on beef exports offered to Botswana by the European Union (EU) since the early 1970s. Like all Third World countries aspiring to export beef to Europe, Botswana was thus required to meet high standards of veterinary hygiene and disease management. The primary concern was foot-and-mouth disease harbored by Cape buffalo populations. Export beef cattle had to be separated from buffalo by an extensive network of veterinary cordon fences. Initiated by the British Protectorate government before independence in 1966, the network of fences were thus greatly extended and consolidated in order to meet stringent disease-control requirements laid down by the Beef Protocol.

As a direct result of these fences, many wild-animal populations found essential seasonal, and more critically drought-related, movements blocked by disease-control fences. Consequently, the severe drought of the 1980s saw an unprecedented decline in Kalahari wildlife populations: approximately 90 percent of wildebeest and hartebeest–approximately one half million animals–perished from 1982 to 1986. Moreover, many antelope, while not actually perishing on the fences directly, were channeled into high-conflict zones with people and livestock, where they inevitably succumbed. The vast Kalahari wildlife resource surveyed in the 1970s, which potentially offered enormous wildlife utilization and tourism potential for rural communities, thus experienced an unprecedented drought-related die-off because of the direct effects of thousands of kilometers of veterinary disease-control fencing.

Recovery of the key Kalahari ungulate species to their 1970s levels was unlikely because

An animal cordon fence in the Okavango Delta, Botswana

(NHPA/Anthony Bannister)

much of the former range had been occupied by livestock expansion, and/or remained blocked by disease-control fencing. Indeed, deep borehole-drilling technology had overcome the age-old problem of the Kalahari, a lack of surface water, thus enabling livestock to move into the desert on a permanent basis. As a result resource use in the Kalahari was changed entirely, displacing the hunters and gatherers who lived there and creating a dependency upon milk and beef products, as wildlife populations and natural food resources declined.

There was much international controversy and criticism of the wildlife conservation policies of Botswana, particularly relating to the wildlife declines that occurred in the 1980s. As a result, the EU funded the provision of boreholes for wildlife in the Kalahari late in the 1980s. Artificial water provision within this ecosystem, however, while appearing to be the logical solution, created fundamental conservation dilemmas, not the least of which was the disruption of a wilderness area.

The ecological integrity of the wilderness was disturbed, especially as water-independent herbivores were disrupted through grazing depletion and the attraction of predators to the watering points–the "canteen effect." The presence of surface water, moreover, threatened to result in the outbreak of such waterborne diseases as anthrax. An even more fundamental threat was that these changes opened the way for the possible removal of land from wildlife protection status for use by livestock.

> New range will be pioneered by traditional cattle-posts. . . . Game will be greatly reduced and displaced into final refuges defined by the one obstacle the stockman cannot yet overcome: lack of suitable groundwater. Such a process cannot be condemned . . . [provided decision makers are] aware of the consequences. In the context of game management there is no case for planned game use if this is only opportunistic pending its substitution by livestock.

The critical question in Botswana was the balance between livestock and wildlife sectors. Cordon fences necessitated the move from conservative "leave it alone, but keep an eye on it" to manipulative wildlife management, and increased conflict between wildlife, livestock, and people. Apart from being expensive to implement, such a policy was also risky. A growing body of ecological theory suggests that intensive management for the stability of large herbivore populations may actually compromise the resilience of the Kalahari system.

The existing wildlife management system, which was increasingly based upon fences and boreholes, appeared to be totally inappropriate for the varied and unpredictable Kalahari ecosystem. Indeed, critical realignments of key cordon fences and a visionary program, protecting essential wildlife refuge areas threatened by cattle, were needed to help redress the imbalance between the sectors. The creation of secure, fenced, disease-free enclaves for cattle around which Kalahari wildlife could freely move constituted a more flexible and sustainable route for both sectors. Instead, disease-cordon fences dissected the whole country, separating key wildlife species from critical refuge areas, threatening the persistence of some key herbivore species and the future of a growing tourism and wildlife-based sector.

Thirty years of desertification rhetoric in the Kalahari also served to reinforce the belief that fenced ranches and increased control of livestock movements were essential management initiatives to curb overgrazing and range degradation. Unfortunately, the substantial body of research pointing to the resilience of the Kalahari ecosystem, as well as the rationality of traditional pastoralists and their disinterest in destroying "the commons," has not been well received in Botswana. Similarly, alternative methods for assessing productivity have not been accepted by policymakers. The more open and flexible (in terms of livestock movements) cattlepost system, is in fact twice as productive as those of fenced commercial ranches–if productivity is assessed in terms on a per-hectare rather than per-beast basis.

Botswana thus appeared locked into a cycle of increasingly intensive management of both wildlife and livestock through increased fencing and borehole provision, as the government continued creating cattle and game ranches. This policy was ironic as surrounding countries in the region were increasingly removing fences in order to increase the spatial scale of wildlife movements, not least through the conversion of former cattle ranches to game reserves (for example, the Madikwe Game Reserve in South Africa) or the creation of large conservancies (for example, Nyae Nyae in northeastern Namibia).

Apart from threatening the resilience of the Kalahari ecosystem, it is also noteworthy that thirty years of livestock expansion under the Beef Protocol led to spiraling poverty and the greatest income disparities in the world. Wildlife presented a viable alternative, as DHV Raadgevend Ingenieursbureau stated in 1980: "Enhanced game use is seen as the best way to raise the standard of living of the greatest number of people in the Kalahari, particularly those who are the poorest." Increasingly intensive management of wildlife and livestock resources in Botswana through fencing and borehole water provision, facilitated to a large degree by the Beef Protocol, has therefore done little but direct the Kalahari along an unsustainable trajectory of development. This policy was unfortunate, as the general uncertainties created by the functioning of a semiarid ecosystem, not to mention a global warming trend, demanded flexibility that could only come from the clear recognition of existing ecological realities, rather than economic expediency. Moreover, a rapidly growing tourism and wildlife-based revenue, increasingly generated through community-based ventures, threatened to totally change the use of resources.

In a conclusion that applies with striking relevance to Botswana, Russell D. Taylor and Rowan B. Martin, in an *Environmental Management* (1987) article, pointed out that

> Under pressure from beef importers, it would be all too easy to adopt a policy that attempted to make the entire country disease free for cattle production, regardless of land capability. Wildlife populations would be reduced to those in a few heavily cordoned enclosures, grudgingly accepted to satisfy the conservation lobby. There is little reason for the developed world to influence land use in the marginal areas [of Zimbabwe] especially if it is short-term economic exploitation at the expense of land.

–JEREMY PERKINS, NATURAL RESOURCES AND PEOPLE, LTD.

References

N. O. J. Abel and P. M. Blaikie, "Land Degradation, Stocking Rates and Conservation Policies in the Communal Rangelands of Botswana and Zimbabwe," *Land Degradation and Rehabilitation,* 1 (1989): 101–123.

M. J. Coe, D. H. Cumming, and J. Phillipson, "Biomass and Production of Large African Herbivores in Relation to Rainfall and Primary Production," *Oecologia,* 22 (1976): 341–354.

J. H. Cooke, "The Kalahari Today: A Case of Conflict Over Resource Use," *Geography Journal,* 151 (1985): 75–85.

Cooke and R. M. K. Silitshena, "Botswana–An Environmental Profile," report prepared for UNEP Desertification Control Activity Centre (Gaborone: UNEP, February 1986).

DHV, *Countrywide Animal and Range Assessment Project,* seven volumes (Gaborone: Republic of Botswana, Ministry of Commerce and Industry, Dept. of Wildlife National Parks and Tourism, 1979–).

E. B. Egner and A. L. Klausen, *Poverty in Botswana* (Gaborone: University College of Botswana, 1980).

Government of Botswana, *National Policy on Agricultural Development* (Gaborone: Government Printer, 1991).

Garrett Hardin, "The Tragedy of the Commons," *Science,* 162 (1968): 1243–1248.

R. Lomba, *Buffalo Fences: Botswana's Shame, The Death Trap.* Collected papers on the Buffalo fence. (1991).

M. Mosienyane, "Livestock Production Impact on the Environment: Botswana's Experience," report of the Workshop on Environmental Impact Assessment Legislation (Gaborone: 2–4 December 1992).

J. Rowton, "Botswana's Wildlife on the Wrong Side of the Fence," *International Agricultural Development,* (1982): 18–20.

C. Skarpe, "Plant Community Structure in Relation to Grazing and Environmental Changes Along a North-South Transect in the Western Kalahari," *Vegetatio,* 68 (1986): 3–18.

Russell D. Taylor and Rowan B. Martin, "Effects of Veterinary Fences on Wildlife Conservation in Zimbabwe," *Environmental Management,* 11 (1987): 327–334.

World Trade Organization, *Report on Tourism* (Geneva: World Trade Organization, 1995).

CHESAPEAKE

Why has the Chesapeake Bay oyster population declined so precipitously during the twentieth century, and what is the best solution to the problem of declining yields?

Viewpoint: The oyster population declined because of natural downward cycles, disease, and poor water quality resulting from estuarine pollution and sedimentation. The best solution to the problem of declining yields is to employ limited, publicly funded repletion techniques that do not threaten the watermen's culture.

Viewpoint: The oyster population declined because of overharvesting, habitat destruction, and failure to implement adequate techniques of science-based management. The best solution is either to privatize the oyster commons and institute intensive cultivation practices or to establish permanent oyster-reef sanctuaries that are off-limits to commercial harvesting.

For more than a hundred years, scientists and watermen have clashed over the question of conserving one of the most renowned natural resources in the world—the Chesapeake oyster, *Crassostrea Virginica.* Throughout the late nineteenth and twentieth centuries, crises precipitated by falling harvest levels prompted passionate debates regarding how best to manage the oyster fishery. Several leading scientists, beginning with Johns Hopkins University zoology professor William K. Brooks, used these opportunities to promote what they believed to be the ideal solution—privatization of the oyster beds through leasing. They were continually frustrated, however, by the resource users—oystermen—who enjoyed disproportionate influence over oyster policy.

Harvesters and scientists have employed vastly different ideas of the natural world, the causes of oyster decline, and efficacy of science-based management. Oystermen's views usually dominated because legislators had everything to gain from defending the men who worked on the water and who possessed political clout. Until the reapportionment programs of the 1960s, commercial-fishing interests enjoyed disproportionately large representation in the Maryland General Assembly because each county possessed one senator, and the fourteen tidewater counties outnumbered the nine nontidal counties. Baltimore, which generated most of the support for oyster reform, suffered a great inequality in representation. Accordingly, politicians were disinclined to heed scientists and urban-leasing advocates because they comprised an insignificant constituency.

For decades the Chesapeake oyster decline provoked extensive interest because of its vital economic importance as one of the leading industries of Maryland and Virginia. For most years from the 1870s through the 1960s the oyster industry of Maryland constituted the largest such endeavor in the United States and one of the largest in the world. Oyster policy took on central importance in Maryland soon after the passage of the first oyster law in

1820, which outlawed dredging and prohibited outsiders from catching and selling oysters from the Chesapeake Bay. Maryland legislators were responding to the influx of New England dredgers who had already depleted their own resource base. Oysters soon became the most legislated topic in Maryland history.

Republication of Brooks's popular book *The Oyster: A Popular Summary of a Scientific Study* (1891) in 1996 confirms his relevance in a controversy that continued to simmer at the end of the twentieth century. In contrast to the multimillion-bushel harvests of previous decades, production levels barely reached half a million bushels per year. Maryland and Virginia harvest levels reached their historical nadir during the 1993–1994 season. Despite improvements in harvests and increased funding for oyster restoration, distinct perceptions of the causes of, and solutions to, oyster decline continued to divide researchers and resource users.

These essays use the terms "watermen" and "oystermen" synonymously, although they are not exactly the same. "Waterman" is an old English word for a commercial fisherman, revealing the long-standing influence of seventeenth-century English settlers in the tidewater region. An oysterman is a waterman, but a waterman is not necessarily an oysterman. Chesapeake watermen historically made their living harvesting a wide range of species, including oysters, crabs, clams, terrapins, eels, waterfowl, rockfish, shad, and other finned fish. Oysters provided the most income for watermen until the 1960s, but since they worked for only eight months of the year (September through April), oystermen usually augmented their pay by gathering other species during the spring and summer interim.

Viewpoint:
The oyster population declined because of natural downward cycles, disease, and poor water quality resulting from estuarine pollution and sedimentation. The best solution to the problem of declining yields is to employ limited, publicly funded repletion techniques that do not threaten the watermen's culture.

During the twentieth century, commercial fishermen of the Chesapeake Bay region pointed to a wide range of causes for the historic declining harvests of the American oyster (*Crassostrea virginica*). Pollution, disease, sedimentation, salinity-reducing spring rains and snowmelt, and natural predators such as skates and crabs have all been blamed for killing off oysters. Watermen also attributed low harvests to circumstances that prevented or dissuaded them from gathering their crop, such as bad weather, governmental regulation, falling market demand, and competition from out-of-state providers of oysters, which may have depressed prices enough to make oystering uneconomical. They even challenged official harvest figures, claiming that actual harvests were much higher but underreported. Fisheries officials questioned the extent of underreporting, the practice whereby watermen sold their catch directly to restaurants rather than seafood dealers, who had to report and pay state taxes on the goods.

Despite the variety of causes cited, oystermen rejected overharvesting and oyster-bar destruction as important reasons for this decline. In fact, many considered themselves "cultivators," arguing that far from destroying oyster habitat, dredging extended the natural beds by reducing overcrowding and competition among young oysters. Dredgers worked in crews to harvest oysters from deeper waters by pulling a heavy metal frame with an attached mesh cage across an oyster bar. By contrast, tongers used a scissorlike instrument with facing rakes at the bottom to retrieve oysters from waters up to six meters deep, usually located in tributaries. Hand tonging is labor-intensive and slow-going, and thus was recognized as less environmentally damaging than dredging. Hydraulic patent tongs, in use since the 1950s, however, also removed chunks of natural oyster bars.

Watermen have blamed bad oyster harvests on poor water quality since at least the 1920s. Responding to complaints that the oil-refining industry in Baltimore was killing oyster, fish, and crab spawn, the Conservation Commissioner of Maryland testified before the U.S. House of Representatives in 1921 on the harmful effects of oil refuse on the oyster and fish industries. Maryland and other East Coast states later persuaded Congress to pass the Federal Oil Pollution Control Act of 1924. Moreover, typhoid outbreaks that were linked to raw oysters led Maryland officials to strengthen sewage-treatment standards and hygienic requirements of seafood processors.

Despite legislative attempts to improve water quality, the Maryland Chesapeake oyster catch continued to decline, from five million bushels in 1920 to less than two million bushels ten years later. Memories of the fifteen-million-bushel catch of 1885, however, highlighted the dreadful state of the oyster fishery. Oyster-

Fishermen bringing in a catch in the Chesapeake Bay, 1954

(Marion E. Warren)

men asserted that chemical pollutants, natural downward cycles, or even God's harsh judgment had rendered the Chesapeake Bay "dead."

Explaining the oyster decline by citing the death of bay waters was a shrewd tactic on the part of the watermen. Their reasoning shifted blame away from the oyster industry to more unmanageable entities: upstream, sewage-spewing industries and municipalities; foreign oil-leaking vessels; or the wrath of God. Such arguments redirected attention from the oystermen's responsibility for overharvesting the bay.

That reasoning is not to say that legislators failed to address the issue of overexploitation. While Virginia legislators liberalized their oyster-leasing laws in the early twentieth century, Maryland policymakers dealt with the problem of declining oyster yields by mandating technological inefficiency. Most Maryland oyster laws aimed to halt the depletion of public oyster bars by constraining technological innovation and entry to the commons through closed seasons, catch limits, cull laws, and bans on motorized boats and large dredges. By the 1920s, however, following steep harvest declines, support for more proactive solutions began to coalesce.

As in the 1890s, Maryland legislators refused to enact strong leasing laws because watermen remained steadfastly against the privatization of public-domain oyster bars. While private oyster culture may indeed have generated greatly increased production and profits for the tidewater people, leasing would have upset long-standing ways of life–altering the Maryland oyster fishery from an open-access resource to a labyrinth of bounded plots and the oysterman from an independent operator to a wage-earning employee. Of course, no waterman is completely independent, for he must rely on dealers to turn oysters and crabs into cash. He deeply values his ability to work for himself, however, and accepts the risks of the unknown.

Privatization would have forced most watermen to foresake oystering as a vocation, because they lacked the disposition and capital assets to farm shellfish. Watermen had no desire to trade their freedom for farming responsibilities. Indeed, aquaculture is more difficult than land farming, since the crops are more vulnerable to environmental changes and hidden beneath the surface of the water. Moreover, underwater farming requires long-term, extensive capital outlays, mainly for the purchase of broodstock. Since seed oysters require three years to reach marketable size, the oyster grower must wait at least that long for a return on his investment, during which time any number of natural disasters could destroy the crop. Commercial fishing in the Chesapeake Bay has historically not been a lucrative profession. Not only could watermen not afford to finance their own leased oyster beds, but also they could not qualify for bank loans, since many lived in virtual poverty.

Faced with the need to take constructive action, the 1927 Maryland legislature adopted the compromise solution of public oyster culture, which entailed seizing empty oyster shells from commercial packers and redistributing them, along with broodstock, on bay bottoms to serve as substrate for floating oyster embryos. The unpaid "acting biologist" for Maryland, Reginald V. Truitt, had recommended reshelling on the basis of large-scale experiments conducted over several years. French scientist Jean Jacques Coste had established the scientific value of shell repletion in the 1850s by showing that larval oysters would attach to shells, tile, or almost any hard substrate when placed near or on spawning oyster beds. Americans first began to return shells to oyster beds on which young oysters (floating embryos, or spat) could attach and grow occurred in Connecticut in 1874. Throughout the 1880s and 1890s Truitt's predecessor William K. Brooks called attention to the importance of reshelling "exhausted" bars.

The decision by the legislature to introduce public oyster culture was not universally accepted. Many watermen retained a great faith in the natural recuperative ability of the oyster beds and contended that all the depleted beds needed was "time to rest." One influential oyster packer, William E. Northam, refused to sell his extra shells to the state on the grounds that "the trouble lies not in the scarcity of shells but in the absence of spat." Blaming "industrial waste" for the absence of embryonic oysters in the Chesapeake Bay, Northam asserted that spreading shells on bottoms was "pure wastefulness" and that the money should be used instead to fund experiments to spreading produce a greater amount of spat in the bay and tributaries.

In his 1929 doctoral dissertation on the Maryland oyster industry, Truitt discerned three attitudes among oystermen regarding the question of oyster rehabilitation. Those people, such as Northam, who believed that either pollution or divine judgment rendered the waters barren, considered attempts to restore the natural bars an extravagant waste of time and money. Others contended that the bay was momentarily dead, but that enormous production would recur once nature had passed through its cyclic depression—thus, it was useless to attempt that which nature would eventually achieve. A much smaller third group considered the bay still potentially prolific; Truitt believed them to be the most open to outreach attempts by conservation agencies.

Intriguingly, as the shell-repletion program continued through the 1930s, oystermen gradually grew more receptive to the idea of oyster rehabilitation. They realized that the planting program helped them doubly by employing them in the off-season to haul and distribute shells and by increasing the number of marketable oysters. During this decade Maryland legislators endorsed oyster-conservation policies that resembled the actions of federal New Deal agencies. Just as the Public Works Administration (PWA) spent millions of dollars on projects to increase employment and stimulate spending, the shell and seed-planting program paid watermen to keep them busy and get oysters into circulation. This experience showed that conservation need not involve leasing, thereby causing many oystermen to temper their opposition toward resource management.

Although they may have grown more sympathetic to the principle and practice of sustainability, that change did not mean that oystermen were willing to surrender management responsibility to university experts. Legislators ensured tidewater dominance of restoration efforts by giving oystermen decision-making authority. Those who accepted the principle of shell repletion believed shells should be planted on barren bars where they or their fathers had taken good oysters. This attitude frustrated Truitt and other biologists, who argued that commissioners should utilize scientific techniques to verify the presence of adequate larvae in areas to be reshelled.

Shell planting achieved legal status because it was substantially preferable to leasing, which was out of the question because of the hostility of oystermen, who comprised a powerful voting bloc. Though some oystermen rejected all cultural operations in the belief that natural bars could revitalize themselves, others grew more receptive toward reshelling and seeding natural beds, since these methods seemed of some use.

Moreover, shell repletion worked from a legislative standpoint because it represented a compromise favoring oystermen at the expense of oyster packers. Oystermen tended to begrudge seafood processors, who profited at their expense. Although packers possessed substantial economic assets, oystermen vastly outnumbered them. Legislators had much less reason, therefore, to oblige packing interests.

Finally, shell and seed planting did not involve calculated methods of resource-use adjustment. States such as New Jersey and New York began to integrate laboratory procedures—

for example, artificial hatching and the breeding of selective strains—into oyster management in the 1920s and 1930s. The system employed by the Maryland Conservation Department, however, left oyster reproduction to chance; humans only helped the process along by supplying the necessary substrate for spat. Legislators believed that dumping shells onto oyster beds did not require special training. Of course, Truitt and other biologists disagreed, asserting that shell repletion was a technical enterprise requiring scientific expertise.

While the shell-planting act incorporated biologists' proposals, policymakers remained receptive to scientific knowledge only to the extent that it did not demand drastic change. Legislators seized upon the reshelling component of Truitt's plan as a low-cost, low-level technology that would maintain production with minimal social disruption. Truitt had argued that public shell planting was useful only as an adjunct, not as the whole program of oyster rehabilitation. Yet, unlike private oyster culture, the state-run shelling and seeding program did not challenge the oystermen's perceived right of virtually unlimited access to the oyster commons. They were only excluded for brief closures of limited reserve areas. When reopened, such areas benefited harvesters in the form of mature oysters that otherwise might not have existed.

Public oyster culture, in the form of shell and seed repletion, represented a compromise effort to resolve the conflicting demands of scientific knowledge and democratic decision making. It combined an inadequately funded fact-finding system and a responsive political decision by those personally concerned with the fate of the watermen, and also represented a compromise effort to reconcile tensions between economic values and social values. Legislators from the tidewater counties abided by their constituents' wishes to maintain the watermen's traditional way of life by disallowing large-scale leasing.

Administrative changes resulting from the 1927 shell-planting law had important effects on oystermen's attitudes. Oystermen's participation in reshelling and reseeding activities integrated them into a system of conservationist and managerial responsibilities for sustaining the fishery. To the extent that shell planting helped maintain oyster reefs by restocking cultch for spat attachment, oystermen saw that they could help restore formerly productive areas on a limited basis, and thus, neither acts of God nor nature alone controlled oyster abundance. Furthermore, replenishing public oyster bars during the spring interim, between the oyster and crab seasons, facilitated their acceptance of seasonal state employment while allowing oystermen to keep their self-identification as autonomous men. Far from reducing oystermen's rights, state-administered cultivation programs began to represent public subsidies to the oyster industry. Watermen accepted the management goal of sustainability through the conservation measures of shell and seed planting, so long as packers and the state paid the majority of the cost and gave them a voice in selecting areas for rehabilitation.

For all these reasons, shell planting became the principal means of oyster restoration in Maryland for seventy years, during which time the fisheries agency prevailed upon the General Assembly to pass a series of laws increasing the amount of shells the state could obtain from packers. The legislature complied time and again because shell planting, and the associated activity of transplanting seed oysters to good growing areas, represented the most politically acceptable resolution to the oyster problem.

Maryland oyster harvests hit rock bottom in the early 1960s; oystermen and packers gathered and processed barely a million bushels a year. The need for better oyster management practices led officials to establish a new repletion policy. Rather than depending on packers for the shells that formed the literal foundation of public oyster culture, officials sought a new source of cultch. The discovery in 1959 of seemingly infinite quantities of fossilized shell beneath the layers of sediment and mud in the Chesapeake Bay was immediately recognized as a godsend. This resource, and the invention of equipment to extract it cheaply, strengthened the intention of the state to greatly expand the public-planting program. Yet, oystermen were skeptical, since fossilized shells tended to disintegrate when handled. They rejected test results indicating that old shells were at least fifty percent effective as fresh ones. As one "old-time Eastern Shore waterman" explained to *The* (Baltimore) *Sun,* "It's throwing good money after bad. Those shells under the mud are blue and black and lifeless. They'll get very little spatting from the likes of that junk. And before they get through stirring up the mud, they'll probably silt up the good rocks and smother the few oysters we now have."

Despite initial resistance, watermen soon accepted the utility of the fossil-shell repletion program, with the aid of substantial subsidies from the Maryland taxpayers. In the 1970s, Maryland began producing disease-free spat and seed oysters in state-owned hatcheries for planting in areas off-limits to commercial harvesting ("sanctuaries"), and on the public-domain oyster bars. At the end of the twentieth century, watermen continued to work as seasonal state employees by stocking hatchery-reared speci-

OYSTER WARS

Watermen (and they are nearly all men) know the locations of most large oyster bars. Many have been charted on maps and almost all have names. Dize says Snake Rip "is just one of the bars we catch oysters on over on this side of the Bay. On the other side, we've got lots of bars to work, too, although there are a lot fewer than there used to be."

No one knows exactly how much of the Bay bottom is covered with oyster bars, but it's thought that the area of the Chesapeake supporting oyster beds has significantly declined over the last 100 years, according to Dorothy Leonard, former director of fisheries at the Maryland Department of Natural Resources (DNR). . . .

This scoop, which watermen call a lick, has brought up nearly 100 oysters, all keepers, meaning they are more than three inches long. "Not every lick comes up like this one," Dize says. "We been out here all morning, got some good licks then but then not much after lunch but about 15 oysters a lick until this one."

"Well, that was the marine police [the DNR] checkin' up on us," Dize says. "It's all pretty friendly with the patrol boats most of the time now, but you should have been out here 30, 50, even 100 years ago. Then, everybody was shootin' at everybody else, the marine police was called the Oyster Navy and murders happened at least once a week, if not once a day."

The oyster wars occurred in the decades after the Civil War. Almost 7,000 men fought on the Bay over oysters until the resource was nearly exhausted in the early 20th century, according to John Wennersten, author of *The Oyster Wars of Chesapeake Bay.*

First, shallow-water tongers, with wood-and-metal tongs that brought up relatively few oysters, fought with deeper-water dredgers, whose scooplike tools nearly wiped out the Chesapeake oyster.

Later, Wennersten writes, "hostilities became more political, with Maryland and Virginia violently disputing their state boundaries for the sake of oyster-fishing rights in the Bay and in the Potomac River."

A boom-and-bust business with the same get-rich-quick spirit of the gold and silver mines of the West, oystering on the Chesapeake knew no bounds in the mid- to late 1800s.

Oyster-packing houses sprang up around the Bay, with the greatest concentration in and around Baltimore. This coincided with the building of the Baltimore & Ohio Railroad.

As trains moved into the hinterlands, packers sent tons of oysters westward as fast as watermen could land them. Before the rail line, oysters had gone by wagons throughout the Midwest, giving rise to a countrywide appetite for the mollusk. The new railroad was a boon to the oyster industry, by 1860 carrying 3 million pounds of oysters a year to points west and to northern cities.

Who was catching all these oysters? Watermen, by the hundreds. In the oyster season of 1869–70, for example, 563 vessels were licensed in Maryland to dredge for oysters. They carried about 800 bushels a load. This lust for Chesapeake oysters led to what Wennersten calls "hell on the half-shell."

With attacks, counterattacks and piracy rampant on the Bay, the Oyster Navy tried to control the looting and shooting. But the conflict raged, with many people on both sides being killed, ambushed in marshy creeks night and day. A worsening lack of oysters finally halted the mayhem.

Only when oyster stocks had been pillaged and too few were left to be worth fighting over, did the oyster wars cease in the mid-20th century.

"There's still guys alive who remember the most recent round," Dize says. "In fact, one of 'em comes down to the dock sometimes when we come in. He's now an oyster buyer for a company, but he used to work for the Oyster Navy in the 1950s and '60s, although I think it was called the marine police by then.

"I know some of these guys got shot at more than once out here. But that never, that I know of, happens nowadays. Now, dredgers and tongers work side-by-side on the Chesapeake, just tryin' to survive. Aren't enough oysters for a squabble."

Source: *Cheryl Lyn Dybas, "Oystering in the Chesapeake Bay: A Proud Tradition Clings to a Scarce Resource,"* Washington Post, *14 January 1998, Internet website.*

mens on the 285,000 acres of public oyster grounds in Maryland.

Since the 1980s watermen have blamed disease as a primary cause of the deterioration of the public oyster fishery. The protozoan parasitic diseases Dermo (*Perkinsus marinus*) and MSX (*Haplosporidum nelsoni*) kill young oysters in high-salinity waters before they reach harvestable size. These two diseases had a major negative impact on the Maryland and Virginia oyster industries in the 1960s and again in the 1980s and 1990s. Maryland fishery officials attempted to minimize their spread by restricting the movement of diseased oyster seed into salinity zones less favorable for Dermo and MSX, and by establishing sanctuaries in areas least susceptible to the parasites.

During the late 1990s, newspaper articles in the Chesapeake region reported that evidence of increasing disease tolerance and slightly rising annual harvests, combined with plans to rebuild oyster bars and increase oyster populations tenfold, sparked cautious optimism among scientists, watermen, environmentalists, and management officials. Popular newspaper and television accounts testified to a growing sense among the stakeholders that oyster restoration needed to be a cooperative effort, and that failure to act would mark the final destruction of the oyster resource.

Yet, distinct perceptions of the sources of, and solutions to, the oyster decline continued to divide scientists and watermen. Scientists asserted that restoring the historic oyster populations in the bay would significantly increase water quality, stimulate submerged grass growth, and prevent outbreaks of toxic microbes such as *Pfiesteria piscicida,* which, unlike Dermo and MSX, can harm human health. Many watermen called instead for controlling sources of pollution and stopping shoreline development, which increases erosion and siltation of the oyster beds. Whereas most scientists approved of establishing oyster-reef sanctuaries, areas prohibited to commercial harvesting where oysters can grow and reproduce unmolested, watermen asserted the need to "work the bars" in order to prevent silt from smothering them. Despite widespread recognition of the immense filtering capacities of oysters, watermen opposed reefs as sanctuaries in Maryland and Virginia because of the enormous expense and, in their words, because "Oysters aren't going to clean up the whole bay." Despite the apparent emergence at the end of the century of a younger generation of watermen who were more inclined to accept scientists' ideas regarding the ecological significance of the oyster, watermen likely will continue to blame reduced stocks upon disease and natural biological cycles rather than overharvesting and will remain suspicious of expensive solutions that impede their free access to oyster beds.

–CHRISTINE KEINER, JOHNS HOPKINS UNIVERSITY

Viewpoint: The oyster population declined because of overharvesting, habitat destruction, and failure to implement adequate techniques of science-based management. The best solution is either to privatize the oyster commons and institute intensive cultivation practices or to establish permanent oyster-reef sanctuaries that are off-limits to commercial harvesting.

Scientists' perceptions of the causes of declining Chesapeake oyster harvests during the twentieth century differed markedly from those of resource users. Scientists deemphasized water quality and disease as crucial causes in favor of overharvesting and habitat loss linked with intensive fishing pressure, actions executed on public-domain oyster bars by oystermen.

Beginning in the late nineteenth century, prominent oyster researchers such as William K. Brooks, Francis Winslow, Ernest Ingersoll, and Charles H. Stevenson reported harvest declines in both the Maryland and Virginia portions of the Chesapeake Bay. From 1882 to 1884 Brooks chaired the Maryland Oyster Commission, which surveyed fifty-nine of the largest oyster bars to investigate allegations of overharvesting. The commissioners concluded that "the worst forebodings" of the imminent destruction of the oyster beds were fully warranted. Rather than condemning harvesters for overfishing, the report blamed consumer demand: "THE DEMAND HAS OUTGROWN THE SUPPLY." To prevent overharvesting, the commissioners recommended better enforcement of the license laws, temporary closures of spawning oyster beds, bans on the sale of young oysters, and shell repletion of worn-out oyster bars.

The most important proposal, however, was science-based oyster cultivation, performed with private financing. Brooks expressed deep concern that oyster beds in Maryland comprised a "commons," free to be exploited by anyone, without regard for the long-term viability of the industry. He assumed that a harvester had nothing to gain by allowing any oysters to remain underwater, since if he did not catch and sell them, someone else would. From his perspective, the Chesapeake oyster fishery personified an early example of "the tragedy of the commons," since such actions accelerated the destruction of natural beds. The "tragedy of the commons" refers to the far-reaching article on the problem of common ownership of natural resources, published in 1968 by biologist and human ecologist Garrett Hardin, who argued that a public pasture ultimately becomes overgrazed as each herdsman places more cows on the commons "to maximize his gain." Hardin's thesis predicts that individual users will maximize short-term gains by exploiting any common-pool resource to the point of environmental ruin. He asserted that the only way to conquer individuals' shortsighted abuse of a common resource is by imposing coercive governmental policies.

Many analysts have applied Hardin's thesis to the public Chesapeake oyster fishery. They argue that it makes economic sense for an oysterman to catch all the bivalves he can. Why leave a hoard of oysters on the bay floor with the expectation of later harvesting more mature, valuable specimens, when they will otherwise be taken by another oysterman, silted over, polluted, or killed by salinity-reducing spring floods? According to the tragedy-of-the-commons model, the common-property status of oysters precludes the development of a conservation ethic because the individual benefits of catching and selling oysters outweigh one's costs. Indeed, the costs of environmental decline to an open-access resource are distributed among all users, not any one individual.

Brooks and many succeeding scientists insisted that the best way to prevent such a tragedy was to impose private property rights upon the public oyster resource. By leasing oyster beds to those who had invested their own assets in "intelligent private cultivation" (he left the question of final sale "for future consideration"), Brooks reasoned that the entire bay could be made to yield billions of bushels. He considered "personal interest . . . the strongest motive which can exist to prevent the needless destruction of property." Carving up the oyster grounds into private holdings, therefore, would prevent the need for protective laws and expensive police enforcement.

After many legislative struggles, the Maryland General Assembly finally enacted a bill in 1906 that allowed individuals to rent up to thirty acres of barren bottom in county waters and up to one hundred acres in the bay beyond county boundary limits for the purposes of cultivation. To appease the oystermen, who feared losing their right of free access, the Haman Act barred corporations and excluded all natural beds. The law imposed so many restrictions on lessees that scientists considered it ineffective. Even so, oystermen felt so threatened that they mobilized to weaken the law further. In 1914 they convinced the legislature to change the definition of a natural bar to include leased areas that had provided oysters naturally five years before the law, thereby undermining the Haman Act.

Following Brooks, a succession of scientists including Caswell Grave, Reginald V. Truitt, Abel Wolman, and Isaiah Bowman—lobbied to privatize the Maryland Chesapeake oyster fishery in line with the actions of such nearby states as Virginia, Delaware, New Jersey, New York, and Connecticut. Because their studies revealed that water quality had not significantly changed since the 1880s, marine researchers of the 1920s declared there was no reason harvest levels could not be restored to the multimillion figures of the late nineteenth century. In 1925 Chesapeake Biological Laboratory director Truitt attacked the Maryland legislature for its failure to institute science-based management. With the exception of the Haman Law, he charged, "there has never been a single constructive forward looking attempt to rehabilitate the Bay." He denounced the General Assembly for merely aiming to "conserve" the oyster industry through restrictive policies regarding equipment and season of capture. Decisive action was needed to develop the natural resource: "Rehabilitation, alone, not conservation, can save the situation."

Truitt asserted that his research, like that of Brooks, suggested that the natural oyster bars of the Chesapeake could be restored within fifteen years so as to produce twenty million bushels a year. If the state would not allow private growers to assume the colossal expense of purchasing and planting shells, then the state should confiscate shells from packers. Failure to act immediately would "undoubtedly . . . be fatal to the industry." The 1927 legislature rejected leasing in favor of the compromise solution of public shell and seed-oyster repletion.

Efforts by scientists to enact strong oyster-leasing laws in 1927, 1935, 1937, 1947, 1949, 1953, and 1988, all failed spectacularly. They based their arguments for leasing on economic rationales, pointing out the immense profits to be made from scientifically cultivating the billions of offspring that would otherwise die. By adopting the economic logic of private oyster culture, the scientists did not realize that watermen had no interest in working for capitalist oyster farmers and that they preferred the gamble of harvesting to the assurance of a steady wage. Such attitudes were implausible within the elite circles of academe, especially during the Progressive Era (1890–1920), when the modern professions emerged along with veneration of the values of efficiency and "professionalism." Moreover, the scientists and their proleasing counterparts refused to consider that private property status might not ensure conservation, that private owners were just as likely to engage in overharvesting. Both during and after the Progressive Era, many scientists regarded private oyster culture as a panacea.

Although Brooks blamed declining oyster harvests on high market demand rather than overharvesting, succeeding scientists were much less hesitant about holding oystermen responsible. Indeed, scientists blamed overfishing long before pollution and disease were recognized as serious problems in the Chesapeake Bay. In the early 1930s scientists at the Chesapeake Biological Laboratory in Maryland, the oldest state-supported facility for biological research on natural resources, announced that water quality had not essentially changed since the peak production years of the 1880s. They suggested that certain areas of the Chesapeake Bay no longer supported oysters not because of pollution, but because oystermen's dredges had stripped the natural beds of broodstock and old shells required for cultch.

The Honga River represented a case in point of oyster-habitat destruction. In the 1880s the area was considered the finest seed bed in the Chesapeake Bay, and as late as 1914 it produced several thousand bushels. Yet, harvests had practically ceased since 1920. The bottom became overrun with eelgrass and algae, but microscopic analyses revealed plenty of larval oysters, presumably coming from a close source of brood oysters. Although some oystermen asserted that the waters of the Honga were dead, biologists viewed the depletion not as "evidence of an angry God, but . . . rather evidence of the greed of man," as one laboratory staffer wrote in *The* (Baltimore) *Sun*. In his words, "Science has established that depleted oyster bars of the Chesapeake can 'come back' if man would only give nature a little assistance." This was a great understatement, given the high costs of shell and seed repletion. Indeed, the tremendous expense of cultivation was the main reason scientists advocated leasing the beds to entrepreneurial oyster growers.

The watermen's accusation of poor water quality appeared to provide a great opportunity for marine researchers to demonstrate the value of their analytic tools and rehabilitative techniques. Testing the idea that the bay waters were "dead" and resistant to restoration efforts required biological, chemical, and physical studies. During the 1930s scientific studies of pollution in the Baltimore waters affirmed their immense assimilative capacity for industrial and municipal waste, thereby undermining oystermen's claims that pollution played a major role in oyster depletion. Yet, Truitt signaled a new consciousness among biologists in 1940 when he announced studies to reveal the possible "accumulative effect" of wastes upon the "delicate biological balance of Bay waters and the relationship of these changes to conservation." As Steven G. Davison and his co-authors observe in *Chesapeake Waters: Four Centuries of Controversy, Concern, and Legislation* (1997), their historical study of Chesapeake water-quality debates, Truitt's statement "sounded, perhaps for the first time, the warning that has been so much a part of the ongoing debate about the quality of the Bay."

The appearance of devastating parasitic oyster diseases in the Chesapeake Bay in the early 1960s helped establish an unprecedented level of respect for marine science, as reflected by greatly increased appropriations to the state biological laboratories. Yet, in their quest to develop disease-free, hatchery-reared spat, researchers focused on narrow aspects of oyster pathology and disease transmission, rather than on the broader relations between oysters and their physical environment. Scientific knowledge of MSX (*Haplosporidum nelsoni*) and Dermo (*Perkinsus marinus*) remained limited in the 1980s and 1990s, when these oyster diseases reemerged in the Chesapeake.

At the same time, however, knowledge of oyster ecology had increased enormously. In 1988 University of Maryland researcher Roger Newell calculated that the oyster population of the late nineteenth century would have filtered a volume of water equivalent to the entire Chesapeake Bay in three to six days, whereas the contemporary oyster population needed a year to filter the same volume of water. He suggested that the reduction of the oyster population to a mere 1 percent of its historic level might have exacerbated the effects of eutrophication (nutrient pollution) on the Chesapeake Bay ecosystem.

By the 1990s, many scientists attributed the enormous reduction of the oyster population, and concomitant declining harvests, during the past hundred years to the mechanical destruction of habitat and stock overfishing, rather than to disease and reduced water quality. As they argued, the decline in oyster landings began decades before parasitic epidemics, toxic pollution, and eutrophication gained recognition as significant problems in the Chesapeake Bay. Some scientists blamed not just overharvesting but also the dominance of fishery management systems by resource users, and the consequent failure of governments to implement needed science-based restoration measures. Such scientists accepted the "tragedy of the commons" model, which holds that resource users lack the incentive to conserve public-domain resources.

Recognition of the extraordinary ability of the oyster to filter impurities and its consequent role as a keystone species of the Chesapeake Bay ecosystem suggested new possibilities for oyster management. To restore the Chesapeake oyster population, scientists in the 1990s outlined four management strategies: implementation of a scientifically regulated fishery to control overharvesting; modernization of the shell repletion program through the use of operations research and system-analysis techniques; habitat replacement in optimal growth and survival areas; and establishment of protected broodstock sanctuaries in areas of high larval production and spat settlement. In January 1999 a group of oyster experts from Maryland, Virginia, and North Carolina developed a "consensus document," which upheld the principle that oyster management should recognize both the economic and ecological role of the bivalve and that the commercial fishery should be placed on a sustainable, nontaxpayer-funded basis.

Reef reconstruction constituted the most innovative and attention-getting strategy for oyster recovery. Scientists sought to incorporate the new recognition of the oyster's pivotal ecological role in water-quality restoration efforts by constructing permanent, three-dimensional oyster reefs. Such reefs consist of piles of shells and broodstock heaped high under the water in intertidal areas with excellent conditions for growing oysters. The reefs would restore healthy oyster populations by increasing the biomass available for water filtration, protecting oysters from smothering sediments, and providing habitat to complex communities of fish, crabs, clams, and other estuarine organisms. Because large oysters that survive disease infestations may be able to pass disease resistance to their offspring, and because a few large oysters clustered together can produce many more eggs than many small oysters, permanent reefs can also help restore the commercial fishery by populating adjacent oyster beds in harvestable zones. For these reasons, in the mid 1990s Maryland and Virginia designated more than 27,000 acres as "Oyster Restoration Areas," where commercial harvesting was prohibited. In addition, hundreds of "oyster gardens" sprang up along the shores of the Chesapeake Bay and its rivers, both in Maryland and Virginia. The state- and privately funded oyster-gardening program utilized the labor of citizens and school groups to restore reefs and promote respect for the role of the oyster as the ecological linchpin of the Chesapeake Bay ecosystem.

Political recognition of the oyster as an ecological asset, rather than as a mere economic commodity, was epitomized by two governmental acts. In June 2000 the governors of Maryland, Virginia, and Pennsylvania, as well as the mayor of the District of Columbia, signed the Chesapeake Bay 2000 Agreement, which among other goals aimed to increase the oyster population in the bay tenfold by 2010. Furthermore, in October 2000 the United States Congress approved more than $3 million for Chesapeake Bay oyster restoration efforts, a nearly fourfold funding increase. The funds were slated to be used to construct oyster reefs throughout the bay and to further develop the system of sanctuaries created by Maryland and Virginia. Such developments seemed to refute the long-standing sentiment first articulated by a *Harper's Magazine* journalist in 1894: "Politics is the bane of the oyster in the Chesapeake."

Educated observers of the "oyster question" in the late nineteenth and early twentieth centuries tended to believe that the disappearance of oystering as a full-time vocation would facilitate the renewal of Chesapeake shellfish populations. As scientist James L. Kellogg predicted in 1910, "But in the course of time—after the natural oyster beds have been destroyed—the tonger and the dredger of the natural crop will have disappeared. All opposition to oyster culture having vanished, the Chesapeake . . . will prove to be of greater value to the people on its shores than mountains full of silver and gold." By contrast, no twenty-first-century scientist would publicly applaud the extinction of traditional resource users; they are much more likely than their turn-of-the-century predecessors to respect watermen's concerns about conservation measures that threaten their time-honored way of life.

Yet, deep distrust persists among the two groups. For example, at one conference seeking to create a "consensus" for oyster recovery efforts, attended by approximately forty scientists and two watermen, the scientists scoffed at one of the watermen who claimed that his colleagues had dredged an experimental oyster bed by mistake. Later, an older researcher stated that his laboratory used to employ armed guards against oyster poachers. Though watermen themselves confess that the temptations of taking mature oysters from sanctuaries are hard to resist, threats of gunfire can hardly be expected to encourage their respect for scientific knowledge and solutions.

Scientists and watermen worked together, along with fishery managers and environmentalists, to formulate the Chesapeake Bay 2000 Agreement. Each side acknowledged that scientific cultivation was crucial to the salvation of both the oyster beds and the oystermen, although all opposition to oyster culture and reef construction had by no means evaporated.

—CHRISTINE KEINER, JOHNS HOPKINS UNIVERSITY

References

Karl Blankenship, "All Sides Agree Sanctuaries Key to Oysters' Recovery," *Bay Journal,* 10 (April 2000): 1, 8–9.

William K. Brooks, *The Oyster: A Popular Summary of a Scientific Study* (Baltimore: Johns Hopkins University Press, 1891; reprinted, 1996).

Brooks, James I. Waddell, and William Henry Legg, *Report of the Oyster Commission of the State of Maryland* (Annapolis: James Young, 1884).

Francis Taggart Christy Jr., "The Exploitation of a Common Property Natural Resource: The Maryland Oyster Industry," dissertation, University of Michigan, 1964.

Steven G. Davison, and others, *Chesapeake Waters: Four Centuries of Controversy, Concern, and Legislation* (Centreville, Md.: Tidewater Publishers, 1997).

Garrett Hardin, "The Tragedy of the Commons," *Science,* 162 (1968): 1243–1248.

William J. Hargis Jr. and Dexter S. Haven, *The Precarious State of the Chesapeake Public Oyster Resource* (Gloucester Point, Va.: Virginia Institute of Marine Science [reprint], 1995).

Tom Horton, *Bay Country* (Baltimore: Johns Hopkins University Press, 1987).

Anita Huslin, "Congress Approves Oyster Funding," *Washington Post,* 21 October 2000.

Ernest Ingersoll, *The Oyster-Industry* (Washington, D.C.: U.S. Government Printing Office, 1881).

E. L. J., "Old Shells, New Oysters," Baltimore *Sun,* 16 January 1960.

George W. Jeffers, "Solving the Secrets of the Bay," Baltimore *Sunday Sun Magazine* (24 July 1932): 3.

Paula J. Johnson, "'The Worst Oyster Season I've Ever Seen': Collecting and Interpreting Data from Watermen," *Journal of the Washington Academy of Sciences,* 76 (September 1986): 199–213.

Christine Keiner, "Scientists, Oystermen, and Maryland Oyster Conservation Politics, 1880–1969: A Study of Two Cultures," dissertation, Johns Hopkins University, 2000.

Keiner, "W. K. Brooks and the Oyster Question: Science, Politics, and Resource Management in Maryland, 1880–1930," *Journal of the History of Biology,* 31 (Fall 1998): 383–424.

James L. Kellogg, *Shell-Fish Industries* (New York: Holt, 1910).

Victor S. Kennedy and Linda L. Breisch, "Sixteen Decades of Political Management of the Oyster Fishery in Maryland's Chesapeake Bay," *Journal of Environmental Management,* 16 (1983): 153–171.

Varley Howe Lang, *Follow the Water* (Winston-Salem, N.C.: John F. Blair, 1961).

Tawna Mertz, "Can Bay's Oysters Make a Comeback?" *Bay Journal,* 9 (September 1999): 1, 10–13.

R. I. E. Newell, "Ecological Changes in Chesapeake Bay: Are They the Result of Overharvesting the American Oyster, *Crassostrea virginica?*" in *Understanding the Estuary: Advances in Chesapeake Bay Research,* edited by Maurice P. Lynch and Elizabeth C. Krome (Solomons, Md.: Chesapeake Research Consortium, 1988), pp. 536–546.

Garrett Power, "More About Oysters Than You Wanted to Know," *Maryland Law Review,* 30 (1970): 199–225.

B. J. Rothschild, J. S. Ault, P. Goulletquer, and M. Héral, "Decline of the Chesapeake Bay Oyster Population: A Century of Habitat Destruction and Overfishing," *Marine Ecology Progress Series,* 111 (August 1994): 29–39.

George D. Santopietro and Leonard A. Shabman, "Can Privatization be Inefficient? The Case of the Chesapeake Bay Oyster Fishery," *Journal of Economic Issues,* 26 (June 1992): 407–419.

"Shell Law is Held Useless by Packer," Baltimore *Sun,* 17 June 1928.

Charles H. Stevenson, "The Oyster Industry of Maryland," *Bulletin of the U.S. Fish Commission,* 12 (1894): 205–297.

Reginald V. Truitt, "Biological Contributions to the Development of the Oyster Industry in Maryland," dissertation, American University, 1929.

Truitt and P. V. Monk, "Oyster Problem Inquiry of Chesapeake Bay," *Third Annual Report of the Conservation Department of the State of Maryland* (Baltimore: 20th Century, 1925), pp. 25–55.

John R. Wennersten, *The Oyster Wars of Chesapeake Bay* (Centreville, Md.: Tidewater Publishers, 1981).

Francis Winslow, *Report on the Oyster Beds of the James River, Virginia, and of Tangier and Pocomoke Sounds, Maryland and Virginia, U.S. Coast and Geodetic Survey Report for 1881* (Washington, D.C.: U.S. Coast and Geodetic Survey, 1882).

COLUMBIA RIVER

Should the federal government have built The Dalles Dam that destroyed an important Indian fishery and cultural site?

Viewpoint: Yes. While The Dalles Dam negatively affected salmon runs and the Indian fishery and village at Celilo, it was a key component of the comprehensive development of the Columbia River Basin, which has formed the backbone of the region's economy.

Viewpoint: No. The Dalles Dam, which destroyed the dipnet fishery at Celilo and inundated old Celilo Village, was an agent of cultural and biological destruction that represented a direct violation of the Indian treaties of 1855.

Wherever dams are constructed, they fundamentally alter a people's relationship to the riparian ecosystem. Nowhere is this situation more true than along the Columbia River watershed of the Pacific Northwest; since the late 1930s, it has been the site of a tremendous investment of financial capital and human energy that has produced a vast network of dams that regulate thoroughly the flow of the river. Channeling its current has redirected human utilization of the biota of the Columbia, in the process transforming social structures and cultural systems.

For many, the development of a mainstem dam such as The Dalles in Oregon was of crucial importance. It enabled agricultural and industrial interests to make use of more-placid waters to barge goods and services between inland ports and the Pacific Ocean; it produced electricity from its hydropower plants that was essential to the industrialization of the Pacific Northwest in the post–World War II era. Without Columbian kilowatts, neither airplane manufacturing, nuclear-weapons production, nor the more-recent boom in computer technology would have been possible. Through massive federal spending, The Dalles and other dams created considerable quantities of high-skilled work in metropolitan centers, and this surge in jobs propelled the region to the forefront of the robust, late-twentieth-century American economy.

There was (and is) much criticism of this new hydraulic river system, and it was (and is) focused on a dramatically different set of outcomes. By controlling the flow of the river, dams such as The Dalles destroyed the rich salmon runs that were an ancient component of Native American life in the Pacific Northwest. Bound up with this destruction was the related devastation of the physical world in which the indigenous people lived. In particular, the Nez Perce, Umatilla, Warm Springs, and Yakima tribes lost their economic access to the river and its former life-sustaining nutrients; the place of the river in indigenous cosmology disappeared as well. As the waters rose behind The Dalles Dam, once-important villages such as Celilo, which lay at the heart of Indian interaction with the river, were inundated; also disappearing from view were venerated burial grounds. The new river buried the old.

Viewpoint: Yes. While The Dalles Dam negatively affected salmon runs and the Indian fishery and village at Celilo, it was a key component of the comprehensive development of the Columbia River Basin, which has formed the backbone of the region's economy.

The Columbia River Basin is the most developed river system in the world. There are more than four hundred dams in the basin, including eleven large projects on the main stem. The federal government led the effort to rationalize the Columbia River, to bring its flow under human control for the benefit of the Pacific Northwest and the nation. Though the majority of residents in the region supported the development of the river, it was still a highly contentious process. The Dalles Dam, a massive power and navigation project just upstream from The Dalles, Oregon, was one of the most controversial of the main-stem dams. This project, finished in 1957, was a key link in regional power and transportation networks and an integral part of the comprehensive development plan of the federal government for the basin. The dam has made important contributions to economic development, creating thousands of jobs and helping to diversify the boom-bust resource economy of the region. It also flooded an important Indian fishery and contributed to the decline of already ailing salmon populations, a trade-off supporters of the project were willing to make.

While electric power was the primary purpose of The Dalles Dam, and the main reason Congress authorized the project, its navigation benefits were equally important to development interests of the region. The stretch of the river upstream from The Dalles, marked by more than ten miles of rapids, falls, massive whirlpools, and narrow channels, was once the most serious obstacle to transportation on the river. As the Pacific Northwest began industrializing in the late-nineteenth century, transportation became more important than ever, especially since the economy of the area was based primarily on resource extraction. After 1883, railroads provided national access to the natural resources, but many Northwesterners believed that full economic development would not be possible without a source of competition to check the monopoly of the railroad companies on transportation. They looked to the great Columbia for solutions. In 1893 the U.S. Army Corps of Engineers concluded that "an unobstructed waterway to the sea will act as a corrective of excessive rates of transportation by rail." Though no river commerce existed above Celilo, the forward-looking agency recommended that a canal be built around the obstructions. "When the obstructions to navigation near The Dalles shall be removed," they argued, "there will be a commerce, although the extent of its development cannot be foreseen."

The Corps was supported in its efforts to improve the river for navigation by an active public constituency. The open-river movement of the late-nineteenth and early-twentieth centuries came primarily from the wheat-producing region east of the Cascades, though Portland, the most populous city in Oregon, also stood to gain from an increase in river traffic. Open-river advocates envisioned the Columbia as their liquid avenue to the markets of the world, and they lobbied hard to obtain the help from the federal government in making their vision a reality. The Corps, charged with regulating and improving navigation on U.S. rivers and streams, was happy to oblige.

The Cascades Canal, built between 1878 and 1896, was the first major navigation project on the Columbia River. Its success in opening the lower river to navigation made the stretch of the river above The Dalles the only major obstacle to river transportation from Astoria to Priest Rapids, a distance of more than four hundred miles. The Corps began work on a project to remedy the problem in 1905, finishing it ten years later. Completion of The Dalles-Celilo Canal was a huge boost to open-river advocates, who equated the taming of the river with human freedom. Joseph N. Teal, a Portland civic leader, investor, and outspoken open-river advocate, remarked at the opening of the canal on 5 May 1915: "This mighty work symbolizes the stern, unfaltering determination of the people that our waters shall be free–free to serve the uses and purposes of their creation by a Divine Providence."

Navigation, however, was not the only element necessary to build up the economy of the region. Power was another essential component of industrial development in the Northwest. Talk of a power dam near The Dalles began in 1912, when John H. Lewis, the state engineer of Oregon, proposed that the state build a 180-foot-high, 300,000-horsepower project to attract new industries. Though Lewis's ambitious proposal, the first for a major dam on the main stem of the Columbia, never got off the ground, another plan for a dam at The Dalles appeared in 1926 as part of a federal survey of water resources in the basin, carried out under the auspices of the 1925 Rivers and Harbors

Act. This act authorized the Corps and the Federal Power Commission to estimate the cost of surveying navigable streams "whereon power development appears feasible and practicable." The federal agencies were charged with developing plans to achieve "the most efficient development of the potential water power, the control of floods, and the needs of navigation." This focus on comprehensive development marked an important departure from previous federal water development, which consisted of projects devoted to single purposes such as irrigation or navigation. Multipurpose river-basin development promised to bring the highest degree of economic development to regions throughout the nation, especially the Pacific Northwest.

Bonneville and Grand Coulee dams, built in response to the Great Depression, were the first federal dams on the Columbia, followed by McNary Dam shortly after the end of World War II. Both Bonneville and McNary are power and navigation projects. River transportation exploded in the late 1930s and early 1940s–in 1935, only 3,631 tons had passed through The Dalles-Celilo Canal, while just ten years later, 632,000 tons of cargo were carried through the project. Wheat and timber products flowed down the increasingly rationalized navigation channel, while oil to power the machines of industry flowed up the river. By the late 1940s, with the rise of river traffic, the already outdated canal at The Dalles, which had seen almost no traffic in the 1920s, became a serious bottleneck. Furthermore, the demands of an escalating Cold War, combined with a massive influx of people into the region, made the need for more power painfully obvious to those interested in postwar economic development of the Northwest.

There was one problem with the comprehensive federal development plan, however–its effect on salmon. The Columbia River was once the greatest salmon producer in the world. Salmon are anadromous, which means they spawn in freshwater, while spending their adult lives in the ocean. Large dams negatively impact both downriver and upriver migrants and ruin important mainstem spawning habitat. Commercial salmon fishing was still one of the most important industries of the region in the 1940s, and, though highly diverse and often bitterly opposed to one another, the various elements of the fishing industry came together in the postwar period to protest the construction of large dams, by the federal government, on the main stem of the Columbia. In a key bid for power in 1947, fish advocates came close to obtaining a ten-year moratorium on dam construction below present-day Chief Joseph Dam, a moratorium that would have stalled, and perhaps prevented, the construction of The Dalles Dam, as well as the John Day Dam and dams on the lower Snake River.

All the major players concerned with the development of the Columbia River attended the June 1947 hearing on the proposed moratorium. Representatives of the Indian tribes, Columbia River Packers Association, Columbia River Fishermen's Protective Union, Washington State Sports Council, Oregon Fish Commission, Oregon Wildlife Federation, Izaak Walton League, and the mayor of Astoria, among others, testified in favor of a moratorium, which many hoped would buy enough time to develop a solution to the problem of fish passage at large dams and to implement a fishery development program in the lower river.

Testifying in opposition to the moratorium were representatives of Tacoma City Light, Pacific Northwest Development Association, Idaho Fish and Game Department, Inland Empire Waterways Association, and the Chambers of Commerce of Portland, Spokane, Pasco, Cascade Locks, and The Dalles, among others. The Portland representatives were especially fierce in their opposition. George LaRoche, general manager of the Portland Dock Commission, argued forcefully that "the economy of this country, this section, does not permit delay or procrastination." He noted the place of Portland as metropolis to the hinterland of the inland Northwest. The expanding port, LaRoche asserted,

> "has played a most vital part in the welfare and growth of the city of Portland; likewise, it has been a beneficial factor in the growth and economical welfare of the Columbia Basin area. . . . The waterways, the carriers and the terminals all make it possible for the producing area of the Columbia Basin to get their products of farm, mine and forest to market on the most economical basis, and conversely those areas are able to obtain the requirements they have to purchase on a like basis." Moreover, "Portland, as a port, occupies a relative position of being the twelfth major port of the United States and as such it is an essential contributor to the needs, stability and economical wellbeing of the country."

F. G. Pender, representing the Port of Vancouver, argued that "I know . . . that for ourselves on the lower river and for these people on the upper Columbia and Snake Rivers we are aspiring to a better way of life, and that can only be accomplished by the development of additional agricultural industry and the further industrialization of this Inland Empire." He noted:

> As far as the Indian problem is concerned, that is tradition with us, and I think those of us in the Northwest who are close to the Indian would wish that we could build a river with the necessary falls and with the necessary

Native American fishermen at Celilo Falls above The Dalles Dam in October 1933

(courtesy of Oregon Historical Society)

recreational opportunities and the necessary life for the Indian, but certainly we don't want it to stand in the way of the development of our own way of life. When we are finally through and done it simply settles down to this: and that is, what do we want for our way of life?

This question was one the federal government decided in the months following the June hearing. While recommending that upstream dams on the Columbia and Snake Rivers, if authorized before 1958, be built before The Dalles, John Day, or Arlington dams, the federal committee charged with making a decision on the moratorium proposal concluded that a rescheduling of already authorized dams would not be in the best interest of the public. Instead of a moratorium, they offered cash compensation for affected Indian tribes and a lower-river salmon-hatchery program to mitigate for upriver fish losses. The Interior Department concurred with the decision of the committee, stating that "the over-all benefits to the Pacific Northwest from a thorough-going development of the Snake and Columbia are such that the present salmon run must, if necessary, be sacrificed." The decision not to institute a moratorium, in combination with a warming of the Cold War, set the stage for congressional authorization of The Dalles Dam three years later.

The Flood Control Act of 1950 authorized the construction of The Dalles Dam as part of the main control plan of the federal government for the Columbia River. Justifications for the project, listed by the Corps in its 1946 cost-benefit analysis, included an increased demand for electricity by electrochemical, electrometallurgical, shipbuilding, and other industries, and the rapid rise of traffic on the mid Columbia. The Corps also emphasized its desire to help integrate the basin into the international economy by making its natural resources more easily accessible, echoing arguments open-river advocates had been making for more than fifty years. "Many resources in the upriver tributary area have lacked adequate transportation facilities, and the high costs of existing transportation have retarded extensive development. These resources are timber products; ores of gold, silver, lead, zinc, iron, copper, and other minerals; and extensive deposits of limestone, phosphates, and clays." They also took into account a projected increase of the population in the basin by two million by 1970 (the population in Oregon and Washington had already risen 40 percent from 1940–1947, compared to a national average of 11 percent).

The Corps did not consider national defense in 1946, but this consideration quickly changed with the advent of the Korean War (1950–1953) and the escalation of nuclear-weapon production at

Hanford Nuclear Reservation in Washington after the successful test of a nuclear weapon by the Soviet Union in 1949. The following year, William E. Warne, assistant secretary of the interior, recommended the construction of The Dalles Dam "if defense requirements demand another additional large block of power," while a 1951 presidential report made mention of the need for four to four-and-one-half million more kilowatts of power to meet critical national-defense programs in atomic energy, chemical production, and the manufacture of aluminum and other metals. The Inland Empire Waterways Association, an influential open-river organization, responded that the completion of just three dams in the Northwest–Ice Harbor, The Dalles, and Hells Canyon–could provide for almost half of these power demands. Although Yakima agent E. Morgan Pryce vigorously objected to The Dalles Dam because it would destroy Celilo Falls, the most productive Indian fishery in the basin, Bureau of Indian Affairs (BIA) Commissioner Dillon S. Myer refused to oppose it "because of urgent national defense need for power." Such arguments served to reinforce predictions by the Bonneville Power Administration and others of imminent brownouts and general economic underdevelopment if additional power sources were not forthcoming.

All four of the Indian nations with treaty-guaranteed fishing rights, the Nez Perce, Umatilla, Warm Springs, and Yakima tribes, opposed the dam, as did unaffiliated River Indians, white supporters of Indian treaty rights, the U.S. Fish and Wildlife Service, and state fish and game agencies. They argued The Dalles Dam would deplete the fish runs on the Columbia, although the U.S. Fish and Wildlife Service and the state agencies also believed that the dam would benefit fishery conservation since it would result in the eradication of the fishery. The Corps agreed with the fishery agencies on the latter point, arguing:

> Inasmuch as the Indians and other fishermen now take about 40 percent of the salmonidae passing Bonneville Dam, prohibiting the commercial take and reduction of the Indian subsistence catch would be a very desirable conservation measure. The construction of The Dalles Dam, therefore, would make a direct and outstanding contribution toward the conservation of the fishery resources in the Columbia River Basin.

The federal government considered the eradication of Indian culture and political autonomy as other positive contributions of the dam. The appendix to the 1950 Rivers and Harbors Act stated that the long-range solution to the Indian fishing problem "lies in the integration and assimilation of these people into society at large" with the goal of "relieving the Government of necessity for supervisions at the earliest practical time." Congress believed that The Dalles Dam, by destroying the Indian fishery at Celilo, would help further the federal policy of terminating relations with Indian tribes and assimilating Native Americans into white society.

Congress appropriated the first funds for the dam in 1951 and the Corps began work on the project early the following year. Five years and more than $300 million later, the contractors completed the work on the initial project, and on 10 March 1957 the engineers began filling the pool of the dam, an event marked by hundreds of mourning Indians, who stood by the side of the road and watched the destruction of their ancient fishery by the manmade flood. It was a telling change in the riverscape, a visual manifestation of the radical economic and political changes the Columbia River Basin had undergone in the previous one hundred years.

In the end, construction of The Dalles Dam, as Pender pointed out in 1947, came down to a question of what kind of life to which local residents aspired. National and international political and economic events played an important role in the federal decision to build a dam at The Dalles, but the majority of local inhabitants genuinely believed that the dam, and other projects in the comprehensive development plan, would raise their standard of living, a belief that has largely been borne out. By the end of the century the Pacific Northwest was considered one of the most livable places in the country, a situation attributable in large part to federal efforts to further regional economic development. The Dalles Dam minimized Indian treaty rights and negatively impacted salmon runs, but the project also must be seen as a key component of the industrial river, which, for better or worse, forms the backbone of the diverse economy of the region.

–CAIN ALLEN, PORTLAND STATE UNIVERSITY

Viewpoint:
No. The Dalles Dam, which destroyed the dipnet fishery at Celilo and inundated old Celilo Village, was an agent of cultural and biological destruction that represented a direct violation of the Indian treaties of 1855.

The calm slackwater pool backed up behind The Dalles Dam offers little evidence of the violent rapids and crowded fishery that once occupied the ten-mile stretch of the Columbia River between The Dalles, Oregon, and Celilo Falls.

While the Nez Perce, Umatilla, Warm Springs, and Yakima tribes, along with unaffiliated River Indians, had protested the construction of previous federal water projects on the Columbia since the 1930s, they worked especially hard to defeat The Dalles Dam, which they considered an agent of cultural and biological destruction. Many Columbia River Indians saw the loss of Celilo in 1957 as a stark symbol of their economic and political marginalization during the century.

A long history of massive basalt flows, Ice Age floods, and the gradual but still powerful force of erosion shaped the ten-mile stretch of the Columbia from The Dalles to Celilo Falls into one of the most-productive inland fisheries in the world. Indians have occupied the area for thousands of years, exploiting the complex structure of The Dalles-Celilo reach with a rich array of harvest technologies suited to the particularities of the natural river. Although dipnets predominated at Celilo, fishermen also employed other tools, including spears, gaffhooks, seines, and traps, to harvest an estimated one million pounds of salmon annually for trade purposes alone after the introduction of the horse in the early-eighteenth century. By the late 1940s the only period for which there is firm harvest data for the Celilo fishery, the tribal dipnet catch averaged 2.6 million pounds annually, about 500,000 pounds of which was for subsistence purposes.

The incredible productivity made possible by the structural complexity of The Dalles-Celilo reach made it a key node in the cultural network of the local tribes. The area was situated in a climatic and cultural transition zone. Wasco/Chinookan-speaking peoples mingled with Sahaptin-speakers just east of the Cascade Range, which soaks clouds coming from the ocean of their moisture, leaving the region east of the mountains relatively bereft of precipitation. This sharp line of aridity can be seen quite clearly in the Columbia Gorge, which acts as a natural and cultural funnel between east and west. The dry, windy conditions of The Dalles-Celilo area made it an excellent place for drying fish, an important trade item in the Native Columbia Basin. The combination of ideal climatic conditions, proximity to the ocean—which meant upriver fish were greater in number and in better condition—and the geological complexity of The Dalles-Celilo reach, made the area an important regional and interregional trading center in the pre-industrial period.

Trade, however, was not the only reason Indians gathered at Celilo. The ten miles from The Dalles to Celilo Falls were a cultural, as well as economic, focal point. Ceremony is an important aspect of Indian culture, and Celilo was the site of one of the largest and most-elaborate First Salmon ceremonies in the region. This ceremony was performed to pay respect to the salmon, which willingly gave sustenance to the people. As important as the First Salmon ceremony was, the Great Rendezvous at Celilo Falls in the autumn was the true highlight of the year. Thousands gathered to make marriage arrangements, perform betrothal ceremonies, meet friends and family, make political alliances, exchange information, race horses, and gamble.

When representatives of the federal government came in 1855 to make treaties with area tribes, the Indians refused to move onto reservations located far from the river unless they could reserve their right to fish at their "usual and accustomed" fishing places, the most important of which was Celilo. Due in part to their belief that fishing would prevent the government from having to feed the Indians during their transition into a settled agricultural lifestyle, and eager to liquidate Indian title to land already being settled by whites, federal representatives Joel Palmer and Isaac Stevens agreed to the Indians' stipulation.

The treaties did not prevent whites from trying to keep Native Americans from exercising their ancient rights, however. Whites were particularly active in their efforts to exclude Indians from the fishery at Celilo during the last two decades of the nineteenth century. For their part, Indians were just as active in trying to defend their rights. In 1886 Billy Parker of the Warm Springs Reservation remarked:

> When we go to the fishery the white people threaten us, and some Indians have been whipped and beaten by the whites; on Sundays, when the whites are not fishing, sometimes the Indians slip in to fish, but when caught are treated rough. The Indian cannot understand why he should be deprived of the sport and food of which he is so fond.

Two years later, J. D. C. Atkins, commissioner for the Bureau of Indian Affairs (BIA), wrote:

> All the lands along the river bank have been passed out of the control of the United States to individual settlers, and the Indians are not allowed to pass from the public highway to the river to fish. Barbed wire fences securely locked or guarded effectually bar their access to the river. This condition of affairs has been maintained for some four or five years, and with each returning season the Indians have made effort to get a foothold at the fisheries. Two years ago they tore down the fences and forced a passage to the river. A public meeting was then held in Dalles City, which resulted in securing to the Indians temporary access to the fisheries at a given point, but they were soon driven off again.

Native fishermen worked with Indian agents and white friends such as Judge T. S. Lang of The Dalles to remedy the situation. Atkins recommended to no avail the purchase of land in the vicinity of Celilo for the Indians' exclusive use. The United States Supreme Court took a major step toward resolving the conflict between white property owners and Indian fishermen in the landmark case *United States* v. *Winans* (1905), which secured the Indians' right to utilize private land when exercising their treaty-reserved rights, but the River People would not secure the land occupied by Celilo Village, a small Indian settlement near the falls, until 1929, when Congress transferred 7.4 acres of land acquired as a right-of-way for The Dalles-Celilo Canal to the Interior Department.

As it was in the preindustrial period, Celilo was the center of the Indian contribution to the Columbia River salmon trade during the industrializing period. Columbia River Indians had gradually entered the market economy by the late nineteenth century as they began to sell some of their harvest to white fish buyers for cash. The currency gained through the sale of salmon and other items allowed them to buy medicine, coffee, flour, sugar, and other basic commodities upon which they had become dependent. Commercialization of the Indian fishery represented economic adaptation without serious cultural erosion. They had always used fish as a trade item–a capitalist market based on a unitary monetary system certainly changed the terms of trade, but not so much that Indians could not adapt their traditional economic and cultural practices to suit the new conditions.

While the commercial fishery allowed Indians to continue to practice their fishing traditions, albeit in the service of an international market, it also meant they had to deal with competing white fishermen. One conflict at Celilo between the Yakimas and the Seufert Brothers cannery went all the way to the Supreme Court. The 1919 case *Seufert Bros.* v. *United States* concerned a dispute between the local cannery and a Yakima man who operated a fishwheel in a spot the company claimed. The court upheld the Yakima's right to fish on both sides of the river, describing the fishery as a "great table where all the Indians came to partake."

In addition to conflicts over access to the fishery, Indians had to defend their right to live next to the river their ancestors had depended on since time immemorial. Local whites resented Celilo Village, considering the settlement not only a blight upon an otherwise beautiful landscape but also a health risk. Though the Wyam, an unaffiliated band, managed to deflect repeated attempts to move them from their homes, the area their settlement occupied was nevertheless reduced by the development of several transportation conduits. In 1883 Henry Villard's Oregon Railway and Navigation Company laid their tracks straight through the ancient settlement. Thirty-two years later the U.S. Army Corps of Engineers cut off the corner of the village with another transportation route, The Dalles-Celilo Canal. This project rendered unusable many usual and accustomed fishing and camping sites on the Oregon side of the river, for which the Indians received no compensation.

In 1916 Oregon paved the Columbia River Highway through the village, adding yet another transportation corridor. While it took additional village land, the highway was not wholly negative for Indian fishermen, as it provided easier access for non-Indian fish buyers from the canneries. It also helped funnel tourists to Celilo, who gladly paid cash to take a picture with a real Indian or to get fish fresh from the river. By the 1940s hundreds of tourists visited Celilo every day during the peak season, buying an annual average of fifty thousand pounds of fish from Indian dipnetters.

In the forty years following the construction of The Dalles-Celilo Canal and the Columbia River Highway, residents of Celilo Village faced several attempts to move them from their home. In 1929, for example, The Dalles Chamber of Commerce launched a plan to eliminate the "unsightly and insanitary" community at Celilo. They considered the village an eyesore and tried to convince the inhabitants to accept a new village with "sanitary facilities conducive to public health." The Wyam successfully resisted this plan and several others in the years leading up to The Dalles Dam. Not until 1957 would the villagers be forced to move from their ancient home by rising waters of the reservoir that would come to be known, ironically, as Lake Celilo.

The tribes in 1945 immediately and unanimously opposed the proposal of a dam at The Dalles upon first hearing of it. Chief Tommy Thompson, leader of Celilo Village, realized early that the rationalization of the Columbia would result in the destruction of his people's fishery. In 1934 he testified against Bonneville Dam, arguing that the structure "not only will submerge the long established fishing grounds but will interfere with the run of salmon, especially the return of the young to the ocean." The Dalles Dam represented an even greater threat to his people's fishery than had Bonneville, which destroyed the Indian fishery at the Cascades, second in importance only to Celilo. Thompson commented in 1945 that "the Great Fear came to me when I heard the white man was takin' a step to build a dam below my fishin' place. My heart

ACCESS TO THE RIVER

The following is a portion of the decision taken from Seufert Bros. *v.* United States *(1919):*

These treaties were negotiated in a group for the purpose of freeing a great territory from Indian claims, preparatory to opening it to settlers, and it is obvious that with the treaty with the tribes inhabiting Middle Oregon in effect, the Untied States was in a position to fulfill any agreement which it might make to secure fishing rights in, or on either bank of, the Columbia river in the part of it now under consideration-and the treaty was with the government, not with Indians, former occupants of relinquished lands.

The District Court found, on what was sufficient evidence, that the Indians living on each side of the river, ever since the treaty was negotiated, had been accustomed to cross to the other side to fish, that the members of the tribes associated freely and intermarried, and that neither claimed exclusive control of the fishing places on either side of the river or the necessary use of the river banks, but used both in common. One Indian witness, says the court, "likened the river to a great table where all the Indians might come to partake."

The record also shows with sufficient certainty, having regard to the character of evidence which must necessarily be relied upon in such a case, that the members of the tribes designated in the treaty as Yakima Indians, and also Indians from the south side of the river, were accustomed to resort habitually to the locations described in the decree for the purposes of fishing at the time the treaty was entered into, and that they continued to do so to the time of the taking of the evidence in the case, and also that Indians from both sides of the river built houses upon the south bank in which to dry and cure their fish during the fishing season. [249 U.S. 194, 198] This recital of the facts and circumstances of the case renders it unnecessary to add much to what was said by this court in United States v. Winans, 198 U.S. 371, 25 Sup. Ct. 662, in which this same provision of this treaty was considered and construed. The right claimed by the Indians in that case was to fishing privileges on the north part and bank of the Columbia river—in this case similar rights are claimed on the south part and bank of the river.

The difference upon which the appellant relies to distinguish this from the former case is that the lands of the Yakima Indians were all to the north of the river and therefore it is said that their rights could not extend beyond the middle of that stream, and also that since the proviso we are considering, is in the nature of an exception from the general grant of the treaty, whatever rights it saves must be reserved out of the thing granted, and as all of the lands of the Yakima tribes lay to the north of the river it cannot give any rights on the south bank. . . .

How the Indians understood this proviso we are considering is not doubtful. During all the years since the treaty was signed they have been accustomed habitually to resort for fishing to the places to which the decree of the lower court applies, and they have shared such places with Indians of other tribes from the south side of the river and with white men. This shows clearly that their understanding of the treaty was that they had the right [249 U.S. 194, 199] to resort to these fishing grounds and make use of them in common with other citizens of the United States—and this is the extent of the right that is secured to them by the decree we are asked to revise.

To restrain the Yakima Indians to fishing on the north side and shore of the river would greatly restrict the comprehensive language of the treaty, which gives them the right "of taking fish at all usual and accustomed places and of erecting temporary buildings for curing them," and would substitute for the natural meaning of the expression used—for the meaning which it is proved the Indians, for more than fifty years derived from it—the artificial meaning which might be given to it by the law and by lawyers.

The suggestion, so impressively urged, that this construction "imposes a servitude upon the Oregon soil," is not alarming from the point of view of the public, and private owners not only had notice of these Indian customary rights by the reservation of them in the treaty, but the 'servitude' is one existing only where there was an habitual and customary use of the premises, which must have been so open and notorious during a considerable portion of each year, that any person, not negligently or willfully blind to the conditions of the property he was purchasing, must have known of them.

Source: FindLaw for Legal Professionals, *Internet website.*

seems to beat and tell me that the white man is trying to destroy our food."

All four of the newly formed tribal governments actively protested The Dalles Dam, meeting with federal officials, testifying at many hearings, and sending statements to legislators. A September 1945 petition from the Nez Perce Business Committee began:

> From time immemorial, the Nez Perce Indians of Idaho have made use of the fishing grounds on the Columbia River at Celilo. Large numbers of Nez Perces have derived a large part of their subsistence from salmon runs there and through the years this has remained a time honored pursuit, particularly in recent years when the dams at Bonneville and Lewiston have severely diminished the salmon runs into the upper reaches and tributaries of the Columbia River. The Nez Perce Indians can only be completely in opposition to the construction of any dam which will destroy in any degree the fishing grounds at Celilo.

The Nez Perce argued that, in addition to the subsistence and commercial value of the Celilo fishery, a "large number of Nez Perce Indians visit Celilo annually for inter-tribal, social and ceremonial activities. This traditional inter-tribal meeting ground is dear to the hearts of the Nez Perce Indians." They concluded: "The Nez Perce Indians have throughout history been consistently deprived of their rights, guaranteed by treaty, and this proposed dam at The Dalles will be another wedge for completely destroying the rights of the Indians in favor of the white man."

In 1947 Thompson joined other Indian leaders and non-Indian fishery interests in a failed attempt to obtain a ten-year moratorium on the construction of dams that threatened salmon runs. Speaking in his native Sahaptin, Thompson told the federal committee charged with making a decision on the moratorium:

> I think I don't know how I would live if you would put up a dam which will flood my fishing places which I have protected and recognized as my accustomed fishing place, and how I am going to make my living afterwards. It is the only food I am dependent on for my livelihood, and I am here to protect that. . . . I want you to treat my people right.

Even after Congress authorized the dam, the Indians tried their best to prevent its construction by lobbying against appropriations. Tribal leaders, however, were in a bind–they wanted to stop the dam, but also had to make sure they were compensated for the loss of their fishing grounds in the likely event Congress appropriated funds for the project. While some leaders such as Chief Thompson refused to accept a cash settlement, others squabbled over the particulars of the settlement, and even over which tribes were eligible. The Warm Springs tribes argued for intertribal unity, though they, like the Corps and Yakima and Umatilla tribes, did not believe the Nez Perce were entitled to a share of the settlement. The Yakima Nation, however, decided to present their claim separately, asserting in 1951 that they were the only tribe to have fishing rights at Celilo. They acknowledged that the Warm Springs tribes used Celilo, but argued that the tribes had sold their rights long ago, pointing to a fraudulent treaty imposed on the Warm Springs in 1865. The Umatillas in turn argued that the Yakimas had sold their rights to the Spokane, Portland, and Seattle Railroad. Another fault line existed between River Indians and reservation Indians–the former believed the latter had sold Celilo out. They were also upset that reservation Indians who had never even dipped a net in the river received the same amount as they did. This disunity played in favor of the Corps, which negotiated separate agreements with the different tribes. The Yakimas, for example, objected to the Oregon tribes' early settlement, arguing that it undermined their attempts to prevent Congress from appropriating funds for the dam.

Although some Native Americans had called for a percentage of the annual income from the dam and enough electricity to power the reservations, the final settlement consisted of one lump-sum payment of just under $27 million. In-lieu fishing sites were not provided, nor was any portion of power revenues from the dam set aside for the tribes. The settlement was divided among the four treaty tribes–$15 million for the Yakimas, $4.62 million for the Umatillas, $4.45 million for the Warm Springs, and $2.5 million for the Nez Perce. Unaffiliated River People were forced to enroll in a tribe to share in the settlement.

Each tribe decided for themselves how to use their portion of the funds. The Yakimas gave every enrolled member a portion of their share of the settlement, while the Warm Springs tribes invested the money in tribal enterprises to develop alternative economic strategies to replace their devastated fisheries. Thompson, who for decades had been an outspoken foe of damming the Columbia River, expressed his final opposition by refusing to accept the money. He did not consider cash to be an acceptable substitute for fish. A 1959 article in the *Oregon Journal* noted that he did not participate in "the agreement which signed away [their fishing] rights. . . . 'I have not signatured away my salmon,' he was fond of saying."

In addition to the cash offer, the Corps helped residents of Celilo Village find new homes, but only because the BIA managed to strike a deal late in the process. In 1955 the BIA, with the support of local officials, convinced the Corps to fund a relocation program in exchange for granting a right-of-way through Interior Department land for the relocation of Union Pacific Railroad tracks. When the relocation effort began in early 1956, Celilo Village had approximately 145 permanent residents, about half of whom were children; another dozen or more were elderly. The villagers relied primarily on fishing for their livelihood, though some worked occasionally on the railroad, in construction, or in the timber industry. Some also owned reservation land that provided a modicum of income. A handful received public assistance.

Residents of the village did not sit passively as their ancestral home was destroyed. They resisted in the ways available to them. Some testified at hearings to stop the dam. Others, such as eighty-two-year-old Teeminway Moses, who insisted on having electrical service, dirt floors, and an outhouse rather than indoor plumbing, battled with the relocation committee over the terms of relocation. Some wrote to government officials, expressing their concerns about the effects of dams on their fishing rights and communities. The youth also did their part. Ed Edmo, who grew up in Celilo Village, later wrote of how he and his friends tried to prevent the destruction of their village:

> When the workmen finished surveying at the end of the day, some of us boys would pull out the stakes from the ground, fill the holes, and make a small fire out of the stakes. Others would climb the cliffs and shoot BB guns at the big dump trucks as they hauled dirt. We would laugh when a driver stopped his truck. In our own small way, we tried to stop the dam.

Eventually, however, the villagers resigned themselves to the fate dominant society had determined for them and began the search for a new home. Most, however, left the village and moved to white communities such as Wishram, Washington, and Gresham, Oregon, or to the Yakima Reservation, where many were enrolled. This exodus pleased local officials, who offered families a $500 bonus if they moved more than ten miles from Celilo. The Corps bought the Indians' old houses for an average of between $500 and $1000 and either built them new dwellings or provided them with funds to purchase homes outside of Celilo. Of the twenty-three families and four individuals who were forced to leave, according to relocation records, only eight families and one individual remained in the village. This meant an exodus of nearly half the total population of the community, paralleling the exodus of residents after the treaties almost exactly a hundred years earlier. Three families and one individual moved to Toppenish on the Yakima reservation, two moved to Gresham, Oregon, three moved to The Dalles, and two moved to Dallesport, Washington.

Living villagers were not the only ones the dam dislocated. Indian burial grounds located on Memaloose and Grave Islands had to be relocated to avoid the manmade flood. The Corps, under the supervision of several Indian representatives, began relocating two of the cemeteries in September 1956, exhuming the remains of 3,000 to 3,500 individuals. Lake Celilo also covered many of the ancient petroglyphs and pictographs in the area. In early 1957 a team composed of members from the Wasco County-Dalles City Museum Commission, National Park Service, Corps of Engineers, The Dalles Chamber of Commerce, and the Universities of Washington and Oregon removed thirty-seven petroglyphs that would be below the water line. There were no Indian representatives present. Salvage effort also sparked a looting spree by "amateur archaeologists." The petroglyphs taken by the professionals ended up in the possession of the Corps. Approximately four hundred petroglyphs were left to be submerged under the reservoir. The salvage team did not save more because of the cost and that there "was considerable skepticism as to whether or not a profit could be made on the project."

The economic base of Celilo Village was also shattered. As Thompson had predicted almost twenty-five years earlier, the flooding of Celilo Falls devastated the fishing-based economy of the River People. While the annual average of the Indians' commercial harvest at Celilo was 2,388,330 pounds in the ten years prior to 1957, the average in the ten years after 1957 was a mere 338,020, less than 15 percent of the pre-dam average. This decline was the result of massive changes in the river and to the discriminatory closure by the state of the commercial fishery above Bonneville Dam. The Corps estimated that four thousand to five thousand Indians were dependent, either directly or indirectly, on the Celilo fishery. With the destruction of their last major dipnet fishery, many Indian fishermen were forced to find some other way to make a living. Some, however, chose to stay on the river and continue to try to make a living fishing. To do this goal they had to invest in boats and drift nets, as one of the indirect effects of The Dalles Dam was to make fishing more capital intensive. Delbert Frank Sr., of the Warm Springs Reservation, commented that, before the dam, "it didn't take a lot of fancy gear or expensive boats to fish. For the cost of one or two balls of twine, about 6 to 12 dollars, I could make the fishing gear necessary for me to catch enough fish to supply my family and many others for a whole year." Though the river and environment had changed dramatically, the River People refused to give up their way of life. They continued to battle the states and federal government for decades after the loss of Celilo. Their tenacity is evidenced by the fishermen, young and old, who continue to dip their nets into the Columbia.

The loss of Celilo remains vivid in the memory of Columbia River Indians. Elizabeth Woody, a writer and educator of Yakima, Warm Springs, Wasco, and Navajo descent, writes in *Seven Hands, Seven Hearts* (1994), that "the unconscionable drowning of Wyam—Celilo Falls—marks a crucial point in our collective history." She notes that, "after nearly four decades, Celilo Falls is still talked about and remembered as the heart of our homeland." Ted Strong, former director of the Columbia River Inter-Tribal Fish Commission and a Yakima Indian, states that the loss of Celilo motivates him and other Indian leaders in their efforts to defend their fishing rights. He wrote: "Our spirit did not perish along with the destruction of Celilo Falls. The greatness of Divine Creation dishonored by the flooding waters of dams has taken refuge in the hearts and minds of the Columbia River Indians." While Celilo may be gone, the River People will never let it be forgotten.

–CAIN ALLEN, PORTLAND STATE UNIVERSITY

References

Cain Allen, "'They Called It Progress': Indians, Salmon, and the Industrialization of the Columbia River," thesis, Portland State University, 2000.

Katrine Barber, "After Celilo Falls: The Dalles Dam, Indian Fishing Rights, and Federal Energy Policy on the Mid-Columbia River," dissertation, Washington State University, 1999.

"Celilo Falls," *Columbia River Inter-Tribal Fish Commission,* Internet website.

Center for Columbia River History, Internet website.

Joseph Cone and Sandy Ridlington, eds., *The Northwest Salmon Crisis: A Documentary History* (Corvallis: Oregon State University Press, 1996).

Wesley Arden Dick, "When Dams Weren't Damned: The Public Power Crusade and Visions of the Good Life in the Pacific Northwest in the 1930s," *Environmental Review,* 13 (1989): 113–153.

William Dietrich, *Northwest Passage: The Great Columbia River* (New York: Simon & Schuster, 1995).

Ed Edmo, "After Celilo," in *Talking Leaves: Contemporary Native American Short Stories,* edited by Craig Lesley and Katheryn Stavrakis (New York: Laurel, 1991).

Dan Landeen and Allen Pinkham, *Salmon and His People: Fish and Fishing in Nez Perce Culture* (Lewiston, Idaho: Confluence Press, 1999).

William L. Lang and Robert C. Carriker, eds., *Great River of the West: Essays on the Columbia River* (Seattle: University of Washington Press, 1999).

Donald L. Parman, "Inconstant Advocacy: The Erosion of Indian Fishing Rights in the Pacific Northwest, 1933–1956," *Pacific Historical Review,* 53 (1984): 163–189.

Roberta Ulrich, *Empty Nets: Indians, Dams, and the Columbia River* (Corvallis: Oregon State University Press, 1999).

Richard White, *The Organic Machine* (New York: Hill & Wang, 1995).

William F. Willingham, *Army Engineers and the Development of Oregon: A History of the Portland District, U.S. Army Corps of Engineers* (Washington, D.C.: U.S. Government Printing Office, 1983).

Elizabeth Woody, *Seven Hands, Seven Hearts* (Portland, Ore.: Eighth Mountain Press, 1994).

COMMUNITY WATER SUPPLY

How important is development of deepwater sources for communities in rural southern Africa?

Viewpoint: Deepwater sources, because they are poorly monitored and often contaminated, have been less important to communities in rural southern Africa than traditional water-abstraction techniques.

Viewpoint: Deepwater abstraction is an established and safe means of providing water for rural southern Africa.

As populations have expanded and water requirements have increased, designers and planners in the water fraternity have ignored people's traditional water supplies and water-management practices. Groundwater-development technology has been introduced in areas of deepwater supplies. Hydrogeological surveys are undertaken, boreholes drilled, and hand pumps fitted in a process that does not involve the end users who are expected to be responsible for the operation and maintenance of the system.

Little consideration or planning has been given to the development of abstraction systems for traditional water supplies. In general, people in disadvantaged areas do not and cannot own their water-supply system and, consequently, since it is communal, there is little effective responsibility and maintenance. Most of the attention and resources have been focused on technically complex solutions of deep groundwater development. Had appropriate systems been developed to improve the abstraction technologies of existing water-supply options, more reliable and sustainable water-supply systems would now be in place and the health and well-being of large numbers of people would have been significantly increased.

Viewpoint: Deepwater sources, because they are poorly monitored and often contaminated, have been less important to communities in rural southern Africa than traditional water-abstraction techniques.

Thousands of people, especially children, in the industrially developing world died annually from waterborne diseases and contaminated water supplies because of badly managed or deficient water-supply systems. Particularly in arid and semiarid areas of deep or unreliable groundwater, hundreds of pumps and water-supply systems were in a condition beyond the means of the state or community to operate or repair. Consequently, many people had to collect water from a great distance. This process led to low rates of both primary and secondary water use and an adverse effect on health. According to a World Bank estimate, some African women used 40 percent of their daily nutritional intake while traveling to collect water. At the domestic level, daily fluid intake was frequently far below recommended minimum-intake levels and sanitation facilities were poor or inadequate. At the secondary level, it was frequently impossible for a family or community to provide themselves with a regular healthy diet.

In southern Africa, up to the 1950s, rural communities relied on traditional methods of water collection, primarily from river pools and water retained in the sand of silted rivers. These systems provided adequate water, were sustainable, and were managed by the communities. As rural populations increased, however, there was a demand for more water and further supply schemes were required.

Improvement of alternate systems such as sand abstraction (the drawing of water from dry silt-laden riverbeds) began in Zimbabwe in the early 1950s and 1960s. No incentive was given to the development of family water-harvesting systems and no thought given to researching traditional systems. The establishment of pumped sand-abstraction systems was a progression from traditional rural technology and was thus highly acceptable to conservative rural societies. Even these schemes, however, were large mechanized systems introduced into the community by a colonial government, with little regard to local input and culture. At the same time that alternative systems began to be improved, deepwater borehole-drilling technology was developing overseas. This innovation curtailed further development of the traditional and alternate systems, and the opportunity for establishing small sustainable schemes was lost.

Despite the introduction of technological improvements, people in a crisis situation in rural areas relied entirely on traditional sand-abstraction systems. When the pumps broke down or the boreholes went dry in a drought year, people turned to the silted rivers for water. The water held in these sands enabled people to survive from one season to the next. In spite of the fact that there was more usable fresh surface water than groundwater (other than behind dams that stored surface water that became quickly and easily polluted), attention was not focused on water-harvesting systems. Even as modern hydrologists began to look into these alternate systems, it was not because of the needs of rural communities but rather as an offshoot of urban requirements. The large amounts of run-off water from urban sprawl (streets, car parks, and roofs) meant that there were vast amounts of dirty water with which to be dealt. Storage systems and infiltration pipes were being devised to regulate flow and separate water from dirt and grime. These designs could be used with equal success for the extraction of water from river sediment or for the collection of water from large compacted earth surfaces in arid areas.

A great potential was lost at the end of the twentieth century. Appropriate technologies were only being developed in the industrialized world, while designers in the developing world were still locked into boreholes and deepwater supplies. Technologies were being developed to meet the changing needs of industrial growth, but they were not being transferred to areas where they could be of primary importance.

Although traditional methods were more dependable and easily sustained, they were not always the first choice of a rural community. The legacy of colonialism, which was so often quoted by African countries, in fact led rural communities to feel that they had been deprived; therefore, they only wanted the "best" new technologies. The perceived best was often groundwater boreholes that commercial farmers and the "developed" world used.

Deepwater sources were utilized for so long that a stigma developed against any other source. Both people and planners frequently considered only deep groundwater supplies as an option. Such sources were costly and difficult to develop as they required complex drilling and installation equipment, as well as technology that the vast majority of people did not know how to operate and could not afford.

Water sources were frequently developed in localities that were not considered suitable by the community. As a result, community members felt little or no responsibility for maintaining the source. People were unable to participate in the siting of deepwater sources because this process required technical equipment to which they did not have access. Such a selection process was also not understood and, in fact, was alien to rural end users. At worst, a borehole might be sited and drilled without the knowledge of local people, who were then expected to accept responsibility for its upkeep.

Historically, state-managed authorities frequently took responsibility for the entire process: site selection, drilling, pump installation, maintenance, and repair. In arid or semiarid areas, water was vital and culturally understood to be free to anyone who requested it. During the latter half of the twentieth century many cash-strapped governments were unable to provide this service and, because water had traditionally been free, the communities were unwilling to take over the financial responsibility. People rationalized that they should not have to pay for community water-supply systems. Therefore, in order to ensure sustainability, people required small-scale family systems, which they could manage and consider to be their own.

Continued pump failures and breakdowns, often for long periods, made it apparent that deepwater sources were neither effective nor sus-

A modern water pump in a Malawi African village in 1992

(PP/David Ree)

tainable at the community level. When there was a breakdown, most communities did not have the knowledge, resources, or equipment to perform the required repairs. In addition, many rural citizens believed that communal water supplies belonged to the government and therefore they felt no onus to either repair them or pay for them to be repaired. When a well pump breaks down, people are still able to draw water with a rope and bucket; in the case of a narrow, deep bore it is not possible to draw water in this manner, and fitted pipes totally preclude all efforts to abstract water. The hole simply becomes an amusement for herd boys who rapidly fill it up with stones.

The installations–and particularly the pumps–on alternate water-supply systems were simple enough for people to operate and maintain for themselves. Similarly, equipment used for the installation, maintenance, and repair of pumps was so basic that expensive specialist tools were not required. People, including technically disadvantaged rural women, were able to undertake their own repairs, although traditionally women were not expected to be involved at a technical level. With small-scale basic schemes women could exercise complete control. Only where there was complex machinery did men wish to be involved. In harsh economic environments, many men moved to towns or other countries seeking work, leaving the women in charge. Systems needed to be developed that would allow women to gain control of and responsibility for their own water requirements.

In contrast, nontraditional systems presented problems of quantity and quality of water supply. Frequently, deep groundwater wells could not provide sufficient water, particularly in a drought year. Because of the depths involved it was physically exhausting to bring water to the surface by hand. Mechanized schemes were costly and nonsustainable, particularly in remote areas. Where recharge was slow, groundwater was frequently contaminated with mineral salts, often to a point where it was sufficiently caustic to be unpalatable and could even burn the skin. It was not unusual for people to pass a brackish deepwater supply on the way to the filtered water from the silt of a seasonal river. A case in point is the Dongamusi area of the Lupane District in northwest Zimbabwe, where thirty-one boreholes were sunk to answer the water needs

UNITED NATIONS AND WATER IN AFRICA

As a key priority of the Initiative, it is intended that the United Nations should play a lead and supporting role in ensuring more equitable and sustainable use of water in Africa, with attention given to the poor majority. The top priority within this effort should be to ensure a basic quantity of safe water for African citizens, and thereby promoting water equity. This "Fair Share" approach advocates water equity across major water uses and users, in national economic development plans, and between countries using shared water resources. The overall goal is to ensure . . . a fair share at affordable prices for water for the poor majority of people throughout Africa.

The question of equity extends to assuring a fair sharing of the use of internationally shared water resources. There are more than 50 international drainage basins in Africa, but few international agreements exist on their use and the protection of water resources in them. Recently, the UN has been helpful in promoting water-sharing agreements. This facilitating role is envisioned to be widely replicated in the following priority.

The programme, while including technological components, focuses primarily on changes in water policies, laws and institutions, in order to ensure that the poor majority of the people in Africa are brought from the margins of the issue to the front of a coherent and sustainable water development agenda. The programme applying the "Fair Share" approach has five key elements:

Assessing all future national and international water policies, plans and programmes in terms of their economic viability, environmental sustainability and equity impacts. If the review indicates the policies, plans and programmes do not lead to at least some improvement in the living conditions and prospects of the poor majority, then a sustainable alternative must be found that does.

Assisting governments to incorporate the "Fair Share" approach in their national water development policies, plans and programmes. The same approach should also be built into and applied to internationally-shared water resources. In both cases, the active involvement of local communities and peoples in water management planning and decision-making must be secured. To implement the above two programme elements would involve a focus first on countries in East and southern Africa with results brought to other areas of Africa, in concert with UNEP, UNDP, FAO, the World Bank and other UN agencies as appropriate, and second, on related additions to current activities.

Assisting governments in implementing the "Fair Share" approach, and in disseminating practical and affordable techniques which can help the majority of people get access to clean water in the shortest possible time. In addition to some large-scale projects, what is now needed is fostering a great many small-scale projects based on community planning and management (e.g., hand-dug wells vs. high-tech boreholes, water tanks, rainwater harvesting, etc.). A series of initiatives to develop and propagate low-cost technologies are proposed along with a number of ongoing activities. UN agency involvement would include UNDP, UNICEF, UNEP, FAO, UNIDO, WHO and WMO in partnership with ECA and SADC.

Accelerating relevant components of existing projects to emphasize and demonstrate application of the "Fair Share" approach (e.g., Zambezi Action Plan) and the advantages of community participation in water management planning and decision-making. This would involve consultations over the next few years and expanded work, basin-by-basin, in 1998–9. Key participating UN agencies would be UNDP, UNEP, and the World Bank in partnership with SADC, NORAD, SIDA and DANIDA. The cost would depend upon the number of basins involved.

Assisting governments to set up more effective drainage basin and regional agreements and institutions for avoiding or settling conflicts over equitable access and use of water resources. The approach here would be workshops on conflict resolution, preparation of an African Guidelines and/or Charter on the Equitable and Sustainable Use of Shared Water Resources, and establishment of a panel of legal experts to advise and assist countries through the peaceful settlement of water disputes via mediation, conciliation and arbitration of disputes. This will involve the UN Secretariat, UNDP, UNEP, World Bank, FAO, ECA, SADC and relevant NGOs.

Source: "The United Nations System-wide Special Initiative on Africa Booklet," *United Nations Development Programme, Internet website.*

of a large rural community. Twenty of these wells yielded water too brackish to utilize, and the people reverted to using water found in the sand of a nearby river.

Rural people were desperate for water for both primary and secondary use. Traditional water sources were neglected and totally underutilized. There were valuable sources, however, in pools, silted rivers, *vleis* (marshes), springs, gravity-supply systems, and other water-harvesting systems. All these sites had great potential and, in the case of sand-abstraction, there was the added bonus of a natural filtration of the water. Tests proved that sand filtered out almost all contaminants, making the water ideal for primary use.

Undoubtedly, there was considerable potential for water supplies to be met from alternate sources, as well as added advantages. For instance, with sand-abstraction systems (such as subsurface storage) evaporation does not take place below 1,000 meters from the surface. Sufficient attention was not paid to these alternatives. Apart from dams that trapped a small percentage of water, the greatest volume flowed unutilized into the oceans. Sufficient studies and resultant systems were not put into place to retain and utilize this lost water.

With a burgeoning world population and, consequently, decreasing and deteriorating water supplies, every aspect of water development needed to be fully investigated. Although there was a greater need for water, water tables continued to drop and boreholes could not be forever deepened. Continuing to deepen the boreholes compounded the problem of sustainability. As the century came to an end, it was clear that for everyone to have access to a reliable and sustainable water supply, alternative systems should have been put in place.

–STEPHEN HUSSEY, BULAWAYO, ZIMBABWE

Viewpoint: Deepwater abstraction is an established and safe means of providing water for rural southern Africa.

The abstraction of water from high groundwater tables was practiced for centuries, and obtaining water from deepwater supplies was a natural progression of this technology. Modern, "appropriate" systems were perceived as being unable to provide total water requirements and were thus little known and little understood by both end users and the water fraternity. Alternative systems did not need to be developed because of the success of groundwater supplies in providing communities with quantities of clean, potable water close to areas of habitation.

"Bore" drilling technologies developed quickly in the United States because of the high demand for the supply of water for ranching and irrigation. Drilling was mainly achieved with augers on the largely alluvial soils of the prairies. With the existing infrastructure readily available, substantial investment, and an ever-increasing demand, drilling systems were quickly developed for more difficult hydrogeological areas. Percussion drilling rigs and air drills were invented and became bigger and faster as drilling technology was improved to deal with every situation from unstable, collapsing sands to drilling through solid basalt. As land was settled, boreholes were put down to provide the water required for ranching and farming. Such highly developed and refined technology and equipment was perceived as appropriate for the agricultural areas of other countries that had a high water demand, even in arid and semiarid areas.

As it became more successful, the technology spread further. In the 1920s and 1930s borehole technology was used for developing water sources for human populations in the Third World. Pressure for land first became a real issue in Zimbabwe (then Southern Rhodesia) during this time as European settlers acquired land. Boreholes were used to open up land for settlement. The introduction of this highly developed drilling technology meant that, in the right conditions, large amounts of water could be provided in a relatively short period of time. An obvious step was to utilize this technology to develop areas for human habitation in increasingly difficult groundwater areas.

The advancements proved appropriate in industrially developed countries where there was easy access to both site-identification technology and the resources to operate and maintain boreholes and pumps. Groundwater drilling became a packaged technology with a known sequence of events from site selection to pump installation and was, thus, only expected to be adopted by emerging countries in the drive for modernization and advancement. Groundwater and boreholes became the preferred means of water supply. The technology came to be seen as clean, reliable, and convenient, as opposed to rather inadequate and underdeveloped traditional technologies.

In order to provide sufficient water for all requirements, groundwater systems needed to be further developed. This water, whether from a shallow or deepwater source, had the advantage of being widely used. The technology and equipment required to develop deepwater sources was readily available. Thousands of users, as well as commercial and state installation contractors, were well equipped to develop groundwater sources through effective site-location equipment, fast and reliable drilling rigs, and appropriate pump systems and reticulation schemes.

At the end of the twentieth century this technology became more appropriate for Third World users. In sandy alluvial soils "jetting" was an easy and practical way of reaching groundwater and, in higher groundwater tables, "sludging" and "tube well augering" were both simple and possible. Similarly, developments in piping, with PVC and plastic, meant that pump maintenance and repair systems were simplified. "Down-the-hole" technology was improved and more-efficient drilling systems were developed. Emulsifiers and wellscreens prevented the collapse of boreholes and the ingress of fine sediment into pumps and pipes. The entire technology was improved in its ease of use and efficiency to a stage where it had considerable support and understanding from the technocrats down to the grassroots user.

More important than an individual's or a community's involvement in site selection was their ability to operate and maintain a pump. Sustainable systems were developed around groundwater-abstraction systems. It was quite possible for one or two women to operate, maintain, and repair deepwater hand pumps, without the need for expensive tools and superstructure. With retractable pump columns and down-the-hole technology, it was easy for one person to operate and maintain a handpump system either on his own or with minimal unskilled assistance.

The use of deep-groundwater technology eased the concentration of populations along rivers and in known water-source areas by enabling people to settle far from obvious sources of water. If the only water source was a river, people either had to move or travel long distances to collect their water; alternatively, an expensive, complex pumping reticulation system had to be devised. So-called appropriate systems generally only provided water in sufficient quantities in the immediate area of collection or storage. Groundwater supplies did not necessitate pipelines to deliver water to population centers. By drilling a borehole close to population centers there was a potential to use deep groundwater. One example could be found in Ntabazinduna, a periurban (settled area on the periphery of a city) area to the east of Bulawayo (southwest Zimbabwe) largely populated by Xhosa people, who arrived from South Africa with the early white settlers in the late nineteenth century. By way of acknowledging their assistance, the Xhosa were "given" some twenty square kilometers of land with little or no surface-water potential. To relieve water stress on the small population, some twenty-seven deepwater boreholes were drilled, largely in the 1950s and 1960s. Approximately nine thousand people lived in the area at the end of the century and were, for the most part, totally dependent on the water supplied from the boreholes.

The technology of groundwater identification and abstraction was well proven. The issue of responsibility and the provision of a maintenance system for the water supply required addressing, rather than the technology itself. Communities needed to be encouraged to take responsibility for their water-supply systems. There were many instances of decentralized water-supply systems in good groundwater areas where all the necessary infrastructure was in place. In too many instances, however, there was insufficient prior discussion or explanation. This poor communication, together with insufficient skills and tools within the community, meant that little responsibility was assumed by the community when the water supplies were handed over to the people. As a consequence, many systems became inoperative. Had the community been better prepared and equipped to undertake service and maintenance, they would have been in a much better position to accept responsibility. A well-known precept suggests that if people do not contribute to the service and maintenance, they do not accept responsibility and will likely call on the implementing agency to effect repairs.

To ensure sustainability in areas where the water-supply system was being decentralized, water-pricing schemes were often introduced to levy users in order to maintain pump systems. With the collapse of centralized maintenance systems, parallel systems of maintenance and repair were developed for rural communities to enable them to take control of their own water supplies. Equipment and training were given to villagers. People were not merely provided with a deepwater supply and then abandoned.

As a result of the proliferation of boreholes, people automatically understood groundwater supplies, and boreholes were often perceived as "the best," if not the only, solution to water-supply requirements. Rural communities were often attracted to the technology, which required little input on their behalf. A drilling rig simply arrived at a community, drilled for water, a pump was installed, and water for the community became available in a short time. The lack of input required from rural communities was particularly apparent when compared to a hand-dug well or the considerable manual labor required in the construction of a dam. Drilling technology was also popular because people believed the deeper the borehole, the more reliable the water supply would be. People generally understood that there would be plenty of water from deep-groundwater drilling through water-saturated rock, such as sandstone, or where the borehole intersected breaks in the rock at several levels through which water flowed.

Water abstracted from deepwater sources was naturally potable, having infiltrated its way from the surface to the water table through sediment and fractured rock. Thus, the water was initially clean and only contaminated after abstraction if it was allowed to form stagnant pools or was placed into unhygienic containers. The development of deep groundwater sources was thus an appropriate, natural, and suitable development of water supplies. The identification of groundwater resources was an effective and relatively easy skill; deepwater drilling a trouble-free technology; and modern pump technology, successful. This technology amounted to a standard and reliable method of providing water across a wide range of hydrogeological and social factors. Because of the prominence and widespread success of drilling and borehole technology, there has been no need to develop traditional or alternate technologies.

–STEPHEN HUSSEY, BULAWAYO, ZIMBABWE

References

Thomas W. Brandon, ed., *Groundwater: Occurrence, Development and Protection* (London: Institute of Water Engineers and Scientists, 1986).

Munyaradzi Chenje and Phyllis Johnson, eds., *Water in Southern Africa: A Report by SADC–Southern African Development Community, IUCN–the World Conservation Union, and SARDC–Southern African Research & Documentation Centre* (Maseru, Lesotho: SADC, Environment and Land Management Sector Coordination Unit; Harare, Zimbabwe: IUCN, Regional Office for Southern Africa, SARDC, 1996).

Lewis Clark, *The Field Guide to Water Wells and Boreholes* (Milton Keynes, U.K.: Open University Press; New York: Halsted Press, 1988).

Fletcher G. Driscoll, *Groundwater and Wells* (St. Paul, Minn.: Johnson Division, 1986).

Peter Fraenkel, *Water Pumping Devices: A Handbook for Users and Choosers* (London: Intermediate Technology Publications, 1986).

E. H. Hofkes, ed., *Small Community Water Supplies: Technology of Small Water Supply Systems in Developing Countries* (The Hague, Netherlands: International Reference Center, 1981).

Charles Kerr, *Community Water Development* (London: Intermediate Technology Publications, 1989).

More Water for Arid Lands: Promising Technologies and Research Opportunities: Report of an Ad Hoc Panel of the Advisory Committee on Technology Innovation, Board on Science and Technology for International Development, Commission on International Relations (Washington, D.C.: National Academy of Sciences, 1974).

Arnold Pacey and Adrian Cullis, *Rainwater Harvesting: The Collection of Rainfall and Run-off in Rural Areas* (London: Intermediate Technology Publications, 1986).

John Pickford, ed., *Integrated Development for Water Supply and Sanitation* (Loughborough, U.K.: Water, Engineering and Development Centre, 1999).

Pickford, ed., *Water and Sanitation for All: Partnerships and Innovations: Selected Papers of the 23rd WEDC Conference, Durban, South Africa, 1997* (London: Intermediate Technology Publications, 1998).

Michael Price, *Introducing Groundwater* (London & Boston: Allen & Unwin, 1985).

H. M. Raghunath, *Ground Water: Hydrogeology, Ground Water Survey and Pumping Tests, Rural Water Supply and Irrigation Systems* (New Delhi: Wiley Eastern, 1982).

EDWARDS AQUIFER

Will thinking of the Edwards Aquifer of south-central Texas as a commons help resolve water conflicts in the region?

Viewpoint: Many citizens do not view the Edwards Aquifer as a commons; instead, they believe its waters are a commodity to be extracted and sold within a regional marketplace.

Viewpoint: The long-term viability of the Edwards Aquifer in South Texas depends on regional water management policies and practices, based upon a shared cultural construct of the aquifer as a commons rather than a simple commodity, subject only to the rules of the marketplace.

The metropolitan center of south-central Texas, San Antonio is located just east of the 100th meridian; that line is often thought to divide the humid American East from the more arid West. The line is not, however, a firm indicator of regional weather patterns. Some years the San Antonio environs receive considerably more rain than in others, and even within a particular year, precipitation may vary dramatically.

Early humans in the area adapted to these cyclical conditions, and not until the late nineteenth century, when the population of San Antonio began to grow rapidly, were pressures on the local (and sole) source of water, the Edwards Aquifer, were first manifest. These problems became even more obvious and worrisome after World War II in response to an interrelated set of factors: the population of the city nearly doubled to approximately five hundred thousand people, residential sprawl to the north of the central core began to encroach on the recharge zone of the aquifer, and the region endured a withering drought that ran through much of the 1950s. Lawns turned brown and foundations cracked, crops and livestock were distressed, and battles over the amount of water the aquifer contained were as pitched as those over which form of consumption deserved priority.

The situation has only worsened. Larger populations in the region, many more houses and commercial developments over the recharge zone, and new state and federal regulations governing the flow of the aquifer dramatically influenced the regional struggle over water. The summer of 2000, for instance, brought yet another intense period of drought that in turn threatened the survival of several endangered species living within the aquifer; in response, extremely tight water restrictions were announced in September, leading to increased complaints about governmental regulations that favored fish over foundations.

These annual, feverish debates over water carry important implications for the proposed resolutions. Some argue passionately that conceiving of water as a market will insure its proper distribution; others believe that only when water is conceived of as a commons, something to which all stakeholders—human and animal—are a part, will it determine survival in the semiarid landscape. Still, others assert that locating new supplies of water, often at some remove, is the only reasonable response to periodic drought. One thing is clear: south-central Texas is running out of time.

Viewpoint:
Many citizens do not view the Edwards Aquifer as a commons; instead, they believe its waters are a commodity to be extracted and sold within a regional marketplace.

The sole source of water for most of the 1.5 million people in the San Antonio metropolitan area is the Edwards Aquifer, which is essential to the economic and physical health of the region. Because every resident in this south Texas city draws from this local resource, the aquifer could be considered as a commons of the sort discussed in Garrett Hardin's 1968 essay in *Science,* "The Tragedy of the Commons." It seems natural that users of the Edwards Aquifer would join together to form a community who would regulate and protect the aquifer, thus averting the fateful tragedy that Hardin predicted. One will see, however, that effective protection of the aquifer will require putting this issue into broader geographical and conceptual contexts.

The Edwards Aquifer is a vast underground lake of water stored within the porous limestone rocks of the Edwards geologic formation. The 160-mile-long formation stretches from Hays County in the east to Kinney County in the west. At its center is Bexar County, the location of San Antonio. The aquifer and San Antonio only exist because of the Balcones Escarpment, the rugged transition zone between the Edwards Plateau to the north and the coastal plains to the south. The karst geologic formation in the drainage and recharge zones collects rainfall and water from the Nueces River, and other rivers, and replenishes the aquifer. The natural outlet for the Edwards is a series of springs, which are the source for the Comal, San Marcos, and San Antonio rivers. The Comal and San Marcos are major tributaries for the Guadalupe River. The springs are an important ecological feature of the Texas Hill Country and are the home of several threatened or endangered species.

Since the late nineteenth century, well discharge has contributed to the annual withdrawal from the aquifer. At its peak in 1989, pumping withdrew 542,400 acre-feet of water from the Edwards. Since the average recharge rate of the aquifer is about 652,000 acre-feet, such large pumping rates could reduce the depth of the aquifer, causing the natural springs to go dry. Reduction in flow, in turn, threatens nine species that live in the springs, as well as downstream ecosystems that depend on the flows in the Guadalupe and San Antonio rivers. To protect these endangered environments and assure an adequate level of aquifer water, the Edwards Aquifer Authority (EAA) was created in 1993. The EAA has the task of reducing annual pumping to 400,000 acre-feet per year by 2007.

Users of the Edwards include agricultural interests, municipal water suppliers, light industry, and the tourist industry on the Comal and San Marcos rivers. For these varied and competing interests, the 400,000 acre-feet pumping limit presents a serious problem that will worsen as population grows. At the current growth rate, the population of the region is predicted to double by 2025. This projection indicates that the San Antonio metropolitan area will have to take steps to avoid significant water shortages in the near future. Periodic droughts that plague the region exacerbate this situation. In the summer of 2000, as in the preceding three years, the area experienced a severe drought. Emergency water-use restrictions were being enforced. In addition, there was concern that global climate change might lead to further reductions in rainfall over the next century.

A threat that is even more serious than the prospect of a water shortage is the potential for pollution of the Edwards Aquifer. Because its recharge zone is composed of karst, it offers little protection against chemical spills and other sources of pollution. The recharge zone is composed of porous limestone and sinkholes, which are efficient at allowing rainfall and river water to enter the aquifer, but it does not filter the water. This open structure means that gasoline from a leaking storage tank, runoff of excess fertilizer from a golf course, or pesticides used to treat residential lawns can seep into the aquifer. Thus, development over the aquifer recharge zone not only diminishes its recharge capabilities by blocking sinkholes and covering porous limestone with blacktop roads and concrete foundations, it introduces toxic chemicals. Part of the recharge zone that lies within Bexar County is crisscrossed by three major freeways (Loop-1604, US-281, and I-10) and is in the middle of the rapidly growing northern suburbs.

Dealing with the dual threat of water shortage and pollution requires careful regional planning. San Antonio has begun to invest in conservation. For instance, the San Antonio Water System (SAWS) developed a successful water-recycling program. Water treated at one of the sewage plants on the south side of town is distributed throughout San Antonio by a network of pipes, allowing golf courses, corporate sites, and university campuses to remain green; this "grey water"

The Riverwalk (Paseo del Rio) in San Antonio, Texas

(photograph © by Mark Langford)

also sustains the booming tourist industry by maintaining the flow of the San Antonio River, thus insuring the continued attractiveness of its fabled (and profitable) Riverwalk. SAWS also encourages water conservation through a public-outreach program. Residential water users are urged to consume less by choosing xeric plants, following sensible lawn irrigation, and installing low-flow showerheads and toilets. San Antonio voters approved legislation in 2000 that will enable the city to spend $45 million in tax money over the next ten years to fund the purchase of sensitive undeveloped land above the recharge zone.

San Antonio is aggressively pursuing the acquisition of additional water resources, a policy that most of its citizens and political leaders believe offers the best solution to local water problems. City officials signed a contract to buy water from Canyon Lake, located to the north, and are considering building a pipeline to transport water from Simsboro Aquifer in East Texas. San Antonio is also reaching southward in search of new water resources. It is considering building freshwater reservoirs and desalinization plants on the Gulf Coast of Texas and pumping the water two hundred miles north to consumers.

These initiatives demonstrate that the community does not find it appropriate to think of the Edwards Aquifer as a commons. One reason for this position is that the water in an aquifer is underground. Living on top of an aquifer is not like residing on the edge of a river or lake. When citizens of Blanco, Texas, a small community to the north of San Antonio, experienced a severe drought, they could walk to the Blanco River and see their dwindling water supply impounded behind a small dam. San Antonians cannot see their water supply because it is stored under hundreds of feet of rock; most residents do not easily connect their wasteful activities with depletion of the aquifer. The disconnection between human consumption and environmental impact explains the general indifference some San Antonians exhibit toward warnings about the link between development above the recharge zone and future degradation of the aquifer.

In San Antonio, water is considered a commodity to be bought and sold within a large geographical region. Planners and ordinary citizens think in terms of regional water supplies that through the careful application of money can be made to flow into the city. The Edwards represents just one of the sources of this valuable and vital resource.

For there to be a true water commons in South Texas, it would have to be defined on a larger geographical scale, and incorporate regional or statewide resources. It would also have to be flexible enough to set water problems in San Antonio within a broader context of environmental decline. The central problem facing the city is not water per se, but population growth and urban sprawl. Together these factors will bring more users of the aquifer–thirsty lawns, industry, highways, and development–into the recharge zone. Currently most of this growth is unregulated sprawl, which not only strains water resources but also destroys wildlife habitat, increases air pollution, and threatens critical species with extinction. Northwestern Bexar County, site of much of the new residential construction, contains critical habitat for the Golden Cheeked Warbler and Black Capped Vireo, two endangered species of birds. As suburban subdivisions spread further away from the center of San Antonio, and commuting distances and air pollution increase, there is greater demand for new highways and the expansion of older roads. A regional plan that addresses the wider problems of environmental despoliation will naturally include water issues. The tragedy to be averted through community action is the destruction of those resources, including the Edwards Aquifer, that help make San Antonio a unique landscape.

–FREDERICK MEERS LOXSOM,
TRINITY UNIVERSITY

Viewpoint: The long-term viability of the Edwards Aquifer in South Texas depends on regional water management policies and practices, based upon a shared cultural construct of the aquifer as a commons rather than a simple commodity, subject only to the rules of the marketplace.

Water, like air, is a commons, a resource that is shared by a group of people. In many parts of the world new land for farming and stock grazing, fish from the sea, and wood for fuel and housing are treated as commons to which each household has access. One of the most popular analyses of the conflicts surrounding the commons is that of Garrett Hardin, first published in *Science* in 1968. Hardin argues that each household can take resources from the commons and deposit wastes into it. Using a calculus of neoclassical economics, Hardin contends that as each household seeks it advantage, the costs to all seem small. Yet, some accumulate resources more rapidly, giving them access to an even larger share of the commons. Add in a Hobbesian view of human nature, and selfish households accumulate wealth from the commons by acquiring more than their fair share of resources and paying less than their fair share of the total costs. Ultimately, as population grows and greed runs rampant, the commons collapses and the end result is "the tragedy of the commons." In semiarid South Texas one does not have to look far to find a freshwater shortage, but the question is whether the commons is leading to tragedy or could such an idea be part of the solution to regional water woes?

Some 1.5 million people across a six-county area depend on water from the Edwards Aquifer, a rechargeable limestone karst that contains more freshwater than all the surface water in Texas. The crescent-shaped aquifer also reflects a cultural landscape: agricultural and ranching interests lie to the west, municipal and industrial needs occupy the central portion, and recreational uses dominate the eastern reaches. Not all of the water, however, is available for human use. In 1993 the Texas legislature set pumping limits and established the Edwards Aquifer

HARDIN'S "TRAGEDY OF THE COMMONS"

The tragedy of the commons develops in this way. Picture a pasture open to all. It is to be expected that each herdsman will try to keep as many cattle as possible on the commons. Such an arrangement may work reasonably satisfactorily for centuries because tribal wars, poaching, and disease keep the numbers of both men and beast well below the carrying capacity of the land. Finally, however, comes the day of reckoning, that is, the day when the long-desired goal of social stability becomes a reality. At this point, the inherent logic of the commons remorselessly generates tragedy.

As a rational being, each herdsman seeks to maximize his gain. Explicitly or implicitly, more or less consciously, he asks, "What is the utility *to me* of adding one more animal to my herd?" This utility has one negative and one positive component.

1. The positive component is a function of the increment of one animal. Since the herdsman receives all the proceeds from the sale of the additional animal, the positive is utility is nearly +1.

2. The negative component is a function of the additional overgrazing created by one more animal. Since, however, the effects of overgrazing are shared by all herdsmen, the negative utility for any particular decision-making herdsman is only a fraction of -1.

Adding together the component partial utilities, the rational herdsman concludes that the only sensible course for him to pursue is to add another animal to his herd. And another. . . . But this is the conclusion reached by each and every rational herdsman sharing a commons. Therein is the tragedy. Each man is locked into a system that compels him to increase his herd without limit—in a world that is limited. Ruin is the destination toward which all men rush, each pursuing his own best interest in a society that believes in the freedom of the commons. Freedom in a commons brings ruin to all.

Some would say that this is a platitude. Would that it were! In a sense, it was learned thousands of years ago, but natural selection favors the forces of psychological denial. The individual benefits as an individual from his ability to deny the truth even though society as a whole, of which he is part, suffers. Education can counteract the natural tendency to do the wrong thing, but the inexorable succession of generations requires that the basis for this knowledge be constantly refreshed.

A simple incident that occurred a few years ago in Leominster, Massachusetts, shows how perishable the knowledge is. During the Christmas shopping season the parking meters downtown were covered with plastic bags that bore tags reading: "Do not open until after Christmas. Free parking courtesy of the mayor and city council." In other words, facing the prospect of an increased demand for already scarce space, the city fathers reinstituted the system of the commons. (Cynically, we suspect that they gained more votes than they lost by this retrogressive act.)

In an approximate way, the logic of the commons has been understood for a long time, perhaps since the discovery of agriculture or the invention of private property in real estate. But it is understood mostly only in special cases which are not sufficiently generalized. Even at this late date, cattlemen leasing national land on the Western ranges demonstrate no more than an ambivalent understanding, in constantly pressuring federal authorities to increase the head count to the point where overgrazing produces erosion and weed-dominance. Likewise, the oceans of the world continue to suffer from the survival of the philosophy of the commons. Maritime nations still respond automatically to the shibboleth of the "freedom of the seas." Professing to believe in the "inexhaustible resources of the oceans," they bring species after species of fish and whales closer to extinction.

The National Parks present another instance of the working out of the tragedy of the commons. At present, they are open to all, without limit. The parks themselves are limited in extent—there is only one Yosemite Valley—whereas population seems to grow without limit. Plainly, we must soon cease to treat the parks as commons or they will be of no value to anyone.

Source: *Garrett Hardin, "The Tragedy of the Commons,"* Science, *162 (1968): 1243–1248, as republished in* An Annotated Reader in Environmental Planning and Management, *edited by Timothy O'Riordan and R. Kerry Turner (Oxford & New York: Pergamon Press, 1983), pp. 291–292.*

Authority (EAA) to issue permits to water users. The legislature acted to protect spring flows in the New Braunfels and San Marcos rivers, which support several species on the endangered list. People who depend on Edwards had to limit consumption even as population above the aquifer grew. Will thinking of the Edwards Aquifer as a commons help resolve water conflicts in South Texas, or is the region headed toward a series of water wars?

Some people have criticized Hardin's "tragedy of the commons" model for failing to distinguish between "common property" and "everybody's property," the latter being a condition of no property rights at all. By contrast, common property is a social institution with agreed-upon rules and rights of access. The Aymara Indians of Peru taught me this lesson early in my capacity as an adviser to the Rural Institute in Puno on Lake Titicaca. My first day on the job I was approached by a group of peasants whose elderly leader asked how we might share the water from the only spring on the ranch. I asked him for a suggestion. He recommended that the Institute use water during the day and the peasants use it at night. We agreed and that was that. Hardin might better have used the term "common pool" rather than "common property" and distinguished between the features of a resource and the ways people choose to relate to it and each other. In other words, the difficulty of bounding or defining a resource such as water or air, does not preclude the ways people under certain conditions may devise to manage the resource themselves. There is good evidence that more participatory and democratic systems of resource management may indeed work well whether under conditions of exclusive property rights (Japanese coastal fishermen) or open access (Norwegian cod fisheries).

The way people relate to a resource and to each other is an empirical question, and not, as Hobbes assumes, a function of a self-centered human nature in which human beings are reduced to predators with no responsibilities for the common good. To his credit Hardin recognized that an individual could be faced with a dilemma when forced to act in his or her own self-interest, while being condemned at the same time for not being a responsible citizen. Yet, Hardin was still stuck in a worldview in which there are only individuals, and communities are no more than the sum of the individual members.

By contrast, social scientists, following in the tradition of French sociologist Emile Durkheim, view communities as fundamentally moral and relational in character. Even a nation, such as the United States, is more than an aggregate of 270 million citizens, but it is an "imagined community," which is symbolically constructed by the moral relationships that bind individuals together. If communities, large and small, are to avoid a "tragedy of the commons," they must be built along the lines of shared meaning, ethical principles, and responsibility for the common good. This effort is not a naive "communitarianism" in which everyone is expected to cooperate. Indeed, in a true community competition and cooperation are not mutually exclusive, as long as everyone abides by accepted strategies and rules, such as "do no harm."

Steps are being taken to create such a moral community among the users of the Edwards Aquifer. The story begins in 1994, when despite the recommendations of two mayoral committees, and the expenditure of hundreds of thousands of dollars promoting the construction of a surface-water reservoir called Applewhite, the citizens of San Antonio rejected the proposal–not once, but twice. After five years of debate not only was there no consensus on a plan to manage the water needs of San Antonio, but the two sides in the conflict seemed to be even further apart. Enter Councilman Bob Ross, who had opposed building the Applewhite reservoir but favored the development of a water-management plan. He concluded that a different approach to the conflict was necessary. Within a week of the second defeat of the referendum, Ross wrote a letter to the *San Antonio Express News,* which read in part: "Now that the Applewhite question has been laid to rest, this will give us an opportunity to concentrate on solutions to overcome the problems that are facing us." He proposed creating a panel of experts who would review existing plans and make recommendations "based on science, hydrology and geology, not on political considerations."

What eventually emerged was the Mayor's Citizens Committee on Water (MCCW), which differed from previous "top-down" efforts at water planning in several ways. First, it included all the players in the former water wars, as well as prominent community leaders and neighborhood groups. The diversity on the committee was to insure public trust and credibility in the outcome of the process–two things not found in the previous water committees. Secondly, the MCCW used professional mediation to forge a consensus on an equitable water plan for the city. Third, the mediators and committee had their own support staff independent of the San Antonio Water System (SAWS). SAWS would be part of the process, but not direct it.

The mediation effort was essentially one of "consensus building." There was no chairperson, since that would endow one of the constituencies with more power than the others. Mediators acted as facilitators to insure that the group abided by the "ground rules," set agendas, met or changed deadlines, and generally moved toward their goal of completing their mission or charge. There were no votes taken, but a topic was discussed until such time as everyone felt they could "live with the decision of the group" whether or not they agreed with everything that was said. One mediator commented that the process demanded, "People had to listen to one another." The committee had a general deadline of January 1997 to report to city council so that the city might have a plan in place before the seventy-fifth Texas legislative session that convened that same month. The committee submitted its final report, "Framework for Progress: Recommended Water Policy Strategy for the San Antonio Area," on 23 January.

As a first step the MCCW set a precedent for building a moral community that could begin to manage its commons. It was only a first step, however, because the commons is much larger than the municipal limits of the city of San Antonio. The EAA is an important next step in constructing a community to oversee the use and conservation of the common pool that the Edwards represents. Still, the EAA has functioned as a permitting agency and has not yet set about creating that moral community and consensus necessary to avoid the tragedies of misuse and abuse of the aquifer. For example, the EAA should be issuing a clarion call about the dangers of aquifer pollution as more homes and businesses are built over the recharge zone.

In 1997 the state legislature established sixteen Regional Water Planning Groups charged with creating a State Water Plan by October 2000. While these bodies are regional and seek local input, their plans to generate new water to meet local needs often include sources outside of their planning region. One such case involves the tapping of the Simsboro Aquifer southeast of Austin to provide water to San Antonio. Farmers, small ranchers, suburban homeowners, and environmentalists in Bastrop County are fighting plans by Alcoa to build a second strip mine and sell underground water to the fast-growing metropolis of San Antonio. Opponents, including the Austin City Council, say the 15,000-acre project will drain underground water supplies from two counties, devastate the land, and force landowners to sell out. Critics of the plan include citizens of San Antonio who argue that to do harm to another watershed to protect one's own is unethical and illustrates the moral weakness of a pure "market strategy." These are of the voices of a community dedicated to avoiding any water-management policy that erodes solidarity, trust, and equality. Their voices, if heard, would turn the commons away from tragedy to hope.

–JOHN M. DONAHUE,
TRINITY UNIVERSITY

References

John M. Donahue and Jon Q. Sanders, "Sitting Down at the Table: Mediation Efforts in Resolving Water Conflicts," in *San Antonio: An Environmental History,* edited by Char Miller (Pittsburgh: University of Pittsburgh Press, forthcoming).

Donahue, "Water Wars in South Texas: Managing the Edwards Aquifer," in *Water, Culture and Power: Local Struggles in a Global Context,* edited by Donahue and Barbara Rose Johnson (Washington, D.C.: Island Press, 1998), pp. 187–208.

Garrett Hardin, "The Tragedy of the Commons," *Science,* 162 (1968): 1243–1248.

Don Hinrichsen, Bryant Robey, and Ushma D. Upadhyay, "Solutions for a Water-Short World," *Population Reports,* 26 (September 1998).

Michael F. Logan, *Fighting Sprawl and City Hall: Resistance to Urban Growth in the Southwest* (Tucson: University of Arizona Press, 1995).

Bonnie J. McCay and Svein Jentoft, "Market or Community Failure?: Critical Perspectives on Common Property Research," *Human Organization,* 57 (Spring 1998): 21–29.

EUPHRATES-TIGRIS BASIN

Who has legal right to the water resources of the Euphrates-Tigris Basin, Syria or Turkey?

Viewpoint: Turkey has the political and legal right to exploit the water resources of the Euphrates-Tigris Basin, though an agreement to resolve a whole nexus of water-related issues should be worked out among Turkey, Syria, and Iraq.

Viewpoint: Syria has strong historical and political claims to the Euphrates waters, though a comprehensive, environmentally and politically sustainable solution should be peacefully negotiated and given the force of international law.

The human population boom of the last half of the twentieth century put the spotlight on the diminishing supply of available freshwater. Water disputes ultimately have graver political, economic, legal, and ecological implications than disputes over any other natural resource, including oil. Without oil, modern industrial life would be crippled; without water, all of humanity would be threatened by thirst and hunger.

The vast majority of water—more than 95 percent of the total world supply—is largely inaccessible to humans. Water found in the oceans and seas is far too salty to be used for drinking or irrigation, and desalinization plants are costly to build and maintain. Freshwater locked in polar ice caps is equally inaccessible, the costs of transporting icebergs to water-poor areas being all but prohibitive. Only lakes and rivers, which contain far less than 1 percent of global water resources, are easily accessed by modern technology.

Agriculture requires the greatest amount of freshwater, even in highly industrialized countries. In arid regions—where rainfall is irregular and unpredictable, and long droughts are a constant threat—access to lakes and rivers takes on an even greater importance. Not surprisingly, therefore, water scarcity is a major source of tension and disputes in the Middle East. Making matters worse is the fact that most rivers in that part of the world cross state boundaries. Resources that are both shared and scarce tend to be viewed by states in zero-sum terms: one state's "gain" is another state's "loss." Water, in fact, is in such short supply in the Middle East that transboundary river issues are matters of the high diplomacy and statecraft. Water politics is even more important than oil politics because, while many Middle East states control an abundance of oil, none has an adequate or secure supply of water.

The following two essays explore one of the most bitter and intractable disputes in the Middle East, the struggle between Turkey and Syria for control of the Euphrates-Tigris Basin. The dispute had political, economic, scientific-technical, and even military dimensions. Both countries rely on rain-fed agriculture to produce their food supplies and both experienced population booms that placed increasing burdens on their water resources. The two nations also understand that rational planning at the regional level provided the best long-term solution to their mutual water problems but were deeply divided along national lines as to how to reach those solutions.

Viewpoint: Turkey has the political and legal right to exploit the water resources of the Euphrates-Tigris Basin, though an agreement to resolve a whole nexus of water-related issues should be worked out among Turkey, Syria, and Iraq.

Many interrelated issues make water a critical element of national security policy in the Middle East. Water resources are important means for achieving economic development, political autonomy, and national unity. Irrigation is the only way to ensure an adequate food supply for one's population, especially during periods of economic and military embargoes. As the birthrate in the Middle East increased each year in the late twentieth century, so too did the demand on available water supplies. Also, in the Islamic religious tradition, water is perceived as a divine gift from God. All of these factors fostered a spirit of competition among the Middle East states for the same water resources, transforming water issues into a central element of national security for each nation.

The Euphrates-Tigris Basin is one of the most conflict-laden river systems of the Middle East. Disputes on the Euphrates and Tigris are inseparable from geography: the territories of Turkey, Syria, and Iraq all lie within their catchment area. The utilization of the Euphrates-Tigris by those three states has been subject to dispute since the dissolution of the Ottoman Empire in 1918. Since the 1950s the most-bitter disputes have centered around differing conceptions in Syria and Turkey as to how to best develop the Euphrates. Most important among these disagreements have been two water development projects, the Euphrates Valley Project in Syria and the Southeastern Anatolia Project in Turkey.

The Tabqa (or ath-Thawrah) hydroelectric dam, built using a Soviet design, is the centerpiece of the Euphrates Valley Project. Completed in 1973, it began filling with water during the winter of 1973–1974 with the aim of being able to generate electricity and providing water to irrigate 640,000 hectares. From the outset, however, it was beset by many technical problems, not the least of which was the fact that it was ill-adapted to the local topography. In summer the reservoir typically gets drawn too low to generate an adequate amount of electricity, and this situation in turn led to power shortages in Aleppo, Damascus, and other major cities.

Turkey began to develop the Euphrates at about the same time Syria did. Construction of the Keban hydroelectric dam began in 1965 and, like its counterpart in Syria, it became operational in 1973. Keban was followed by other more-sophisticated projects, all of which were later subsumed under the Southeastern Anatolia Project. Turkish engineers and construction companies oversaw all of the planning and development.

Tensions between Syria and Turkey over the Euphrates waters began to multiply as both developed their projects independently of one another. Syria took the position that the Euphrates and Tigris were separate entities, and that the subject of talks between two states should be limited to the Euphrates. According to Syria, the Euphrates was an international river that had to be treated as an integral entity throughout its basin; all of the riparian states had inherent and equal rights that could not be infringed on by the upstream state of Turkey. The Turkish argument, by contrast, was based on the standard definition of an international watercourse, which has both a geographic and legal dimension. Strictly speaking, both the Euphrates and the Tigris were transboundary, not international, watercourses. International watercourses are boundary rivers, that is, rivers whose left and right banks belong to two different states. Typically these states divide the river along an in-stream line known as the *thalweg*. A transboundary watercourse, by contrast, is one that begins in the territory of one state and subsequently passes through one or more states as it flows downstream. Both the Tigris and Euphrates are such watercourses. They are therefore governed by the obligation of each state not to cause appreciable harm to another state, and by the principle of equitable and reasonable use of available waters without prejudice to sovereignty rights—but not by the specific rules that govern international watercourses.

The Turkish government argued that the Euphrates and Tigris constituted a single hydrological system, not only because they merged before reaching the Persian Gulf to form the Shatt al Arab, but also because Iraq used the waters of both rivers interchangeably through its Tharthar Canal Project, which transferred waters from the Tigris to the Euphrates. There was yet another reason Turkey insisted that the two rivers be linked diplomatically: its decision to proceed with the Southeastern Anatolia Project was perceived as aggressive and insensitive by both Syria and Iraq. Both countries feared that the consumptive use of the Euphrates waters by Turkey would disrupt both the consumption patterns and future plans of two downstream countries. From the Turkish perspective, therefore, a resolution of the water question with Syria was inseparable from a resolution with Iraq.

The Ataturk Dam across the Euphrates River in southeastern Turkey. One of the largest earth- and rock-fill dams in the world, it became fully functional in 1990.

(Select/JB Pictures [Ed Kashi])

It must be stressed, however, that the Southeastern Anatolia Project did not significantly diminish Iraqi and Syrian water supplies. Turkey used only a small amount of the total debit of these rivers. In the winter and spring months a vast quantity of water unused by Turkey, Syria, or Iraq would flow into the sea. The water that is now in dispute is in fact that which otherwise flowed unused into the sea. The Turkish dams actually benefited neighboring states because they regulated seasonal fluctuations, particularly by helping to prevent water shortages in Syria and Iraq by changing the fickle natural flow into a near-continuous one. In addition, calculations showed that a belt of thirty to fifty kilometers bordering Turkey and Syria might benefit from this project with minimum investment. In fact, Syrians would benefit from the huge Turkish projects without having to pay any of the costs.

The heart of the dispute, however, revolved not around water-flow regulation, but water allocation. Syria and Iraq claimed that the 1987 protocol signed between Turkey and Syria on allocating the Euphrates waters to the downstream countries was an interim one, and interpreted the five-hundred-cubic-meters-per-second clause in that protocol as a prelude to a final partitioning of the waters. They insisted on increasing the minimum quota to seven hundred cubic meters per second, which is about 70 percent of the average flow of the Euphrates River, until a definitive allocation of the waters among the riparians was agreed upon.

These demands were excessive. Syria and Iraq received plenty of water from the Euphrates and Tigris, only to squander most of it through wasteful irrigation methods rooted in past traditions. Moreover, they continued the practice of irrigating infertile land even though it inevitably resulted in an uneconomic crop yield. Both countries must improve their methods of water consumption before they return to the negotiating table to demand more water based on need and equity.

When viewed from a larger perspective, Syrian water politics reveal themselves to be contradictory. Syria is a lower riparian state on the Euphrates, but an upper riparian state on two other river systems, the Yarmuk and Orontes. On the Yarmuk, Syria built a series of dams upstream that significantly decreased the flow reaching Israel and Jordan. It does the same on the Orontes, which flows from Syria to Turkey. In fact, Syria made use of 90 percent of the total flow of the Orontes–and is expected to take even more if the planned reservoirs of Ziezoun and Kastoun are built. Even as Syria accused Turkey of overutilizing the Euphrates, it took the lion's share of the Orontes leaving Turkey almost none.

Additionally, Syria supported the activities of an anti-Turkish terrorist organization, the Kurdistan Workers' Party (PKK). By tolerating the PKK and their training facilities in the Bekáa Valley, Syria employed international terrorists in its water dispute with Turkey. PKK operations from the Bekáa Valley continued throughout the late 1980s and 1990s, causing thousands of deaths and injuries. PKK activities dangerously increased tensions between Turkey and Syria, and the two countries came to the brink of war in 1998. War was only avoided when Syria signed the Adana Declaration and agreed to cut its support to PKK. In February 1999 Abdullah Öcalan, the leader of PKK, was captured in Nairobi, Kenya, and subsequently imprisoned on Imrali Island in the Sea of Marmara. Öcalan was tried and sentenced to death on 29 June 1999. With the PKK issue seemingly resolved, economic relations between the two countries began to improve, and relations between Syria and Turkey were expected to improve further under the leadership of the new Syrian president Bashar al-Assad.

Turkey preferred cooperation over conflict in its relations with Syria and Iraq. To achieve this cooperation, since the 1980s it was taking important steps toward resolving the transboundary river issues. The first step toward cooperation came with the formation of the Joint Technical Committee (JTC). In the meeting of the Turkish-Iraqi Mixed Economic Commission in December 1980, the two sides agreed on the formation of the JTC to study matters relating to regional waters, in particular the Euphrates-Tigris Basin. The first meeting was held in May 1982. In 1983 Syria joined the meetings, and from then on the JTC convened on a trilateral basis. The JTC was not, however, able to resolve the underlying political and legal disputes. After sixteen technical and two ministerial meetings, the JTC talks came to a deadlock, having failed to produce the outline of its report. The seventeenth meeting, scheduled for June 1993 in Ankara, was canceled at the last minute when Syrian officials announced their decision not to attend.

The second Turkish initiative was the Peace Water Pipeline Project. On a visit to the United States in February 1987 the former Turkish prime minister Turgut Özal proposed the construction of a huge pipeline to transport water from the Seyhan and Ceyhan Rivers of Turkey to various countries in the Middle East. The prime minister suggested that Syria, Jordan, Saudi Arabia, and the Gulf States could be supplied with water through two pipelines. The Peace Pipeline was aimed at creating interdependence among countries of the region and establishing regional peace and stability. Although it was financially and technically feasible, the Saudi and Kuwaiti officials did not accept Özal's request on political grounds as well as on the argument that the price of water delivered through the pipelines would be too high compared to local desalinization. Failure of the Peace Pipeline indicated that the states in the Middle East were not yet ready to accept and implement models that created a peaceful interdependence among them.

One of the major obstacles to the efficient use of water in the region was the lack of reliable data on flows, quality of water and land in the basin areas, and current crop and irrigation patterns. The paucity of reliable information stood in the way of finding more efficient ways of utilizing water by the riparians. Turkey therefore proposed a plan—called the Three-Staged Plan for Optimum, Equitable, and Reasonable Utilization of the Transboundary Watercourses of the Tigris-Euphrates Basin—at the second tripartite ministerial meeting on 26 June 1990 in Ankara. The plan mainly used the terminology developed by the International Law Commission of the United Nations and used in the Law of the Non-Navigational Uses of International Watercourses (1997).

The three stages of the plan are: water-resource inventory studies designed to determine evaporation, temperature, and rainfall patterns; land-resource inventory studies to determine soil and leeching conditions; and water-and-land evaluation studies to determine the irrigation type and system for planned projects aiming at minimizing water losses and to investigate the possibility of modernization and rehabilitation of the projects in operation. After these studies were complete, the total water consumption of each state was to be determined.

The plan was not only designed to facilitate negotiations among the parties by providing a common set of data, but it allowed for a more efficient use of water. For example, after preparing a standardized soil classification of possible irrigation sites on the Euphrates and Tigris, it was possible to work out an agreement to irrigate the higher-quality lands, irrespective of the country in which they were located, before commencing irrigation of lower quality lands because the former would produce higher yields using the same amount of water. Despite its virtues, the plan was rejected by the downstream riparians. One of the main reasons was the refusal of Syria to negotiate on the Orontes River as well as the Euphrates-Tigris Basin.

Of course, water disputes constituted only one aspect of regional ethnic, religious, economic, and strategic issues—all of which are interrelated. To a certain extent problems of water resources cannot be tackled independently from other issues that divide the region. Precisely

VISIT TO ILISU-BARAJI (HASANKEYF)

The Ilisu-dam is to be built at the Tigris about 65 km upstream the border of Syria and Iraq nearby the town Dargeçit having a length of 1820 m and a height of 135 m. This will form a reservoir with a surface area of 313km^2 and a capacity of 10.4 km^3. Main goal of this structure is the generation of energy. . . .

During the round travel could be visited the part of the project area in and around the town Hasankeyf and the surroundings of Batman and Siirt. Together with its architecture, the cave buildings, the ruins of the old bridge across the Tigris and the steep bank of the Tigris—sometimes changing with gentle slopes—the town Hasankeyf forms a magnificent landscape. Short before reaching the town one passes several military areas. The town itself makes a rather neglected impression. Obviously no considerable investments have been made for several years. The numerous buildings under historical preservation are as well heavily neglected. But though, the historical value of the buildings and the whole ensemble is still unmistakable. A planned taking apart of some of those monuments and their rebuilding at another place would not cope with the demand for preservation. Besides, considering the type of construction and the state of these monuments of architecture this way to preserve them would cause enormous damages to the original buildings. Along the Tigris river many people are to be seen. Women do the laundry, children are playing in the water, adults are as well bathing. Along the riverbank at the side of the town are situated several restaurants in the water—formed by simple wooden constructions with a roof of leaves. The people are living on and with the river. The river could not ever be replaced by the planned reservoir. The water quality of the reservoir would be in any case worse than that of the running river. With regard to the aesthetics the reservoir could not compete with the living Tigris either. In the stagnating water waste water would concentrate and it would be a habitat to mosquitoes.

Following the optical impression the water in the Tigris is of good quality. In spite of the low water level no pollution, waste pipe discharge or concentrations of eutrophic algae are recognisable. The river seems to be rich in fish.

The alluvial valley of the Tigris at that section is relatively narrow. Especially along the right hand side and sometimes at both sides the river is restricted by rock face. Tributaries often form deeply carved gorges. Upstream of Hasankeyf there are many woody plants, prevailingly willow. Above the regularly flooded area are situated fields and gardens. Especially downstream of Hasankeyf can be found large agricultural areas in the flooding designated area of the Ilisu reservoir. Due to the season only few birds could be observed around Hasankeyf. But one can expect that the manifold countryside of the river valley houses a biodiversity that by far exceeds the one of its environs. This is valid as for the flora as for the fauna. Different habitats are to be found close to each other due to the rapidly changing conditions in a river environment. . . .

The structure will dam up the Tigris on a stretch of 120 km. This will have enormous ecological consequences. The ecological functions of the river will be lost. The waste water discharges by the cities Diyarbakir, Batman and Siirt will even more pollute the river as the self cleaning ability of the river will be considerably reduced on this long stretch. The population of these cities has massively grown in the last few years. Diyarbakir with about 1 million has doubled its population since 1995. This means large problems with rubbish and waste water. Until now no water treatment plants do exist. Merely Diyarbakir is planning the construction of a water treatment plant. As this is the only plan of such a plant in the whole region it is rather unlikely that this will solve the problem of water pollution. An other danger to the Tigris as well for the planned Ilisu reservoir is the oil production around the city of Batman. The hauling plants are situated close to the planned Ilisu reservoir, their surroundings are heavily contaminated with oil which would make a pollution of the reservoir very likely.

That dam would have massive impacts on the household of sediment of the whole Tigris river. Downstream of the dam an increased side and depth erosion of the river bed can be foreseen. A deepened riverbed can lead to a dropping of the ground water level. The intensified side erosion would mean a loss of agricultural land and an increased danger for buildings and bridges. The interruption of the sediment transport would have impacts on the whole river down to the estuary in the Gulf of Persia.

Source: *Stefan Michel, "A Travel Report," translated by Alfred Olfert (Summer 1999), Dam Projects in Turkey, European Rivers Networks, Internet website.*

because these issues are interlinked, however, it is important that progress be achieved. The innovative Turkish initiatives designed to resolve water problems in the Middle East were put forth in the hope that they would hasten progress on other fronts as well.

–IBRAHIM MAZLUM,
MARMARA UNIVERSITY

Viewpoint:
Syria has strong historical and political claims to the Euphrates waters, though a comprehensive, environmentally and politically sustainable solution should be peacefully negotiated and given the force of international law.

Syria is only modestly endowed with natural resources, but it is rich in historical experience. That legacy explains the desire of Syria for self-sufficiency, its wariness with regard to its wealthier and more-powerful neighbors, and its insistence on comprehensive and negotiated settlements. Of all the countries of the Middle East, Syria is one of the poorest in water resources. While southern Turkey (its driest part) receives more than 650 centimeters of rainfall annually, Syria is lucky if it receives 300 centimeters. The Turks utilize 2,300 cubic meters of freshwater per capita per year, while Syrians use only 270 cubic meters. When water is so scarce, it is understandable that it would be a coveted and sacred resource.

Repetitive cycles of growth and decline have etched lessons in the Syrian communal memory. At the crossroads of the Middle East, and thus of three continents, the location of Syria has determined a survive-to-prosper strategy that linked agriculture and trade through the political economy of its cities. When demographic and environmental conditions permitted, cultivation and settlement were extended outward from the cities and their oases. This strategy has been successful: Damascus and Aleppo are considered to be the oldest continuously inhabited cities on earth.

Beginning in the late eighteenth century, when Syrian lands were part of the Ottoman Empire, a noticeable growth and revival of civilization occurred. Though continuing into the twenty-first century, this process has not always been easy. The borders of the modern Republic of Syria were drawn by European colonial powers—boundaries that curtailed and disrupted agriculture and trade. Aleppo, the most important Syrian city in the north, lost its agricultural hinterland in the west, north, and northeast to Turkey. Syria also lost to Turkish control the headwaters of the rivers that supplied Aleppo and its oasis with water. These rivers were subsequently laid dry by Turkey, necessitating major engineering projects in Syria to transport water from the Euphrates for the rescue of the thirsty city.

To the west the colonial powers created Greater Lebanon, trebling the size of Lebanon by attaching to it the Mediterranean coastal strip of central Syria and the agricultural lands of the Bekáa Valley. Both of these areas contained important water resources and some of the best agricultural soil of the Fertile Crescent. Palestine was separated from Syria in the south. The new Syro-Lebanese and Syro-Palestinian borders separated Damascus from its ports of Tripoli, Beirut, Saida, and Haifa.

An especially painful situation took place in 1938 when the French ceded the water-rich province of Alexandretta to the Republic of Turkey in an unsuccessful diplomatic maneuver to win Turkey as an ally in the approaching conflict with Germany. In contravention of United Nations (U.N.) resolutions, Israel has occupied a good deal of Syrian agricultural land. The Golan, a water-rich agricultural region that, like the Bekáa Plain, was formerly attached to Damascus, was taken by Israel in 1967. While the rain- and river-rich western coastal regions of northern Syria, Lebanon, and Palestine were detached from the interior, the tribal steppe-lands of the eastern and southeastern interior were divided between Syria and the new states of Iraq, Kuwait, Saudi Arabia, and Trans-Jordan. Syria thereby became an arid rump of its former self, a country in which only 8 to 12 percent of the land receives sufficient rainfall for cultivation.

Only one small river originates and ends within the borders of the Republic of Syria. This river is the Barada, which only partially meets the needs of the Damascus oasis. The Yarmuk (400 million cubic meters), a tributary of the Jordan River, is shared with Jordan and Israel. The Orontes (1.1 billion cubic meters) rises in Lebanon, flows through Syria, and ends in the disputed province of Hatay. Compared to the two rivers disputed by Turkey, however, these three rivers are mere streams whose combined volume is minuscule.

On average, the Euphrates carries an approximate annual total of thirty-two billion cubic meters at its fullest point and the Tigris carries fifty billion cubic meters. One hundred percent of the waters available to Syria of both the Euphrates and Tigris collect in Turkey, either in the form of rain, upland springs, or tributaries. Thus, Syria is sandwiched between Turkey, where the water originates, and the Republic of Iraq, where more water is added. Modern political geography has given both Turkey and Iraq mountains that capture the precipitation that sustains the rivers. As the middle partner, and as the country with the greatest scarcity, the position of Syria is precarious.

It is a paradox that while losing so many important territorial and hydrological assets to neighboring countries on all sides, Syria simultaneously became the substitute homeland for the large numbers of refugees victimized by these territorial transfers. The flow of water was replaced by a flow of refugees. Already in the nineteenth century the Syrian lands had been the receptor for thousands of refugees from other parts of the Ottoman Empire. At that time the peasants who came to Syria from Algeria, Greece, the Balkans, the Caucasus, and other lost Ottoman territories were welcome additions to the rapidly developing agricultural economy.

By the beginning of the twentieth century, during peasant uprisings and pogroms against the Armenians, however, the Syrian economy was no longer in a position to absorb more refugees. Available cultivatable land was settled, the return on cultivation no longer profitable, and entrepreneurs invested in the importation of grain. The huge numbers of Armenians forcibly deported from Turkey during and following World War I arrived at a time when Syrians were already starving. Reliance on the world market for its food supply led to the starvation of at least half a million people in Syria between 1915 and 1918.

With the creation of the state of Israel (1948), Syria received yet more refugees as thousands of dispossessed Palestinian peasants fled their homeland. Then, in 1967, when Israel occupied the Golan, ethnic cleansing generated yet another wave. During the late 1990s, in the north and northeast, large numbers of Kurdish peasants (experiencing a fate similar to that of the Armenians and the Jaulanis) have also fled to Syria from Turkey and Iraq. It is an irony of history that Syria is held responsible for the irredentist political movements of these refugee populations, which confuses cause and effect.

By the end of the twentieth century Syria was still a developing country. The rate of capitalization and industrialization lagged; Syria lacked the water resources of Turkey, oil reserves of Iraq, and the foreign aid assistance given to Jordan and Israel. At the same time, a sustained high birthrate combined with an increase in the average life span gave Syria one of the highest population growth rates (at 4.7 percent in the 1980s, dropping to 3.8 percent in the 1990s) in the world. More than half of the population was under the age of sixteen.

There was insufficient economic opportunity in agriculture for large rural populations. This situation was exacerbated in Syria because of population growth and the limited amount of arable land. Syria had a huge unemployed and underemployed former-peasant population in its cities, making food security a social and political imperative. The urban population of 6.2 million in 1990 was expected to grow to 29.1 million by 2025. Understandably, the Syrians wished to reverse the land-flight trend, grow their own food, and limit their dependence on imports for the basic staples. Past experiences with politically induced famines (such as during World War I), and also their food dependency on Egypt, Jordan, and Iraq, colored Syrian perspectives.

The agricultural boom following World War II was largely the result of the introduction of groundwater pumps along the Euphrates in the north and northeast of the country and the extension of irrigation to new acreage. Because Syria had only limited oil resources, the harnessing of hydroelectric power became a developmental imperative. Emulating Egypt, Syria negotiated long-term loans and technical assistance to build a high dam on the Euphrates. The Tabqa Dam was completed in 1974. As in Egypt, however, the dam in Syria brought many new and unforeseen problems. Though dams were ideal solutions in colder, wetter climates, the creation of a large exposed basin of water was not ideal in the hot dry climate of Syria. Water loss to evaporation was exacerbated by seepage. Leeching brought mineral residues to the surface. Before long, a good deal of the newly recovered land was endangered by salinization, and yields have not improved as was anticipated.

Against this background the importance of the High Dam at Tabqa as an energy producer must be assessed. Increasing amounts of hydroelectric energy could power more efficient irrigation systems and ease the transition of Syria from agriculture to agriculture-related industry. Unforeseen was the possibility that the water would be stopped upriver. As Turkey began its extensive damming of the Euphrates, beginning with two, but eventually controlling the flow at more than a dozen points, the Syrian water supply became increasingly vulnerable. When the basin of the largest Turkish dam, the Attaturk Dam, was filled in 1990, the flow to Syria was interrupted for nearly a month, causing electricity shortfalls and blackouts. An estimated ten billion cubic meters of river water were removed for Turkish irrigation projects. In addition, Turkish hydroelectric planning indicates that water release to Syria (related to snowmelt surpluses) would take place at a time in the agricultural cycle when Syria cannot utilize it, requiring the construction of additional dams in Syria.

During the early and mid 1990s the flow was reduced to the point that it stopped operation of seven of the ten turbines at Tabqa, causing severe power outages throughout Syria. In 2000 Turkey announced it would permit water to flow over the dam—even though it did not need the electricity during the holidays—so that the power supply in Syria would not be interrupted. Because Turkey took these steps without consultation, it became painfully clear to Syrians that not only their industrial future, but the very water itself, was at the mercy of Turkish water diplomacy.

From the Syrian point of view, the Turkish record did not inspire trust. Ever since the collapse of the Ottoman Empire, Turkey has repeatedly turned its back on the rest of the Middle East. It laid rivers dry that provided the main supply of one major Syrian city. The promises from Turkey that 50 percent of the former Euphrates flow would be released to Syria proved to be a unilateral pronouncement rather than a mutually agreed amount, and it was not tenable. Although both Syria and Iraq are watered by the Euphrates, their joint claim for 70 percent flow was rejected by the Turks. The Syrians felt that Turkey sidestepped international and Islamic law, as well as breached both the spirit and letter of bilateral agreements.

Some Turkish politicians held that just as the Arabs sell their oil, Turkey can sell "its" water. Water cannot, however, be equated with oil as a resource. Unlike oil, water is a renewable resource restored annually by global weather trends. In other words, to say that Turkey owns the water would be like saying Turkey owns its clouds. The Turkish position was also in contradiction to Islamic law, which is clear on the point that water, like air, belongs to God and therefore to everyone.

Countries to the southwest and north of Syria were the greatest military powers in the region. The Israel military was guaranteed by the United States to exceed that of all the Arab states combined. As a member of the North Atlantic Treaty Organization (NATO), Turkey had the added advantage of access to superior technology. The expressions of friendship between Turkey and Israel were threatening from the Syrian perspective. It was easy enough for the "big guys on the block" to feign a cooperative spirit, while continuing to help themselves to generous portions of the regional resources. Syrians felt that Turkish water diplomacy was thinly disguised hegemonic ambition.

Syrians asked: could it be that Turkish water initiatives were intended not to serve the interests of the Middle East but those of NATO, as well as those of the European Union (EU), to which Turkey aspired to belong? It should be noted that, when refused funding by the World Bank (because the project was not acceptable to all riparian states), Turkey nonetheless raised the necessary money for the Southeastern Anatolia Project. This project was said to be the only economic policy that could pacify and revitalize the southeastern region of Turkey, by bringing prosperity to the neglected and rebellious Kurds living there. Syrian observers point out, however, that this concern for the Kurds came rather late. Beyond that, the World Bank created a commission to study the economic effectiveness of large dams. At some point, they noted, Turkey would have to make a choice between using the Euphrates for irrigation or for the generation of hydroelectric power.

In any case, large-scale engineering remedies to social and political problems were proven to be impolitic as well as environmentally dangerous. Though ostensibly serving the local and national economy, these projects were implemented over the heads of the populations affected, ignoring grassroots input and basic human rights. As for the environment, the increasing amounts of water withdrawn from the Euphrates by Turkey was likely to be to the detriment of Syria. Downstream waters and the groundwater that returns from the Southeastern Anatolia Project into Syrian reservoirs were likely to be increasingly polluted. Thus, there was not only the issue of the quantity, but also of the quality, of this water.

The political motivations behind Turkish irrigation projects may have been intended to overcome European misgivings with regards to the poor human-rights record of Turkey vis-à-vis the Kurds. The Peace Water Pipeline Project of Ozal was, ostensibly, a Turkish contribution to a solution of the Arab-Israeli conflict. Even if Turkish intentions were genuine, however, Syrians observed that both of these measures would be achieved at the expense of Syria, or would further reduce its bargaining position in the Euphrates waters dispute. Therefore, Syrians argued that a comprehensive, environmentally and politically sustainable solution, peacefully negotiated and given the force of international law, had to be negotiated. The division of the Euphrates waters had to be fair and respectful of all developmental needs. Such an agreement would assure that the Euphrates would provide the basis of friendly and cooperative relations between all three riparian states.

–L. S. SCHILCHER, UNIVERSITY OF CALIFORNIA, LOS ANGELES

References

J. A. Allan and Chibli Mallat, eds., *Water in the Middle East: Legal, Political, and Commercial Implications* (London & New York: I. B. Tauris, 1995).

Asit K. Biswas, ed., *International Waters of the Middle East: From Euphrates-Tigris to Nile* (Bombay & New York: Oxford University Press, 1994).

John Bulloch and Adel Darwish, *Water Wars: Coming Conflicts in the Middle East* (London: Gollancz, 1993).

Norman Frankel, "Water and Turkish Foreign Policy," *Political Communication and Persuasion,* 8 (1991): 257–311.

Farhad Kazemi and John Waterbury, eds., *Peasants and Politics in the Modern Middle East* (Miami: Florida International University Press, 1991).

Gün Kut, "Burning Waters: The Hydropolitics of the Euphrates and Tigris," *New Perspectives on Turkey,* 9 (Fall 1993): 1–17.

Miriam R. Lowi, "Rivers of Conflict, Rivers of Peace," *Journal of International Affairs,* 49 (Summer 1995): 123–144.

Erol Manisali, "Two Cornerstones of Turkey's Foreign Relations," *Middle East Business and Banking,* 9 (March 1990): 7–10.

Thomas Naff and Ruth C. Matson, *Water in the Middle East: Conflict or Cooperation?* (Boulder, Colo.: Westview Press, 1984).

Robert Olson, "Turkey-Syria Relations Since the Gulf War: Kurds and Water," *Middle East Policy,* 5 (May 1997): 168–194.

Gencer Özcan and Sule Kut, eds., *En Uzun Onyil: Türkiye'nin Ulusal Güvenlik ve Dis Politika Gündeminde Doksanli Yillar* (Istanbul: Boyut, 1998).

Peter Rogers and Peter Lydon, eds., *Water in the Arab World: Perspectives and Prognoses* (Cambridge, Mass.: Harvard University Press, 1994).

Greg Shapland, *Rivers of Discord: International Water Disputes in the Middle East* (New York: St. Martin's Press, 1997).

John Spagnola, ed., *Problems of the Modern Middle East in Historical Perspective: Essays in Honour of Albert Hourani* (Reading, U.K.: Ithaca Press, 1992).

Joyce Starr, *Covenant over Middle Eastern Waters: Key to World Survival* (New York: Holt, 1995).

Starr and Daniel C. Stoll, eds., *Politics of Scarcity: Water in the Middle East* (Boulder, Colo.: Westview Press, 1988).

Richard G. Tarasofsky, "International Law and Water Conflicts in the Middle East," *Environmental Policy and Law,* 23 (April 1993): 70–73.

Mehmet Tomanbay, "Sharing the Euphrates: Turkey, Syria and Iraq," *Research and Exploration–Water Issue* (1993): 53–61.

Ilter Turan, "Turkey and the Middle East: Problems and Solutions," *Water International,* 18 (1993): 23–29.

Turan and Gün Kut, "Political-Ideological Constraints on Intra-Basin Cooperation on Transboundary Waters," *Natural Resources Forum,* 21 (1997): 139–145.

Water Issues Between Turkey, Syria and Iraq (Ankara, Turkey: Ministry of Foreign Affairs, 1995).

FINLAND

What were the factors that forced pulp-and-paper mills in Finland to stop polluting the lakes and rivers?

Viewpoint: Regional and local environmentalists were the driving force behind the cleanup of the lakes and rivers of Finland. National legislation would have been ineffective without this push "from below."

Viewpoint: The environmental cleanup of the forest industry of Finland was a consequence of several factors, including national legislation, new paper-production technologies, and the greening of the international paper market.

Historically, water pollution problems in Finland have been closely connected to its forest industry, especially its pulp-and-paper mills. As late as 1984, timber production accounted for 96 percent of the biological oxygen demand (BOD) in Finnish waters. The government tolerated these high pollution levels in large part because forestry was seen as the economic locomotive that drove the entire industrial production of the country. Fearing that strict regulations would undermine this industry and thus cripple the national economy, the Finnish parliament was reluctant to force its pulp-and-paper mills to modernize and adopt green practices. The Second National Water Act of 1961, for instance, ostensibly established new standards for water policy and water administration. In practice it exempted any firm that could demonstrate a potential economic harm as a consequence of these new regulations. This elastic clause was written with the forest industry in mind and allowed the pulp-and-paper mills to avoid the new environmental regulations. As a consequence the lakes and rivers around the mills got dirtier, even as the waters around urban centers got cleaner.

A step forward was taken in the 1970s with the establishment of the National Board of Waters. This board brought regional and local water administrations under one roof for the first time, allowing for a more efficient and uniform application of national water laws. Initially, however, it too had little effect, for all it did was usher in an era of "instant permits" that allowed forest enterprises to continue to pollute national waters as long as they reduced their production of solid wastes such as clay and lime. By the late 1970s the "instant permits" gave way to stricter ones, known as "up-to-date permits." Once again the forest industry was able to evade strict regulation, this time because the 1973 oil crisis and subsequent recession served to remind legislators of the fragile dependence of the country on its forest products. Old mills were allowed to stay in production as long as they were economically profitable, regardless of the amount of pollution that they caused. As late as 1984 there were aged paper mills in production that emitted BOD levels twenty times higher than new mills.

Over the last twenty years of the twentieth century, Finland clamped down on its forest industry and the results were impressive: the rivers and lakes in general were cleaner than they had been for decades. Esa Konttinen and Jarmo Kortelainen debate whether this cleanup was primarily a result of pressures "from below," in the form of local and regional environmental movements, or whether it was primarily a consequence of pressures "from above," in the form of national legislation and international pressures.

Viewpoint: Regional and local environmentalists were the driving force behind the cleanup of the lakes and rivers of Finland. National legislation would have been ineffective without this push "from below."

A modern environmental movement came into being in Finland in the late 1960s and early 1970s, much as it did elsewhere around the globe. Part of the impulse came from Rachel Carson's influential book *Silent Spring* (1962) and part from the broader social radicalism of the era. The impact of the first environmental wave, however, was mainly limited to politicizing the pollution issue for the first time. The movement was still powerless to effect changes in environmental policy. For instance, a Ministry of the Environment, demanded by the Finnish Association for Nature Conservation (FANC), was not established at that time; and the most serious polluter, the forest industry, was too strong to be forced to make essential advancements in its wastewater policies. The second environmental wave in the late 1970s and early 1980s marked a turning point in national environmental policy. The environment became a major social issue during this time, making it impossible for Finnish industries to continue their polluting practices of the past. A clear change of values took place, known as a move toward "soft values." Industrial development was no longer the sole concern; environmental issues were also high on the social agenda.

Spurred by the environmental group Club of Rome and Donella H. Meadows's *The Limits to Growth: A Report for the Club of Rome's Project on the Predicament of Mankind* (1972), the concept of "zero-growth" won broad support in Finland. The focal point of protest was the threat that the national economy caused to local milieus. Even the most important industries—including the forest-related ones—became a target of criticism. Protests were held throughout the country in opposition to plans to build new power plants along the rivers. There were also strong demands to protect bird life around the lakes. These protest actions often enjoyed broad public support. People were ready to protect their local environments, which they perceived as an important element of their way of life.

This new attitude manifested itself in a major environmental conflict in south-central Finland. Central Finland had long been one of the chief forest-industrial centers in the country and therefore was one of its most highly polluted regions. In fact, the stretch below the Äänekoski pulp mills counted among the worst-polluted areas in the country. This region included the northern part of Lake Päijanne, the second biggest lake in Finland. The water there was brown and smelly. Salmon had long ago vanished from the entire watershed.

Criticism against pollution had been voiced decades earlier by a few local inhabitants and fishing associations, but without success. Economical interests of the forest industry were considered more important. By 1982, however, the situation began to change. The existence of a strong national environmental movement emboldened local activists and other environmentalists to take a stance against the water-pollution policies of the massive Äänekoski mills. This outburst caught company officials off guard, for they were one of the largest forest firms in the country and were therefore accustomed to function without such disturbances. Adding to their surprise was the fact that the company had recently announced plans to construct a new mill, one that promised to replace old ones and thus significantly reduce emissions. Company officials presumed—wrongly as it turned out—that activists would be satisfied with these advancements. The local population and their environmental allies, however, were anything but satisfied with the promises.

Protests continued for the next three years as a legal case ensued. The struggle brought together citizens who had long suffered from the wastewater, researchers from the university, activists from the regional branch of FANC, various voluntary associations, and local waterworks organizations. Local legislators from the Finnish parliament even joined the protesters. Representatives of the company used their all-too-familiar argument in response: the extra costs for more-effective cleaning equipment would lead to a situation where the competitive edge of the company would be severely endangered.

This time their contention did not work: the final decision by the Superior Administrative Court in 1985 came much closer to satisfying the demands of environmentalists than mill representatives. The company had to build an activated sludge facility similar to the one already in use for cleaning local wastewater. Not only was enforcement of old measures tightened, but also new limits were set, and for the first time attention was paid to phosphorus and chlorical phe-

A pulp mill and paper factory in Häme province

(courtesy Embassy of Finland, Washington)

nol emissions. In the event of massive or accidental dumpings, the company was obligated to make an immediate announcement to the community. Furthermore, a wastewater permit was issued only for a limited period of time, which represented a real departure from previous practices.

The new purification system of the Äänekoski pulp mill was far more effective than that of any mill in the country at the time. Water downstream from the mill started to get cleaner almost immediately. In fact, the system was so effective that the results were clearly better than norms set by the official permission. Within a few short years, biological oxygen demand (BOD) indicators showed values that were only a tiny fraction of what they had once been—and this improvement occurred despite the fact that production had remarkably increased during the same time period. Trout and whitefish returned to the northern part of Lake Päijanne, and within ten years the rapids below the Äänekoski mills recovered their past reputation as one of the finest fishing places in the middle and southern parts of the country.

More importantly, Äänekoski was not an isolated case. The legal dispute had a far-reaching impact on wastewater policy. The immense publicity that the Äänekoski issue generated contributed to a change in attitude among water officials. This change can be clearly seen in yet another conflict in the same district in 1985, one that broke out when it was revealed that an old pulp mill near Lake Lievestuore had exceeded its wastewater limits. The atmosphere was already charged because of the Äänekoski conflict, and water authorities faced strong criticism for failing to control wastewater permissions tightly enough. Under pressure, the national water-control authorities took a more-critical stance toward the mills and started insisting on solutions similar to those imposed at Äänekoski.

Forest-industry officials, moreover, began to learn from these conflicts and became aware that certain economic benefits could accrue from practicing environmentally sound policies. Paper produced in the Äänekoski mills, for instance, received a Nordic Environmental Certificate (the first paper product to get such a designation in Finland), which the mill owners skillfully exploited in their advertising campaigns. Other companies saw the handwriting on the wall and followed suit. Yet, another proof of changing times came when a new pulp mill was built in Rauma in the early 1990s, constructed by the same company that had been in charge of the Äänekoski mills during the environmental agitation. This time around company officials announced that they had learned their lesson and built a model plant with the most-sophisticated new equipment—one that led the environmental activist organization Greenpeace to recommend it to U.S. companies as a model.

Occurring at the level of national policy was a change in the interpretation of the Second National Water Act by the authorities. They now

interpreted these regulations more strictly, as did the Water Rights Courts. This new orientation signaled an end to the era when pulp-and-paper mills could openly flout the regulations, safe in the knowledge that they would find protection from the authorities. Nonetheless, environmental progress was not smooth and uniform, but instead gradual and uneven, with each local region having to push its own cleanup causes. For instance, at the Uimaharju pulp mill in eastern Finland, citizens were forced to launch a campaign every bit as determined as those at Äänekoski and Päijanne before they met with success. This struggle suggests that much of the driving force came "from below" and not "from above."

Of course, it would be an exaggeration to argue that the environmental movement was the sole factor that influenced the cleanup of the pulp-and-paper mills. Pollution levels from the forest industry peaked in the late 1960s and early 1970s and were already on the decline by the mid 1970s, when the environmental movement was gaining steam. Environmental awareness, however, ensured that the cleanup continued. Most remarkably, pollution levels decreased from the mid 1980s onward, despite a continuous rise in production. These positive results were possible because the industry was forced to shut down older plants and install newer, cleaner ones. The local environmental movement contributed to that process by putting the spotlight on forest-industry practices.

–ESA KONTTINEN,
UNIVERSITY OF JYVÄSKYLÄ

Viewpoint: The environmental cleanup of the forest industry of Finland was a consequence of several factors, including national legislation, new paper-production technologies, and the greening of the international paper market.

Finland has been called the "land of thousands of lakes," a phrase that highlights the high number of lakes and rivers in the landscape. The country is also known, however, as a "forest-sector society," for its extensive forests are of incalculable importance to its modern economy. These two features of the Finnish landscape–water and forests–are tightly interlinked with the national political and social life. Because of its economic importance, the forest industry was the most significant utilizer and manipulator of the lake-and-river systems during the twentieth century.

The forest industry became an important activity in Finland in the second half of the nineteenth century. Dozens of sawmills and paper mills emerged in the span of a few short decades. Rapid industrialization in Finland was led by forestry interests. Two important environmental preconditions made the large-scale forest industry possible. First, there were seemingly inexhaustible forest resources available for exploitation; second, there was a vast network of lakes and rivers to transport cut timber. Logs were floated throughout the lake-and-river systems to mills downstream.

Even the most peripheral regions of Finland were connected to the production systems of the forest industry by the beginning of the twentieth century. The emergence of the forest sector also led to the mobilization of national water resources. Companies established associations to manage and develop log-driving, which in practice meant turning the lake-and-river systems into transportation routes. Rivers were dredged to avoid logjams, and large shore facilities were built to sort the logs. Log-driving was a labor-intensive activity, and hundreds of men worked along the riversides or on log-sorting sites. For decades, floating equipment was one of the most prominent man-made features of the Finnish waterscape.

Extensive log-floating is a thing of the past. It diminished gradually after the 1950s, mostly because trucks replaced water routes as the primary means of timber transportation. The construction of hydroelectric stations also helped bring an end to log-driving in the major rivers (though even at the end of the twentieth century one could see tugboats towing log bundles on some Finnish lakes in the summer). Log-sorting plants were closed down and most of the floating equipment dismantled.

Hydropower was the second resource that water bequeathed to the forest industry. The locations of the early sawmills and paper mills were determined by the availability of hydroelectricity. As a result, dozens of water-driven sawmills and paperboard mills were established near rapids. Proximity to waterpower lost its importance at the end of the nineteenth century when long-distance wires made it easy to transfer electricity. Energy needs of the forest industry, however, increased along with production, and thus hydropower remained an important source. Timber companies actively supported the construction of hydroelectric stations in order to guarantee their energy supply through low-cost water power. Most of the large rivers in Finland were dammed, and about one-third of all lake areas were affected to one degree or another

FINLAND AND ENVIRONMENTALLY FRIENDLY POLICIES

At the Conference on Environmental Economics at Hyvinkää on 29 March 1998, Finnish prime minister Paavo Lipponen gave a speech on sustainable development, a portion of which appears below:

The theme of the conference is highly topical: economic incentives for environmentally friendly policies, energy taxes and the possible creation of markets for greenhouse gas emissions to curb global warming. These themes are high on the agenda in environmental debate world-wide. . . .

The Union is presently engaged in debating burden sharing among the member states. Fulfilling the target of an overall reduction of 8 per cent from the year 1990 level is an ambitious task. It requires major adjustments in production and consumption of energy in member countries. For Finland the current proposal to cut our emissions back to the level where they were in year 1990, is simply too much with the figures that have been used to calculate the so called baseline. The figure for year 1990 does not reflect adequately the fact that Finland imported bigger than usual share of her supply of electricity.

There are some fundamental principles that Finland stressed when agreeing to adopt the very ambitious target for emission reductions of the European Union. These include equitable burden sharing, co-operation in developing common rules for energy taxes and the principle of joint implementation.

The agreement in Kyoto includes the possibility of joint implementation between developed countries and it allows signatory countries to use the practice of emissions trading to meet greenhouse gas reduction targets. The clean development mechanism plays a role in assisting developing countries to achieve sustainable development and in contributing to the objectives of the Kyoto Convention. The idea of emissions trading is a new one and requires some thinking. It is a promising alternative and we should be able to make progress with it before the next important meeting on Climate Change in Buenos Aires at the end of this year.

All this makes economic sense and helps to achieve the intended results. Climate change is a global threat and the effects are borne by all nations alike, but not all countries are in the same position when it comes to energy efficiency, technological capability and financial possibilities to pay for the costs of reducing greenhouse gas emissions. International co-operation is needed–not only in agreeing what to do to curb the emissions, but also in the practical implementation of emission reductions.

For Finland it is of utmost importance that we are able to use joint implementation in practice. The Baltic countries and Russia would be obvious partners for us. It makes sense to co-operate in emissions reductions with countries that lag behind when it comes to efficient use of energy. Countries in the Baltic Sea region have for a long time co-operated in cleaning the sea and the coastal environment. Now we should be able to extend co-operation to the protection of our climate from excess warming.

Joint implementation is needed, but that alone is not enough. Finland has for a long time championed agreement on minimum levels of energy taxes within the European Union. International efforts to fight global warming are making this goal even more important to achieve. It is simply not possible for one single country to introduce substantial energy levies that affect the competitiveness of her industry in the common market.

The European Commission is preparing a report on sustainable development for the Cardiff European Council. The Nordic countries were active in promoting environmental issues in the IGC discussions and we are satisfied that the Amsterdam Treaty now includes sustainable development as a goal for the Union. Cardiff should be a start for a process which Finland will also take forward during our own presidency. The EU should also keep environmental concerns high on the agenda in her external relations, including the WTO.

To make good policy that is both environmentally, economically and socially sustainable we need a scientific basis for our approach on environmental problems and an open debate. I am sure that this conference will contribute to this debate in a positive way.

Source: *The Finnish Council of State, Internet website.*

from water regulation. Nearly two-thirds of hydropower potential in the country has been harnessed.

The construction of mills and hydroelectric plants caused extensive changes in the water environment. Dredging and damming caused the most damage to fish. Migration routes of salmon, for example, were cut and most of their spawning beds destroyed. This problem was not confined to Finland alone: most of the salmon rivers in the Baltic Sea were harnessed or polluted to such an extent that salmon and other migratory fish could no longer spawn in them. In the past, as many as seven to ten million salmon fry hatched naturally in the Baltic region each year, compared with only a half million by 1999. Although populations were maintained with the aid of stocking, the naturally reproducing Baltic salmon was endangered. Also threatened were subspecies of salmon that spawn in the rivers flowing into the largest Finnish lake, Saimaa. Hatcheries were established to keep salmon populations alive on many Baltic rivers.

Rivers also provided the forest industry with a cheap method of waste disposal. Historically, the mills utilized the lake-and-river systems of Finland as sewers, making the industry the worst water polluter in the nation. The growth of paper production during the decades following World War II led to an extensive increase in water pollution levels. Almost untreated sewage was typically discharged into water systems, and the growth in production resulted in an increase in waste output for the whole period between 1945 and the 1970s. Because most Finnish lakes are shallow and have a slow flow, the effects of the pollutants were often dramatic, sometimes resulting in oxygen depletion and fishkills. Water near the mills was the most polluted, but sewage spread over a much wider area. Pulp-and-paper mills were scattered along the lake-and-river systems in different parts of the country; therefore, a majority of Finns suffered from a decline in water quality to one extent or another. One example of this pollution involved the Uimaharju pulp mill, originally constructed in 1967, in eastern Finland. The most obvious environmental consequence was a change in the smell and color of the water, which sometimes made fish inedible. High phosphorus loads, which created a favorable environment for algae and thus caused eutrophication (the process by which a body of water becomes enriched with dissolved nutrients), were a serious problem. The sewage works were far too small and inefficient to deal with the output of the mill. Although the plant was relatively small, the pollution it produced affected aquatic systems and impacted the recreational opportunities of people more than fifty kilometers downstream.

The 1970s, however, marked a turning point in water protection. More stringent water and environmental policies came into being, which forced the mills to emphasize pollution control. Production of pulp and paper increased three-fold, jumping from around four million tons in 1970 to more than twelve million tons in 1999. The output of effluents, however, started to decrease rapidly. During the same period forest industry biological oxygen demand (BOD) loads dropped from around a half million tons to less than twenty thousand tons per year. First, the use of water became more efficient. Most mills were able to decrease their waste emissions by recycling water in the production process, by improving their spill controls, and by making other changes in production systems. Wastewater discharges decreased from 1.8 million cubic meters per year in 1973 to six hundred thousand cubic meters in 1993. Second, purification plants became much more efficient. This development was particularly fast after the mid 1980s, when the forest industry started to build effective biological-chemical sewage treatment plants. Third, the use of elementary chlorine, which dropped from two hundred thousand tons in 1980 to twenty thousand tons in 1993, was replaced by less harmful chemicals in pulp production in the early 1990s.

All these changes led to an improvement in water quality in the lakes and rivers that were previously heavily polluted by the forest industry. This improvement, in turn, offered the industry the opportunity to utilize water in a totally different way. Paper mills capitalized on the lake-and-river systems as a symbolic resource, playing up their effective environmental protection; that is, they highlighted the fact that paper production had become a "clean" industry. This transformation improved their standing in the international paper markets, where the green label gave them a competitive edge. The greening of international paper markets was the result of growing public environmental awareness and the globalization of economies and communications. People became increasingly conscious of the environmental consequences of both producing and consuming goods and services. As consumers became more aware, they began to think not just of their local concerns, but also about the environment in faraway places where many consumer goods were produced. Finnish paper producers started reporting on effluent levels to their customers and environmental organizations. Sales agencies in countries the Finns exported to, in turn, reported back to the forest-company officials on public environmental debates and attitudes.

While the price and quality of products were formerly the most significant factors in sales, in the global market of images, forest companies began to build a positive environmental image for themselves in the 1990s. They started publicity campaigns in which they issued annual environmental reports and other publications for their customers and other interested parties. Company managers convinced their stockholders that environmental issues would play a key role in the international paper markets and that a positive image was necessary if a company was to increase its market share. At the same time, companies constructed environmental markets with these images: it was not only a question of conquering ecological markets, but also creating them and making them bigger, as well.

Water quality played an essential role in the development of the new environmental image. Forest-industry leaders put much effort into publicity campaigns, seeking to create an impression that their companies were responsible for cleaning up lakes and rivers in Finland and that they worked in harmony with nature. In leaflets, environmental reports, and newspaper articles, and on web pages, company managers pointed out that, although production grew significantly, the discharge of effluents had decreased markedly. Research results from biologists and limnologists were used, often selectively, to support industry claims. The most successful mills were portrayed as examples of the new environmental policy of the companies.

The relationship of the forest industry with the water environment in Finland changed dramatically during the three last decades of twentieth century. Until the 1970s these companies utilized lake-and-river systems as transport routes, energy producers, and sewers–transforming and polluting them practically without any external control. As environmental policy became more stringent in the 1970s and 1980s it forced companies to put more efforts into wastewater treatment. Not environmental policy, however, but the greening of the paper markets changed forest industry policies. Until the 1990s environmental protection was seen purely as an economic burden that caused extra expenses for the forest companies. This view changed when customers–publishers, printing houses, and consumers–started to respond to the environmental problems of the forest industry. Clean water became a valuable resource that could be utilized in the construction of positive environmental images for the companies. Pollution control was not an extra expense anymore; it became a necessary part of production in order to clean both the water and the images of the companies.

–JARMO KORTELAINEN,
UNIVERSITY OF JOENSUU

References

Environmental Statistics 1980 (Helsinki: Official Statistics, 1981).

Eeva-Liisa Hallanaro, *The Environment in Finland: Current Status and Measures to Protect It* (Helsinki: Ministry of the Environment, 1999).

Tapio S. Katko, *Water!: Evolution of Water Supply and Sanitation in Finland from the Mid-1800s to 2000* (Helsinki: Finnish Water and Waste Water Works Association, 1997).

Esa Konttinen, "From Industrial Consensus to Environmental Regulation: The Coming of the Finnish Industrial Waste-Water Policy," *Water Policy*, 1 (1998): 305–319.

Jarmo Kortelainen, "Environmental Questions and the Forest Industry: A Case Study of the Uima-harju Pulp Mill," in *The Changing Circumpolar North: Opportunities for Academic Development: 3rd Circumpolar Universities Cooperation Conference, November 30–December 3, 1992, University of Lapland, Rovaniemi, Finland,* edited by Lassi Heininen (Rovaniemi, Finland: Arctic Centre, University of Lapland, 1994), pp. 123–134.

Kortelainen, "The River as an Actor-Network: The Finnish Forest Industry Utilization of Lake and River Systems," *Geoforum,* 30 (1999): 235–247.

Tarmo Koskinen, "Finland–A Forest Sector Society? Sociological Approaches, Conclusions and Challenges," in *Problems in the Redescription of Business Enterprises: Proceedings of the First Summer Seminar of the Group on the Theory of the Firm, 7–8 August 1984, Espoo, Finland,* edited by Kari Lilja, Keijo Räsñen, and Risto Tainio (Helsinki: Helsinki School of Economics, 1985), pp. 45–52.

Scott Lash and John Urry, *Economies of Signs and Space* (London & Thousand Oaks, Cal.: Sage, 1994).

Jarmo J. Meriläinen and Virpi Hamina, "Recent Environmental History of a Large, Originally Oligotrophic Lake in Finland: A Paleolimnological Study of Chironomid Remains," *Journal of Paleolimnology,* 9 (1993): 129–140.

Olli Saastamoinen, "New Forest Policy: The Rise of Environmental and Fall of Social Consciousness," *Maaseudun Uusi Aika,* 3 (1996): 125–137.

Jukka Tana and Karl-Johan Lehtinen, *The Aquatic Environmental Impact of Pulping and Bleaching Operations–An Overview* (Helsinki: Finnish Environment Institute, 1996).

FRANCE

Was hydroelectric development an "ecological" choice in the context of post–World War II France?

Viewpoint: Hydroelectric development of the Rhône River demonstrates that ecological thinking played an appreciable role in post-1945 energy policies in France.

Viewpoint: Hydroelectric development in postwar France was geared toward remolding and disciplining a nation and its resources. French technocrats viewed untamed rivers and unruly people as enemies.

France has played a leading role in European water politics and hydraulic affairs for the past three hundred years. Two of the most prominent French military-engineering schools—the *École des Ponts et Chaussées* and the *École Polytechnique*—served as model educational institutes for the rest of Europe in the eighteenth century; French engineers provided many of the most important theoretical and practical textbooks for everything from bridge construction to river engineering. "Necessity, convenience, or luxury cannot do without the help of water," wrote Pierre Louis Georges Du Baut in one of the great engineering classics of the eighteenth century, *Principes d'hydraulique* (1779). "Water must be brought into the very center of our dwellings; we must protect ourselves from its ravages, and make it work the machines that will ease our discomforts, decorate our dwellings, embellish and clean up our cities, and transport from province to province (or from one end of the earth to the other) everything that is precious to us; large rivers must be contained; the beds of smaller rivers must be changed; we must dig canals and build aqueducts."

Napoleonic France pioneered in the establishment of the first river commission, the *Magistrat du Rhin,* out of which emerged the Rhine Commission (1815) and similar river commissions around the globe. France also led in the development of national water agencies, not only at home but also elsewhere in Europe. The Department of Public Works and Water Management (*Rijkswaterstaat*) of the Netherlands—one of the largest and most important water agencies in the world—originated as the *Comité Central du Waterstaat* in 1809, at a time when the Dutch were under Napoleonic occupation.

These two authors debate whether the French government pursued ecologically sound engineering practices on the Rhône River in the immediate post-1945 period. Sara B. Pritchard suggests that the French proclivity for thinking in grand terms—in this sense in terms of the Rhône's entire watershed—demonstrates a holistic approach to river management that is at core "ecological," even if the practices they followed in the 1940s and 1950s were considered outmoded by the end of the century. Robert L. Frost contends that Rhône River management reflected the centralizing tendencies of the French state, that is, the desire of national administrators to "develop" the waterway according to their own dictates regardless of its impact on the local inhabitants and environment.

Viewpoint: Hydroelectric development of the Rhône River demonstrates that ecological thinking played an appreciable role in post-1945 energy policies in France.

Between 1934 and the late 1980s the Rhône River Authority (*Compagnie Nationale du Rhône,* or CNR) developed the Rhône according to multipurpose objectives. The vast majority of the eighteen CNR projects included a hydroelectric dam for energy production, locks to facilitate navigation, and irrigation networks to promote agriculture. Until the 1970s CNR projects received backing from a broad coalition of politicians, engineers, writers, and citizens. By the late 1970s, however, just as the CNR began to develop the upper Rhône, the stretch between Lyons and the Swiss-French border, this coalition fell apart. In the late 1980s the French government even canceled the final CNR project, Loyettes, shortly before it was to be built. Why?

The growing critique of the CNR and its projects, apparent by the late 1970s, emerged in large part from a growing environmental movement in France. Furthermore, this movement became institutionalized in the government during the 1970s with the creation of a Ministry of the Environment and the passage of new environmental laws. Within this broader context of the mainstreaming of environmental concerns, the cancellation of Loyettes can be specifically traced to growing pressure from activists who, along with scientists, academics, outdoor enthusiasts, and residents of the region, hoped to preserve this section of the Rhône. They argued that this stretch represented the last undeveloped and pristine part of the river, and, consequently, should be saved from development. The efforts of this diverse coalition of environmental and social activists proved successful. Within fifty years, France had moved from the wholesale development of the Rhône to its protection and preservation. The cancellation of Loyettes therefore serves as an important reminder that national ideals and attitudes can change quite dramatically over time.

The arguments expressed by opponents of Loyettes exemplified many of the central tenets of modern environmentalism. What about the ideas, however, of those who supported the development of the Rhône during previous decades? Could they, too, be considered "environmental"? Looking at ideas of nature in the context of their time, and the implementation of these ideas into the design features of CNR projects, demonstrates that even the development of the Rhône can be understood as "ecological."

After World War II much of France was in ruins. Thousands of soldiers, prisoners, deportees, and citizens had been killed. Some cities had been bombed beyond repair. Food was scarce. Inflation was spiraling out of control. The war had also damaged important industrial infrastructure including transportation networks, energy sources, and production sites. In the context of this political and economic decimation, French political leaders and technical experts attempted to get the economy and nation back in order by targeting key industries for reconstruction. At the top of the list was energy production. The CNR was in a good position to play an important role in achieving this goal. In 1934, only a few years before the outbreak of war, the French government had created the CNR and granted it the authority to develop and manage the river. Hydroelectricity was one of the three mandated directives of the new agency. After the war the government helped to jumpstart the economy by actively promoting the development of the Rhône.

Ideas about the river, and nature more generally, helped to further justify the development of the Rhône. Amid the decimation of war and the efforts to reconstruct the nation, politicians, engineers, and writers across France celebrated the efforts of CNR to "tame" and "harness" the unruly river. They extolled the so-called domestication of nature by man and machine. In addition, they described the waterway as a resource for people's use. The Rhône's waters could be tapped for their productive potential. A coalition of political, intellectual, and technical experts thus portrayed the river as an engine for economic and political growth that would return France to its former greatness.

There was, nevertheless, disagreement among these parties over the meaning of growth. Labor leaders and unions disagreed with industrialists and some French politicians over how work should be organized at the construction of the first postwar CNR project, Donzère-Mondragon, built between 1947 and 1952. Cooperation tended to be the rule, however: although they might disagree over who should benefit, nearly everyone across the political spectrum agreed that the Rhône could and should be remade to serve the social, economic, and political agenda of postwar reconstruction. They supported the idea of controlling and harnessing the river

The dam at Tignes in the French Alps
(David Wright)

and shared confidence in large-scale technology as providing the proper solution to this objective. Diverse groups in postwar France thus conceptualized the river as a resource and tool for human use and betterment.

Many politicians, writers, and engineers also naturalized CNR projects. One journalist wrote, for example, in the popular magazine *Science and Life,* that "nature designated [the Rhône], therefore, to give the greatest hydroelectric powers to France." In this view, the authority for river development came from nature itself. Not surprisingly, the CNR deployed similar arguments in order to bolster support for its projects. One top administrator emphasized the symbiosis between the Rhône and projects of the agency when, taking on the supposed voice of the river, he wrote in 1957 that the "palaces where your engineers capture my power, I find them worthy of my dignity." Other journalists underscored the natural fit between the regional environment and CNR projects. One concluded that "here, nature and men seem–for once–to be allied to attempt a new adventure." These journalists and CNR officials portrayed, then, the "naturalness" of the projects, which helped to justify their construction. These two concepts–the idea of the river as a resource and the view of CNR projects as inevitable extensions of nature–together helped to naturalize the projects. In the process of making this argument, politicians, engineers, and journalists conceptualized CNR projects and technology as part of the ecosystem of the Rhône.

These ideas shaped the design of CNR projects and their technical features. Nature also affected the engineers' plans. For instance, the topography of the Rhône valley influenced the overall CNR approach to development. All but one of the projects shared a common design element: each had a lengthy diversion canal, which channeled most of the waters through the hydroelectric plant located on a dam on the canal. Downstream of this dam, the diversion canal rejoined the original riverbed. In part, the CNR selected the diversion approach, rather than choosing a high dam and huge reservoir system, such as those at the Hoover Dam (in Nevada and Arizona), in order to avoid flooding rich agricultural areas and towns upstream of their projects.

In addition to these political and agricultural benefits, the diversion system allowed natural processes to continue to shape the Rhône valley in several ways. For one, unlike the reservoir system, the diversion canal preserved the original riverbed close to its pre-project characteristics and dimensions. This design feature thus allowed the preservation of river ecology by allowing river flows in the original riverbed, known as reserved flow, to vary during the year. The CNR guaranteed a minimum amount of water to flow in the original riverbed at all times, with larger flows allotted during floods. The diversion canal thus permitted the river to have flow in a manner similar to before the projects, albeit with important modifications. For example, the constant reserved flow was much less than its rate before the construction of the CNR project. At Donzère-Mondragon, the CNR regulated the reserved flow at a constant sixty cubic meters per second. Before the project, this flow would have varied daily, seasonally, and annually, but it averaged fifteen hundred cubic meters per second. With the completion of Donzère-Mondragon, most of this water now passed through the diversion canal.

The CNR therefore regularized, standardized, and controlled the natural processes of the river. Overall, however, the diversion canals allowed natural processes to continue to transform the river valley to a limited extent, preserving river ecosystems to a greater scale than the alternatives considered. A large reservoir system would have entirely wiped out the ecological and human communities of the valley. The diversion-canal approach preserved these communities while modifying them. For example, prompted by the Water and Forest Agency, the design of Donzère-Mondragon included technical features to help maintain fish populations. In the early 1950s the CNR built a large-fish ladder on an additional dam constructed at the beginning of the original riverbed. The Water and Forest Agency and the CNR worked together to ensure that a large percentage of the reserved flow would pass through, and then pour out of, the base of the ladder in order to attract fish. Even in the early 1950s, then, the CNR attempted to address the needs of nature in their design, construction, and operation of the project.

Ecological thought also undergirded the hydroelectric development of the Rhône in that the CNR treated the entire river as a single, comprehensive system. When the French government passed a law permitting construction on the Rhône in 1921, it stated that "the development of the Rhône between the Swiss border and the [Mediterranean] sea be undertaken for three objectives: 1) use of hydroelectric power; 2) navigation; 3) irrigation, drainage, and other agricultural uses." This fundamental law required a plan that took the entire river into account. The French government thus decreed that development be comprehensive and systematic, not piecemeal. The CNR followed the intent of the law. In 1935, only a year after the creation of the CNR, engineers drafted a plan proposing twenty projects to be built over the entire length of the river. This plan was modified over time, but most of the projects originally conceived in 1935 were built. As the plan indicated, the CNR conceptualized the relationship of any single project to all other proposed projects and to the entire Rhône itself. As a former CNR president stated in 1946, "the process of planning and building Donzère-Mondragon must be considered, in addition, as the point of departure for a larger whole even more vast, which will consist of canalizing the entire central third of the lower Rhône." One top administrator even characterized the CNR program as an "organic plan," suggesting that the agency envisioned not only an entire program for the river, but also that it derived, partially, from nature itself. The CNR approach to development thus depended upon a comprehensive view of the Rhône basin as a system of which each project was one component.

When considered within its historical context, hydroelectric development of the Rhône River by CNR can be understood as "ecological." Yet, even outside of their specific historical context, these development projects displayed elements more closely associated with modern environmentalism. Even in the 1940s the CNR incorporated natural processes into the design of the project. The agency allowed nature a much greater role in reshaping valley ecology and history than some of the possible alternatives. The projects were also based on watershed management. In addition, the CNR addressed the needs of fish. Certainly, much more could have been done. In fact, the CNR began to implement ecological thinking to a greater degree in its projects on the upper Rhône. Built from the late 1970s on, these efforts incorporated natural processes, sustained river ecology, and protected fish and wildlife populations to a greater degree than earlier CNR projects such as Donzère-Mondragon. These design changes suggest how the definition of environmental concerns were widened and implemented more fully than just three decades before. Still, even the early CNR projects embodied concerns that are often only associated with the late twentieth century. The challenge then, as now, was creating a sustainable world in which the technological, cultural, and natural coexist.

–SARA B. PRITCHARD,
STANFORD UNIVERSITY

CALL TO ACTION International Day of Action Against Dams and for Rivers, Water & Life March 14, 2000

Dear Friends,

We urge you to join us on March 14th as part of the International Day of Action Against Dams and for Rivers, Water & Life. Over the last year, the anti-dam movement has gained huge momentum—from nonviolent mass resistance in Asia to unprecedented networking in Latin America and Africa to dam removals in Europe and North America. Let's keep this momentum growing. Plan an event on March 14 as part of the Day of Action.

By acting together we:

- Strengthen local groups by linking them to the global network of dam fighters and river protectors.
- Show the world a strong, diverse worldwide movement dedicated to the health of rivers and the people that depend on them.
- Publicize the need to move towards equitable and sustainable ways to manage our rivers.

As our movement grows, so has the number of groups fighting for reparations. Reparations are measures taken to mitigate or compensate people for damages suffered because of already existing dams. Worldwide, people are demanding that institutions and dam builders not be let off the hook once a project is completed—and that they be held accountable for social and environmental damages. Let's work together to send institutions and dam builders our message.

Another exciting trend is the growing movement to decommission dams. In the US and France, governments and dam building agencies have acknowledged that the era of dam-building is over and are starting to tear dams down. We need to push this message forward around the world that dams do not last forever. It's time to create a new vision for managing our rivers for the next millenium.

It is also time to force policymakers to implement real solutions for meeting water, flood management and energy needs. We need to spread the word about alternatives, starting with the use of demand side management strategies for water and energy and true renewables such as solar and wind energy.

Let's work together to strengthen the movement. Organize an event on March 14, 2000 for the International Day of Action Against Dams and for Rivers, Water & Life. Reparations, decommissioning and alternatives are just some of the many issues around which to organize your event. Below is some information on the Day of Action, including additional resources, background information and examples of previous events.

We look forward to your involvement in the International Day of Action.

Susanne Wong,
International Rivers Network

Source: *"International Day of Action Against Dams and for Rivers, Water & Life,"* International Rivers Network, Internet website.

Viewpoint: Hydroelectric development in postwar France was geared toward remolding and disciplining a nation and its resources. French technocrats viewed untamed rivers and unruly people as enemies.

It is ahistorical to judge the technological practices of fifty years ago by the environmental values, knowledge, and sentiments of the twenty-first century. It is also ahistorical, however, to alter earlier notions of "river systems" to fit modern conceptions of "ecosystems." It may well be that the Rhône River Authority (*Compagnie Nationale du Rhône,* or CNR) technocrats possessed a laudable sensitivity toward democratic participation and a nascent "ecological" viewpoint, but a parallel group of French actors–the technocrats of the French National Electrical Company (*Électricité de France,* or EDF)–framed their ideas of river and political systems in a narrow, technocratic fashion. They built hydroelectric facilities with a determination to enact a ritual of environmental and social violence.

France in 1944–1945 was in the midst of a consensus-driven shift in basic political, technical, and economic decision making. The order that had dominated France from 1870 to 1940—a constitutional democracy in which access to political power and economic resources was in practice controlled by a small number of wealthy families—collapsed with the defeat of June 1940. Compounding the problem, many of the elites who were broadly held responsible for the defeat were perceived to have been rather too cozy with the Germans during the wartime occupation. The vast majority of the French people after the war therefore sought a thoroughgoing renewal of their society, economy, and polity.

In its "Democratic Charter" (*La Charte nationale,* 1943), an underground publication, the National Council of the Resistance (*Comité National de la Résistance*) explained the changes needed in the postwar system:

> the installation of a true economic and social democracy, compelling the eviction of the great economic and financial castes from the direction of the economy; a rational organization of the economy, assuring the subordination of particular interests to the general interest and exempt from the dictatorship of the professions installed in the image of the fascist states; the intensification of production along the lines of a plan set by the state after consulting the representatives of all of the elements of that production; the return to the nation of the great monopolized means of production and the fruit of collective labor, of the sources of energy, of mineral wealth, of insurance companies and large banks; the development and support of consumers' and producers' cooperatives, both agricultural and artisanal; the right of access, in the framework of the enterprise, to the functions of management and administration for the workers possessing the necessary qualifications, and the participation of the workers in directing the economy.

Such statements articulated ambitious goals, but they remained vague and ambiguous. First, one must note the Rousseau-like language of the "general interest," that the legitimate core of decision making resides abstractly in "the people" who, by their contribution to the nation, enjoy an immutable claim to power. Indeed, these fine words in all of their ambiguity betray the practical meaning of French political "ecology" in the postwar era.

The key concept here is, of course, that of democratic participation, but of a sort that goes beyond traditional parliamentary democracy. Indeed, on one level, CNR was already a model for a new form of economic democracy. With a board of directors composed of the major stakeholders in the Rhône Basin, substantive decisions about the use of resources were made in a far more democratic fashion than those made by capitalist firms in their profit-maximizing mission. If one extends Rousseau's idea of "natural law" further, nature itself was and is what the people define it to be. In short, in the collective frame of postwar French political thought, nature and democracy were inextricably intertwined: what was good for France was good for nature. In addition, the concept of participation, according to the Charter, meant involving workers and consumers in decision making.

EDF, founded in 1946, was an institutional outcome of that political context. The de facto founder of the firm, Minister of Industry Marcel Paul, was a member of the Central Committee of the French Communist Party (*Parti Communiste Français,* or PCF). In those halcyon days of national unity before the onset of the suffocating fog of Cold War politics in 1947, EDF not only had a Board of Directors composed of stakeholders (including a large share of Communist unionists, as well as leaders of agricultural cooperatives), everyday management within the firm was to embrace a similar sort of stakeholder democracy. One might imagine that the Cold War meant closing the Communists out of political power within EDF, but that is a mistaken notion: the Communists formed a key base of support for the efforts of EDF managers to harness and control nature. Criticism from outside the firm, such as that initiated by industrial conservatives in a report of 1952 (which accused the hydroelectricians of cornering far too much capital for their projects), usually compelled EDF to close ranks and defend its "higher" mission—the renovation of France.

Were one to draw comparisons between the hydroelectric projects in France and those of the Soviet Union and the United States, the vision and approach of EDF more approximated that of Joseph Stalin than Franklin D. Roosevelt. Several factors made this so. First, one must note within EDF a sense of urgency to build infrastructure in order to have industrial (and, by implication, military) capacities commensurate with the "rightful" place of France in the world; the sheer scale of the projects would symbolize a nation rising from ruins. Secondly, though the French vision of conquering nature was guided a bit more gently by Rousseau-like notions of nature as an ally rather than an enemy, Soviet visions of "progress," directly inherited from Marxism, belonged much more to a view (at root, biblical) that progress arose from man's dominion over nature. A common Stalin-era image was that of a muscled, heroic worker wielding tools to conquer nature for the peoples' progress. It is no coincidence that after 1989 the worst zones of environmental damage were in the former Soviet bloc. Therefore, though the role of Communists within EDF seemed to reflect a participationist conception of democracy, it was in that place bereft of any notion of a compromise with nature–it was to be conquered to save France.

The modernization plan adopted by the first elected post-1945 French government stressed a basic industrial strategy. Seven sectors–among them steel, cement, electrical power, rail, fertilizer, and coal–were targeted in the foundation-building stage of economic planning. Not only was electrical generation to focus on hydroelectricity, it was to serve industrial customers. Enjoying the honeymoon for an elected government that succeeded the Nazi occupation, planners believed that consumers could be left out of the initial modernization equation: new output was intended to serve industry exclusively.

Marching orders for EDF were clear: to build dams as quickly as possible in order to help industrial development and free the nation from power rationing (which continued until 1949). Enjoying access to relatively generous financing through a combination of state-backed borrowing and Marshall Plan dollars from the United States after 1948, EDF had the human and financial resources it needed for a truly heroic dam-building effort. The promotional pamphlets of the company made it clear that the goal was to "correct the mistakes of nature" and "harness the wistfully feminine force of flowing water." Workers and managers, so it was claimed, selflessly dedicated themselves to work long hours in concrete-pouring "campaigns."

The state divided the tasks between the CNR and EDF in a relatively straightforward and clear manner: the CNR was to build low-drop dams on the Rhône, while EDF was to help save coal by building reservoir dams high in the French Alps and Pyrenees. The people who lived within the designated geographic scope of EDF, however, were among the most remote (in the minds of technocrats: backward) French peasants, whose goats and cider apples were symbolic of a past that the technocrats were determined to escape. This conception of "primitives" and their concerns about local environmental quality thus excluded the local folks from decision making at the outset.

How, then, did EDF decide which sites to build upon? The papers of the EDF Alpine Regional Hydroelectric Group explicitly state the criteria as entirely economic and technical. Usable sites had to be topological bowls with streams at the bottom, with downstream openings in the bowl suitable for anchoring the dams. If fill material for the dams could be had by gouging out nearby mountainsides, so be it. Financially, the experts calculated the electricity available by taking into account the drop and size of the (artificial) lake, the time of day when the power would be used, the overall anticipated cost of each project, and losses on power lines used to move electricity to sites of consumption. As a consequence of the latter consideration, EDF strongly advocated extending the electrochemical and metals industries in the Alps–industries that had already had a negative impact in the Isère, Arc, and Durance River basins. It is important to note, therefore, that places at the decision-making table were set only for technocrats and that the basis for decisions excluded considerations of the local population or of the local environment. At many sites, the style of dam installed meant that river flowage below the structure had water whose temperature dropped often as much as five to ten degrees centigrade, destroying streambed ecosystems and the local villages dependent upon them.

EDF was not to succeed so easily, however, and it met formidable opposition throughout the Alps, particularly at Tignes. EDF officials arrived in 1946 at Tignes and announced their intention not only to build a dam over the village, but to put the community under up to fifty meters of water. The peasants were not asked to approve the project. Instead they were just told what was going to happen. No legal recourse was possible–not even over the valuation of the land seized by EDF. Pleas for a voice in the process were ignored. The peasants protested sullenly and refused to accept the property settlements. EDF still did not respond, so on one spring night in 1948, the peasants rioted, burning much of the site and closing off Highway 202 by the deliberate felling of trees. It was a declaration of war against the technocrats, but power resided firmly in the hands of EDF. Riot police were dispatched to the site and occupied it continually until the village was flooded in March 1952. The peasants first became foreigners in their own valley, then a diaspora. In an attempt to annihilate memory of what was an Alpine "Shangri-La," EDF even dynamited the village so that its ruins would not reappear each year as the lake was emptied for power production.

The incidents at Tignes caused a flurry of romantic "sturdy peasant" commentaries in the press, but they were soon lost to public memory. EDF did not, however, forget. Until the 1970s, the firm restricted environmental considerations to questions of public perceptions and protest. Once most hydrosites were equipped and engineers refocused toward nuclear facilities (in the early 1960s), the old vision survived: each facility, conceived and built by technocrats, was an "environment" unto itself. To EDF the desirable environment was the engineered one, even (and often) at the expense of later notions of the natural environment.

–ROBERT L. FROST, UNIVERSITY OF MICHIGAN, ANN ARBOR

References

Jean-Paul Bravard, *The French Upper Rhône: Historical Geography and Management of a River* (Denver, Colo.: U.S. Bureau of Reclamation, 1988).

Robert L. Frost, *Alternating Currents: Nationalized Power in France, 1946–1970* (Ithaca, N.Y.: Cornell University Press, 1991).

Frost, "The Flood of 'Progress': Technocrats and Peasants at Tignes (Savoie), 1946–1952," *French Historical Studies*, 14 (Spring 1985): 117–140.

Gabrielle Hecht, *The Radiance of France: Nuclear Power and National Identity in France After World War II* (Cambridge, Mass.: MIT Press, 1998).

Richard F. Kuisel, *Capitalism and the State in Modern France: Renovation and Economic Management in the Twentieth Century* (Cambridge & New York: Cambridge University Press, 1981).

Bryan Pfaffenberger, "The Harsh Facts of Hydraulics: Technology and Society in Sri Lanka's Colonization Schemes," *Technology and Culture*, 31 (July 1990): 361–397.

Langdon Winner, *The Whale and the Reactor: A Search for Limits in an Age of High Technology* (Chicago: University of Chicago Press, 1986).

GABCIKOVO DAM

Were environmentalists who opposed the Gabcikovo-Nagymaros Dam project politically naive?

Viewpoint: Yes. The Gabcikovo-Nagymaros project was a potent symbol of Slovakian independence in the 1990s, and those Slovak environmentalists who opposed the project on ecological grounds lost their popular support.

Viewpoint: No. The Slovaks made a conscious decision to pursue their narrower nationalist interests or their broader goal of joining the European Union (EU).

In 1977 the communist governments of Hungary and Czechoslovakia signed an agreement to construct two hydroelectric power dams on the Danube River. The first was built at Gabcikovo in Slovakia (part of Czechoslovakia until the Velvet Divorce in late 1992, the two countries officially being separated on 1 January 1993). The second hydrodam was to be built at Nagymaros, in the Danube Bend area of Hungary. Before work commenced there, however, the Soviet bloc collapsed and the Hungarian government decided against the project on the grounds that it would result in "catastrophic, long-term environmental damage." The Slovaks, however, remained firmly convinced that the Gabcikovo power station offered safe and clean energy at an affordable price. After much argumentation with their Hungarian counterparts, they decided to complete their half of the project. Eventually they implemented a plan known as Variant C, which diverted the Danube onto Slovak territory as a temporary solution. Hungary protested this move and demanded a halt to the operation of the Gabcikovo Dam. Frustrations on both sides finally brought the conflict to the International Court of Justice (ICJ) in The Hague in 1993.

In September 1997 the ICJ handed down a decision that was as carefully worded as it was politically ambiguous. It stated that Hungary had violated the 1977 treaty by pulling out of the project in 1989, but that the construction of the Nagymaros Dam was not an absolute necessity, and that Czechoslovakia had been entitled to proceed with Variant C in 1991, but was not entitled to divert the Danube without Hungarian consent or an ICJ ruling.

Both sides claimed victory after receiving the court's verdict, a fact that clearly underscores the politically charged context of this water controversy. In fact, however, the verdict was anything but a clear-cut victory for either side: it obliged both governments to return in good faith to the negotiating table to continue the negotiations. Furthermore, the court hinted that, if the two sides could not find a modus vivendi on this issue, they would be jeopardizing their chances of joining the European Union (EU) in the foreseeable future. Nationalistic rancor, so the court seemed to suggest, had no place in the new Europe.

The Gabcikovo-Nagymaros dispute is a case where history and politics played significant roles in the social construction of the natural environment and the technology that transformed it. These two authors explore the interlocking problems that brought Hungary and Slovakia into this diplomatic dispute, and the dilemmas they faced as they tried to find a mutually acceptable solution.

Viewpoint: Yes. The Gabcikovo-Nagymaros project was a potent symbol of Slovakian independence in the 1990s, and those Slovak environmentalists who opposed the project on ecological grounds lost their popular support.

The initiative for the Gabcikovo-Nagymaros project first originated in 1951 during the Soviet period, a time when massive construction efforts to reshape the natural landscape went hand in hand with the communist ideology of social and technical progress. The joint Czechoslovak and Hungarian dams were conceived to improve the navigability of the Danube River and supply energy to the industrializing economies of both Eastern-bloc countries. By the terms of the treaty that finally materialized in 1977, Czechoslovakia and Hungary were to share the costs and construction of two power plants. Like other large-scale works of the Soviet period, implementation did not always follow precise planning. While construction was started almost immediately in Czechoslovakia at Gabcikovo in 1978, the project was postponed on the Hungarian side because of a lack of available funds. By 1988, however, Hungary had secured an agreement with neighboring Austria to finance the building of the Nagymaros Dam and the government resolved to realize its commitment to the joint treaty.

The issue of timing played a crucial role in the development of the dispute. The controversy only emerged during the astonishing collapse of the communist regimes in Eastern Europe. It was in the context of the highly dynamic and divergent political transitions in both Hungary and Czechoslovakia that the dam project began to carry different meanings for the countries involved. By 1988 communist Hungary had been slowly reforming politically and the government started to tolerate public criticism of state policy. By contrast, during this same year, few would dare openly challenge the hard-line regime in Czechoslovakia.

In Hungary, fueled by the brave efforts of Janos Vargha, a Hungarian biologist who had studied the potential ecological effects of the planned Nagymaros project, an environmental organization called the Danube Circle challenged the government to rethink the dam project. By 1989 the Danube Circle had gained increasing public support. The democratizing government issued a moratorium on construction after Vargha and the Danube Circle successfully mobilized thousands of individuals in protests and petition campaigns against Nagymaros.

Meanwhile, in reform-resistant Czechoslovakia, construction at Gabcikovo proceeded with little public opposition. While Slovak environmentalists had gained popularity by exposing a wide range of environmental maladies since 1987, they did not clearly single out the Gabcikovo project as a major problem. Moreover, the strongest opposition to the regime in Czechoslovakia had come from Czech dissidents who rallied around broad-based human-rights issues, burying environmental issues in a long list of grievances against the communist state. As democracy arrived on the doorstep of Czechoslovakia during the Velvet Revolution (1989), the Gabcikovo dam was nearly 90 percent completed.

Only after the collapse of communism did Hungary begin to put real pressure on Czechoslovakia to halt the project at Gabcikovo. The Hungarian government challenged Czechoslovakia with projections of increased flood dangers and a reduced water supply for nearby inland areas. It argued that a vital and unique ecosystem in Central Europe, the result of years of human nonintervention on this section of the Danube River, would be destroyed for a power station that would only provide limited energy production. Moreover, the Hungarian government (backed by a growing number of international ecological activists) charged that there had never been a proper environmental impact assessment of the waterworks.

Again, the political context played an important role in shaping the dispute as Czechs and Slovaks began to discuss the breakup of Czechoslovakia into two independent postcommunist states. The Czechs responded to Hungarian attacks on Gabcikovo by insisting that the dam was not a Czech problem, leaving Slovak officials to defend the project alone. Slovaks countered the Hungarians by arguing that many other sections of the Danube had been altered in the past with some twenty dams in operation in Germany and Austria. Why should the new Slovak state be deprived of using the Danube as needed? At the same time, the environmental legacy of communism included more-immediate ecological problems, such as the burning of low-grade coal that caused unhealthy air pollution throughout much of the country: was the dam project truly the most pressing ecological threat in Central Europe in light of these other environmental issues?

The economic arguments launched by Slovakia to counter Hungarian opposition were also criticized in the increasingly public debate. According to John Fitzmaurice in *Damming the Danube: Gabcikovo and Post-Communist Politics in*

The Gabcikovo Dam under construction, circa 1991

Europe (1996) the dam proponents' projection of three billion kilowatt-hours of electrical output from the Gabcikovo station would "produce no more than 10–15 percent of the expected Slovak electricity consumption of about 20 billion kilowatt hours per year." Hungary pointed out that the high cost for such a low energy output was inefficient and Slovakia would still need to use other sources of energy, such as coal and nuclear power, to fulfill its energy demands.

While each side used environmental or economic arguments to defend its position internationally, it was the symbolic linking of the project to Slovak independence that successfully mobilized the support of the Slovak public. Clearly, the Danube was not simply a natural resource, but a political resource as well. For Slovaks (and for Hungarians) the river served not only as an historical border or commercial waterway, but also as a cultural landmark and symbol of identity. These symbolic roles of the river in the cultural life of the populations on both sides became important rallying points as the dispute heated up in the early 1990s.

While the dam was labeled by Hungarian demonstrators in 1991 as a "monument to Stalinism," government officials in Slovakia touted Gabcikovo as a shining example of Slovak engineering. The politically savvy Julius Binder, director of Hydrostav, the water management company involved in the building of Variant C, described Gabcikovo as a site of national pilgrimage and suggested that Hungarian opposition to the dam was influenced by Hungarian nationalism. Slovakia had never been an independent state, and words such as these invoked visions of its long nine-hundred-year history under Hungarian rule. Every political party in Slovakia openly supported the dam, including the Slovak Green Party, whose rank-and-file members opposed the principles behind the project—only one of its members, Mikulas Huba, openly challenged its completion. Even in the United States, Slovak-American periodicals included articles in favor of the dam, labeling it crucial to Slovak membership in the New Europe. At a time when Slovakia was starting on the road to independence, these lively characterizations of concrete and steel played well to a public that was struggling in a new and uncertain economy, and was looking for a monument of certainty and achievement.

In Slovakia the Gabcikovo dam did not simply function to supply energy or improve navigation on the Danube. After the completion of Variant C, many tourists and schoolchildren visiting Bratislava boarded boats to travel down the famous waterway for an excursion to see the dam and ride through the lock system. Many of these Slovak visitors from the countryside had never seen the previously untouched banks of the mighty Danube. As a cultural resource, the dam became intimately linked to Slovak national identity in the new postsocialist Europe.

The dam project, as a symbol, was vulnerable to the political situation in each country. While the ecological arguments of the Danube Circle and other environmental groups looking to shut the dam down worked well in Hungary, they carried no weight in Slovakia. For Hungarians, the unfinished dam at Nagymaros was a clear example of an ineffective communist regime, and pressure from environmentalists perhaps provided a convenient excuse for a financially strapped government to shelve an expensive project. Conversely, for Slovakia the nearly completed dam at Gabcikovo, despite its high cost and technical shortcomings, serves as a convenient monument of independence in a dynamic and uncertain political environment.

While it is true that most of the Slovak population came out in favor of Gabcikovo, it is important to note that there was a concerted effort on the part of Slovak environmentalists to fight the dam system shortly after the collapse of communism. Along with their counterparts in Hungary, the Slovak Union of Nature and Landscape Protectors (known by its Slovakian acronym, SZOPK) joined protests in 1991 for a monthlong campaign at the dam site, enduring forced removal by police and security guards. Slovak environmentalists, however, had miscalculated the symbolic value of Gabcikovo for the new nation, and the price of protest was severe. "When we demonstrated against the dam, we were labeled 'traitors of Slovakia' by some politicians. And after our campaign, the government reduced our organization's budget," noted Lubica Trubiniova, a SZOPK activist. In a 1997 article in *Environmental Politics,* Juraj Podoba, an academic and former SZOPK activist, remarked that during the Gabcikovo protests, "the attacks on the [Slovak] environmental movement were more aggressive than the campaigns in the communist press" launched against activists before 1989.

Like the political posturing of Slovakia and Hungary, the ruling of the International Court of Justice (ICJ) in The Hague in 1997 can also be viewed as a political move. The ICJ placed relatively equal blame on each of the parties and executed no substantive penalties, assuaging any criticism of the court from both sides. Is such an outcome a testament to the inevitably political role the ICJ must play in resolving international disputes? This decision simply achieved a return of the dispute back to the parties involved, leaving it up to them to find a compromise. In this sense, both Slovakia and Hungary could rightly claim victory after the ruling, and not fear any real international intervention. This reality, however, does not bode well for international and local environmental organizations seeking to challenge state governments and private multinational corporations regarding transboundary ecological issues.

After their defeat over Gabcikovo, environmentalists in Slovakia attempted to turn their attention to other ecological issues, such as the still-unfinished nuclear-power plant at Mochovce and the Chernobyl-style reactors in operation at Jaslovské Bohunice. The latter posed a clear environmental danger to the region. The neighboring state of Austria, which has no nuclear-energy plants (and had helped finance the Gabcikovo project), came out in full support of Slovak activists against nuclear energy. It appeared that Slovak environmentalists would always be associated with their stance against the Gabcikovo dam. Was not Gabcikovo "the lesser of two evils?" remarked one villager at an antinuclear rally. "Is there anything that environmentalists in this country are 'for'?" asked another villager. The lesson to be learned from the Gabcikovo case is that ecological questions are often tightly connected to cultural and historical environments, and quite vulnerable to the power of symbolic representations in dynamic political arenas.

—EDWARD SNAJDR, FLORIDA STATE UNIVERSITY

Viewpoint: No. The Slovaks made a conscious decision to pursue their narrower nationalist interests or their broader goal of joining the European Union (EU).

Among the many dams designed and built on the Danube River, the Gabcikovo-Nagymaros system is certainly the most gigantic in size as well as the most disputed. The twentieth century brought about severe disturbances in the delicate ecological balance of the Danube through sand excavation, channelization, deforestation, and pollution even before the dam was built. The main site of the Gabcikovo hydroelectric dam was one of the few remaining safe havens for wildlife and unspoiled natural scenery. The largest drinking water reserve in Central Europe, presently supplying the needs of about three million people, also happens to be near the dam project. Situated on a section of the river that forms a state boundary, this project not only posed an environmental catastrophe but also threatened the sociopolitical stability of the region. Beyond doubt, only a holistic approach can produce a valid evaluation of this multifaceted problem. Technical details need to be analyzed in light of the conditions the natural environment and regional economy dictate. Similarly, sociopolitical implications demand sensitivity toward the entire historic legacy and interests of the region.

Originally "inspired" by Joseph Stalin's leadership in 1951, the Gabcikovo-Nagymaros project was in line with all elements of the Soviet-style industrialization ideology. As a monumental installation, it meant to expand human control over the land and convey a message of accomplishment in conquering the forces of nature. Another intention was to engender better relations among two neighboring countries, which were historically at odds over the location of the boundary separating them, by introducing a joint scheme that would necessitate mutual reliance on cooperation over the river they share. The project was also strongly supported by the Soviet Union because it would have stabilized the navigability of a waterway connecting the Black Sea with the North Sea through the Rhine-Main-Danube Canal (completed in 1992), a strategic Soviet interest. As the project evolved, increased incentives appeared for energy self-reliance and mutual economic development among communist-bloc countries; therefore, the original focus on navigation, flood control, and irrigation was gradually reoriented toward energy production.

According to the original plan, the flow of the Danube was to be diverted near Dunakiliti, Hungary, into a newly created 60-square-kilometer reservoir extending over both Hungarian and Slovak territory. Then a 17.5-kilometer-long artificial channel was to be built above ground to transport the water to the turbines of an electric power station near Gabcikovo, Slovakia. At this location, the embankments of the 300-meter-wide sealed channel would be situated eighteen meters above the level of surrounding plains. Below the turbines, an 8-kilometer-long channel, carved deeply into the ground, would then carry the water back to the original riverbed. As a consequence, a 30-kilometer section of the original river and its surrounding branches would be left with only a fraction of the original discharge–roughly 15 percent–resulting in the level of the water table dropping by at least two meters on average.

In other words, the classic model of damming rivers by closing off a section of a valley and simply letting the water fill it up was not feasible in Gabcikovo since a valley did not exist on this flat land area. Consequently, a "valley" had to be built in the form of an artificial channel that could carry the flow until there was a sufficient drop in elevation to generate electricity. Variant C (implemented when Hungary backed out of the project) changed the original plan: water was diverted at Čunovo instead of Dunakiliti so that the entire artificial reservoir and channel rests on Slovak soil.

In order to maximize the value of electricity output, the original plans called for the Gabcikovo station to be a "peaking plant," operating mainly during the high-demand hours of the day that are most expensive to cover. This plan necessitated the construction of a second dam farther downstream in order to counterbalance the massive fluctuation of water flow. The proposed site for this dam was Nagymaros, about a hundred kilometers away, lying entirely on Hungarian territory in the mountainous Danube Bend area. The two dams would have had a total output of 878 megawatts, with the Gabcikovo station contributing 720 megawatts and the smaller Nagymaros plant 158 megawatts. The main significance of these figures is that 70 percent of the output was to be during peak hours.

One of the chief complaints on the Slovak side, therefore, had to do with economics: as a result of the Nagymaros Dam having been abandoned, the Gabcikovo station is only a "base plant" without an ability to generate valuable extra power during peak hours. The Hungarians argued that the action was absolutely necessary in order to prevent an even graver ecological catastrophe. In the absence

DECLARATION OF CURITIBA

On 14 March 1997 conference members meeting at the First International Meeting of People Affected by Dams, at Curitiba, Brazil, published a declaration of position and goals, a portion of which is reproduced below:

We, the people from 20 countries gathered in Curitiba, Brazil, representing organizations of dam-affected people and of opponents of destructive dams, have shared our experiences of the losses we have suffered and the threats we face because of dams. Although our experiences reflect our diverse cultural, social, political and environmental realities, our struggles are one. Our struggles are one because everywhere dams force people from their homes, submerge fertile farmlands, forests and sacred places, destroy fisheries and supplies of clean water, and cause the social and cultural disintegration and economic impoverishment of our communities. Our struggles are one because everywhere there is a wide gulf between the economic and social benefits promised by dam builders and the reality of what has happened after dam construction. Dams have almost always cost more than was projected, even before including environmental and social costs. Dams have produced less electricity and irrigated less land than was promised. They have made floods even more destructive. Dams have benefited large landholders, agribusiness corporations and speculators. They have dispossessed small farmers; rural workers; fishers; tribal, indigenous and traditional communities. Our struggles are one because we are fighting against similar powerful interests, the same international lenders, the same multilateral and bilateral aid and credit agencies, the same dam construction and equipment companies, the same engineering and environmental consultants, and the same corporations involved in heavily subsidized energy-intensive industries. Our struggles are one because everywhere the people who suffer most from dams are excluded from decision-making. Decisions are instead taken by technocrats, politicians and business elites who increase their own power and wealth through building dams. Our common struggles convince us that it is both necessary and possible to bring an end to the era of destructive dams. It is also both necessary and possible to implement alternative ways of providing energy and managing our freshwaters which are equitable, sustainable and effective. For this to happen, we demand genuine democracy which includes public participation and transparency in the development and implementation of energy and water policies, along with the decentralization of political power and empowerment of local communities. We must reduce inequality through measures including equitable access to land. We also insist on the inalienable rights of communities to control and manage their water, land, forests and other resources and the right of every person to a healthy environment. We must advance to a society where human beings and nature are no longer reduced to the logic of the market where the only value is that of commodities and the only goal profits. We must advance to a society which respects diversity, and which is based on equitable and just relations between people, regions and nations.

***Source:** "Declaration of Curitiba," International Rivers Network, Internet website.*

of an appropriate environmental impact assessment on the stretch of the river that would face a daily flood wave between the two power stations, Hungary opted for putting a halt on construction in May 1989 rather than risk having to employ expensive measures of mitigation at a later stage (not to mention public outrage looming in a state of political transition). Specialists from local and international bodies later produced conclusive reports questioning the project and arguing that the financial resources invested could be much better used toward improving energy efficiency in the old and wasteful communist-style industries.

Austria, for example, abandoned the Hainburg Dam Project for environmental reasons in 1984. This decision did not stop Austrian legislators, however, from voting to participate in the Gabcikovo-Nagymaros project through technical and financial assistance. It may sound like absurd economic reasoning, but the financially strapped Hungarian government of the 1980s offered to repay its debt to Austria with electricity the dam system would produce. Based on estimates, the power plant would therefore not have produced much energy for Hungary during the first twenty years of its operation, largely defeating the purpose of economic self-sufficiency. The tab the unfinished project produced was added to the Hungarian national debt, since Austria requested monetary repayment.

Even without the prospect of a fluctuating Danube, the Gabcikovo station raised serious concerns over water quality. Like most other European rivers, the Danube has been used as a convenient way for discharging municipal sewage. Only 14 percent of the sewage entering the Hungarian-Slovak stretch of the Danube and its tributaries was treated in sanitation plants. Still, groundwater quality had not deteriorated to the extent that it might have because the river moves fast enough, and dissolves enough oxygen, to go through a process of self-cleaning. Slowly moving or completely stagnant bodies of water, however, result in the deposition of polluted silt on the riverbed, creating anaerobic (oxygen-deficient) conditions, iron and manganese mobilization, and infiltration of toxic organic materials into the aquifer below.

The geological makeup of the surface of this region consists of gravel (alluvial cone) several hundred meters thick, which acts not only as a reservoir but also as a filter. Damming the river puts a tremendous burden on this natural-filtration mechanism. Evidence showed that pollution had already begun in the reservoir near Gabcikovo, and based on examples of similar projects elsewhere in Europe, there was reason to believe that the long-term effects would be detrimental unless serious measures were taken to install appropriate sewage-treatment facilities upstream (which would still be only a partial solution as incidental spills were also likely to pollute the water). While it is true that many other dams were built on the Danube, it was also commonly accepted that constructions in flat land areas carry more drawbacks than benefits. New democracies need to learn from the mistakes of other countries.

The effects on ecological stability in the inland delta near Gabcikovo are alarming, to say the least, though ecosystem deterioration can take anywhere from a few years to several decades to show, making it difficult to prove a case to the International Court of Justice (ICJ) in The Hague. Before the diversion, an ecological balance in this area had been reached through periodic floods that supplied water and nutrients to plant life. The gravel aquifer acted as a reservoir for the redistribution of water during droughts. A lowered water table near the old riverbed, however, has already caused native flora to perish. In an attempt to counterbalance this process, weirs were constructed to try to hold the water within the river branches. Not only was this policy an imperfect solution, it also resulted in fish communities being sectioned off, facing deterioration of their genetic stock.

The Gabcikovo dam system leaves many technological questions unanswered as well. It is near the Rába geologic fault line, which marks the meeting point of the Transdanubian and Alpine tectonic plates. Although this area is not a particularly active seismic zone, studies show that the expected intensity of historic quakes exceeds the security threshold the dam was designed to handle. Furthermore, experts contend that many elements of the project are structurally inferior and have questionable reliability.

The reason the Slovak government still decided to move ahead with the construction and implementation despite all the difficulties is well known and understood. This dam symbolizes Slovak independence and nationhood, which is a long-awaited dream come true after many centuries of Hungarian rule. This fact was skillfully used to rally citizen support by Prime Minister and President Vladimir Meciar, notorious for his cloudy affairs and dubious conduct as the leader of Slovakia. Meciar was able to stir nationalist sentiments among Slovaks whenever the Hungarian government expressed concerns over the rights of the sizeable ethnic Hungarian minority living in southern Slovakia, many of whom were also affected by the dam project. Granted, some of this upheaval might have been avoided by better diplomacy from the Hungarian government, which between 1990 and 1994 was also made up of a right-wing coalition. Agreement became a far-fetched dream under these circumstances.

Accepting the maximized operation of a project with these many adverse effects for the sake of its status as a Slovak monument is still inconceivable, not just from a Hungarian but also from a regional point of view. One national symbol may become a malady for the region. The implications of a project such as this one rise far above and beyond national boundaries and the interests of a single nation. Furthermore, the interpretation of a monument is a function of available information. The monumentality of the Gabcikovo Dam is partly the legacy of the Meciari propaganda machine, and it is up to the Slovak people to decide how much of it they wanted to preserve. Increasingly, many Slovaks blame Meciar for tainting the image of their country internationally and slowing the process of Euro-Atlantic integration.

At the end of the century, the question is: what alternatives could both sides accept? A common denominator is imaginable, since both Hungary and Slovakia applied for accession into the European Union (EU). The Europe of the future had been declared to be "The Europe of Regions." These regions are no longer defined by the old, artificially drawn boundaries, but rather by smaller subregions shaped after the natural human environment. It is certainly unrealistic for Hungary to expect the demolition of the Gabcikovo plant. Most environmental groups, among them the World Wildlife Fund (WWF), would be happy with a middle-of-the-road solution, although they may assert that only a complete abandonment of the dam would be ideal. What is most important is for enough water to flow through the branches of the inland delta in order to reinstate the original conditions as much as possible. One WWF measure, included among a series of remedial ones, calls for at least 65 percent of the original flow to be redirected into the old riverbed and also for allowing periodic floods to occur.

As renowned California naturalist John Muir said: "When we try to pick out anything by itself, we find it hitched to everything else in the universe." Gabcikovo-Nagymaros in its complexity should not have any elements singled out whether they are technical, environmental, or sociopolitical. The energy generated cannot be considered renewable because this form of electricity production degrades and depletes resources of ever-increasing global scarcity: drinking water and biodiversity. Similarly, a broader examination of the sociopolitical implications suggests that endangering the stability of the region is an unreasonable price to pay for a monument of questionable origin. How acceptable can it be for regional inhabitants to approve of a gigantic, ill-conceived project in their backyard that not only symbolizes Slovak independence but also serves as a reminder of the socialist-style coerced industrialization amplified by the Meciari self-serving politicking? Slovakia needs to invent a national monument that is more forward-looking and less tainted with the unwanted legacy of the past.

–GÁBOR BIHARI, BUDAPEST, HUNGARY

References

G. Berrisch, *Construction and Operation of Variant C of the Gabcikovo-Nagymaros Project under International Law* (Brussels: WWF, 1992).

Julius Binder, "Damning Evidence?" *East European Reporter,* 5 (September–October 1992): 76–78.

Sharon Fisher, "Gabcikovo-Nagymaros Dam Controversy Continues," *RFE/RL Research Report,* 2 (September 1993): 7–12.

John Fitzmaurice, *Damming the Danube: Gabcikovo and Post-Communist Politics in Europe* (Boulder, Colo.: Westview Press, 1996).

Karoly Okolicsanyi, "Slovak-Hungarian Tension: Bratislava Diverts the Danube," *RFE/RL Research Report,* 1 (December 1992): 49–54.

Juraj Podoba, "Rejecting Green Velvet: Transition, Environment and Nationalism in Slovakia," *Environmental Politics,* 7 (Spring 1998): 129–144.

Jaromir Sibl, ed., "Damming the Danube: What Dam Builders Don't Want You to Know," *A Critique of the Gabcikovo Dam Project Prepared by Slovak Union of Nature and Landscape Protectors and Slovak Rivers Network* (Bratislava: April 1993).

Gábor Szabó, "Hágai vízlépcsoper: Ítéletido" (The Hague Hydro-Station Courtcase: Judgment Time), HVG (Hungary) (4 October 1997): 9–12.

Ludovit Tuba, *Mesiac na hradzi* (A Month on the Dam) (Bratislava: Central Committee of the Slovak Union of Nature and Landscape Protectors, 1991).

GRAND CANYON

Should the Colorado River have been dammed?

Viewpoint: Yes. Arizona politicians believed that diverting water from the Colorado River would ensure the growth of the state economy and proposed building two dams in an unprotected section of the Grand Canyon to generate power and create water recreation for millions of people.

Viewpoint: No. Dams would threaten the Grand Canyon, one of the seven wonders of the natural world. There are many other ways to generate power, but there is only one Grand Canyon.

The long-running battle over the proposal in the 1960s to build dams on the Colorado River to generate water for agriculture and urban consumers, as well as to generate hydropower, sparked an array of environmental, legal, political, and social dilemmas. Each revolved around a question of competing sets of values and priorities that drove the public struggle and private debate over the future of the river and the fantastic canyon through which it flows.

Those who favored the dams included federal and state officials, Arizona farmers, and others who believed that the water resources of the Colorado River should be better employed. They were convinced that the proposed Central Arizona Project (CAP)—one of many colossal water-development projects that the federal government initiated during the 1950s and 1960s—would have a dramatic impact on the lives and living standards of many Arizona citizens. By storing the water in vast reservoirs, it could be more easily distributed to irrigators and city water purveyors, allowing greater rural and urban growth. The reservoirs would provide unparalleled opportunities for recreationists to boat, fish, and swim in these captured waters. This form of tourism in northern portions of the state would enhance the capacity of local Native American peoples to expand their incomes. Once completed, CAP would transform Arizona, enriching its diverse population as well as diversifying and strengthening its economy.

Opponents cast doubt on the financial windfall that the supporters of CAP touted as the reasons for the project. Public-interest groups such as the Sierra Club challenged the estimates of economic growth and denounced the hitherto unacknowledged environmental costs associated with the project. Through a letter-writing and public-relations campaign, they focused national attention on the degree to which the proposed dams and reservoirs would damage the Grand Canyon, now heralded as the gem of the National Park system. In the end, the environmentalists' arguments—however heatedly contested—proved successful, in part benefiting from and expanding on the larger social debates then swirling through the American political landscape. Like protests over civil rights and the Vietnam War, those that erupted over CAP depended on different social values and public-policy agendas.

Viewpoint:
Yes. Arizona politicians believed that diverting water from the Colorado River would ensure the growth of the state economy and proposed building two dams in an unprotected section of the Grand Canyon to generate power and create water recreation for millions of people.

The state of Arizona has sought to obtain what it believed was its "rightful" share of the Colorado River for much of the twentieth century. Early plans envisioned a series of aqueducts to bring water to the fertile valleys in the central part of the state near Phoenix. Other western states, however, most notably California, also desired to utilize the water of the river for agriculture and the growing cities of Los Angeles and San Diego. Although Arizona and California contested Colorado River rights bitterly for much of the century, there was one point of agreement: the plans of each state required tremendous amounts of electric power to be generated by hydroelectric dams in the Grand Canyon.

In 1919 U.S. representative Carl Trumbull Hayden (D-Arizona) sponsored the law that created Grand Canyon National Park. Envisioning the future needs of his native state, Hayden inserted a provision within the statute that provided for the construction of water projects within the Grand Canyon, so long as they did not "impair the purposes of the park"–the preservation of the scenic beauty of the canyon. This provision was scarcely debated because most of the American public in the early twentieth century did not feel that the creation of a lake in a national park would damage the scenery it was designed to protect. The statute protected 100 miles of the Colorado River within Grand Canyon National Park, while an additional 177 miles of the canyon lay unprotected outside of the park boundaries. This unprotected section of the Grand Canyon became the focus of important public debates in the years to come.

In the American West, courts have recognized a doctrine of water law called "prior appropriation," where the first person to put water to use establishes a right that is superior to those of other users. As a result, Arizona and California attempted to divert as much of the water as possible to establish a legal right to it. At the same time, Arizona and California attempted to prevent each other from using Colorado River water. In 1922 representatives from seven Western states signed the Colorado River Compact and agreed to divide the water among themselves. Arizonans, suspicious of California's motives, refused to sign it and remained a holdout until 1944. Meanwhile, Congress allowed California to initiate construction of Boulder (Hoover) Dam, a structure that would enable California to divert great quantities of water for agricultural and urban uses. Arizona protested in vain and even called out the National Guard to prevent California from building still another dam in 1935.

Arizona and California also contested each other's Colorado River rights in the federal courts and in the Congress of the United States. The Supreme Court ruled in favor of California three times and Arizona once prior to World War II. After the war, Arizona, a state with a relatively small population, found itself in a powerful political position in Congress. Senate majority leader Ernest William McFarland (D-Arizona) and Hayden, who had moved to the Senate from the House, sponsored bills in 1950 and 1951 for federal construction of a water diversion, called the Central Arizona Project (CAP). Though it passed the Senate overwhelmingly, the project, which included a dam in Grand Canyon, was derailed in the House of Representatives by twenty-three representatives from California, who then rammed a bill through the Congress forbidding further consideration of the project until the water rights in the lower Colorado River had been determined by the U.S. Supreme Court.

In 1963 the Supreme Court handed down its ruling granting Arizona a large portion of the water from the lower Colorado River. Hayden, in the last great political fight of his career, along with Representative Morris King Udall (D-Arizona) and his brother Stewart Lee Udall, who was secretary of the interior, pushed for congressional approval of the CAP. The proposal now contained two dams slated for construction in Grand Canyon: Bridge Canyon Dam, rivaling Boulder Dam in height, would have been located seventy-eight miles downstream of the park, and its reservoir would have backed water through Grand Canyon National monument and along thirteen miles of the park boundary; and Marble Canyon Dam, which would have been built twelve miles upstream of the park.

To gain backing from California, whose support he deemed indispensable, Secretary Udall proposed a grand scheme designed to unite Arizona and California: The Pacific Southwest Water Plan, of which the CAP was an integral part. Seeking to ensure enough water for everyone, Udall proposed that water be imported to the Southwest from the Columbia River. The two Grand Canyon dams constituted the critical components of this scheme, for these structures were designed to be "cash registers" to generate funds from the sale of hydroelectric power to finance the massive pumping stations, tunnels, and canals necessary to move water 1,200 miles from the Pacific Northwest.

For the first time California and Arizona stood united, and federal officials, such as Bureau of Reclamation chief Floyd Dominy, embarked on a massive public-relations campaign that touted the economic benefits the project would bring to the Southwest. These officials also contended that Native American groups in the region would benefit greatly, because the south abutment of each dam would rest on the Hualapai and Navajo reservations. Dominy and others contended that the Grand Canyon dams would open the scenic wonders of the inner canyon to millions of sightseers and boating enthusiasts, just as the recently completed Glen Canyon Dam had provided recreational opportunities in the stunning setting of Lake Powell further upstream.

By 1965 the proposals to build the Grand Canyon dams were the subject of rigorous debates in Congress. Arizona officials believed that they would gain congressional approval within two years provided that the Arizona/California alliance held. These supporters of the Grand Canyon dams, however, who had so painstakingly hammered out a seemingly workable political coalition after decades of fighting, now found themselves confronted by a new adversary, a growing activist environmental movement, which had begun to mobilize public opinion against the Grand Canyon dams.

By the mid 1960s the environmental movement, along with civil-rights, free-speech, and antiwar movements, was remaking the social and moral consciousness of the United States. Holding to early-twentieth-century perceptions of resource usage that stressed efficiency and economic benefit, supporters of the Grand Canyon dams were mystified and angered by environmentalists who contended that other, noneconomic values should also be considered in debates over resource usage. David Ross Brower, executive secretary of the Sierra Club, spearheaded opposition to the dams and began to publish books that focused upon the destruction of U.S. environmental treasures. Brower contended that the 1960s constituted a crucial point in the history of the nation in terms of environmental protection, because development was occurring at such a prolific rate that there would be little left worth saving if another decade were allowed to pass without certain restrictions.

Supporters of the CAP pointed to the 1919 law that had created Grand Canyon National Park and argued that the construction of dams within the Grand Canyon was allowed by the statute. These officials also gained the support of the Hualapai Nation, and eventually eight other Native American groups in the region, by promising the impoverished Hualapai a large annual payment in exchange for the use of the Bridge Canyon site. Scoffing at the idea that the Grand Canyon would be flooded or desecrated, CAP supporters contended that environmental groups, which consisted of mostly upper-middle-class whites, were attempting to reserve the Grand Canyon for themselves, while excluding millions of Americans from recreational opportunities, as well as discriminating against the Hualapai who sought to utilize the only resource available to them.

In June of 1966, after a contentious round of congressional hearings, the nature of the debate changed. In response to the Sierra Club advertising campaign, in which full-page advertisements opposing the dams were placed in *The New York Times* and other newspapers, the Internal Revenue Service (IRS) revoked the tax status of the Sierra Club. Relying on Supreme Court opinions dealing with similar situations, the IRS contended that the club was engaging in lobbying by trying to influence the legislative process, an activity that nonprofit organizations were forbidden to do by federal statute. The Sierra Club had used its advantaged status as a nonprofit organization as a platform from which it was trying to manipulate public opinion and influence the debate now occurring before Congress.

The alliance between Arizona and California, meanwhile, had begun to come apart during the heat of battle, threatening the entire project. To break the deadlock, Secretary Udall decided to remove the controversial dams from the legislation in the fall of 1966, opting instead in favor of coal-fired powerplants, a solution supported by the Sierra Club. Although some support for the dams remained, Congress eventually passed a damless CAP bill over the objections of California, and President Lyndon B. Johnson signed it into law on 30 September 1968.

Deleting the Grand Canyon dams from the CAP bill resulted in environmental and human consequences that have had far-reaching effects. Because of the efforts of the Sierra Club, the Hualapai Nation remains mired in poverty, forbidden from developing the only natural resource on their reservation that promises substantial economic benefits. Even the recent foray of the tribe into gaming has not assuaged the plight of the people. Furthermore, the Navajo Nation, the only Native American group in the region to oppose the

GRAND CANYON ENLARGEMENT

Below are some portions of the Grand Canyon National Park Enlargement Act, passed 3 January 1975.

It is the object of this Act to provide for the recognition by Congress that the entire Grand Canyon, from the mouth of the Paria River to the Grand Wash Cliffs, including tributary side canyons and surrounding plateaus, is a natural feature of national and international significance. Congress therefore recognizes the need for, and in this Act provides for, the further protection and interpretation of the Grand Canyon in accordance with its true significance.

Sec. 3 (a) In order to add to the Grand Canyon National Park certain prime portions of the canyon area possessing unique natural, scientific, and scenic values, the Grand Canyon National Park shall comprise, subject to any valid existing rights under the Navajo Boundary Act of 1934, all those lands, waters, and interests therein, constituting approximately one million two hundred thousand acres, located within the boundaries as depicted on the drawing entitled "Boundary Map, Grand Canyon National Park," numbered 113-20, 021 B and dated December 1974, a copy of which shall be on file and available for public inspection in the offices of the National Park Service, Department of the Interior.

(b) For purposes of this Act, the Grand Canyon National monument and the Marble Canyon National Monument are abolished.

(c) The Secretary of the Interior shall study the lands within the former boundaries of the Grand Canyon National Monument commonly known as the Tuckup Point, Slide Mountain and Jensen Tank areas to determine whether any portion of these lands might be unsuitable for park purposes and whether in his judgement the public interest might be better served if they were deleted from the Grand Canyon National Park. The Secretary shall report his findings and recommendations to the Congress no later than one year from the date of enactment of this act.

Sec. 4. (a) Within the boundaries of the Grand Canyon National Park, as enlarged by this Act, the Secretary of the Interior (herein referred to as the "Secretary") may acquire land and interest in land by donation, purchase with donated or appropriated funds, or exchange.

(b) Federal lands within the boundaries of such park are hereby transferred to the jurisdiction of the Secretary for the purposes of this Act.

Sec. 5. Notwithstanding any other provision of this Act (1) land or interest in land owned by the State of Arizona or any political subdivision thereof may be acquired by the Secretary under this Act only by donation or exchange and (2) no land or interest in land, which is held in trust for any Indian tribe or nation, may be transferred to the United States under this Act or for purposes of this Act except after approval by the governing body of the respective Indian tribe or nation.

Source: *Public Law 93-620, 16 USC 228.*

dams, has been victimized by the "damless" Sierra Club proposal. Peabody Coal Company has inflicted enormous environmental devastation upon the four corners region and Navajo country strip-mining for coal. Perhaps the most ironic indictment of all, haze produced by the coal-fired power plants is so dense that visitors to the Grand Canyon itself are unable to see the opposite rim for more than half of the year.

None of these negative effects need have occurred. Hydroelectric power is nonpolluting; Grand Canyon National Park would not have been threatened; and scenery of the inner gorge of the Grand Canyon would have been greatly enhanced with two beautiful lakes in a spectacular setting. More than one hundred miles of free-flowing river would have remained protected. The air and land of the Navajo country would have remained pristine. The Hualapai have been denied a decent living and the control of their own resource. Millions of Americans have been prevented from enjoying a natural spectacle that now is only accessible to a privileged, selfish elite who have the physical stamina and can afford the equipment to see it.

–BYRON E. PEARSON,
WEST TEXAS A&M UNIVERSITY

Viewpoint: No. Dams would threaten the Grand Canyon, one of the seven wonders of the natural world. There are many other ways to generate power, but there is only one Grand Canyon.

In 1913 the United States Congress authorized the construction of a dam in Hetch Hetchy Valley, a spectacular place of waterfalls and soaring cliffs within Yosemite National Park. From that point forward, developmental interests have assumed that economic value should, in the final analysis, take precedence over the intangible values of beauty and wilderness preservation during debates over resource use in the United States. Even though the National Park Service was created in 1916 to oversee the protection of places of natural beauty in the United States, the statutes creating new national parks often reserved the right for future development of resources contained within their boundaries. Such was the case of Grand Canyon National Park in 1919.

Most environmental organizations were originally created to promote hiking, camping, and the preservation of local areas of pristine beauty. The Sierra Club, for instance, was formed to preserve the beauty of the Sierra Nevada Mountains in California. Many environmental groups were made up of members who differed on issues such as wilderness preservation and activism. In the case of the Sierra Club, it was to remain an organization devoted to its original mission into the post–World War II era.

When the war ended, Americans began to take to the outdoors in ever-increasing numbers, spurred on by postwar prosperity and the availability of surplus camping gear and automobiles. By 1950 the Sierra Club stood at an important crossroads in its history. Older, established members such as Sierra Club president Bestor Robinson did not believe that the construction of dams and other developments were necessarily bad in (and for) national parks. A new generation of activists, however, most notably David Ross Brower of the Sierra Club and Howard Zahniser of the Wilderness Society, began to try to convince the members of their organizations that they needed to become national advocates for environmental protection, because they feared the environmental consequences of postwar development.

In the early 1950s the U.S. Bureau of Reclamation planned to construct two dams within Dinosaur National Monument in Utah and Colorado as a part of a massive proposal called the Colorado River Storage Project (CRSP). The Sierra Club and other organizations banded together and through an intense public-relations campaign managed to persuade Congress to delete the controversial dams from the bill in 1956. Environmentalists rejoiced, for now it appeared as though the harmful precedent of Hetch Hetchy had been reversed and that the scenic grandeur contained within the national parks and monuments stood a good chance of protection from development.

In the wake of the Dinosaur victory, however, lay the seeds of future controversies. As a part of the compromise over Dinosaur National Monument, environmentalists had agreed not to oppose the raising of the proposed Glen Canyon Dam, which was also a part of the CRSP. Only after defeating the Dinosaur dams did activists such as Brower venture to Glen Canyon. To his eternal regret, though, Brower discovered that the place he and others had agreed to sacrifice was arguably more beautiful than the canyon they had saved. From the late 1950s until January 1963, environmentalists fought a poignant but futile battle against the filling of Lake Powell. On 21 January 1963, with Brower waiting in his outer office, Interior Secretary Stewart Lee Udall gave the order; the gates were closed; and the flooding of Glen Canyon, one of the most beautiful places in the world, began.

Having learned the bitter lessons of compromise during the Glen Canyon battle, Brower, the Sierra Club, and other environmentalists vowed never to allow similar losses to occur again. When Senator Carl Trumbull Hayden (D-Arizona) and other supporters of the Grand Canyon dams began to seek congressional approval, the Sierra Club and other environmental organizations launched a counteroffensive in the fall of 1963. Driven by the memory of the inundation of Glen Canyon, environmentalists mobilized behind a grassroots strategy of letter writing, hoping that a massive public outcry would convince Congress to delete the dams from the proposed legislation.

Throughout 1964 and 1965, environmentalists sponsored workshops and public symposiums to try to counter the promotional efforts of Central Arizona Project (CAP) supporters. Arguing that scenic and psychological values–what author Wallace Stegner called "the geography of hope"–should take precedence over economic gain, opponents of the dams stated in clear unequivocal terms that this fight should be finished. Sierra Club member Martin Litton, writing in the October 1963 issue of the *Sierra Club Bulletin*, called environmentalists to arms saying: "But are we resigned? Shall

The Grand Canyon

(Gene Ahrens)

we fail to go into battle because it is hard to win? . . . Could not 22,000 Sierra Club members, without strain turn out 22,000 letters a day for a week? . . . . Three letters each . . . and more to follow . . . could assure the Canyon's interim survival and rescue the opportunity for reason to prevail."

The letter-writing campaign became the focus of the environmentalists' efforts, and beginning in late 1963 a trickle of mail began to arrive in the mailboxes of federal officials. Sierra Club leadership contended that the club was exercising its First Amendment rights of free speech and petition. Environmentalists also began to appear on Capitol Hill and the Sierra Club published two books: Eliot Porter's *The Place No One Knew: Glen Canyon on the Colorado* (1963), a requiem for Glen Canyon; and Francois Leydet's *Time and the River Flowing: Grand Canyon* (1964), to warn the public of the scenic grandeur that would be lost forever if the Grand Canyon dams were approved. Beautifully photographed and written, these widely read and hotly debated books presented stunning visual evidence of the intangible values environmentalists believed ought to be considered in debates over resource usage. Even hard-boiled House Interior Committee chairman Wayne Norviel Aspinall (D-Colorado), a strong dam supporter, wept openly after reading the prologue to *The Place No One Knew.*

Environmentalists also testified at congressional hearings in 1965 and 1966, and argued that alternative sources of energy such as coal-fired and nuclear-power plants could generate the electricity required by the CAP at relatively little environmental cost. Sierra Club members also held a forum on the rim of the Grand Canyon in March 1966 and aired their views to the national press. Representative Morris King Udall (D-Arizona), Senator Barry Morris Goldwater (R-Arizona), and other dam supporters crashed the gathering and tempers got so hot that some Sierra Club members threatened to duke it out with their uninvited guests. Cooler heads prevailed, but the political heavyweights in favor of the dams managed to garner most of the press coverage.

After the congressional hearings in May 1966, with the rhetoric and intensity of the debate increasing, the Sierra Club unleashed another powerful broadside at the pro-dam interests; on 9 June 1966, it took out full-page ads in *The New York Times, The Wall Street Journal,* and other national newspapers, accusing the Interior Department of "flooding Grand Canyon for profit." The next day, the constitutional rights of free speech and petition of the club were violated by the Internal Revenue Service (IRS), which revoked its tax-deductible status. Although he denied it for the rest of his career, all the evidence points to Morris Udall as the person who instigated the IRS investigation. The purpose of the IRS action was for nothing other than the destruction of the Sierra Club, because it depended on tax-deductible dues and contributions for its very existence.

The American public reacted angrily to the heavy-handed tactics of the federal government. A flood of letters protesting the Grand Canyon dams and the IRS action arrived in Washington, D.C., during the summer of 1966–the volume grew so great that the postal service pressed dump trucks into service to haul the mail to Capitol Hill. Contributions and requests for Sierra Club membership soared. The IRS action turned out to be a blunder of colossal proportions. Instead of crippling the club and stopping its advocacy against the dams, the action gained an unprecedented amount of publicity for the Sierra Club and its causes. Millions of Americans learned of the Grand Canyon fight and tens of thousands of people joined the Sierra Club as a result.

Supporters of the Grand Canyon dams also used deceptive tactics to gain the support of American Indians in the region in an attempt to portray environmentalists as racist. In the summer of 1966, Arizona officials, pretending to be the chiefs of the Hualapai Nation and other Native American groups, sent tens of thousands of letters to prominent Americans and the national press, in which the "chiefs" pleaded with Congress and the American people to fight the attempt by the Sierra Club to hold the Hualapai people in "racial and economic subordination." Yet, despite these outright lies on the part of CAP supporters, the Navajo Nation, the largest tribal organization in the United States, sided with the Sierra Club and called for a deletion of the dams in favor of construction of coal-fired powerplants that would utilize the plentiful supplies of coal found on their reservation.

With the public in a furor, in 1968 Congress bowed to the inevitable and passed a CAP bill that deleted the Grand Canyon dams, and in 1975 extended national-park protection to the entire canyon. Because of the efforts of the Sierra Club and other dedicated organizations, the Grand Canyon remains free of dams. It only remains so, however, by the whim of Congress, which could change its mind at any time and reconsider the dams. Environmental groups must remain vigilant to stop the destruction of what is left of the scenic beauty of the United States.

In saving the Grand Canyon the Sierra Club earned a global reputation as a vigorous and uncompromising environmental advocate, a reputation it has used to gain the leadership of the modern environmental movement. While it is true that most people will never have the chance to view the inner gorge of the Grand Canyon in person, it is equally true that millions are comforted just by knowing that it and other wild landscapes still exist. Once they are gone, they can never be replaced. Although economic development is necessary for the health of the United States, it should not come at the price of destroying natural treasures. Those who sought to build dams in the Grand Canyon were shortsighted and greedy, while the environmentalists sought to protect it for future generations. There are occasions where compromise is not an option, because in the end, one cannot put a price on a Grand Canyon where the river runs freely.

–BYRON E. PEARSON,
WEST TEXAS A&M UNIVERSITY

References

Mark W. T. Harvey, *A Symbol of Wilderness: Echo Park and the American Conservation Movement* (Albuquerque: University of New Mexico Press, 1994).

Francois Leydet, *Time and the River Flowing: Grand Canyon,* edited by David Brower (San Francisco: Sierra Club, 1964).

Roderick Nash, *Grand Canyon of the Living Colorado* (New York: Ballantine, 1970).

Byron E. Pearson, "'People Above Scenery,' the Struggle over the Grand Canyon Dams, 1963–1968," dissertation, University of Arizona, 1998.

Eliot Porter, *The Place No One Knew: Glen Canyon on the Colorado,* edited by Brower (San Francisco: Sierra Club, 1963).

Marc Reisner, *Cadillac Desert: the American West and its Disappearing Water* (New York: Viking, 1986).

Stewart Lee Udall, *The Quiet Crisis and the Next Generation* (Salt Lake City: Peregrine Smith, 1988).

U.S. Department of the Interior, "Pacific Southwest Water Plan Report" (Washington, D.C.: U.S. Government Printing Office, 1964).

U.S. Department of the Interior, Bureau of Reclamation, *Lake Powell, Jewel of the Colorado* (Washington, D.C.: U.S. Government Printing Office, 1965).

GREAT LAKES

How did federal agencies in Canada and the United States respond to declining water quality in the Great Lakes?

Viewpoint: In Canada, the need to present a united front when dealing with the United States helped the provincial and federal governments to overcome their differences.

Viewpoint: In the United States, the federal government ignored the cautious attitude of state-level authorities and promoted more-rapid abatement progress. The presence of another developed nation in the Great Lakes Basin also acted as a positive force for pollution control.

Canada and the United States share a lengthy 5,525-mile border, a good portion of which runs through the aptly named Great Lakes. These five lakes encompass nearly 95,000 square miles, form the largest series of interlocking bodies of freshwater in the world, and contain 20 percent of the earth's freshwater. Although this basin is demilitarized, in the War of 1812 its waters and shores were the scene of bloody naval and military engagements between the United States and Great Britain. Those political tensions evaporated, but the Great Lakes remained the source of serious binational concern, specifically over their water quality. In 1909 the United States and Great Britain signed the Boundary Waters Treaty, which created a regulatory body of Americans and Canadians, the International Joint Commission (IJC), to resolve disputes over the use of shared waters and pollution concerns. The IJC consists of six members, three each appointed by the U.S. president and the Canadian cabinet, with three main functions: the authority to approve obstructions, dams, and other diversions of boundary waters and water crossing the border; an arbitrational role, which has never been utilized; and an advisory role on any matter referred to it by the two federal governments. Before 1972 the investigative powers of the IJC were rarely invoked through the formal reference mechanism—there were only three such requests between 1912 and 1972—a consequence largely of complex domestic politics. Neither the Canadian province of Ontario, which envelops the five lakes, nor its counterparts in the United States were willing to grant authority to their respective national governments over environmental problems.

This situation changed in the post–World War II era. The Great Lakes Basin had been the heart of the prewar industrial economy for both nations, and so it remained in the rapid economic development and urban population growth that followed. Toronto, along with Cleveland, Detroit, and Chicago, exploded in size and manufacturing productivity. As more natural resources were processed, chemicals refined, steel manufactured, and automobiles constructed, there were escalating environmental consequences. The lakes and their many tributaries were befouled—deterioration that became glaringly obvious when, in the late 1960s, the Cuyahoga River, which flows into Lake Erie in the heart of Cleveland, erupted into flames.

To stem the destructive assault upon the basin required new thinking about pollution and its costs and a new form of governmental oversight. These concepts emerged within differing national contexts as environmental activists brought intense pressure on their respective political authorities to control the flow of effluent. Aiding the cause was the realization that only federal legislatures and administrations could raise the funds necessary to clean up the lakes; only they could wield the kind of regulatory clout needed to monitor and regulate industrial pollution that flowed across state, provincial, and national boundaries. To restore the water quality of the Great Lakes required once-reluctant governments to develop more environmentally sensitive policies and responsible governance.

Viewpoint: In Canada, the need to present a united front when dealing with the United States helped the provincial and federal governments to overcome their differences.

To comprehend the Canadian response to Great Lakes water-quality issues, it is necessary to understand how the federal-provincial relationship, established under the British North America Act (Constitution Act, 1867), developed in the twentieth century. Federal-provincial jurisdictional maneuvering related to water-resource issues cannot be viewed in isolation. Both levels of government took this situation as an opportunity to address the larger issue of provincial economic and policy independence. Nevertheless, because of the constitutional division of powers, the reality was that the federal and provincial governments had to work closely when addressing pollution in the international Great Lakes, and this cooperation helped them present a strong front when working with the U.S. federal government, as well as states that bordered the Great Lakes, on water-resource issues.

The signing of the Boundary Waters Treaty (1909) placed Canadian domestic responsibility and international obligations for water resources into conflict. The British North America Act delegated primary responsibility for a range of issues related to water resources to the provinces, which had jurisdiction over municipal-sewage and water-treatment facilities. They regulated public health and were responsible for setting and enforcing controls over industrial wastewater quality. The constitution gave only modest water-resource responsibilities–for fisheries, navigation, and shipping–to the federal government. Yet, under the treaty, the Canadian government was committed to avoid polluting the water on its side of the border to the detriment of health and property of the Americans. This policy meant identifying and controlling sources of municipal and industrial pollution. To meet their international obligation, the federal government required considerable support and cooperation from the provinces.

The province of Ontario cooperated with the federal government and participated in Great Lakes pollution studies led by the International Joint Commission (IJC). The province allowed its technical experts to be seconded to the IJC and adopted, where possible, the resulting conclusions. Provincial support for IJC recommendations was important because of constitutional limitations to the water-resource management authority of the federal government. Although the federal Parliament debated several times between 1910 and 1915 bills to ban pollution in the nation, a majority of legislators believed any such legislation would be ruled ultra vires, or outside its legal scope of authority, and refused to pass the proposed laws. In 1915 Ontario amended its Pollution Control Act to require provincial approval before municipalities could issue debentures to fund water-treatment and sewage-control plants. This step was an important legislative one because it gave the province direct control over those municipalities that chose to construct pollution-control infrastructure.

The support of Ontario for federal obligations and initiatives could not always be expected, however. Beginning in the late nineteenth century, successive premiers asserted the broadest possible independence over provincial economic development and growth. As the wealthiest province in Canada, Ontario provided more tax dollars to the federal government than it received in federal programs or transfer payments. Ontario premiers sought better fiscal relations with the federal government and resisted federal involvement in areas constitutionally delegated to provinces, such as education and health care. As general practice, the premiers jealously guarded the legislative authority granted to the province under the constitution. While they saw the advantages in cooperating with the federal government and IJC in addressing boundary-waters pollution, they clearly would not meekly allow the federal government to overstep its jurisdiction.

Given the responsibility of provincial leaders for regulating industrial and municipal effluent, the participation of Ontario in implementing programs to meet the Objectives for Boundary Water Quality (1951) proposed by the IJC after World War II was key. Municipalities located on the connecting channels proved to be the primary polluters of boundary waters. While they recognized the need for sewage-treatment facilities, these communities were unable to act because the wartime boom and postwar economic expansion left them with overtaxed infrastructure and more-immediate priorities. Throughout the early 1950s the border municipalities appealed to the province for financial help. Premier Leslie M. Frost refused to help because he was afraid to establish a precedent that would force him to support sewage-treatment facilities provincewide. Under pressure from the United States, the federal government brought what political leverage it could to prod the province to address municipal pollution. The premier used this federal concern as an opportunity to address his longstanding desire to redress federal-provincial fiscal relations and to insist that pollution abatement be considered under that category. The prime minister refused to consider municipal sewage treatment as anything other than a provincial responsibility.

Officials from Ontario participated on IJC-appointed Technical Advisory Boards monitoring binational water quality. In an effort to achieve the Objectives for Boundary Waters Quality, the provincial sanitary engineer's office urged municipalities to plan and build sewage-treatment facilities, but there was little progress. In the mid 1950s a water shortage in southwestern Ontario provided the premier with an opportunity to address the municipal sewage problem in border communities. Initiated by the drought, an assessment of water infrastructure needs across the province revealed that municipalities required some $2.5 billion in water- and sewage-treatment plant construction and upgrades. This situation provided the government an opportunity to develop a program that would serve the entire province, thus in the process providing badly needed resources to the border municipalities.

In 1956, therefore, the provincial government created the Ontario Water Resources Commission (OWRC). Until that time, responsibility for water quality resided in the sanitary engineer's office under the Department of Health. Other aspects of water-resource management were scattered among various departments. With the creation of the OWRC, the province concentrated responsibility for all aspects of water-resource management in one agency. The OWRC was responsible for regulating both the water supply and municipal and industrial pollution control. The commission developed water sources, managed groundwater, and approved, financed, and/or built municipal water-purification and sewage-treatment systems. It monitored water quality in provincial lakes and streams and set standards for the industrial and municipal effluent released into them. The government charged the OWRC to update the aging water and sewerage infrastructure and authorized a $2.5 billion construction program in the province.

Although the OWRC construction program addressed the infrastructure needs in border municipalities, it did not end the boundary-waters controversy. There had not been a comprehensive assessment of Great Lakes pollution since early in the century and the federal governments were anxious to determine the state of the Great Lakes. Under the Boundary Waters Treaty, the federal governments could ask the IJC to investigate any issue along the common boundary. Although the treaty did not require consultation with either the provinces or states on a pollution study, it was a necessary courtesy by the 1950s to secure their participation. The IJC would also require the services of provincial and state water-resource managers. In Canada the majority of recommendations emerging from the survey would have to be implemented by the province—without the participation of Ontario there was little point in beginning.

The Frost government was reluctant to approve the study and ignored it for several years. Officials knew that conclusions arising from it could prove embarrassing to the province, because they had just created the OWRC expressly to manage pollution problems and feared that the new program, admittedly inadequate along some significant portions of transboundary waters, was not yet ready to withstand public scrutiny. Frost's successor, John P. Robarts, finally agreed to the study in 1963 when the OWRC program was sufficiently advanced.

In 1964 the IJC began investigating the state of the lower Great Lakes. The postwar industrial boom provided an unparalleled period of growth and prosperity to most of North America, particularly the Great Lakes Basin, which was the industrial heartland of both Canada and the United States. Development and associated urban growth, however, had not been accompanied by similar expansion of pollution abatement infrastructure, and by the mid 1960s the lakes were a mess. Excessive nutrient loading from municipal effluent and agricultural runoff created massive algae blooms on Lake Ontario and Lake Erie each summer. The algae died and washed up on the beaches—thick, stinking, black masses of slime. Industrial effluent left an oily sheen on the harbors and beaches near the cities of the Great Lakes. Oil spills and other flammable materials were so thick on one tributary river, the Cuyahoga, that it caught fire several times, most spectacularly in 1969.

The pollution study marked the beginning of several binational and domestic initiatives to control Great Lakes pollution. By the

Firefighters in Ohio working to put out a blaze on the Cuyahoga River, a tributary of Lake Erie, November 1952

(The Cleveland Press Collection)

mid 1960s governments across North America began to hear increasing public concern about the state of the environment. In Ontario the postwar economic boom that had damaged the natural beauty of the province ironically provided more people with the leisure time and resources to leave urban centers and enjoy the beaches, hiking trails, and rivers. Watching these beloved areas deteriorate around them caused environmentally aware activists to demand government action to protect and restore the natural beauty of Ontario. Bowing to these demands, the federal government in particular undertook a series of initiatives designed to address public concern.

The federal government began to adopt a more proactive role in water-resource management. Clearly there were resource-management issues for which the provinces were unable or unwilling to assume responsibility. In 1966 the government created the Department of Energy, Mines and Resources to develop and coordinate national programs addressing these issues. One of the first initiatives was to develop a Great Lakes research program based upon needs identified by the IJC. At this point, federal involvement consisted of research and did not yet address pollution-abatement efforts directly.

In 1969 federal authorities took the next step and introduced the Canada Water Bill for debate in Parliament. This legislation was designed to allow the federal government more direct involvement in water-resource management in partnership with the provinces. It enabled the government to establish formal federal-provincial consultative committees and cooperative agreements on the development and implementation of watershed plans. The bill also gave the federal government the authority to enter into agreements with the provinces to address water-quality issues of urgent national concern. The government would then be free to develop the regulatory tools necessary to address water-quality issues. Finally, the proposed legislation banned the manufacture and import of phosphate-based detergents.

Led by Ontario, the wealthy provinces rejected the bill outright for political and technical reasons. While the federal government viewed it as an example of cooperative federalism, the provinces knew that the legislation had been written so the federal government could assert responsibility over interjurisdictional waters when a province failed to meet its obligations. Both Quebec and Ontario expressed concern that the federal government had not consulted with the provinces while developing the new legislation.

Ontario also opposed the Canada Water Bill because it did not propose uniform national effluent and water-quality standards. Since its inception, the OWRC had worked toward meeting the Objectives for Boundary Water Quality and was philosophically committed to common interjurisdictional standards. The OWRC also believed that the legislation would add another, unnecessary layer of bureaucracy in the Great Lakes Basin without providing any obvious advantage in addressing pollution problems. Ontario controlled the entire Canadian portion of the watershed, and therefore felt that there was no need for internal coordination; instead, the province asserted that the unmet need was for greater coordination between the two countries. If the federal government wanted to pursue that objective, the province would cooperate fully. Despite these objections the legislation was passed in 1970.

Aware that the IJC was close to completing its report, which would recommend some kind of binational initiative beyond the existing Technical Advisory Boards and the Objectives for Boundary Water Quality, U.S. and Canadian water resource managers began meeting early in 1970. The initial conference involved ministerial-level participants and achieved a basic understanding that a working group of water-resource managers would investigate the possibility of a bilateral agreement. From the outset, representatives from OWRC played an important role in this process. The provincial and federal governments might not agree on how to implement pollution-control initiatives within Canada, but they were united when facing their U.S. counterparts. This strong cooperation impressed U.S. officials, who had initially been reluctant to consider a binational agreement. With increasing pressure coming from the Canadians, the public, and the Great Lake states, U.S. water-resource managers began to cooperate enthusiastically by the fall of 1970.

Part of the new U.S. federal interest in an agreement with Canada stemmed from increased state and provincial activity in this area. In September 1970 Ontario hosted officials from the Great Lake states and governments of Manitoba and Quebec at the Great Lakes Environmental Conference. There the representatives, in many cases governors and premiers, discussed opportunities to develop interjurisdictional initiatives to address pollution control. On one hand, it was logical for this type of discussion to occur at the state and provincial level; on the other, anxious federal observers hoped that this initiative would not overshadow the efforts of the Working Group to develop a binational response to pollution. Thus, when the Working Group met again after the Ontario conference, officials from Michigan represented the Great Lake states.

The Working Group, governors and premiers conference, and the final IJC report all came to the same conclusion: Canada and the United States had to develop a binational agreement on water quality in order to address the range of pollution issues in the Great Lakes. Unlike when it negotiated the Boundary Waters Treaty, the Canadian federal government could not conclude such an agreement without first coming to terms with the province of Ontario. In the resulting Canada-Ontario Agreement (COA) the federal government pledged substantial resources to accelerate municipal sewage-treatment programs in the province and committed additional resources to water-quality research. Significantly, COA was based upon the assumption that Canada and the United States would conclude a Great Lakes agreement. If no such agreement occurred, COA would lapse. COA demonstrated to the United States that both the provincial and federal governments were committed to the development of a binational agreement. The built-in expiration date only added pressure to conclude it.

Finally, on 15 April 1972, President Richard M. Nixon and Prime Minister Pierre E. Trudeau signed the Great Lakes Water Quality Agreement. This event was the culmination of two processes: careful negotiations between Canada and the United States, and equally vigilant discussions between the Canadian government and the province of Ontario. With the agreement and the development of COA, federal-provincial water-resource relations that had been in conflict since the Boundary Waters Treaty were finally harmonized. COA reconciled conflicting domestic responsibility and international obligations and provided the mechanism for better integrated federal-provincial programs related to Great Lakes water quality.

–JENNIFER READ, GREAT LAKES INSTITUTE FOR ENVIRONMENTAL RESEARCH, UNIVERSITY OF WINDSOR AND THE GREAT LAKES COMMISSION

THE POLLUTION IN THE GREAT LAKES

On 9 February 1972 Representative Abner Joseph Mikva (D-Illinois) spoke to his colleagues in the U.S. House of Representatives about pollution in the Great Lakes.

Mr. Speaker, the Great Lakes are being poisoned. Slowly but surely, they are dying off—losing their oxygen and their vitality—and slowly but surely, the quality of life for the people who live around them is deteriorating. Together the five lakes cover 95,000 square miles, comprising an area often described as the world's largest body of "fresh" water. Today, at least part of that description is no longer accurate. Every year, more beaches are closed because there is too much bacteria in the water. Every month, the water is stained and fouled with new pollutants and sewage and, every day, the lakes yield a bit more to the pollution of progress. Lake Erie already is a dead sea where there is no recreation, no fishing, and virtually no life—except perhaps for the scavenger fish, the sludge worms and the algae which seem to thrive on the municipal and industrial waste. Lake Michigan and Lake Ontario are not far behind.

The last few years have seen the beginning of a new national awareness on the problems of the environment. But despite that, the Great Lakes have lost ground in their struggle with the pollution of man and industry, because every hour another billion gallons of waste is dumped into them. Every one of the Great Lakes is more polluted today than it was 5 years ago. It is almost futile to discuss "progress" in the fight against pollution—we have not even been able to keep up with it. As a nation, we still are spending more time and money polluting the Great Lakes than we are spending to revitalize them. It is simply a losing battle.

On February 8, 1971—almost precisely 1 year ago today—the President sent Congress a message on the environment. In it, he outlined a sweeping program that covered water pollution, air pollution, the recycling of wastes, pesticides, and national parks. . . .

It is a sad and troubling story. The Environmental Protection Agency recently asked the administration for $141.3 million to support a proposal which assigned "national priority" to the fight against pollution in the Great Lakes. It was a comprehensive proposal—bold and innovative with a clear-cut goal and a good chance of meeting it—but the Office of Management and Budget rejected the request and the proposal. With a national budget of $246.3 billion, and a deficit of more than $25 billion, it seemed that $141 million to fight pollution in the Great Lakes was too much of a fiscal burden for the country to bear. As a result, the battle against pollution will continue to be a losing battle. . . .

We are not making sure the anti-pollution technology is being used in the Great Lakes, and I am afraid that the results of the gap between promise and performance will become clear in the next 5 or 10 years. By then, Lake Michigan and Lake Ontario may have joined Lake Erie on the list of dead seas, and Lake Erie will not be the only body of "fresh" water in this country which has, in the words of the EPA report:

> A mat of algae two feet thick and a few hundred square miles in extent that floats in the middle of the lake in mid-summer.

That is the prospect for the other four Great Lakes, and I simply cannot understand the refusal of this administration to set aside $141 million to help save them. The 30 million people who live in the Great Lakes Basin are going to find it difficult to understand too. . . .

The EPA realizes the danger. It realizes that Lake Michigan and Lake Ontario will not die suddenly. Rather, it will be a death from a long and lingering illness, an illness that might have been cured had it not been for the indifference and inactivity of people and government.

Source: Congressional Record, *volume 118 (3 February 1972 to 14 February 1972), pp. 3463–3464.*

Viewpoint:
In the United States, the federal government ignored the cautious attitude of state-level authorities and promoted more-rapid abatement progress. The presence of another developed nation in the Great Lakes Basin also acted as a positive force for pollution control.

At the beginning of the 1960s, the states bordering the Great Lakes remained the core of industrial America. Residents of lakefront cities such as Milwaukee, Detroit, Chicago, and Cleveland took great pride in the manufacturing output of their steel mills, auto plants, chemical factories, and other industries. This impressive industrial production, however, took its toll on the local environment, especially the waters of the Great Lakes and their tributary rivers that acted as waste conduits for both industrial effluent and sewage of the large urban centers that had grown up with these industrial complexes.

The polluted waters of Lake Erie and some of the other Great Lakes had become a national disgrace by the late 1960s, when a burgeoning environmental movement helped raise Americans' consciousness about the downside of unrestrained economic growth and development. Concerted pollution abatement efforts on the part of industry, government, and concerned citizens eventually resulted in significant progress in cleaning up some of the worst pollution, although significant problems remained. This progress would not have been possible without a reordering of government responsibility that allowed the federal government to take on a much larger and direct role in regulating environmental practices in the region. In addition, the need to coordinate activities with a neighboring country–at a comparable stage of economic and social development–also played a positive role in prompting a more determined pollution-control effort.

Government officials, business executives, and other parties at the state level strongly resisted greater federal involvement in water-pollution control. Until the 1960s most people in a position to influence policy believed that water-pollution control was best left to those who were intimately familiar with local problems and circumstances. In practice, state agencies were responsible for regulating wastewater discharges within their borders. Federal water-pollution control laws explicitly recognized the "primary responsibilities and rights of the states" in regulating waste discharges.

The state officials responsible for water-pollution control in the Great Lakes Basin and other parts of the United States practiced a form of regulation that emphasized cooperation and voluntarism. In the Great Lakes region, the control boards and commissions did all that they could to avoid issuing formal abatement orders or engaging in litigation. Instead, they relied on informal cooperation with waste dischargers to work out "reasonable" solutions. State regulators were usually satisfied with the results of these negotiations because they believed in the importance of balancing other considerations with the need to control pollution. In their view, pollution itself was a relative concept. As the sanitary engineer who directed the water-quality program in Illinois put it, "Pollution as it affects water quality is objectionable only in relation to the intended use of the water." In other words, a river in a highly developed industrialized area did not need to be as clean as a section of a lake that was used mainly for recreation. In practice, this perspective led to a kind of de facto zoning in which some waterways were subject to a fairly high degree of protection, while other waters were allowed to deteriorate.

This approach to regulation can be traced, in part, back to the Progressive Era, when specially trained experts assumed a leading role in many areas of public life. Sanitary engineers, who were largely responsible for administering the water-pollution laws, saw themselves as disinterested experts who were uniquely qualified to balance the needs of competing interest groups and select rational policies that would best serve the public interest. There was another important factor at work. State and local officials believed that they were locked in a continual struggle with other states to attract industry and hold on to existing jobs. Adopting more-effective pollution-control practices was an expensive proposition, especially for older factories that had been constructed before environmental practices were a major concern. Because regulations varied by state, officials worried that tough water-pollution regulations might drive industry out of the region, or at least make it more difficult to attract new development. A member of the Wisconsin State Committee on Water Pollution explained that they saw "our work as serving the best interests of the most people. This means we can't stop pollution completely. It would hurt the state too much economically."

Not everyone shared the belief that water pollution control was best left to the states. Traditional conservation groups, such as the Izaak Walton League of America, had long been critical of state governments for not being aggressive enough in their regulation of major pollution sources. With the emergence of the environmental movement in the 1960s, established conservation groups experienced membership growth, while new organizations focused their activities on addressing pollution problems. Even the League of Women Voters adopted water-pollution control as one of its top concerns. All of these groups expressed impatience with the handling of water-pollution problems and looked to the federal government for leadership on this issue.

Environmentalists in the Great Lakes region found powerful allies in Congress, the federal bureaucracy, and among local news media who also viewed an enhanced federal role as the key to greater progress in controlling water pollution. The decade was in many respects the heyday of liberal activism, and both the Kennedy and Johnson administrations viewed pollution control as an important component of a political agenda aimed at improving Americans' quality of life. Liberal Democratic members of Congress from the Great Lakes states were among the strongest voices calling for federal intervention and new legislation to provide enhanced regulatory powers. In addition, major metropolitan newspapers in the Great Lakes Basin, a powerful voice in an era when newspaper readership remained high, fueled this discontent with heavy coverage of local pollution problems and editorials that usually supported critics of the state programs. For example, a 1960 front-page article in the Cleveland *Plain Dealer* on the Cuyahoga River, which runs through downtown Cleveland and drains into Lake Erie, warned that "Industry Waste Turns River Into a Menace."

Liberals in Congress and their allies believed that economic competition among the states prevented them from imposing tough pollution control regulations on their industries. Senator Gaylord Anton Nelson (D-Wisconsin), who helped establish Earth Day, recalled that when he had been governor the powerful paper industry had successfully used the argument that more stringent regulation would put manufacturers in Wisconsin at a competitive disadvantage with firms in more lenient states. Nelson, Senator Robert F. Kennedy (D-New York), and other Democrats believed that national standards and a greater federal regulatory role were the only means to undermine industrial polluters' leverage and ensure a level playing field in which significant progress in pollution abatement could be achieved. Proponents of national regulation noted that industry executives had long been strong supporters of maintaining pollution-control authority at the state level.

The erosion of state authority was a gradual process. Prior to the creation of the Environmental Protection Agency in 1970, federal officials were forced to rely on a procedure known as the enforcement conference when they wanted to intervene in badly polluted areas. These conferences brought together national and state regulatory officials with representatives from the municipalities and industries responsible for the pollution. Federal administrators used this tool sparingly, in part because of resistance from state officials who deeply resented federal intrusion. Moreover, an enforcement conference could only be convened to address "intrastate" (as opposed to interstate) pollution problems at the request of a state governor. Even so, as a result of growing public pressure that was skillfully orchestrated by environmentalists and their allies, five enforcement conferences were convened prior to 1970 to deal with different areas of the Great Lakes. These conferences were relatively informal proceedings, with only limited provisions for legal action against polluters. In the Great Lakes region, however, they produced valuable studies of polluted areas, helped mobilize public opinion, and initiated comprehensive abatement programs that—eventually—resulted in significant improvements in water quality.

At the national level, the Water Quality Act of 1965 represented an important step toward federal control. Under this law, the states were required to adopt quality standards for their interstate waters, subject to the approval of the federal government. The law was an example of what scholars term "partial preemption." The concept refers to laws that require state governments to implement regulatory programs created by the federal government. Such laws, in effect, create national minimum standards that all states are required to meet. The Water Pollution Control Act of 1972 represented the final culmination of this trend in water-quality policy. The law established a national permit system that gave federal officials the authority to regulate directly the effluent leaving outfall pipes. Instead of such requirements being set by state officials based on local conditions, they would be established by federal officials based on nationwide industry guidelines and technological feasibility. The law included a provision for state governments to eventually assume control of the program, but federal officials would maintain a veto over individual permits.

The growth of federal power in water-pollution control was of critical significance across the United States, not just in the Great Lakes region. Pollution-control efforts in the latter region also benefited from the fact that it is bordered by another country, Canada. Both nations, but especially the United States, had long been reluctant to surrender any sovereignty to international agencies, so the role of the International Joint Commission (IJC) was confined to that of investigation and coordination. Even so, IJC scientific studies were a source of unassailable information about the health of the lakes, and thus its recommendations, while carrying no legal weight, exercised a benign pressure on various levels of government in both countries. With the signing of the Great Lakes Water Quality Agreement in 1972, the mutual obligation of the two countries to achieve and maintain certain levels of water quality became even more pronounced.

In addition, significantly, on certain issues the Canadian governments appeared willing to take more aggressive action to control pollution than their American counterparts. Such was the case when the Canada enacted legislation restricting the phosphorus content of detergents, which had been determined to contribute significantly to the problem of lake eutrophication (accelerated nutrient enrichment, leading to excessive algae growth and other conditions). In this case and others, American environmentalists could point to their northern neighbor as a shining example of what could be done, if only U.S. public officials had the courage of their convictions. It is interesting to contrast this situation with that on the southern border with Mexico. In this case the disparate economic and social conditions of the two neighbors made environmental cooperation an altogether trickier endeavor, where future progress relied to a great extent on the development of the Mexican economy and the continued growth of a strong and politically active middle class.

–TERENCE KEHOE, MORGAN, ANGEL & ASSOCIATES

References

Christopher Armstrong, *The Politics of Federalism: Ontario's Relations with the Federal Government, 1867–1942* (Toronto & Buffalo: University of Toronto Press, 1981).

Theodora E. Colborn, and others, *Great Lakes, Great Legacy?* (Washington, D.C.: Conservation Foundation, 1990; Ottawa, Ontario: Institute for Research on Public Policy, 1990).

Samuel P. Hays, with Barbara D. Hays, *Beauty, Health, and Permanence: Environmental Politics in the United States, 1955–1985* (Cambridge & New York: Cambridge University Press, 1987).

Terence Kehoe, *Cleaning Up the Great Lakes: From Cooperation to Confrontation* (DeKalb: Northern Illinois University Press, 1997).

Clarence Klassen, "Water Quality Management–A National Necessity," in *Proceedings of the National Conference on Water Pollution in Washington, D.C., December 12–14, 1960* (Washington, D.C.: U.S. Department of Health, Education, and Welfare, Public Health Service, 1961).

Earl Finbar Murphy, *Water Quality: A Study in Legal Control of Natural Resources* (Madison: University of Wisconsin Press, 1961).

Jennifer Read, "'Let us heed the voice of youth': Laundry Detergents, Phosphates and the Emergence of the Environmental Movement in Ontario," *Journal of the Canadian Historical Association,* 7 (1996): 227–250.

Read, "Managing Water Quality in the Great Lakes Basin: Sewage Pollution Control, 1951–1960," in *Ontario Since Confederation: A Reader,* edited by Edgar-Andre Montigny and Lori Chambers (Toronto & Buffalo: University of Toronto Press, 2000), pp. 339–361.

Read, "'A Sort of Destiny': The Multi-Jurisdictional Response to Sewage Pollution in the Great Lakes, 1900–1930," *Scientia Canadiensis,* 51 (1999): 103–129.

INDIAN DAMS

Have large dams in India contributed to social and economic development in a sustainable and equitable way?

Viewpoint: Large dams in India have provided some benefits, but have also had many negative consequences, with a doubtful balance between costs and benefits. More equitable and environmentally benign ways of conserving and managing water resources are available and need to be given serious consideration.

Viewpoint: While failing to achieve projected benefits for social and economic development in a sustainable and equitable way, large dams in India have led to disastrous social, economic, environmental, and human consequences, including the loss of opportunities to develop alternatives, as well as the destruction of traditional water-harvesting technologies and management systems.

India has three major landforms: mountain ranges (the Himalaya in the north, Aravalli and Satpura in the central areas, and Western and Eastern Ghats in the south), plains (Gangetic in the north), and plateau (Deccan in the south). The Thar Desert is in the northwest, while coastal plains (deltas) are in the east and south. With altitudes ranging from sea level to five thousand meters, temperatures vary depending upon altitude and latitude. Large parts of western, central, and southern India have semiarid to arid climates, but the east is prone to recurring heavy floods. Rainfall occurs largely during the southwest monsoons of June to September and to a limited extent the northeast monsoons from November through January in southern India. During the monsoon, rain is concentrated in just a few weeks, ranging in amount from one hundred millimeters in western desert areas to eleven thousand millimeters in the extreme northeast. As a result, recurring droughts and floods threaten agriculture, buildings, and life.

In response to these conditions, the ancient civilizations of the subcontinent developed sophisticated mechanisms for water harvesting, storage, and irrigation. The Grand Anicut, a diversion structure built by the Chola kings (9th–13th century A.D.) on the Kaveri River more than a thousand years ago in Tamil Nadu, has often been restored and renovated. Southern Indian irrigation systems of the Vijayanagar kings (1336 A.D.–1614 A.D.) were extant, and were admired by the British in the early nineteenth century. There were also extensive tank systems in the south, water-harvesting structures in Gujarat and Rajasthan, and canals built by the Moghuls in the north. These systems were largely based upon local and community control, had financial incentives for construction and maintenance, and depended upon social consensus for the fulfillment of commitments. With the advent of British rule, modernity, and engineering education, traditional water-management systems tended to fall into a state of neglect and deterioration, along with the knowledge upon which they were based.

At India's national independence in 1947, its industrial base was still developing, food production of fifty million tons did not satisfy the national need, poverty was widespread, and electricity was scarce. Indians wanted the benefits of education, science, and technology. There was a debate about how to achieve these goals. Jawaharlal Nehru, the first Indian prime minister, was driven by a belief in centralized economic planning and the application of western science and technology as the means of making his county prosperous and modern. He embraced the engineers' faith in the construction of large dams to produce electricity, irrigate crops, supply water to distant locations, and control flooding. This stance gave voice to modernism in India and had a major influence on public opinion. In the latter part of his seventeen-year rule Nehru became disenchanted with large-scale multipurpose river-basin projects. Nehru's changed attitude was less well publicized and was, therefore, less influential.

India has more than four thousand large dams and more than fifty years of experience with their short- and long-term consequences. Popular resistance movements emerged to advocate the cause of those whose lives had been adversely affected by dams, to prevent further dam construction, and to urge alternative approaches to water management and energy production. Throughout the country water use and management in general, and dams and river control in specific, were being debated—dams were no longer seen as an unqualified benefit to society.

Viewpoint: Large dams in India have provided some benefits, but have also had many negative consequences, with a doubtful balance between costs and benefits. More equitable and environmentally benign ways of conserving and managing water resources are available and need to be given serious consideration.

India has a long history of water management. There were large numbers of widely varied water-harvesting and conservation structures and systems in different parts of the country. While the rulers built some relatively large structures (for instance, the Grand Anicut built by the Chola kings in Tamil Nadu over a thousand years ago, or the canals built by the Moghuls in the north), the systems were largely local and community-managed. All this changed with the advent of the British period and of "modernity." Control over water resources passed from the hands of the community into those of the state. While the ownership of natural resources was claimed by the state, management passed into the hands of engineers and bureaucrats. The induction of Western engineering ushered in the era of large dams and there was a concomitant decline of traditional forms of small-scale, local, community-managed systems. The new projects became symbols of "development" and came to be regarded as "the temples of modern India" in Nehru's famous (but somewhat misinterpreted) phrase.

India has over four thousand large dams as defined by the International Commission on Large Dams. At the beginning of the twentieth century India had forty-two large dams. By 1950 a further two hundred and fifty had been added. The rest came up in the second half of the last century. A large number of them, roughly half of the total number of large dams in the country, were undertaken in the period 1970 to 1989. Why were these dams built?

With an estimated quantum of "available" water resources of 1,953 billion cubic metres (BCM), or the same number of cubic kilometres (km^3) which is an alternative way of putting it, a "usable" component of 1,086 BCM, and a current level of use of around 600 BCM, the position does not seem uncomfortable in national terms at present, though this may change in the future. However, national aggregates and averages are misleading. There are wide variations, both temporal and spatial, in the availability of water in the country. Much of the rainfall occurs within a period of a few months during the year, and even during that period the intensity is concentrated within a few weeks. There are also variations from year to year. Spatially, there is a wide range in precipitation from one hundred mm in parts of Rajasthan to eleven thousand mm in Cherrapunji. Apart from the desert in Rajasthan, there are arid or drought-prone areas in parts of Gujarat, Maharashtra, Karnataka, Andhra Pradesh, and Tamil Nadu; and the eastern parts of the country experience devastating floods from time to time.

The standard engineering response to these temporal and spatial variations was to propose (a) the storing of river waters in reservoirs behind large dams to transfer water from the season of abundance to that of scarcity (as also from good years to bad), and (b) long-distance water transfers from "surplus" areas to water-short areas. Both large "storages" (that is, reservoirs) and the "linking of rivers" (that is, "inter-basin transfers") have played an important part in the thinking of our water resource planners, and both need large dams. In energy planning, hydroelectric power is considered a necessary component of total generating capacity, and it is also perceived as "clean," that is, nonpolluting; and large-scale hydropower generation implies big projects.

What has been the contribution of large dams to the country? The production of food grains increased from fifty-one million tons in 1950–1951 to almost two hundred million tons by 1996–1997. The increase was the result of a combination of several factors such as high-yielding varieties of seeds, chemical fertilizers and pesticides, credit, extension, support prices, and so on, but clearly irrigation played a crucial role, and some of that irrigation came from large dams while the rest came from other sources ("minor" surface water irrigation and groundwater). On the question of how much of the increase in food production can be attributed to dams, there are different estimates ranging from 10 percent to 30 percent. As for hydroelectric power, about two-thirds of the installed hydropower capacity of 21,891 MW in March 1998 (out of a total generating capacity of 89,000 MW) is attributed to dams, with one-third coming from run-of-the-river schemes. Turning to flood control, the contribution of dams has been very modest. (Dams are not often planned with flood moderation as a primary aim, and even where they are, the competing claims of irrigation and power generation often override the flood moderation function. Further, while dams may indeed moderate flood flows to some extent under normal conditions, they may aggravate the position if, in the absence of a flood cushion, water has to be suddenly released in the interest of the safety of structures.) Public water supply is not often a stated objective of large dam projects, but in many cases reservoirs and canals are in fact made use of for this purpose. There are a few projects which meet industrial demands for water. As regards navigation, this has not so far played a significant role in the planning of dam projects, except in the case of the Damodar Valley Corporation; even there it did not develop as originally envisaged.

Thus it can be said that dams have contributed (along with other factors) to an increase in food production, added to hydropower capacity, provided water for domestic, municipal, and industrial uses, and (to some extent) helped in flood moderation. However, disenchantment with large projects has been growing during the last two decades or so. The Silent Valley Project in Kerala was abandoned. The Narmada (Sardar Sarovar) Project in Gujarat and the Tehri Hydro-Electric Project in the Himalayan region have been facing strong antiproject movements. (These movements, and in particular the "Save the Narmada Movement" or Narmada Bachao Andolan (NBA), have become internationally known, and were among the factors that led to the establishment of the World Commission on Dams.) Projects proposed long ago in the Northeast of India (Dihang, Subansiri, and Tipaimukh) and in Bhutan (Manas and Sankosh) have made hardly any headway because of opposition on diverse grounds. The earlier tacit consensus on such projects has clearly broken down; the statement that they are "the temples of modern India" no longer commands universal assent. How did this happen? The answer lies in a convergence of dissatisfactions with such projects from diverse points of view:

Indian officials inspecting the Rihand hydropower station

(i) financial/economic ("time and cost overruns"; an insatiable demand for resources; the failure of many projects to achieve the projected benefits; their inability to generate revenues for reinvestment or even for proper maintenance, partly because of the poor pricing of irrigation water);

(ii) "political economy" aspects (the widespread perception of the prevalence of corruption and of the influence of vested interests in the planning and implementation of projects; serious inequities in the incidence of costs and benefits);

(iii) environmental/ecological concerns;

(iv) concern about the displacement of people and dissatisfaction with rehabilitation policies and practices; and so on.

All these strands are important, but the environmental and displacement aspects are at the heart of the controversy. The environmental impacts will of course vary in range and severity from case to case, but most such projects have some common and inescapable consequences, such as:

• violent disturbance of pristine areas; varying degrees of submergence of land including forests in some cases;

• impacts on flora and fauna, leading to a reduction in biodiversity;

• in particular, severe impacts on the fish population in the river;

• the stilling of flowing waters leading to temperature stratification as well as variations in nutrient content and dissolved oxygen, rendering the water inhospitable to aquatic life;

• drastic changes in the river regime downstream of the dam (reduced flows affecting aquatic life and riparian communities, reduced capacity for self-regeneration, increased pollution levels, reduced recharge of groundwater aquifers, adverse impact on estuarine conditions).

Some of these effects cannot be remedied or even mitigated; and in some cases efforts at the mitigation of or compensation for environmental impacts may in turn create further problems. Further, it is clear from past experience that all the consequences and ramifications arising from the damming of a river cannot really be fully foreseen and planned for.

In most cases, there will also be varying degrees of displacement of human settlements, with the attendant problems of resettlement and rehabilitation; this impact often falls on poor and disadvantaged sections, particularly tribal communities. There are inherent difficulties in resettlement and rehabilitation: a lack of full knowledge of the numbers and categories of people likely to be affected; separation of communities from the natural resource base on which they are dependent; inadequacy of land for land-based rehabilitation; scattering of well-knit communities; resettlement in distant and unfamiliar areas; difficulties with the host communities in the resettlement areas; major transformation in ways of living and loss of old coping capabilities and the need to learn new skills and ways of living; and so on. However good and enlightened the rehabilitation policies and 'packages,' there will inevitably be great hardship and suffering, to which the response of the governmental machinery is rarely adequate, much less imaginative.

The usual answer to these criticisms is to say that all this can be taken care through comprehensive environmental impact assessment (EIA) studies (including the rehabilitation aspects); proper cost-benefit analyses based on such EIA studies, and investment decisions with reference to such cost-benefit analyses; and remedial and/or compensatory measures to counter the expected impacts.

Unfortunately, EIAs are not dependable. When they are undertaken in-house by the project planners, the desire to get the project approved may influence the EIA and render it suspect. Even when a reputed external consultancy firm is engaged (as is often the practice), the thoroughness and objectivity of the study cannot be taken for granted. The insidious pressure on the consultant to be "positive" about the project could be very strong: to say this is not to imply that there is collusion between the project-planner and the consultant. The latter has an interest (not necessarily conscious) in coming to the conclusion that the adverse impacts of the project can be remedied or mitigated or compensated for; that the project will still remain viable; and that the overall balance of costs and benefits will be favorable. A consultant who says "The impacts of this project are too grave to be mitigated or offset: the project should not be undertaken" is unlikely to secure many assignments. It is only a disinterested examination by an independent appraisal agency, say, the Ministry of Environment and Forests or an agency appointed by it, that could be expected to be truly neutral and objective. But even that agency could come under strong pressure from other agencies within the Government to be "positive" and supportive of "development." Further, as already mentioned, it is impossible to foresee all the consequences of such major interventions in nature; nor is it always possible to remedy or mitigate or compensate for the ill effects of such projects. As for cost-benefit analysis, it is a flawed basis for decision making because (i) it is susceptible to manipulation (costs are usually understated and benefits overstated); (ii) it is necessarily incomplete and inadequate (not every aspect or dimension can be brought within the ambit of the calculation); and (iii) it is morally blind (the infliction of misery on some people is often sought to be justified on the ground that a larger number elsewhere will be benefited). Moreover, the rationale of a cost-benefit analysis is that the benefits (direct and indirect) justify the costs (financial and social); and that justification tends to get undermined by the fact that the costs are certain to be incurred and are almost always higher than projected, whereas the claimed benefits are often problematic and may not be fully realized.

In regard to the "political economy" aspects of such projects, it could be argued that inequities, injustices, corruption, collusion, and so forth, arise from the sociopolitical milieu and cannot be attributed to dams; but some of the inequities and ills are perhaps facilitated by or at any rate associated with large-dam projects.

However, given the projected magnitudes of demand for water (linked to rates of growth of population and urbanization), are such projects avoidable? A widely held view is that they are not. This way of thinking holds that future needs cannot be met without massive "water resource development," that expression being treated as synonymous with large "storage" (that is, dam and reservoir) projects, and that local rainwater harvesting and watershed development schemes, while very necessary, are bound to remain secondary and supplementary to large projects and cannot be a major component of water resource planning. However, there are others who see great potential in water-harvesting and watershed development and are convinced that these activities, undertaken in several thousands of locations all over the country, are capable of making a substantial contribution toward future needs, while being environmentally benign, people-centered, and conducive to equity. That potential needs to be carefully assessed, but it is clear enough that a major push needs to be given to these activities; there is no justification for assuming a priori that they can play only a small, supplementary role in water-resource planning. If in fact they can make a significant contribution, the need for large projects can be minimized; only a small number may be needed, and the environmental, social, and human impacts will be correspondingly reduced.

A seemingly powerful argument for large dams is that even if there is no need for them for irrigation, they are definitely needed for the generation of hydroelectric power. However, it has been argued by some that through a combination of demand management, energy-saving, technological improvements, and getting more generation out of capacities already installed, the need for additions to capacity can be greatly reduced; that significant additions can be made through extensive decentralized generation; and that if this approach were adopted very few large projects would be needed. This proposition, which runs counter to the establishment view, has not been given serious consideration.

The question is not whether large "water resource development" projects should be allowed or ruled out, but whether they should be the first choice or the last option. That question, if rigorously pursued, will take us beyond the domain of water resources into larger issues. The examination must necessarily include a questioning of the demand projections (particularly in the case of energy) and of the lifestyles they are derived from, and a redefinition of what constitutes development. Large dams are only one aspect or feature of the modern world. It is possible to marshal an impressive array of evidence against dams; but it is equally possible to build up a strong case against other symbols of "development": coal-burning and nuclear power plants; metallurgical, chemical, hydrocarbon and petrochemical industries, and mining complexes; monstrous megalopolises; the exploding automobile population; vast networks of railways and highways built by trenching into floodplains, drainage channels, fields, forests, and wildlife habitats, and by blasting hillsides and tunnelling through mountains; the onslaught on aquatic life by giant trawlers and whaling vessels; the staggering global trade in oil and the everpresent threat of oil-spills; and so on. All these are manifestations of a certain conception of "development" and a related attitude to nature. At the moment it is difficult to see how a change of direction is going to be brought about and doom averted. However, instead of perplexing ourselves with large and unanswerable questions, we could perhaps consider what can be done in practical terms and in limited contexts. From that point of view, and in the context of water resources, it seems very necessary to explore all nondam possibilities of meeting future needs before we consider recourse to large-dam projects.

—RAMASWAMY R. IYER, CENTRE OF POLICY RESEARCH, NEW DELHI

Viewpoint: While failing to achieve projected benefits for social and economic development in a sustainable and equitable way, large dams in India have led to disastrous social, economic, environmental, and human impacts, including the loss of opportunities to develop alternatives, as well as the destruction of traditional water-harvesting technologies and management systems.

India's rich tradition of water resources development and management skills is well documented. But the story of India's water-resources development over the last five decades is a story of the rise of dams and also a story of the fall of this rich tradition. In 1947, when India became independent, it had 293 completed large dams.

By 1994, this number had gone up to 3,596 completed large dams as per the definition of International Committee on Large Dams. According to the World Commission on Dams, India has the largest number of large dams under construction in the world today at about 695 large dams, which is about 40 percent of total large dams under construction in the world. Out of the total investment of Rs. 2313.87 billion spent on water resources in India over the last fifty years, by March 1997, over two-thirds, that is Rs. 1567.76 billion (both the figures at constant 1996–1997 price level) have been spent on large projects.

The story of large-dam building in India is accompanied by huge social and environmental costs, undemocratic and manipulated decision making with exaggerated projected benefits and underestimated costs, unrealised dreams, shattered houses, families, communities and cultures, silenced rivers, and dead forests. The most significant evidence of unaccountable process is the fact that comprehensive ex post facto analysis is not available for a single of the thousands of projects completed over the last fifty years. Here are deafening stories of a few of the celebrated large dams of India:

Bhakhra is the most celebrated of Indian Dams. Let us look at it in some detail. Nehru, India's first Prime Minister, at one stage called such projects "Temples of Modern India." Few, however, care to know that the same person told India's dam builders in the latter stages of his life, "For some time past, however, I have been beginning to think that we are suffering from what we may call, 'disease of gigantism' . . . the idea of having big undertakings and doing big tasks for the sake of showing that we can do big things is not a good outlook at all. . . . It is, as you also referred to it, Mr. President, the small irrigation projects, the small industries and the small plants for electric power, which will change the face of the country far more than half a dozen big projects in half a dozen places." This less well-known outlook of Nehru is even less practiced.

The people who were displaced by this dam are still struggling to get the bare minimum compensation due to them. Many years after the construction of the project, when India's Water Resources Minister K. L. Rao visited affected villages, he saw that they had neither drinking water nor electricity, the main selling points of the project. He admitted, "we handle our projects without sparing a thought for the affected people." Contrast this with what Nehru said in the mid-1950s while inaugurating Konar project in Damodar Valley: it will be alright if the electricity does not reach the factories, but it must reach the affected people first.

That the benefits from Bhakhra are unsustainable is evident from the story of agriculture in Punjab, Haryana, and Rajasthan today. The farmers are so impoverished that they are unable to pay for water or power they use for irrigation. The debt-ridden farmers are committing suicide by the hundreds. The food grain stores of the government are so full that the government is unable to purchase farmers' crops. As a result, in September 2000 the government contemplated giving away the stored food grain almost free to the poor. Millions of hectares of land are waterlogged and salinised. The Government is thinking of getting another series of World Bank loans in order to sustain the present level of production, despite the fact that the rate of crop yield increase has already flattened and started to decline. Instead of controlling floods, as Nehru claimed in 1963 while inaugurating the Bhakhra dam, the dam is known to have created most damaging floods repeatedly (for example, in 1978 and 1980).

The Pong Dam on the Beas River in Himachal Pradesh is another site of dislocation. The people displaced by this project are still fighting for rehabilitation, thirty years after displacement.

The foundation stone of the Hirakud Dam was laid by Nehru in 1948—years before the detailed technical appraisal of the project was completed and detailed project reports were prepared. When asked about this lapse later in his life, Nehru said he had been "overcome with a sense of adventure." Fifty years later the tribals and other oustees of the project are still fighting for minimum compensation promised to them. The flood control performance of the project is worse than that of Bhakhra. There are more frequent, more prolonged, and more destructive floods today then there were before the project.

The words of Nehru, spoken while laying the foundation stone for this project, are most prophetic in their failure to see the future: "It can be said that not only the future of Orissa, but the future of India as a whole, is going to be affected by the success of this scheme. . . . Orissa, which is the poorest of our provinces in spite of its notable past history, developing into one of our foremost provinces . . . will make that prosperity endure for a thousand years." Orissa remains one of the poorest states of India, and the project's remaining lifetime would be no more than another fifty years due to much higher amounts of siltation than predicted. Higher than predicted rates of siltation is a "disease" that is prevalent among almost all large dams of India.

The Damodar project, the first one in India to be modeled after the famed Tennessee Valley Authority of the United States, was one of the most expensive and yet least successful of India's

FREEING THE RIVERS

Large dams have engendered much environmental protest, including the establishment of Living Rivers: The International Coalition for the Restoration of Rivers and Communities Affected by Dams, which published the following founding statement on 25 July 1998.

Free-flowing, living rivers are an essential, life-giving feature of our natural and human environment. They fulfill a multitude of ecological, economic, spiritual, cultural and aesthetic needs and wants.

Worldwide, these invaluable rivers are now degraded by hundreds of thousands of dams, which have flooded huge areas of the world's most beautiful and ecologically rich habitats and the homes and lands of tens of millions of people. Dams have impoverished countless communities which were dependent on the bounty of free-flowing rivers and riverside lands, and endangered public health.

Dams have blocked flows of nutrients and sediments and the passage of fish and other aquatic lifeforms. Dams have contaminated river water. Dams have eliminated essential natural flooding regimes thereby degrading the ecosystems, farmlands and fisheries which depend on floods. And dams have caused the decline and extinction of riverine species and the ecological degradation of estuaries and coastlines.

Many dams provide services for society, including the generation of electricity, the storage and diversion of water, flood protection, navigation and flat-water recreation. But we now know that these services come at a high economic, ecological and social cost and often can be met in other less damaging ways. We also have learned that costs and benefits of dams are unequally shared–those who reap the rewards are rarely those who must bear the costs.

After decades of experience, we now know that the promised benefits of many dam projects have never been realized, and their adverse effects are more serious than predicted. Trying to recreate artificially the complex natural cycles and functions of undammed rivers has proven to be far more difficult than was once thought. Efforts to mitigate the adverse effects of dams have often proven expensive and ineffective.

The knowledge learned over the past decades has led to the continuing improvement of standards for planning, designing, and operating dams. This has included social and environmental impact assessments, access to information, public participation in decision-making, and periodic re-evaluation of a dam's impacts and operations.

Many existing dams would never have been built if they had had to comply with current best-practice planning principles, procedures and standards. Some are illegal because they were constructed in violation of existing laws, or because required environmental mitigation and social compensation measures were never implemented.

Many dams are now obsolete. Many have reached the end of their functional life span and no longer serve a purpose that justifies their negative impacts. Many are unsafe, threatening the lives of millions of people, as well as property, fish and wildlife.

For many dams the cost of maintenance and of environmental and social mitigation exceeds the benefits to be gained from dam operation. The cost of removing dams is in many cases proving less than the cost of continuing to operate them, even without taking full account of the social and ecological benefits of dam removal.

A movement is now growing around the world which recognizes the vital importance of living rivers. People are calling for major changes in the operating patterns of dams to lessen their negative impacts, the decommissioning and removal of obsolete and dangerous dams, the restoration of rivers and the provision of reparations for past damages suffered by riverine communities affected by dams.

Source: *"Walker Creek Declaration,"* World Rivers Review, *13 (August 1998), Internet website.*

large-dam projects. Damodar Valley, whose historical prosperity was linked to its celebrated traditional system of diversion canals from flooding river, is today one of the poorest regions of the country. The myth of flood control is totally shattered as the region experiences increasing flood damage. Today Damodar Valley Corporation is not known for the hydropower that it was formed for, but for its thermal power stations. The people affected by the project, like those of other projects mentioned above, continue to fight for the promised compensation, decades after their displacement.

The Rajasthan Canal project was heralded to green the deserts. Instead, it is best known for the destruction and waterlogging it caused in some otherwise cultivable areas. Thousands of hectares of land made irrigable in other areas finds no takers because irrigated agriculture is known to be unsustainable in these hardpan areas. When questioned about this, the irrigation planners agreed they had "forgotten" to check the drainage capacity of the soils.

The Narmada Valley Development Project with over 30 major projects, 125 medium projects, and over 3000 minor projects, was said to be the world's largest river valley project when planned through the 1970s and 1980s. Today it is known for everything that has gone wrong with India's water resources development. The most well known of the battles fought by the movement Narmada Bachao Andolan (NBA) has exposed the projects for their exaggerated and unsustainable benefits, underestimated costs, lack of options assessment, nonparticipation of people, destructive and unacceptable social and environmental impacts, unjustifiable financial expenses, corrupt and unaccountable practices, drowning out of more viable options, and nonviable economics. It is well known that after a long battle the World Bank was pushed out of the projects, and that the Sardar Sarovar Project stands stalled due to ongoing legal battle in the Supreme Court of India and ongoing agitation in the Narmada Valley.

One of the bitterest antidam struggles is being fought against the upstream Maheshwar project. In an unequal battle between global capital and local resistance, the latter had, as of September 2000, succeeded in pushing out at least four international funding agencies, including German and U.S. multinationals. Even further upstream, in the Bargi project, following a sequence that can best be described as a tragedy of errors, 162 villages were submerged in the reservoir that was supposed to submerge only 101 villages. Less than 10 percent of the displaced were resettled in a project that is unable to irrigate more than 5 percent of projected irrigated lands. The struggle of the affected population here has achieved some historic wins, including handing over the reservoir fisheries to a federation of cooperatives formed by affected communities.

The large dams in India over the past fifty years are known to have displaced over forty million people. Millions of hectares of forests have been submerged or deforested for the projects. A large number of rivers can no longer be called perennial. There are more drought-prone communities, more annual average flood damages, more villages without an adequate source for drinking water, more rivers with nonpotable water, and more poor people in India today than there were fifty years ago. That, in short, should be a good scorecard of large dam-centered water resources development.

There is no doubt that installed hydropower capacity has gone up some forty-three-fold in the last fifty years. But where has all this power gone? 95.9 percent Schedule Caste (SC) and Schedule Tribe (ST) population of Bihar, 93.5 percent of SC and ST population of Orissa, 90 percent SC and ST population of West Bengal, and 87.5 percent SC and ST population of Uttar Pradesh, for example, still do not have access to electricity. In the process of building big hydropower stations, the biggest loss has been missing the opportunity to develop alternative power systems.

It is claimed that India has become a food surplus nation due to large-dam-based irrigation. It is true that India's food production has gone up over four-fold in the last fifty years. But when we looked at the net contribution of lands irrigated by large dams, their contribution was found to be less than 5 percent of India's food production today. It is claimed that famines have been eradicated from India due to large dams. But research by Amartya Sen and Jean Dreze have shown that the real reasons for this success are not in increased food production or large dams, but elsewhere, in political processes that have no relation to the large dams.

Finally, in the process of building the world's largest irrigation area, Indian water resources managers have totally neglected the traditional water technologies and systems. That, by far, must be counted as one of the biggest losses. As the World Bank and others have noted, the Indian irrigation system is in a state of serious degradation and India's agricultural production is unsustainable if continued as present.

Waterlogging and salinisation of millions of hectares of large dam-based, canal-irrigated lands on the one hand, and fast-depleting groundwater levels in adjoining areas on the other hand, are drowning the watery dreams of the green revolution. Even more resounding testimony of failure of this system is available in the overflowing food grain warehouses of India. India's food grain stock is over forty million tonnes today, even as India has the world's largest number of poor people not being able to buy two square meals a day. The whole strategy of creating a few islands of surplus through large projects has failed. In a country where over two-thirds of the population continues to live in villages and depend on agriculture, a development strategy would have to take care of the employment needs and purchasing capacities of this big segment of the population. Rainfall is as decentralised as the land; the amount varies from place to place. Given the rich tradition of indigenous water management, local water systems, developed and managed by the communities all across the country, would be the most likely solution for agriculture's water needs.

Studies show that in agricultural systems based on local water systems more employment is generated than in the case of systems based on large dams. This is true both with respect to the construction phase and employment generated in agriculture per hectare of irrigated land. This wisdom was simply ignored when large projects were designed. There is, indeed, cruel irony in the fact that more grains are destroyed in post-harvest losses in India than what large dams based irrigated lands contribute.

Besides large dams, the other central strategy followed by the Indian water resources sector is that of tubewells and pumps. This strategy, followed without really assessing the implications, has lead to greater inequities across India. Thus, whoever has the land can dig wells as deep as they want to, drying up the surrounding wells and aquifers. Thus, the phenomena of parched throats and drought-struck villages could be found amidst green fields and water guzzling industries across India. In the summer of 2000, over five thousand villages in the highly irrigated state of Punjab had no adequate source of drinking water.

All available evidence would suggest that the environment assessment and mitigation policies have totally failed in India. A study by a member of an expert committee of India's Central Ministry of Environment and Forests found that

> Environmental impacts have rarely been fully anticipated or understood, let alone prevented or ameliorated. A national assessment of the state of dams cleared in the 1980s and 1990s shows that in 90% of cases, the environmental conditionalities under which clearance was given by the central government, have not been fulfilled by the project authorities.

No action was taken in a single case to cancel the clearance. The study concluded "If this is the case, making big dams environmentally viable may simply not be possible."

"WCD India Country Study: A Study of Economic Performance of Indian Large Dams," done for the World Commission on Dams in 2000, has a number of important conclusions:

• The impact of these factors on actual benefit-cost ratios and internal rates of return are obvious; the actuals have not only been lower than the projected ratios/rates but they have also reached levels that show that direct agricultural benefits fall short of costs.

• Yet, the conclusion seems to be uncomfortably true: by the early 1990s, major and medium projects may have become unviable if irrigation benefits alone are considered. On the margin, the benefits from bringing one hectare of land under irrigation through M & M [major and medium] projects falls short of the direct costs involved.

• There is possibly no net gain to the economy from major and medium irrigation projects.

• Costs are systematically underestimated and benefits exaggerated so that the requisite benefit-cost ratio is shown to have been arrived at. Further, during actual implementation, there are enormous escalations in costs, considerable delays, and changes in design and scope of projects. Benefits, on the other hand, fall well below anticipated figures as actual irrigated area and achieved yields fall below projected levels.

• Given the high capital cost, long gestation periods, and the environmental and social costs, a (large) hydropower development (project) is not the preferred option for power generation compared to other sources.

The constant refrain of the dam promoters that there is no alternative to such projects is best answered by what is happening when communities are given the right to follow their own path. The most interesting of several such cases is that of the work of communities in the Alwar district in Rajasthan. There, over the last fifteen years, communities have constructed over 2,500 small water-harvesting systems. As a result of these works, groundwater levels have come up by over twenty-five meters; a food deficit region now has surplus food; people migrating out for employment have stopped; and many people are going back to the district. The most eloquent testimony is that five of the local rivers that used to dry up soon after monsoons have become perennial. The President of India, for the first time in Independent India, on 28 March 2000 went to honor the community for their path-breaking work.

Similarly, following the summer 2000 drought in Gujarat, it was clear that rainwater harvesting was the only solution to water problems of this region. The lies of propaganda surrounding the Sardar Sarovar Project, under construction on Narmada River, were laid bare.

A lot of blame for India's present water resources and related crisis is attributed to population explosion, as it is called. But a number of researchers, including Sen and Dreze, have noted that if water and energy resources development are done in a way that would empower local communities, it would actually lead to self-management of population rates by communities and reduced national population rates. By pursuing large water and energy resource projects, India has disempowered communities, instead of adding alternative empowering development. Development projects that had actually contributed to the population problem were being justified in the name of population growth.

The solution is clear: follow the alternative, decentralised, small-scale, participatory, sustainable, equitable, and cost-effective path of water and energy resource development and management. Large dams, if at all, should be the last option after exhausting all local options, after achieving optimum returns from existing infrastructure, and after doing all other kinds of demand-and-supply management.

–HIMANSHU THAKKAR, SOUTH ASIA NETWORK ON DAMS, RIVERS AND PEOPLE

References

Anil Agarwal and Sunita Narain, eds., *Dying Wisdom: Rise, Fall and Potential of India's Traditional Water Harvesting Systems* (New Delhi: Centre for Science and Environment, 1997).

Roy Arundhati, *Greater Common Good* (Bombay: India Books, 1999).

Kothari Ashish, "Environmental Aspects of Large Dams in India: Problems of Planning, Implementation, and Monitoring," presentation at South Asia Public Hearing organized by the World Commission on Dams, Colombo, Sri Lanka, December 1998, in *Large Dams and Their Alternatives: South Asia Consultation from SANDRP, South Asia Network on Dams, Rivers and People* (New Delhi: 1999), pp. 20–32.

Government of India, National Commission on Integrated Water Resources Development Plan, 1999.

Patrick McCully, *Silenced Rivers: The Ecology and Politics of Large Dams* (London & Atlantic Highlands, N.J.: Zed Books, 1996).

Modern Temples of India: Selected Speeches of Jawaharlal Nehru (New Delhi: Central Board of Irrigation and Power, April 1989).

Sandra Postel, *Pillar of Sand: Can the Irrigation Miracle Last?* (New York: Norton, 1999).

Iyer Ramaswamy, and others, *Large Dams: India's Experience: A Report for the World Commission on Dams* (Cape Town: World Commission on Dams, 2000).

Amulya K. N. Reddy and Girish Sant, "Electrical Part of the Sardar Sarovar Project," Submission to the Five Member Group on the Sardar Sarovar Project, Report of the FMG, Vol.II, Appendices (New Delhi: Ministry of Water Resources, 1994).

Sangvai Sanjay, *The River and Life: People's Struggle in the Narmada Valley* (Mumbai: Earthcare Books, 2000).

Amartya Sen, Jean Dreze, and Athar Hussain, eds., *The Political Economy of Hunger: Selected Essays* (Oxford: Clarendon Press; New York: Oxford University Press, 1995).

Satyajit Singh, *Taming the Waters: The Political Economy of Large Dams in India* (New Delhi: Oxford University Press, 1997).

World Bank, *Round Table on Water Sector Strategy Review,* New Delhi, 11–12 May 2000, *The World Bank Group,* Internet website.

World Commission on Dams, Internet website.

JORDAN RIVER BASIN

What caused the water crisis in Israel and the Middle East?

Viewpoint: The water crisis in Israel and neighboring countries occurred because of the Israeli misappropriation and overuse of the resources of the region.

Viewpoint: A combination of climatic, demographic, economic, and political factors caused the water crisis in the Middle East.

Since 1948, when its statehood was established, Israel has held the upper hand in controlling water resources within its boundaries. Twenty years later, following the Six-Day War (1967) and failures to achieve peace, Israel extended its control over the territories of the West Bank (formerly part of Jordan), Gaza Strip and Sinai Peninsula (formerly part of Egypt), and Golan Heights (formerly part of Syria). After 1973 and yet another war and failure to achieve peace, Israel established several Jewish settlements on the West Bank, Gaza, the Sinai, and Golan Heights; later, as part of a peacemaking effort, Israel returned the Sinai to Egypt and removed its settlements there.

With each extension, from the establishment of its initial borders to its occupation of territories won in war, Israel also took control of both surface and underground water resources and applied national policies to them. These policies involved complex engineering and technology, as well as centralized planning and allocation. The total quantity of water available for use was increased dramatically and the distribution of water was altered.

Water supplies did not, however, keep pace with demand, and this imbalance lay at the root of a crisis in the Middle East. Furthermore, the Arab population of the region had much less access to water, and used much less per capita, than the Jewish population. Water quantity and quality changed for the worse in many areas, particularly those resources serving Arab populations.

Viewpoint: The water crisis in Israel and neighboring countries occurred because of the Israeli misappropriation and overuse of the resources of the region.

Disenfranchisement of the Palestinian people began before the establishment of the state of Israel in 1948, when Zionist immigrants began to settle Palestine in the late nineteenth and early twentieth centuries. Zionist organizations purchased large landholdings from absentee landlords, in many cases displacing farmers who did not hold titles but who tilled the land. As the Zionist settlers became organized, they incorporated plans for use and control of water resources that were alien to the traditions of local agriculture. French and British colonial regimes had done nothing to assist the emergence of Palestinian autonomy or the formulation of any overall economic-development strategy. By contrast, Zionist settlements, with the assistance of European and American backers, had a strategy in place at the time of statehood.

After Israel was established, the state began a program of expropriation of Arab land and water resources. Lands and villages that had been evacuated were taken over by Israelis. There was a massive influx of Jewish settlers, first from Europe, then from North Africa and the Middle East. The emphasis of Israeli policy was to find land and water for them, and this policy was carried out at the expense of the indigenous Palestinian population.

The Israelis immediately nationalized all water resources, contrary to traditions in the region. Its second move was to develop through immense engineering projects the transportation of water from where it was relatively plentiful to areas of scarcity, primarily to benefit settlers in the south of the country. This policy also was contrary to local traditions, which held it illegal to transport water from one basin to another. Of course, these engineering works had tremendous impacts on localities that had once supplied their own water from streams and wells. Diversion of streams and intensive use of natural reservoirs increased salinity levels of water sources. The draining of swamps to transform them into arable land deprived indigenous populations of yet other resources they traditionally used and altered the hydrological balance of the land. In all, the initial Israeli program of intensive development of water resources was an ecological disaster. They drained Lake Huleh in the north, destroying the lake and surrounding wetlands; lowered the amounts of water in the Sea of Galilee to dangerous levels for the health of this lake; reduced the water table in many areas, causing the drying up of wells; raised the water table in other areas through irrigation, causing higher salinity levels in the upper aquifers; polluted water supplies through applications of chemical pesticides and fertilizers; and endangered coastal aquifers by overpumping, which led to incursions of seawater.

These activities had a direct impact on the indigenous Palestinians who remained in their villages. Their standard of living was far lower than that of the Jewish population, and while they were accorded citizenship, their treatment by the state was always discriminatory. Water for irrigation and domestic consumption was delivered to them as it was to Jewish communities, but in far lower proportions. Non-Jewish localities received no more than 2 percent of the total amount of water consumed in Israel throughout the history of the state, even though they constituted approximately one-third of the rural population. At the same time, those Palestinians who left Israel in 1948 were largely consigned to refugee camps in the West Bank and Gaza. Their lives were a constant misery, a result of Israeli occupation of their lands.

With the capture by Israel in 1967 of the West Bank and Gaza came the expropriation of water resources in these occupied territories. Israel claimed that control over the resources, particularly those of the mountain aquifers under the West Bank, was essential to its national security. It began pumping water from these aquifers for its own purposes, essentially a theft of resources from conquered territory. After the 1973 war with its Arab neighbors, Israel began a massive settlement program in the occupied West Bank and Gaza (it had annexed the Golan Heights after 1967). Israel used water resources in these areas to benefit these new settlements.

In the course of more than thirty years of governing the occupied territories, Israel did virtually nothing to improve the water supply or sanitation facilities of the Palestinians in the West Bank and Gaza. As a result, water facilities deteriorated; water pollution and salinization became severe problems; and people became enraged at their unfair treatment. Even after the creation of the Palestinian Authority, with its own branch of water administration, the Israeli government prevented Palestinians from exploiting their own water resources by denying permission to dig wells, assigning the right to produce water to the national water company, Mekorot, and pricing water at outrageously high levels.

Israeli critics of these water policies agree that they have led to environmental and economic disaster. Israel subsidizes the cost of water to farmers, favoring those agricultural settlements it wishes to promote and those with the most political influence. Consequently, water is wasted on endeavors that are not economically sound or environmentally suitable; farmers are encouraged by the low price of water to produce what they would not if they were made to pay higher prices. Furthermore, mismanagement of the water system has led to severe deterioration of resources, including the Sea of Galilee and coastal aquifers, as well as pollution of many wells. Finally, Israeli obsession with capturing every source of water by elaborate engineering devices has led to the destruction of beautiful natural areas that might be enjoyed by the wider public as recreation areas and should be preserved as part of the national patrimony.

Israel was able to overexploit these water resources for political purposes, thanks to its command over the technology of exploitation and the financial means to apply it, as well as its military power to sustain its ability to defend its

THE ARABS REJECT THE JOHNSTON PLAN

On 10 August 1955 Muhammad Amin al-Husayni, president of the Arab Higher Committee for Palestine, rejected the attempt by U.S. Ambassador Eric Johnston to mediate the use of water from the Jordan River Basin. A portion of his letter appears below:

There is no question but that the most important of these means and factors is "water," which is needed by the Zionists to consolidate their existence and to irrigate the extensive lands which they have usurped from Palestine but which they cannot cultivate and exploit except by ensuring (the existence of) water especially in the Negev and the southern parts of Palestine.

The Zionists had previously put forth a number of schemes to exploit the water resources of the Jordan River Valley foremost among which is the well-known project of Mr. Lowdermilk. They have been trying to control these water resources ever since the British Mandate was imposed on Palestine after the First World War.

The scheme of Unified Development, the subject of the present study, has been meant to fulfil for the Zionists all the water schemes which they put forth many years ago and for the fulfilment of which they have waited for the opportune time.

The Zionists admit that their possession of water resources is a fundamental factor in the life of their State and their continued existence. They consider themselves (to be engaged) in a fierce battle with the Arabs, which is the "battle of water."

One of the most conspicuous indications of the importance attached by the Zionists to the water problem is what their Prime Minister Ben-Gurion stated in the course of a speech made by him on 14 May 1955 in Tel Aviv, in commemoration of the establishment of their State. He said: "The Jews are today fighting the Arabs in the 'battle for water.' On the outcome of this battle depends the future of the Jewish existence of Palestine. If we were not to win this battle, it would be as if we had done nothing in Palestine, and we should (then) admit (our) failure."

There is no question but that the Johnston Scheme will be the strongest weapon in the hands of the Zionists if they succeed in carrying it out, (and this), despite the objections which they are raising (now) against some aspects of the scheme, and (notwithstanding) the disinterestedness which they are feigning concerning (the scheme) because it (supposedly) does not fulfil their wishes. . . .

The scheme mentioned will realize for the Zionists their ambitions of seizing the (water) resources and exploiting them to irrigate the southern areas and the Negev. For it will make the waters of the tributaries of al-Hasbani, Banias, Tall al-Qadi and al-Yarmuk (and all these lie outside Palestine and outside its occupied part), as well as the Jordan River itself, within the reach of the Zionists and subject to their exploitation for their own interests. This is confirmed by (the fact that) there is (now) a study about the Unified Development Scheme (Johnston's Scheme), showing that the tragedy, to which the tragedy of Andalusia, or indeed any other tragedy which has befallen the Arab nation, cannot (by any means) be comparable.

It is undeniable that the Jewish State, which was established by imperialism and Zionism on the wreckage of the Arabs in Palestine, is dominated by economic crises, by (special) political circumstances, and by party differences which it can hardly stand. (This is) in addition to its being subject to the pressure of the Arab economic blockade. It is as if the advocates of the Johnston Scheme are asking the Arab nation to harness its water resources and wealth to the service of such an aggressive Jewish State and to lend it their support, thereby saving it from its plight and willingly handing over to it their effective weapon which it will use to destroy them in the near future.

For this reason, the Arab Higher Committee considers that the interest of the Arab nation, in general, and that of the Palestine problem and the refugees, in particular, necessitate the outright rejection of the scheme of "The Unified Development of Water Resources in the Jordan River Valley", as well as the rejection of any co-operation concerning it.

The Arab (Higher) Committee is certain that the esteemed Arab States, having made accurate studies of this scheme, share in its opinion regarding the great extent of its danger and the great harm it will bring to Palestine and the neighbouring Arab countries, and consequently, to the whole Arab nation. There is no doubt that the Arabs will lose nothing by rejecting that scheme, for, (by doing so), they will keep their water power for themselves, at a time when the Israelis alone will suffer loss. . . .

Source: *"Arab Higher Committee for Palestine Rejects Johnston Plan," The Jewish Student Online Research Center (JSOURCE), Internet website.*

activities. Neglect of the rights of Palestinians and Israeli Arabs, the nonfarming Israeli public interest, and the natural environment led to both environmental and political crisis.

Profligate Israeli exploitation of water resources resulted in deficits in neighboring countries as well. Israel annexed the Golan Heights, it claimed, for security purposes; in fact, the Golan provided great quantities of water in the winter that could be used by Jordan or Syria. Jordan shared water resources with Israel but was impeded in its development of hydraulic works by Israeli opposition. Israel bombed Jordanian waterworks as part of military hostilities and prevented the construction of new ones. Ultimately, Israel acted as a giant "sponge," soaking up a hugely disproportionate share of the linked water resources by immoderate extraction. Whether this policy was intended to deprive its enemies of water or simply to furnish its own citizens with a luxurious lifestyle, the outcome was the same: its neighbors suffered. This injustice has been decried not only by its victims, but also by Israeli citizens in various public media.

Water in the Middle East is truly limited. By the end of the twentieth century, all the available resources were tapped as fully as possible. Israel, Palestine, Jordan, Syria, and Lebanon were all vulnerable in drought years, yet Israel far exceeded the other nations in per capita water extraction and use. It became clear that only by Israel relinquishing its policies and practices regarding water extraction could some measure of security and comfort be achieved by its neighbors.

Various proposals for the international sharing of water in this region have been made. The best known was the Johnston Plan, named for Eric Johnston, U.S. president Dwight D. Eisenhower's special envoy to the Middle East, who was sent in 1953 to mediate a settlement among the users of Jordan River Basin resources. Many return to this plan as a basis for an equitable allocation of water resources, albeit in modified form. Israel has intransigently refused the notion of equitable distribution, however, arguing that its history should be taken into account, and in any case, has refused to cede hegemony while in a state of armed conflict with its neighbors. Israel claims the need to control water for security reasons, neglecting the welfare of her neighbors. In the meantime, Israeli overuse of this resource has caused considerable damage to the ability of the system to recover from pollution and the degradation of the aquifers, lakes, streams, and wetlands that once fed them. If Israel were to agree to share common international water sources equitably, it would be obliged to use water more prudently to the benefit of the entire region.

—DANIEL MORGAN, LOS ANGELES, CALIFORNIA

Viewpoint: A combination of climatic, demographic, economic, and political factors caused the water crisis in the Middle East.

When the first pioneer Zionist settlements were established during the Ottoman regime of the late nineteenth and early twentieth century, Jews were prohibited from purchasing land in most of Palestine and restricted from nearly all remaining areas. They were permitted to purchase tracts of land that were largely nonarable or extremely marginal. In order to make these parcels habitable and arable, the settlers had to invest enormous efforts. Where they settled in or near malarial swamps, farmers had to drain the land for both their safety and their ability to produce crops; where there was no water, they had to sink wells. The hilly areas of the Galilee and West Bank were inhabited by Druze, Christian, and Muslim villages dependent largely on rain-fed crops, mainly olive and fruit trees, and field crops such as barley. Limited areas were irrigated by flood waters and stream-fed earthen canals. Jewish settlers had little access to such arable land or water resources. They saw water as a serious problem to be solved by engineering, improved farming practices, modern technology, and social control. None of these solutions, although considered a priority, came easily. Jewish settlers negotiated cooperative arrangements among themselves and assisted one another in sustaining a precarious existence in a hostile land.

These settlements were steps toward a realization of a dream that consisted of the creation of a Jewish state for a nation in exile, the revival of a prosperous rural economy in Palestine, and the establishment of a radical new society based on social equality, respect for labor, and the sharing of wealth—in other words, a socialist ideal. Land would not be privately held; it was purchased by the Jewish National Fund and leased to farming communes or cooperatives. Water also was not private property but a public utility.

While the Jewish population grew with new waves of immigrants and refugees, the rural

The Jordan Valley

(Reproduced courtesy of the Ministry of Information, Jordan)

segment of society remained a minority, but because of its symbolic and political importance, the public nurtured it through special support. With the establishment of Israel in 1948, this special support became official policy. Agriculture was to have the greatest share of water produced by the state and was to receive subsidies, especially those communities located in remote arid areas in the south of the country. Although agriculture never contributed more than 10 percent of the gross national product (GNP), its importance was symbolic, social, and political. Rural communities defended national borders, produced essential foodstuffs, and spread the population over the land.

Israelis quickly started developing technology to secure as reliable and plentiful a water supply as possible. Engineers planned an elaborate national network of interconnected water-supply and water-delivery arteries, fed by both surface and underground resources. As the network was built, some communities lost older, shallower sources of water, and these were replaced by deliveries from the national grid. Planning was done by a semigovernmental engineering firm, TAHAL Consulting Engineers Ltd.; implementation was accomplished by another semigovernmental corporation, Mekorot, the national water-supply company.

Before the first Zionist settlements were established in Palestine, Arab farmers had a well-developed system of agriculture, which used irrigation in some areas–though minimally. This system involved the diversion of streams into open earthen canals. Most agriculture, however, depended on rainfall. Farming was done in hilly regions, which were safer from malarial infestation and militarily secure. Farmers invested slowly, over the centuries, in terracing, canal construction, stone removal, and the planting of trees. This type of agriculture worked reasonably well for a small population with limited economic demands. The population of Palestine, however, began to increase in the latter part of the nineteenth century, placing pressure on the land even before the influx of Jewish settlers and refugees. Palestinians did not take the initiative, however, to change their system of irrigation, either from a technical or a sociopolitical point of view. The reason may be the inherited social system: *fellahin* (landless or small landholder peasants) were subservient to overlords who owned the productive land and water. As a result, the Palestinians fell far behind the Israelis in developing a modern system of water exploitation and distribution. Although Palestinians often blamed colonial domination before the establishment of the Jewish state and Israeli occupation afterward for their problems, the Israelis and their predecessors worked under harshly adversarial conditions to plan and implement their program of hydraulic development, and should not be blamed for having succeeded. Moreover, the welfare of Arab Israelis was not, for the most part, taken into consideration–they received less water for a variety of reasons, although these were not malicious in intent.

The domination by Israel of the Palestinians in the occupied territories was something different. It is difficult to say what their rights were because their position was ambiguous. Clearly water was scarce and they suffered as a consequence. The Palestinians were quick, however, to blame the Israelis for their troubles and far too slow to assume any responsibility. They repeatedly rejected Israeli offers of assistance because they feared loss of sovereignty down the road and that any improvement in the lifestyle of the Palestinian population would reduce ardor for resistance to the occupation.

At the same time, unlike the Israelis, the Palestinians were slow to face the need for an organized plan for how to use their water. This policy would have meant confronting inequities in the traditional allocation of land and water, specifically challenging the powerful families that dominated the landscape of the West Bank and owned much of the land and water. The Israelis developed a system based on democracy and equality on idealized owner-operated farms (even though the ideal was not always entirely carried out in practice). Such a radical change would have struck at the heart of Palestinian tradition–not what their leadership wanted to face at the moment. Instead, they turned outward at their enemy to obscure internal problems, and the ongoing war allowed them to evade internal self-examination. Cooperation with Israel, along with internal change, might have permitted the kind of technical and sociopolitical nation-building that Israel underwent more than half a century earlier and could have provided a better standard of living for the Palestinian people.

To be sure, there were faults in the implementation of the Zionist dream: for instance, there was some environmental destruction, much of which was corrected. Since the late 1970s, with changes in the national government and society, the rural sector became less influential politically, and as a consequence, political decisions about the water system resulted in management practices that Israelis themselves greatly criticized. Essentially, a succession of coalition governments after 1977 was vulnerable to pressures from various interest groups, and the implementation of water policies was undermined. It was too hard for politicians to "just say no," so discipline sometimes wavered, which was detrimental to the system in hard times–during drought conditions. Palestinians defied the system by sinking illegal wells and taking water without permits; these actions also endangered water resources.

Nevertheless, the Israeli system of water exploitation and distribution was never a "free-for-all." All water belonged to the state and therefore could not be taken without a license. Permits were issued according to policy dictates and were renewed only after serious review of the capacity of the system and competing demands for limited water. Distribution was implemented according to a complex rationing system based on prior-use patterns; standards for various crops were set by the Ministry of Agriculture for various regions, as well as according to the size and structure of communities. Every drop was monitored: stiff penalties, in graduated price increases and fines, were levied for overuse of allocated quotas; and delinquent communities risked having their water turned off altogether. Israeli farmers paid much higher prices for water than farmers in other comparable countries, and the Israeli public still demanded reductions in subsidies to agriculture. Furthermore, there was elaborate monitoring for salinity and pollution; penalties for polluters; and intensive cleanup efforts where decreases in water and soil quality were discovered.

This system was costly. Not only did it require initial investments in the planning and construction of the water-supply network, as well as continued investments in its expansion and maintenance, it also demanded investments in management and political implementation. Water would nearly always be scarce–as the single most valuable input into agriculture–and an increased water supply is a desirable component in raising standards of urban living. In years of low rainfall, competition for water was fierce; maintaining discipline was politically costly. After 1977, when the dominant Labor Party was for the first time voted out of office, a series of coalition governments were formed, which were, because of their dependence on fragile alignments, relatively weak. Succeeding governments had a varying impact on the effectiveness of discipline regarding water administration.

Israeli policies were designed to realize a larger vision of a prosperous and secure Israel. This policy discriminated against Arab communities that did not engage in Israeli political-movement politics and were not involved in such types of communities as kibbutzim and moshavim. Israeli Arab farming communities, however, were not altogether neglected and did increase their water supply–they benefited from the national grid. Furthermore, Palestinian farmers on the West Bank and Gaza increased their water use, as well as their utilization of Israeli technology that allowed them to make better use of this resource.

Israel invested intensively in technology not only to extract water but to use it more efficiently. They developed irrigation industries and practices for this purpose. Consequently, their efficiency rose dramatically, and so did the water use of Arab farmers in both Israel and Palestine. Open canals were eliminated: drip and sprinkler irrigation became the norm. Productivity rose dramatically.

Israel provided a ready market for Palestinian products, and Israeli technical experts were eager to provide Palestinian farmers with technical assistance of various kinds. Israel engaged in such assistance through its Agricultural Extension Service and other agencies since 1967, following the Six-Day War, and repeatedly offered other help–only to be rejected in many instances for political reasons. International agencies were prepared to assist in developing cooperative ventures between the two parties, but political interests often placed obstacles in the way.

Increased population and standards of living, especially in urban areas, placed enormous demands on water, a limited resource. In drought years, which are frequent in the Middle East, failures of discipline undermined the effectiveness of both the technology of water extraction and systematic replenishment, and the political process of allocating water fairly and sensibly. For Israel, the vision was in place and just needed to be applied. Democracy was the basis for what was designed to be a nationally equitable system of distribution; ineffectiveness could be laid at the door of relatively weak coalition governments in a multiparty political system. For its neighbors, however, an effective managerial system had yet even to be devised.

–SUSAN H. LEES, HUNTER COLLEGE, CITY UNIVERSITY OF NEW YORK

References

David Amiran, *Rainfall and Water Management in Semi-Arid Climates: Israel as an Example* (Jerusalem: Jerusalem Institute for Israel Studies, 1995).

Saul Arlosoroff, "Efficient Use of Water: Policy and Problems," in *Water in Israel* (Hakyira, Tel Aviv: Ministry of Agriculture, Water Commission, Water Allocation Department, 1973).

Arlosoroff, *Israeli Experience in the Achievement of Efficiency in the Use and Re-Use of Water* (Tel Aviv: Israel Water Commission, 1976).

Arlosoroff, *Legal, Administrative and Economical Means for the Preservation and Efficient Use of Water in Israel* (Tel Aviv: Israel Water Commission, 1974).

Isaac Arnon and Michael Raviv, *From Fellah to Farmer: A Study on Change in Arab Villages* (Rehovot: Settlement Study Centre, 1980).

Sharif S. Elmusa, *Negotiating Water: Israel and the Palestinians* (Washington, D.C.: Institute for Palestinian Studies, 1996).

Izhak Galnoor, "Water Policymaking in Israel," in *Water Quality Management Under Conditions of Scarcity: Israel as a Case Study,* edited by Hillel I. Shuval (New York: Academic Press, 1980), pp. 287–313.

Rosina Hassoun, "Water Between Arabs and Israelis: Researching Twice-Promised Resources," in *Water, Culture, and Power: Local Struggles in a Global Context,* edited by John M. Donahue and Barbara Rose Johnston (Washington, D.C.: Island Press, 1998), pp. 313–338.

Daniel Hillel, *Rivers of Eden: The Struggle for Water and the Quest for Peace in the Middle East* (New York: Oxford University Press, 1994).

Jad Isaac and Hillel Shuval, eds., *Water and Peace in the Middle East: Proceedings of the First Israeli-Palestinian International Academic Conference on Water, Zürich, Switzerland, 10–13 December 1992* (Amsterdam & New York: Elsevier, 1994).

Susan H. Lees, *The Political Ecology of the Water Crisis in Israel* (Lanham, Md.: University Press of America, 1998).

Lees, "Socialism, the Moshav and the Water Crisis," in *Rural Cooperatives in Socialist Utopia: Thirty Years of Moshav Development in Israel,* edited by Moshe Schwartz, Lees, and Gordon M. Kressel (Westport, Conn.: Praeger, 1995), pp. 63–79.

Stephan Libiszewski, *Water Disputes in the Jordan Basin Region and Their Role in the Resolution of the Arab-Israeli Conflict* (Zürich: Center for Security Studies and Conflict Research, Swiss Federal Institute of Technology; Bern: Swiss Peace Foundation, 1995).

Stephen C. Lonergan and David B. Brooks, *Watershed: The Role of Fresh Water in the Israeli-Palestinian Conflict* (Ottawa, Canada: International Development Research Centre, 1994).

Miriam R. Lowi, *Water and Power: The Politics of a Scarce Resource in the Jordan River Basin* (Cambridge & New York: Cambridge University Press, 1993).

R. Nativ and A. Issar, "Problems of an Over-Developed Water System: The Israeli Case," *Water Quality Bulletin,* 13 (1988): 126–132.

Hillel I. Shuval, "Conclusions: The Impending Water Crisis," in *Water Quality Management Under Conditions of Scarcity: Israel as a Case Study,* edited by Shuval (New York: Academic Press, 1980), pp. 315–337.

MED PLAN

Why has the Mediterranean Action Plan (Med Plan) failed to achieve its stated goal of ridding the Mediterranean Sea of its most pernicious pollutants?

Viewpoint: The Med Plan was shaped by internationally organized scientists and environmental activists. The absence of state capacity in that region has constrained cooperation and pollution control.

Viewpoint: The Med Plan was a half-hearted measure to clean up the environment that was continued primarily because tourist dollars were at stake.

The Mediterranean Sea is the largest inland sea in the world. Its catchment area is home to about two hundred million people divided among nearly two dozen countries. It is a salty sea because evaporation is high and the freshwater influx from rivers is low. At Gibraltar its heavier, salty water flows out to the Atlantic beneath an incoming current of lighter, less salty ocean water. On average it takes about eighty years for the water to flush out the Mediterranean fully. Pollutants linger longer here than in the North Sea, where they stay about 2 years, though not so long as in the Black Sea, where they can persist for about 140 years. Biologically, the Mediterranean is both rich and poor. It is rich in species diversity, home to about ten thousand animals and plants. Because its waters are normally thin in nutrients, its total biomass and biological productivity are extremely low. This situation is why, where it is not polluted, the water is so clear. Over the past hundred years, however, the number and variety of pollutants have far outpaced the ability of the sea to flush and clean itself, and as a consequence it has become one of the most contaminated bodies of water in the world.

Authors Stacy D. VanDeveer and J.R. McNeill agree that too little progress has been made over the past forty years in cleaning up the Mediterranean, despite the promises of the Med Plan. They disagree, however, on what brought the Mediterranean states to the negotiating table in the first place and on the extent of progress that has been achieved. VanDeveer highlights the role of the international scientific community in putting the spotlight on pollution issues and blames the states themselves for not implementing the plan. He is disappointed that the potential of the Med Plan has not been fully realized. McNeill, on the other hand, points out that the Med Plan only survived the torturous path of international negotiations in the first place because the future of the all-important tourist industry in the region was at stake. He is impressed that the states have managed to work together on pollution issues at all.

Viewpoint: The Med Plan was shaped by internationally organized scientists and environmental activists. The absence of state capacity in that region has constrained cooperation and pollution control.

Most analysts of regional environmental cooperation around the Mediterranean Sea, and participants in such efforts, agree that scientific knowledge and the producers of this scholarship played important roles in developing and maintaining cleanup activities in the region. Yet, international relations analysts often treat scientific and technological information as objective or exogenous knowledge that informs policymakers, who are assumed to "learn" passively from science and technological experts. Regional Mediterranean environmental cooperation, however, demonstrates that scientific experts must be politically organized to achieve international consensus and act collectively in international arenas.

The dominant theoretical approach to the study of scientific and technical information in international relations–particularly international environmental cooperation–focuses on "epistemic communities." Peter M. Haas, in *Saving the Mediterranean: The Politics of International Environmental Protection* (1990), developed the idea of knowledge-based communities in his examination of international environmental cooperation around the Mediterranean Sea. Haas separates the construction of scientific knowledge from his treatment of institutional bargaining at the international and domestic levels and the organizational politics of the United Nations Environment Programme (UNEP). "Science" and "politics" are treated as separate, but interactive, spheres. The interaction occurs after scientists have established "what they know," that is, after they have reached a consensus. This "international science" does not, however, exist in a separate sphere from international or transnational "politics." The "scientific knowledge" utilized at the international level in the Mediterranean region was circumscribed and shaped by at least three factors: the organizational values, goals, and preferences of UNEP; a set of fundamental principles and policy norms associated with regional environmental cooperation, especially a statist bias against perceived violations of sovereign independence; and the "politics" among scientists as part of the collective (social) production of knowledge. Consensus among scientists and/or policymakers is intersubjective. Transnational scientific consensus building within international ("political") organizations such as UNEP and the Med Plan results in overlapping processes of "scientific" and "political" consensus building. One sphere does not simply inform the other; the two spheres constantly interact.

In the early 1970s, when regional pollution treaties were under discussion, many states in the Mediterranean basin lacked the expertise, equipment, and administrative capacity for environmental and pollution monitoring and regulation. Most environmental research in the region conducted prior to the early 1970s focused on local areas; almost no regional research existed. In this politically volatile region, scientists steered clear of research that might incite an international incident. Early concern focused on visible and topical environmental problems. Oil pollution from tanker traffic, visible on beaches as tar balls, became a central issue. Beach closings, some as a result of disease outbreaks, had the effect of increasing awareness of existing and potential economic costs of environmental degradation. High-profile oil spills such as the 1967 *Torrey Canyon* accident and other environmental disasters also illustrated the vulnerability of regional and local marine ecosystems.

By the early 1970s environmental concern was rising in the region, and in France and Italy urban environmental protest movements emerged. International organizations launched initiatives to raise awareness and to expand knowledge about pollution and its effects in the Mediterranean. These organizations included the United Nations Food and Agricultural Organization (FAO), the Intergovernmental Maritime Consultative Organization, the World Health Organization (WHO), United Nations Educational, Scientific and Cultural Organization (UNESCO), and the European Community (EU), as well as nongovernmental organizations such as the United Towns Organization and the International Commission for the Scientific Exploration of the Mediterranean Sea (CIESM). These organizations sponsored international scientific conferences, workshops, and reports explicitly attempting to organize and codify regional scientific consensus about emerging environmental threats and needed research.

Organized under the auspices of UNEP, representatives from the Mediterranean states formulated the Med Plan and negotiated and adopted the 1976 framework for the Barcelona Convention (Convention on the Protection of the Mediterranean Sea against Pollution). The Med Plan was the first official regional cooperation forum to encompass the entire region. State officials subsequently negotiated seven pollution-control and environmental-management protocols to the Barcelona Convention. Over

PROTECTING THE MEDITERRANEAN, 1976

A portion of the Convention on the Protection of the Mediterranean Sea against Pollution (Barcelona Convention)—"Protocol for the Prevention of Pollution of the Mediterranean Sea by Dumping from Ships and Aircraft," *appears below:*

CONSCIOUS of the economic, social, health and cultural value of the marine environment of the Mediterranean Sea area,

FULLY AWARE of their responsibility to preserve this common heritage for the benefit and enjoyment of present and future generations,

RECOGNIZING the threat posed by pollution to the marine environment, its ecological equilibrium, resources and legitimate uses,

MINDFUL of the special hydrographic and ecological characteristics of the Mediterranean Sea area and its particular vulnerability to pollution,

NOTING that existing international conventions on the subject do not cover, in spite of the progress achieved, all aspects and sources of marine pollution and do not entirely meet the special requirements of the Mediterranean Sea, area,

REALIZING fully the need for close cooperation among the States and international organizations concerned in a coordinated and comprehensive regional approach for the protection and enhancement of the marine environment in the Mediterranean Sea area . . .

Article 4 General undertakings

1. The Contracting Parties shall individually or jointly take all appropriate measures in accordance with the provisions of this Convention and those Protocols in force to which they are party, to prevent, abate and combat pollution of the Mediterranean Sea area and to protect and enhance the marine environment in that area.

2. The Contracting Parties shall cooperate in the formulation and adoption of Protocols, in addition to the protocols opened for signature at the same time as this Convention, prescribing agreed measures, procedures and standards for the implementation of this Convention.

3. The Contracting Parties further pledge themselves to promote, within the international bodies considered to be competent by the Contracting Parties, measures concerning the protection of the marine environment in the Mediterranean Sea area from all types and sources of pollution.

Article 5 Pollution caused by dumping from ships and aircraft

The Contracting Parties shall take all appropriate measures to prevent and abate pollution of the Mediterranean Sea area caused by dumping from ships and aircraft.

Article 6 Pollution from ships

The Contracting Parties shall take all measures in conformity with international law to prevent, abate and combat pollution of the Mediterranean Sea area caused by discharges from ships and to ensure the effective implementation in that area of the rules which are generally recognized at the international level relating to the control of this type of pollution.

Article 7 Pollution resulting from exploration and exploitation of the continental shelf and the seabed and its subsoil.

The Contracting Parties shall take all appropriate measures to prevent, abate and combat pollution of the Mediterranean Sea area resulting from exploration and exploitation of the continental shelf and the seabed and its subsoil.

Article 8 Pollution from land-based sources

The Contracting Parties shall take all appropriate measures to prevent, abate and combat pollution of the Mediterranean Sea area caused by discharges from rivers, coastal establishments or outfalls, or emanating from any other land-based sources within their territories.

Article 9 Cooperation in dealing with pollution emergencies

1. The Contracting Parties shall cooperate in taking the necessary measures for dealing with pollution emergencies in the Mediterranean Sea area, whatever the causes of such emergencies, and reducing or eliminating damage resulting therefrom.

2. Any Contracting Party which becomes aware of any pollution emergency in the Mediterranean Sea area shall without delay notify the Organization and, either through the Organization or directly, any Contracting Party likely to be affected by such emergency.

Source: *Eur-Lex, Internet website.*

time, these protocols expanded the scope and increased the specificity of state commitments. Regional activities and environmental organizations have grown in number, as have interstate cooperation programs for research, information exchange, and pilot and demonstration projects.

In the 1990s state representatives amended the Barcelona Convention and three of its protocols, expanding coverage of the convention to include coastal areas and incorporate important new concepts in environmental governance and management into the agreements. Med Plan participants established a Coordinating Unit for the Med Plan and eight Regional Action Centers (RACs) administering various Med Plan programs and facilitating implementation of the Barcelona Convention and its protocols. State parties developed a highly specified set of rules, procedures, and mandates for regime-sponsored conferences, meetings, Med Plan administration, RACs, and other regime programs and activities. Additional accomplishments included "action plans" to protect monk seals, marine turtles, and cetaceans, and to encourage sustainable development.

The success of international cooperation within the Med Plan regime was limited, however. Environmental "improvements" resulting from this international cooperation remained small, few in number, and controversial. Oil spillage and biological contamination of beaches have decreased, but eutrophication, beach tar, and solid litter appear to be increasing. Coastal development remained largely unplanned and unconstrained by environmental concerns; habitat losses continued. Policies to encourage "sustainable tourism" remained (at best) merely in the planning stages. While sewage treatment capacities grew, so did populations, economies, and waste generation. Environmental protection of the dune and wetland ecosystems, ancient harbors and historical sites, and threatened species and marine parks remained poor or nonexistent. The Med Plan lacks comprehensive implementation plans for the growing number of international commitments within the regime. In fact, little assessment of national implementation existed on which such plans could be based and states failed to agree on the annexes and common measures necessary to assess implementation of existing protocols.

Regional environmental cooperation and implementation of international commitments was constrained by limited, often declining, state organizational capacity in many Mediterranean countries. Nations facing low levels of organizational capacity cannot increase environmental protection. Such states do not lack commitment to regional environmental goals: they lack the ability to institutionalize and administer environmental policy. Few international assistance programs in the region attempted to build administrative or implementation capacity. Most capacity-building programs focused only on the enhancement of technical capacity through activities such as education, training programs, and equipment provision. Merely increasing the technical skills of some individuals or improving their access to particular types of technology is unlikely to improve science advice to policymakers. Nor will it automatically improve policymakers' capacities to act on such advice.

Informed by scientific community members, for example, Algeria, Egypt, and Turkey embarked on efforts to incorporate many aspects of the regional environmental discourse into law and policy in the 1970s and 1980s. These states passed basic environmental laws, ratified international environmental agreements, established administrative bodies for pollution control, and participated in several Med Plan regime activities. In the wake of stagnant or declining state environmental policy capacity, little environmental policy development or implementation occurred in Algeria, Egypt, or Turkey since the 1980s–despite a growth in international environmental policy commitments. Collapsing governments in Albania, Bosnia, and Lebanon have left these countries devoid of any meaningful environmental policy–let alone Med Plan implementation. Libya and Syria also lack sufficient environmental policy capacity to comply or implement the Med Plan commitments.

In many Mediterranean states, only pilot programs and projects with international funds appear to be influenced significantly by internationally agreed upon environmental standards. Without a minimum level of state capacity, there is no policy development for experts to influence, nor any place to institutionalize environmental principles and policy norms. While Med Plan programs are often models for scientific and technical capacity building, Mediterranean environmental cooperation did little to address the lack of public sector capacity in many troubled and failing states. Furthermore, the Med Plan had little ability to increase resources dedicated to marine and coastal protection in wealthier and more capable states such as France and Italy.

Staff and budgets for the Med Plan Coordinating Unit and the RACs remained small and the activities of each organization fell well short of the goals tasked to it. For most of the 1990s, the Med Plan budget was well below the $10 million states were supposed to contribute

A polluted beach on the Mediterranean shore of Egypt

(PEPS/Keith Scholey)

annually. To put these figures in perspective, one estimate of the Med Plan implementation costs for the four Mediterranean members of the EU (France, Greece, Italy, and Spain) totaled almost $20 billion–and even this high figure did not include the costs of implementing other international environmental commitments nor expenses to be borne by consumers.

While regional international environmental cooperation agreements and scientific research can be accomplished with relatively few resources, implementation of higher standards costs much more. Even the wealthiest states (those on the European side of the sea) have not invested in Mediterranean environmental protection. Nor have these nations applied the "polluter pays" principle to the activities and economic sectors that often did great harm to the marine environment: tourism, transportation, agriculture, energy, industrial production, and fishing. Both the World Bank and EU stepped up funding for Mediterranean environmental protection, but these contributions represented only a small portion of economic development assistance given by these bodies. One positive sign, however, was the EU effort in the 1990s to force compliance with its environmental standards on its Mediterranean member states.

Mediterranean environmental cooperation offers guidelines for regional environmental management needs. Yet, the Med Plan lacked a comprehensive implementation plan or programs to build state capacity. Furthermore, none of the states pushed for a more serious implementation effort. In short, the regional effort to protect the Mediterranean marine environment from pollution and overexploitation remained largely an internationalist project. Little local- and state-level implementation occurred and major marine-resource users, such as the tourism and shipping industries and municipal sewage systems, contributed few resources toward regional environmental protection. While users of the marine environment appeared interested in regional environmental protection, they failed to invest in ecological quality. Regional scientists shaped environmental protection agreements and benefited from them, yet most major Mediterranean polluters (economic sectors, states, and municipalities) did not dedicate significant resources to environmental protection of the sea. Environmental protection requires more than scientific advice. It requires capable states.

–STACY D. VANDEVEER, UNIVERSITY OF NEW HAMPSHIRE

Viewpoint: The Med Plan was a half-hearted measure to clean up the environment that was continued primarily because tourist dollars were at stake.

Marine pollution in the Mediterranean Sea is not new. The ancient harbors of Ostia, Piraeus, and Alexandria were strewn with wastes and garbage. Bays, estuaries, and inlets close to population centers–the Golden Horn, Venetian lagoons, and the Bay of Naples–were unsanitary long before the industrial age. In the twentieth century, however, the waters of the Mediterranean grew progressively less clear and more polluted.

Since 1960, the main pollutants in the Mediterranean have been much the same as elsewhere around the aquatic world. Microbes, synthetic organic compounds such as dichlorodiphenyltrichloroethane (DDT) or polychlorinated biphenyls (PCBs), oil, litter, and excess nutrients topped the list. In the most general terms, by 1990 about a quarter of the total land-derived pollution contaminated the northwestern Mediterranean coasts from Valencia to Genoa, and another third plagued the Adriatic. The main sources were the big cities, large rivers, and a few coastal industrial enclaves.

Microbial contamination from sewage existed in rough proportion to human population until the twentieth century, because sewage treatment scarcely existed. By the end of the twentieth century, about 30 percent of the raw sewage splashing into the Mediterranean received treatment, but the total quantity had tripled or quadrupled since 1900. So the risks of gastrointestinal ailments, typhoid, or hepatitis to people bathing or eating seafood increased significantly. By the late 1980s, when the European Union (EU) developed guidelines for permissible levels of microbial contamination, beach closings became routine from Spain to Greece. In any given summer in the 1990s, about 10 percent of Mediterranean European beaches failed EU standards, although they were not necessarily closed.

Oil became a major pollutant with the emergence of the Persian Gulf oilfields after 1948. The existence of the Suez Canal and the energy demand of European transport and industry ensured that the Mediterranean would become one of the oil highways for the world. About a quarter of world oil shipments crossed the Mediterranean (1970–1990), leaving behind a sixth of the oil pollution in the world. Of that, one-third washed up on the beaches.

Industry did more than oil to sully the Mediterranean. Many factories sprouted on the water's edge, taking advantage of the low costs of seaborne shipping. Others emerged on rivers that flow into the sea, for transport reasons or because industrial processes required fresh water for cooling or cleaning. Even factories far from the water polluted the Mediterranean through airborne deposition. Whatever the avenue, the Mediterranean received significant amounts of synthetic compounds and heavy metals from industry. Industrialization proceeded spectacularly in the Mediterranean basin in the late twentieth century, as regional countries accounted for about 5 percent of international industrial production in 1929, about 3 percent in 1950, but 14 percent in 1985. A great surge came after 1960. For the next quarter century industrial production in Mediterranean countries rose by about 6 to 7 percent annually.

This expansion caused greater pollution, which was concentrated near industrial centers: in Italy, France, and Spain. Despite the rapid growth of industry in North Africa, by 1990 it still accounted for only 9 percent of Mediterranean industry; several countries, ranging from Israel to Croatia, represented another 10 percent. Italy generated two-thirds of the industrial production of the Mediterranean basin; Spain–mostly around Barcelona–a tenth; France (where little industry is in the Mediterranean catchment) only a twentieth. The greatest pollution problems therefore arose in the northwest of the Mediterranean basin, around the mouths of rivers with industrialized basins, such as the Ebro, Rhône, and Po, and around the centers of heavy industry, such as Barcelona, Genoa, and the northern Adriatic coast from Mestre to Trieste. Industries poured the usual pollutants (PCBs and heavy metals such as mercury, lead, or arsenic) into the air, rivers, and Mediterranean itself.

Outside of these primary hot spots, additional pollution problems developed in the late twentieth century. In Greece, for example, two industrial clusters developed around Athens and Thessaloníki. Between them, they contained all major Greek industry, except for power plants. Neither city, as late as 1990, had sewage treatment plants. In Greece, the pollution from almost all of its metallurgical industry, all of its refineries, paper mills, and shipyards, three of its four fertilizer plants, and half its human population were concentrated in the vicinity of Athens or Thessaloníki. The increasing severity of pollution, and perhaps a decline in the Greek public's tolerance for pollution, combined to produce remedial measures after about 1980, which took the form of incentives (some existed since 1965) to relocate industries and of limited pollution control.

Counterparts to these troubled Greek waters existed. The Gulfs of İzmir, İskenderun (once Alexandretta), Tunis, Trieste, and many others all developed major pollution problems. The Golden Horn of Istanbul, which had suffered from biological pollution for many centuries, added growing concentrations of toxic metals to the mix after 1913. Indeed, wherever urban and industrial centers grew up on bays, gulfs, or inlets exempted from the general counterclockwise currents of the Mediterranean, pollution accumulated.

Eutrophication, the accumulation of excess nutrients that allows algae blooms, derived less from industry than from agriculture and municipal sewage. From time to time algal blooms, often called red tides, occurred naturally in the Mediterranean, as elsewhere in enclosed waters. They happened much more often in the twentieth century, because of urbanization and its untreated sewage, and because of the burgeoning use of chemical fertilizers. The most affected areas were the Gulf of Lion (France), which suffered its most serious blooms after 1980; the Saronic Gulf around Athens, which experienced its first recorded red tide in 1978; and the northern Adriatic. Between 1872 and 1988 the northern Adriatic recorded fifteen eutrophication blooms: the first large outbreak occurred in 1976, the biggest in 1988. Their frequency increased after 1969, which probably reflected increased nutrient loadings, or warmer water temperatures–perhaps both. Algal blooms played havoc with fish populations, seabed life in general, and the tourist trade.

Despite a century of intensifying marine pollution, the Mediterranean Sea in the 1990s was no cesspool. Long stretches of coastline in southern Turkey and North Africa, and smaller ones elsewhere, retained clean waters. The Mediterranean was cleaner than the Baltic Sea, Black Sea, Yellow Sea, or Sea of Japan. Two reasons explain this situation. First, the size of the Mediterranean, its lively mixing of deep and surface waters, and its currents helped to dilute pollution. Second, the total pollution load paled beside other unfortunate bodies of water, in part because Mediterranean societies after 1975 made some concerted efforts to reduce contamination.

As in much of the world, explicit environmental awareness and politics around the Mediterranean dates mainly from the 1970s. Most countries by 1975 had tiny bands of ecologically concerned citizens, such as those Corsicans, who in 1973 demonstrated against an Italian chemical plant that had polluted and disfigured their island shores. By 1980 some countries had green parties. The general political and cultural milieu–if one can generalize–did not favor environmental movements. In none of this activism, or lack thereof, were Mediterranean countries exceptional.

They were exceptional after 1975 for developing the Med Plan. Under the auspices of UNEP, all Mediterranean littoral countries except Albania convened in Barcelona and agreed to an ongoing process of environmental management for the entire basin. The Med Plan supported scientific research and integrated development planning. It produced several agreements and protocols to limit pollution. Enforcement, however, normally left something to be desired. For instance, about two thousand kilometers of coastline were sacrificed to development through lax enforcement or special dispensations. The Plan, together with national regulations and EU restrictions, however, helped limit Mediterranean pollution from 1976. The agreement aided in the construction of sewage-treatment plants for Marseilles, Cairo, Alexandria, Aleppo, and several other cities. At the end of the 1980s work began on sewage works for Thessaloníki and Athens. While the Sea twenty-five years later was more polluted than when the agreement began, it surely would have been much more so without the Med Plan.

Any accords involving Greece and Turkey, Syria and Israel, and other pairs of sworn enemies (as of the 1970s) must rank as high political achievement. In this case some of the credit should go to scientists who forged something of a Pan-Mediterranean community. Scientific wisdom, normally quickly ignored when hard bargaining begins in international environmental politics, carried unusual weight for one reason:

hundreds of billions of tourist dollars were at stake. In the last quarter of the twentieth century, about one-third of international tourism involved visits to Mediterranean countries, usually to coasts and beaches. Greece, Italy, and Spain hosted the most visitors, who numbered in the tens of millions annually. The economic health of these countries depended on tourist receipts. Israel, Turkey, Egypt, Tunisia, and Morocco also derived significant income from tourism, although in Morocco not from Mediterranean beaches. No country could achieve clean beaches alone, given the circulation of the Mediterranean. Greek islands received Turkish sewage, and needed Turkish commitments to enjoy uncontaminated beaches. Syria needed Israeli cooperation, and Israel needed Egyptian assistance. The quest for tourists, who contributed mightily to pollution, paradoxically helped stabilize, and in cases improve, the quality of coastal waters of the Mediterranean. This circumstance, while not unique (consider the Caribbean), is rare, and so the model, and partial success, of the Med Plan is not readily transferable to other settings.

–J. R. MCNEILL, GEORGETOWN UNIVERSITY

References

Serge Antoine, "18 pays riverains dans le même bateau: le souci d'environnement et de developpement durable," *Peuples méditerranéens,* 62–63 (1993): 255–277.

Patricia A. Bliss, "Review of the Mediterranean Action Plan," *Ocean Management,* 3 (1978): 315–335.

Baruch Boxer, "Mediterranean Pollution: Problem and Response," *Ocean Development and International Law Journal,* 10 (1982): 315–356.

Boxer, "Societal Contexts of Ocean Pollution Science: Cross-National Comparisons," *Global Environmental Change* (March 1991): 139–356.

L. Anathea Brooks and Stacy D. VanDeveer, eds., *Saving the Seas: Values, Science and International Governance* (College Park: Maryland Sea Grant College, 1997).

Michel Grenon and Michel Batisse, eds., *Futures for the Mediterranean Basin: The Blue Plan* (Oxford & New York: Oxford University Press, 1989).

Peter M. Haas, "Do Regimes Matter: Epistemic Communities and Mediterranean Pollution Control," *International Organizations,* 43 (Summer 1989): 377–404.

Haas, *Saving the Mediterranean: The Politics of International Environmental Protection* (New York: Columbia University Press, 1990).

L. Jeftic, "The Role of Science in Marine Environmental Protection of Regional Seas and Their Coastal Areas: The Experience of the Mediterranean Action Plan," *Marine Pollution Bulletin,* 25 (1992): 66–69.

Basil D. Katsoulis and John M. Tsangaris, "The State of the Greek Environment in Recent Years," *Ambio,* 23 (1994): 274–279.

Gabriela Kutting, "Mediterranean Pollution: International Cooperation and the Control of Pollution from Land-based Sources," *Marine Policy,* 18 (1994).

Philippe Le Lourd, "Oil Pollution in the Mediterranean Sea," *Ambio,* 6 (1977): 317–320.

A. Manos, "An International Programme for the Protection of a Semi-Enclosed Sea–The Mediterranean Action Plan," *Marine Pollution Bulletin,* 23 (1991): 489–496.

Roberto Marchetti and Attilio Rinaldi, "Le condizioni del Mare Adriatico," in *Ambiente Italia: lo stato di salute del paese e le proposte per una società ecologica,* edited by Giovanna Melandri (Milan: Mondadori, 1990), pp. 33–37.

Ramón Margalef, ed., *Western Mediterranean* (Oxford & New York: Pergamon Press, 1985).

J. R. McNeill, *The Mountains of the Mediterranean: An Environmental History* (New York: Cambridge University Press, 1992).

Erdal Özhan, ed., *MEDCOAST 93: Proceedings of the First International Conference on the Mediterranean Coastal Environment, November 2–5, 1993, Antalya, Turkey* (Ankara: MEDCOAST Permanent Secretariat, 1993).

Geoffrey Pridham, "Towards Sustainable Tourism in the Mediterranean? Policy and Practice in Italy, Spain and Greece," *Environmental Politics,* 8 (Summer 1999): 97–116.

Evangelos Raftopoulos, *The Barcelona Convention and Its Protocols: The Mediterranean Action Plan Regime* (London: Simmonds & Hill, 1993).

David Stanners and Philippe Bourdeau, *Europe's Environment: The Dobris Assessment* (Copenhagen: European Environment Agency, 1995).

United Nations Environment Programme (UNEP), *Report of the Ninth Ordinary Meeting of the Contracting Parties to the Convention for the Protection of the Mediterranean Sea*

Against Pollution and Its Protocols (Athens: UNEP, 1995).

United Nations Environment Programme (UNEP), *The State of the Marine and Coastal Environment in the Mediterranean Region* (Athens: UNEP, 1996).

Stacy D. VanDeveer, "Changing Course to Protect European Seas: Lessons after 25 Years," *Environment* (July/August 2000): 10–26.

VanDeveer, "Normative Force: The State Transnational Norms and International Environmental Regimes," dissertation, University of Maryland, 1997.

VanDeveer and Geoffrey D. Dabelko, eds., *Protecting Regional Seas: Developing Capacity and Fostering Environmental Cooperation in Europe, Conference Proceedings* (Washington, D.C.: Woodrow Wilson International Center for Scholars, 2000).

F. B. de Walle, M. Nikopoloulou-Tamvakli, and W. J. Heinen, eds., *Environmental Conditions of the Mediterranean Sea: European Community Countries* (Dordrecht & London: Kluwer Academic Publishers, 1993).

World Bank, *The Environmental Program for the Mediterranean: Preserving a Shared Heritage and Managing a Common Resource* (Washington, D.C.: World Bank; Luxembourg: European Investment Bank, 1990).

MEXICAN WATER TREATY

What were the motivations behind regional support of the Mexican Water Treaty?

Viewpoint: Arizona politicians supported the Mexican Water Treaty in an effort to expand irrigation and encourage development throughout the state.

Viewpoint: Mexican officials viewed the Mexican Water Treaty and construction of Morelos Dam as important, yet incomplete, steps to liberating Mexicali Valley from dependence on water from the Colorado River.

Prior to the twentieth century the turbulent and muddy-red Colorado River sustained a vibrant wetlands in its delta. Situated on the edge of the Sea of Cortez and the Sonoran Desert, this improbable oasis provided food for birds migrating along the Pacific Flyway, as well as for Cocopah and Quechan natives who lived near the mouth of the river or along its fertile banks. For hundreds of years, members of these two native bands cultivated a wide variety of crops on the floodplains and waited for annual floods to irrigate their crops. As one early American observer remarked, "The Cocopahs, although so wild in many respects, have become agriculturists to such an extent that nearly every family plants a garden after the June rise of the Colorado River, and raises considerable quantities of corn, beans, squash, and melon." In the 1920s, as native bands lost control of the river to Anglo and Mexican communities in the region, Juan Grant, president of the Quechan tribe, noted to a congressional committee, "The Colorado River has been flowing from the Rocky Mountains to the sea for many generations, long before the white man come [sic]. We Indians were farming along its shores, raising corn, pumpkins, beans, and watermelons to support ourselves."

At the dawn of the twentieth century, however, American and Mexican developers created different visions of the desert landscape that deeply altered the ecology of the region. Instead of continuing to farm along the banks, where floodwaters were unpredictable and often destructive, American and Mexican developers looked to the fertile soil—if only it could be irrigated—in the Mexicali, Imperial, and Yuma valleys. William A. Smythe, a respected journalist and promoter of irrigation, announced his visions for an irrigated oasis in the region in *Sunset,* a new magazine sponsored by the Southern Pacific Railroad. The magazine promoted the areas through which the railroad carried tourists and potential inhabitants of the region. Smythe contended that with irrigation, the desolate desert floors of the region could be made to resemble the "beauty of Damascus." Citrus groves and olive trees would adorn this "new Damascus to rise under our southwestern sky . . . fairer than that in the Syrian desert . . . with the life of a new time and blessed with American liberty."

Particularly in the years since 1940, Mexicans and Americans brought Smythe's dreams for the region to fruition. Intensive agricultural development and competition for water resources caused the irrigated agricultural oases of the valleys to flourish. Two factors contributed to the success of

those pursuits, which radically altered the ecology of the lower delta. First, the irrigated oases never could have flourished without a controlled supply of water. Dams upstream on the Colorado River, including the Hoover and Glen Canyon Dams, regulated the flow of water to the delta and the farming communities. Second, domestic and international treaties played a large role in determining how much water each state and nation in the Colorado River Basin received from the river.

Demand for an international treaty to divide water from the river between the two nations began during discussions for the Colorado River Compact (CRC) during the 1920s. With congressional approval of the treaty secured in 1928, President Herbert Hoover signed the CRC into law the following year. The compact apportioned the water from the Colorado River among the seven basin states in the United States but failed to guarantee Mexico any water. Nevertheless, Mexican officials continued to press for U.S. recognition of their claims for water from the river. Agricultural development in Sonora and Baja California depended on the availability of this water.

At the same time, Mexican water policy in the delta illustrated a clear movement toward economic independence. Prior to 1937 the Colorado River Land Company, an American-held company, owned most of the arable land in Mexicali Valley. The Imperial Irrigation District (IID), also controlled by Americans, owned and operated the water distribution system in the valley. After President Lázaro Cárdenas's expropriation of Colorado River Land Company lands in 1937, and their subsequent distribution to Mexican peasants and farmers, national and regional policymakers took steps toward controlling every aspect of agricultural production in the valley. Reaching that goal meant the Mexican government ultimately needed to take control of the water distribution system. In an effort to force the United States to offer a water treaty, Cárdenas encouraged as much development in the region as possible.

Lack of water during 1944–1945 further compelled Mexico to seek an international treaty that would divide waters from the Colorado, Rio Grande, and Tijuana—all international rivers that crossed the boundary between the two nations. As the following two essays illustrate, however, international water treaties were often viewed as much more than simply devices to divide water between nations that shared access to a river. Instead, they were often used as tools to either limit development by an opposing nation or decrease the dependence of one nation on the other to access to the water.

The Mexican Water Treaty (1944) elicited a wide spectrum of responses, both negative and positive, on the national, state, and local levels in the United States. The Franklin D. Roosevelt administration hoped that the treaty would assure Mexican support for the Allied cause during World War II. Most members of the Senate, who would be called upon for approval, supported the treaty. They felt that it would illustrate U.S. goodwill toward its southern neighbor. Senators from California, however, feared that the treaty would limit the amount of surplus water they could take from the Colorado River under the provisions of the CRC. While Arizona was as water-hungry as California, its senators supported the treaty. While they had no intention of giving water to Mexico out of the goodness of their hearts, they hoped that a treaty would place a ceiling on the amount of agricultural lands that could be developed south of the border.

The Mexican Water Treaty provided Mexicali Valley farmers with a firm baseline of how much water they could expect from the Colorado River on an annual basis (1.5 million acre-feet of water; an acre-foot represents the amount of water needed to fill one square acre twelve inches deep). In order to make delivery of that water more efficient, the treaty also made provisions for Mexico to build a new diversion dam that would augment water supplies in the valley. Morelos Dam provided a conduit for channeling water into the Alamo Canal, which was still owned by the IID. The push to take control of the Alamo Canal ended the hold of the IID on the Mexicali water supply and vindicated efforts by Mexico to decrease their reliance on U.S. institutions for an adequate water supply.

Viewpoint: Arizona politicians supported the Mexican Water Treaty in an effort to expand irrigation and encourage development throughout the state.

Arizona water politics underwent subtle transformations during the 1940s. While they had always been leery of the amount of water used by California, they quickly became aware of new developments after Mexican president Lázaro Cárdenas pushed to increase agricultural production in the Mexicali Valley. Prior to the 1940s, politicians in Arizona refused to support the Colorado River Compact (CRC), primarily because of the large amount of water awarded to California. After 1940, however, Governor Sidney P. Osborn and other state officials recognized that if they were to have any luck realizing additional development in central Arizona, it would have to approve the compact and a treaty guaranteeing Mexico a minimal amount of water from the Colorado River. The Arizona legislature subsequently ratified the compact, which guaranteed the state 2.8 million acre-feet of water each year. Following approval of the CRC, most Arizona officials offered support for the Mexican Water Treaty (1944) in an effort to limit water appropriations south of the border in the Mexicali Valley.

The U.S. Senate determines whether or not to approve international treaties, and senators from Arizona played a crucial role in enunciating the position of their constituency. Junior senator Ernest William McFarland emphasized the precarious situation of the state:

> It is plain that in Arizona we shall be forced to reduce the number of acre-feet of water pumped each year. This simply means that acreage already cultivated and prosperous will have to become a part of the desert unless we in Arizona can supplement our water supply from another source–and the only remaining source is the Colorado River.

McFarland's plea for help illustrated the hope for additional funding for irrigation and water supply projects, even in the context of discussing a treaty to supply another nation with water. McFarland believed that much of the development of Arizona achieved during the first half of the twentieth century would return to desert unless Congress approved the Central Arizona Project, a canal that would carry water from the Colorado River to the Phoenix metropolitan area. Not only would lands already under production be rejuvenated, but also thousands of new farms and homes could be established. McFarland believed that for continued growth to occur in Arizona, Mexican water use from the Colorado River had to be limited to 1.5 million acre-feet of water.

The Senate hearings focused specifically on the quality of water that Mexico would receive as a result of the treaty, and the implications of water quality on future relations. McFarland's requests adhered to the letter of the treaty, which stated that any type of water could be used to satisfy the treaty: whether it was drainage water or from a reservoir on the river. This position illustrated the hope of Arizona officials that greater amounts of water would be available for use in the state if poorer quality drainage waters from farms close to the river could be counted on to contribute to the obligation of the United States to Mexico.

Coincidentally, McFarland was the only member of the U.S. Senate who had previous judicial experience in determining issues of water quality in agricultural production. As a state judge earlier in his career, McFarland had ruled in one case that farmers upstream had to assure that the water downstream was of suitable quality for use in farming. Two opponents of the treaty, Senators Patrick Anthony McCarran (D-Nevada) and Sheridan Downey (D-California), pointed out that his previous ruling and current position on the treaty were incongruent. Nevertheless, McFarland maintained that Mexican officials understood the intent of the treaty, which stipulated that any water "regardless of quality" could be used to fulfill the treaty. Senator Edwin Carl Johnson (D-Colorado) warned against the long-term consequences of acting rashly. Johnson himself had once "sustained a considerable loss in connection with irrigated lands because of the saline content of the water." Despite the silence of the treaty on the issue of water quality, Johnson feared that if the Senate failed to add an amendment guaranteeing Mexico high-quality water, "the whole matter [would] be thrown into an international controversy." In fulfillment of Johnson's fears, Mexico complained in 1961 that highly saline water from the Colorado River, delivered as part of the U.S. obligations under the treaty, had damaged farmlands in Mexicali Valley. The controversy lasted until 1974 when the United States pledged to provide Mexico with better quality water under an agreement known as Minute 242 of the Mexican Water Treaty.

For those living close to the Mexican border in the delta, the Mexican Water Treaty also elicited strong emotions. Farmers in Yuma County and San Luís Rio Colorado (a community in northwestern Sonora) had cooperated with each other over the years on water issues. In the 1920s prominent lobbyist and booster

A dredge in operation on the Imperial Canal, circa 1910

(Bancroft Library)

Benjamin Franklin Fly presented the Yuma County Water Users Association (YCWUA) with a proposal to sell their wastewater to farmers across the border in San Luís Rio Colorado. The wastewater, which was delivered to the Mexican farmers by way of drainage pipes that reached the border, helped transform the desert lands near San Luís Rio Colorado into productive agricultural farmland.

As Senate debate over the Mexican Water Treaty grew closer in 1944, YCWUA officials did not object to the amount of water that Mexico would receive under treaty. They were concerned, however, about the method that would be used to deliver the 1.5 million acre-feet to Mexicali Valley and San Luís Rio Colorado. They were particularly concerned about the provision in the treaty that gave Mexico the right to build a dam that would lift water into the aging Alamo Canal. Increased farming and demographic growth in the region made a more efficient water-diversion system necessary. The proposed dam, YCWUA officials believed, would be located near the site of Hanlon's Heading. The Imperial Irrigation District (IID) had previously used a diversion structure at Hanlon's Heading to divert water into the Alamo Canal, which then passed through Mexicali Valley on its way to the Imperial Valley. When the All-American Canal was completed in 1942, however, Alamo Canal became obsolete as a water-delivery channel. Mexico continued to use the structure, although it quickly became inadequate for the needs of farmers and residents.

YCWUA leaders feared that the new dam would allow water to seep into the water table beneath valuable farmlands of Yuma Valley. The waterlogged lands would then have to be drained at the farmers' expense and the excess water would stunt the growth of crops. YCWUA president Henry Fraunfelder noted at a 6 March 1944 Board of Governors meeting that the chairman of the International Boundary and Water Commission (IBWC) had informed him that: "the cost of a Mexican diversion dam and protective works which would meet American requirements would be so great that it would not be built." Lawson suggested that Mexico could receive water deliveries to the Alamo Canal from the newly built All-American Canal.

Thereafter, YCWUA officials encouraged McFarland and Carl Trumbell Hayden (D-Arizona) to favor delivery of water through the All-American Canal instead of supporting the provision for a new dam near Yuma Valley. To McFarland, Fraunfelder stressed the approval of his organization for the quantity of water awarded to Mexico under the treaty. He emphasized, however, that if the proposed dam were built near Hanlon's Heading, it might allow Yuma Valley to become "seeped in a relatively short time." Not only would diversion through the All-American Canal avoid seepage problems, but also it might place greater regulatory control on the IID over the Imperial Dam (located above Yuma, Arizona, where the All-American Canal received water from the

Colorado River). Yuma Valley farmers received water from the All-American Canal through a siphon that carried water below the body of the Colorado River. Arizona farmers feared that the IID, granted authority over the dam by the Department of the Interior in 1931, might limit water apportionment to Yuma at some future date. Federal control, Fraunfelder believed, could check this potentially arbitrary exercise of power. He concluded by suggesting that amendments be added to the treaty to "obviate Mexico's need for a diversion dam." If such a measure could not be secured, he observed, "it might be well to defer ratification of the Treaty pending further study of the effects dams are having on the lower Colorado and adjacent lands."

While Hayden and McFarland sympathized with the concerns of Yuma Valley farmers, greater political pressure from the more populous interior to secure additional water for central Arizona explained their unwillingness to object to the provision for the dam. The senators also knew that the dam would catch drainage water from Yuma Valley and divert it to Mexicali Valley. During Senate hearings on the treaty, Hayden pressed C. M. Ainsworth, engineer for the International Boundary and Water Commission (IBWC), for assurances that water backed up by the diversion dam would not harm Yuma Valley farmlands. Ainsworth observed that the dam would not accelerate seepage or flooding in Yuma Valley. He also noted that the dam, as Arizona officials had calculated, would "assure credit to the United States for the return flow and other flows that will appear in the river." He further reminded Hayden that U.S. officials, not Mexican leaders, had suggested construction of the dam. They had done so in an effort to reduce the amount of higher quality water, destined for Mexicali Valley, held behind reservoirs upstream.

Ainsworth's responses alleviated Hayden's fears related to the potential damage to farms in Yuma Valley by the proposed dam. Hayden subsequently added an amendment to the treaty that required Mexico to pay for levees to protect Yuma and Imperial Valley farms from any damage the dam might occasion. While Yuma Valley farmers were pleased that lower-quality wastewater would be counted toward U.S. treaty obligations, they were still uneasy with the prospect of a new dam being built so close to their lands.

On 18 April 1945 Senators Hayden and McFarland voted in favor of the treaty. For the most part, the seventy-six to ten vote conveyed a gesture of goodwill to Mexico. Senate approval made the treaty operative between the two nations. Subsequently, the Mexican government began planning for construction of Morelos Dam at the previous location at Hanlon's Heading on the Arizona-Mexico boundary. Construction began in 1948 and was finished in 1950.

—EVAN WARD, UNIVERSITY OF GEORGIA

Viewpoint: Mexican officials viewed the Mexican Water Treaty and construction of Morelos Dam as important, yet incomplete, steps to liberating Mexicali Valley from dependence on water from the Colorado River.

Construction of Morelos Dam did not completely extricate Mexicali farmers from dependence on U.S. facilities to provide water for the valley. It only raised water into the Alamo Canal, which then carried it to distribution systems. The dependence of these farmers on water infrastructure owned by U.S. companies or organizations traces its roots back to the beginning of the twentieth century, when the privately financed California Development Company (CDC) won the right from the Mexican government to transport water from the Colorado River to the Imperial Valley through the Alamo Canal. The CDC diverted water into the Alamo Canal on the California side of the river near the Mexican boundary. Gravity then carried the water into Mexicali Valley and then back north (even further below sea level) to the Imperial Valley. Mismanagement and a series of floods ruined the CDC, whose rights to deliver water then passed into the hands of the Southern Pacific Railroad, which had taken control of the company in exchange for help in stemming the floods in the delta. In 1916 the Imperial Irrigation District (IID) purchased the Alamo Canal and waterworks in Mexicali Valley from Southern Pacific. The *Compañía de Terrenos y Aguas de la Baja California, S.A.*, a Mexican subsidiary for the IID, continued to deliver water from the Colorado River to Mexicali Valley. Since the *Compañía* was owned almost exclusively by U.S. citizens, the Mexican government stipulated that they would only enjoy that right until 1960.

Despite the push to "Mexicanize" agricultural infrastructure in the Mexicali Valley during the Lázaro Cárdenas presidency, the following administration confirmed the right of *Compañía* to deliver water to Mexicali Valley. As development of the valley proceeded in the 1940s, however, the Mexican government began to entertain

SENATOR DOWNEY ON THE MEXICAN WATER TREATY

On 9 April 1945 Sheridan Downey (D-California) made the following remarks about water relations with Mexico to his colleagues in the U.S. Senate:

What I wish to make clear to the Senate is this: It is the claim of the State Department that Mexico is obligated to take 1,500,000 acre-feet of water, regardless of its quality or salinity, or whether it is usable or nonusable. In my opinion it is wholly within the bounds of possibility that every acre-foot of the 1,500,000 acre-feet might be return flow, and might be so saline as to be utterly worthless to Mexico.

So far as I am concerned, I have too high a regard for Mexico and for the honor and integrity of my own country, to vote for a treaty containing a provision which our State Department says might, under certain conditions, obligate Mexico to take perfectly useless water.

I am much more deeply concerned over another phase. I know that no court of international arbitration would ever stultify itself by so interpreting this treaty. Furthermore, I know that a court of international arbitration might set up salinity standards which would prove so disastrous for every State in the Colorado River Basin that we should never recover from the shock of what might happen.

Mr. President, that issue can be clarified simply and easily by one understanding—the most important reservation which I shall present. I propose to suggest that Mexico be granted 1,500,000 acre-feet of water, at least 750,000 acre-feet shall be the best water we have in the lower basin States, out of Lake Mead. That is all we can give her. I do not know how saline that water is going to be; but we can at least guarantee Mexico the best water we have. She should not be compelled to take more than 750,000 acre-feet of return flow. The only thing I ask is that it be precisely stated in the treaty that with respect to the return flow, Mexico shall agree to take it regardless of quality.

The distinguished junior Senator from Colorado [Mr. Millikin] stressed on the floor what was emphasized and repeated before the Committee on Foreign Relations, namely, that it is expected that in excess of 1,000,000 acre-feet of this water will be return flow. I think perhaps all of it might be return flow. Under the reservation which I am suggesting, Mexico would be in a far better position, and so would we, because we would limit our obligation to deliver water out of Lake Mead to 750,000 acre-feet. That would enable us to plan definitely for the future, without the unhappy problem of salinity being left unresolved.

I have made a rather concentrated study of this treaty for months. I have said heretofore that even yet I am not definitely prepared to pass on the treaty. Over the week end I discovered certain facts with reference to salinity which are most alarming to me. I rather understood from what the distinguished junior Senator from Colorado said that he had considered the implications of that situation before I had done so.

The present salinity in Lake Mead is approximately 750 parts of salt per million, which is very good water. The prognosis of the Bureau of Reclamation and of other instrumentalities is that in the future we may expect that degree of salinity to increase to 1,000 parts per million, which is still very good water. I am now led to believe—I can not state it as a certainty, but I believe it to be true—that the estimate that in the future the salinity in Lake Mead will be 1,000 parts per million was based upon the assumption that in Colorado the transmountain diversions will be 500,000 acre-feet.

I am also informed now that Colorado has certain plans for diversion, which are perfectly proper—I have no objection to them—far exceeding that amount. I have heard the figure 2,000,000 or 3,000,000 acre-feet of diversion discussed by representatives of the Bureau of Reclamation.

What is the importance of that? The importance of it, Mr. President, is that it would mean, I assume, that the very freshest, cleanest water in Colorado would go over to the eastern slope—snow water, rain water, and other water up in the pines, with almost no salinity.

Source: Congressional Record, *volume 91 (27 March 1945–4 May 1945), p. 3175.*

the need to extricate itself from U.S. control—either private or public—in the development of the valley. As a result, the *Compañía,* despite its ties to the politically and financially powerful IID, experienced various challenges to its dominance over regional water supplies. Accordingly, the *Compañía* discussed selling Alamo Canal and the rest of its holdings to the Mexican government as early as 1942.

The forces of change that eventually led to Mexican control of the Alamo Canal began long before the Mexican Water Treaty (1944) was conceived. For example, long-term disputes over water tariffs between the *Compañía* and the Mexican government complicated administration of Alamo Canal. Whether or not Mexico used the tariffs as a lever to force the hand of the IID in relinquishing control of water infrastructure in the Mexicali Valley is not known. Disputes over price control, as much as the treaty or construction of Morelos Dam, convinced the IID to get out of the transnational water business.

During the 1920s the Mexican government largely allowed the *Compañía* to control water pricing in the valley. During the Great Depression (1929–1941), however, the government required the *Compañía* to cut water rates by 30 percent. Further cuts were made in 1931, including an agreement to freeze the price for water at one peso per cubic meter of water during a twenty-four-hour period. Eleven years later the government allowed the *Compañía* to raise the rate to 1.20 pesos. A devaluation of the peso (or an increase in the number of pesos required to equal an American dollar) in 1954 prompted the government to allow the *Compañía* to increase water rates to $1.60 per cubic meter. The *Compañía* suffered heavy losses as a result of this tightfisted control over water prices. Nevertheless, the Mexican government continued to deny *Compañía* requests for tariff increases, even though it was required to pay for its water from the IID in American dollars.

As a result of control over water prices, the *Compañía* increased pressure on the Mexican government to honor its commitment to pay for 50 percent of its capital investments (Alamo Canal, the levees, and other infrastructure), as well as 5 percent interest for payments they had not yet made. Pressured by financially strapped farmers in Mexicali Valley to keep water rates low, and influenced by the belief that the *Compañía* was financially successful, the Mexican government refused to let the *Compañía* raise water rates in order to recoup capital investments. Instead, Mexican officials promised to make payments for the capital expenses directly to the organization and its creditors. Subsequently, the government set up a Valuation Commission to determine its share of the capital investments. As engineer M. J. Dowd observed in 1959, however, the commission "had only one or two meetings [between 1941–1959] and failed to reach any conclusion by reason of the withdrawal of the representatives of the Mexican government." To add insult to injury, Dowd noted, the Mexican government removed the railroad system from the levees and "converted the levees into highways, which are main arteries leading from Algodones down through the farming areas into the delta." "Thus, by using the investment of the *Compañía* in the levees," he continued, "the Mexican government has provided highways at a tremendous saving over the cost if the levees had not been used. This hardly seems fair to the *Compañía.*"

Compañía officials experienced additional frustration when the Mexican government argued that the International Boundary and Water Commision (IBWC) would have to determine how much it owed on the structure, since the levee occupied territory in both nations. The *Compañía* valued the levee at $5 million and had been reimbursed $3 million for the system by the U.S. government. In contrast, Dowd noted in 1959 that "the *Compañía* has never received from the Mexican government any payment representing rental for [or construction of] the levee system."

Despite these financial problems, the IID still wanted to hold onto Alamo Canal. Its interest in controlling the Mexicali water supply probably influenced its attitudes toward the Mexican Water Treaty. The amendment that gave Mexico approval to build Morelos Dam, as well as the fear of losing surplus waters from the Colorado River that California had been using since the CRC was enacted, explain the opposition of the IID to the treaty.

Construction of Morelos Dam preempted the need for Alamo Canal as a water intake from the Colorado River. At the same time, the Mexican government built Matamoros Check, a structure that would guide water from the dam into Alamo Canal. Quite simply, Mexico appropriated the Alamo Canal by an engineering sleight of hand. Ever since the early 1940s, Mexican officials had been frustrated by the inability of the canal to provide sufficient water to irrigate crops in the Mexicali Valley. Furthermore, valley officials were put off by the unwillingness of the IID to allow the Colorado River Irrigation District, or CRID (the water authority in Mexicali Valley), to build a temporary dam to lift additional water into the canal. The manager of the irrigation district, Eligio Esquivel Méndez, observed that the new structures were adapted to interface with Alamo Canal because "your Company was not able to comply with the demands requested by the CRID in order to satisfy its farmers users." Furthermore, "As this is considered a public service, this Management found itself obliged to operate the canal above mentioned, constructing the works that it considered necessary in order to be able to satisfy the demands of the Mexican farmers for irrigation."

With completion of Morelos Dam and the Matamoros Check, the *Compañía's* dissolution was a fait accompli. The *Compañía's* legal counsel in Mexico City, José Barcenas, informed the company lawyer in Mexicali that with the new dam, "the company considers that the most appropriate and convenient settlement for both parties would be the purchase by the Government of all the properties of the Company." Barcenas also pointed out that operation of Morelos Dam infringed on the rights of the *Compañía*. Furthermore, the new dam reduced the company delivery revenues by "approximately 25 to 30 percent." Barcenas informed Arturo Orcí that the company would push for an increase in tariffs while negotiating for the sale of capital assets in order to recoup some of its losses. In September 1951, *Compañía* manager W. K. Bowker met Orive Alba, Mexican Secretary of Hydraulic Resources, to inform him that he wished to arrange for the sale of company assets to the Mexican government. He also suggested that the government temporarily raise the water tariff so that the *Compañía* could recoup some of its previous expenses and capital investments. Alba committed to pay for 20 percent of the levees in the delta constructed by the *Compañía*.

In accordance with the move to dissolve *Compañía*, the IID took stock of its losses associated with the organization. Dowd noted that devaluation of the peso since the company was purchased in 1916 complicated the process of obtaining an equitable settlement. Between 1917 and 1957, the dollar was approximately equal to two pesos. By 1957, however, the value of the peso had slipped to 12.50 pesos per dollar. Dowd also observed that Mexico had made only one payment for water delivery after 1942, and still owed the district 3,823,771 pesos. The IID had offered to sell the *Compañía* to Mexico as early as 1941 for 50 percent of the cost of its capital assets. That offer would have yielded 1,707,000 U.S. dollars in 1941. By 1957 the devaluation of the peso dropped the value of that offer to $662,000. IID officials felt that any subsequent offer should take the historical devaluation of the peso into account. In all, Dowd calculated that the IID had invested $5,092,370 in the company, equivalent to 17,793,494 pesos. Adjusted to the 1957 exchange rate, the amount skyrocketed to 63,654,625 pesos.

Legal issues also signaled the end of the *Compañía's* operations in Mexicali Valley. The organization operated under a concession that granted it the right to deliver water until 1960. The Board of Directors appealed for a five-year extension, fearing that they would not be able to sell their property to the Mexican government. Mexico denied their request for an extension but reassured the company that expiration of the concession would not affect the liquidation of its assets. The concession expired on 25 August 1960, when company interests were controlled by Richard B. Brissenden, Robert García Martínez, and Bowker.

The Mexican government emphasized that it practically owned the Alamo Canal by virtue of its location between Morelos Dam and the lateral canals of Mexicali farmers. Secretary of Hydraulic Resources Alfredo Del Mazo informed Attorney Orcí that "in private and as a friend he would state that he was not in favor of buying the said assets, advising me that that opinion was not to be taken as that of the Government, nor as final, adding that with a 'much' smaller amount the canals and other works which the Company is selling could be built, all more modern and adaptable to the present, reducing the width of the canals and avoiding the great loss of water by evaporation." While Del Mazo's statements had the air of a threat, the CRID was already considering rehabilitation of the irrigation system. Those plans also included many of the propositions set for by Del Mazo, who also pointed out that the Mexican government felt no obligation to buy the works "if the price did not suit it." Del Mazo reiterated this ambivalent position in February of 1961, citing the opinion of the Legal and Advisory Board that the *Compañía* "had become liable to the loss of all the rights, assets, and properties related to the concession, because of its expiration." He also stressed to Orcí and Bowker that the lowest possible price should be assigned to the *Compania's* holdings. This policy would facilitate a decision as to "whether [or not] the Government would buy the assets of the Company and [provide] . . . something concrete for the decision of the President of the Republic." He noted that the federal government was strapped for funds and that "it would have to be for a very low price (mentioning seven million pesos)."

In March 1961 Orcí presented Del Mazo with an offer of fifteen million pesos for company property valued at $49,461,640. On 8 May 1961, Del Mazo made a counterproposal for 4.5 million pesos in three payments. The contract of sale was completed on 9 August 1961. The payments were used to reimburse IID for part of its losses related to the enterprise, pay workers three months wages and seniority rights, and reimburse stockholders for their shares in the company. On 29 September 1961 control of the Alamo Canal passed from the company to the

Department of Hydraulic Resources. Curiously, members of the Water Workers and Distributors Union of Baja California (CROC) parted with the *Compañía* by comparing their separation to "that of the moment of the GREAT CAPTAIN and his LOYAL OFFICERS who bring the BELOVED SHIP to the dock to leave it there, and its crew bids farewell to all." This affectionate message was highly ironic given the labor strife of the previous fifteen years. Nevertheless, the poetic expression of gratitude marked a turning point in U.S.-Mexican relations in the delta region. Mexico had finally taken control of the water-supply infrastructure that supplied its farms and homes. While Mexicali residents would still be dependent on U.S. dams upstream to prevent floods and deliver water to Morelos Dam, Mexico gained an important advantage in controlling the future of agribusiness in the region by purchasing the rights to Alamo Canal.

–EVAN WARD, UNIVERSITY OF GEORGIA

References

William DeBuys and Joan Meyers, *Salt Dreams: Land and Water in Low-Down California* (Albuquerque: University of New Mexico Press, 1999).

M. J. Dowd, ed., *Compañía de Terrenos y Aguas de la B.C., S.A., Correspondence Water Tariff, volume 1, 1942–1959* (Imperial, Cal.: Imperial Irrigation District Research Library, n.d.).

Dowd, ed., *Compañía de Terrenos y Aguas de la B.C., S.A., Negotiations with Mexico re: Water Service to All American Canal and Sale of Assets* (Imperial, Cal.: Imperial Irrigation District Research Library, n.d.).

Dowd, ed., *Compañía de Terrenos y Aguas de la B.C., S.A., Various Subjects–1911–1957* (Imperial, Cal.: Imperial Irrigation District Research Library, n.d.).

James B. Greenberg, "The Tragedy of Commoditization: Political Ecology of the Colorado River's Destruction," *Research in Economic Anthropology*, 19 (1998): 133–149.

Norris Hundley Jr., *Dividing the Waters: A Century of Controversy between the United States and Mexico* (Berkeley: University of California Press, 1966).

U.S. Senate, Committee on Foreign Relations, *Water Treaty with Mexico. Hearings before the Committee on Foreign Relations*, 79th Congress, 1st Session (Washington D.C.: U.S. Government Printing Office, 1945).

Evan R. Ward, "Two Rivers, Two Nations, One History: The Transformation of the Colorado River Delta since 1940," *Frontera Norte*, 22 (July–December 1999): 113–140.

Anita Alvarez de Williams, *Travelers Among the Cucapa* (Los Angeles: Dawson's Book Shop, 1975).

MISSISSIPPI RIVER

Who and what were responsible for the massive 1964 fishkill along the lower Mississippi River?

Viewpoint: Federal scientists determined that sloppy environmental management of the pesticide Endrin by a chemical company was to blame for the fishkill on the Mississippi River.

Viewpoint: No one was entirely responsible; but by focusing on management errors of a single company, the federal government avoided developing a broader public policy to protect overall water quality.

In March 1964 something killed more than five million fish in the lower Mississippi River, and Louisiana officials sought assistance from federal authorities in determining the cause. As they searched for a culprit, *The New York Times* reported that pesticides draining from farms were responsible. Coming on the heels of smaller fishkills in previous years, and shortly after the acclaimed publication of *Silent Spring* (1962), Rachel Carson's popular portrayal of the dangers of pesticide use, this deadly event sparked a debate that reverberated far beyond the cane and cotton fields of Louisiana. It revealed the contentiousness of environmental issues at the time and the sometimes inconclusiveness of science in resolving them.

This fishkill became a watershed event in environmental policy for several reasons and is thus worthy of closer consideration. It led public officials to discount the ability of massive streams such as the Mississippi to dilute unchecked releases of contaminants and shifted the focus from agricultural users of pesticides to manufacturers. Furthermore, the use of recently developed analytical techniques to detect organic chemicals in the water initiated a new era in water-quality assessment by acknowledging pollution was regional, and not just local, in its impact. As public officials sought to determine the cause of the fishkill, and unwittingly pushed through to another phase of water-quality protection, they encountered opposition and criticism. Using somewhat untested methods, scientists became key players in a subtle, but significant, public-policy shift.

Viewpoint: Federal scientists determined that sloppy environmental management of the pesticide Endrin by a chemical company was to blame for the fishkill on the Mississippi River.

Sugarcane farmers in Louisiana began applying Endrin to their fields in 1958. Used to combat the cane borer, this organic chemical offered exceptional control of the pest when applied several times during a growing season. Not long after its initial use, fishermen complained to the state wildlife agency that runoff was killing fish in the small streams that drained the sugarcane-growing region of the state. Typically, these events occurred when heavy rainfall washed the recently applied poison off the

Poisoned fish on the Mississippi River, circa 1964

cane plants and into adjacent creeks and bayous. As early as 1959 the Louisiana Stream Control Commission, the pollution-control body in the state, received almost daily reports of fishkills in waterways that drained the cane-producing region. Since these events were largely confined to the growing season (May to September) and to smaller streams, there was little official response. The lone adjustment called for by a government agency had little to do with environmental concerns. The U.S. Department of Agriculture, however, prohibited Endrin application forty-five days prior to the cane harvest to prevent any of the toxic chemical from finding its way into processed sugar.

Large fishkills that occurred outside the normal period of application called the lenient policies of the state into question. Beginning in November 1960 (during the cane-harvest season) and lasting into the following February, a spectacular kill wiped out more than three million fish in the Mississippi River and its principal distributary, the Atchafalaya. Affecting fish from as far north as the Arkansas-Louisiana border to near the mouths of the rivers, this event was much greater in terms of the number of fish affected, its geographic extent, and its duration. Since much of the damage occurred upstream from the cane-growing region, officials discounted the likelihood that Endrin was responsible. Lacking adequate analytical methods to test for trace quantities of this chemical, state and federal investigators were unable to pin the blame on the pesticide. In the absence of any other explanation, biologists reasoned that bacteria spreading downstream caused the fish to die off.

Smaller fishkills during the summers of 1961 and 1962 prompted Louisiana to restrict Endrin application, but this policy response did not halt environmental damage. The 1963–1964 event, the largest by far, captured the public's attention nationwide and prompted a more-vigorous response by state and federal officials. Beginning in late October

1963, fishermen and other observers began reporting that fish were acting "crazy" and dying in both the Mississippi and Atchafalaya Rivers. Fish mortality extended from near the northern boundary of Louisiana to marine waters beyond the mouths of the two rivers. By the end of February 1964, Louisiana biologists estimated that more than 5.1 million fish had died. Since the problem extended to the upstream extent of state boundaries, pollution-control officials called on the federal government to assist in determining the origin of the fishkill.

Armed with new analytical techniques unavailable in 1960, federal investigators set out to determine if Endrin, or other chemicals, were responsible. They initiated a three-pronged analysis for Endrin in fish flesh, river water, and streambed sediments. Water samples showed Endrin was present at West Memphis, Vicksburg, and New Orleans in fall 1963 and spring 1964. Bed sediment samples revealed concentrations much higher than in the water, with particularly high readings at locations in the vicinity of Memphis. Endrin also appeared in the blood and flesh of fish, sometimes at levels sufficient to cause a toxic reaction. The most perplexing element of the study was that the Endrin readings existed far upstream from the sugarcane-growing region. Indeed, the highest concentration from the fall of 1963 occurred at the West Memphis sampling station. U.S. Public Health Service (USPHS) scientists also considered other sources of the die-off, such as oxygen depletion, viruses, or other contaminants. No evidence supported the other possible causes.

The upstream reading led the USPHS to consider nonagricultural sources—namely Endrin producers. Velsicol Chemical Company was the only manufacturer of Endrin in the lower Mississippi River Valley and they came under immediate scrutiny. Investigators dispatched to the Memphis plant discovered that the company sent large quantities of industrial wastes, containing Endrin, in barrels to a nearby landfill. They observed that the containers leaked wastes that flowed into a Mississippi River tributary. Furthermore, Velsicol discharged liquid wastes into ditches and sewer lines that also drained into the river. High Endrin levels were found in the sediments of these drainage systems as well. Based on these observations, the USPHS concluded that the industrial wastes from Velsicol, and not agricultural runoff, were the principal cause of Endrin-related fishkills in Louisiana.

The timing of this discovery was fortunate for the agricultural chemical industry as a whole, but unfortunate for Velsicol in particular. Rachel Carson's account of environmental damage tied to agricultural chemicals, *Silent Spring* (1962), had put the public and U.S. Congress on alert. If the fishkills on the lower Mississippi resulted from agricultural runoff, then the entire industry was at risk. If sloppy housekeeping by one manufacturer was the cause, then the industry stood less chance of major policy revisions. Public hearings conducted in the wake of the fishkill allowed the USPHS to lay the blame on one company and its waste-management practices, thereby greatly softening the negative impact of the event.

Velsicol mounted an aggressive, although solo, counterattack, accusing the USPHS of shoddy science. How, it asked, could there be no major fishkill near the point of alleged release—where the chemicals would have been more concentrated? What mechanisms allowed the chemicals to travel a great distance before killing any sizable number of fish? Furthermore, they challenged the decision by USPHS to analyze bottom dwellers, such as catfish. They charged that this technique was misleading, since 96 percent of the affected fish were menhaden (*Brevoortia tyrannus*), a marine species. Although their arguments were compelling, there was little Velsicol could do or say to alter the government scientists' opinions.

In testimony before Congress and at public hearings conducted in the region, Velsicol made its case alone. Treated as a sacrificial lamb, Velsicol found no support from industrial trade groups. Facing pressure to reduce environmental threats, the industry as a whole embraced the discovery of trade wastes as the culprit. This approach meant that normal chemical application was not killing millions of fish and that Congress would not likely tighten regulations.

Following the government study, Tennessee authorities forced Velsicol to redirect its wastes to a remote land dump to prevent further fishkills. Even in the absence of regulation, production and use of Endrin dropped after 1964. This change eliminated potential problems that resulted from accidental releases or runoff, and indeed there were no subsequent events on the scale of 1963–1964.

Early concern with Endrin fishkills assumed that local releases caused the resulting damage. Officials paid little attention to distance sources. With the massive kill of 1963–1964, a distant source proved to be the culprit and this discovery forced public-health officials to reconsider the scale of analysis. Armed with new analytical methods, they were able to detect small quantities of toxic substances originating hundreds of miles from where fish were dying. This method demon-

ENDRIN POLLUTION IN THE LOWER MISSISSIPPI RIVER BASIN

Summary of Significant Findings

1. The solubility of endrin in water is difficult to determine; for the purpose of the study, 260 µp/1 was accepted as the "solubility" of endrin in water realizing that all of this was not true molecular solubility.

2. Endrin degrades at a slow but significant rate in cold or warm water under aerobic or anaerobic conditions.

3. Endrin is toxic to certain species of non-resistant fish (e.g. fat head minnow and channel catfish) in water concentrations of from 0.10 to 0.40 µg/1 as determined in field and laboratory tests.

4. Endrin is toxic to certain species of non-resistant fish (e.g. gizzard shad and bigmouth buffalo) where concentrations in the blood reach 0.10 to 0.28 µg/g depending on the species.*

5. Some fish develop a resistance to endrin and can survive with endrin concentration in their blood much higher than concentrations which kill non-resistant fish. Resistant fish were found at times at all sampling stations on the Mississippi and Atchafalaya Rivers.

6. The condition of endrin when it enters an aquatic environment is an important fact in determining its availability to the aquatic biota and, therefore, its potential toxicity to fish.

7. There were two significant sources of endrin in the study area: (1) the waste discharge of the Velsicol Chemical Corporation and (2) agricultural runoff.

8. Process waster discharges of the Velsicol Chemical Corporation were a more significant source of endrin pollution to the Mississippi River prior to November 1966 than thereafter.

9. A study of pesticide formulating plants and raw sugar factories showed that the wastes from these plants were not a significant source of endrin pollution to the Mississippi River.

10. Endrin concentrations in the Lower Mississippi River reached a maximum during the 1964 water year (Oct. 1, 1963 to Sept. 30, 1964).

11. On the average, endrin was relatively uniformly distributed over the length of the Lower Mississippi and Atchafalaya Rivers but was randomly distributed in the cross sections of these rivers.

12. Endrin concentrations in the waters of the estuarine areas of the Mississippi River were of the same magnitude as the water concentrations of the Mississippi River.

13. The production and use of endrin declined after 1964.

14. Mean concentrations of endrin in the blood of fresh water fish declined after March 1966 as compared to most previous sampling periods.

15. Endrin concentrations in the blood of salt water fish taken from the estuarine area of the Mississippi River were of the same magnitude as endrin concentration in the blood of fresh water fish taken from the same river.

16. No endrin caused fishkills occurred in the Mississippi or Atchafalaya Rivers after the fall and winter months of 1963–64.

17. In the tributaries to the Mississippi River, two fishkills occurred in the waters of the Wolf River in 1965 where the endrin in the blood of dead or dying fish exceeded the minimum lethal concentrations. However, in both instances, the dissolved oxygen in the river was zero.

18. A three year fish survey of the Mississippi an Atchafalaya Rivers showed that the fish populations of these two rivers have recovered from any effects of the 1963–64 fishkills except for an apparent paucity of fish in the larger size groups of the more long lived species.

19. A favorable commercial and sport fish population exists in the Mississippi and Atchafalaya Rivers.

20. Endrin was found in oysters taken from the Louisiana estuarine areas but in concentrations reported as insignificant from a public health standpoint.

22. The shallow burial of waste endrin at a farm in Hardeman County, Tennessee, has contaminated portions of both the surface and subsurface environment at the disposal site and in Pugh Creek as far as 1½ miles downstream from the site. A substantial portion of the local water-table aquifer, which is the potential source of local domestic water supplies,+ is exposed to the hazard of contamination from the water disposal pits.

* All blood data are reported on a wet weight basis.

+ There are no known domestic water wells in this 150 acre area.

Source: *U.S. Department of the Interior, Federal Water Pollution Control Administration,* Lower Mississippi River Technical Assistance Project, Baton Rouge, Louisiana, *June 1969.*

strated that the Mississippi was unable adequately to dilute these potent toxins and that monitoring had to involve a substantial territory. Subsequent policy sought to incorporate these critical ideas about toxic pollutants.

Despite massive evidence, government scientists encountered strong opposition—but from only one party. In the absence of an industry-wide objection, the contested conclusions of the government stood.

–CRAIG E. COLTEN, LOUISIANA STATE UNIVERSITY

Viewpoint: No one was entirely responsible; but by focusing on management errors of a single company, the federal government avoided developing a broader public policy to protect overall water quality.

Federal and state authorities apparently were satisfied when they concluded their hearings on chemical contamination in the lower Mississippi in the early 1960s. Diligent investigations had identified a lone culprit, and subsequent local action prompted the polluting party to divert its waste away from the river. Indeed, no comparable aquatic calamities occurred in subsequent years. Yet, one must question the effectiveness of this "sacrificial lamb" policy. Public concern with agriculture chemicals was mildly distracted by this situation; redirecting the waste of Velsicol Chemical Company to a land sink ultimately contributed to groundwater contamination; and drinking-water supplies continued to carry the chemical to households in New Orleans. The discussion of the 1963–1964 fishkill and the events it spawned should not be read as success in environmental management, but as delay in formulating other water-related public policies. Indeed, there were contrasting viewpoints to the actions taken in the wake of the massive pollution incident.

Velsicol offered the most vocal dissent and emphatically argued that the government scientists overlooked glaringly obvious evidence in their rush to identify a culprit. First, the company challenged the use of gas chromatography to pinpoint the chemical responsible for the die-offs. The vice president for research for Velsicol claimed that at best the technique yielded only estimates of unknown materials and not conclusive readings of a particular pesticide, as the government alleged. He charged that government analysis of sludge from the company indicated a pesticide that they did not produce in greater concentration. By implication, in his view, this analysis undermined the Endrin reading.

Velsicol also critiqued the U.S. Public Health Service (USPHS) scientists' work on the absence of fishkills near Memphis—where the concentration, in theory, should have been greatest. Endrin is not water soluble, but it could be absorbed by solids such as the sediments in the river. Extremely high concentrations existed in the drainage ditch that carried the waste to the Mississippi, but within a few miles downstream, Velsicol argued, the river water thoroughly dissipated the chemical. The producers' strongest point on this issue was the absence of fishkills in the vicinity of Memphis. Government scientists, indeed, did not specifically respond to this argument—other than to assert that they found Endrin in dead fish's flesh far downstream.

Velsicol offered testimony of an aquatic biologist who had examined the symptoms of dead river fish that he compared to fish killed by Endrin in a laboratory experiment. The fish in his aquarium did not exhibit similar symptoms to the dead fish in the Mississippi River, and therefore he concluded that the actual fishkill resulted from another cause.

Although Velsicol put forward considerable other evidence and took its stand against the government agencies alone, they were unsuccessful in their challenge—despite offering some reasonable doubts. Most importantly, the arguments of Velsicol suggested there were other chemicals at work in the environment and hence additional sources that were at least involved, if not wholly responsible, for the situation. At the time, their argument was largely ignored. Policy, consequently, ignored other chemicals for the time.

The scapegoat remedy produced questionable public policy responses to the Mississippi River fishkill. Two major outcomes were: the diversion of the waste to a landfill far from the river and the downplaying of public-health threats presented by chemicals in drinking water.

Velsicol, at the prompting of local officials, redirected its effluent to a landfill in nearby Hardeman County, Tennessee. Almost immediately, citizens in the area expressed concern. They challenged the safety of waste-hauling trucks passing through their rural neighborhood and government officials questioned the advisability of land disposal in an area where residents drew their drinking water from wells. Despite dumping millions of gallons of liquid chemicals in highly permeable sandy soil, Velsicol contended its disposal site was geologically "tight" (impermeable) and that its wastes resembled asphalt. Later proved wrong, these contentions suggested the wastes would remain where buried and not cause environmental damages. Only a few years after Velsicol commenced land dumping, and in response to public concern, the U.S. Geology Survey sent a team to scrutinize the relationship between these wastes and groundwater. Federal scientists concluded in 1967 that a sizable plume of contaminants had already spread from the dump and that the main rural aquifer was endangered. Subsequent legal action against Velsicol further demonstrated the impact of its action to domestic wells and the groundwater near its disposal site. Yet, the policy that forced Velsicol to divert its waste from the river to the land had not found the "ultimate sink" and had already done its damage by the time the courts became involved.

The Louisiana Department of Wildlife and Fisheries hosted the principal water-pollution-control authority in the state—the Stream Control Commission. As the lead investigative agency of the Endrin situation, it focused exclusively on the fishkill. Even though federal investigators went beyond the aquatic species and tested drinking water in New Orleans, where they found a small concentration of the pesticide, this discovery did not alarm state officials. Instead, they took the position that the concentration was inconsequential. This ruling remained a pat response to pollution, as demonstrated by the battle of the city and state against evidence of organic-chemical contamination in the city water supply a decade later. By attributing the Endrin damage to one source and then making that company divert its wastes to a land dump, federal officials deflected concern about any and all chemicals finding their way into urban drinking water. They also downplayed the general impact of agricultural chemicals on public water supplies.

Even though completely overwhelmed by the massive damage of the fishkill of 1963–1964, Louisiana officials accepted the federal argument that controlling wastes from Velsicol would eliminate the problem. Jointly, the government agencies sacrificed one producer to offset a larger environmental problem. The arguments of Velsicol, although dismissed by government scientists, illustrated the need to take other chemicals and sources into consideration. Moreover, despite the fact that the Endrin fishkill effectively enlarged analysis to larger stream basins and directed attention to industrial wastes, it undercut the momentum of other efforts to regulate agricultural chemical use and to protect drinking-water supplies. Finding one culprit was the easy solution and delayed effective policy on other fronts. Yet, Velsicol was not pure and beyond blame. Certainly its actions and deceptions at its Hardeman County dump called into question its prior accusations of bad government science. Nonetheless, the actions of the public agencies was narrow and missed an opportunity to link, rather than separate, environmental problems with policy solutions.

—CRAIG E. COLTEN, LOUISIANA STATE UNIVERSITY

References

Rachel Carson, *Silent Spring* (Boston: Houghton Mifflin, 1962).

Craig E. Colten, ed., *Transforming New Orleans and Its Environs: Centuries of Change* (Pittsburgh: University of Pittsburgh Press, 2000).

T. A. DeRouen and J. E. Diem, "The New Orleans Drinking Water Controversy: A Statistical Perspective," *American Journal of Public Health,* 65 (October 1975): 1060–1062.

Robert H. Harris and Edward M. Brecher, "Is the Water Safe to Drink?" *Consumer Reports,* 39 (June 1974): 436–443.

Donald R. Rima, and others, *Potential Contamination of the Hydrologic Environment from the Pesticide Waste Dump in Hardeman County, Tennessee* (Washington, D.C.: U.S. Geological Survey, Administrative Report to the Federal Water Pollution Control Administration, 1967).

Sterling v. *Velsicol* (1986), 647 F. Supp. 303.

Joel A. Tarr, "The Search for the Ultimate Sink: Urban Air, Land, and Water Pollution in Historical Perspective," *Records of the Columbia Historical Society of Washington, D.C.,* 51 (1984): 1–29.

U.S. Department of Health, Education and Welfare, *Proceedings: Conference in the Matter of Pollution of the Interstate Waters of the Lower Mississippi River,* volumes 1–4 (Washington, D.C.: U.S. Department of Health, Education, and Welfare, 1964).

U.S. Department of the Interior, Federal Water Pollution Control Administration, *Endrin Pollution in the Lower Mississippi River Basin. Dallas, Texas* (Washington, D.C.: U.S. Government Printing Office, 1969).

NATIVE AMERICAN RESERVATIONS

Should Native Americans govern water and land resources on reservations that are home to a significant number of non-Indians?

Viewpoint: Non-Indian people who live within the exterior boundaries of Indian reservations should not be subject to the jurisdiction of tribal governments without their consent.

Viewpoint: Native Americans, who were forced to give up most of their land, should exercise jurisdictional sovereignty over their reservations.

On 8 September 2000, at a ceremony marking the 175th anniversary of the Bureau of Indian Affairs (BIA), Kevin Gover, head of the agency and a member of the Pawnee Tribe, issued a formal apology for the mistreatment of Native Americans by the BIA for its complicity in what Gover called "the ethnic cleansing that befell the Western tribes." Somehow American Indians managed to survive these oppressive policies and today inhabit over three hundred reservations. They consider these reservations to be their permanent homelands, and they want to exercise jurisdiction over these lands and their associated water resources. However, Indian reservations have for more than a century also been home to many non-Indians; almost as many non-Indians live on reservations as Indians.

Because they lack a voice in tribal decisions, these people feel threatened by tribal control over their lands, and they oppose efforts by tribes and the federal government to give tribal governments sovereign control throughout reservations: "Many thousands of non-Indians are being driven from their homes, lands, and businesses just as Indians were forced from theirs over a century ago," argues Darrel Smith in *Indian Reservations: America's Model of Destruction* (1997). "Federal Indian policy is patiently cleansing reservations of non-Indians. This country is engaged in a quiet, legal, bloodless, politically-correct form of ethnic cleansing." Thus, both sides raise the specter of ethnic cleansing to justify their position. In addition, both sides want to control the one resource that makes Western land valuable and productive: water.

In an oft-arid landscape, who controls "white gold" controls the fate of the land and the people it sustains, a matter of considerable concern ever since the conclusion of the U.S. Civil War in 1865. In the postwar years, the U.S. Army moved out onto the Western Plains to assert control over indigenous populations. Through military power, and the creation of a system of reservations in which Indians were forced, along with the destruction of the buffalo, the construction of railroads, and the vast surge of population into the newly "liberated" terrain, new forms of land-use management had come into play. This transformation accelerated with the enactment of the General Allotment (or Dawes) Act of 1887, which marked the conclusion of the reservation period. The act allotted 160 acres to each Indian and declared the remaining lands to be "surplus," and thus open to sale to non-Indians. In doing so, it began to shrink the amount of land under individual ownership, which many white reformers justified by noting that with the introduction of irrigation to the arid West, Native American tribes required even less land for their maintenance. Moreover, these irrigated and independent farmsteads were supposed to assimilate the Indians into American culture.

Under the BIA's direction, Indian laborers constructed hundreds of miles of ditches and canals, but the chief beneficiaries of these irrigation projects were the white farmers who had purchased "surplus" allotments on the reservations; whites owned approximately two-thirds of the 700,000 acres that the BIA made arable. The Dawes Act, one U.S. senator concluded in 1914, had relegated the Indian to labor "with his bare hands. The white man could not make a success under similar circumstances."

Since 1887 disputes on reservations over water and property rights have intensified. The sources of tension are many, and depend in part on historic inequities between white and Indian irrigators. There are also deep concerns about political equity: tribal governments that seek greater control over resources such as water often are constrained by Western and federal laws; whites who live on the reservations chafe at the imposition of tribal authority over their irrigation practices, for they do not have representation in the governance of the reservations. To develop an equitable distribution of water and power will require Indians and whites to confront the past, mitigate its shameful legacies, and fashion new, cooperative ventures.

Editor's Note: Christopher Columbus mistakenly named the peoples he encountered in 1492 *Indians,* a term that persists in modern statutes, case law, and use on many reservations. Recent literature sometimes replaces *Indian* with the term *Native American.* For consistency, the authors of the essays that follow have generally used the word *Indian.* No endorsement of Columbus is intended.

Viewpoint: Non-Indian people who live within the exterior boundaries of Indian reservations should not be subject to the jurisdiction of tribal governments without their consent.

About twenty-five miles north of Missoula, Montana, Highway 93 comes over the crest and descends into the Jocko Valley. The crest marks the southern border of the Flathead Indian Reservation, home of the confederated Salish, Kootenai, and Pend Oreille tribes. Traveling north in September 1999, I was drawn back to my prior travels on Highway 93. Each venture into the reservation teaches me more about the Flathead Irrigation Project, which sprawls over 125,000 acres south of Flathead Lake. Each trip underscores the contradictions of federal Indian history and the looming disputes over management of reserved water rights. More than 85 percent of the land in the Flathead "Indian" Irrigation Project is owned by those who do not belong to the tribe. Fewer than one-fourth of the 25,000 residents on the reservation are tribal members. Like the glacial moraines that underlie its rich farmland, confused landholdings and water-rights disputes in Flathead defy simple explanation. How did our history deposit such confusion and conflict on the land? Who should control the destiny of this project–its waters, lands, and people? These increasingly urgent questions afflict Indian irrigation projects throughout the West.

To understand the present, one must look first at the evolution of federal Indian law. The laws of the young United States attempted to separate Indian and non-Indian cultures. In the early nineteenth century "Indian Territory" was an enclave beyond state boundaries and set aside for the exclusive use of Native Americans. In Indian Territory only federal officials and federally licensed Indian traders could look for protection from the United States. As westward settlement unfolded, conflict broke out between tribes and between tribes and settlers. The "enclave" policy gradually changed to one aimed at assimilating Indians into the national fabric. In 1887 the Dawes Severalty Act sought to "advance the civilization and improvement of the Indians and to encourage habits of industry and thrift among them." For many reservations in the Northwest, a key mechanism was to grant land allotments to Indians to encourage settlement and farming. The individual allotment would remain protected in federal trust for twenty-five years, after which it would become subject to state taxes and other laws. In addition, large amounts of reservation lands were opened to homesteading by non-Indians. The policy of the Dawes era was the eventual assimilation of the Indian population and a gradual elimination of reservations. On the Flathead Reservation, these land policies led to a growing non-Indian population. In the irrigable lands of the reservation core, land ownership became a "checkerboard," with Indian lands interspersed among non-Indian towns and farm districts.

In the Indian Reorganization Act of 1934, Congress halted the allotment process and sought to strengthen tribal governments. Federal oversight of the reservations, however, continued. Land-claims legislation in 1946 allowed courts to award per capita payments to individual Indians, based on the loss of land and water rights. Flathead tribes recovered substantial amounts for lost lands and water rights.

Flathead Lake in western Montana

(Photograph by Marc Gaede)

World War II and the postwar economic growth revived the assimilation process. Many Indians relocated to the cities. Congress declared that they should be subject to the same laws as all other citizens, and, through "termination," sought to end federal wardship for tribes. Along with several other reservations dominated by nonmembers, the Flathead Reservation was proposed for termination, with proceeds from sale of tribal trust lands to be distributed among individuals. Flathead was eventually dropped from the termination list, but the tribe continued to assimilate into Montana politics, sending a Supreme Court justice and several legislators to the state capitol. Because of increased intermarriage with the nonmember population, the tribe reduced the quantum of tribal blood required for membership.

While Congress modified the law of reservation lands, courts developed a water rights doctrine intended to encourage Indian agriculture. The theory of federal "reserved water rights" is inconsistent with water law of the western states. Under both federal and state law, no one owns water in a stream. State water rights, however, must be used continuously and beneficially, which generally means diversion and consumption for irrigation, domestic, or industrial purposes. Federal public-land law encouraged settlers to irrigate the arid West and specifically protected state water rights based on continuous beneficial use–for example, diversion, irrigation, or consumption.

The reserved-rights doctrine emerged during the Dawes Act period to protect Indian irrigators from adjacent non-Indian use. The decision in *Winters* v. *United States* (1908) protected potential future tribal water use by implying a reserved-water right that would be quantified by the purpose of the reservation, rather than history of actual beneficial use. In 1963 the Supreme Court, in *Arizona* v. *California,* quantified the reserved right for five Lower Colorado River reservations based on their "practicably irrigable acreage." The Court has never required the federal government, however, to build or fund irrigation projects on Indian reservations so that irrigable acreage can practicably be used. Federal funds for new irrigation projects are increasingly unlikely. The result is that the reserved right remains inchoate and unrealized and is a cloud on non-Indian water use.

Early in the twentieth century, federal funds were secured to allow tribes to begin irrigation of reservation lands. On Flathead, as on other Dawes Act (or "open") reservations, Indian irrigation projects were begun in the 1920s. On those reservations with robust agricultural activity, however, most "Indian" irrigation projects that obtained federal funding actually turned out to have non-Indians as principal beneficiaries of the federal program.

A 1928 federal survey found that 68 percent of the acreage in western Indian irrigation projects was farmed by non-Indians. The survey criticized the Dawes Act policy of trying to force Indians into farming:

> Another defect in the allotting system is that it is based on the assumption that it is possible to make of every Indian a farmer. This is no more possible or desirable among Indians than it is among people of our own race. . . . All the larger and more prosperous of the Indian Irrigation Projects are as a matter of fact, not Indian, but white projects. On such projects as the Yakima, Flathead, Crow, Wind River, Uintah and Fort Hall, most of the farming is being done by whites.

From the start, irrigators chafed at Bureau of Indian Affairs (BIA) control of these projects. In 1928 "the universal complaint more less insistent on the part of the non-Indians on every project is 'taxation without representation.' They bewail the fact that they are required to pay irrigation charges but have no voice in the management of the work." These complaints–of lack of control and faraway decision making based on old policies–were mirrored by those of the tribes. Objections on both sides have only deepened through the twentieth century.

The tribes and the irrigators both rely on the rhetoric of "self-determination." I first heard these complaints in July 1986, when I attended a public hearing on the Flathead Indian Irrigation Project held by then Senator John Melcher (D-Montana). Melcher's meeting in the Ronan high-school gym attracted some six hundred angry irrigators. Speaker after speaker attacked the BIA for ignoring irrigator concerns in a report on the Flathead Indian Irrigation Project. Few of the irrigators were tribal members. The biggest concern was control of canal maintenance, roads, and water deliveries. In addition the tribe had recently obtained control of $9 million in Kerr Dam hydroelectric revenues, threatening the repayment capacity of the irrigation project. From the irrigators' perspective the tribe was seeking to control the water, revenues, and operations of an irrigation project in which the tribe had little economic stake. Hard questions were asked: how could a federal government dedicated to racial equality allow a genetically defined minority to assert control over the local majority? What about self-determination for the farmers whose livelihood depended on the irrigation project? Was not the country founded on the consent of the governed?

After a few hours, I left Melcher's meeting with the irrigators and went to a similar angry rally at tribal headquarters in Pablo, ten miles up Highway 93. Tribal members were frustrated because Melcher was meeting with the irrigators and not with them. The tribe had used its Kerr Dam hydroelectric revenues to hire fishery biologists to document the effect of irrigation diversions on bull trout in the Jocko River. When the BIA curtailed irrigation diversions benefit fish, the tribe helped defeat the irrigator's lawsuits. The tribe had its own hard questions. Should the irrigators be allowed to use a statewide and national political majority to control local resources–water, fish, and land–that rightfully belonged to the tribe? If the tribe was a sovereign government, where was the respect it was due from federal agents? Should not the tribe have self-determination within its own reservation?

The bitter Flathead dispute will lead again to court battles. After twenty years of preparation, the Flathead tribes and the irrigators are now on the verge of a general stream adjudication that will quantify thousands of water rights in the Irrigation Project, including federal reserved-water rights. This massive lawsuit, likely to last for decades and cost millions, will quantify the amounts of water to which different categories of checkerboard land are entitled: allotted lands owned by tribal members subject to federal trust, lands owned by tribal members not in trust, fee lands owned by nonmembers derived from an Indian allotment, and fee lands based on early homestead claims. However the quantification lawsuit comes out, a key unsettled legal issue is the inherent sovereign powers of the tribe to administer or regulate non-Indian water use on the lands within the project. Should the tribe have regulatory authority over 85 percent of the project owned by non-Indians? The doctrinal roots of that unsettled legal issue reach back to the earliest Supreme Court Indian law decisions.

Two conflicting and unresolved views of inherent tribal authority to regulate nonmember lands on the open reservations weave through two hundred years of federal Indian law. Both have a basis in history and reflect the present diverse population patterns on reservations. One, the "internal regulation" doctrine, limits tribal powers to its members and trust lands. A competing doctrine, the "territorial regulation" view, extends tribal powers to the entire reservation, including the lands of nonmembers.

Both the internal and territorial views of tribal power conflict with some aspects of modern reservation life. The internal doctrine is inconsistent with tribal self-governance on traditional enclave reservations, such as Hopi or Pyramid Lake. On these reservations the dominant Indian culture may conflict with non-Indian concepts of governance. For example, some Pueblos maintain a theocracy, or have little intermarriage with non-Indians. With few nonmember residents and minimal fee lands, these reservations encompass a uniquely Indian culture and economy. If these

TRIBES EYE CONTROL OVER WATER RIGHTS

HELENA (AP) — The Confederated Salish and Kootenai Tribes proposed Wednesday that tribal government take jurisdiction of water rights for all people on the Flathead Indian Reservation, including rights now administered by the state.

The tribes' proposal is the first step in negotiating a water-rights compact involving the state, tribal and federal governments.

The proposal Wednesday surprised state officials, who were meeting with tribal representatives for the second time to negotiate a water-rights compact.

Tribal officials said the proposal will be put in writing by Nov. 1, and they requested a meeting in December to hear the state's response.

Chris Tweeten, chairman of the Montana Reserved Water Rights Compact Commisssion and the state's chief representative in the water-rights negotiations, said that the time frame was far too short.

Tweeten said the issue requires the public have an opportunity to comment, and the commission cannot schedule public meetings until after the 2001 legislative session, which begins in January and will end this spring. During the next few months, the commission will be busy preparing another water agreement, involving the Fort Belknap tribes, for presentation to the Legislature.

A federal negotiator at the meeting, Chris Kenny of the Bureau of Indian Affairs, said the proposal by the Salish and Kootenai tribes merits serious consideration and appears consistent with federal policy on tribal sovereignty.

The tribes indicated they can be trusted to look out for nontribal interest. They cited their record in managing Mission Valley Power—the Flathead Indian Reservation's federally owned electric utility—and their management of fishing and upland bird hunting for non-Indians on the reservation.

"We want a level of protection for (water) users that currently exists under state law," Tweeten said.

Source: The Billings Gazette, *15 September 2000.*

tribes exercise self-determination, they will generally affect only those non-Indians who have chosen to have consensual relations with the tribe.

Conversely, the territorial doctrine is inconsistent with the demography of open reservations such as Flathead, where nonmembers predominate. These reservations have towns incorporated under state law. For example, the Agua Caliente reservation includes checkerboard tribal lands under the hotels in downtown Palm Springs. As Justice Anthony Kennedy has noted, "a basic attribute of full territorial sovereignty is the power to enforce laws against all who come within the sovereign's territory, whether citizens or aliens. . . . The tribes can no longer be described as sovereigns in this sense. Rather . . . the retained sovereignty of the tribes is that needed to control their own internal relations and to preserve their own unique customs and social order." Because tribal governments are not subject to the Bill of Rights, and nonmembers cannot vote for or sue the tribe, the Supreme Court has rejected "an extension of tribal authority over those who have not given the consent of the governed that provides a fundamental basis for power within our constitutional system." The Court has allowed a limited exception that allows the tribes to protect self-government if the nonmember conduct has a direct effect on the health or welfare of the tribe. The scope of this exception is unclear, particularly as applied to water-rights administration, which should follow hydrologic boundaries. The question is whether state law or tribal law should be the background for regulation of non-Indian lands. One court recently allowed the Flathead tribes to set water-quality standards for the entire reservation. Elsewhere in the West, courts have rejected a tribal claim to enforce water quantity or quality regulation directly against a nonmember's lands.

Can the mistakes of history be resolved to benefit future generations? Indian water settlements elsewhere in the West have finessed the issue of water-rights administration by setting it aside. Water settlements on Fort Peck and Fort Hall reservations, for example, have allowed dual water administration both by the state (for the substantial non-Indian populace) and by the tribe (for its members), along with a dispute resolution process. Conversely, on the open Wind River Reservation, litigation over water-rights administration continues twenty years after the general stream adjudication began.

One thread of Indian policy is to encourage tribal self-determination. How that policy is applied on an open reservation such as Flathead is a recurrent question. What is the duty of the federal government to ensure that tribal self-determination does not impair the water rights of the nonmembers who have lived on the reservation for many generations? Does a federal obligation for mutual self-determination arise where conflicting federal policies have engendered a century of conflict?

Although the Flathead Reservation is relatively productive, its lands and people bear the scars of changing federal Indian policies. On Flathead there is no agreement about the history of the land and its waters, rather, a deepening polarization between the tribe and the irrigators. Neither seeks permanent harm to the Flathead Irrigation Project; neither is likely to abandon lands occupied by earlier generations. The struggle over water is really a struggle for control. The important decisions about intensely local issues–water use, environmental protection, and personal governance–are made in distant cities, based on policies of the past. One result is a bitter victim mentality for both Indians and irrigators. Success in this polarized context has meant "end running" neighbors to influence a decision in Denver, Helena, Portland, or Washington, D.C. If past patterns continue, local polarization will deepen each time one side seeks out a decision maker somewhere else.

Novelist Wallace Stegner challenged westerners to outgrow their origins in individualism by learning cooperation. Perhaps the tribes and the irrigators will find a common destiny in wresting local control of water from distant bureaucracies and courts. Perhaps it will be possible for the people who live on Flathead to preserve and enhance their rich water resources without seeking dominion over each other. On the Flathead checkerboard, as elsewhere in the West, the challenge remains: Can one respect the past without repeating its mistakes?

–PETER W. SLY, OAKLAND, CALIFORNIA

Viewpoint: Native Americans, who were forced to give up most of their land, should exercise jurisdictional sovereignty over their reservations.

The view of Flathead Lake from KwataqNuk Resort in Polson, Montana, is spectacular. The lake is sandwiched between the rocky massif of the Mission Range on the east and the dark green slopes of the Salish Mountains on the west. The Flathead Valley, verdant and well watered, is the picture of peace and serenity. But that is an illusion. The land splayed out between the mountains appears to be a continuous sweep of forest and field, but in fact it is an irrational checkerboard of Indian, private, state, and federal land. A greater administrative and political nightmare could hardly be imagined. How did this seemingly peaceful valley become such a bewildering patchwork of conflicting jurisdictions?

The Salish and Kootenai people once lived throughout a large region in the northern Rockies. When Meriwether Lewis and William Clark encountered the Salish in 1805, they found them to be friendly and generous. Joseph Whitehouse, a member of their expedition, wrote that the Salish Indians were "the likelyest and honestst Savages we have ever Seen [sic]." The irony that these amiable, good-hearted people were referred to as savages was apparently lost to Whitehouse, but it is indicative of conflicting American attitudes toward Native Americans.

Despite their generosity to Lewis and Clark, the Salish people did not escape the gradual loss of land and freedom that befell every Native American tribe in the United States in the nineteenth century. Through purchase, fraud, or force of arms, Indian land became non-Indian land until only small remnants remained. These small remnants, called Indian reservations, were set aside for Native Americans, and in most cases, were promised as permanent homelands for the exclusive use of a specific tribe or tribes. These promises, however, were broken in nearly every case, as land-hungry settlers demanded that Indian land be made available to white people.

One of the instruments facilitating this massive land grab was the General Allotment Act of 1887 (the Dawes Severalty Act). This law provided for the subdivision of Indian reservations into 160-acre private parcels for individual tribal members, the remaining "surplus" land was to be sold to whites; often this land was the best farm acreage on the reservation. Subsequent laws "opened" Indian reservations to white settlement, thus allowing even more tracts of land to become white-owned. These laws were a disaster for Native Americans and clearly violated many treaties and guarantees that the United States had made to Indian people.

The loss of Native American land in Montana was particularly severe. The following table indicates the total acreage of Indian reservations in Montana, and the amount of land that remains in trust status, meaning land that is held by the tribe as a whole and has not been sold or allotted. The table also shows the relative population of whites and Indians on these reservations:

Indian Reservation	Total Acreage	Trust Acreage	Non-Indian Population	Indian Population
Blackfeet	937,838	302,072	8,549	7,025
Crow	1,517,406	408,444	6,370	4,724
Fort Belknap	588,756	188,017	2,508	2,338
Fort Peck	904,683	391,769	10,595	5,782
Rocky Boy's	108,334	108,334	1,954	1,882
N. Cheyenne	436,948	318,072	3,923	3,542
Flathead	627,070	518,907	21,259	5,130

Some reservations, such as Rocky Boy's and Fort Belknap, lost little land because there was not much acreage that was suitable for farming (and therefore attractive to white settlers). But reservations that contained well-watered lands with agricultural potential lost enormous tracts, which were even greater if an "Indian" irrigation project had been constructed, providing even greater inducement for white politicians to demand that the government sell that land to non-Indians, with the accompanying water supply. Thus, in a perverse way, water became an inducement to land loss—the better the water supply, the more non-Indians coveted Indian land.

This situation is what happened at Flathead Lake, a reservation that has a much better water supply, because of higher rainfall and a government irrigation project, than many other reservations. Nearly all irrigation project lands (85 percent) at Flathead ended up in the hands of non-Indians—a process the Indian commissioner in 1915 called a "great injustice." As a result, much of the reservation now belongs to non-Indians, and the Native American population is overwhelmed by whites. Under such conditions, how can Native Americans protect their land and water rights and still maintain a meaningful level of control over their reservation? The answer, in regard to land, has been the development of a form of government that extends tribal controls over the territorial limits of the reservation, thus giving them powers over lands that lie within the outermost boundaries of the reservation.

In regard to water, tribal control has been supported by the development of a doctrine of water law, decided in *Winters* v. *United States* (1908), of federal reserved-water rights. It is important to understand that the Winters Doctrine, as it came to be known, was created to help Native Americans survive on the remnants of their traditional lands. It states that, when lands were reserved for Indians, sufficient water was also reserved to meet the purposes of the reservation. Without reserved-water rights, Native American tribes would be overwhelmed by their non-Indian neighbors both on and off the reservation.

The ability to control water goes hand in hand with control over land—a basic fact anywhere in the world. That is why tribes place such great emphasis on territorial sovereignty; it gives them the power to resist the loss of cultural and political identity, and protect the natural resources that are necessary to life and a viable economy.

The Salish and Kootenai of the Flathead Reservation feel that they should have control, exercised through a federally recognized tribal government, over their reservation and its water resources. The policy of Indian self-governance, authorized in the 1975 Indian Self-Determination Act, replaced a much more repressive and paternalistic policy where the BIA ruled the reservations as a virtual dictator. Self-determination provided a new horizon for Native Americans, allowing them to preserve their culture and their homelands in a manner that best met their needs.

This movement toward Native American control of Indian reservations was vociferously opposed by some non-Indians, especially those who lived within the exterior boundaries of reservations. According to the 1990 census, about three hundred thousand non-Indians lived on reservations in the United States. With innocuous sounding names such as Dakotans for Equal Rights, and Totally Equal Americans, these groups sought to dramatically limit the power of tribal governments; indeed, some of them would have liked to see tribal governments dismantled altogether. Although there were legitimate concerns expressed by these groups, a tone of anti-Indian racism ran through much of their public discourse. At a public meeting at Flathead Lake, regarding hunting and fishing rights on the reservation, one local Anglo said: "I will guarantee the state and the tribe that if I see and catch an Indian officer . . . on my land, they can expect to not survive. Maybe this sounds like I'm racist and a radical. I'm just a white landowner who has been pushed into a corner by a minority of Indian assholes, dictating to a majority of whites." I doubt most whites living on or near reservations embody such racist and violent sentiments, but this quote illustrates the hostility that exists between many whites and Indians.

In regard to Indian water rights, this high level of hostility was expressed through a long series of legal confrontations. The courts have attempted in vain to clearly define and quantify Indian rights to water. These decisions pleased no one and simply resulted in more litigation. Beginning in the 1980s, the federal government initiated a policy of negotiating settlements to these vexing water conflicts. By the end of the century, fifteen settlements had been signed, and although about half experienced serious difficulties, there have been success stories.

Negotiated water and land settlements have made it obvious that seemingly intractable conflicts can be resolved if a proper forum for dispute resolution is provided. The first step in this process is to recognize the legitimacy of both sides' claims. In regard to water negotiations, non-Indian users and their allies in state and local governments have, in many cases for the first time, acknowledged the Winters Doctrine and the legitimacy of tribal claims. This situation was necessary before any progress could be made. Western states have finally recognized that Indian reservations are permanent players in the high stakes game of Western water resources.

Lessons learned from the settlement negotiations, and the continuing debate over tribal sovereignty and related land and water issues, indicate that significant policy innovations are in order. Some possible remedies might include:

1) The federal government should pursue an aggressive policy of purchasing non-Indian land on reservations to help mitigate the damage done by the allotment era and the opening of reservations. Lands purchased from willing sellers at market price would give non-Indians the option of removing themselves from tribal rule and allow tribal governments to consolidate their holdings.

2) In situations where there is a significant concentration of non-Indian lands on a reservation, especially town sites and private homes, agreements should be negotiated with tribes to remove these areas from the reservations in exchange for land of equal or greater value adjacent to or near the reservation.

3) The federal government, as part of its trust responsibility, should act to prevent further diversions of water that are clearly a threat to future reserved-water-rights claims, which could be done through either negotiated settlements or litigation.

4) Federal water policy should encourage more efficient use of water resources and eliminate subsidies for water-intensive irrigation. Economically viable farming operations would survive this change in policy; money-losing operations would not. This situation would free up significant amounts of water, to be used to mitigate past damage, and to provide the water "currency" necessary for successful settlement negotiations.

There will be no easy or cost-free solutions to the mistakes of the past. Americans must recognize that the past mistreatment of Native Americans was, in many respects, shameful. They must begin to mitigate the impact of those policies through an assertive policy of protecting Native American land, water, and tribal sovereignty. America took 99 percent of what the Indians had; the least we could do is help them protect the 1 percent that remains.

–DANIEL MCCOOL, UNIVERSITY OF UTAH

References

Lloyd Burton, *American Indian Water Rights and the Limits of Law* (Lawrence: University Press of Kansas, 1991).

Elizabeth Checchio and Bonnie G. Colby, *Indian Water Rights: Negotiating the Future* (Tucson: Water Resources Research Center, University of Arizona, College of Agriculture, 1993).

Indian Data Center, Internet website.

Daniel McCool, *Command of the Waters: Iron Triangles, Federal Water Development, and Indian Water* (Berkeley: University of California Press, 1987).

Thomas R. McGuire, William B. Lord, and Mary G. Wallace, eds., *Indian Water in the New West* (Tucson: University of Arizona Press, 1993).

John Shurts, *Indian Reserved Water Rights: The Winters Doctrine in its Social and Legal Context, 1880s–1930s* (Norman: University of Oklahoma Press, 2000).

Peter W. Sly, *Reserved Water Rights Settlement Manual* (Washington, D.C.: Island Press, 1988).

NUCLEAR-POWER PLANTS

How did water issues affect the regulation of nuclear-power plants in the United States?

Viewpoint: Water-quality issues significantly altered the character of nuclear regulation in the United States by generating new federal legislation and industrial reform, as well as undermining confidence in the environmental benefits of nuclear power.

Viewpoint: The system of local and state laws and regulations that governed water use in the United States democratized and decentralized the regulation of nuclear power.

In the United States of the late 1940s the use of atomic power was at once appealing and repellent. The detonation of atomic bombs over Hiroshima (6 August 1945) and Nagasaki (9 August 1945), and the subsequent obliteration of those Japanese cities, brought World War II (1939–1945) to an end. It also sparked a dangerous arms race, however, as many nations poured billions of dollars into the construction of nuclear weapons and then launched atmospheric and underground tests of these weapons of mass destruction. The billowing, radiant gases of the mushroom cloud became one of the most discordant images of the era.

Out of this discordance emerged a small antinuclear movement to challenge the spread of these weapons; other citizens and scientists called for the peaceful control and use of nuclear energy. Among the beneficial uses of the atom that the federal government and utility corporations envisioned was the generation of electricity; nuclear-power plants would replace those fueled by oil and coal. Moving away from fossil fuels was to have brought cleaner air and cheaper power, a peacetime dividend of considerable import to the booming Cold War economy.

Because water was used to cool the steam that powered the turbines of the reactors, these new nuclear facilities were sited along inland waterways and seacoasts; the plants easily could pump water into their systems and subsequently flush the effluent back into the nearby river or ocean. Though cooled, this water remained warmer than that into which it was reintroduced, leading to thermal pollution that elevated temperatures and had the potential to harm fish and other species.

Worries about the threats these plants posed to humans also surfaced in the 1950s and escalated with the rise of the environmental movement in the 1960s. The nuclear power industry, and its regulatory agency, the Atomic Energy Commission (AEC), came under increased scrutiny and political attack. In the late 1960s Congress began to respond to the controversy and, with the 1970 passage of the Water Quality Improvement Act, gave the AEC new authority to regulate the industry and the growing problems associated with thermal pollution; utility companies soon developed new technologies to reduce thermal pollution.

The impetus for change was not only top-down, as the successes of environmental activists in California demonstrated. They raised regional awareness of the issues associated with nuclear power, launched effective protests against new construction, and helped create the California Coastal Commission, designed to protect the seascapes and beaches from development. To resolve the potential (and varied) environmental threats nuclear energy posed required a range of political responses.

Viewpoint: Water-quality issues significantly altered the character of nuclear regulation in the United States by generating new federal legislation and industrial reform, as well as undermining confidence in the environmental benefits of nuclear power.

As the problems of industrial pollution and the deteriorating quality of the natural environment in the United States became increasingly visible during the 1960s, the federal government gradually took steps to meet the growing crisis. Congress enacted a series of measures to combat air and water pollution and of protect natural resources. The control of water pollution had long stirred controversy over the relative powers of state and local governments, which had traditionally exercised responsibility, and of the federal government. In 1965 Congress substantially strengthened the role of federal agencies. The Water Quality Act created the Federal Water Pollution Control Administration and empowered the federal government to establish quality standards for interstate waterways if the states did not set sufficiently rigorous standards. This law and others passed in the 1960s were cautious and limited measures, however, that fell short of ensuring effective federal action against water pollution.

The laws also failed to provide clear authority to deal with one of the most troubling perils to water quality–thermal pollution. During the latter half of the 1960s thermal pollution emerged as the source of a major controversy that centered on the threat that the growing number of nuclear-power plants would dump large amounts of waste heat into the national waterways. Thermal pollution resulted from cooling the steam that drove the turbines, which produced electricity in either a fossil-fuel or nuclear-power plant. The steam was condensed by the circulation of water, and in the process the cooling water was heated, usually by ten to twenty degrees Fahrenheit, before being returned to the body of water from which it came. This problem was not unique to nuclear-power plants but it was more acute in them, largely because fossil-fuel plants use steam heat more efficiently. Thermal pollution created more anxiety during the 1960s than previous decades because of the expanding number of steam-electric plants and greater size of these plants. Utilities built huge new fossil-fuel plants and, for the first time, also ordered nuclear-power stations in large numbers to try to keep up with anticipated demand for electricity. Although the severity of the consequences of thermal pollution remained a subject of debate among scientists, the potential damage generated considerable alarm. An article in *Scientist and Citizen* in 1968, for example, declared that "we cannot continue to expand our production of electric power with present generating methods without causing a major ecological crisis."

Thermal pollution caused concern because it was potentially harmful to many species of fish. A rise in water temperature could alter their reproductive cycles, respiratory rates, metabolism, and other vital functions. It could also disrupt the ecological balance in rivers and streams, allowing plants to thrive that made water look, taste, and smell unpleasant. Technical solutions to deal with this problem were available, but they required extra costs in the construction and operation of steam-electric plants. Cooling towers of different designs or cooling ponds, for example, would greatly alleviate the release of waste heat to the source body of water. Utilities resisted adding cooling systems to their planned facilities, however, because of the considerable expense and appreciable loss of generating capacity. Advocates of stronger federal action to protect the environment urged the U.S. Atomic Energy Commission (AEC), the agency primarily responsible for regulating the safety of nuclear-power plants, to require its licensees to guard against the effects of thermal pollution.

The AEC insisted, however, that it lacked the statutory authority to require applicants for nuclear-plant licenses to build cooling towers or other means of reducing the temperature of condensate water before it was returned to its source. The agency argued that the 1954 Atomic Energy Act, from which it drew its jurisdiction, restricted its regulatory authority to radiological dangers. Its authority did not apply to condensate water, which did not circulate through the core of the reactor and was not radioactive. The position of the AEC was upheld by the Department of Justice and federal courts. When several members of Congress introduced legislation to grant the AEC legal authority to combat thermal pollution, agency officials opposed the measures unless fossil-fuel units had to meet the same conditions. The Atomic Energy Act gave the AEC a mandate to promote the nuclear-power industry as well as to regulate it. The AEC feared that nuclear power would be placed at a competitive disadvantage if plant owners had to provide cooling equipment that was not required of fossil-burning facilities.

The position taken by the AEC triggered a great deal of criticism. As early as 1965 the Fish and Wildlife Service, an agency of the U.S. Department of the Interior, complained about the potential effects of thermal pollution from nuclear plants and the refusal of the AEC to regulate against them. Members of Congress, particularly Representative John David Dingell Jr. (D-Michigan) and Senator Edmund Sixtus Muskie (D-Maine), sharply questioned claims by the AEC that it had no regulatory jurisdiction over nonradiological effects of nuclear-power production. The agency also incurred attacks in the popular media. The most prominent and vitriolic review appeared in *Sports Illustrated* in January 1969. Writer Robert H. Boyle assailed the AEC for failing to regulate against thermal pollution and attributed its inaction to a fear of the "financial investment that power companies would have to make . . . to stop nuclear plants from frying fish or cooking waterways wholesale."

The growing debate left the AEC in an awkward position. It had clear judicial support for its argument that it lacked jurisdiction over thermal pollution, but it was the subject of withering rebukes from critics who accused it of indifference to the environment. Eventually, as the AEC sought a way out of its dilemma, new developments largely defused the thermal-pollution controversy. In January 1969 Muskie introduced new legislation that required applicants for nuclear-power plant construction permits or other federal licenses to present certification that their plants could meet water-quality standards. The bill did not apply specifically to nuclear power or thermal pollution, but it promised to give the AEC statutory authority to regulate against the effects of waste heat from nuclear-power facilities. It also applied to most fossil-fuel plants, which alleviated the concern about legislation that discriminated against nuclear power. For those reasons the AEC and others who had opposed previous proposals backed Muskie's bill. Congress passed the final version of the bill as the Water Quality Improvement Act in March 1970. The National Environmental Policy Act, signed into law on 1 January 1970, offered further assurance that federal agencies, including the AEC, would treat the problem of thermal pollution.

The most important reason that the controversy faded from prominence was that utilities increasingly took action to curb the consequences of discharging waste heat. Although they initially resisted the calls for cooling systems, they soon found that the costs of responding to litigation, enduring postponements in the construction or operation of new plants, or suffering a loss of public esteem were less tolerable than those of building cooling towers or ponds. By 1971 most nuclear plants being built or planned for inland waterways, where the problem was most acute, included cooling systems.

Nevertheless, the legacy of the thermal pollution debate lingered. The growing concern about the effects of steam-electric plants on water resources led to legislation that expanded the regulatory authority of federal agencies, including but not limited to, the AEC. In the case of nuclear power the thermal-pollution issue played a key role in wakening public doubts about the environmental impact of the technology. One reason that utilities had ordered nuclear plants in unprecedented numbers in the 1960s was that, unlike coal units, they did not spew millions of tons of noxious chemicals into the air annually. Power companies regarded nuclear reactors as a promising means to meet the demand for electricity without contributing to air pollution. In comparing coal-fired plants to nuclear ones, AEC chairman Glenn T. Seaborg once declared, "there can be no doubt that nuclear power comes out looking like Mr. Clean." The thermal pollution controversy, however, pointed up the environmental damage that nuclear plants could cause; and the reluctance of the AEC and utilities to take prompt action to prevent it curbed public support for nuclear power. Rather than being seen as a solution to the problem of providing power without causing air pollution, nuclear power became increasingly viewed as a threat to the environment. Water-quality issues, both by inspiring new legislation and undermining confidence in the environmental benefits of nuclear power, made a major impact on nuclear regulation.

–J. SAMUEL WALKER, U.S. NUCLEAR REGULATORY COMMISSION

Viewpoint: The system of local and state laws and regulations that governed water use in the United States democratized and decentralized the regulation of nuclear power.

Given access to cooling water, a nuclear-power plant can be built practically anywhere. There have been proposals to place plants near downtown Manhattan; in underground caverns,

THE SIERRA CLUB PROTECTS THE COAST

In 1972 the Sierra Club opposed the construction of a nuclear-power plant by Pacific Gas and Electric Company (PG&E), which they argued threatened the coastline. Several excerpts from a pamphlet produced by the Sierra Club are included here:

A "Major Factor"

The difference between thermal output and electric generating capacity at the turbines shows that the plant is expected to be about 33% efficient; the difference is the waste energy that must be disposed of. To dump these vast amounts of waste heat, cold ocean water would be drawn through condensers to cool the spent steam at a rate of 3,880 cubic feet per second (16,000 acre-feet per day). It would be heated approximately 18 degrees F. above intake (Ambient) temperature and discharged back to the ocean. Periodically the water will be heated to 50 or 60 degrees F. above ambient to "boil out" marine growths in the cooling system. Although the company promises to design the cooling water discharge structures "to recognize environmental and ecological concern as a major factor," the design submitted to the Atomic Energy Commission does not even disclose whether heated water will be discharged at the shoreline or in deep water.

During normal operation, the plant will discharge low-level gaseous and liquid radioactive wastes into the sea and atmosphere: PG&E insists that these contaminants will be kept within AEC guidelines.

While acknowledging that "some biological organisms may reconcentrate the dilute radioactive material," and conceding that the degree of such concentration cannot be determined at present, PG&E promises only that this phenomenon "will be studied experimentally at the Mendocino site . . . prior to plant start-up." The company indicates no intention to modify its construction plans if these studies indicate serious environmental or public health hazards, such as reconcentration in marine food organisms.

The Dirtiest Reactor

In addition to its unreliability as a power source, the Humboldt plant has been a serious source of radioactive contamination of the downwind environment. According to the U.S. Environmental Protection Agency, during 1965 and 1969 leakage of liquid and gaseous radioactive wastes exceeded those for any other plant operating in the United States. AEC Director of Regulation Harold Price is reported to have described the Humboldt plant as the "dirtiest" reactor in the country. Yet the company's public relations office has continued to crank out misleading material, strenuously asserting that the plant "has been producing kilowatts for Californians at a steady, reliable pace" and if radiation measuring instruments near the plant indicate a "significant increase [in releases] PG&E would immediately take action to correct the situation." But when serious problems of cracking in the fuel elements led to record releases of radioiodine and other fission products, beginning in 1966 and continuing into 1968, the company deferred corrective action until the normally scheduled time for refueling.

The Pacific Picket Fence

If the risks of an earthquake-triggered catastrophe are so great, why does PG&E insist on building the reactor at Point Arena? The answer depends on politics, economics and corporate inertia.

PG&E has an important stake in the California coastline. Other utilities across the country must try to persuade the citizenry that dumping waste heat into local rivers and lakes is harmless. It is not surprising that they are increasingly less successful and have begun planning power plants to be cooled by the atmosphere with specially constructed towers. Even in California, the Sacramento Municipal Utility District is constructing cooling towers for its 800 megawatt nuclear plant nearing completion at Rancho Seco in the Central Valley.

But PG&E has too long enjoyed the luxury of dumping waste heat into bays, estuaries and the ocean—at Humboldt Bay, San Francisco Bay, Moss Landing, Morro Bay, and very soon, Diablo Canyon. If the company can nail down two or three more major sites on the coast, its political demands will be secured. The Point Arena plant is the first major generating facility proposed on the north coast since the Bodega project was abandoned; it represents a major move in the company's strategy to retain the freedom to dump waste heat into the ocean.

Source: *David E. Pesonen,* Power at Point Arena *(San Francisco: Sierra Club, 1972).*

marshes, and deserts; and on barges and artificial islands. Despite this versatility, few issues so bedeviled the nuclear industry as siting, and often the Gordian knot was water. By the late 1960s industrial, agricultural, and recreational demands on water resources turned a once promising nuclear future into a regulatory quagmire of competing federal, state, and local bureaucracies and interests. Promoters of the peaceful atom could not have predicted such a result. The Atomic Energy Commission (AEC) emerged in a secretive Cold-War climate with almost exclusive authority to regulate nuclear-power plants and to limit public input. Federal regulators considered public objections to a facility only if such concerns related directly to radiation safety. Nonnuclear issues, including those related to water–such as thermal pollution, coastal protection, and irrigation rights–were left to industry-friendly public-utility commissions (PUCs). These officials, however, often dismissed nonnuclear problems, claiming they were only interested in the cost effectiveness of a facility. Nuclear critic Ralph Nader charged that in establishing this impenetrable regulatory scheme the AEC subverted the democratic process by "concentrat[ing] political and economic power in a few hands." However, the power of Nader's leviathan proved illusory and fleeting. In particular, the decentralized system of laws and regulations that governed water use offered a way to unlock the closed system enjoyed by electric utilities, PUCs, and the AEC. Several nuclear-plant controversies in California over coastline protection and irrigation rights are instructive in demonstrating the limits of centralized power in a nation founded on a federal system of governance.

The first misstep of electric utilities in California with nuclear power began with their ambition. In the late 1950s companies such as the Pacific Gas and Electric Corporation (PG&E) developed massive nuclear-construction projects. Avoiding potential conflicts with agribusiness over freshwater resources, PG&E executives eyed the Pacific Ocean. In the early 1960s PG&E proposed stringing scores of white, monolithic reactors along the California coastline like a "picket fence," as one opponent put it. By seizing the best coastal locations, PG&E could control access to cooling water and power production in the region and squeeze out its smaller competitors in the electric market. The utility constructed a small prototype plant near Eureka and appropriated another site at scenic Bodega Head, a peninsula near San Francisco that the state had planned to turn into a park. Further south the Los Angeles Department of Water and Power (LADWP) followed a similar strategy and purchased a nuclear-plant site along the famous beaches of Malibu.

In choosing Bodega and Malibu, PG&E and LADWP officials were dismissive of the exploding demand for coastal recreation and the power of the environmental movement. In the 1960s environmental activists lobbied to create Point Reyes National Seashore, halted the filling of San Francisco Bay, and developed legislation to protect open space along the coastline. As power plants began to crowd the coastline, environmentalists raised objections to the new facilities. With 85 percent of the burgeoning population of the state living within thirty miles of the coastline, these efforts were met with wide public support.

While they tried to save the Bodega and Malibu sites for their scenic value, plant opponents discovered that neither the PUC nor AEC was interested in the issue of scenic shoreline preservation. Blocked in their initial efforts, plant opponents instead convinced the AEC to reject both power plants because of their close proximity to earthquake faults. These episodes left an important political legacy. Environmental activists decided to lobby for a regulatory agency independent of the PUC to protect open space near the coast. "The lesson of Bodega should be shouted from the housetops," journalist Harold Gilliam wrote, "There is no agency in the State of California to protect the people's interest in maintaining open space." State resource officials, too, watched with alarm as utilities, the PUC, and federal regulators moved forward with nuclear construction. Wildlife officials could do little more than write letters to the PUC and AEC protesting their lack of consultation. In the late 1950s officials in the Department of Fish and Game objected to permission given by the AEC to an independent operator to dump radioactive wastes near the Farallon Islands. State officials further complained of the approval of the Eureka nuclear plant "before the state has any indication that a site is being considered, " and joined environmentalists in demanding that a state agency regulate coastal and environmental issues.

The environmentalists' victory at Bodega Bay forced utilities to agree to limited state supervision of coastal siting, but the new system proved unworkable. Utilities consented to informally consult state agencies and conservative environmental leaders, and to carry out mitigation efforts in areas of concern. In the late 1960s PG&E used this arrangement to win approval of its Diablo Canyon nuclear facility. In exchange the utility sold a site in the Nipomo Dunes to the state for use as a park. This new system, however, still limited public

A drawing of the proposed San Joaquin Nuclear Project, including its cooling towers

(Courtesy of Los Angeles Department of Water and Power)

input and was unacceptable to nuclear opponents. The defeat of nuclear projects continued as local residents and radical environmentalists fought any coastal power-plant proposal. Unable to use an informal arrangement, utility executives tried to bypass the opposition with state legislation vesting environmental and coastline regulatory authority in the friendly hands of the PUC. The strategy backfired.

By 1970 the surging popularity of the environmental movement checked the drive for utility-friendly legislation and led to a new coastline regulatory agency that operated independently of the PUC and AEC. In 1972 a voter initiative created the California Coastal Commission, which was passed despite strenuous and well-funded opposition from utility, oil, and real-estate interests. To slow development the new commission placed a temporary moratorium on new power-plant projects on the coast. As one power-plant opponent argued, "no more coastal sitings should be permitted in California. PG&E has a duty to explore the technology of alternate sources of energy and alternate inland siting of thermal plants, fossil and nuclear." The initiative forced utilities to tackle the vexing problem of building power plants in the arid interior of California.

In approaching this dilemma, utility companies did not fail for a lack of effort or imagination. Engineers with the LADWP developed a creative solution to an ironic problem in the Central Valley—too much water. In areas of the valley where drainage was poor, irrigation waters pooled leading to salt buildup that ruined agricultural land. In 1973 the LADWP proposed a nuclear facility, to be built near Bakersfield, that included a wastewater-collection system that would drain the poisonous runoff from nearby farms for use as power-plant cooling water.

Rather than sensing opportunity, however, many agribusinessmen saw in the LADWP proposal a Trojan horse. LADWP officials assured farm interests that they would not intrude on the share of water from the California Aqueduct that was dedicated to agriculture, but many operators were nonetheless suspicious. The LADWP, they alleged, had once "stolen" water from the nearby Owens Valley in the early-twentieth century and destroyed the agrarian economy of that community. Already distrustful, agribusinessmen reacted negatively to flaws in the wastewater plan. "I realized this was a P.R. job," one remembered. "They weren't negotiating for wastewater, they were after [our] freshwater." Plant opposition quickly coalesced around the issue of protecting Central Valley water supplies for agriculture.

Activists turned to local water districts for help. Historically, quasigovernmental water districts served and protected farming interests by raising money and federal support for local irrigation projects and by helping set water policy. Any project that touched on water use came under the scrutiny of these districts. Antiplant activists convinced district boards to publicize their opposition to the wastewater system and force the Kern County Water Agency to end its cooperation with the LADWP on the wastewater plan. The growing public outcry forced county supervisors to sponsor a referendum in March 1978 on whether to allow construction of the plant. Responding to the plant opponents' claim that "LA wants to gobble up our valuable farm land and water and leave us with the wastes!," 70 percent of county residents rejected a construction permit.

The defeat of nuclear projects in the name of coastline preservation and irrigation rights reveals the limits of the federal government to sponsor policies that intrude on local interests. Despite their initial tight control and avid promotion of the nuclear industry, federal officials could not prevent the decentralization of nuclear regulation as states and citizens were aroused to assert their traditional authority over land and water use. Not limited to California, water issues had the same effect in a host of nuclear controversies around the country regarding thermal pollution, wetland protection, and scenic preservation of shorelines. Highly valued as a recreational and economic resource, water played a significant role in democratizing atomic regulation.

–THOMAS R. WELLOCK, CENTRAL WASHINGTON UNIVERSITY

References

Joan Aron, *Licensed to Kill?: The Nuclear Regulatory Commission and the Shoreham Power Plant* (Pittsburgh: University of Pittsburgh Press, 1997).

Brian Balogh, *Chain Reaction: Expert Debate and Public Participation in American Commercial Nuclear Power, 1945–1975* (Cambridge & New York: Cambridge University Press, 1991).

Henry F. Bedford, *Seabrook Station: Citizen Politics and Nuclear Power* (Amherst: University of Massachusetts Press, 1990).

Robert H. Boyle, "The Nukes Are in Hot Water," *Sports Illustrated,* 30 (20 January 1969): 24–28.

John Cairns Jr., "We're in Hot Water," *Scientist and Citizen,* 10 (October 1968): 187–198.

Marc K. Landy, Marc J. Roberts, and Stephen R. Thomas, *The Environmental Protection Agency: Asking the Wrong Questions from Nixon to Clinton* (New York: Oxford University Press, 1994).

Martin V. Melosi, *Coping with Abundance: Energy and Environment in Industrial America* (Philadelphia: Temple University Press, 1985).

Daniel Pope, "'We Can Wait. We Should Wait': Eugene's Nuclear Power Controversy, 1968–1970," *Pacific Historical Review,* 59 (August 1990): 349–373.

J. Samuel Walker, *Containing the Atom: Nuclear Regulation in a Changing Environment, 1963–1971* (Berkeley: University of California Press, 1992).

Thomas Raymond Wellock, *Critical Masses: Opposition to Nuclear Power in California, 1958–1978* (Madison: University of Wisconsin Press, 1998).

OGALLALA AQUIFER

Are farmers on the western plains of the United States in danger of running out of water?

Viewpoint: Yes. Continued heavy consumption of groundwater from the Ogallala Aquifer will deplete the resource and threaten future agricultural prosperity on the western plains.

Viewpoint: No. The irrigation that revived the Plains can continue indefinitely through more efficient technologies and careful management.

Beginning in the 1880s, large numbers of energetic and ambitious eastern U.S. farmers arrived on the unplowed but fertile great western plains of North America—nearly three hundred thousand square miles of flatland that faced the eastern slope of the Rocky Mountains. This area was known to receive far less rainfall than the Midwest or East. Settlers were urged into the region by railroad boosters and the patriotic notion that Americans could succeed anywhere. They believed the popular saying, "rain follows the plow," a claim supported by some prominent scientists, as well as politicians and entrepreneurs. The region, once called the Great American Desert, was turned into the Great American Garden. Newly arrived settlers ignored the contrary but rare warning from scientists such as John Wesley Powell that the land west of the one-hundredth meridian was too dry for successful farming.

More often than not, however, these farmers could not eke out a bare existence, failed, and moved away. It simply did not rain enough, nor at the right season, for their crops to grow. The occasional good year meant twenty inches of rain at the most, still not enough to grow corn. Plains farmers soon learned instead to plant winter wheat, which had been introduced by Russian Mennonites, and sorghums (animal feed). Both of these crops, unfortunately, were often a glut on the market and brought unacceptably low prices. The climactic event was the Dust Bowl of the 1930s, but it was only one of the worst of totally rainless periods of two to five years that also hit the western plains in the 1890s, 1950s, 1970s, and 1990s.

Rumors of a vast body of underground water had tantalized these dryland farmers since they first heard of it early in the twentieth century. It was impossible to reach with windmills or early pumps. The enormous Ogallala Aquifer is groundwater trapped in gravel beds below 174,000 square miles of fertile, but otherwise dry, Plains farmland. This territory covers large parts of Texas, Oklahoma, Kansas, and Nebraska, and extends into New Mexico, Colorado, and South Dakota. The aquifer—the crown jewel of the Plains environment—was later discovered to be the largest underground body of water in the United States. More than three billion acre-feet (an acre-foot is a foot of water across one square acre, or 325,851 gallons) were deposited under the Plains. Unlike most underground water supplies in the world, Ogallala groundwater is mostly irreplaceable "fossil water," because its sources were cut off thousands of years ago and virtually no water trickles in from surface rivers or rainfall.

Not until the late 1950s would a combination of deep well-drilling, efficient pumps, cheap energy, irrigation devices, and better hydrological knowledge bring a boom in remarkable yields of wheat, corn, alfalfa, and sorghums. The problem of the Plains seemed solved; irrigation farmers prospered; and the plains entered the American mainstream. In 1950 Ogallala water was being flooded onto 3.5 million acres of farmland using old-fashioned furrow irrigation. After 1960, center-pivot irrigators sprinkled fields in large circles, and by 2000, irrigated fields had grown to 16 million acres, although down from 17 million in the heyday 1970s. The lack of rain could be ignored, and the farmland was transformed into a fabled "breadbasket [and feedbag] of the world."

Once reached, Ogallala groundwater profoundly affected surface events. An irrigated cornfield produces 115 bushes an acre, compared to 89 bushels on an eastern humid-land farm, and 48 bushels on a dryland acre. The modern Plains farmer, on his typical 1,280 to 1,920 irrigated acres—eight to twelve quarter sections—is now bound on each quarter section to a gushing steel umbilical, six to eight inches wide, drilling down 100 to 250 feet through layers of rock to the wet gravel beds, and raised to the surface by impeller pumps driven by powerful engines. In 1990 a center-pivot sprinkler system, from drilling the well to watering the wheat or alfalfa, would cost a farmer $70,000 to $100,000 per 160 acres, depending on well depth and field needs. Most irrigators need 12 wells, pumps, and center-pivot irrigation systems, which will cost him more than $1 million dollars. He will want to pump furiously to assure high crop yields to pay for this irrigation miracle. Fortunately, for each unit he will only pay $15 to pump an acre-foot using natural gas and $30 using electricity (1990 dollars). Not the least, the irrigator needs good wheat or sorghum prices, which in the last two decades of the twentieth century were half of what they were in the 1970s. From any rational perspective about Plains farming, irrigation is a marvelous technology, and alternatives are gloomy.

This artificially induced friendly environment—"land of underground rain"—appears to be nearing its end, however, because the water is running out. A third of the groundwater had been consumed by 1990, and another third was inaccessible. Drought is still the dominant feature of the region during 130 years of human migration on and off the Plains.

Viewpoint: Yes. Continued heavy consumption of groundwater from the Ogallala Aquifer will deplete the resource and threaten future agricultural prosperity on the western plains.

The list of problems created by farmers' decisions on the Plains over the last 120 years seems endless. The region was planted in the wrong crops for a semiarid zone with less than 20 inches of normal rain a year. Corn demands the most water during the season, an astonishing 900,000 gallons laid on 130 acres of a 160-acre quarter section, wheat and sorghum half that amount. In one growing season, a single acre of alfalfa needs up to thirty inches of water, equivalent to 2½ acre-feet or almost a million gallons. Between 1960 and 1990 about one billion acre-feet of Ogallala water were consumed by irrigation farmers, mostly in western Kansas, eastern Colorado, the Oklahoma Panhandle, and western Texas. Western and central Nebraska holds more than 60 percent of the remaining aquifer water, but that region is less fertile and is mostly cattle country. Another billion acre-feet are inaccessible because of high pumping costs and high saline quality. The remaining billion gallons are coming under stress. Ogallala groundwater does not recover naturally and artificial replacement remains unlikely.

It is far too costly to pipe water onto the Plains from the Mississippi or Missouri Rivers, and grandiose plans to transfer water from the great rivers and lakes of Canada would run to hundreds of billions of dollars. Farmers can afford up to $70 (1990 figure) an acre-foot; such imported water would cost, conservatively, $500 to $800 an acre-foot. Using modern techniques, many local irrigators say they will be happy to hold on for another decade. At the end of the century, more than half of the usable water is gone and levels still decline on the average of two feet a year. At the edges of the aquifer, irrigation has taken all but five or ten feet of usable Ogallala water, and some farmers are reverting to dryland farming with questionable results. Few irrigators face up to the fact that pumping water is a mining operation as much as coal, gold, or oil. United States Geological Survey (USGS) hydrologist John Bredehoeft stated it clearly: "To the extent that we are mining groundwater, we are running out of water."

There are other quagmires. Most major irrigators on the Plains are now older men and a few women. Their sons and daughters are leaving the farm. "It was too many hours at too much hard work." New irrigation start-ups are far too costly. Equipment is also getting old; costs have skyrocketed to $75,000 (1990 dollars) to replace pumps, piping, and center-pivot irrigators for a quarter section, when the farmer needs eight to twelve quarter sections to stay in business. Overall, consumption of Ogallala water can soon double or triple to compensate for such problems. Aging, less-efficient equipment wastes water. Reduced government supports means a farmer has to plant more crops, which he has to water. An eroding soil produces lower yields on the same amount of water. In the last decade of the twentieth century, a vertically integrated agribusiness in beef or pork became the most reliable operation. Such corporate operations need copious water to serve its demand for high yields. The threat of the next drought (possibly intensified by the greenhouse effect) would triple water consumption. Cutbacks in irrigation are likely to mean the end of family farming on the western plains.

Without the discovery of the Ogallala Aquifer and its pumping for irrigation, the semiarid western plains, often down to twelve inches or less of rain a year, would have remained a hostile and unproductive frontier environment. It still experiences hot windy summers and harsh winters. Dryland farming remains high-risk farming over which the best local producers have serious doubts. The label, Dust Bowl, is apt. The arid climate of the western plains may once again have the direct impact it has not had for fifty years. With yields three times higher at the turn of the century, together with unprecedented capital investment, the stakes are far higher than during the 1930s Dust Bowl. Not only would grain production be ended by desertification, which global warming is likely to bring to the Plains, but also all-important cattle feedlot operations would be halted by sun, wind, and temperature extremes. As water levels decline, Plains agriculture is subject once again to unpredictable interruptions from its old enemy, climate. The Great American Garden would revert to the Great American Desert.

The concept of sustainable development offers a useful perspective by which to examine the golden age of irrigation from 1960 to 1990 on the High Plains, and the extreme difficulties that farmers are having in their attempts to switch away from high consumption. What is the balance between human needs and the "carrying capacity" of a geographical region? Sustainability gives priority to preservation and improvement of fertile soils; maintenance and expansion of supplies of clean water; and protection and regeneration of a satisfying quality of life for the workforce. The Ogallala is in truth an environmental resource that is mostly nonrenewable and is being used up at a high rate. Even with well-meaning local control, groundwater mining is still ten to twenty times any recharge. Energy costs from gasoline, natural gas, or electricity are expected to go up four to ten times every decade. New problems that arose in the 1990s included threats to water quality from factory-sized hog and cattle confinement operations that consume vast amounts of water and, for the first time, threaten contamination from the waste produced by thousands of animals in a small space.

As a water crunch continues, the historically independent family farm is likely to succumb. Only corporate farming, with deep pockets, can afford the costs of technological "fixes" and marginal commodity prices, but its managers and shareholders demand high productivity that consumes water and soil. Sustainable development emphasizes the on-site balance between agriculture and natural conditions that is likely to come from small family farms committed to quality of life instead of quarterly profit reports. Kenneth A. Cook of the Center for Resource Economics calls for "a new social contract between farmers and society. For its part, society will have to recognize the enormous cost farmers already bear to conserve natural resources and protect the environment. Taxpayers will have to be willing to share more of that burden–probably a great deal more–as external costs of agricultural production becomes internalized." That is, the total costs of soil erosion, water consumption, energy use, and human labor cannot be taken for granted. Stable, self-maintaining ecological systems of farming can be tailored to suit local variations in knowledge, climate, soils, and biological diversity. Instead of sacrificing land, water, and energy to serve market value alone, sustainability lays emphasis upon lowest possible consumption of soil and water, as well as keeping good people on the land.

–JOHN OPIE, NEW BUFFALO,
MICHIGAN

Viewpoint:
No. The irrigation that revived the Plains can continue indefinitely through more efficient technologies and careful management.

Consumers of High Plains groundwater have the good fortune to enjoy it as a "free good," available to whomever owns the land above reservoir at no cost for the water itself, but requiring an equipment cost of approximately $100,000 to irrigate a 160-acre quarter section. The Plains farmer found it wonderful that he could schedule rain for the dry land because he could irrigate his crops by the start of a pump. The Desert became the Garden.

DROUGHT IN THE SOUTHWESTERN UNITED STATES

On 12 July 1996, host Steve Curwood, reporter Sandy Tolan, Texans K. T. McLeaish and Jud Chevront appeared on Living on Earth, *a Public Broadcasting System radio show, a portion of which appears below:*

CURWOOD: Recently the mayor of San Angelo, Texas, proclaimed a day of organized prayer. For rain. Hot, dry weather across much of the western and plains states and northern Mexico for the past 3 years has devastated the planting and livestock industries and brought new pressures to fragile landscapes and the aquifers beneath them. *Living on Earth*'s Sandy Tolan recently traveled to West Texas, where many people are comparing this drought to the devastating dust bowl of the 1930s.

TOLAN: In West Texas people love to watch the sky.

MC LEAISH: That's something we sure have a lot of is sky. There's not a lot of things to block our view. And the sky can be incredibly entertaining, to watch a dust storm roll in from the north when it's got a 3,000-foot ceiling on it and it looks like a giant red rolling wave just coming at you. Or watch the big thunderstorms roll in. The lightning can be just—fantastic to watch, beautiful. This is the time of year we get those storms.

TOLAN: Ordinarily. But for the last 3 years, says K. T. McLeaish, longtime resident of the West Texas town of Odessa, there have been precious few thunderstorms to watch. Almost nothing but hot, dry winds and clear, sunny skies, unrelenting.

MCLEAISH: I think it's really starting to grate on people's nerves. Everybody's—testy. I think there's a prevailing bad attitude right now. You hear it constantly no matter where you go, the minute you step out of the nice air conditioned car and you're hit with the wind or the dust or just the heat, and somebody's going to say God, I'm so tired of this. It's constant. And the wind has been relentless. And of course with all the dryness and then it instantly kicks up the dust.

TOLAN: It's bad enough in town, but out on the land 3 years of this heat and wind and no rain has brought devastation. Nothing will grow on the dry land farms, which rely entirely on the rains. Some are lucky enough to have a little income from small oil wells on their land. Other dry land farmers are completely out of business, and much of the topsoil is blowing away. And now the drought is threatening even farmers who irrigate their fields from the underground aquifers. . . .

TOLAN: Sitting in the back office of Seminole's John Deere dealer, Chevront lays out his financial woes. His dealer Paul Condit looks on in sympathy. No rains mean more farmers have to reach deeper and pump harder from the Ogallala Aquifer, the underground lake which stretches down to West Texas from way up in Nebraska. Chevront's spending an extra $40,000 a month on electricity to pump water, and he's already laid out half a million since last spring on new wells. Costs like this, he says, may drive his family out of business.

CHEVRONT: It's a disaster right now and—I don't know what'll happen. Just trust in the future. I guess I'll make it some way or other. Very stressful right now; we just had our first child in December and—wasn't a good time to bring one in, I don't think, but you know, he's a joy in our life right now. (Laughs) It's good to come home and see him.

TOLAN: And so while they pray hard, the farmers of Seminole keep pumping the hidden waters into their fields, and the great Ogallala Aquifer drains down.

CHEVRONT: We ain't had the rains so we've had to run the wells all the time. Didn't run the wells would pull the water table down, and nothing's replenished it. It's very low, the aquifer has dropped extremely where I live. Even some of my good wells, they're starting to pull air instead of water.

Source: *"Impact of Drought on Southwestern United States,"* Living on Earth, *12 July 1996, Internet website.*

Local irrigators have not stood around wringing their hands over thirty- to sixty-foot declines in their well levels during twenty years of irrigation. In 1970, farmers around Sublette in western Kansas concluded they had three hundred years of water left in the aquifer, based on current pumping and known supplies. By 1980 their estimate had fallen to seventy years as pumping rose dramatically, and by 1990 that figure dropped to less than thirty years. When Plains farmers found their groundwater levels in continuous decline they applied a variety of conservation strategies that mixed traditional and innovative ideas—converting to specialized drip irrigation, irrigation scheduling to water a crop at an ideal growth period, a shift to genetically engineered drought-tolerant crops, and special tillage procedures used since Dust Bowl times. Efficiency in laying the water into the ground can rise dramatically under ideal conditions, from the miserable 45 percent in flood-the-furrow irrigation (the rest lost to evaporation) to 75 percent with scheduled center-pivot sprinkling. Drip irrigation directly to the roots of plants claims 90 percent efficiency, but it is more costly.

Not the least, many irrigation farmers also joined regional water-management districts in Kansas and Texas, or formed their own independent associations, as in Oklahoma, to control the number and spacing of wells and pumps, to measure consumption, and to foster conservation and fight waste. The pathbreaking Texas Groundwater Management District No. 1 opened its doors in Lubbock in 1952. In February 1953 the district set out its first regulations that eventually included more than 8,000 full-scale irrigation wells (each pumping 100,000 gallons per day or more). The district manages 8,149 square miles, or 5,215,600 acres, spread across 15 counties. Compliance to the regulations was voluntary, a critical feature for fiercely independent farmers. Popular representation is also evident in its structure: a five-member Board of Directors supported by five-member committees from each of the counties, "a grassroots network of 80 elected officials."

The Texas precedent was followed by the statewide Oklahoma Water Resources Board and Western Kansas Groundwater Management District No. 1 in 1972, the Southwest Kansas Groundwater Management District No. 3 in 1976, and the Northwest Kansas Groundwater Management District No. 4 in 1977. Similar districts also appeared in Colorado and Nebraska. On the western plains, "groundwater management" is still a surrogate phrase for "economic development." The original mission of Texas District No. 1 was to promote controlled development of Ogallala Aquifer water. It has now shifted policies to protect the remaining supply for only "beneficial use" to slow down the decline of aquifer levels. These groundwater management districts have a common goal—not always well served—to provide a structured means by which to continue indefinitely the development of Ogallala water for profitable agriculture.

The trend in Texas District No. 1, like most other districts, is away from historic overpumping and toward minimum-water-use conservation. One major goal in Texas is to assure that future crops can be irrigated even when pumping rates decline below fifty gallons per minute (gpm), compared to the usual five hundred to one thousand gpm. This policy includes new low-pressure overhead sprinklers, soil-moisture monitoring, irrigation scheduling, tailwater (runoff) and other water-reuse systems, possible recharge through local small "rainwater storage" lakes called playas, furrow dikes (rediscovered from 1930s conservation practices), low- or no-tillage practices (also employed since the earliest dryland farming days), and the science of crop-water consumption.

One pioneering and controversial effort is weather modification (cloud-seeding by aircraft) by Kansas District No. 1 in Scott City, Kansas District No. 4 in Colby, and Texas District No. 1, to reduce groundwater consumption by inducing more rain. Weather modification, when it is successful, could increase rainfall by 9 percent and thus reduce pumping by 6 percent. Cloud seeding can also control the threat of disastrous hailstorms, which, for example, cost almost $5 million in Sherman County, Kansas. Another direction is suggested by animal-confinement operations in cattle or hogs, by which more dollars can be squeezed from each gallon of water by raising livestock instead of feed. In addition, Ogallala groundwater is expected to stay dedicated to food production. The Plains is not likely to find itself embroiled, as is happening in the Southwest, over water for heavy industry or metropolitan sprawl.

The typical Plains irrigator is aggressively independent and individualistic. When the groundwater-management districts first appeared, these libertarians often lashed out at any attempts to control their free consumption of Ogallala water at any pace they pleased. The *Cross Section*, the newsletter for Texas District No. 1, in March 1956 promised suspicious local farmers that "Hitlerism" was not on the way: "The Water District was not created to do away with the rights of the individual but rather . . . to maintain those . . . rights and . . . provide for orderly development and wise use of our own water." Even while Ogallala waters showed large and continuing declines in the territory, local irrigators still had mixed feelings about extensive water management. "When you start talking about a man's water, you get into real trouble." According to a 1975 survey, seven out of ten irrigators supported the way the local district was doing its job, although one farmer reflected the minority view when he said, "All I want is to be left alone. If

A 1912 map designating an underground water site

(Courtesy of Southwest Collection, Texas Tech University)

I can't make it on my own I'll go out of the farming business. This is the way it ought to be with everything. Survival of the fittest."

Any control or regulation is vigorously scrutinized. In 1975, Texas District No. 1 distributed a policy paper that emphasized that "Groundwater management is not prohibiting groundwater development; it is finding equitable means for making reasonable use of groundwater supplies." It continued, "What is groundwater management? The individual extracting water from a well constitutes groundwater management–whether his use of the groundwater is for a beneficial or wasteful purpose." The formation of the district in 1952 had little to do with environmental protection. Instead it meant the protection of farmers' groundwater as valuable private property. The goal of the district, according to local irrigators, was to protect the profit motive for individual farmers by assuring water to guarantee high yields.

A radical step bears watching. The Northwest Kansas Groundwater Management District Four, established in 1977, set in 1990 a zero-depletion goal to be reached in as little as ten years. The founding director, Wayne Bossert, argued that the logic was simple: despite sophisticated water-management strategies, groundwater levels continued to decline. Declining levels meant zero depletion anyway, so why not opt to reach the same goal earlier while retaining an acceptable quantity of water for future management options?

Bossert noted that the 3,600 wells in his district were drawing levels down averaging two feet a year. Some wells had declined nearly sixty feet between 1966 and 1990. He courageously (some said it was foolhardy) redirected emphasis away from consuming all the water needed for highest possible crop yield toward less water consumption. He persuaded his district board to give priority to protection of aquifer levels instead of highest yield. After all, he concluded, individual farmer security based on irrigation was one of the major improvements compared to an earlier frontierlike, high-risk lifestyle. Nonirrigated agriculture–dryland farming–is less desirable because it varies greatly from year to year depending upon rainfall and climate. Not the least, the average value of crop production in northwest Kansas between 1985 and 1989 was $43 higher for an irrigated acre than for a nonirrigated acre.

The district is experiencing great difficulty, however, in matching its draconian goal with the immediate needs of local farmers to irrigate for their year-to-year survival. Farmers found that their survival depended upon consuming more water than zero depletion allowed: more water pumped than was replaced at any given well site. A tough-minded compromise was reached in 1992 that permitted ten more years of decline, sacrificing 22 percent of Ogallala groundwater to protect the remaining 78 percent.

Agricultural policy analyst Earl O. Heady believes that the advent of new efficient technologies, despite lower water levels, will continue to support current food production, and probably surpass it. "I am optimistic about our ability," despite declining water levels, "to continue growth in agricultural productivity and food production." Heady argues for a bullish future at least as productive as the past, based on more efficient management of existing farming instead any move toward unknown and untried alternatives.

It is hard to argue against the productivity of the Plains, despite the price paid in depletion of water and soil. Industrial farming plays a major role in the ability of each American farmer to feed a whopping eight dozen people, compared to four dozen when the nation began. This success story, perhaps the most important in all of modern history, does much to define U.S. prosperity. It is remarkable that less than 2 percent of Americans work on the farm, compared to 30 or 40 percent of populations in other nations. Half of these remarkable U.S. farmers, about a million, live on the Plains.

–JOHN OPIE, NEW BUFFALO, MICHIGAN

References

Mark Fiege, *Irrigated Eden: The Making of an Agricultural Landscape in the American West* (Seattle: University of Washington Press, 1999).

Gilbert C. Fite, *The Farmer's Frontier, 1886–1900* (New York: Holt, Rinehart & Winston, 1966).

Donald E. Green, *Land of the Underground Rain: Irrigation on the Texas High Plains, 1910–1970* (Austin: University of Texas Press, 1973).

John Opie, *Ogallala: Water for a Dry Land*, second edition (Lincoln: University of Nebraska Press, 2000).

John Wesley Powell, *Lands of the Arid Region of the United States* (Washington, D.C.: U.S. Government Printing Office, 1878).

James Earl Sherow, *Watering the Valley: Development along the High Plains Arkansas River, 1870–1950* (Lawrence: University Press of Kansas, 1990).

Walter Prescott Webb, *The Great Plains* (Boston: Ginn, 1931).

Donald Worster, *Dust Bowl: The Southern Plains in the 1930s* (New York: Oxford University Press, 1979).

PACIFIC NORTHWEST

Was the Municipality of Metropolitan Seattle's effort to save Lake Washington a success?

Viewpoint: Yes. The rescue of Lake Washington in Seattle is an example of how political, scientific, and technological solutions to declining water quality seemed to create a regional identity centered on protecting nature and an outdoor lifestyle.

Viewpoint: No. By enabling uncontrolled suburban growth in the Seattle area, regional wastewater treatment worsened water pollution in the long run while falsely suggesting that deeply rooted environmental problems in the United States were easily solvable.

At the end of World War II (1939–1945) the urban American West boomed. The wartime emergency had pumped money and immigrants into urban centers, fueling a new affluence. Seattle, Washington, was no exception. Allied orders for planes and ships caused local industries such as Boeing to explode almost overnight. As postwar peace turned into Cold War readiness, still more people came to the urban Puget Sound area in quest of high-paying jobs, spectacular scenery, and low housing prices. As elsewhere in the United States, postwar prosperity translated into urban growth.

Rapid growth in the postwar urban West, however, as in other metropolitan centers across the nation, yielded a new wave of environmental problems. One of the more dire concerns was worsening water pollution. Industrial expansion put more pollutants into urban watersheds. The postwar housing boom taxed aging sewer systems. When new subdivisions expanded beyond existing municipal boundaries, many contractors used septic tanks instead of building sewers. For a city such as Seattle, which is surrounded by water, these problems became acute. As suburban sprawl began to surround Lake Washington, a large body of freshwater to the east of the city, water quality deteriorated rapidly. By the early 1950s scientists warned that sewage dumped into the lake was creating an ecological nightmare. For old-time residents and new arrivals alike, the postwar boom in Seattle now threatened the very qualities that made living there attractive.

In 1958 Seattle and King County voters, after a sustained campaign, approved the creation of the Municipality of Metropolitan Seattle, or Metro, to save Lake Washington. Metro was one of the first publicly approved regional agencies in the nation to address environmental concerns. In a remarkably short time, engineers and planners built a series of gigantic interceptor sewers that diverted sewage out of the lake. By 1970 scientists proclaimed that the lake had been saved and Metro was a resounding success. Despite its achievements, though, Metro could not stop continued growth in the region or solve all of its water quality problems. The limited mandate of Metro prevented regional solutions to growth, while it simultaneously pursued avenues to alleviate the worst effects of pollution.

The Lake Washington story is a case study of the problems that water pollution posed for cities across the United States. Before 1945, pollution was seen by most urbanites as one of the many prices of material affluence. After

World War II more and more citizens questioned if pollution was truly the cost of progress. Urbanites across the continent pursued political, regulatory, economic, and technological solutions to reduce or eliminate pollution, with varying success. Their quest to preserve what environmental historian Samuel P. Hays has called "beauty, health, and permanence" is the focus of the stories that follow.

Viewpoint:
Yes. The rescue of Lake Washington in Seattle is an example of how political, scientific, and technological solutions to declining water quality seemed to create a regional identity centered on protecting nature and an outdoor lifestyle.

Seattle and water are nearly synonymous, but their relationship to one another has changed over time. Ocean and lakes surround the city, built on a narrow isthmus, on nearly all sides. Lake Washington, the second-largest body of freshwater in the state, lies to the east of the city at the foot of the Cascade Mountains. Human alterations to the lake over the past century have changed its hydrology and residents' perceptions toward it. In 1917 engineers opened the Lake Washington Ship Canal, which connected the lake to saltwater Puget Sound, hoping to spur industrial growth and control flooding around its shores. The canal lowered the lake by nearly twelve feet, eliminating its original drainage through the Duwamish River. Most Seattleites at the time celebrated the canal because they saw the lake as an engine for economic progress. Later generations came to appreciate the natural attributes of Lake Washington as well. Like Mount Rainier, the lake came to symbolize the scenic virtues of Seattle. Passions for Lake Washington grew steadily after the opening of the canal, helping to shape a new environmental consciousness. When pollution threatened the lake after 1945, residents appealed again to engineers, planners, and scientists to change the lake for the better.

Understanding that its human inhabitants have always altered Lake Washington, area residents embraced the Municipality of Metropolitan Seattle, or Metro, as a solution to the pollution problem. Earlier alterations to the lake helped later Seattleites to make the case for another intervention. A coalition of private and civic leaders, eager to promote continued regional prosperity, played upon residents' desires to preserve environmental quality without sacrificing material affluence. By casting Lake Washington as an ecosystem susceptible to human control, Metro renewed local people's faith in science and technology to save nature and protect their livelihood.

Rapid suburban growth in the postwar West yielded widespread problems with water pollution. As early as the 1930s, state and local authorities noted with alarm that water quality in Lake Washington was declining rapidly. Urban watersheds were increasingly being polluted because of industrial expansion. Aging sewer systems, which spilled untreated sewage into the lake, were taxed by the postwar housing boom. Although Seattle had diverted most of its sewers into Puget Sound by 1936, smaller communities on the eastern side of the lake, such as Bellevue and Kirkland, continued to use the lake as a sink. Storm-sewer overflows from Seattle plants contributed to the problem; so did older, inefficient plants in the newer northern suburbs. Homebuilding also added to the litany of problems. Real-estate developers, eager to sell lots and homes, built inexpensive septic tanks to promote new subdivisions. Most of these leaked into the watershed, adding still more pollution to the lake. By the early 1950s scientists were predicting that sewage would literally kill the lake by the end of the decade.

Scientists such as W. T. Edmondson, a professor of zoology at the University of Washington, were the first to sound the alarm that Lake Washington was dying. Edmondson and his colleagues linked the rising level of nutrients in the lake to increased sewage flows. This effluent was an extremely effective fertilizer for aquatic plants, such as algae, which bloomed and died quickly in the lake, fouling the water and nearby beaches. The nutrients liberated by dying algae perpetuated the cycle. Moreover, scientists and public-health officials noted, untreated sewage could also promote the growth of fecal coliform bacteria at municipal swimming beaches. Although health was a major worry for public authorities, scenic and recreational amenities were the immediate concern for residents. During the hot, dry summer months, people complained that stinking mats of decaying algae stuck to boats, swimmers, and water skiers. Newspaper editorials called for officials to correct the problem, but in the mid 1950s protecting the regional environment was a jurisdictional jungle. The Washington State Pollution Control Commission, created in 1942, had limited enforcement powers over

A staged photo used by Metro in 1958 to dramatize pollution of Lake Washington, Seattle

(courtesy of the Municipality of Metropolitan Seattle)

polluters. The problem, Edmondson and his colleagues argued, would only be corrected with the complete diversion of sewage effluent out of the Lake Washington basin.

Edmondson's warnings found willing support among a group of local civic activists who wanted to control the meteoric but chaotic growth of the region. James R. Ellis, a rising Seattle attorney who later spearheaded the Metro campaign, was a typical activist. Nearly all were white-collar professionals and members of civic associations such as the Municipal League of Seattle and King County. Many were women who had experience as political activists for a variety of women's and social organizations, such as the League of Women Voters. The Municipal League, in particular, was a meeting place for residents who wanted to consolidate county government under an executive branch to give it more control over regional planning, growth management, and transit. An earlier League attempt to reform the King County charter to handle such issues was defeated in a 1952 election. As concerns over Lake Washington began to rise, this coalition of concerned citizens saw an opportunity to promote regional government again. The eventual nickname of their plan would be Metro, and saving Lake Washington would become its rallying cry.

Proponents of metropolitan government employed a two-phase approach to insure passage of their plan. The first was legislative; the second went directly to the public. The political campaign for Metro began in 1956 with the election of reform-minded politicians at the local and state level. The newly elected governor, Albert D. Rosellini, a Seattle native and Democrat, appointed a "Metropolitan Problems Advisory Committee" and agreed to share expenses with local communities to clean up the lake. Seattle mayor Gordon S. Clinton appointed a similar committee and drew heavily upon Ellis and his reformer allies for assistance. This latter committee drafted legislation to create a metropolitan government for King County and submitted it to the state legislature in Olympia for approval. This new metropolitan government would be responsible for three issues only: sewage, mass transit, and land-use planning. Nonetheless, many suburban legislators feared that the proposal was a Seattle-led plot for regional dominance. After a heated debate, a bipartisan coalition passed the bill and placed it on the King County ballot for March 1958.

The second phase of the campaign focused on convincing area residents that the absence of metropolitan government spelled the end of Lake Washington. Before the election, the Metro Action Committee (MAC), countering charges that metropolitan government would give Seattle too much power over its adjacent towns, launched a massive public-relations crusade. Advertisements in local newspapers pointed to the miserable quality of Lake Washington waters. Pro-Metro reporters for the *Seattle Times* and *Seattle Post-Intelligencer,* the two largest papers, wrote editorials and articles supporting the measure. Government allies released reports listing the dangerous conditions at beaches throughout King County. One famous image (later found to be a staged photograph) pictured five young children facing the lake next to a sign declaring the water unfit for swimming. Pro-Metro rhetoric focused on the fact that new political systems, empowered with the latest science and technology, could reverse the trend.

Despite the coordinated efforts of the pro-Metro camp, the measure failed to pass by the necessary majority. In Seattle, Metro passed by nearly a six-to-one margin, but in the rest of King County it lost by nearly seven thousand votes. Opponents of Metro, largely from small towns at the southern end of the lake, feared that the proposal would elevate taxes and benefit Seattle at their expense. Alarmed at the prospect of losing yet another chance for municipal reform, Ellis and his allies transformed Metro and put a revised version on the ballot for that September. The new Metro encompassed a smaller geographical area (excluding those areas that voted against the March 1958 version) and limited itself to one function: collecting, treating, and disposing sewage. Metro proponents lined up support from the mayors of major suburbs, notably Bellevue and Kirkland, and renewed their public campaign to save Lake Washington. Opponents again charged Metro supporters with promoting a centralized government, suggesting that the new "super government" was a kind of communist-inspired plot. An unusually hot and dry summer, however, coupled with newer scientific evidence that the health of the lake was even more imperiled than previously believed, helped the MAC to make its case for a clean lake. On 9 September, in spite of a low turnout, voters endorsed Metro 59 to 41 percent. Suburban voters approved the measure by nearly two-to-one. Metro supporters had convinced voters that a new political institution, supported by good science and efficient technology, could work.

At first, residents' confidence in Metro seemed justified. By early 1959, Metro engineers and planners fanned out across the Lake Washington Basin to build the most comprehensive sewerage system in the region. The first phase, completed in 1963, came in under budget and before schedule. Although Metro was not especially large when compared to other sewerage systems of the era, it attracted nationwide attention for its speed of construction, low cost, and widespread public support. Although some continued to complain about high sewerage bills and increased taxes, most felt that Metro had lived up to its promise: environmental quality at an affordable price. It also proved remarkably effective in arresting algae and pollution troubles in Lake Washington. By 1968 the direct dumping of municipal sewage into Lake Washington had completely stopped; by 1971 Edmondson proclaimed that water quality was better than it had been in nearly two decades.

Metro was not without its costs, however, and they were not insignificant. In order to divert effluent from the Lake Washington basin efficiently and inexpensively, engineers dumped treated sewage directly into the Duwamish River–the former outlet for the lake. Sewage outfalls, combined with industrial waste and residential pollution, threatened salmon runs and water quality along the lower Duwamish. When sportsmen and local residents complained that Lake Washington sewage was hurting the salmon, Metro officials deflected blame onto the Muckleshoot Indians, who were beginning to assert their treaty fishing rights on the upper reaches of the river. Metro also put more effluent into Puget Sound, following the old engineering dictum of "solving pollution with more dilution." The treatment plant at West Point, in the minds of some locals, now was affecting fragile marine life and hurting recreational fishing in Elliott Bay. Metro was not a panacea for the environmental woes in Seattle.

Despite the shortcomings of Metro, its successes pointed to how proponents both played upon and fostered a regional identity centered upon protecting nature and outdoor recreation. Convincing residents that nature could and must be improved was central to their campaign. Before Metro, Seattleites and their suburban neighbors had seen the lake as an amenity that would endure forever. They also understood that earlier residents had manipulated the lake for human benefit. Concerned reformers–led by politicians, engineers, and scientists–demonstrated how

MISCONCEPTIONS ANSWERED

University of Washington

Department of Zoology

Seattle 5

January 13, 1958

Metro Action Committee

507 Green Building

Seattle, Washington

Attn: Mrs. Lemere

Dear Mrs. Lemere:

On Friday I had a long telephone conversation with Nicolas A. Maffeo, who is chairman of a committee against Metro. This was not a very satisfactory conversation because he was not receptive to my contention that the interpretation is fully as important as the facts.

In thinking about the matter I suddenly realized the nature of a misconception about the lake that seems to be fairly widespread and could result in people deciding against an action like Metro, whereas would not if they realized the true situation. Therefore, I thought I had better tell you about the misconception so that you could inform your associates to be on the lookout for it and spike it whenever it comes up. The point is that some people are impressed by the fact that it appears that a large fraction of the income of dissolved phosphorus to the lake cannot be attributed to sewage. The misconception is that it would be necessary to reduce the phosphorus income to nothing in order to solve the algae problem. This is absolutely untrue and cannot be supported by scientific knowledge of lakes. The point is that all lakes receive phosphorus through their inlets and all lakes produce algae. In Lake Washington we are dealing with an overfertilisation and overproduction of algae. If a large fraction of the phosphorus income is removed from the lake, then the production of the algae must necessarily be reduced. I am convinced that the diversion of sewage alone would be adequate to push the condition of the lake back to something like the way it was before 1950 and hence perfectly acceptable. The evidence upon which I base this conclusion is very bulky, but includes in part the fact that Lake Washington has already demonstrated its ability to absorb large quantities of nutrients without producing algae nuisance conditions. Now we are getting to the point where the Lake is noticeably beginning to deteriorate. Nobody has ever claimed that it would be possible or necessary to prevent Lake Washington from growing any algae at all.

I asked Mr. Maffeo what would happen to him if he started eating only half as much and drinking only half as much water as he was used to. This question seemed to startle him and I think this question might well be asked anyone who proposes that cutting almost half of the nutrition of the lake would not have any effect. To my mind "solving the alga problem" means merely reducing the nutrient supply enough to reduce the production of algae to an acceptable condition such as that existing before 1950. I believe that diversion of sewage is adequate to accomplish this end.

Of course, I recognize that we must have reasonable land-use policies in the area, but on the basis of my present knowledge I do not think that anything more elaborate than sewage diversion is necessary to maintain the lake in good condition. If conditions were to develop in the future which required some control of erosion or land drainage, the problem would have to be solved on a regional, not a local basis.

Sincerely yours,

W. T. Edmondson

Professor of Zoology

Source: *W. T. Edmondson to Metro Action Committee, 13 January 1958, James R. Ellis papers, Box 1, Acc. 2146, Manuscripts, Special Collections, University Archives, University of Washington Libraries.*

human activity was hurting the lake and how human intervention could save it. In a sense, the success of Metro helped to forge the identity of Seattle as an environmentally conscious city. Whether this image continues to reflect the true condition of the local natural environment remains open to debate, but for the millions who enjoy the clear waters of Lake Washington, the legacy of Metro may lie in the message that some environmental catastrophes are partially reversible.

–MATTHEW W. KLINGLE,
UNIVERSITY OF WASHINGTON, SEATTLE

Viewpoint:
No. By enabling uncontrolled suburban growth in the Seattle area, regional wastewater treatment worsened water pollution in the long run while falsely suggesting that deeply rooted environmental problems in the United States were easily solvable.

In the 1950s development pushed out from Seattle and into the cutover forests and farmland surrounding Lake Washington. Suburban growth requires people willing to pay for housing, but also services such as streets, water, garbage collection, and sewers to serve the needs of an affluent lifestyle. In this boom a limiting factor to growth was often not input but output: new development was sometimes stymied not by a lack of consumer items but by places to put the waste. Since the mid 1940s the Washington State Pollution Control Commission had required that sewage be treated according to increasingly strict standards. By the mid 1950s real-estate developers and state water-pollution regulators both favored large trunk sewers in the Lake Washington area that would intercept smaller lines from homes and deliver the raw sewage to centralized treatment plants. By building only a few large plants, wastewater could be treated to higher standards at lower overall cost. Who would pay, however, the billions of dollars needed for these sewers and treatment plants? Cost-conscious developers and city officials balked at the idea of taking on that kind of debt. By the mid 1950s state pollution authorities warned that Lake Washington would soon be unsafe for swimming, and cities and builders insisted they could not pay for new sewers.

Sewage disposal was the major limiting factor to the continued growth of suburbs in Seattle. Too many people already lived in the basin, and their waste flowed downhill into Lake Washington. State regulators and civic officials recognized that to preserve this key suburban environmental amenity, they would have to remove effluent from the lake. The issue was most pressing for lakeside towns such as Bellevue, whose sewage commissioners proposed a united plan in 1956 to collect waste from all Eastside communities, present and future, and pipe it to a central treatment plant for disposal outside the basin. At first, the proposal received little support from developers, who wanted immediate, if temporary, drains for their new houses.

At its core, solving the pollution problem in the urban Puget Sound region was a political and regulatory task. State regulators played a major role in bringing together recalcitrant developers and Eastside mayors. The state Pollution Control Commission (PCC) instituted a new policy in July 1956: all effluent should be removed from Lake Washington, and all towns and new developments should work toward this goal. It also pushed the governor of Washington to hire a consulting engineer to design a comprehensive sewer report for the region, which was completed in March 1958. The report echoed earlier Eastside proposals for trunk sewers to collect waste from the lake basin and carry it far away for treatment and dumping. Backed by prominent engineers, scientists, and the PCC, the sewer report suggested a plan to solve the problem of continued Eastside growth at minimal cost and without further damaging Lake Washington.

To pass a public-sewage authority, backers had to gain the support of a majority of city and county voters. Eastside interests teamed up with Seattle civic reformers, who planned an ambitious new governmental authority that would take over delivery throughout the region of urban services such as planning, garbage, water, and public transit, as well as sewage treatment. These reformers sought more orderly development of the region, which they regarded as inevitable and even desirable. Many residents of the small towns around Seattle, however, felt differently about growth and metropolitan government. Opponents of the measure described Metro as a monster that would burden taxpayers with heavy assessments while enabling Seattle to swallow its neighbors. Their message resonated with enough voters and the ambitious initiative lost in the March 1958 elections.

Immediately after the election, a coalition of Eastside interests acted to salvage a sewage utility from the wreckage of the defeated measure. In a compromise, Eastside cities, Seattle officials, and suburban developers backed a new initiative that formed an institution solely dedicated to sewage treatment and disposal. Proponents dangled a carrot in front of tightfisted voters: the new sewage authority would save lots of money by achieving economies of scale. The PCC added a stick: any further sewage produced in the region would have to be disposed of on land, effectively blocking further construction. Civic activists stepped forward to promote this measure as a means to come together around a treasured local resource, Lake Washington. Advertisements, like a poster crying "Clean up our filthy waters!" appealed to voters' sense of communal responsibility for their environment.

Whether this campaign and the subsequent election was a mandate to save the environment is questionable. When the measure passed that September, backers proclaimed it a victory for a new kind of regional identity. Yet, if Metro was a referendum on a regional identity, it is remarkable how few residents even bothered to vote. An even lower percentage of area residents voted in the September election than had in March, despite the increased publicity by the Metro Action Campaign and opponents. Saving Lake Washington had crystallized the campaign for Metro proponents, but many prospective voters seemed ambivalent about rescuing nature.

Nonetheless, metropolitan sewage treatment did succeed in diverting the wastes choking Lake Washington. Within a few years the lake was noticeably cleaner. Yet, Metro succeeded by exporting the pollution into neighboring watersheds, particularly to Puget Sound. Regional wastewater treatment failed in its more ambitious goals. Metro did not solve the animus between Seattle and its suburbs, which complicated efforts at regional planning into the twenty-first century. Metro did not take seriously the objections of its opponents, who tapped into a deep resentment of the booming growth in the region. Instead, Metro built a myth of a false consensus and patched over the nagging issue of the costs of growth with a technological fix.

The complicated history of regional wastewater treatment in greater Seattle tells us much about the American relationship to nature since 1945. Voters in 1958 were cajoled by a wave of publicity to "Clean up our filthy waters" in a manner that foreshadowed the environmentalism of later decades. A majority of those few who voted did choose to tax themselves to save their lake, but many more people were influenced by years of public discussion about a cost-effective way to provide sewage disposal for a booming region. The regional waste-treatment authority of Seattle solved the practical needs of builders and homeowners, not simply the conservationist urges of an enlightened public.

Therein lies the irony of this solution to regional water pollution. Metro was an initiative sold as a means to clean up a lake and was passed by cost-conscious consumers, but it ultimately aided the pollution of the lake it was supposed to protect by encouraging further growth. In retrospect, Metro seems like an environmental catch-22. The Metro campaign has been valorized as a successful solution and the beginnings of environmental activism in Seattle. History suggests that this past, however, was far more complicated. Lake Washington was not endangered in 1958 by the lack of sewage treatment and disposal, but by a highly consumptive American society that damaged the environment it fed upon. Rather than addressing the root cause of pollution, regional sewage treatment permitted further suburban sprawl. Postwar growth carried a built-in paradox: the more that suburbs expanded, the more they threatened the very qualities that made living there attractive. The message of the Lake Washington story may be that there are no easy technological solutions to pollution.

–MATTHEW BOOKER,
STANFORD UNIVERSITY

References

Carl Abbott, *The Metropolitan Frontier: Cities in the Modern American West* (Tucson: University of Arizona Press, 1993).

W. T. Edmondson, *The Uses of Ecology: Lake Washington and Beyond* (Seattle: University of Washington Press, 1991).

Sarah S. Elkind, *Bay Cities and Water Politics: The Battle for Resources in Boston and Oakland* (Lawrence: University Press of Kansas, 1998).

John M. Findlay, *Magic Lands: Western Cityscapes and American Culture after 1940* (Berkeley: University of California Press, 1992).

Joel B. Hagen, *An Entangled Bank: The Origins of Ecosystem Ecology* (New Brunswick, N.J.: Rutgers University Press, 1992).

Samuel P. Hays, with Barbara D. Hays, *Beauty, Health, and Permanence: Environmental Politics in the United States, 1955–1985* (Cambridge & New York: Cambridge University Press, 1987).

Andrew Hurley, *Environmental Inequalities: Class, Race, and Industrial Pollution in Gary, Indiana, 1945–1980* (Chapel Hill: University of North Carolina Press, 1995).

Hurley, ed. *Common Fields: An Environmental History of St. Louis* (St. Louis: Missouri State Historical Society, 1997).

Kenneth T. Jackson, *Crabgrass Frontier: The Suburbanization of the United States* (New York: Oxford University Press, 1985).

Terrence Kehoe, *Cleaning Up the Great Lakes: From Cooperation to Confrontation* (DeKalb: Northern Illinois University Press, 1997).

Martin V. Melosi, *The Sanitary City: Urban Infrastructure in America from Colonial Times to the Present* (Baltimore: Johns Hopkins University Press, 2000).

Metropolitan Seattle Sewerage and Drainage Survey: A Report for the City of Seattle, King County, and the State of Washington on the Collection, Treatment, and Disposal of Sewage and the Collection and Disposal of Storm Water in the Metropolitan Seattle Area (San Francisco & Seattle: Brown & Caldwell, 1958).

Adam Ward Rome, "Prairie Creek Hills Estates: An Environmental History of American Homebuilding, 1945–1970," dissertation, University of Kansas, 1996.

Carlos A. Schwantes, *The Pacific Northwest: An Interpretive History,* revised edition (Lincoln: University of Nebraska Press, 1996).

R. Bruce Stephenson, *Visions of Eden: Environmentalism, Urban Planning, and City Building in St. Petersburg, Florida, 1900–1995* (Columbus: Ohio State University Press, 1997).

Jeffrey K. Stine, *Mixing the Waters: Environment, Politics, and the Building of the Tennessee-Tombigbee Waterway* (Akron, Ohio: University of Akron Press, 1993).

Joel A. Tarr, *The Search for the Ultimate Sink: Urban Pollution in Historical Perspective* (Akron, Ohio: University of Akron Press, 1996).

Richard White, *"It's your misfortune and none of my own": A New History of the American West* (Norman: University of Oklahoma Press, 1991).

PACIFIC SALMON

Why are the Pacific salmon in crisis?

Viewpoint: For more than a century, Pacific Northwesterners have refused to recognize limits to their consumption of salmon, and the rivers they depend upon, treating them as inexhaustible resources and ruining both.

Viewpoint: Over-reliance on hatcheries and the belief that technology can provide a remedy to declining habitat quality have been responsible for the decline of Pacific salmon.

In 1992 only two sockeye salmon (*Onchorynchus nerka*) returned to their spawning grounds along the upper Snake River in western Idaho. That same year a federal agency declared the sockeye an endangered species according to the Endangered Species Act of 1972. The Snake River sockeye were the first of many populations of Pacific salmon (*Oncorhyncus*) on the West Coast to reach critically low levels in the 1990s. Throughout the second half of the twentieth century, many populations (or stocks, in fishery parlance) of salmon declined throughout their range from Alaska to Mexico.

With the reduction in salmon numbers came a human crisis as well. Commercial, sport, and subsistence fisheries were cut back or eliminated, throwing thousands of families out of work. Hydropower dams on western rivers, major producers of cheap power and light throughout the region, were indicted for blocking salmon from free passage from the streams to the ocean. Billions of dollars were spent in efforts to adapt the dams to allow fish passage. The regional economy was threatened directly when federal agencies, empowered by the Endangered Species Act, ordered changes in land use that might affect salmon habitat in rural and urban areas alike.

What caused the twentieth-century decline in Pacific salmon? Since the 1940s this question has led to heated exchanges in the West. Every user of the rich resources of the region found a reason to blame every other user. Fishers and biologists charged that the burgeoning construction of dams for power, irrigation water, and navigation—more than one hundred were built in the Columbia Basin alone—doomed salmon to a certain death. Barge companies, power users, and irrigators noted that an ever-more-efficient fleet of fishermen scooped up salmon from an ever-shrinking population. Both groups accused logging companies of ruining spawning and rearing habitat in mountain streams following the removal of timber.

Fishery managers increasingly relied on hatcheries to replace the fish that were disappearing from rivers. Critics noted with alarm that hatchery salmon interbred with, and sapped the natural vitality of, wild fish. Hatchery and wild salmon mingled in the ocean too, further confusing predictions of abundance. In the end, all the finger-pointing did not stop the slide toward extinction of the Pacific salmon. The real cause of the decline was a mixture of many factors, some of which are poorly understood.

The complicated life history of Pacific salmon is one important factor in understanding the history behind their decline. "Pacific salmon" is a broad term that refers to a complex and varied genus of seven species, each of which has a different form adapted to life in specific rivers. The sockeye salmon of the upper Snake River, for example, have a different life history than the sockeye salmon of Bristol Bay, Alaska. All Pacific salmon, however, require clean, cold freshwater streams to lay their eggs. The young fry then remain a varying time in freshwater—from days to a year or more—before migrating downstream, where they spend from one to five years feeding on fish and shrimp in the ocean. Guided by still mysterious forces, the adult salmon then return to precisely the stream where they were hatched, completing the cycle. After reproducing, Pacific salmon die, and their carcasses provide an important source of nutrients for their offspring. Remarkably well adapted to their environments, populations of salmon evolved to fit most streams draining into the Pacific from the Arctic to Mexico.

Yet, the same diversity that fits them into so many niches means that Pacific salmon are highly susceptible to anthropogenic—or human-induced—changes to their environment. Dependent on both pristine streams and favorable ocean conditions, salmon are vulnerable throughout their life cycle. Individual salmon populations have fluctuated widely from abundance to scarcity, but only in the last few decades of the twentieth century were salmon threatened throughout their range. In asking "what caused this salmon crisis?" it is important to revisit the natural and human history of this species before suggesting any answers.

Viewpoint: For more than a century, Pacific Northwesterners have refused to recognize limits to their consumption of salmon, and the rivers they depend upon, treating them as inexhaustible resources and ruining both.

More than a century after fisheries expert Livingston Stone called for the dedication of salmon parks to protect spawning grounds in 1892, no major river system between Alaska and Mexico remained unblocked or was completely protected from fishing. The Columbia River, once filled with salmon from the Pacific to the Rocky Mountains–one thousand miles inland–is now an obstacle course of concrete dams backing the river up into a series of stagnant pools. Despite the fact that salmon lost most of their spawning grounds and freshwater habitat, fishing pressure remained intense. Columbia River salmon were pursued in the high seas by drift netters, along ocean shores by seiners and trollers, and in estuaries and rivers by gillnetters and sportfishers. Not coincidentally, the huge runs of all seven Pacific salmon species in the Columbia shrank to a fraction of their former glory. The remnants of famous chinook salmon, fish weighing one hundred pounds or more, spawn only in the last remaining unblocked reach. All along the Pacific slope, salmon must run a gauntlet of nets and dams to reach their spawning grounds. The combination of excessive harvesting by fishermen and dams blocking migration was at the heart of the salmon crisis. It was a crisis of consumption, not production. No matter how many salmon were caught or kilowatt hours produced, there were never enough salmon or hydroelectricity to satisfy the demands of consumers.

As long as there have been people in the Pacific Northwest, they have harnessed the salmon and the energy of rivers. Native people for millennia tapped the abundant salmon and used a variety of plants and animals in the extensive forests. Salmon are like bolts of electricity when attached to the end of a line. Their flesh is fat and protein-rich: they are concentrated repositories of nutrients from the Pacific Ocean, which they burn as they make their long way upstream against powerful river currents. The first people to live in the Pacific Northwest recognized that salmon were an ideal source of energy. Over millennia, the Native Americans built dense and complex societies supported by the abundant and predictable salmon runs, and evolved highly adapted methods of fishing for the seven species of salmon in both fresh and saltwater.

American settlers who entered the Northwest in the nineteenth century also relied on the bountiful salmon and powerful rivers of the region. Few conceived of limits to their use: anyone could see that the Indians, despite taking millions of fish annually from the rivers and bays, had barely touched the tremendous salmon resource. Fish were among the first regional products to be shipped to distant markets, and they became a key food source for burgeoning cities such as Portland and Seattle. Beginning in 1866 with a cannery on the Columbia River, salmon canneries appeared on almost every major river in the region. By 1884 thirty-seven canneries processed forty-two million pounds of salmon from the Columbia River alone.

Unrestrained salmon fisheries quickly overexploited their resource. Unlike traditional native fisheries, which had taken salmon at many points throughout the rivers and in the ocean, whites concentrated at only a few spots where access was easiest and the fish were most easily canned and shipped. The imperative of an expanding global market drove their ambitions. Unlike the natives, who recognized and fished for many distinct species and runs of salmon, whites concentrated on a few populations, such as the enormous "June hogs," an exceptionally large and flavorful run of Columbia River chinook salmon that entered the river in the easy-to-fish summer months. Finally, while native people had evolved a set of religious practices toward salmon that effectively placed limits on exploitation, whites faced no barriers to their consumption. Late-nineteenth-century salmon fisheries were, furthermore, efficient only at catching salmon, not at processing them: sometimes canneries, when already working at full capacity, dumped boatloads of dead salmon.

By the turn of the century, salmon catches on the Columbia River were sharply lower than previous decades. In a declining fishery, users began to fight for access to this dwindling resource. Often, stronger users pushed out weaker ones. Fish-wheel operators fenced native people, who held treaty rights to fish, out of their traditional sites. State and federal courts upheld white fishers over Native Americans in a landmark 1905 case on the Columbia River. Increased competition also attracted the attention of legislators, who created state agencies to regulate the fisheries.

While often in conflict, both fishers and regulators wanted more fish. Hatcheries promised to produce more salmon than could reproduce in the degraded streams, and despite many problems, they sometimes succeeded. Even successful hatchery programs, however, rarely replaced the fish lost by blockage of streams or met the demands of consumers. Despite the widespread wastage of salmon in the early fishery and increasing pressures on their survival because of habitat degradation, few people seriously considered restricting the consumption of what was regarded as a public resource. In a pattern that held true throughout the twentieth century, regulations on the fisheries came too late, faced much resistance, and rarely reduced pressure on salmon populations.

The same attitude of natural abundance without limits toward salmon dominated discussion and use of the regional waterways. At first the streams that drained the Pacific slope served as convenient transportation routes for shipment of products to distant markets. Indian canoes, sailing ships, and eventually steamboats plied the inland waterways in the nineteenth century. Even after the advent of railroads and trucking in the twentieth century, the rivers remained important and inexpensive highways for bulk goods such as grain, lumber, and produce.

With the widespread diffusion of hydroelectric technology, Northwesterners envisioned another way to extract value from rivers. In the 1930s federal planners pointed out that the Columbia River alone contained 40 percent of the potential hydroelectric energy of the entire nation. An alliance of local boosters and federal engineers set out to realize that potential, beginning with Grand Coulee and Bonneville Dams. When completed in the desolate emptiness of eastern Washington in 1938, Grand Coulee Dam was the biggest man-made structure on earth. It harnessed so much electricity from the pooled force of river water that even boosters wondered what to do with it. Promoters promised that Grand Coulee would turn a million acres of desert into lush farmland, providing farms for tens of thousands of industrious Americans.

The hydroelectric facilities built in the 1930s were actually not the first dams to be built on Northwest rivers and streams. Nineteenth-century loggers constructed temporary "splash" dams on small streams. After filling the streambed with cut trees, loggers blasted the dams to wash the timber down to mills and markets. Miners, factories, and some cities also built reservoirs to store water for drinking and industrial use. Hydroelectric dams, however, were the first to entirely block the main stems of the major Northwest rivers, which also happened to be salmon highways.

Despite its many benefits, hydroelectricity was not without its costs. As early as the 1930s, critics pointed out that the dams blocked upstream migration of spawning salmon, while the reservoirs behind them replaced cold, fast-flowing rivers with tepid and stagnant pools in which disease flourished and predators thrived on weak and confused juvenile salmon. These small fish were ground up in hydroelectric turbines and swept onto irrigated fields by diversion dams. Despite vociferous protests from some fishermen, dams went up at almost every possible site during the decades after 1945.

The postwar Northwest quickly became addicted to the cheap hydroelectricity that flowed from the dams. Aluminum smelters and defense plants used all the energy that could be produced in the 1940s, and postwar planners called for new structures to meet projected demand for power. Dam building proceeded apace through the 1970s. From 1961 to 1984, despite years of experience with the devastating impact on salmon, more than twenty additional multipurpose dams were built on the Columbia River and its tributaries. Perhaps more would have been built if there had been sites for them, but engineers were running out of river. The main stem of the Columbia, once a pipeline for millions of salmon, by the early 1980s was a series of still lakes punctuated by concrete monoliths.

A consistent decline in salmon numbers during the twentieth century continued to foster bitter competition among fishers. Earlier debates had pitted fishermen against each other on the basis of the gear they used or their ethnicity. By the 1960s these same struggles were resurgent. Sportfishers blamed commercial fishermen and Native Americans for reducing the runs of fish. Both commercial and sportfishers blamed Native Americans, despite the fact they were taking a tiny percentage of the overall catch. Fishery managers often agreed, further restricting traditional Indian fishing locations and methods. In the 1960s Native Americans fishermen began to stage "fish-ins" to protest their mistreatment by authorities. They also went to court. In the 1970s federal appellate courts reaffirmed Native Americans' rights to fish in common with whites, which the court interpreted to mean that they should have 50 percent of the catch. Led by presiding judge George Boldt, the federal court even briefly took over management of Northwest fisheries when the state of Washington refused to comply. The Boldt decisions were dramatic federal interventions that prefigured the power of Endangered Species Act (1973) listing of salmon in the 1990s, but ultimately they merely redistributed an ever-shrinking pie. As Native American fishermen bitterly noted, half of nothing is still nothing.

The steady decline of salmon was publicly discussed for nearly all of the twentieth century. Their disappearance preoccupied residents of a region where salmon had long been a key part of the good life, an existence that also included an economy based on the abundant and cheap hydroelectricity. Pacific Northwesterners came to rely on the two forms of energy taken from rivers–electricity and salmon–but few accepted that one comes at the expense of the other.

–MATTHEW BOOKER,
STANFORD UNIVERSITY

Viewpoint:
Over-reliance on hatcheries and the belief that technology can provide a remedy to declining habitat quality have been responsible for the decline of Pacific salmon.

Fish ladder at the Bonneville Dam on the Columbia River, Oregon

(Oxford Scientific Films/Mike Birkhead)

Salmon symbolize the good life along the north Pacific coast. Beautiful and delicious, they stand for the natural abundance of the region, but consuming salmon has put them at risk. In order to keep the good life going, residents have repeatedly turned to science and technology to manufacture more salmon. They came to rely upon hatcheries to produce salmon and help them to coexist with industries (such as logging and grazing) that often destroyed their habitat. The residents' faith, however, changed over time as salmon populations continued to decline. By the post–World War II period, science and technology were criticized for driving salmon into extinction–even as most residents continued to look to scientists and engineers for solutions. The historical relationship between science, technology, society, and the physical environment illustrates how maintaining the good life that salmon represented has always been under debate.

The roots of the contemporary salmon crisis extend to how nineteenth-century Euramericans in the far West understood their relationship to the natural world. Settlers coming to the Pacific slope carried two stories with them across the continent: one invoked the Fall from

PUT THE FISH BACK INTO THE RIVERS

The salmon's spirit–Wy-Kan-Ush-Mi Wa-Kish-Wit–is sacred life. The salmon has provided a perfect world in which to enjoy its existence. For thousands of years, the salmon unselfishly gave of itself for the physical and spiritual sustenance of humans. The salmon's spirit has not changed; the human spirit has.

Today the perfect world of the salmon is in total disarray. Even its very existence and worth are being debated. Human arrogance has brought the salmon to the brink of extinction.

Rather than a dignified cultural icon, the salmon is being redefined as a problem, as something that makes unacceptable the human laws designed to protect the environment. In spite of the state of crisis, crude science and perilous politics have reduced the salmon and its habitat to a struggling species living in a polluted and life-threatening home.

The four Columbia River treaty tribes, who are keepers of ancient truths and laws of nature, employ the depths of their hearts and expanse of their minds to save the salmon. . . .

If the salmon are to survive in the Columbia River Watershed, we must face the challenges before us with our goals clearly in mind, in heart, and in spirit. We must now begin to respect, to reestablish, and to restore the balances that once enabled this watershed to perform so magnificently.

Wy-Kan-Ush-Mi Wa-Kish-Wit: The Columbia River Anadromous Fish Restoration Plan of the Nez Perce, Umatilla, Warm Springs and Yakarna Tribes provides a framework to restore the Columbia River salmon, simply stated: put the fish back into the rivers. Yet making this happen has become increasingly difficult because of the decades of poorly guided and deeply entrenched fish management policies. More than science and its limits, the problems have almost always involved people and their institutions–whether government, business or otherwise.

Much of what is recommended to benefit the salmon is what has been needed and known for a long time. More than 50 years ago, Federal biologists warned that the consequences of continued habitat degradation and additional hydroelectric development would be devastating to the salmon populations. They were joined by tribal leaders and through the years, by government commissions and citizen groups.

However, until the enactment of the Pacific Northwest Power Planning and Conservation Act of 1980 and its fish and wildlife program, there was no comprehensive salmon restoration program for the Columbia Basin. Had the Northwest Power Planning Council's salmon plan been implemented, the people of the Northwest would not be today facing a salmon crisis. . . .

Wy-Kan-Ush-Mi Wa-Kish-Wit is the culmination of the leadership and wisdom of the Nez Perce, Umatilla, Warm Springs and Yakarna fish and wildlife committees and the technical work of reservation fisheries and the Columbia River Inter-Tribal Fish Commission staffs. This tribal salmon restoration plan outlines the cultural, biological, legal, institutional and economic context within which the region's salmon restoration efforts are taking place. This long-term plan addresses virtually all causes of salmon decline and roadblocks to salmon restoration for all anadromous fish stocks: chinook, coho, sockeye, steelhead, chum, eels (Pacific lamprey) and sturgeon, above Bonneville Dam. This area, encompassing about three quarters of the Columbia River Basin, is where most of the tribes' treaty-reserved fishing places and fish resources are located.

The Columbia River treaty tribes take a holistic "gravel-to-gravel" approach to the management of the salmon, which differs from approaches of many other groups in a variety of respects. This approach focuses on the tributary, mainstem, estuary, and ocean ecosystems and habitats where anadromous fish live. The focus on passage, habitat, harvest and production requires substantial changes in current practices and specific actions to recover from historical destructive impacts.

Source: *"Wy-Kan-Ush-Mi Wa-Kish-Wit: Spirit of the Salmon,"* Salmon in the Columbia River Basin: Review of the Proposed Recovery Plan, Hearing Before the Subcommittee on Fisheries, Wildlife, and Drinking Water of the Committee on Environment and Public Works, *United States Senate, 23 June 1999 (Washington, D.C.: Government Printing Office, 2000), pp. 61–63.*

Eden, arguing that humans inevitably destroyed nature; the other looked at nature as a kind of garden, with humans improving the environment. The tensions between these two representations of how Americans interact with nature deeply affected the Pacific salmon fisheries. Residents in the region have always feared that salmon were a finite resource, but they have also believed, with equal fervor, that they could make salmon last forever.

By the late nineteenth century these two visions were on a collision course as extractive industries transformed the Northwest. By 1900 mining, grazing, agriculture, and logging significantly reduced salmon habitat. Mining was especially destructive. Placer operations in Oregon, Idaho, and California rerouted streams, leaving spawning salmon high and dry. Hydraulic mining amplified such effects by using pressurized water to wash down entire hillsides, burying salmon nests, or redds, beneath the rubble. Irrigated agriculture, like mining, also mangled salmon streams. Farmers living in the arid expanses of Idaho, California, Washington, and Oregon diverted water to their fields during the dry summer months when spawning salmon needed it the most. After the passage of the Newlands Act (1902), which promoted federally-subsidized irrigation, large-scale farms further transformed streams and rivers into deadly mazes of ditches and canals that trapped confused salmon. Remaking the rivers of the Northwest to the benefit of mines and farms spelled disaster for the Pacific salmon.

Other extractive industries also destroyed salmon habitat. Livestock, raised for hungry miners and city dwellers, trampled grasses and soils that held stream banks in place and exacerbated erosion while polluting waters with their excrement. Logging completed the gauntlet of challenges facing spawning salmon. Loggers, who cut nearly a billion board feet annually in Oregon by the late 1880s, initially used streams to move raw timber to mills. In order to expedite timber shipments, they built splash dams to hold water back until enough logs could be flushed downstream. The resulting floods scoured streambeds, uprooting any redds in their path. Removing trees from stream banks also exposed spawning beds to direct sunlight, elevating water temperatures to fatal levels. Downstream, lumber mills dumped tons of sawdust into the waters, smothering spawning beds. As extractive industries such as these expanded across the Pacific Northwest landscape, it seemed that the nightmare of Eden despoiled had arrived.

Hatcheries seemed to offer salvation from this impasse. Political culture at the time believed in the principle of multiple use abetted by minimal regulation. Resource managers and early conservationists thus saw artificial propagation as a panacea that would prevent salmon extinction while keeping extractive industry intact. Hatcheries also avoided increasingly complicated debates over how best to regulate fishers and reduce conflict between them. State governments, unwilling to restrain fishing or restrict habitat destruction, were also able to put the onus on the federal government instead.

The United States Fish Commission (USFC), created in 1870, was the federal agency that first brokered a deal between these interests by promoting hatcheries. Spencer Fullerton Baird, the first USFC commissioner, championed artificial propagation as a way to prevent salmon extinction, while also improving natural runs even further. Fish culture in the United States dated back to the 1850s, but Baird proposed a network of hatcheries to produce salmon all along the Pacific Coast. In his mind, hatcheries evoked the promise of unlimited bounty for all without sacrifices by any. Technology, in the form of hatcheries, became politics by proxy.

Natural occurrences beyond human control also inadvertently made hatcheries seem necessary. In 1877 fishers along the Pacific coast faced one of the worse salmon seasons in memory. As everyone started assigning blame, Baird pointed to hatcheries as the best way to save the fisheries without unnecessary regulation. Scientists and historians later suggested that El Niño–an atmospheric and oceanic phenomenon where warmer waters from the equatorial Pacific push northward into colder coastal waters likely decimated Northwest runs. The event left commercial fisheries along the Columbia River with empty nets and unfilled cans. Frustrated at a nature they could no longer control, the industry accepted the premise that making salmon would solve their problems.

By the turn of the century, hatcheries became the primary instrument in Pacific salmon management despite evidence questioning their effectiveness. Federal, state, and private hatcheries sprouted along the rivers and streams, manufacturing salmon in an industrial process. Hatcheries trapped spawning female salmon, stripped their eggs, fertilized them artificially, and raised the juveniles in ponds before releasing them. As early as the 1890s, however, local operators questioned whether hatcheries worked. Federal fisheries biologist Willis Rich produced damning evidence during the 1920s that hatcheries had not saved one declining fishery. Rich's findings, along with other criticisms, were ignored or actively suppressed in a political and economic climate that promoted multiple use. Arguing against hatcheries was akin to arguing against progress.

The Great Depression (1929–1941) only sharpened the dependence of the region upon hatcheries to counteract habitat destruction. The 1930s was a boom period for the Pacific slope. Federal investment poured into the region as part of President Franklin D. Roosevelt's New Deal. The Bonneville Power Administration and the Columbia Basin Project, two of the largest hydroelectric and irrigation systems in the nation, helped to reinvigorate the sagging local economy by remaking the Columbia River. Despite their important economic benefits, gigantic dams and irrigation diversions blocked salmon from their historic spawning grounds. Protests from commercial and sportfishers pressured the U.S. Congress to pass the Mitchell Act in 1938, instructing the Bureau of Reclamation and Army Corps of Engineers to make dams more salmon friendly. Devices, such as ladders, to carry spawning fish past the dams, however, proved woefully inadequate at maintaining runs. In the midst of an economic and social crisis most residents felt that hatcheries would lessen the consequences. By 1945 most streams in the western United States and Canada had at least one state, provincial, or federal hatchery along their banks.

Dependence upon hatcheries continued into the postwar period as economic expansion fostered the sense that humans had remade Northwest nature into a perpetual growth machine. Postwar affluence led to an increased population and a demand for raw materials to fuel still more growth. Extractive industries continued to exact high tolls upon salmon habitat in order to meet consumers' wishes. Logging skyrocketed after World War II to fuel the construction boom. New homes and industries depended upon big dams for hydroelectricity and food. As more urbanites turned toward outdoor pursuits, such as sportfishing, they insisted upon more fish to catch. Hatcheries became a way to satisfy everyone, and scientists promised even more spectacular results. Salmon biologists and hatchery operators experimented with new foods, breeding techniques, and rearing methods to boost production. To paraphrase environmental historian Richard White, in *The Organic Machine* (1995), humans had transformed the salmon fisheries into an "organic machine" where the man-made and the natural blurred.

Many individuals felt that this organic machine was beginning to break down, as concerns sharpened over still-declining salmon runs. Attention focused on both known causes, for example habitat destruction, and newer culprits, such as hatcheries. The rising power of the environmental movement signaled the growing skepticism of many Americans toward the effects of technology upon nature. Newer kinds of science and technology, such as evolutionary biology and genetics, gave critics the tools to evaluate the effects of hatcheries on native salmon. Some researchers argued that artificial propagation had diluted genetic diversity, leaving salmon more vulnerable to disease and environmental changes. Hatchery proponents discounted such claims as political posturing. As Lauren Donaldson, a fisheries scientist at the University of Washington, insisted in a 1991 interview, hatcheries were unimpeachable. "The technology is there," he proclaimed, "just tell us how many fish you want." Others were not so sure that manufacturing Frankenstein-like salmon for dying rivers was the best way to keep the fisheries viable.

By the 1990s the critics of technological fixes had prevailed, but awareness of the crisis did not prevent some salmon runs from declining even further. The intense El Niño seasons of 1983–1984 and the late 1990s hammered some runs into near extinction, proving conclusively that hatcheries alone could not forestall disaster. A growing sense of urgency spread across the region, culminating in the 1999 Endangered Species Act listing of salmon runs in the Seattle and Portland metropolitan areas. It was the first time that the salmon crisis directly affected the cities. Businesses, homeowners, and municipal governments now faced strict limits on building, water usage, and pollution control. More residents than ever could now lay claim to salmon, their habitat, and the best ways to protect both.

Ultimately the same politics of blame that had made hatcheries so desirable also made eliminating them completely all but impossible. By the 1980s battle lines had reemerged between environmentalists favoring logging bans and breaching dams, Native Americans asserting fishing-treaty rights, farmers and industries fighting against dam removal and water restrictions, and sportfishers wanting fish in their creels. Too many demands on too little fish meant that some still saw hatcheries as the only solution. Native American tribes along the Columbia River, for example, opened their own hatcheries to ensure steady runs. Sportfishers supported government hatcheries while condemning Indian fishers for taking or producing too many fish. Even some environmentalists admitted that some hatcheries might be necessary to keep dying runs on life support in lieu of habitat restoration. Residents wanted to remake the machinery of the salmon fisheries, but they were now dependent upon it as well.

As the salmon emergency continued into the twenty-first century, the two prevailing stories that guided fisheries management in the region continued to shape its future. Residents saw that technological fixes and habitat destruction despoiled the once great fisheries in the Northwest. Yet, they also acknowledged that without human intervention some salmon runs may not survive at all. Any solution will ultimately have to address the complex history that has made the plight of Pacific salmon one of the most durable environmental crises in the United States—that rests, in part, upon untangling the snarled connections between science, technology, society, and an unpredictable natural world.

—MATTHEW W. KLINGLE,
UNIVERSITY OF WASHINGTON, SEATTLE

References

Charlene J. Allison, Sue-Ellen Jacobs, and Mary A. Porter, eds., *Winds of Change: Women in Northwest Commercial Fishing* (Seattle: University of Washington Press, 1989).

Daniel Boxberger, *To Fish in Common: The Ethnohistory of Lummi Indian Salmon Fishing*, revised edition (Seattle: University of Washington Press, 1999).

Bruce Brown, *Mountain in the Clouds: A Search for the Wild Salmon* (New York: Simon & Schuster, 1982).

Committee on Protection and Management of Pacific Northwest Anadromous Salmonids, Board on Environmental Studies and Toxicology, Commission on Life Sciences, *Upstream: Salmon and Society in the Pacific Northwest* (Washington, D.C.: National Academy Press, 1996).

Joseph Cone, *A Common Fate: Endangered Salmon and the People of the Pacific Northwest* (New York: Holt, 1995).

Cone, and Sandy Ridlington, eds., *The Northwest Salmon Crisis: A Documentary History* (Corvallis: Oregon State University Press, 1996).

Chris Friday, *Organizing Asian American Labor: The Pacific Coast Canned-Salmon Industry, 1870–1942* (Philadelphia: Temple University Press, 1994).

C. Groot and L. Margolis, eds., *Pacific Salmon Life Histories* (Vancouver: University of British Columbia Press, 1991).

Blaine Harden, *A River Lost: The Life and Death of the Columbia* (New York: Norton, 1996).

Jim Lichatowich, *Salmon Without Rivers: A History of the Pacific Salmon Crisis* (Washington, D.C.: Island Press, 1999).

Irene Martin, *Legacy and Testament: The Story of Columbia River Gillnetters* (Pullman: Washington State University Press, 1994).

Arthur F. McEvoy, *The Fisherman's Problem: Ecology and Law in the California Fisheries, 1850–1980* (Cambridge & New York: Cambridge University Press, 1986).

Diane Newell, *Tangled Webs of History: Indians and the Law in Canada's Pacific Coast Fisheries* (Toronto & Buffalo: University of Toronto Press, 1993).

Newell, ed., *The Development of the Pacific Salmon Canning Industry: A Grown Man's Game* (Kingston, Ontario: McGill-Queen's University Press, 1989).

Courtland L. Smith, *Salmon Fishers of the Columbia River* (Corvallis: Oregon State University Press, 1979).

Joseph E. Taylor III, *Making Salmon: An Environmental History of the Northwest Fisheries Crisis* (Seattle: University of Washington Press, 1999).

Roberta Ulrich, *Empty Nets: Indians, Dams, and the Columbia River* (Corvallis: Oregon State University Press, 1999).

Richard White, *The Organic Machine* (New York: Hill & Wang, 1995).

RHINE CANAL

Is the ecological cost of the Rhine-Main-Danube Canal to the Altmühl Valley justified by the economic benefit it promises?

Viewpoint: The future economic benefits that the canal might bring to Central Europe have to be balanced against the ecological damage that it caused to the Altmühl River valley.

Viewpoint: The canal was designed and constructed in an ecologically sensitive manner and should serve as a model for future canal construction.

Since 1992 the Rhine-Main-Danube Canal (RMD Canal) has linked three of the most commercially important European rivers, allowing goods to pass freely from the North Sea to the Black Sea. First envisaged by Charlemagne in 793 A.D., it proved to be far beyond the technological capabilities of his time and was quickly abandoned. King Ludwig I of Bavaria took up the challenge anew in the early nineteenth century, and from 1845 to 1945 the Ludwig Canal was open to a limited amount of ship and barge traffic. Never a money-maker, it was originally designed to handle horse-drawn barges with a maximum weight of 120 metric tons and was thus too small to handle even the modest-sized steamships of the day, let alone the massive push-tug systems of later years. Damaged when Allied bombs struck Nuremberg in World War II, the canal was never rebuilt.

The idea of linking the Rhine and Danube did not die with World War II, and in 1960 engineers of the Rhine-Main-Danube Company (RMD Company) began constructing a new 171-kilometer-long canal designed to handle the most modern ships and barges. Controversial from the outset because of its impact on the surrounding landscape, it was not completed until 1992, the delays almost wholly owing to environmental concerns. It had yet to prove to be economically viable by the end of the 1990s, though traffic on the canal increased yearly.

The canal stretches from Bamberg, a port town on the Regnitz (a Main tributary), to Kelheim, a port town on the Danube River. Engineers built the so-called Northern Route first, a 72-kilometer-long canal that links Bamberg with the town of Nuremberg. It took twelve years to complete and went into operation in 1972. The 99-kilometer-long Southern Route was more challenging, both from an engineering and environmental perspective, for it required the construction of a series of massive locks to create an artificial waterway over the Continental Divide. It also entailed extensive reengineering of both the Main and Danube Rivers in order to create a uniform trans-European waterway. Construction began at both ends simultaneously, with one engineering team working from Nuremberg southward and another northward from Kelheim. From the outset, however, a huge controversy arose between planners and environmentalists over the environmental impact of the Southern Route because building it meant cutting through the Franconian Jurassic Upland by way of the Altmühl River valley, the Ottmaring valley, and then the Sulz valley to the saddle of the Continental Divide 406 meters above sea level. Saving the stunningly beautiful Altmühl River valley from destruction became the main objective of a fast-growing, widespread, and massive resistance movement against the canal project.

Both authors agree that the RMD Canal did not yet prove its economic worth by the end of the century. It was much cheaper to ship goods between the North Sea and Black Sea through the Mediterranean, and it is not clear that a sufficient amount of inland trade will develop between the western and eastern halves of Europe to justify the high costs of the construction of the canal. The authors differ, however, as regards their assessment of its impact on the landscape. For Reinhold Schneider, the costs to the Altmühl valley were substantial and need to be taken into account in any assessment of the economic pros and cons of this project. Mark Cioc sees the new canal as an innovative approach to inland transport and argues that it might serve as a model for future canal construction.

Viewpoint: The future economic benefits that the canal might bring to Central Europe have to be balanced against the ecological damage that it caused to the Altmühl River valley.

What did the Altmühl River valley look like before the construction of the Rhine-Main-Danube Canal (RMD Canal) changed it? Originally formed by the Danube itself more than 11 million years ago, the valley cuts 100 to 150 meters deep into the limestone bed as it winds its way through a beautiful plateau. The valley is naturally curvaceous, owing to the gigantic meanders of the former Danube pathway. After the Danube changed course and abandoned the valley, its former course was taken over by the Altmühl River, a relatively small tributary merely 15 to 20 meters wide, which flowed through a valley floor 250 to 400 meters in breadth. It carried its crystal clear waters slowly through the various meanders and loops, its slow rate owing to the slight gradient of the valley bottom. Steep, wooded slopes flank the Altmühl valley. Occasional outcroppings of dolomite (rock composed of coral reefs left over from the Jurassic-era sea that once covered the area) stick out of the woodland cover. Medieval castles still adorn many cliffs.

The valley had already been affected by river engineering before the RMD Canal was built, for it had been part of the route selected by King Ludwig I of Bavaria when he commissioned construction of the Ludwig Canal in the 1830s. The Ludwig Canal, however, was only one-fourth the size of the RMD Canal and its many locks had an average lift of less than two meters. For this reason the impact on the environment was kept to a minimum. Cuts in the valley bottom near the locks only scratched the terrain, and the adjacent dams did not stick out distinctly. The Ludwig Canal also did not impose a uniform bed on the valley: in part it simply used the original bed of the Altmühl, and in part it relied on an artificial lateral channel. The moderate size of the Ludwig Canal also meant that the dynamics of the natural river (especially seasonal flooding) were not significantly altered. Abandoned in 1945, the Ludwig Canal was quickly reclaimed by nature and became a haven for many rare and endangered species.

The slight slope of the Altmühl valley meant that it was rich in riparian habitat. Slight differences in elevation and soils, along with frequent inundations, created ideal preconditions for habitat diversity. Meander loops, though nominally cut off by the earlier canal, remained connected to the main watercourse, creating zones of retreat and reproduction for fish and amphibians. In fact, the Altmühl region was known for its high level of species diversity, for its populations of rare and endangered species such as kingfisher and blue butterflies of the Nymphalidae family, and for the outstanding quality of its ecological habitats—at least until the new canal was built. The local Bavarian farming communities, moreover, utilized the valley for cattle-farming, grain-growing, fishing, and forestry, all without an appreciable impact on the local ecology. Small market towns supplied the locals and travelers alike. A modest number of tourists—hiking groups, families on vacation, and anglers—also appreciated the charms of the valley.

The sheer size of the proposed RMD Canal made it problematic from an ecological perspective: with a width of fifty-five meters, a depth of four meters, and two lock lifts of eight meters or more, it threatened to completely swallow up the relatively small valley, consuming the river and old canal along with it. This kind of massive construction was bound to totally change the scenic, richly structured, and diverse landscape formed by nature and maintained by local inhabitants. The nearly natural Altmühl River was to be replaced by a wide artificial channel, with two large basins, locks, weirs, and high dams. The deep cuts in the terrain, backlog of water, and regulated current would undermine the natural dynamics of the river, preventing seasonal flooding and therefore the natural benefits of silt and sediment. A reduction in the flow of the water was also bound to change the water quality and therefore the mix of fish species. A drop in the groundwater would also create a drier soil in the vicinity of the cuts of the canal. This change, in

The Leerstetten Lock on the Nuremberg-Altmühl section of the Rhine-Main-Danube Canal

turn, would lead to a reduction in the size and extent of wetlands and, therefore, in the population numbers of rare species. The green fields of the valley would turn to gray. Leaching fertilizer and a lack of oxygen would further deteriorate water quality and reduce capacity for fish and amphibian populations.

At first, the local population was skeptical but not overtly hostile to the new canal project: farmers were more concerned with issues of compensation than issues of ecology; fishermen focused on the loss of fishing holes and species; and others worried about the noise, dust, and detours that five years of construction would undoubtedly entail. Only a small group of locals, organized as the "Friends of the Altmühl Valley," were prepared to fight the project. This group was soon supported by the Bavarian nature group, *Bund Naturschutz in Bayern* (BUND).

The BUND, which ultimately spearheaded the protest against the canal, is a nongovernmental organization of conservationist-minded activists, with many local branches. It thrived in the 1970s and 1980s, an era of growing consciousness of the value of natural resources and concern over pollution and depletion of the environment, after the rapid industrial development of the postwar German "economic miracle." BUND had gained many members and much support by fighting major projects such as nuclear-power plants along the Isar, Main, and Danube, and by taking the lead in fighting against acid rain and Waldsterben (forest death). The campaign against the canal lasted from 1972 to 1983 and penetrated into every German-speaking household in Central Europe by virtue of its tremendous media coverage. BUND united everyone who opposed turning the Altmühl River into an oversized canal with a standardized riverbed and banks, that is, into an ugly monstrosity in an otherwise scenic valley.

The BUND and its allies had an impact. To help address the growing concern and awareness of environmental issues, the Bavarian government established the Ministry for Development and Environmental Issues in 1972 (the first of its kind in Europe). It also put in place state-of-the-art environmental regulations, which obligated investors to take into account the impact that the new canal would have on the surrounding landscape. The new legislation made it possible for the RMD Company to get approval to utilize the Altmühl valley as part of the Southern Route. In 1972 the RMD commissioned Reinhard Grebe, a Nuremberg-based landscape architect, to draw and implement a landscape plan. Grebe began with a simple proposition: that the canal follow the path established by nature rather than a straight line, which was typically favored by canal engineers. First, an inventory of the existing landscape was undertaken to gather all available information about local flora and fauna. Based on this data, Grebe prepared a set of guidelines on how to keep the impact on the most sensitive parts of the valley as low as possible, by altering the originally proposed canal line. The banks, dams, levees, roads, backwaters, and channel were to imitate nature as much as feasible. Engineers and landscapers, by working together, learned to understand each other's needs and to reach compromises. For instance, the engineers originally planned to apply an even standard to the profile of the canal, but backed off in light of the objections of the landscapers. Eventually, the landscape plans were laid out in legal documents binding on all parties.

The RMD Company's planning authority, moreover, was restricted to the course of the canal and to the surrounding land that had to be acquired in order to compensate for the unavoidable impact. To ensure that the whole area of the valley bottom came within Grebe's plans, all communities (led by the Kelheim district) formed a legal planning association and promised to adhere to Grebe's landscape plans within their area. Preparation of the landscape plan also helped produce a certain amount of rapport between the canal planners and the opposition; and the enormous costs associated with implementing the plans helped reconcile otherwise divergent viewpoints. By 1982 the canal extended halfway through the valley, which allowed critics to examine the positive impact Grebe's proposals were having on canal construction. To be sure, the canal course meant a tripling of the water surface and the loss of the Altmühl River as a natural entity, but engineers preserved (and in some cases built new) backwaters, wetlands, and similar river-edge habitats into the new riverscape—thus creating and preserving a variety of niches meant to foster a diversity of species. The banks were built so that plant life could establish itself. Permeability to the aquifer was ensured wherever possible. Unusually designed bridges added to the aesthetics of the construction. Water quality was maintained at Class 2 ("slightly polluted") on a sliding scale ranging from Class 1 ("clean") to Class 4 ("heavily polluted")—a remarkable accomplishment given that neither the Rhine nor Danube maintain that level of cleanliness through their entire courseway.

In 1980 a new dispute erupted, this time over transport policy and differing economic interpretations of cost-benefit analyses. Would the canal ever find enough cargo to justify its existence? Would it not make more sense to transport any additional future cargo on railroads? Did one need the canal to divert Danube water across the divide into the dry land of northern Bavaria (which counted for half the benefits) instead of using a pipeline at a lower cost? This discussion peaked when Volker Hauff, the Minister of Federal Transportation in then-West Germany during Chancellor Helmut Schmidt's administration, called the canal "the most stupid construction project since the Tower of Babel." In January 1982 the Schmidt government ordered that the work immediately cease, at a time when only two-thirds of the project was completed. In the fall of 1982, however, Helmut Kohl took over as chancellor and lifted the government moratorium, allowing work to resume. Meanwhile, in the Ottmaring and Sulz valleys, similar landscape plans were developed and implemented. Ten years later—in 1992—the canal was finished.

Despite Grebe's innovative planning, the canal placed a heavy ecological burden on the valley by its very size. As feared, the natural dynamics of the valley were permanently changed, not the least because the Altmühl was a fickle river that inundated the landscape frequently, whereas the new canal is wholly tamed. When one balances the impact on the environment against the compensation measures, and when one takes into consideration the growth and traffic created to support infrastructure, one must conclude that the canal has undermined much of the natural beauty of the Altmühl valley. To be sure, the valley was not destroyed, but it has suffered.

Compensation measures mellowed the impact a great deal. The local population gained in exchange by various spinoffs of the construction. As a transport facility the canal paid back to the environment in saved energy, less pollution and noise, fewer accidents, and reduced external costs of transport. There was an opportunity for growth and development along the new route through Europe from northwest to southeast, especially after the Soviet Union had collapsed. Seizing the opportunity to transform and integrate the formerly communist Eastern European economies within the European Union (EU) will significantly improve the economic record of the link. The canal construction even earned an international reputation for landscaping, with much justification. Yet, one cannot help but ask if the economic benefits outweighed the ecological costs involved with spoiling a unique stretch of landscape; the answer to that question by an optimist viewing of the economic dimension is yes.

—REINHOLD SCHNEIDER,
REGENSBURG, GERMANY

Viewpoint: The canal was designed and constructed in an ecologically sensitive manner and should serve as a model for future canal construction.

The Rhine-Main-Danube Canal (RMD Canal) is, in many respects, a hideous monstrosity. It cuts a wide swath across several beautiful

A WORTHY PROJECT?

On the edge of a sunny field in an almost forgotten corner of Bavaria there stands an incongruous sight; a stone monument built around an old-fashioned, long-handled pump from which water flows in two directions—to the left and to the right. Set on Europe's continental divide, it is there to make a point. Water flowing to the right will find its way to the Main River and onward to the Rhine and the North Sea, 600 winding miles to the north. Water draining to the left will run in a contrary direction, heading south and east for the Danube and on to the Black Sea, 1,350 miles distant.

The pump was erected by the Bavarian state government as a diversion for passers-by, but for well over a thousand years people have known that this is, geographically speaking, an almost magical spot: a place where two great river systems come tantalizingly close to touching.

A canal running only three miles between the Rivers Altmühl and Schwäbische Rezat would connect the two. For the sake of 5,500 yards of digging, you would get access to 2,000 miles of navigable waterway. In A.D. 793, Emperor Charlemagne decided the mathematics were too tempting to ignore. He set an army of men to work digging an eight-foot-deep-trench just outside the present-day village of Graben (the name means "trench" in German).

Today, his project, the Fossa Carolina, can still be seen, just a hundred yards or so from the watershed pump. It inhabits a wild and oddly melancholy stretch of woodland, a curving pool of still, green water cut off from the world by a dense overhang of leaves and a tangle of thorny undergrowth. For all its forlornness, it still looks remarkably navigable, but this is an illusion.

The Fossa Carolina was never deep enough to accommodate the difference in elevation between the two small rivers it was intended to connect. Charlemagne's men dug and dug, but as the trench repeatedly filled with water under heavy rains, the banks turned into an unstable ooze. Frustrated, and with more pressing problems, beckoning from elsewhere within his empire, Charlemagne abandoned the project after just two months.

Now, 1,199 years later, Charlemagne's dream is about to be realized on a scale beyond his wildest imaginings. The Main-Danube Canal, nearing completion 30 miles east of Graben, will link not only the Rhine and the Danube river systems but also (thanks to other canals already in existence) much of the European waterway network. In September, for the first time, a heavy barge will be able to travel from, say, Strasbourg to Bucharest without ever turning to the sea. The question is whether anyone much will want to.

"A canal is used not because it is there, but because there is a need for it," says Eugen Wirth, a professor of physical geography at the University of Erlangen-Nürnberg and one of many vocal critics of the project. "And the need for this canal has never been demonstrated."

Where the Main-Danube Canal proves to be a prescient and lucrative conduit to the newly emerging markets of Eastern Europe, as its builders hope, or a costly white elephant, as many others believe, it is certainly an impressive engineering achievement.

Running for 106 miles between Bamberg, where the Regnitz feeds into the Main River, and Kelheim, on the Danube, and climbing and dropping a total of 800 feet as it crosses the Fränkische Alb, it winds through some of the most challenging, scenic, and environmentally sensitive landscape in Germany. It is this last factor that lies beneath a long and often passionate ground swell of opposition.

"It is the biggest *Sauerei* of the century," Eduard Steichele, director of tourism for the picturesque cathedral town of Eichstätt told me, employing a piece of porcine Bavarian slang that is as emphatic as it is inelegant. "Even if the canal is an economic success, and that is by no means certain, the cost in terms of destruction to the Altmühl Valley is unforgivable."

Source: *Bill Bryson, "Main-Danube Canal: Linking Europe's Waterways,"* National Geographic, *182 (August 1992): 3-31.*

valleys as it winds its way from Bamberg to Kelheim. Sixteen massive locks—some of the largest in the world, with lifts of nearly twenty-five meters—are used to raise ships a total of 243 meters over the continental divide. The RMD Company had to build nearly sixty hydroelectric dams in the nearby vicinity in order to help cover construction costs and to keep the canal supplied with electric power. Thousands of gallons of water are withdrawn from the Danube at night and then pumped uphill to special storage facilities in order to keep the lock-and-canal systems functioning. Yet, for all its artificiality, the canal is a thing of beauty and ought to serve as a model for future canal construction and river rectification.

The beauty of the canal lies in its radically new design, for it breaks with four hundred years of European river-engineering and canal-construction practices. Since the Renaissance, Europeans have actively manipulated and altered their major rivers to improve navigation. In practical terms, this process has meant nothing short of turning navigable rivers into canal-like structures. Everything that interfered with the smooth transport of goods—meanders, loops, braids, islands, and the like—were systematically removed from the channel. Typically engineers would simply develop a blueprint that foresaw a straight path through the floodplain and then begin digging a ditch that would become the main channel. Rectification work also usually entailed the erection of artificially high banks to keep the water in its channel during high water periods. Finally, dam-and-lock systems were usually installed in order to compensate for, and help stabilize, the natural gradient of the river.

These practices had a negative impact on the local flora and fauna, for these construction methods blocked both the longitudinal and lateral passageways. Longitudinal passageways refer to the ability of organisms, especially migratory fish, to reach all stretches of a river to which they are adapted. Dam-and-lock systems, unless constructed with fish ladders, block these passageways and thus interfere with a fish's life cycle. Lateral passageways refer to the connections that naturally exist between a river channel and the wetlands at its edges. Artificially high banks undermine this connection, making it difficult or impossible for organisms to find spawning and nursing sites.

A naturally flowing river provides a multitude of small econiches for a wide variety of flora and fauna. These niches include the main, secondary, and seasonal channels, as well as braids, backwaters, pools, riffles, wetlands, islands, and innumerable other sites. River engineering, unless undertaken in an ecologically sensitive manner, invariably destroys or diminishes most of these microhabitats. Fewer islands and trees means fewer birds. Fewer back channels means fewer amphibian and insect species. Fewer deepwater pools and braids mean fewer fish. The effect, moreover, is cumulative: as the number of insect species drops, so does the number of higher invertebrates and vertebrate species that depend on them for sustenance.

Harnessed rivers all tend to have a similar look. They have one main channel with few, if any, secondary channels or braids. This main channel is shorter and straighter than nature intended and its flow is faster, owing to the steeper gradient that comes when a river is shortened. They are all tamer than they would otherwise be. While no engineering project has ever completely tamed a river—flooding will nearly always occur under certain conditions—almost all rectification work fundamentally undermines the natural ebb and flow of the river. Naturally flowing rivers can, under high-water conditions, attain a breadth of many kilometers across their floodplains. Rectified rivers, by contrast, seldom attain such a breadth owing to the dams and weirs that straitjacket the water into their main channels. This level of manipulation opens up the floodplain space for urban, industrial, and agricultural use, at least until the occasional "hundred year" flood wipes it all away.

In the past, navigational improvements inevitably brought with them a diminishment of riparian biodiversity. The Rhine, Main, and Danube—all of which count among the most rectified rivers of Europe—are also among the most biologically impoverished rivers in the world. Rectified rivers look alike and exhibit a uniformity of plant and animal life. Flora and fauna depend on a diverse, not uniform, habitat. Every missing island and braid represents a microhabitat lost to some species, and if enough microhabitats are lost, so too are the species that once inhabited them. Flora and fauna, well adapted to the natural rhythms of a river, can withstand seasonal variations ranging from ice to drought. Few can survive, however, a geometric assault by river engineers. Migratory fish are almost always hit the hardest: dependent as they are on all stretches of a river, from its delta to its headwaters, their numbers decline as the number of hydroelectric dams and locks increase. The Rhine and Main, once famous for their salmon, shad, and sturgeon runs, now support only one main migratory fish, the eel. The Danube, a much larger river, has been less affected, but it too has only a fraction of the fish species it once supported.

The original blueprints for the RMD Canal were based on the old engineering practices. Engineers envisaged a straight route, one that did not take into consideration the natural contours of the Altmühl valley. Fortunately, however, the *Bund Naturschutz in Bayern* (BUND) and its environmental allies forced a rethinking before it was too late. Reinhard Grebe's reformulated blueprints transformed a canal into a riverlike entity. To be sure, the RMD Canal cuts a wide swath across the Altmühl valley, one that is sure to dismay those who grew up with the tiny Altmühl. The valley is broad precisely because it once housed the mighty Danube, so the new canal does not seem overly out of place to those who come with fresh eyes. The canal, moreover, snakes through the valley, following the hillside contours. It has been outfitted with backwaters, wetlands, and many other river-edge habitats. As a consequence it has managed to maintain and even attract an astonishing amount of biodiversity. The contrast is all the more striking when one compares it to the rivers that it links: the Rhine, Main, and Danube would all be able to maintain a greater biodiversity if they were retrofitted to look more like the RMD Canal. One of the greatest ironies of the whole waterway from the North Sea to the Black Sea is that its most artificial stretch is also its most "natural." The Rhine, Main, and Danube are all natural rivers that have been transformed into canals. The RMD Company, once environmentalists forced them to rethink their project, constructed a canal that resembles a river.

The political will to construct the RMD Canal was there from the outset. The Bavarian state government subsidized the project by offering generous hydroelectric licensing agreements to the RMD Company. The German federal government, except for a brief moment in the early 1980s, also backed the project. The real question was not whether the RMD Canal would be built, but under what conditions: would it be a traditional canal like all its predecessors, or would it be an innovative canal that took into consideration the valley and its original biodiversity? That the BUND and its affiliates managed to force the RMD Company to construct an ecologically sensitive canal has to be considered one of the great triumphs of the German environmental movement to date.

–MARK CIOC, UNIVERSITY OF CALIFORNIA AT SANTA CRUZ

References

Bill Bryson, "Main-Danube Canal: Linking Europe's Waterways," *National Geographic,* 182 (August 1992): 3–31.

Ian G. Cowx and Robin L. Welcomme, eds., *Rehabilitation of Rivers for Fish: A Study Undertaken by the European Inland Fisheries Advisory Commission of FAO* (Oxford & Malden, Mass.: Fishing News Books, 1998).

Raymond H. Dominick III, *The Environmental Movement in Germany: Prophets and Pioneers, 1871–1971* (Bloomington: Indiana University Press, 1992).

David M. Harper and Alastair J. D. Ferguson, eds., *The Ecological Basis for River Management* (Chichester, U.K. & New York: Wiley, 1995).

Patrick McCully, *Silenced Rivers: The Ecology and Politics of Large Dams* (London & Atlantic Highlands, N.J.: Zed Books, 1996).

Brian Moss, *Ecology of Fresh Waters: Man and Medium* (Oxford & Boston: Blackwell Scientific Publications, 1988).

Hans Peter Seidel, "Landscape Architecture and Ecology," in *Planning and Construction of the Main-Danube Canal,* edited by Rhein-Main-Donau AG (Munich: RMD, n.d.), pp. 30–34.

RIPARIAN ECOSYSTEMS

Are Southwestern riparian ecosystems being managed effectively?

Viewpoint: Yes. Management promoting naturalized abiotic factors, particularly the restoration of river flows and floods, is arguably the most appropriate course of action for reestablishing riparian ecosystems.

Viewpoint: No. Current management of riparian ecosystems, based on both protected and controlled species, has resulted in an unproductive outcome.

Ecosystem management is a tricky process; the science of it is not yet well enough understood to insure a sustainable outcome, and the politics of it is fraught with innumerable difficulties. Some of these problems are fully manifest in an analysis of a series of attempts to restore damaged watersheds and riparian environments in the American Southwest.

Since the mid 1940s it has become increasingly clear that the costs of traditional river-management practices have outweighed their benefits. For instance, building levees and other flood-control devices has substantially altered riverbeds and stream flow, often intensifying the very flood damage they were designed to prevent; this fact is as true for major rivers such as the Colorado, Mississippi, and Missouri as it is for smaller systems, such as those in the Southwest that often are dry. Other alterations that have compromised the flow of water, and the biota that depends on it, are the use of floodplains for agriculture or settlement, unregulated grazing, diversion, and impoundment. With few exceptions, in the Southwest (and elsewhere) "natural" rivers are almost nonexistent.

How to repair this situation and to restore a more traditional flow of water is open to much debate. Some conservation scientists and environmental activists have filed the Endangered Species Act (ESA), which has inspired legal challenges to seek to compel the preservation or restoration of riparian systems. Framed around a particular threatened species—and there are many in the region—these lawsuits generally target federal land-management agencies to repair portions of the public land they regulate; the Southwestern willow flycatcher is the "poster child" of campaigns to rebuild riparian woodlands in Arizona.

Such campaigns are also complicated, however, for the ecosystemic changes that have occurred as a result of altered rivers make it difficult to restore native species and habitat; it is invariably easier to promote protection of an endangered species or attacks on an invasive exotic plant than it is to organize a systemic restoration of ecological functions. Moreover, rescuing degraded ecosystems that have only recently been acknowledged as valuable may require significant changes in the expectations of society of regionally limited natural resources. To reconstruct riparian woodlands, for instance, will require the reestablishment of more free-flowing rivers, which in turn would mean that human consumers would not have uncontested (and first) rights to regional water supplies. That is a proposal of revolutionary dimensions.

Viewpoint:
Yes. Management promoting naturalized abiotic factors, particularly the restoration of river flows and floods, is arguably the most appropriate course of action for reestablishing riparian ecosystems.

Riparian ecology, like any other, concerns the interrelationships of organisms and their environments. Riparian ecosystems consist, then, of biotic and abiotic factors. This characteristic holds true on the prairies and in the arid West, where a distinct "green line" of water-loving vegetation winds with rivers among the upland grasses, scrub, and cacti; and in the boreal forests and high altitude intermountain West where conifers give way to broadleaf species along canyon-bottom streams. This development is also true in the temperate eastern deciduous woodlands where the change to riverside vegetation seems more subtle, from oaks and hickories to poplars and sycamores.

Early riparian ecology discussions were one-dimensional, concentrating on the postulated benefits (to downstream water customers) of removing "phreatophytes," literally "pump plants," from riversides to eliminate a source of water "loss." Subsequent riparian-ecology-research issues attracted botanists and zoologists sooner than geologists, hydrologists, climatologists and others who concentrate on abiotic factors. Particularly in arid regions, riparian areas supported the greatest concentration and variety of animals, served as corridors for migratory songbirds, and harbored rare aquatic and semiaquatic species. As a result, the first wave of publications specifically addressing riparian-ecological function concentrated on biotic factors. Habitat studies of major native plants and animals supported a mostly "gray literature" of agency reports and plans for grazing and timber-harvest management. As detailed inventories of riparian woodlands were conducted it became clear that the overall acreage of riparian vegetation had been seriously reduced. A variety of causes produced the effect; clearing floodplains for agriculture, diversion of stream flows, water impoundment, urbanization, flood-control channelization, and uncontrolled intensive grazing by domestic and feral livestock had each taken a toll.

The effect was again most obvious in the arid West where perennial streams are small, few, and far between and riparian zones are narrowest. By the early 1980s lines were drawn on maps and many remaining stands of native riparian trees were marked for protective custody by government agencies and conservation organizations. Resource-management planners considered potential impacts to standing woodlands and specific methods were developed for avoidance or mitigation.

Meanwhile, autecological information about major riparian woodland components such as cottonwoods (*Populus deltoides, Populus fremontii, Populus angustifolia, Populus nigra,* and so forth) and willows (*Salix gooddingii, Salix exigua, Salix bonplandiana,* and many others) began to quantify what had long been casually observable: these species were short-lived pioneers on repeatedly disturbed floodplain substrates. Protecting existing stands provided only a temporary respite. Riparian woodlands live and die by river dynamics, and their species have adapted to both the advantages and disadvantages of floods and low flows. New stands cannot become established under old ones. Cottonwoods and willows eventually give way to longer-lived mesquites (*Prosopis spp.*) at low elevation or ashes and oaks (*Fraxinus* and *Quercus spp.*) higher up, as long as major disturbance by flooding never occurs.

With the early twentieth-century construction of so many power-generation and water-storage projects in the West, river dynamics had been seriously revised. The same could be said for levees, navigational dredging, small dams, urbanization, and floodplain farming farther east. There was nothing experimental about this program of wholesale change, and unimpacted reference systems, the "controls" by which effects could be judged, really no longer existed. A few minor rivers in the West remained undammed, or at least only temporarily and unsuccessfully dammed, and provided a small-scale glimpse of the old regime (such a "river" in Arizona, for example, the Hassayampa northwest of Phoenix, can often be crossed in one bank-to-bank hop by a healthy adult during normal low flows). No large rivers, however, remained in unaltered states. What little is known comes from comparing live or recent tree-ring data to flood records. Given the short lives of riparian trees (often one hundred or fewer years), the mid-twentieth-century die-off of so many riparian woodlands following construction of big dams, and the fairly recent establishment of systematically recorded river-gauge data (mainly since 1900), the history of flooding and riparian woodland development has been written based on a relatively small sample of remaining trees and streams.

Even with such a caveat, the results of studies on "natural" rivers, plus observations after the fact of flooding during El Niño springs (1983 and 1993) that overwhelmed the Southwestern water-storage infrastructure, appear to paint a robust picture of the relationship between riparian woodland establishment and

BABBITT ON THE INVASION OF ALIEN PLANT SPECIES

On 8 April 1998, Secretary of the Interior Bruce Babbitt gave the following statement to a Denver, Colorado, symposium on alien weed invasions into the United States, a portion of which appears below:

The invasion of noxious alien species wreaks a level of havoc on America's environment and economy that is matched only by damage caused by floods, earthquakes, mudslides, hurricanes, and wildfire. These aliens are quiet opportunists, spreading in a slow motion explosion.

Each year noxious weeds exact an ever-heavier toll: Farmers and ranchers spend more than $5 billion just for control. Losses to crop and rangeland productivity exceed $7 billion. Weeds infest 100 million acres in the U.S., spread at 14 percent per year, and—on public lands—consume 4,600 acres of wildlife habitat per day. They diminish or cause the extinction of native plants and animals, a third of all listed species. They homogenize the diversity of creation. They ignore borders and property lines. No place is immune.

Consider the damage done by purple loosetrife, a beautiful, seemingly harmless flower one might be pleased to find in a meadow. But not for long. For this species, found in 36 states, costs $45 million to manage. To bring this into a statewide perspective, consider that Florida spends $11 million each year to manage water hyacinth. Tropical soda apple, first reported in Florida, now covers 370,000 acres and costs the state $28 million. . . .

Conservative estimates count 2,000 alien plant species, 350 of which experts say are serious and dangerous invaders. Each day, new cargo ships arrive in American ports, and new shipments of tropical fish and plants are sold on the open global market. Some noxious weeds were introduced with the best of intentions, shipped to make a garden colorful, to dry up wetlands, to provide ground cover. Obviously, we cannot and should not shut down that global trade in an effort to grind the weed invasion to a halt.

What we can and must do is unite and prepare for that invasion both early and thoroughly. We can establish a responsive and comprehensive network, a network that will stop and someday even reverse the spread of invasive alien weeds, a network that efficiently shares all human and economic resources rather than keeps them working alone in isolation.

It must be a network forged by scientists and land managers, by local, state, and federal officials, by Eastern nurseries, Southern foresters, Midwestern farmers, Rocky Mountain cattlemen and Western irrigation engineers. . . .

Invasive alien species will never have the power to capture the imagination, the headlines, or the nightly news in the same way El Niño has. But we can do something about it. For I have seen the spread from the Great Lakes to Glacier and Everglades National Park. I recognize the dangers, and scope, and impact of the spread of weeds. And my resolve and determination only hardens. We can beat this silent enemy. We can beat a threat that erodes our soil, spreads wildfire, and damages our critical water supply and property values. We can tackle a force that is toxic and painful to humans, livestock, and wildlife habitat.

But we cannot ignore it any longer. We must act now, and act as one. We owe it to ourselves and to the next generations that will seek to live from a healthy, stable landscape. Too much is at stake. I look forward to working with you.

Source: *U.S. Department of the Interior, Internet website.*

flow dynamics. Finally, and particularly in the 1990s, hydrologists, hydrogeologists, and geomorphologists entered the riparian-management picture. The first major manifesto of the partnership between students of the biotic and abiotic aspects of riparian ecology appeared as a seven-author article in the peer-reviewed journal *BioScience* in 1997. Emerging from workshops funded by the organization *Trout Unlimited* and titled "The Natural Flow Regime: A Paradigm for River Conservation and Restoration," the piece summarized what was known about the ecology of riverine and riparian ecosystems. It also made the simultaneously obvious, inevitable, and revolutionary claim that maintaining viable riparian and riverine biota depended on maintaining natural abiotic dynamics.

The implications of such a statement are far-reaching. Natural flows follow the vagaries of climatic trends and cycles. They have traditionally been considered wild and in need of taming and do not lend themselves to the precision regularities of modern commercial or agricultural practice. The United States was built on the premise of using rivers as highways, pipelines, sewers, and powerhouses, and all of these uses require considerable predictability to function.

The development of large-scale, precision-engineered river infrastructure coincided with a mid-twentieth-century climatic quiescence, during which North America, and particularly the West, experienced a relatively narrow range of conditions that tended toward the dry side. That coincidence lulled river-project engineers and managers to expect and plan for similarly narrow future tolerances. The locally and regionally catastrophic floods of 1993 in both the greater Mississippi and lower Colorado River watersheds provided a harsh reminder that climate-scale factors take no notice of cultural expectations. According to the 1993 annual report of the Council on Environmental Quality Rainfall, more than 260,000 square miles of the upper Midwest that summer was locally "200–350 percent of normal," which might better be put as "two or three times what we thought we could expect." Economic damages were estimated at $15.6 billion and thirty-eight people died from flood-related causes. Earlier in the spring of 2000, the entire state of Arizona was declared a disaster area as flows exceeded storage capacity by about three million acre-feet, economic damages totaled $392 million, and the death toll reached seventeen.

The same federal report concludes:

> As a result of 1993 floods and the damage and loss of life that occurred, the effectiveness of the traditional levee-drainage-diversion approach to alleviating flood risk in flood-prone basins is under review. In 1993 the [Clinton] Administration formed several interagency working groups to consider alternative ways to reduce flood risks in the future, such as programs that protect, restore, and enhance wetlands, thus reducing the rate of inflow from the watershed, and movement of dwellings out of hazard zones. For example hazard mitigation projects funded by the Federal Emergency Management Agency following these recent flooding disasters are removing development from floodplains and restoring some areas of the floodplains to open space and natural areas. . . . The White House also appointed the Administration Floodplain Management Task Force to make recommendations on changes in current policies, programs, and activities of the federal government that most effectively would achieve risk reduction, economic efficiency, and environmental enhancement in the floodplain and related watersheds.

Suddenly, river control looked prohibitively expensive and increasingly unreliable. There was so much investment in flood-prone areas and such a traditional attachment to many sites that most people and governments felt little choice but to rebuild in situ. After the summer 1993 Midwest floods, towns such as Cape Girardeau, Missouri, constructed massive floodwalls and hoped for the best. Others learned differently. In Valmeyer, Illinois, 460 residents of low-lying areas rebuilt their homes and businesses uphill of the floodplain and out of foreseeable harm's way.

In the usually arid Southwest, the response was also mixed, but for somewhat different reasons. In states where every gallon of surface flow is allocated and reallocated (even overallocated) according to the prior appropriation doctrine, someone must come up the loser if water goes uncaptured. In central Arizona, Roosevelt Dam on the Salt River upstream of Phoenix was raised to provide additional flood control and "conservation" storage capacity, mainly for irrigation and hydroelectric generation. Below the major irrigation works, otherwise perennial Arizona rivers are usually reduced to sandy wastelands. In metropolitan Phoenix, where Salt River flooding circa 1900 reached into central downtown, the river has since been extensively channelized, the floodplain mined for aggregate, the gravel pits used for dumping municipal and industrial waste, and development has encroached to the edges of the floodway. Abandoning the floodplain in anticipation of a someday megaflood has hardly been mentioned, much less seriously considered. Just the cost of cleaning up more than fifty historic and poorly documented landfills to avoid exposure by and contamination of floodwaters appears nightmarishly expensive. Encouraged by major subsidies from the U.S. Army Corps of Engineers, the cities of Phoenix and Tempe are now occupied in constructing a $90 million project to make the flood-control channel look something like a natural riparian corridor, by installing an irrigation system and planting thousands of nursery-grown trees. At best, if the trees survive, this project may literally be for the birds. Meanwhile, twenty-five miles downstream, unconstrained 1993 floodwaters had something like their normal effects. In reaches of the Salt and confluent Gila River, where municipal effluent provides a minimal base flow, millions of cottonwoods and willows germinated and in 2000 the survivors of the shading-out contest are reaching maturity, and not one had to be transplanted or irrigated. Riverine marshlands reappeared and beavers built dams. Visiting the site annually during National Audubon Society-sponsored Christmas bird counts has provided an invaluable firsthand look at the process of natural riparian reestablishment.

Whether the general lesson that floodplains are integral parts of rivers, and rivers will occasionally "out," will ever be compatible with cultural expectations is an open question, but at least that question is on the table. Whether dewatered Western rivers will be rewatered and allowed to exhibit natural seasonal fluctuations has not yet been asked seriously at levels where such decisions can be implemented. Comprehensive, or even piecemeal, rewatering presupposes fundamental changes in the social and economic strategies of the region. More-subtle changes in the timing of some releases may be the best hope for riparian ecosystems in the near future.

Cottonwoods, willows, and other arid-Western riparian trees shed their diminutive seeds in synchrony with the typically high-water periods of late spring, while floods are renovating the riverine landscape by transporting and redepositing sediments. Such seeds are viable for about a month. The moist sandbars left behind by these receding floods are the seedbeds for new stands of riparian trees. It is a precarious opportunity, subject to flash flooding later during summer monsoons or subsequent spring flooding; channel migration and flood variability among sites and years combine to allow enough trees to survive in enough places to keep the recruitment cycle intact. Rivers that have been impounded for agriculture lose their spring floods to reservoir storage and have their highest flows during the summer irrigation season.

Both the geomorphic work of redeposition and the receding spring-flood limb are likewise lost, along with an entire potential annual cohort of trees. Adding to the problem, exotic riparian trees such as salt-cedars (*Tamarix spp.*) produce seed during most of the year, allowing them to germinate when summer conveyance flows are "turned off" at the spillways. Salt-cedars grow more slowly than native trees, and these, where present, can often shade-out the imported competition. In many places, though, they never get the chance.

Without the cottonwoods and willows there are relatively few structural and trophic opportunities for establishment of their coadapted fauna and understory flora. Exotic-dominated riparian woodlands are, at best, depauperate ecosystems. Given a few thousand years, this situation will doubtless improve. There are already signs of adaptation to salt-cedar domination among some native plants and animals. Whether that is an adequate outcome, whether we want to wait that long, and coping with whatever else may occur during the interim all require more serious and thoughtful attention.

MATT CHEW, ARIZONA STATE PARKS

Viewpoint: No. Current management of riparian ecosystems, based on both protected and controlled species, has resulted in an unproductive outcome.

Public lands in the western United States are increasingly managed on a species-by-species basis. This trend includes policies directed at both specially protected and specially disfavored taxa. Protections include international treaties, proposal or listing under the federal Endangered Species Act (ESA), and similar designations under federal and state laws and regulations. Special disfavor includes formal "noxious weed" status or any of a variety of formally and informally negative classifications, such as "invasive" or "invasive exotic"; and unlimited take and possession of certain animals under state game and fish regulations. Southwestern riparian areas are particularly susceptible to the effects of such designations, being particularly species-rich and relatively rare components of the arid landscape.

Both positive and negative designations profoundly influence federal, state, local, and private managers of riparian resources. Federal protection of riparian species under the ESA has been pursued through the internal administrative processes of the U.S. Fish and Wildlife Service (USFWS), citizen petitions, and the courts through special-interest lawsuits. Arizona provides a good example of the way ESA-listed species influence riparian management. The tally is a long one, including birds such as the Southwestern willow flycatcher (*Empidonax traillii extimus*), a neotropical migrant and riparian obligate; the cactus ferruginous pygmy owl (*Glaucidium brasilianum cactorum*), a denizen of mesquite woodlands; bald eagles (*Haliaeetus leucocephalus*), recently downlisted but still protected under ESA and their own individual federal act; and the Yuma clapper rail (*Rallus longirostris yumanensis*). Other significant riparian birds, such as the Western yellow-billed cuckoo (*Coccyzus americanus occidentalis*), seem well on their way to joining the list.

Fish listed by ESA in Arizona include the "big river" pike-minnow (*Ptychocheilus lucius*), razorback sucker (*Xyrauchen texanus*), bonytail (*Gila elegans*) and humpback chub (*Gila cypha*),

***Empidonax traillii extimus*, or the Southwestern willow flycatcher**

(Brian E. Small)

cold-water Gila and Apache trouts (*Oncorhynchus gilae* and *Oncorhynchus apache*), and a variety of smaller, perhaps less charismatic, species such as the Gila and Yaqui topminnows *(Poeciliopsis occidentalis occidentalis* and *Poeciliopsis occidentalis sonoriensis*), Little Colorado spinedace (*Lepidomeda vittata*), and spikedace (*Tiaroga cobitis*). ESA riparian amphibians in Arizona include the (proposed threatened) Chiricahua leopard frog (*Rana chiricauhensis*), most likely soon to be joined by the Lowland leopard frog (*Rana yavapaiensis*); the narrowly endemic Ramsey Canyon leopard frog (*Rana subaquavocalis*) escaped listing by virtue of protection under a conservation agreement with the U.S. Department of Defense and private landowners. No riparian reptiles or mammals are presently listed, although the Mexican and narrow-headed garter snakes (*Thamnophis eques* and *Thamnophis rufipunctatus*) are foreseeably in the running. Only two Arizona riparian plants have been listed; the Huachuca water umbel *(Lilaeopsis schaffneriana var. recurva*) and the extremely rare Kearney blue-star (*Amsonia kearneyana*). Of the ESA species specifically mentioned above, three were listed in the 1960s, one in the 1970s, five in the 1980s, and six in the 1990s, with one more proposed in 2000.

ESA listing is most likely to affect management on federal lands, but much of the West and most of the Southwest falls under federal ownership, and many large projects that affect riparian areas, such as flood control and water storage and distribution, qualify as federal actions. Multiple-use management on U.S. Bureau of Land Management (USBLM) and U.S. Forest Service (USFS) properties entails review of ESA species, and many uses, such as cattle grazing, have historically had particular impacts on riparian vegetation, stream-bank stability, and water quality, leading to recurring review of potential impacts to both riparian and aquatic species.

By virtue of its obligate riparian nesting and formerly region-wide distribution, the most important of these species at present to riparian managers has been the Southwestern willow flycatcher, often (and herein) abbreviated "SWWFL," which comes into play whenever a lowland federal grazing lease or permit is reviewed for modification or renewal. It also significantly affected the Bureau of Reclamation project to increase the height of the Roosevelt Dam and thereby the storage capacity of its reservoir on the Salt River in central Arizona. Mitigation plans for replacing lost SWWFL habitat on the shores of the lake required the purchase, protection, and restoration (through The Nature Conservancy) of three hundred acres of potential habitat on the lower San Pedro River, where irrigated flood-plain farm fields are to be actively returned to native riparian vegetation. In addition, a $1.25 million SWWFL "management fund" was created and a SWWFL "Conservation Coordinator" position was established and funded for ten years. More problematically, it also calls for efforts to reduce populations of brown-headed cowbirds (*Molothrus ater*), a brood parasite often observed using SWWFL nests.

Cowbirds introduce the second suite of species, those that are particularly disfavored–that is, targeted for reduction or eradication in Southwestern riparian environments. Native species such as cowbirds are relatively scarce on the roster, and it remains to be seen whether expanding cowbird populations are a symptom of ill-advised grazing management and woodland fragmentation or a legitimate target of management action. One other bird on the riparian hit list is the European Starling (*Sturnis vulgaris*), which competes with native birds for nest cavities in the western United States as much as it does elsewhere on the continent. The problem of nest-site competition can be locally acute where riparian woodlands are particularly fragmented.

Bullfrogs (*Rana catesbeiana*) and several crayfish species, as well as game and forage fishes from the eastern United States (and even a few saltwater types) have been introduced into Southwestern reservoirs. These inevitably escape both upstream and downstream into rivers and are transported by "bait bucket Charlies" into locations otherwise inaccessible to them. The legal and popularity status of many of these species is complex. Introduced fish are hardy in artificial ponds, reservoirs, and other modified systems, but do not cope as well with natural river conditions. They have been widely stocked to provide recreational opportunities, but are now considered unwelcome in certain river systems. Crayfish, apparently once unknown in the Gila River watershed, have more successfully adapted, have a smaller political constituency, and are in the process of receiving whipping-boy status as the Arizona Game and Fish Commission is changing the wildlife rules to prohibit the sale or transport of live crayfish. Bullfrogs already hold such a distinction, including a provision allowing the legal possession of an unlimited number of these animals–as long as they are dead. Each of these transcontinental imports is reasonably presumed to prey on or displace native species, many on the ESA lists. Each has to be considered when proposing federally enacted or funded river- or riparian-management changes.

Most of the species on the "bad plant" list are exotics, introduced on purpose or by accident from similar ecosystems in Africa, Eurasia, or South America. Quite a few are European agricultural weeds that can only survive in arid regions under irrigation or in the relative damp of riparian zones. These are mostly herbaceous annuals such as black mustard (*Brassica nigra*). Others, mostly African grasses, are grazing "improvements" gone awry. Bermuda grass (*Cynodon dactylon*), still popular and widely sold as a warm-season turfgrass, is now almost ubiquitous in desert riparian areas. Johnson grass (*Sorghum halpense*), now a prohibited noxious weed, is almost as common. Literally hundreds of exotic plant species have now been collected from riparian ecosystems, where they often compose the bulk of the biomass.

The plants with the worst reputation for riparian impacts are salt-cedars (*Tamarix spp.*), shrubs, and small trees mostly from western Asia that were promoted by the federal Soil Conservation Service early in the twentieth century for use as windbreaks and ornamental plants. Salt-cedars are peculiarly well adapted to Southwestern rivers that have been impounded for power-generation and water-supply purposes; in fact, far better so than their native counterparts, which have, for a variety of reasons, locally failed and given way to the exotics. They are accused of everything from actively displacing native trees, to lowering water tables, to poisoning soils with salty excretions. Salt-cedar eradication has become a rallying point for riparian ecosystem managers, for whom spraying or burning a monotypic salt-cedar stand makes an impressive photo opportunity. The Animal and Plant Health Inspection Service (APHIS), a federal agency charged with some responsibility for controlling invasive exotics, has spent years collecting and testing biological control agents, mainly insects, from native salt-cedar habitats in hopes of finding a "killer bug" to release on stands in the United States.

The picture is more complicated, however, than a first glance might suggest. Most SWWFL nests now occur in salt-cedar stands. In circumstances where the native trees favored by breeding SWWFL cannot be sustained by altered rivers, there is no practical alternative to letting the exotic trees remain in place. At a recent conference on SWWFL management held at Arizona State University, one speaker suggested that salt-cedar planting might be an appropriate management tool for encouraging the recovery of SWWFL populations in certain areas. The draft FWS recovery plan for the SWWFL is nearing completion and may be released for public review before the end of 2000. The SWWFL recovery team has requested that APHIS suspend release of anti-salt-cedar bugs within the bird's critical habitat. The most hated exotic plant in Southwestern riparian ecosystems is on its way to becoming an integral component of strategies to save the most protected bird.

Whither ecosystem management amidst the welter of individual species considerations? There is not enough time, money, or expertise available to similarly treat every species. Whether the outcome of all these efforts will be positive or negative remains to be seen, and lies in the eye of the beholder.

–MATT CHEW, ARIZONA STATE PARKS

References

Arizona Game and Fish Commission, *Arizona Fishing Regulations 2000* (Phoenix: Arizona Game and Fish Department, 1999).

Arizona Game and Fish Commission, *Arizona Reptile and Amphibian Regulations 2000* (Phoenix: Arizona Game and Fish Department, 1999).

Arizona Game and Fish Commission, *Wildlife News*, 48:27 (Phoenix: Arizona Game and Fish Department, 2000).

Arizona Heritage Data Management System, *Status Designations–Biological Elements of Arizona* (Phoenix: Arizona Game and Fish Department, 1998).

Executive Office of the President, Council on Environmental Quality, *Environmental Quality: The Twenty-fourth Annual Report of the Council on Environmental Quality (1993)* (Washington, D.C.: Government Printing Office, 1994).

T. D. McCarthey and others, *Arizona Partners in Flight Southwestern Willow Flycatcher 1997 Survey and Nest Monitoring Report,* Technical Report 130 (Phoenix: Arizona Game and Fish Department, 1998).

C. E. Paradzick and others, *Southwestern Willow Flycatcher 1998 Survey and Nest Monitoring Report,* Technical Report 141 (Phoenix: Arizona Game and Fish Department, 1999).

Kittie F. Parker, *An Illustrated Guide to Arizona Weeds* (Tucson: University of Arizona Press, 1972).

D. T. Patten and others, "Assessment of the role of effluent dominated rivers in supporting riparian functions," in *Final Report to Arizona Water Protection Fund* (Phoenix: Arizona Department of Water Resources, 1998).

N. L. Poff and others, "The Natural Flow Regime: A Paradigm for River Conservation and Restoration," *BioScience,* 47 (December 1997): 769–784.

John N. Rinne and W. L. Minckley, *Native Fishes of Arid Lands: A Dwindling Resource of the Desert Southwest* (Ft. Collins, Colo.: U.S. Department of Agriculture, Forest Service, Rocky Mountain Forest and Range Experiment Station, 1991).

S. J. Sferra and others, *Arizona Partners in Flight Southwestern Willow Flycatcher Survey: 1993–1996, Summary Report,* Technical Report 113 (Phoenix: Arizona Game and Fish Department, 1997).

J. C. Stromberg and Matt K. Chew, "Foreign Visitors in Riparian Corridors of the American Southwest: Is Xenophytophobia Justified?" in *Invasive Exotic Species in the Sonoran Region,* edited by B. Tellman (University of Arizona Press, forthcoming).

Stromberg and Chew, "Herbaceous Exotics in Arizona's Riparian Ecosystems," *Desert Plants,* 13 (1997): 11–17.

Stromberg and Chew, "Restoration of Riparian Ecosystems in the Arid Southwest: Challenges and Opportunities," in *Riparian Ecosystem Restoration in the Gila River Basin: Opportunities and Constraints,* Workshop Proceedings, Issue Paper 21, edited by P. B. Shafroth, B. Tellman, and M. K. Briggs (Tempe: University of Arizona Water Resources Research Center, 1999), pp. 11–18.

U.S. Army Corps of Engineers, South Pacific Division, *Rio Salado Salt River Arizona Feasibility Report and Environmental Impact Statement* (San Francisco, 1998).

U.S. Bureau of Reclamation, *Final Environmental Assessment, Potential Impacts to the Southwestern Willow Flycatcher at Roosevelt Lake, November 1996* (Phoenix: 1996).

U.S. Fish and Wildlife Service, *Proposed Rule to List the Southwestern Willow Flycatcher as Endangered with Critical Habitat,* Federal Register, 58:140 (23 July 1993), (Washington, D.C.: Government Printing Office, 1993), pp. 39495–39519.

SALMON POPULATIONS

Should the dams built on the Snake River be removed to revive the salmon runs?

Viewpoint: Although not all hydroelectric dams along the Columbia River basin will be removed, four along the Snake River, part of the Columbia watershed, can and must be breached to save salmon populations.

Viewpoint: Removing the dams might reverse the decline of salmon and restore the ecology of rivers, but for political and social reasons the dams are here to stay for the foreseeable future.

Pacific salmon are a remarkable fish, having adapted to a life cycle that flows through three habitats—riparian, estuarine, and marine. Their ability to live and reproduce within the diverse waters of the Pacific Northwest has been the key to their success as a species. Their durability and ubiquity, argues fisheries biologist Jim Lichatowich in *Salmon Without Rivers: A History of the Pacific Salmon Crisis* (1999), is striking: "They are like silver threads woven deep into the fabric of the Northwest ecosystem."

That these threads are unraveling is beyond dispute. After more than fifty years of intensive human manipulation of the Columbia River Basin, including the construction of an extensive series of hydroelectric dams, the varied habitats of the salmon have in good measure disappeared—and so have seven affected species of fish: the pink, coho, Chinook, chum, and sockeye salmon, as well as the steelhead and cutthroat trout. Beyond dispute, too, is that this dire situation needs to be rectified and soon, if it is not already too late. That is the only conclusion to be drawn from the tens of millions of dollars spent trying to preserve the fish, and the hundreds of thousands directed to research into what is called the "Pacific Salmon Crisis."

There is considerable debate—for all the capital, energy, and time expended pinpointing the many elements of this crisis—about how to restore the devastated habitat. Actually, the controversy is less about ends than about means. A growing chorus of voices is demanding that the massive dams constructed along the Columbia and its many tributaries be decommissioned or breached; only by tearing them down will the rivers begin to return to their more natural state; only then will the salmon have a chance to regenerate along streams they have populated for perhaps ten thousand years. In sharp opposition to this plan are those who profit from the continued presence of the dams. Prominent among these are the power companies and their many commercial and residential customers who rely upon cheap electricity; others include the agricultural interests who reap considerable benefits from the barge traffic that plies the now-placid waters of the Columbia.

In this contest the insights of biology and ecology clash with the dominant social organization and political structure of the Pacific Northwest. The outcome of this contest is uncertain and is perhaps best framed in a paired set of questions that Lichatowich poses to the local citizenry: "Are they willing to save the salmon even if it means changing the way the industrial economy uses the region's land and water? And if they are not willing to make the necessary changes, will a Pacific Northwest without salmon retain its appeal as a high-quality environment for people?"

Viewpoint: Although not all hydroelectric dams along the Columbia River basin will be removed, four along the Snake River, part of the Columbia watershed, can and must be breached to save salmon populations.

Shortsighted decisions to dam the Snake River in the Pacific Northwest brought the greatest runs of salmon and steelhead in the world to the brink of extinction. Such a permanent consequence deserves careful consideration of the choices that were made and paths still open to decision makers. One measure of a sane and intelligent society is the ability to admit when mistakes were made and to correct the course of action when new information becomes available. If this is done, then salmon can be restored—but corporations, heavily subsidized by the current system of federal dams, have stonewalled needed reforms.

Consider, first of all, the fish. They begin their lives in the headwaters of rivers, migrate to the Pacific Ocean as smolts a few inches in length, fatten themselves off the fruits of the sea, then return to spawn and start the next generation in a new cycle of life. Mysteriously finding their way home after ten thousand miles of roaming, evading the multiple hazards of predators and anglers, swimming upriver for nine hundred miles to the very stream where they were born— these fish are truly astonishing creatures.

The Columbia River once hosted the greatest runs of Chinook in the world. Sixteen million fish of several species historically made the journey upriver, blanketing the surface of the tributaries. This was the quintessential American wealth, like the buffalo of the plains. For the salmon of the Columbia basin, however, it is not too late to bring the wealth back.

Native Americans lived off these fish and still revere them in religious traditions. White settlers built impressive industries in commercial and sportfishing, and an entire system thrived on the returning salmon as a basic building block. From grizzly bears and bald eagles to aquatic insects and microbes, the fish directly fed scores of species. Even more important, the transfer of nutrients from ocean-to-headwaters nourished an intricate ecosystem in the Northwest. One study showed that 35 percent of the carbon in insects on the floodplains was derived from the rotting flesh of spawned-out fish. Salmon have been nothing less than the keystone species and cultural icon of this great region.

Because of damage to the streams where the fish spawn, overharvesting by commercial fleets, and use of hatcheries—that ironically jeopardize the very species they sought to enhance—the salmon are in deep trouble. Causing far greater mortality than any of these other hazards, however, dams block the passage of the fish as they strive to reach the sea and later return to their natal homes.

Salmon and steelhead of the Snake River basin in Idaho, Oregon, and Washington—where the runs were once the greatest—are confronted by eight main-stem dams. Four large structures span the Columbia, while another four smaller ones block its largest tributary, the Snake. The combined effect is to kill up to 40 percent of the adult fish bound upriver. Even more devastating, up to 88 percent of young smolts starting out to sea die because of the dams and related flatwater reservoirs. The losses are cumulative: 8 to 15 percent of the smolts perish at each dam.

While the big Columbia dams provide hydroelectric power and open the river for commercial barging to the desert city of Pasco, Washington, the Snake River dams serve little purpose in comparison. Biologists opposed their construction, but the dam builders promised that they could meet the needs of fish. Even the U.S. Army Corps of Engineers disagreed with the building of these dams because they were deemed uneconomic. Although Lewiston, Idaho, is 460 miles from the ocean, businessmen there wanted their town to be a seaport and eventually got a $1 million appropriation. Annual budgets in the 1970s were justified to "complete" construction of the four dams.

As the biologists feared, the fish indeed plunged toward extinction. Many runs—meaning separate populations of fish uniquely adapted to certain streams—are extinct. All the remaining runs are federally listed as endangered. Total populations of around one hundred thousand Snake River salmon in the 1960s, before the last four dams were built, plummeted to three thousand or less. The dams not only bar the passage of fish, but the water in the reservoirs heats up beyond their tolerance. In 1999 the Environmental Protection Agency (EPA) found that the dams violated the federal Clean Water Act (1977). Compliance could cost $900 million if the dams are not removed.

In an effort to prevent extinction of the salmon, as well as meet federal laws, about $400 million per year was being spent in the Columbia basin, most of it fruitlessly. As of the year 2000, $3 billion had been used trying to counteract the deadly effect of the dams. Big money has gone to hatcheries, to modifying the dam structures, and to hauling fish on barges. Because it requires little change in the other functions of the dams, the barging of salmon remained the cornerstone of recovery attempts. Pulled out of the river at the uppermost dams, the young fish are piped onto a barge and motored hundreds of miles out to tidewater. The most salient fact related to this $52 million-a-year taxpayer enterprise is that after decades of such effort the fish are nearly extinct. Meanwhile, salmon on undammed tributaries, such as the John Day River in Oregon, survive respectably well.

Businesses involving commercial barging, aluminum smelting, irrigated agriculture, and hydroelectricity benefit from government subsidies related to the dams and so push to maintain the status quo. Barging, for example, is almost 100 percent subsidized; taxpayers contribute $16 million a year for maintenance and operation of the locks, not counting $11 million worth of water that is lost from hydroelectric generation. Taxpayers pay to dredge the river so the barges do not run aground. Subsidies to the other industries are even greater. Altogether, dam subsidies to the four industries total $500 million a year.

With time running out for these important fish, the authorities should stop wasting money. This emblem of the Northwest that once provided twenty-five thousand fishing jobs can be restored. A fishery worth $250 to $500 million a year can be reinstated, allowing a whole circle of life to grace the living once again—and it can all be done by saving money. Partial removal of four dams is the solution advocated by fishermen, biologists, Native American tribes, and some state and federal agencies. Breaching these earth-fill structures would restore the lower Snake River to its free-flowing condition and allow the fish to pass. The other dams on the Columbia, along with its hydropower network, can remain intact. The four Snake River dams provide only 5 percent of electricity to the region, an amount that can be saved or replaced. Irrigators can be served without the dams by withdrawing water from the adequate flow of the undammed river itself. The bargers' allies in the hydropower and agribusiness industries would scarcely be affected by dam removal, except to get endangered-species requirements off their backs.

Because barging to Lewiston is the main reason to keep the dams in place, one would think that whatever is being transported must be important. Yet, surplus grain bound for Asia is the main commodity in this fishkilling complex. Meanwhile, thousands of farmers are paid not to grow the same crops. While shipping surplus grain abroad, another source of food—the salmon—are pushed to ruin. Even without the four dams, barges could still travel from Pasco, just 130 miles from Lewiston. Less than five of the thirty-eight million tons of commodities on the Columbia system are shipped above Pasco. Trucks and rail can fill the gap; indeed, until the late 1970s that was how all the transport was done.

The federally owned dams could be breached for a total cost of about $1 billion, amortized at $75 million a year according to engineers hired by the Army Corps. Conservative projections by economists for Idaho Rivers United document that taxpayers could save $183 million a year by laying these four white elephants to rest.

People who oppose removing the dams rely on several basic arguments. Dam proponents contend that recovery of the salmon would not be certain even if the dams were removed, although panel after panel of scientists since 1996 have concluded that returning the river to a more natural state is the only way the fish will survive. The multiagency Plan for Analyzing and Testing Hypotheses agrees that the fish would benefit from a free-flowing river. They put the odds at 80 to 95 percent that dam removal would restore a viable fishery. No other alternative rated higher than 70 percent. Moreover, two hundred prominent scientists wrote to President Bill Clinton urging him to expedite dam removal. There was growing agreement that bypassing the four dams was the most certain means to bring back the fish and also the easiest, cheapest, and only way to tackle the job.

To avoid taking action because no one guarantees certainty is like staying home all the time because no one will guarantee that you will not get hit by a car when crossing the street on your way to the grocery store. In their public-relations campaigns, however, dam proponents do not have to prove that they are right—they only have to confuse the public. Doubts raised about dam removal are corroborated not by biologists working on behalf of the fish and paid for by federal, state, and tribal fishery agencies but by scientists who work for the industries or by bureaucrats influenced by big money that the industries pour into political campaigns for politicians who then lean on agency chiefs. These contributions are documented under campaign finance laws. Nothing else can explain why top officials of the National Marine Fisheries Service (NMFS) stated in 1993 that the dams posed "no jeopardy" to the enormous numbers of fish that unquestionably died while trying to get past the dams.

Defenders of the dams also point their fingers at other causes of the demise of salmon. They blame hatcheries, insufficient upstream spawning habitat, and overharvesting in order to obscure the fact that the dams are killing fish. They blame sea lions or Arctic

Dead salmon smolts in a Yakima Valley irrigation ditch in the early 1900s

(John Nathan Cobb Papers, Special Collections, University of Washington Libraries, neg # 18300)

terns for feeding on the few salmon that remain after most have perished at the dams. They argue that fixing the dam problem should not be done without first correcting other problems, as if a patient needing open-heart surgery should forego the operation because, even if it were successful, she would still have a bad case of athlete's foot. The other difficulties of the salmon do need to be addressed, but that is no reason to avoid fixing the worst offender.

Dam defenders furthermore argue that the region would be economically destroyed if the structures were removed. Study after study, however, shows otherwise. Even with the modest residential rate increase of $1 to $3 per month to accommodate the slight reduction in hydropower, northwesterners would still have the lowest power rates in the nation–roughly half of what people in many eastern cities pay. And the rate increase will be needed without dam removal because the alternatives are even more expensive. The small amount of lost electricity could be replaced by conservation and natural gas. Some jobs, of course, really are dam related, such as the twenty-five people who work at the port of Lewiston and perhaps the 4,830 jobs that are "influenced" by the dams. These people, however, would be reemployed by the more labor-intensive replacement industries of trucking and rail, and the twenty-five thousand jobs lost in the fishing industries would begin to return when the fish reappear. Even the Army Corps estimated that dam removal would create twelve thousand new jobs.

The economic losses of keeping the dams in place will be far greater than the costs of taking them out. Consider that the demise of the fishery will constitute a treaty violation with the Native Americans who were guaranteed the right to fish on the Columbia River forever. The NMFS predicted that the settlement for loss of the fishery could exceed $10 billion. To avoid this and all other costs of extinction, the economic pill of reform need not be bitter. It will be far cheaper for the government to aid in the economic transition from these four ill-conceived dams than to continue subsidies that kill fish by violating endangered-species and clean-water laws. Lewiston could be the biggest winner by upgrading from a fourth-class barge depot to a world-class fishing destination.

Finally, opponents of dam breaching say that this solution is politically unfeasible. They contend that elected officials do not support the plan and never will. Ending slavery and gaining women's suffrage, of course, were once considered profoundly unviable. Indeed, Oregon governor John A. Kitzhaber was the only major political official of the region supporting breaching in the autumn of 2000. Few southern politicians, however, supported the Civil Rights Act in 1964. Furthermore, the fundamental tenet of a democracy is that people can change politics–they have done it repeatedly when common sense and economics were on their side, as they are in this case. Growing public support is evident in the unanimous vote for dam removal by the Seattle City Council–the largest city in the Northwest and also the governing board of the largest public utility. In

2000 more than 212,000 Americans contacted the administration urging dam removal. Most important in this regard, since breaching is likely the only real solution to the demise of the salmon, to give up on this proposal may be tantamount to consigning the fish to extinction. Deciding consciously to do so would signal a profound vacuum of hope, a relinquishment of ideals as fundamental as those that founded the United States and that guide humans toward biological survival.

By getting rid of four unneeded dams several great species of fish will be allowed to remain on earth. The Snake River will again flow free, and the greater ecosystem will brim with life. Sport anglers from all over the world will again journey to the heart of the domain of salmon and steelhead. Businesses that support fishing will thrive in scores of towns across the three-state region. Commercial fishermen will again be able to do the work they have done for centuries, once again going out to sea to procure one of the finest sources of food the world has to offer. By bringing back the river whole tribes of Native Americans will be restored their treaty rights and their ability to live and celebrate life as they have for millennia. Once this river is restored everyone can celebrate with a genuine sense of reverence and wonder the same creation that blessed their ancestors—a world that is still within grasp but that is quickly slipping away for reasons that their descendants will judge as unconscionable.

In the nineteenth and twentieth centuries people either lacked the knowledge or will to choose the correct course of action for both the salmon and economy of the region. At the turn of the twenty-first century people had the knowledge, and many citizens the will—therefore, the leaders must look beyond subsidies for their corporate constituents and, instead, save taxpayers' money and the salmon.

—TIM PALMER, BEAVER, PENNSYLVANIA

Viewpoint: Removing the dams might reverse the decline of salmon and restore the ecology of rivers, but for political and social reasons the dams are here to stay for the foreseeable future.

"Elephants in the Room" is the title of a cartoon depicting a group of people at a cocktail party ignoring that the columns they are leaning against are the legs of pachyderms. The plight of the Pacific Northwest salmon is related to the failure to recognize the "elephants"—the dams that are responsible for dramatically altering the Columbia River basin and harming the salmon. Many of the surviving salmon runs are on the path to extinction, and dam removals might increase their chances of survival. Because of the interaction of economic, social, and political factors, however, dam removal is not likely.

Historically, seven different species of salmon and trout occupied the Columbia River basin. These included the chum, pink, coho, Chinook, and sockeye salmon, as well as the steelhead and cutthroat trout. Although many people associate the dams on the Snake, Skagit, Rogue, and Trinity Rivers with the demise of salmon, there are several other factors responsible for their decline, such as timber harvest, mining, agriculture, smaller dams, commercial overfishing, and rapid urbanization. After all, more than thirty-two dams were built on tributaries of the Columbia River basin before 1930. These smaller dams may have been responsible for destroying more than half of the salmon habitat before the major dams were constructed as part of the large public-works programs of the New Deal (1932–1941).

Large or small, dams harnessed the Columbia River to irrigate dry basins, illuminate cities, power factories, generate rural electrification, and transport goods by barge. Along the Columbia River and its tributaries run railroads, roads, and interstate highways; their channels are periodically dredged; cattle pound their banks into bare ground; irrigation pumps suck water from the rivers; and runoff into the watersheds is laced with herbicides, insecticides, and fertilizer. The river system itself, that for decades produced considerable income for the regional economy, has undercut the chances for survival of the salmon.

One of the reasons the salmon issue is so complex is that many different people, agencies, and groups are involved in their management. The primary agencies include the National Marine Fisheries Service (NMFS), whose responsibilities include enforcing the Endangered Species Act of 1973 (ESA) for anadromous fish, in addition to developing a recovery plan for the salmon. The NMFS has the authority and mandate to stop any federal action that could harm the salmon, which includes increasing water flows or changing or removing the dams. The Bureau of Reclamation built and operates dams on the upper Snake River and the Grand Coulee Dam on upper Columbia River, while the U.S. Army Corps of Engineers built and operates federal dams on the lower Snake and Columbia. The Bonneville Power Administration is one of three federal hydro agencies that markets the electricity produced by the dams. The Fish Passage Center monitors salmon populations, making requests to change dam management, and is operated by three state fishery agencies and four Columbia River

Indian tribes. Although the White House could be involved, through the Council for Environmental Quality, presidential actions, or the Endangered Species Committee (the so-called God Squad), they have only been observers.

Since the dams provide a significant source of income and energy to this region, it should come as no surprise that there was no significant resistance to dam-based development. Efforts to improve salmon populations included actions such as barging the juvenile salmon around the dams, supplementing wild stocks with hatchery fish, and increasing upstream releases to increase water flow. Despite these and other measures, however, salmon populations continued to decline. The Snake River salmon were listed by the NMFS as "endangered" in 1992. The dams have been estimated to be responsible for about 95 percent of all human-caused mortality to the fish. It was not until 1992, when federal judge Malcolm Marsh ruled against the NMFS for its annual Biological Opinion (decision-making document that determined whether or not the dams would affect the fish), that the plight of the salmon gained national attention. Marsh stated that NMFS had been "arbitrary and capricious" when it determined in 1993 that federal dam operations on the Columbia and Snake Rivers posed "no jeopardy" or threat to the sockeye and two Chinook salmon species, adding that "the situation literally cries out for a major overhaul."

Idaho governor Cecil D. Andrus (1971–1977, 1987–1995) developed a proposal that called for drawdowns, a method of diverting water over dam spillways to prevent the fish from passing through hydroelectric turbines, to re-create river-like conditions. Drawdowns seemed like a good idea until a 1999 Army Corps of Engineers assessment showed that lowering the reservoirs for part of the year would adversely affect the barging industry and reduce per-capita availability of electrical power. Some $5 billion would be required to retrofit the dams under Andrus's plan, compared to the $900 million to breach four dams, specifically those on the lower Snake River. (The latter plan has long been considered a radical solution. With the ruling of Judge Marsh and the cost of Andrus's plan, however, dam breaching suddenly seemed more viable.)

Breaching the dams and/or reducing salmon harvests had little federal support. In 1999 federal officials released the "4H Paper," which examined four key factors for salmon survival: harvest, hatcheries, habitat, and hydropower. None of the options called for dam breaching. Instead, they suggested increased spending on additional measures to aid in salmon recovery. Some of the measures included increasing water released from Idaho reservoirs for young migrating salmon headed for the sea, limiting commercial harvest levels, expanding hatcheries, and enforcing state and local rules to protect streams. Federal officials acknowledged that such efforts might cost more and be no less controversial than breaching the dams. Brian Gorman, an NFMS spokesman, stated: "The political pressure that is being put on decision-makers not to breach dams is going to be transferred from dams to habitat. Those people whose oxen will be gored by the decision to put the burden on habitat improvement will complain as loudly as those that were worried about the dams," but they are considerably less in numbers and power.

Breaching the dams will not be prevented because of economic costs, but political issues. For example, in May 2000 Oregon governor John A. Kitzhaber, the first major political proponent of breaching and a supporter of Vice President Al Gore, criticized Gore for his "continued silence" on the issue. The potentially volatile situation for Democratic presidential candidate Gore was defused when President Bill Clinton announced, in July 2000, that any request to Congress to remove the dams was at least eight years away. This declaration allowed Gore to sidestep the issue for two more elective cycles. Republican presidential candidate George W. Bush criticized Gore and expressed adamant objections to dam removal.

One of the biggest issues surrounding the salmon is the political reality that this brief, national focus on the plight of the salmon in the Columbia River basin has not gained the national attention that the old-growth forests and the spotted owl received in the early 1990s. Why? The costs of addressing the issue are dramatically higher in both economic and social terms and too controversial to provoke significant action. Ultimately, congressional authority will be needed to breach or remove the federal dams and Congress would likely require either regional consensus (which is obviously lacking) or a strong national compulsion (which is no more evident).

Another substantial issue standing in the way of dam removal is the daunting task of determining the costs and benefits of breaching the dams. More than $1 billion is spent each year on efforts to save the salmon. Dam removal would save some of that expense, but citizens of the Pacific Northwest would also have to give up a fair percentage of electrically generated power at a time of significant increases in the regional population, which comes coupled with an increasing per-capita rate of energy consumption and dramatically rising energy costs. There are no plans for any new large-scale energy sources in the near future. With the passage of time, the prospects for dam breaching only get dimmer.

SAVING THE SALMON GENE POOL

Before a U.S. Senate subcommittee hearing on the recovery of salmon on the Columbia and Snake Rivers, University of Idaho zoology professor Joseph Cloud proposed establishing a gene bank for endangered fishes:

Many fish populations around the world are declining. Some of the causative factors that have contributed to these declines include over-fishing, habitat destruction or degradation, pollution and genetic introgression. Regardless of the causes, a decrease in the size of a population can result in a decrease in the diversity of genes within the population. Because many of the unique characteristics of the various fish stocks are genetic adaptations to local conditions, the loss of phenotypic characteristics within a population can be detrimental to the long-term survival of the population in its natural habitat. Since a number of the causes for the declines in fish populations are due to the activities of the human population, many of the problems that contribute to these declines in fish populations can be corrected, but these corrective actions may require extended periods of time.

In order to reduce or reverse the declines in fish populations, fish hatcheries have been established to mitigate the loss of native spawning habitat and to enhance the reproductive output of fish stocks. Although fish hatcheries have generally been very successful in the production and rearing of fry, the resultant gene pools of the hatchery populations are not always the same as the native stock from which they were derived. Thus, although hatcheries have been an important tool in the enhancement of fish populations, they have some inherent weaknesses relative to the maintenance of the original genetic composition of fish stocks.

Therefore the establishment of germ plasm repositories for fish populations provides (1) a means to reestablish a population when factors that resulted in the population decline are corrected and (2) a backup for the inadvertent change in the genetic makeup of a population with the development of hatchery programs. . . .

The establishment of gene banks for fish populations is not a hypothetical suggestion; it is a program that has a successful track record. This technology has been utilized successfully by a number of different countries in the establishment of fish germ plasm repositories around the world as a component of efforts related to fish genetic conservation. Norway, for example, has initiated an extensive effort to collect and preserve the germ plasm of Native Atlantic salmon that spawn in their rivers. In 1986 the Directorate for Nature Management in Norway established a national gene bank program for their native salmon. At present, their repository contains frozen milt from over six thousand individuals from 155 salmon stocks. Although there is no national program in the United States, there are regional programs involved in the collection and cryopreservation of fish sperm. In the Northwest, our laboratory at the University of Idaho in partnership with Washington State University and the Nez Perce Tribe has initiated the development of a gene bank for chinook salmon that spawn in tributaries of the lower Snake River. At present, our efforts have resulted in the cryopreservation of sperm from over 500 males from 12 tributaries. Our efforts were initiated in 1992 and continue to the present. Although our efforts have been limited by funding, we are determined to save at least a portion of the gene pools of these stocks.

The major disadvantage of a gene bank based on frozen sperm is that the reestablishment of an extinct stock requires extensive backcrossing or the use of androgenesis with eggs from a related stock. This problem has a simple solution—preserve both sperm and eggs. However, the cryopreservation of fish eggs, because of their relatively large size, has not been successful to date. Support for research efforts in this area is needed; however, this is a very challenging problem and will not be solved quickly.

It is my belief that the human population has intrinsic need and responsibility to preserve the genetic legacy of our fish populations. Genetic conservation of existing fish stocks is an important goal in itself, and is a component of programs designed to insure a viable and sustainable fishery under changing environmental conditions.

Source: *"Statement of Joseph Cloud, Professor of Zoology, Department of Biological Sciences, University of Idaho,"* Salmon Recovery on the Columbia and Snake Rivers, Hearing Before the Subcommittee on Drinking Water, Fisheries, and Wildlife of the Committee on Environment and Public Works, United States Senate, *8 October 1998 (Washington, D.C.: Government Printing Office, 1999), pp. 90–91.*

What are the social and economic costs to the people whose livelihoods depend on the dams? Farmers of eastern Washington plead that breaching will increase shipping costs, reduce land values, and bankrupt some farms at a time when wheat markets are at a thirty-year low. Environmentalists are calling for the government to spend more than $300 million to increase road and railway systems to replace lost barge transportation, as well as the outright purchase of farms. Breaching the dams would also bring economic hardships to the booming inland ports such as Lewiston, Idaho, and Clarkston, Washington. Together these ports handle about 3.8 million tons of grain annually. One study predicted that breaching the dams would cost the Lewiston-Clarkston area between 1,580 and 4,800 jobs. Potlatch Corporation, with more than two thousand employees, uses barges to ship their paper, pulp, and lumber. Experts have estimated that seven hundred thousand more truck-miles a year would be needed to ship agricultural products if barging were not available. The dams provide about 4 percent of the comparatively cheap power (enough to supply the city of Seattle) of the region. Dam breaching would cost up to $291 million annually and result in an individual monthly power-bill increase of up to $5.30 a month. Power bills for the aluminum companies would rise by $758,000 monthly. Additionally, proponents of the dams argue that they are a major tool for flood control and associated water-based recreation.

Simply put, as costs to save the salmon skyrocket, the salmon will continue to slide toward extinction. The struggle to develop coherent policy and approaches among federal, state, tribal, and public players continues. Regulatory agencies pretend to act forcefully, exaggerate the limiting factors not related to the dams, and focus on easier targets (which are, regretfully, comparatively insignificant to salmon recovery), while avoiding the truly significant issues (dam breaching). Clearly, agency managers are driven by the Endangered Species Act to act out their roles in this passion play in the face of one failure after another. Is there another instance where such ongoing failure to comply with the ESA would be tolerated? Meanwhile, environmentalists who fought the tough battles over the northern spotted owl simply do not demonstrate the heart for this battle. The risk of backlash is simply too high for them to deal with. Instead, they settle for incremental changes while ignoring accumulating failure in salmon recovery. Though these actions are not saving salmon, they do result in a better environment, such as the reduction of mine wastes and abusive grazing, and improvement in riparian zones and water quality.

The ESA was designed to "provide a means whereby the ecosystems upon which endangered and threatened species may be conserved, [and] to provide a program for the conservation of such endangered and threatened species." The Columbia system has been so dramatically and irreversibly changed since 1850, however, that "conservation" in any semblance of its original state is impossible. Even draconian actions such as removal of dams almost certainly will not occur because of astronomical direct costs and associated social, economic, and political consequences. Any vision of the return of a long-vanished ecosystem collapses before the reality of the dams, hatcheries, and barging of fish; the dredging, road building, and transportation networks, along with the stream-flow diversion and effluents from many varied sources; and the influences of urban development and industrial electrification. The pitiful remnant salmon runs of what Aldo Leopold called the "noumenon," as the animal spirit of the place, hang on to remind us of what once was. Many of these runs of these magnificent creatures exist only in dreams and fading memories.

The Columbia, for good or ill, is a working river and will remain such. The dams cannot be removed without giving up significant sources of electricity. Unless there is a replacement, citizens of the Northwest will not be willing to accept such a sacrifice. Hydroelectric power has consequences, but what are the options? Nuclear? Natural gas? Coal? Alternative sources of energy are also fraught with difficulties. As the National Energy Plan of 1995 stated: "Although everyone has a stake in the energy future, energy policy tends to receive national attention only in crisis situations. But policies fashioned in response to a crisis tend to focus narrowly on the immediate predicament, while failing to recognize and deal effectively with the underlying cause of the crisis itself." Without another source of energy and a proactive national-energy policy, the nation will not remove the dams.

It is not likely that new energy sources will be substituted, so what should/could happen? It is time to apply "triage" techniques, to face up to what are likely irreversible declines in some salmon runs, and direct resources to those runs where the odds for long-term survival are realistic. This policy would entail identifying lands whose management can no longer be conceived as having an impact on salmon. Regulatory agencies should reduce their arena of influence to habitats that can realistically help the salmon.

Although the Columbia River salmon issue is far more complex ecologically, politically, economically, socially, legally, and administratively than its predecessor crisis in the Pacific Northwest involving the spotted owl, there are similarities.

Delays in developing a coordinated response have eroded management options. The old-growth forest issue festered until a series of teams were appointed with a leader who was given the necessary resources and authority to work, without political meddling, to derive and evaluate options for a decision.

Scientists and technical support personnel must be chartered under a single leader with the authority, reputation, intellect, and fortitude to face the situation, form the necessary teams, deliver options, and defend the results. Any such process that is guided by a "board of directors" from the involved agencies will be so organized and conducted as to produce compromises before they should be made. Support teams will be sent back to the drawing board, time after time, for more analysis in hope of politically viable answers–producing significant delays.

There is another elephant in the room: who, finally, is to make the momentous decisions as to how much protection is afforded and who absorbs the economic, social, and political consequences. The mix of missions, mandates, pressure groups, constituencies, personalities, and political loyalties involved does not produce a suitable cultural medium for a solution. Given that the issue has international and interstate connotations with enormous magnitude of ecological, economic, and social impact, there is only one logical choice for the decision maker–the president. A precedent, in the form of the old-growth issue, exists for the president to make such a decision. There would be no appeal possible internal to the administrative branch, and the opposition would have to turn to the courts. Given the consequences, the president would cut the finest possible line in choosing an option that would minimize impacts on human welfare and affording salmon a chance for survival.

A loss to the environmentalists or the tribes would require either more attention to salmon welfare with associated increases in social and economic impacts or trigger an immediate appeal to the Endangered Species Committee (the so-called God Squad). Congress would then be able to bless the decision by appropriating the funds necessary to execute the plan; or, by refusing funding, veto the plan and open the door for certain legal action for failure to adhere to the requirements of the ESA. Such a "veto" would run the risk of a judge-ordered action that could have dramatic impacts on the economy in the Northwest. It seems implausible that Congress would exercise such a veto without instituting legislation predicated on the phrase "all other laws not withstanding" that would legislate a solution to the impasse.

It does not seem possible that the ESA was written, debated, and passed with any inkling that an issue of the magnitude of the Columbia salmon would arise. Magnified by the collateral issue of tribal fishing rights, this set of circumstances makes the spotted-owl/old-growth issue pale into relative insignificance. So there is likely to be no immediate recognition of the elephants in the room. That leaves no room for bold strokes even to be suggested. What sane official, agency, or politician would take on a "lose/lose" situation of this magnitude?

The likely outcome of plodding along the current path is continued "wink-outs" of the salmon runs, a buildup in expenditures, accumulated restrictions on landowners–whether effective for salmon or not–and drawn-out assessments and evaluations. Oddly, this all-too-likely scenario will produce an answer to the quandary. The salmon will dwindle and disappear in place after place. It will be bemoaned, but they will be gone and that will be that.

Americans have become too complacent, accustomed to extant processes, mired in political rituals, and addicted to disjointed "showpiece" actions to change their ways, as the salmon runs drift, seemingly inexorably, into the shadows of history, to become one of the myths of what once was in this land near the sea.

The situation for salmon is getting worse. It is not likely to improve unless dams are breached–and not just the four in the lower Snake River. The truth is there is no politically acceptable way that compliance with the ESA as it relates to salmon in the entire Columbia River system can be achieved. Americans are not yet willing to come to grips with the fact that the Columbia is a working river harnessed to provide the cheapest electrical energy in the world. What can be done to save the remnant population of salmon is to direct a combination of money and resources to the places that will do the most good and to let others off the hook. There should be no shame and much honor in facing the facts and telling it like it is.

Americans should do better. The law says so; land ethics say so; consciences say so. As people ponder what the Columbia River would be like without its noumenon, they would do better if they recognized and dealt with the elephants in the room.

–JACK WARD THOMAS AND STEPHANIE GRIPNE, UNIVERSITY OF MONTANA

References

J. Brinkman and J. Barnett, "Habitat Restoration Gains Emphasis Over Breaching Dams," *Oregonian,* 7 November 1999.

The Cost of Doing Nothing: The Economic Burden of Salmon Declines in the Columbia River Basin (Eugene, Ore.: Institute for Fisheries Resources, 1996).

Elizabeth Grossman, "Endgame: The Future is Now for Salmon and the Four Lower Snake River Dams," *Cascadia Times,* November/ December 1999.

Independent Scientific Group, *Return to the River: Restoration of Salmonid Fishes in the Columbia River Ecosystem: Development of an Alternative Conceptual Foundation and Review and Synthesis of Science Underlying the Columbia River Basin Fish and Wildlife Program of the Northwest Power Planning Council* (Portland, Ore.: Northwest Power Planning Council, 1996).

Jim Lichatowich, *Salmon Without Rivers: A History of the Pacific Salmon Crisis* (Washington, D.C.: Island Press, 1999).

Char Miller, ed., *Water in the West: A High Country News Reader* (Corvallis: Oregon State University Press, 2000).

Tim Palmer, *The Columbia: Sustaining a Modern Resource* (Seattle: The Mountaineers, 1997).

River of Red Ink (Washington, D.C.: Taxpayers for Common Sense, 1996).

Save Our Wild Salmon Coalition, *Wild Salmon Forever: A Citizen's Strategy to Restore Northwest Salmon and Watersheds* (Seattle: Save Our Wild Salmon Coalition, 1994).

Joseph E. Taylor III, *Making Salmon: An Environmental History of the Northwest Fisheries Crisis* (Seattle: University of Washington Press, 1999).

SALMON 2000

Will the Salmon 2000 Project make a significant contribution to the ecological restoration of the Rhine?

Viewpoint: Salmon 2000 is largely a public relations effort on the part of the riparian states. The money would be better spent on restoring the lost floodplain of the Rhine.

Viewpoint: Salmon 2000 has helped draw public attention to the plight of the Rhine and thus has won support for more extensive projects in the future.

The Rhine River, the busiest commercial waterway in Europe, links the economies of Switzerland, Germany, France, and the Netherlands. With nearly fifty million people living on its banks, it is a classic example of a "multiuse" river—one used simultaneously for transportation, energy generation, industrial production, and urban services. Some of largest European chemical-pharmaceutical firms (Bayer, Hoechst, BASF, Ciba-Geigy, Sandoz, and Hoffmann-La Roche) are located on its banks, as are many of the biggest automobile companies, aluminum factories, pulp-and-paper mills, and nuclear and conventional power plants. Among the water routes in the world, only the Mississippi carries more freight each year.

The Rhine is not by nature an easily navigable river. Left to its own devices, it flows too low in summer, freezes over in winter, and meanders wildly across its floodplain (especially in the expansive Rift Valley at the base of the Alps between Basel and Strasbourg). It is also prone to severe and unpredictable flooding. In the nineteenth century, however, the riparian states straightened and shortened the river in order to make it better suited for ship and barge transportation. They reinforced its banks; usurped its floodplain to provide space for farms, factories, and cities; added dams to tap it for electricity; and built locks and reservoirs to ensure a more even day-to-day flow. The result was a "tamed" river—one that more resembles a canal than a free-flowing stream.

This industrial and commercial development came with an environmental price tag. Biodiversity on the river dropped precipitously in the late nineteenth and early twentieth centuries. Many aquatic and semiaquatic species vanished as a consequence of the river rectification work. Bird, mammal, amphibian, and insect numbers began to drop as the floodplain upon which they relied for their sustenance disappeared. Hardest hit, by far, were fish populations, especially migratory species, for they needed access to all stretches of the river and were therefore adversely affected whenever the river was modified. Most prominent among the migratory fish were the salmon, the most celebrated and coveted natural resource of the river. The annual salmon catch peaked in 1885 at around two hundred thousand, then dropped to under a hundred thousand by 1905. By 1935 the annual catch fell below fifteen thousand, and after 1945 the industry (and salmon) gradually disappeared completely from the river.

These two authors debate whether it makes sense to lavish so much public attention on the reintroduction of salmon into the river. Mark Cioc sees the Salmon 2000 Project mostly as a public-relations stunt and argues that more attention should be paid to floodplain restoration than fish repopulation. Bruce Thompson contends that in-stream habitat restoration is an important first step in river rehabilitation and that it makes sense to focus on a "charismatic" species such as salmon because it will help generate interest in other more-extensive restoration projects in the future.

Viewpoint: Salmon 2000 is largely a public relations effort on the part of the riparian states. The money would be better spent on restoring the lost floodplain of the Rhine.

The origins of the Salmon 2000 Project can be traced back to one event: a massive industrial accident at the Sandoz chemical plant in Basel-Schweizerhalle. A fire broke out at a storage facility there on 1 November 1986, igniting more than a thousand metric tons of insecticides, herbicides, fungicides, fertilizers, and other agrochemicals. Because the facility was not equipped with sprinklers, firefighters doused the blaze, containing it in a matter of hours, with hundreds of thousands of gallons of water that flushed tons of unburned chemicals into one of the sewers. From there the chemicals found their way to the Rhine and began to scour the riverbed as they journeyed downstream. Within days of the spill, the entire eel population from Basel to the Lorelei lay dead or dying. Grayling, pike, zander, and other fish species within a few hundred kilometers of the spill survived only if they happened to be in a few sheltered backwaters and tributaries when the accident occurred. Even the fish that survived struggled in the aftermath, since the chemicals wiped out most of the macro-organisms upon which they depended for nourishment. It took several months before the macro-organisms mounted a comeback and many years before the eel population returned to normal levels.

Sandoz was the worst industrial accident to strike the Rhine in the twentieth century and proved to be a public-relations nightmare for industries and governments along the Rhine. Most Europeans had long been aware that the river was heavily polluted; its nickname, after all, was "Europe's sewage dump." The Sandoz spill, however, taught many for the first time just how vulnerable the entire ecosystem of the river was and how little had been done to protect it from degradation.

Out of this scandal emerged the Rhine Action Plan of 1987, complete with plans to create an effective early-warning system to guard against future accidents and plans to improve the quality of the water through the construction of purification plants. One of the most important—and highly publicized—aspects of this plan was the Salmon 2000 Project. It set out an ambitious agenda: to reestablish a small but viable and self-sustaining salmon population in the river by the year 2000. Work commenced almost immediately. Researchers began by identifying those Rhine tributaries and subtributaries that still possessed a sufficient amount of gravel bed for use as salmon spawning and nursing grounds. Eventually the Sieg, Saynbach, Lahn, Moselle, Kinzig, Main, Ill, and a handful of other tributaries were selected as test sites. Then, researchers identified the main in-river barriers (dams, weirs, locks, and the like) that blocked migration to these streams and began constructing fish passages and ladders.

The results have, in some instances, been impressive. After fish passageways were added to weirs in the Netherlands, migratory routes from the North Sea to the Rhine opened up not just for salmon but also for sea trout, lampern, shad, sturgeon, and eel. Efforts are now under way to retrofit the Iffezheim dam-lock and Gambsheim hydrodam-lock systems so that fish can reach the upper stretches of the river as well. Researchers have so far identified around 150 hectares of available spawning grounds and 630 hectares of nursery grounds in the entire Rhine system—a sufficient amount of space to ensure that at least 600,000 smolts can survive long enough to make the journey downstream. Based on an average return rate of 1 to 2 percent, the Rhine could potentially support an annual run of 6,000 to 12,000 adult individuals. Twelve thousand fish can be considered a stable and self-sustaining population.

It is still too early to tell whether Salmon 2000 will achieve this goal. As of 1999, researchers had only been able to verify a total of 180 returning salmon, but they estimate that only 5 to 10 percent of returning salmon are actually detected as they swim upstream. That would suggest that somewhere between 1,000 and 2,000 adult salmon returned to their nursery grounds between 1988 and 1999. Evidence of natural reproduction has been found so far only on the Sieg (since 1994) and Ill (since 1997).

Has this project been worth all the time and effort devoted to it, or has it just been a convenient and high-profile way of diverting attention from the Sandoz scandal and from more pressing ecological matters? Even the most optimistic researchers believe that the Rhine will never sustain more than a remnant salmon population—twelve thousand individu-

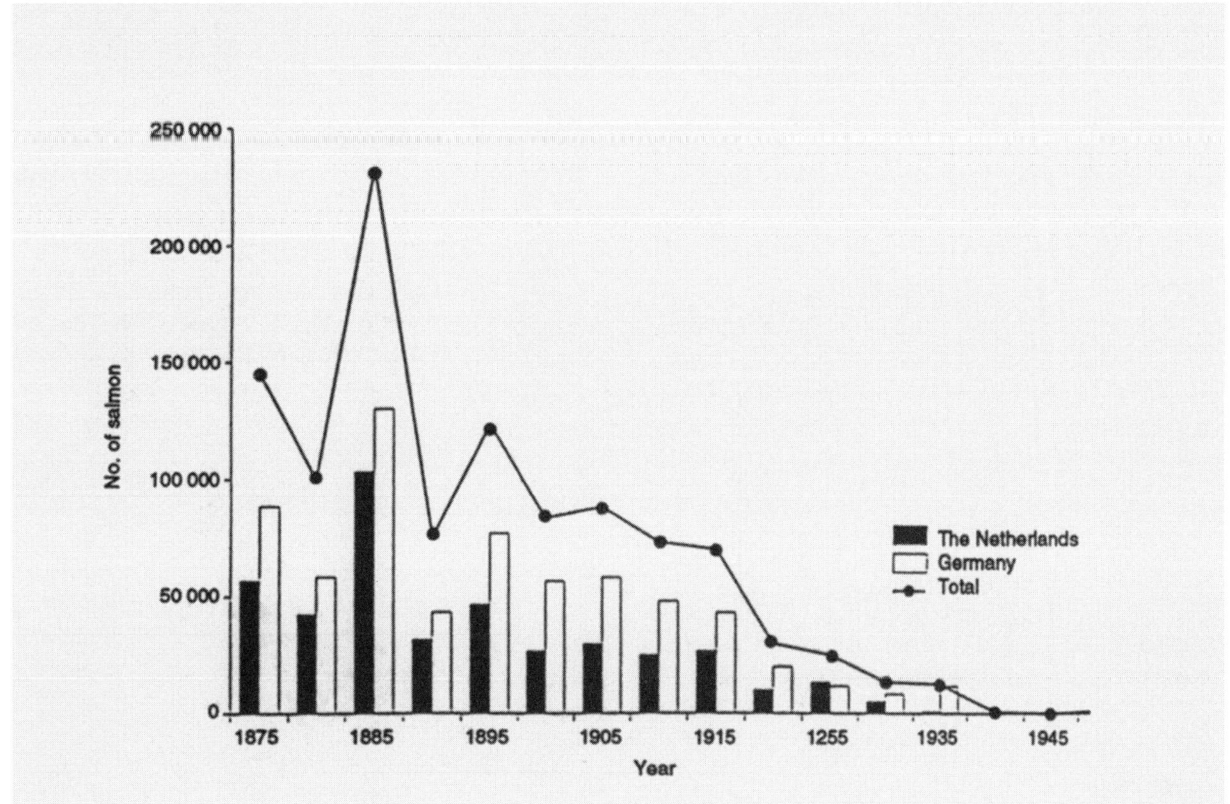

A graph showing the salmon catches in Germany and the Netherlands for a seventy-year period

als is, after all, only a tiny fraction of the half million that once swam in its waters. Salmon 2000 will not, in other words, turn the Rhine into a true "salmon river" again, with annual migrations reaching into the hundreds of thousands. There are too many dams, weirs, and other in-river obstructions that are considered indispensable to river management and navigation for anyone to contemplate reopening all of the longitudinal pathways of the river. There has, moreover, been far too much sand and gravel extracted from the riverbed for fish to flourish in great numbers. At best, Salmon 2000 will reestablish a symbolic presence of migratory fish on the river, and nothing more.

Meanwhile, a far more pressing issue–floodplain restoration–took a backseat in the 1980s and 1990s. Even as Salmon 2000 captured all the media attention, the river was struck four times in twelve years (1983, 1988, 1993, and 1994) by so-called hundred-year floods, that is, by inundations of such intensity that they normally occur only once a century. Simply put, the river is missing its floodplain more than it is missing its salmon. More than 75 percent of its former floodplain has been usurped for industrial, agricultural, and urban use during the past two hundred years. In 1815 the river had more than two thousand square kilometers of floodplain, which formed a single continuous corridor, varying in width from a few hundred meters to fifteen kilometers and stretching over one thousand kilometers from Lake Constance in the Alps to the mudbanks of Hoek van Holland. By 1975 less than five hundred square kilometers were still subject to periodic flooding–and even most of that space no longer belongs to nature but to the human-built environment.

The forests, meadows, marshes, and reeds of the floodplain once gave the Rhine its geographic breadth, biological diversity, and ecological dynamism. Only fish and a handful of other organisms live their entire lives in the river channel itself, and even they are highly dependent on the surrounding nonaquatic environment for organic nourishment. Most riparian organisms cling to the riverbed or bank, or dwell in the wetlands, grasslands, hills, trees, bushes, meadows, and valleys around the flowing water. Wetlands are especially important because they serve as nursery grounds for fish, shellfish, aquatic birds, and other animals. They also remove excess phosphorus, nitrogen, and other pollutants from the river. The roots of trees and bushes help stabilize the banks and even out the flow of water during drought and flood periods. Foliage provides shelter, shade, and nesting spots for birds and other animals. Thus, when the Rhine lost most of its floodplain it also lost most of the living space upon which its biodiversity depended.

Where once there was a continuous river corridor, there now remains just a few natural or near-natural stretches, tiny dots on a riverscape otherwise dominated by human enterprise. That any of these patches managed to survive long enough to get official protection in the 1960s and 1970s was more a matter of luck than planning: usually it just meant that no city or industry had yet reached that spot, or that the cost of reclamation exceeded the prospect for development. The two largest protected areas—Kühkopf-Knoblochsaue and Taubergiessen—are only around six thousand and four thousand acres in size, respectively. Most of the rest are much smaller. Yet, only on these tiny spaces can the full range of original biodiversity on the river still be found. These spaces also provided many organisms their only refuge from the Sandoz spill.

After much public outcry over the flooding, the Rhine states finally implemented "The Rhine Action Plan on Flood Defense" in 1998. The chief purpose of this plan was to "compensate for the ecological deficits of the past" by undoing the "human interferences with the river regime, as far as possible." To accomplish this task, five new guiding principles were laid out. Principle One states that "water is part of the natural ecological cycle of all surfaces and of land use and must be taken into account by all fields of policy." Principle Two states that "water must be stored in the catchment area and along the Rhine as long as possible." In other words, much of the former floodplain is to be restored by removing dikes and taking agricultural fields out of production. In areas where the floodplain has been permanently lost to cities and industries, overspill basins and other artificial storages are to be constructed. Principle Three states simply "let the river expand." Instead of following the old dictums of straight, fast, and harnessed, the trunk river and its tributaries were to be redesigned as much as possible to allow the channels to overspill their banks during high-water periods once again. Principle Four highlights the impossibility of providing complete flood protection to humans and their property: "We must again learn to live with this risk." Principle Five emphasizes the need for "integrated and concerted" action: flood control will require the cooperation of all governments within the Rhine's drainage basin.

Recognizing the limitations of floodplain restoration, the Rhine states initiated the "Habitat Patch Connectivity Project" at the same time that it announced its new flood-control plans. This project will focus on reconnecting the alluvial corridor that once stretched uninterrupted from Lake Constance to Hoek van Holland. One goal is to create natural and near-natural regions large enough to provide adequate living space for individual species, especially endangered ones. A second goal is to re-create as much habitat variation as possible, including riverbank vegetation with soft woods (willows, and so forth) and hard woods (oak and elm), and river-edge spaces with reed plains and marshlands. The third goal—and the one that gave the project its name—is to reconnect these patches to provide migration and colonization paths for animals and plants. "Envisaged is a riverscape in which the most ecologically valuable and near-natural core areas are linked together so that every organism can reach every biotope," stated the Habitat Reconnectivity Project declaration, "for this will ensure the largest populations and the greatest variation. The Rhine's bed, bank, and floodplain are once again to become aquatic and terrestrial habitats that function as viable living space for animals and plants."

One can only wish that the Rhine states had implemented the Flood Defence Plan instead of the Salmon 2000 Project. The fastest and most effective way to restore the viability of the ecosystem is to return usurped river-edge space of the Rhine to native flora and fauna, that is, to restore as much of the natural floodplain as possible. Such a program is good for humans and nonhumans alike, for it has the effect of reducing flooding while augmenting the diversity of the river.

—MARK CIOC, UNIVERSITY OF CALIFORNIA AT SANTA CRUZ

Viewpoint: Salmon 2000 has helped draw public attention to the plight of the Rhine and thus has won support for more extensive projects in the future.

Why are salmon so important to us? Why do we tend to associate great rivers with this species? What features of this fish and its life cycle account for its extraordinary "charisma" and potent symbolic value?

The salmon is not only a migratory fish, it is also an anadromous one: it lives most of its life in the sea, then returns to the stream in which it was born in order to spawn. Such a journey "home," over long distances and past many hazards and obstacles, is one of the wonders of nature. The life cycle of the salmon, in other words, is more dramatic than that of most fish. Humans admire the salmon not so much because it is a successful predator at the top of a food chain—an "apex species" such as the shark, eagle, wolf, or tiger—but rather because it seems to symbolize sheer persistence and stamina in the struggle to propagate the next generation. The salmon is a marathon swimmer: not only is it a determined uphill

SALMON RETURN TO THE RHINE

By 1970, the Rhine was dead. Vast amounts of untreated waste depleted its oxygen, and much of its aquatic fauna had vanished. Mercury and cadmium levels in the sludge soared off the charts. Contamination was so profuse near Cologne, Germany, that a 10-mile stretch was declared a danger zone.

But last November, an extraordinary discovery provided evidence that the river's fortunes have undergone a dramatic change: A group of French biologists found that salmon and sea trout had returned to the upper Rhine for the first time in 50 years.

"We were amazed and delighted. We knew the water was getting cleaner, but we did not expect this kind of result for several more years at least," said Pascal Roche, leader of the team that captured nine salmon and 35 trout at the Iffizheim Dam north of here.

"Some trout were tagged with markers by Dutch colleagues, so we knew they had successfully migrated all the way up river to spawn," Roche said. "These fish are very sensitive to all kinds of pollutants, so the fact they made it this far proves the entire river has been transformed."

The resurrection of salmon and sea trout in the Rhine was hailed as a spectacular victory for the emergency rescue project launched in 1986 by Switzerland, France, Luxembourg, Germany and the Netherlands. The nations drained by the vast Rhine River system have long bickered over who was guilty of poisoning its waters and who should pay for the cleanup, but it took a near catastrophe to stop the finger-pointing and produce serious action. . . .

The program has been so successful that most goals already have been achieved. Lead, mercury and dioxin levels have been cut by 70 percent, while those of chrome, nickel and other poisonous heavy metals have declined by half.

Modern waste treatment plants have made treated river water safe enough to drink again. Industrial accidents have become rare because of the tight controls and because many factories that generate dangerous materials have been moved away from the river. International patrols now scour the Rhine to clamp down on clandestine polluters. . . .

Nonetheless, experts say the fight against pollution has not yet been won. Nitrogen and phosphorous concentrations are still too high because of the large amounts of fertilizers and pesticides that drain from farms into the river. About one-third of all nitrogen discharged into the North Sea comes from the Rhine.

"I would say the Rhine is out of the emergency ward but not yet out of the hospital," said Rodolphe Greif, the international commission's president. "We have to watch out for new poisons and to make the river safer against floods. It will be a long time before we can advise eating fish from the Rhine, but the fact that they are back already is a remarkable success."

The salmon's reappearance after an absence of nearly a half-century has restored an essential actor to the lore and legend of the continent's main artery. The celebrated fish extolled as early as the 4th century by the Roman poet Ausonius, at last appears poised for an enduring comeback in what used to be its favorite European habitat. . . .

"Now that the salmon and trout have returned, we are awaiting the imminent arrival of shad and sturgeon," Roche said. "By the year 2000, we may achieve the kind of diversity in flora and fauna that will tell us the Rhine has finally returned to a healthy state of life."

Source: *William Drozdiak, "'Sewer of Europe' Cleans Up Its Act,"* Washington Post, *27 March 1997.*

swimmer, but also it can leap high in the air to overcome an in-stream barrier. Of course the fact that it is a large and handsome fish, delicious to eat and a particularly healthy source of protein, also contributes to its reputation. Because it thrives in free-flowing, clear streams, it is associated with freshness and purity as well.

For a river such as the Rhine to be able to support even a modest population of salmon would symbolize an astonishing recovery. Much of the great river was transformed over the nineteenth and twentieth centuries into an industrial canal and sewer. Engineers altered its flow and industrialists polluted its waters with little regard for the ecological consequences of their activities: in particular, the loss of habitats capable of supporting a wide variety of species. Large stretches of the banks were encased in concrete and stone, and some of its tributaries were "sacrificed" as they became overloaded with a toxic soup of chemical wastes. At its nadir in the 1970s, the Rhine was one of the most heavily polluted rivers on the planet. Because of its relatively rapid flow and large size, polluters claimed that they could dump huge quantities of waste into the river without significant costs or consequences. The result was a classic example of "the tragedy of the commons": what appeared to be rational calculations by local authorities and particular enterprises produced disaster for the river as a whole. A witch's brew of poisons made life in the river intolerable for all but the hardiest of native species. The navigable stretch of the river from Basel to Rotterdam was most affected. Between Basel and Mainz, river quality was down to Class II/III (as measured on a sliding scale from I to IV), meaning that the levels of dissolved oxygen were so low and of organic pollutants so high that many key river organisms could not live in it. Between Mainz and Rotterdam, river quality was down to Class III/IV, bad enough to make it impossible for most fish species to survive.

Much of that damage was reversed in the late twentieth century, as the riparian states cooperated to limit the amounts of effluent discharged into the river. By 1991 the Basel-to-Mainz stretch was nearing Class II ("slightly polluted") and the Mainz-to-Rotterdam stretch was up to Class II/III ("moderately polluted"). So successful was the cleanup effort that it was possible for most native species (including salmon) to survive in the river once again. Branches of the river with their gravel beds intact—the sort of habitat in which salmon can spawn—were unfortunately few and far between. Access to these sites was almost always blocked by a daunting obstacle course of dams and locks designed to facilitate flood control and navigation. In most cases these man-made structures could not easily be dismantled, but they could be equipped with artificial ladders to assist migratory fish. This effort, in accordance with the Salmon 2000 agenda, signaled the fact that the era of indifference to the ecology and biodiversity of the river was over.

Moreover, Salmon 2000 (despite its name) focused on the restoration of all migratory fish, not just salmon. Sea trout and lampern populations have begun to stabilize, and sea lamprey, fintis shad, and North Sea houting are all mounting slow comebacks. Every acre of restored gravel bed provides additional space not just for spawning and nursing fish, but also new habitat for riparian plant and animal communities. As superfluous dams and weirs have been eliminated, the natural hydrological and morphological features of the Rhine have been partially restored. These developments, in turn, have opened up new possibilities for bank stabilization, habitat variation, and species diversification throughout the Rhine basin.

Certainly the broader goal of restoring the floodplain is more important than the recovery of a few migratory fish species. Environmental restoration on such a large scale, however, does not occur in a vacuum: it requires the mobilization of public opinion. In order to do so, it is enormously helpful to highlight the status of a species whose fortunes can symbolize recovery. It is important to acknowledge the significance of what biologist Edward O. Wilson calls "biophilia," the human capacity for empathy with other species. Although this feeling is not entirely rational, and no doubt involves a certain element of anthropomorphism, the projection of human concerns and aspirations onto the natural world—a generous dose of biophilia—may play a useful role in engaging public support for wider efforts of restoration.

In Great Britain, salmon have been successfully reintroduced into the Thames and its estuaries. Like the Rhine, the Thames suffered catastrophic degradation by the middle of the twentieth century, so that when the river reached London it was foully polluted. The Thames is a much smaller stream than the Rhine, however, and since most heavy industries were concentrated in the northern part of Britain they did not have the opportunity to discharge their wastes into the river. Nor is the Thames an international river with seven states along its banks. Improving the quality of water in the Thames was therefore a far easier task than cleansing the Rhine. Nevertheless, the return of salmon to the Thames, a river with a long history of severe pollution, was a great achievement and a remarkable symbol of ecological recovery—and one that helped spawn greater public awareness of the virtues of clean streams everywhere in Great Britain.

A similar case in the United States was the dramatic recovery of the bald eagle. By the 1970s the national symbol of America was well on the way to extinction. The culprit was the pesticide dichlorodiphenyltrichloroethane (DDT), whose concentration in the food chain threatened the capacity of the bird to reproduce. The banning of DDT and other similarly persistent chemicals (chlorinated hydrocarbons) saved the eagle and other large predatory birds and helped to demonstrate to the American public that negative ecological trends were not necessarily irreversible. Similarly, the return of salmon to the Rhine would demonstrate the resolve of Europeans to bring a dying river back to life. Just as the disappearance of salmon by the middle of the twentieth century signaled the inexorable loss of biodiversity, so the return of salmon would advertise the resurrection of a great river. There are, to be sure, limits to what can be achieved. Salmon runs in the hundreds of thousands are unlikely, but the very difficulty of the project is a sign of the seriousness of the commitment. The real lesson, of course, is that the river is not merely an industrial canal and sewer, but also a functioning (if not a flourishing) ecosystem.

The problem of biodiversity, which has only recently begun to receive the attention it deserves, will surely be one of the crucial issues of the twenty-first century. Wilson estimates that ten thousand species a year, one per hour, are being lost and that over the first thirty years of the century a million species might disappear. The rate of extinction is probably greater than it has been since the dinosaurs disappeared sixty-five million years ago. The Rhine, to be sure, is not and never has been as biologically diverse as the Amazon; in fact, European rivers in general are not particularly rich in species and thus make only a small contribution to the biodiversity of the planet. Moreover, protection of relatively intact ecosystems is undoubtedly a more pressing concern than the restoration of degraded ones. In Europe, however, virtually all ecosystems have been seriously degraded. Here, restoration is the name of the game, and if salmon can once again swim in the Rhine and spawn in its tributaries, then Europeans can have some confidence that the effort is worth making.

–BRUCE THOMPSON, UNIVERSITY OF CALIFORNIA AT SANTA CRUZ

References

Action Plan on Flood Defense (Koblenz, Germany: ICPR, 1998).

International Commission for the Protection of the Rhine, *The Rhine: An Ecological Revival* (Koblenz, Germany: Internationale Kommission zum Schutze des Rheins, 1993).

Roy E. H. Mellor, *The Rhine: A Study in the Geography of Water Transport* (Aberdeen, Scotland: University of Aberdeen, 1979).

G. E. Petts, H. Möller, and A. L. Roux, eds., *Historical Change of Large Alluvial Rivers: Western Europe* (Chichester & New York: Wiley, 1989).

Goronwy Rees, *The Rhine* (New York: Putnam, 1967).

Royal Institute of International Affairs, *Regional Management of the Rhine* (London: Chatham House, 1975).

Salmon 2000 (Koblenz, Germany: ICPR, 1994).

A. Schulte-Wülwer-Leidig, "Outline of the Ecological Master-Plan for the Rhine," *Water Science and Technology*, 29 (1994): 273–280.

Norman Smith, *Man and Water: A History of Hydro-Technology* (New York: Scribners, 1975).

J. A. van de Kraats, ed., *Rehabilitation of the River Rhine: Proceedings of the International Conference on Rehabilitation of the River Rhine, 15–19 March 1993, Arnhem, The Netherlands* (Oxford, U.K. & Tarrytown, N.Y.: Pergamon, 1994).

B. A. Whitton, ed., *Ecology of European Rivers* (Oxford, U.K. & Boston: Blackwell Scientific, 1984).

Edward O. Wilson, *Biophilia* (Cambridge, Mass.: Harvard University Press, 1984).

SOUTHERN AFRICA

Did the construction of large-scale hydroelectric dams and water-diversion projects benefit the people of southern Africa?

Viewpoint: Yes. Dams and water-diversion projects made possible the expansion of European agriculture, industrial and mining enterprises, and the creation of modern nation-states in southern Africa.

Viewpoint: No. Africans were not involved with the decision-making processes of dam and water-diversion projects in southern Africa and suffered serious negative consequences from their construction.

The southern African region is generally considered to include the nations of Angola, Zambia, Malawi, Zimbabwe, Mozambique, Namibia, Botswana, Swaziland, Lesotho, and South Africa. Until the middle of the twentieth century all of these nations were ruled by Britain, Germany, or Portugal. Zambia, Malawi, and Zimbabwe were British colonies; South Africa was a semiautonomous Dominion of the British Empire; and Botswana, Swaziland, and Lesotho were British Protectorates. Each of these territories had British government officials as heads of state—and all of the people were subjects of the Queen of England. After World War II the German colonial status of Namibia ended and, as a United Nations (U.N.) Trust Territory, it was administered by South Africa. There had long been an assumption among Europeans that one day the South Africa borders would be expanded to include Lesotho, Botswana, Swaziland, and Namibia. In contrast, Angola and Mozambique were ruled by Portugal. Official language and economic ties isolated these territories from their neighbors.

Most of southern Africa is semiarid to arid bush savannah or grassland, and many rivers are seasonal or ephemeral. Much of the landscape is watered by springs. There are no natural lakes, but both seasonal and perennial marshes and wet spots (called *vleis*) occur. The largest and most well known is the mouth of the Okavango River, the Okavango Delta, at the edge of the Kalahari Desert in northern Botswana. The few perennial rivers flowing the dry southern African landscape have their headwaters in upland areas with higher rainfalls: the Zambezi, Okavango, and Cunene Rivers rise in the Angolan highland plateau and the Orange River (called Senqu in Lesotho) in the Drakensburg Mountains of Lesotho. Most of these rivers are international rivers, since they drain or traverse more than one nation. It is not surprising, therefore, that reliable water supplies for agriculture, mines, industry, and urban areas have been—and continue to be—a primary concern in southern Africa.

In the 1950s the amount of water and electricity required by industry and urban areas exceeded the capabilities of local production. Large-scale damming and diversion of regional rivers to serve distant cities seemed to be the obvious solution. Dams could serve a dual function—collecting and storing water and generating electricity. New technologies had been developed that allowed both large-scale engineering construction projects in remote locations and the long-distance transfer of electricity and water. As a result, dams were constructed on all major southern African rivers in the last half of the twentieth century, and water was diverted across the landscape. Plans exist for further dams and diversion projects in most southern African nations for construction in the twenty-first century.

Viewpoint: Yes. Dams and water-diversion projects made possible the expansion of European agriculture, industrial and mining enterprises, and the creation of modern nation-states in southern Africa.

Large dams were built for power on the Zambezi, Orange, and Cunene Rivers in southern Africa from the mid 1950s through the 1980s. The demand for water and electricity had increased as regional mining, industry, and municipalities expanded. Demonstration of the political power of the state, however, through the conquest of nature, rather than the generation of hydroelectric power or the supply of water, guided construction decisions. Dams were built to assert the claims of European colonial governments and settlers to the African landscape. These structures were understood to be necessary demonstrations of the technical and cultural superiority of European civilization. The dam sites were all remote from European settlements and, from a European perspective, populated by backward cultures that education, Christianity, and other civilizing influences could only improve.

This essay will describe the political contexts of the construction in Africa of the first large dam at Kariba Gorge on the Zambezi River between Zambia and Zimbabwe, the Cahora Bassa Dam further down the Zambezi in Mozambique, the Kafue Dam on the Kafue River, the drawing up of plans for the Epupa Dam as part of the Cunene River Scheme in Namibia, the Orange River Project with its Gariep Dam in South Africa, and the contemporary Lesotho Highlands Water Project (LHWP) Katse Dam. Preindependence names of nations and projects were used during the colonial era. Zambia was Northern Rhodesia, Zimbabwe was Southern Rhodesia, Malawi was Nyasaland, Namibia was South-West Africa, Lesotho was Basutoland, the Cahora Bassa Dam was called Cabora Bassa, and the Gariep Dam was called Verwoerd. Mozambique, Angola, and South Africa have not had name changes.

There was shock in southern African colonial and settler societies when the Gold Coast (modern Ghana) was granted self-rule under Kwame Nkrumah in 1951. The granting of self-rule status by the British Colonial Office was a major step toward achieving complete political independence. This recognition of African capabilities to form and run a government threatened the white settlers, especially those in territories where the settler population was small and the infrastructure undeveloped. Their claims to the land seemed tenuous, at best. Settlers in the British territories of South Africa, South-West Africa (Namibia), Southern Rhodesia (Zimbabwe), and Northern Rhodesia (Zambia) sought to consolidate and strengthen their industrial base. Portugal needed both to increase white settlement and develop infrastructure in Angola and Mozambique to strengthen its claims to those territories.

The Portuguese territories of Angola and Mozambique were not part of the British Empire, but their economies were linked to that of South Africa through corporate interests and, after 1960, a shared political vision. European settlement had never been a priority in Mozambique. Instead, Portugal saw the territory as a collection of natural resources whose extraction would finance the growth of the Portuguese economy. In contrast, Angola had a history of conscious Portuguese settlement. For three centuries it was the destination for Portuguese murderers, rapists, and thieves sent into exile under the *degredado* system. A settler population of traders, administrators, and soldiers grew up around this enforced-settler population. Prior to World War II, South Africa and Angola were the only African territories with white populations greater than 1 percent. Almost all of the European settlement of Angola, however, had occurred along the coast. Not until the 1940s did Portugal become interested in white settlement for agriculture and ranching.

After World War II many British veterans and their families immigrated to the Rhodesias and South Africa, while Portuguese citizens immigrated to Mozambique and Angola, to claim land and establish farms, mining operations, and businesses. Infrastructure was developed to serve the expanding white, urban populations. Reliable supplies of water and electricity were fundamental to this growth. The settlers and their governments were confident that they were constructing new and permanent societies, taking European culture to a new continent. African societies were displaced to accommodate the new arrivals, while individual

LESOTHO DAMS PROTEST

On 23 January 1998, several environmental and reform groups, including the Group for Environmental Monitoring (GEM) and International Rivers Network, issued a joint statement on dam development in Lesotho, a portion of which appears below:

Today marks the inauguration of the first water supply from Lesotho to South Africa. However, it is not a day to celebrate. Today as President Mandela, King Letsie the III, Namibian President Sam Nujoma and President Kelumile Masire of Botswana celebrate the transfer of water from the Katse dam to South Africa they are neglecting serious outstanding social, environmental and economic issues from the construction of the phase 1A Katse dam. Today, four of Southern Africa's leaders are celebrating the completion of a project which has and could continue to adversely affect a great number of people, directly cause significant harm to the environment and set a damaging precedent for water management in southern Africa. If this region is to meet the challenge of sustainable development, we must learn to use our precious resource efficiently before forcing poor people and the environment to make sacrifices.

Large dams, such as the Lesotho Highlands Water Project (LHWP), force people from their homes, submerge fertile farmlands, forests and sacred places, destroy fisheries and cause the social, cultural and economic impoverishment of affected communities. In addition, because large dams often cost more than the benefits they produce, they divert funding away from the provision of important basic needs such as the provision of sanitation, safe drinking water, affordable and efficient irrigation systems, health and education. . . .

Phase 1A [Katse Dam] of the LHWP directly affected 2000 people—approximately 300 households— and indirectly affected at least 20000 more by their losing the use of common resources or income through the loss of 925ha of arable and 3000ha of grazing land.

The compensation program for affected household was intended to offset losses caused by the project. Major elements include the annual delivery of foodstuffs as compensation for the loss of arable land, single cash payments for gardens, baled fodder for lost rangeland, cash and replacement seedlings for trees, and incidental repairs and replacement of damaged property. Since its inception, there have been problems with the program and its implementation, causing affected people anguish for many years. A new program, mostly untried is now underway.

In late 1997 the Highlands Church and Solidarity Action Group (HCSAG) conducted a qualitative study of 93 households in the villages of Khohlontso, Ha Nkokana, Ha Mensel, Ha Theko, Ha Ramanamane, Ha Seshote, and Ha Lejone. All of these villages are in close vicinity to the Katse Reservoir. They found that:

•40% of the grievances lodged 3 years ago were not addressed in any way whatsoever; 55% of the grievances were, to varying degrees, partially addressed; and 5% of the grievances were fully addressed. It is worth noting that two of the four households whose grievances were fully addressed claimed not to be satisfied with the compensation.

•Only 2 of the 93 households reported to be satisfied with their compensation. Of the 38 claims that were not addressed in any way whatsoever, 26 (68%) received no reason from LHDA as to why this was the case; 10 (26%) received promises of compensation, but nothing was ever delivered; and 2 (5%) received an explanation as to why no action had been taken.

The LHWP Treaty signed in 1986 guarantees that people will "be enabled to maintain a standard of living not inferior to that obtaining at the time of first disturbance."

Contrary to the commitment established in the 1986 agreement, the HCSAG survey of affected households found that,

•75% felt that their standard of living had decreased since the beginning of the project;

•15% felt that they were living at the same level and

•10% felt that their standard of living had been raised since the beginning of the project.

Source: *"Lesotho Water Transfers—No Cause for Celebration: Groups Call for a Halt to Project Until Problems Resolved," Africa Policy Information Center, Internet website.*

Africans were expected to provide labor for the various enterprises undertaken.

Between 1960 and 1964 African political parties were formed and challenged colonial and settler authority. The South-West African People's Organization (SWAPO), the Mozambique Liberation Front (FRELIMO), the Zimbabwe African People's Organization (ZAPU), and the Zimbabwe African National Union (ZANU) in Southern Rhodesia were formed. In South Africa a peaceful demonstration against Pass Laws resulted in the Sharpeville Massacre (21 March 1960), the banning of the Pan-African Congress (PAC) and the African National Congress (ANC), and the first declaration of a State of Emergency. The Federation of Northern and Southern Rhodesia and Nyasaland broke up, and ZAPU was banned and went into exile in the newly independent nation of Zambia (former Northern Rhodesia). *Umkhonto we Sizwe* (MK), the military wing of the ANC, made its first attack and the armed struggle against settler governments began in Angola, Rhodesia, and Mozambique. By 1968 Rhodesia, Mozambique, Angola, and the northern border of South-West Africa were active guerilla war zones. After South Africa invaded southern Angola in August 1975, northern South-West Africa and southern Angola were more or less continually occupied by South African troops and subject to full-scale military battles and bombing through the 1980s.

Government officials saw southern Africa as "the last bastion of western civilization in Africa"; regional political and economic cooperation was essential to erect a bulwark against black liberation forces. Large hydroelectric-power dams and water-diversion schemes were essential for the development of settler societies. Like the struggles for independence, the dams and water-diversion projects had both national and regional contexts. Projects were financed by national, regional, and international governments and banks, and most of the projects were meant to benefit the infrastructure requirements of more than one country, as well as address the regional concern for a bulwark of white civilization. The construction of dams and water projects began in the late 1950s, expanded in the 1960s and 1970s, and continued through the 1980s.

The notion in Northern and Southern Rhodesia of a future union with South Africa ended when the Afrikaner Nationalist Party won the South African elections in 1948 calling for reduced ties with Britain. By 1953 the legislatures of Nyasaland, Southern Rhodesia, and Northern Rhodesia had agreed to the formation of the Federation of Rhodesia and Nyasaland. The federal government developed a policy of stimulating industrial growth and expansion through the development of essential infrastructure. One of the first tasks assigned to the newly created Federation was the construction of a massive hydroelectric-power dam at Kariba Gorge on the Zambezi River to provide power for both Southern Rhodesian industry and Northern Rhodesian mines.

From a European perspective the Zambezi River was a remote and wasted resource that, if harnessed, could ensure the development of industrial societies. The Tonga who lived in the Zambezi Valley were shocked and angered by the idea of changing the flow of the river. Because of their fear of the police, most south bank (Southern Rhodesian) Tonga did not resist the order to move. In Northern Rhodesia, however, there were both national political opposition and local resistance. The Queen of England was petitioned to appoint a Commission of Enquiry and one group of valley residents refused to move, resulting in an armed confrontation with Northern Rhodesian police. Construction of Kariba Dam began in 1955, and the largest man-made lake in the world was created in 1959.

While the central African territories pulled away from South Africa, South-West Africa became increasingly linked to it. South African corporations exploited the mineral deposits, South African settlers established ranches, the South African legal system and currencies were used, and the South African police patrolled the cities and territorial boundaries. The Odendaal Commission into South-West African Affairs was convened from 1962 to 1963 to make plans for socioeconomic development and future administrative structure of the region.

The Commission proposed a scheme to exploit the Cunene River, which formed the northern border with Angola, to be implemented in cooperation with the Portuguese government. This plan included a series of thirteen dams, including one at Epupa Falls that would regulate the flow of the Cunene River and provide water and electricity in southern Angola and northern South-West Africa. It could not be implemented without the active support of Angola. A cooperative agreement between South Africa and Portugal was worked out in conjunction with the construction of the Cabora Bassa Dam in Mozambique.

Construction of the first dam, called Gove, near the headwaters of the Cunene began in 1969. The second dam, Calueque, also on Angolan territory but downstream and closer to the South-West African border, was begun in 1971. The last structure to be built before wars of independence halted this project was the Ruacana Diversion Wier, which generated electricity for South-West Africa, where it had been constructed in 1972–1973. The dam at Epupa Falls was part of the Cunene River Plan, but was not implemented because of war. Independent Namibia, however, resurrected and promoted the 1960s apartheid-era plans for a hydroelectric dam at Epupa Falls as essential for national development.

The decision to build the Kafue and Itezhitezhi Dams was the Zambian response to the Rhodesian Unilateral Declaration of Independence (UDI) in November 1965. Since the hydroelectric generating plant of Kariba Dam had been built on the Southern Rhodesian side of the gorge, Zambian mines and industry relied upon Southern Rhodesia for power. Seeking an independent source, Zambian officials revived the plans first drawn up in the late 1950s for a dam on the Kafue River at the Kafue Gorge, with the Itezhitezhi storage dam four hundred kilometers upstream.

In March 1957 the Portuguese government established the *Missao do Fomento e Povoamento do Zambeze* (MFPZ) to study the potential for development and settlement in the upper Zambezi Valley in Angola and lower Zambezi Valley in Mozambique. One of its 1959 reports gave preliminary assessment of the hydroelectric potential of the Cabora Bassa gorge in Mozambique, and a strategic assessment was published in 1966. A dam at Cabora Bassa was seen as a source not only of electricity but also of revenue for development of the lower Zambezi Valley. A foreign customer was required, and South Africa was approached. South Africa had no need for more electricity but was concerned about the development of hydroelectric projects on the Cunene River. Negotiations between South Africa and Portugal began in 1965. In 1969 the South African government agreed to purchase electricity from a dam at Cabora Bassa and invest in its construction if Portugal would agree to participate in the Cunene River Project.

Soon after its construction began in 1969, the Cabora Bassa Dam became a political symbol. To the financial and settler communities it was "synonymous with an increasing struggle against terrorism." For African nationalists and their international supporters the dam became a symbol of colonialism. In 1968 FRELIMO leader Eduard Chivambo Mondlane stated that if Cabora Bassa were not destroyed, it would destroy Mozambique. The dam site became a military target, protected by the Portuguese army and attacked by FRELIMO troops.

Internationally, the dam was recognized as a political, rather than economic, project. Opposition to it mounted at multilateral, government, and nongovernment levels. The Cabora Bassa Dam was condemned by the Organization of African Unity (OAU) and the NonAligned Movement. A 1970 United Nations General Assembly resolution condemned foreign investment. Campaigns to mobilize public opinion against the project and stop government investment and corporate participation were mounted by church groups, liberation support groups, and others in Sweden, West Germany, Italy, Britain, the United States, and Canada.

The Orange River Development project was the South African response to African nationalist protests of the apartheid system. "The white *platteland* is largely the pivot of western civilization. . . . [a strong farming community] is a prerequisite to the continued existence of Christian civilization in our country," stated a 1959 commission on the rural white population in South Africa.

The 1928 suggestion that water be diverted from the Orange River through tunnels to the Great Fish River Valley for irrigation was given new life after the Sharpeville massacre. When this project was first formulated in 1962, almost the entire area to be developed had been designated as a "white group" area. Most whites supported the project; dissent came in discussion of the high cost of the project. The Lower Orange River flowed through arid land that had been set aside as "Coloured" reserves; here ten thousand acres would be irrigated. The inclusion of these reserves in the project was seen as a mechanism to cultivate goodwill and loyalty among the "Coloureds," preventing them from becoming aligned with the "Africans."

The largest interbasin water-transfer project in South Africa was constructed. A series of dams (including Gariep Dam) were built to collect water and transfer it to municipalities and through more than 51 miles of tunnels, 50 miles of canals, and 120 miles of pipeline to agricultural land. The project created a 40 percent increase in total irrigated land in South Africa and provided permanent water supplies to the Afrikaner hinterland in the Cape Province.

The 1976 uprising by South African schoolchildren, the subsequent publication of the Total Strategy White Paper, and the financial impact of the international economic-sanctions campaign gave impetus to the last major regional dam and water-diversion scheme to be initiated, the LHWP. In South Africa, the major industrial area defined by the towns of Pretoria and Vereeningen and the mineral-laden hills of the Witwatersrand developed because of proximity to mineral rather than water resources. The closest perennial river to the region (formerly called PWV, currently Gauteng) was the Vaal. The potential limitation of the region by water availability was recognized in the 1920s, and the solution seemed to be diverting water from the Orange River one hundred kilometers to the south, which flowed from the mountains of adjacent Basutoland (modern-day Lesotho). Incorporation of Basutoland into South Africa gave South Africa unlimited access to the headwaters of the Orange River.

As the concept of incorporation lost impetus, plans were devised for the transfer of water between an independent Lesotho and the Vaal River catchment area in South Africa. Although the possibility of diverting water from the Orange River to the Vaal River catchment had been discussed since the 1950s, not until May 1979 did the governments of Lesotho and South Africa formally agree to prepare a feasibility study for such a project. Specific plans for the LHWP were formulated in the early 1980s.

A consortium of British and European engineering and electricity firms prepared a feasibility study between August 1983 and August 1986. Negotiations between Lesotho and South Africa continued during this time. Prime Minister Leabua Jonathan insisted that Lesotho should be able to regulate the flow of water to South Africa, but a South African-backed military coup in January 1986 removed him from office.

The feasibility study was completed in August 1986. Lesotho would not control the flow of water. The twenty-four volume final report included not only designs for dams, tunnels, and pumping stations to reverse the flow of the Orange River and its tributaries in Lesotho and the construction of a small hydroelectric plant, but also an outline of the bureaucratic structures required to manage such a scheme, draft legislation to create the Lesotho Highlands Development Authority (LHDA) to implement the project in Lesotho, and a draft of the Treaty between Lesotho and South Africa.

The treaty implementing the LHWP was signed on 24 October 1986, nine months after the coup. Neither government had international legitimacy. South Africa was subject to an international embargo at the time, and the Lesotho government had come to power by a coup and was, therefore, unconstitutional. Namibia (whose southern border is formed by the Orange River) was, at that time, under the control of South Africa as South-West Africa. According to LHDA authorities, the United Nations (U.N.) Council for Namibia said that there would be no impact–and SWAPO was not consulted.

The LHWP was described as a Lesotho Development Project, and finance was arranged through the World Bank and international contractors in order to circumvent the international anti-apartheid economic sanctions against the South African state. Construction began on the access roads to the remote mountain site of Katse Dam (the first of five major dams) in 1988, construction of the transfer tunnel and Katse Dam began in 1991, and water first flowed to South Africa on 22 January 1998.

Dams and water-transfer schemes were built in southern Africa to strengthen fledgling European settlements and growing industrial enterprises. Government archives, international treaties, and contracts document not only the engineering concerns and details, but also the larger political objectives of these projects. It was well understood by local and international governments that the future of European domination of southern Africa was threatened by an educated African elite no longer contented with colonial status. Substantial infrastructure to support the promotion of European immigration was required.

The design specifications of projects drawn up in the late twentieth century reflected the interests of the governments that commissioned them. The evidence remains in the landscape. Transmission lines pass over rural villages to deliver electricity to urban, mining, and industrial sites. Water is similarly available to areas in which white settlement was concentrated at the time of construction. While there is no doubt that dams and water diversions in southern Africa have provided water and electricity, clearly these benefits did not and do not extend to most of the population. Engineering plans drawn up in that era but implemented at the turn of the century can only reflect the priorities of colonial governments, rather than the more inclusive goals of independent states.

–KATE B. SHOWERS, BOSTON UNIVERSITY

Viewpoint: No. Africans were not involved with the decision-making processes of dam and water-diversion projects in southern Africa and suffered serious negative consequences from their construction.

The story of dams in Africa, like many twentieth-century tales, depends on the perceptual lens with which the storyteller views the world. For the last century, these storytellers have had many things in common. They have mostly been men; they have mostly been educated; they have mostly come from the cities; they have mostly viewed development to be in the national common interest; and they have mostly been paid a high salary that has been linked in some way to serving the needs of that national interest. There are many other stories, however, that have been murmuring as a faint background noise, throughout the rural areas of Africa–stories that are spoken in many different languages, by women and children, as well as by men, and by those whose education lies in the lay of the land, the flow of the rivers, and the cycle of the seasons.

More than 1,200 large dams have been built in Africa, with two-thirds of these located in the southern continent. It is, therefore, apt that many of the stories shared here come from the presentations that were made at the Southern African Hearings for Communities affected by Large Dams. The hearings were held in November 1999 to ensure that the voices of the affected peoples of southern Africa would be heard by the World Commission on Dams (WCD); representatives of the Tonga, Zulu, Basotho, Himba, Swazi, Xhosa, and Tswana each told their story. The WCD was, at the time, half the way through its mandate of evaluating the development effectiveness of large dams. Perhaps the following excerpt from the Final Declaration of the Hearings conveys, in the words of the delegates themselves, reveal the true cost of large dams:

> The history of large dams and affected communities in Southern Africa has been one of broken promises and incalculable losses:
>
> - We lost our livelihoods and cannot regain them
> - Our land where we grew food was taken from us and not replaced
> - Our homes were demolished and drowned
> - Our livestock was taken from us
> - We lost control of our natural resources
> - Our wildlife has disappeared
> - Our cultural values, functions and roots have been destroyed
> - Our ancestors graves have been buried under deep waters, and
> - The lives of some of our communities and family members were violently taken from us.
>
> We have been forced to move against our will without knowing when or where we would be going without a way for our concerns or objections to be heard. We have not been treated with dignity, nor with respect for our customs, our ancestors or our children. We have shouldered the burden of large dams but we have enjoyed very few of the benefits. In short, large dams have been devastating to many of our communities.

This essay will explore the impacts experienced by African communities around the themes of flawed and unjust decision-making processes, and the nature and extent of negative social impacts, using the testimonies of effected people as evidence. This experiential knowledge is used to make the concluding recommendations for policy and process changes, so essential for making reparations for past injustices and to prevent injustices from recurring in the future.

Chief David Syankusule asked for a minute's silence in remembrance of the forty Tongans who were shot, and the eight who were killed, by the "soldiers who were sent by the Federal Government to kill our people who did not want to move away from the river." This incident occurred in the 1950s and the people were killed to make way for Kariba Dam, which straddles the border between Zambia and Zimbabwe. While not all the experiences were so violent, all the presentations made at the hearings, except for one, gave evidence that decisions to build dams were made unilaterally, and communities did not participate in the decision-making process in any meaningful way. Syankusule spoke for everyone when he said: "An African had no say." More than 57,000 Tongans had no say when they were forcibly moved to make way for the Kariba Dam, built to supply copper mines with cheap electricity. The year the dam was built is remembered by the Tongans as the "Year of Eating Bones." According to Fanuel Cumanzula, people were starving and had to resort to digging for roots to stay alive.

In South Africa the situation was more complex as the apartheid regime had transformed much of the landowning population into farm laborers. When dams were built, these farm workers had no claim to the land. In the case of Gariep Dam, Mrs. Mbalula spoke of how she used to work on a white-owned farm that was to be flooded by the Gariep Dam. "We were never consulted. We were only told that we had to move out because the farmer has sold his farm. We had a car, a donkey car. We had also cattle. When we were along the road, staying there, I was highly pregnant by then. I gave birth to a baby son along the road."

If colonial and apartheid governments paid little heed to the rights of communities effected by dams, so too did the postindependence democratic governments. Motjinduiko Kapika, a Himba from Namibia, who lives near the site of the proposed Epupa Dam on the Cunene River in Namibia, said he had been sent by his Headman to the southern African hearings to give the message to everyone who would hear that the Himba people did not want the dam. He further went on to describe how community meetings held to discuss the Epupa Dam were broken up by armed police and how people who opposed the dam were threatened.

Similarly, in Lesotho decisions for the Lesotho Highlands Water Project (LHWP) were made unilaterally at high levels and the communities were told that resettlement was compulsory. According to Anna Moepi, who originally came from the village of Molikaliko, "Our lives before the Lesotho Highlands Water project came was a nice one. We were living in peace and harmony. We were planting maize, wheat and everything that sustains our lives. And then the project came and told us that we were to leave our places whether we liked it or not."

In looking at the reasons why these large dams have been built in southern Africa, it appears that many are built for short-term geopolitical goals and multinational corporate interests. In the case of the Gariep and Van der Kloof Dams, the decision was motivated by the goal of the Nationalist Party government toward "building a political symbol to Afrikaner Nationalism and a monument to the grand scheme of apartheid at a time when South Africa had just withdrawn from the British Commonwealth." Patrick Bond, in "Paying for Southern African Dams" (1999), found similar evidence of the political economy of dam building in his analysis of the rationale for constructing Kariba Dam and LHWP. In particular, he asserted that "the LHWP was biased towards the needs of the then apartheid state for financial resources and African allies, the unsustainable water consumption practices of mining, industrial and wealthy domestic users, and a corruption-ridden construction industry." He concludes that financing of the dams has exacerbated these problems by adding debt loads and curtailing affordability for those citizens who most need electricity and water.

Olive Sephuma gave testimony of the only case where community participation was taken seriously–that of the Southern Okavango Integrated Water Development Project in Botswana. A special community meeting called a *kgotla* was held in January 1991 in the area where the people lived. More than seven hundred people came to the meeting. According to Sephuma, "each and every community member stood up and talked about how they did not want the plan and how it was not the right thing to do because you cannot fiddle with the environment in that way and expect not to suffer some consequences." The Botswana government took these concerns seriously and undertook further studies, which corroborated the community perspective that the project would be a disaster. The project was stopped despite the investments already made.

At the hearings the importance of burial grounds and the issue of separating an African from his/her ancestors brought the strongest emotional response from so many people. Western dam builders do not understand the role that ancestors play in the daily lives of many African cultures. Patrick Maphalala (Woodstock Dam, South Africa) spoke about how one woman had to spend a night's vigil with her deceased relative because the construction workers left at the end of the day with the grave opened. Anna Moepi (LHWP, Lesotho) described how the host community to which her family had moved to would not allow the newcomers to use the local graveyard. When Moepi's mother died they had no choice but to bury her at their place of residence. The authorities subsequently told them that they had to exhume her body. This event she describes as "the saddest thing I have come across." Mbalula cried when she spoke of her children who had died on the farm inundated by the Gariep Dam and how they "are in the water now, where the dam is."

This issue, more than any other, forms the core of the Himba's opposition to the Epupa Dam. For the Himba a grave is not just the location of the physical remains of a deceased person; it is a focal point for defining identity, social relationships, and relations with the land, as well as being a center for important religious rituals. A person's status with respect to access to land and decision-making powers is based on the number of ancestral graves he has in a particular area. The key point is not the physical fact of the graves themselves but the connection between the graves, the family's history, and the community's system of land tenure and decision making. This connection cannot possibly be preserved if graves are relocated. When told that the Epupa Dam will flood large numbers of gravesites, many Himba have asked, "Who will then know who is owning the land?"

The thread of broken promises was woven throughout the testimonies at the hearings. From South Africa, O'Brien Gabasche, Paulos Gwala, and Maxwell Meyiwa told the story of how their three communities had been forced off their tribal land for the Inanda Dam in 1986 and how they are still waiting for the land they were promised as compensation. According to Meyiwa, "Up until today, every promise has been broken. The community feels unheard." From Zimbabwe, Cumanzula spoke of the promises that were made but never materialized, a result in part of the lack of any contract or agreement between the government and the people. Despite the promises that water would follow them, it never did, and the "People of the Great River" are still waiting for water in the dry places they were forcibly removed to four decades ago. From Lesotho, Benedict Leuta spoke of the promises for compensation and employment that never

Kenyan girl waters cattle near Lorugumu

(Images of Africa)

came; and Didian Malisemelo Tao spoke of the promised compensation for gardens, fruit trees, forest and wood trees that was never paid, of water never provided, and indoor stoves never delivered.

Social impacts are many and varied. At the hearings people spoke of their standard of living dropping, of how they were once self-sufficient and now depend on handouts, of how HIV and AIDS are spreading through their communities, of how conflict has increased in once-peaceful communities. In the words of a young boy from Lesotho, Lipolelo, when asked about the impact of Katse Dam (LHWP) on his family: "The LHWP has also destroyed very much. Our sisters are out of control. They are pregnant. My mother left my father alone and stayed at Katse with another man. Our brothers are drinking beer and making young girls pregnant. Girls are killing their babies. They throw them in tins and in toilets. LHWP has been bad because girls were drinking beer and they were going in cars of foreign engineers and contractors; especially my sister." How can one quantify the legacy left behind for decades to come?

Worse still is that people do not understand the full extent of the impacts of the dams and are assured by the consultants and officials that whatever they might be, they will be mitigated. Many people from rural areas cannot conceive of what a large dam actually is. The Himba's experience of dams is a 100-meter farm dam, and it was a while before they realized that the Epupa Dam would cover 180 square kilometers of fertile riverine landscape and 6,000 trees upon which their lifestyle depends. It is impossible to mitigate this loss, and yet the consultants are confident.

The Resettlement Policy of the World Bank advocates that the lives of resettled people should be better off than they were before being moved. It is particularly pertinent therefore, in the case of LHWP, which the World Bank partly funded, that people's lives have deteriorated. In this case, LHWP has been an active agent in the collapse of self-sufficiency of the mountain communities as the severe land shortage in Lesotho precludes land-for-land compensation. The authorities have been naive or callous to think that rural people who live off the land can, in such a short space of time, learn to survive within an urban cash-based economy. The narrative of Moepi described the promises made by the authorities that their lives would improve, that they would receive compensation for all the assets lost, training for new lives, water, and that they would be better off than they were before. This situation has not happened, and she concluded her submission by saying: "Our lives are in danger and we have not been compensated. When compensation does finally come, it comes very late and only once a year. You see our lives as deteriorating day by day. We are worse off." Her community has asked to be resettled again. They can never go home to Molikaliko.

The Phongolapoort Dam highlighted the critical issue of downstream impacts of large dams, which have throughout the world devastated the downstream food security of riverine communities. In this case, the dam was built to supply white-owned sugar farmers with irrigation water. Like many apartheid-era developments, it was badly planned and the purpose for which it was built never materialized. The dam nonetheless completely altered the natural flood regime. Community testimony reflected the devastating impact that this dam had on the indigenous economic activities consisting of flood-plain agriculture, fishing, and animal husbandry.

While promises were made and broken in the past, this does not mean that the story has ended. The World Commission on Dams briefing paper, titled "Reparations and the Right to Remedy" (2000), makes a case for reparations for dam-affected communities in order to acknowledge and attempt to repair, make amends, and compensate for past failure. While this right to reparation is clearly defined in several United Nations treaties dealing with human-rights issues, it is not clearly understood by dam-affected communities in southern Africa. The final declaration of the hearings urged for mechanisms or institutional arrangements to be found to address these past injustices. In the case of Kariba Dam, they strongly felt that the Commonwealth and the Queen of England were still culpable. The Zambezi River Authority acknowledged in 1999 that the current situation of those resettled by Kariba Dam is even worse now than it was decades ago, and in order to address these outstanding issues they initiated the Zambezi Valley Development Fund. Thus, a start has been made on making reparations, and this policy is setting a strong regional precedent for other dam-affected communities.

We live in a new decade, a new century, and a new millennium. According to Richard Falk, in a speech at the World Commission on Dams Forum Meeting in Prague (March 1999), "We are coming out of a long period of immoral and unethical decision making." The role of the state has changed from being a pivotal authority to being a pawn of global and market forces. In tandem with these changes comes an increasing endorsement of human rights, as well as the recognition that development must be both sustainable and human-centered for us to survive. The rights of civil society to participate in decisions that affect their lives are paramount in this new democratic order. In southern Africa, the story of dams has been tragic for those most affected. The testimonies are powerful in their expression of powerlessness. We have been powerless, but it is not so anymore.

To tap into this power to play a role in the decisions which affect lives, and to regain a quality of life that was stolen, residents in the affected communities have made a range of demands, requests, and suggestions. This is what they want:

- Reparations for past injustices, and for their governments to pay the debts they owe, for example compensation for outstanding losses and damages caused by large dams;

- To be treated in a just, equitable and dignified manner through participation in decision making processes as equal partners, particularly with regard to whether a dam is built or not. (This is in line with the global civil society position that communities effected by dams should have the right to prior, informed consent, which has been discussed in the World Commission on Dams process);

- To be able to participate in a meaningful and capacitated manner. Mechanisms to build community capacity include being informed of their rights, support from NGOs, development of community structures; access to information (in understandable languages), and access to funds for ensuring informed participation such as being able to pay for legal expertise;

- To sign negotiated legal contracts which are enforceable when governments and authorities break their promises and the projects are not implemented properly, particularly with respect to resettlement and compensation;

- Resettlement and compensation should be finalized before construction begins. Families should be kept together and graves must be moved with families. Facilities such as health and education should be in place before resettlement begins. Compensation should be fair and adequate and characterized by land for land, and a structure for a structure. Further, effected people who pay the costs should be the first in line to receive benefits.

Dams should be seen as a means to development, not an end in themselves. As such, dams should be a last resort and more-sustainable alternatives should be prioritized. The Southern African Hearings was the first public gathering at which the voices of people affected by large dams had been heard in southern Africa. Cumanzula, on behalf of the Tonga people of Kariba, said thank you for listening, as it "provides an opportunity to try and restore our dignity and humanity which were lost from the time when we faced the problems of resettlement and relocation." Mbalula was grateful for the door that was open for the first time in three decades. Chief Syankusule, in preparation for the hearings, had met with his seven chiefs, and they had told him: "this is our time when we as a people could be heard." Listening is not enough. We listened. We heard. Now it is our responsibility to act.

–LIANE GREEFF, ENVIRONMENTAL MONITORING GROUP, CAPE TOWN, SOUTH AFRICA

References

Patrick Bond, "Paying for Southern African Dams: Socio-Economic-Environmental Financing Gaps," EMG / GEM / IRN, Submission to the World Council of Dams, 1999.

Renfrew Christie, *Electricity, Industry and Class in South Africa* (Albany: State University of New York Press, 1984).

Christie, "The Political Economy of the Kunene River Hydroelectric Schemes," thesis, University of Cape Town, South Africa, 1975.

Richard Falk, speech made at the World Commission on Dams Forum Meeting in Prague, March 1999.

Kornia Horta, "The Mountain Kingdom's White Oil: The Lesotho Highlands Water Project," *The Ecologist,* 25 (1995): 227–231.

David Howarth, *The Shadow of the Dam* (London: Collins, 1961).

Dianne Hubbard, *The Epupa Debate: A Summary of Some of the Key Issues Around the Proposed Hydropower Scheme on the Lower Cunene River* (Windhoek, Namibia: Legal Assistance Centre, 1998).

Brigitte Lau and Christel Stern, *Namibian Water Resources and Their Management: A Preliminary History, Including Excerpts from Unpublished Sources* (Windhoek, Namibia: National Archives of Namibia, 1990).

D. C. Midgley, "Water and Electric Power to Develop Southern Africa," *Executive Intelligence Review,* 17 (1990): 34–37.

Henry Olivier, *Great Dams in Southern Africa* (Cape Town & New York: Purnell, 1976).

Save the Children Fund (U.K.), "Since the Water Came: Kids in Lesotho Talk About Katse Dam," in collaboration with Transformation Resource Centre, Lesotho, 1999.

Georg Schreyogg and Horst Steinmann, "Corporate Morality Called Into Question: The Case of Cabora Bassa," *Journal of Business Ethics,* 8 (1989): 677–685.

Kate B. Showers, "Colonial and Post-Apartheid Water Projects in Southern Africa: Political Agendas and Environmental Consequences," Working Paper No. 214 (Boston: Boston University African Studies Center, 1998).

H. J. Simons, "Harnessing the Orange River," in *Dams in Africa: An Interdisciplinary Study of Manmade Lakes in Africa,* edited by Rubin Neville and William M. Warren (London: Cass, 1968), pp. 128–145.

"The Story of Cabora Bassa," *Barclay's National Review* (March 1973): 10–13.

World Commission on Dams, "Orange River Case Study Pilot Project," Draft Report, October 1999.

World Commission on Dams, "Reparations and the Right to Remedy," briefing paper prepared by Barbara Rose Johnston, Center for Political Ecology, California, 2000.

World Council of Churches, *Cunene Dam Scheme and the Struggle for the Liberation of Southern Africa* (Geneva: World Council of Churches, Programme to Combat Racism, 1971).

TISZA CHEMICAL SPILL

What lessons can be learned about transboundary environmental conflicts from the January 2000 Tisza chemical spill in Romania?

Viewpoint: Diplomatic and economic pressures make governments poor guardians of the environment. The best guarantors of environmental safety are regional, national, and international nongovernmental organizations (NGOs).

Viewpoint: International mining companies view the environment as an "externality" and therefore do not calculate pollution and accidental spills into the costs of doing business in foreign countries. They do not put environmental safety first because they know they likely will not be held financially accountable.

On 30 January 2000 the tailings dam at a gold-processing pond owned by Aurul SA in Baia Mare, Romania, breached and allowed around a hundred thousand cubic meters of water containing high levels of cyanide, copper, zinc, and other heavy metals to spill into the nearby Sasar and Lapus streams. Within three days the toxic plume had flowed into Hungary, where it reached the Tisza River, a major tributary of the Danube. Within a month the spill had passed through Hungary, Serbia, Bulgaria, and back into Romania before entering the Black Sea at the Danube Delta.

Cyanide is highly toxic to humans, animals, and plants; its effects are immediate and acute (it blocks cells from uptaking oxygen), but it then disperses from the environment rapidly. Heavy metals, by contrast, accumulate in sediments and bioaccumulate in plants and animals, increasing in toxicity over time. In this accident, the cyanide immediately killed thousands of tons of fish, poisoned waterfowl, and threatened the drinking water supplies of many communities, although few injuries to human beings were reported. Meanwhile, heavy metals were deposited in the sediment, where they will continue to affect life forms for many decades. The disaster affected about two thousand kilometers of the Danube basin. "After Chernobyl, this is the largest ecological disaster ever to hit Eastern Europe," stated Zoltán Illes, chairman of the environmental committee of the Hungarian parliament.

The cyanide concentration measured 32.6 milligrams per liter when the pollution plume reached the Romanian-Hungarian border on 1 February 2000, a concentration level three hundred times higher than the 0.1 milligrams per liter level recognized as "heavily polluted" by the Hungarian Ministry for Environmental Protection. When the plume met the Tisza River in northeastern Hungary on 3 February, the cyanide level had dropped to 13.5 milligrams per liter, still a highly lethal dose. In Szolnok, a city of one hundred thousand people, the water-intake system was closed down and clean drinking water was brought in trucks. When the spill reached the Hungarian-Serbian border on 11 February 2000, the cyanide concentration had dropped to 1.49 milligrams per liter, still almost fifteen times the "heavily polluted" level.

While the catastrophic fishkill was predominantly confined to Hungary, Serbian fishermen reported seeing dead fish on the Danube as far south as Belgrade. At the end of February, a research team of the United Nations Environmental Program (UNEP) detected the plume at the Danube Delta in Romania, registering at 0.058 milligrams per liter, almost six times the permissible concentration level for cyanide allowed by the Romanian Environmental Protection Agency.

Aurul SA was a joint venture begun in 1992 between the private Australian mining company, Esmeralda, and the state-owned Romanian mining concern, Remin. The Romanian government had heralded the involvement of Esmeralda as an opportunity to introduce more environmentally sound mining and extraction practices in the already heavily mined region. The plant received an operating permit, following an environmental impact assessment, and began processing in April 1999. At the time of the accident, Aurul SA was operating in accordance with Romanian regulations. Governments, nongovernmental organizations (NGOs), and citizens communicated well enough about the chemical spill to prevent widespread poisoning of people, although some episodes of illness were reported.

Troubles for the Tisza did not end with the Aurul SA cyanide spill, however. In spring 2000 additional toxic spills and catastrophic flooding sent more contaminants down the river. On 10 and 15 March 2000, tailings dams containing high concentrations of heavy metals broke at a Remin-owned mining facility in Baia Borsa, north of Baia Mare, releasing more than twenty thousand tons of mud contaminated with lead, zinc, and copper. These spills did not contain high levels of cyanide, nor did they match the scale of the Aurul SA disaster. The heavy-metal spills did, however, damage the upper reaches of the Tisza that had been spared in the earlier cyanide spill. The plume of polluted mud traveled through Romania, Ukraine, and Slovakia before reaching Hungary. While the cyanide broke down chemically and dispersed after several weeks, the heavy-metal contamination from the three toxic spills settled into river sediment and will eventually accumulate in living tissue, posing a long-term health hazard in the region. In April, following the second wave of toxic contamination, a record-breaking flood struck the Tisza basin in Romania, Hungary, and Yugoslavia. This "flood of the century" spread sediment from the earlier spills across the Tisza floodplain, endangering soil safety and making it difficult to monitor the long-term effects of these toxic disasters.

In the aftermath of this flooding, officials, activists, and scholars have continued to debate how to apportion blame and how to assess (and collect) damages for the spill. They also worry about the level of preparedness in states such as Romania for other environmental accidents.

Viewpoint: Diplomatic and economic pressures make governments poor guardians of the environment. The best guarantors of environmental safety are regional, national, and international nongovernmental organizations (NGOs).

The break in the tailings dam occurred at 10 p.m. on 30 January 2000. At 10:30 p.m. the Aurul SA plant notified the Baia Mare Environmental Protection Agency, which allowed ten hours to pass before notifying the Romanian Waters Authority. This delay placed residents in the immediate area of the spill at great risk, though fortunately no fatalities were reported. The Romanian Waters Authority moved quickly when told of the spill, contacting local authorities downstream from the spill, alerting national environmental bureaucracies in Bucharest, and informing the Hungarian Environmental Protection Agency at Nyíregyháza, just over the border. By 11 p.m. on 31 January, the Romanian Department of Waters, Forests, and Environmental Protection activated the Principle International Alert Center environmental early-warning system, sending news of the spill to the Hungarian Ministry of Environmental Protection. While communication at the national ministerial level moved slowly, local environmental and water authorities in Hungary and Romania exchanged information quickly and effectively. Cooperation between Hungarian and Yugoslavian water authorities also proceeded smoothly.

One international response to the Tisza crisis was the creation of the Baia Mare Task Force, convened by the European Union (EU) and composed of regional environmental NGOs. Together with the task force, the United Nations Environmental Program (UNEP) undertook an assessment of the Tisza spill remarkable for both its rapid collection of data and its quick publication. The UNEP mission entered the field on 23 February, only about three weeks after the spill. It completed both its chemical and biological assays, as well as interviews with government agencies, NGOs, and other affected parties in three countries, by 6 March and published its report later in the month.

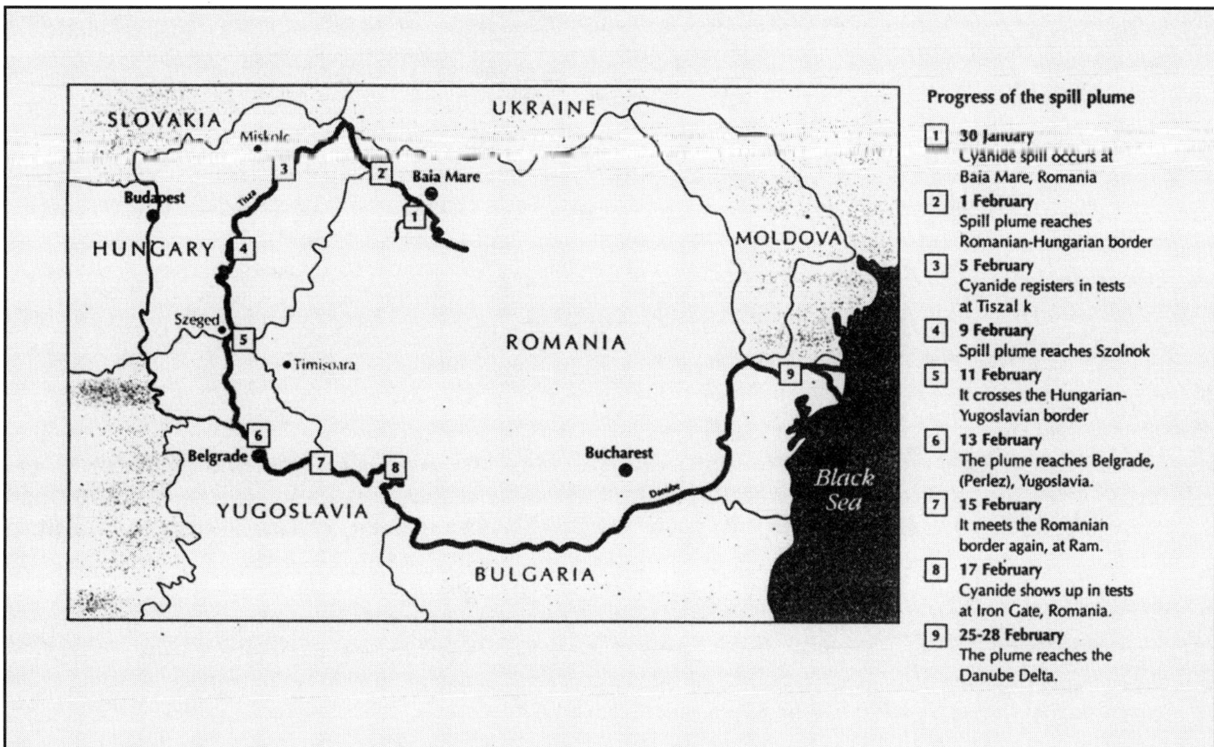

A map showing the spread of the Tisza cyanide spill

(MTI, Ministry for Environmental Protection [Hungary], Environmental Inspectorate, United Nations Environmental Program)

In its report the UNEP mission expressed the importance of the rapid response in this incident: "The UN mission was unique and represented a useful model for inter-agency, multi-disciplinary rapid assessment missions. It was limited in size, scope and time and meant to assist in clarifying the facts around the Baia Mare accident. As such, it may help the Governments concerned and international partners in their further investigation and assessment of the spill and its impact, with a view to addressing longer-term rehabilitation needs of the area. It may also help clarify points of concern amongst NGOs and the local population."

The UNEP report concludes that Romania, Hungary, and Yugoslavia have "professional and reliable laboratories which in principle generate internationally comparable data." Yet, the report notes that contamination levels measured in Romania were below those registered downstream in Hungary. Among some Hungarian environmentalists, the discrepancies were described alternatively either as evidence of incompetence on the part of Romanian laboratories or as suggestive of intent to minimize the reported damage. Similarly, Romanian officials claimed that Hungarian measurements exaggerated the effects of the spill. The UNEP report remarked that "discrepancies in measurement findings of concentrations of the pollution between Romanian and Hungarian scientists cannot be fully explained but might have occurred because of differences in locations and the time intervals of the sampling." Similarly, Hungarian and Romanian depictions of fish deaths diverged.

The villages immediately abutting the Aurul SA plant rely on groundwater from shallow wells that are connected with the Sasar and Lapus streams. Television news reports showed villagers testing the water supply by lowering live fish into their wells and waiting to see how much time passed before the fish died. Wells in Bozanta Mare, the village closest to the leaching pond, registered cyanide concentrations eighty times the legal limit on 10 February. By the end of February the cyanide level dropped below the permissible limit, but well water in Bozanta Mare and the surrounding area continued to register unacceptable concentrations of copper, cadmium, and other heavy metals that present a long-lasting health hazard. As the wave of pollution passed through Hungary, the water supply of the city of Szolnok was threatened. Local authorities shut down the surface-water treatment facility while the spill passed through the city. Clean drinking water was brought by truck for one hundred thousand inhabitants. Groundwater in Hungary was not acutely threatened because most wells are deep enough to avoid surface contamination. Drinking water supplies in Yugoslavia were not endangered by the spill, according to the UNEP report.

The Aurul SA cyanide disaster revealed the complexity of transboundary environmental problems in the context of postsocialist Eastern Europe. That Hungarian officials were hesitant to pursue compensation claims reveals some of the place-specific limitations of the regulatory and legal environment for dealing with transboundary conflicts. Members of NGOs claim that not only regulation and enforcement systems need to change, but also national-level models of development. Until states do their job of protecting citizens from health and environmental threats, "social watchdogs" and whistleblowers have an important role to play in monitoring industrial development. Recognizing the need for cooperation between upstream and downstream neighbors, NGOs throughout the region are initiating transboundary relationships to deal with these problems.

In mid July 2000, the Hungarian government filed a claim against the Esmeralda corporation for 179 million Australian dollars (106 million U.S. dollars) in damages, claiming that it was pursuing reparations from Esmeralda because the company was the project manager for the tailings pond (polluted water) at Aurul SA. Meanwhile, Hungary has been slow to pursue compensations from Romania for the spill for reasons that reflect shortcomings in the institutional setting and a history of transboundary conflicts with neighboring countries.

Institutional oversight of the cyanide spill in Hungary was split among several ministries: Water and Transportation, Environmental Protection, and Foreign Affairs. While the Ministry of Water and Transportation is widely believed to have handled the disaster effectively, the cyanide spill provoked a crisis in the Ministry of Environmental Protection that eventually led to the resignation of Minister Pál Pepó in June 2000. Pepó did not make a public statement regarding the cyanide spill until three days after the ministry received news of the disaster. He also did not declare a state of emergency after the spill, a decision that left local governments and civil organizations with the task of cleaning up without adequate financial support from the government. The problem of harmonizing the various ministries in the weeks following the disaster was so intractable that the Hungarian prime minister appointed a government commission on the Tisza to oversee the activities of the ministries involved, to monitor environmental "hotspots" along the river, and to handle compensation claims. Some Hungarian officials feared that pressing the case for compensation could irreparably harm the domestic agricultural and tourist industries by reinforcing western Europeans' perceptions of the region as polluted.

Hungary was furthermore reluctant to get embroiled in a transboundary conflict that could potentially whip up nationalist tensions. Both Hungarian activists and several officials indicated that pursuing the matter with Romania could create a nationalist backlash and pose difficulty for the substantial Hungarian minority population in Romania. The experience of the country in a previous international water dispute, the decade-long lawsuit with Slovakia over Hungarian withdrawal from a treaty to dam the Danube, left officials with little taste for another prolonged European Court case. In pursuing EU accession, Hungarian officials wanted to present the country as having harmonious relationships with its neighbors, in distinct contrast to the Balkan states immediately to the south.

Beyond the question of compensation, the Aurul SA cyanide spill highlights the question of what constitutes development for Romania and postsocialist Eastern Europe as a whole. Citizens mobilizing for environment and public health in Romania and Hungary challenge the notion that industrial disasters are the price communities must pay in exchange for jobs and regional development. According to these activists, regulations and enforcement will continue to lag behind until the state recognizes health and the environment as key priorities for development.

On the one hand is the concept of development that calls for foreign direct investment and for public-private partnerships to increase output and income. The Esmeralda-Remin partnership, backed by international financing that created the Aurul SA facility–in this case Dresdner Bank of Germany–is a characteristic example of this framework for development. In the postsocialist period, Romania attracts foreign investment not only with its minerals, but also with its relatively lax environmental standards for extracting that wealth. This drive shares a curious commonality with the Nicolae Ceausescu-era productivist impulse. In both periods, this notion of Romanian development emphasized mineral extraction and processing, although the character changed somewhat from domestically financed and state-driven before 1990 to foreign direct investment, financed and managed by public-private partnerships in the period since transition.

On the other hand, development has more recently come to mean ecologically sustainable development. Concepts of sustainable development call for better environmental standards, democratic public participation, and good relations with one's neighbors. In Romania, Hungary, and elsewhere in Eastern Europe, this vision of development is increasingly associated with the desire to join the EU. In an essay on the Tisza cyanide disaster, Romanian activist Viorel Lascu, president of the Regional Center for Ecological Supervision of the Apuseni Mountains, criticized Romanian politicians for not taking the environment seriously enough in the country's plan for EU accession. "Romania's journey towards Europe passes through Hungary, and

TRAGEDY ON THE TISZA

On 17 February 2000 Commissioner Chris Patten spoke about the Tisza spill to European Parliament at its meeting in Strasbourg:

An objective assessment of the facts is not easy at this stage. But early reports suggest that the poisoning of the Lepos, Somes [Szamos] and Danube rivers is a very serious environmental tragedy. It had destroyed an entire ecosystem in a matter of days. No living organisms, from microbes to otters, have been spared.

Several Members have set out what seems to have happened. We have all seen some of the consequences on our television screens. In terms of destruction to an ecosystem some environmental experts have put the environmental consequences of this disaster, at least so far as the damage to the ecosystem is concerned, on a par with Chernobyl.

It has affected the peoples of three countries—Romania, Hungary and Yugoslavia. It is the Tisza, Hungary's second river, perhaps its most beautiful and most loved by its people, that has borne the brunt. As with all such disasters it is the long-term consequences that are the most pernicious. Some estimates suggest that it could take up to five years to restock the river. There is a continuing threat to other wildlife from eating toxic fish.

We plainly have a responsibility to do everything we can, as rapidly as we can, to help cope with this catastrophe. That is certainly the view of my colleague, Commissioner Wallstrapm, who I know would have wished to respond to this resolution in person today. The reason she cannot do so is because, as some honourable Members have pointed out, she is in Hungary and Romania to see for herself the extent of the damage and how best we can help the Hungarian and Romanian authorities to tackle the crisis.

We stand ready to do so. We contacted the Romanian Government and the International Commission for the Protection of the Danube River about the accident earlier this month to seek more information urgently. The Romanians have approached UNEF and OCHA, in Geneva, for an assessment of the damage in the Danube catchment area by an independent and international team of experts. We stand ready to assist in this assessment if there is a joint request from Hungary and Romania and if access to the sites for nationals of both countries can be guaranteed, that is obviously crucial. It is plainly essential to establish as rapidly as possible an accurate picture of the scope of the damage so that we can decide exactly how best to tackle it. It is to that end that our efforts are now engaged.

There is also a need to clarify the legal responsibilities of the mining company and of the Romanian authorities. This is an important point, as several speakers have suggested. The polluter-pays principle is a cornerstone of European Union environmental policy. It is mirrored in the International Convention for the Protection and Sustainable Use of the Danube River and it should be applied in this case.

The European Union could not substitute itself for the mining company for any compensation payments due. The Union has mobilised some EUR 20 million over the past seven years to support protection of the Danube River basin. In the context of pre-accession aid to the region it may be possible to redirect some of the assistance we are giving under ISPAR and PHARE to tackle the most severe impact of this accident, as long as the polluter-pays principle is fully respected.

We will want, in the longer term, to see what lessons can be learned from this disaster, above all to see how to prevent such disasters happening in the first place. The incident reinforces the case for a strengthening of European civil protection, along the lines suggested by Mr. Prodi in his recent speech and as suggested by one or two Members today. But for now the priority is to cope with this crisis. As I have said, my colleague, Commissioner Wallstrapm, is on the spot today. She will want to keep Parliament closely in touch with the action she proposes as a result of her visit.

This has been an appalling tragedy for Europe, and Europe has to respond and do all it can to ensure that incidents as dreadful as these do not continue to blight our future.

Source: *Gusztavv Kosztolavnyi, "Aquatic Chernobyl: Requiem for the Tisza and the Szamos: Part Two: Anatomy of a Disaster,"* Central Europe Review, *2 (27 February 2000), Internet website.*

this is why European integration means the two countries working together," he stated.

For other activists in Romanian and Hungarian civil organizations, the cyanide spill revealed the need for citizens to defend their right to a clean and healthy environment in the face of strong economic pressures to disregard ecological considerations. József Hamar, president of the Tisza Club in Szolnok, Hungary, stated that "Aurul is the perfect example of eco-colonialism taking advantage of the lack of regulations and unemployment. It was an accident, but the causes are not mysterious, they are precisely these." In Romania, members of the Association of Professional NGOs for Social Assistance in Baia Mare (ASSOC) lobbied the local government to force Aurul SA to clean up agricultural lands previously contaminated with heavy metals from the facility. Educating Baia Mare residents about the toxic hazards around them, ASSOC activists resist "economic blackmail" that demands the public to sacrifice its health and environment for employment opportunities.

Because the postsocialist governments of Eastern Europe face the task of massive economic restructuring, members of NGOs envision their own mission as keeping citizens' demands for participation, public health, and a clean environment on the political agenda. A representative of a Romanian NGO participating in the Baia Mare Task Force described the importance of NGOs in coordinating information flow among governments, NGOs, and citizens, for example, providing warnings to villages along the Tisza against drinking contaminated water. In this crisis, however, she identified an additional and extraordinary role for Romanian NGOs–the actual creation of scientific knowledge about the disaster in the absence of adequate government capability. Throughout the spring, NGOs in Romania had to take a direct role in collecting data on water quality, interpreting those data, and informing both governments and citizens of the results. The task-force participant expressed alarm that such responsibilities had fallen upon NGOs but indicated that they had performed well under the circumstances.

Hamar stated that in keeping the state aware of its responsibilities, the role of "social watchdogs" cannot be overstated. Beyond domestic politics, transboundary environmental problems call for transboundary citizens' actions. The Tisza Club, for example, has teamed up with environmental NGOs from Ukraine, Romania, Slovakia, and Yugoslavia to monitor toxic "hotspots" in the Tisza basin. Hamar continued: "The lesson of the Tisza disaster is that citizens in the five countries of the Tisza catchment area have to cooperate to protect their health and the Tisza basin environment." Hamar mentioned sharing information, exchanging expertise, and understanding each other's problems as upstream/downstream neighbors as key examples of the kind of cooperation that could help NGOs work more effectively in their home countries. These exchanges emphasize the commonalities of citizens of the bioregion, rather than play up nationalist tensions for short-term political gain.

While transboundary environmental conflicts occur all over the world, analysts must attend to the place-specific dimensions of environmental regulation and enforcement, competing definitions of development, and the interpretations of local citizens. In postsocialist Eastern Europe, citizens facing economic pressures for "eco-colonialist" forms of development have made international alliances to prevent further threats to their health and environment.

–KRISTA HARPER, UNIVERSITY OF MASSACHUSETTS, AMHERST

Viewpoint: International mining companies view the environment as an "externality" and therefore do not calculate pollution and accidental spills into the costs of doing business in foreign countries. They do not put environmental safety first because they know they likely will not be held financially accountable.

Until the cyanide spill of 30 January 2000, the Tisza River system was an area of impressive biodiversity. Prior to the disaster several stretches of the Tisza had chronically high concentrations of heavy metals because of upstream industrial plants and agricultural runoff. Yet, despite a century of river pollution, the river remained home to more than sixty species of fish, including the sterlet (a unique species of sturgeon) and the Danube salmon, as well as more-common freshwater varieties such as carp, pike, and catfish. The Tisza basin wetlands provide food and habitat to endangered bird and mammal species as well, including the white-tailed sea eagle and European river otter. The European mayfly, a rare insect that lives for only a few hours, disappeared from the rivers of western Europe one hundred years ago but persists along the Tisza in Hungary, where the species is called the tiszavirág, or "Tisza flower."

Hungarian officials recorded the collection of more than one thousand metric tons of dead fish as the cyanide spill passed through their country. Yugoslavian sources reported major fishkills along the Tisza, and dead fish were observed on the Danube as far south as Belgrade. Fish-eating birds and mammals were among the first casualties. A white-tailed sea eagle, one of a small population painstakingly reintroduced to the Hortobagy National Park, died from eating poisoned fish. Several European otters and bears were poisoned. From the source of the spill to the point where the Tisza meets the Danube, the wave of cyanide destroyed the plankton and small insects upon which the food chain in the Tisza depends. Although many of these microorganisms returned after the passage of the plume, whether the riverine ecosystems can be restored remains to be seen.

The Tisza cyanide spill had far-reaching social and economic effects in Romania, Hungary, and Yugoslavia. It revealed social tensions over environmental decision-making; economic vulnerability in the agricultural, fishing, and tourism sectors; and concerns about the future of this culturally significant river. In the communities near the Aurul SA plant in Baia Mare, Romania, citizens complained of officials' dismissal of environmental and health threats posed by the mining industry. The area has been a significant metallurgical center for centuries, and at least seven major mining sites are currently located in Maramures County. Tailings dams and smelters regularly pour effluents into the air and water, and the World Health Organization (WHO) characterized the region as the environmental health "hotspot" with the highest human exposure to lead ever recorded. Residents near the Aurul plant have lodged complaints about fumes and dust since the facility began operation, with little response from the Baia Mare Environmental Protection Agency. For local residents, the Aurul SA cyanide disaster was simply the latest chapter in a long history of environmental suffering.

The cyanide spill affected the agriculture sector in several countries. Farmers reported the death of cows following the disaster, and they were unable to sell eggs, apples, or milk as public perceptions of pollution in the region were heightened. The spill passed through the Tokay wine region of northeastern Hungary, and winegrowers feared that the reputation of their vineyards would be compromised. Commercial fishermen in both Hungary and Yugoslavia also suffered great losses in the short term as a result of the massive fishkill. Fishing on the river was officially suspended for several months, resulting in the unemployment of more than two hundred fishermen in Hungary, and it was again permitted in mid June, as new stocks of fish were released into the Tisza. Hungarian fishermen fear, however, that demand for fish will be low because consumers worry about contamination.

In Hungary, the tourist industry has also been impacted. Recreation areas and parks along the river have attracted a growing number of German and Austrian tourists since the change of political systems in 1989. The Tisza has become a major site for the promotion of "eco-tourism," with many travel agencies offering birdwatching expeditions, as well as kayak and canoe tours of the wetlands. This incipient tourist industry is especially threatened by public perceptions of the river as a disaster area, and industry representatives fear a drop in visitors and, consequently, employment as a result. Finally, the cultural importance of the Tisza generated tremendous public concern. The Tisza runs through the Great Plain and is associated with the Hungarian war of independence and late-nineteenth century peasant life in the national imagination. The river is celebrated in lyrical poems memorized by Hungarian schoolchildren. When news of the cyanide spill reached Hungary, thousands of citizens flocked to funeral processions for the Tisza.

That the disaster occurred at all, and that it had such far-reaching ecological and social impacts, is owing to the fact that industries treat the environment as an "externality," an outcome of an economic activity that primarily affects parties that are not directly participating in that activity. River pollution is quite literally the textbook example of an externality. In the Tisza case, the economic activity is the gold extraction of Aurul SA, and the externally affected parties are all of the communities along the Tisza water system that runs through four different countries. Ninety-five percent of the rivers of Hungary, for example, originate in other countries. Externalities generate distress because the parties causing the damage think almost solely in terms of the profit to themselves and do not adequately consider the negative effects on other parties; hence, they tend to impose this bad outcome on others. The profits of Aurul SA might not suffice to compensate the wronged parties, even if such compensation were attempted.

One textbook solution to the externality problem assigns property rights and stipulates their enforcement through contracts or litigation. The alternative approach would implement effluent taxes on the polluting party to bring its accounting of the economic cost of the pollution in line with the actual social cost to the victims. Economic theory shows that either approach can achieve an economically optimal level of externality production (including no production, if that is optimal). Neither approach is feasible, however, without an appropriate set of institutions to assign and enforce the solution. In the case of the spill at Baia Mare, the complexity of the public-private partnership in the extraction concern and the transboundary character of the accident may render these approaches inadequate both for restitution and for creating appropriate incentives to avoid future accidents.

The difficulty in implementing adequate regulation before the accident and in assessing damages afterward points up a grave difficulty for regulators, posed by public-private partnerships. When the state simultaneously undertakes the conflicting functions of both promoting industrial growth and protecting public health and the environment, the competing claims are unlikely to result in a happy compromise. Regulation of public-private partnerships curiously echoes the difficulties of environmental oversight during the socialist period. An explanation for the poor performance of the socialist countries in environmental protection is that the constituency for such protection was unable to press its case against the industrial-growth constituency. The Baia Mare region was already highly contaminated from mining activity from the Nicolae Ceausescu-era, with serum lead measurements in adults and children well in excess of accepted safe levels.

The curiosity is that public-private partnerships–a symbol of the twilight of big government–share this difficulty with state-socialist enterprises. In both cases the competing demands on the sovereign power of the state to provide both growth and safety create an internal tension with disastrous consequences. In both periods Romania has seen the demand for industrial growth defeat the calls for public health and safety. The state does poorly as simultaneous promoter of economic growth and guarantor of environmental health and safety. Public-private partnerships may pose systematic difficulties for regulators and substantial risks for people and wildlife as the private partner may seek to exploit the sovereignty of the state in avoiding firm regulation.

The Aurul SA project at Baia Mare had complied with the Romanian permitting process and had been inspected by some Romanian authorities. A policy implication for the transition era is that in the context of a market economy, the state may be more effective in an exclusively regulatory role than in a partnership with private, profit-driven parties. Furthermore, the Baia Mare experience suggests a role for nongovernmental organizations (NGOs) in enforcing environmental regulations both to avoid accidents and to address them when they occur. The fine levied on Aurul SA by Romanian authorities was a paltry $166, obviously an insufficient sum to cover the existing damage or to deter irresponsible behavior in the future. The fine was small because Aurul SA was deemed to be in compliance with Romanian standards. Indeed, Aurul SA was considered a model facility. The management of transboundary environmental externalities requires both a realistic assessment of the fines and regulations necessary to give incentives for accident prevention and regulatory institutions capable of implementing them.

In the absence of an adequate regulatory apparatus, the burden of sanction and disincentive may fall to litigation and tort law. The litigation approach also can be problematic where it depends on the enforcement of rulings across national boundaries. Both Hungary and Romania are party to the 1992 Helsinki agreement that stipulates the "polluter pays principle," but there is little recourse if the polluter refuses to pay and the host government refuses to extract payment. Furthermore, the tort process requires complainants. NGOs may play an important role in identifying, informing, and coordinating aggrieved parties, indeed in transforming parties that have suffered damages into damaged parties in the sense of warranting legal accountability.

The former Yugoslavian Republic is among the parties demanding compensation from Aurul SA. The government of Serbia was for the most part cooperative with international task forces, although UNEP reported some resistance to inquiries for its report. Yugoslavian NGOs, through their participation in the Baia Mare Task Force, may be substituting in important ways for government activity constrained by the United Nations (U.N.) sanctions over the Kosovo crisis. Through the Baia Mare Task Force, Yugoslavian NGOs are communicating scientific data about the effects of the spill to the international community. These NGOs have played an important role in both informing Serbian citizens of and protecting them from the contamination.

The Aurul SA cyanide spill, as well as the heavy-metal spills and catastrophic flooding that followed, demonstrates the multilayered character of environmental disasters. Esmeralda executives denied responsibility for the spill; citing the heavy rains and cold weather as the cause, they claimed it was a natural disaster. Environmentalists consider this evasion outrageous because the dam had actually broken–rather than merely overflowed, as Esmeralda executives initially claimed. Indeed, environmentalists consider the entire Marmures County landscape to be a human-made disaster. The floods can be seen as a product of earlier river regulation, ongoing mineral extraction, and forest clearcutting in the Ukrainian and Romanian Carpathian Mountains; and some environmentalists go so far as to cite human- induced global warming as a cause of catastrophic flooding.

Policy solutions to the externality problem require well-defined criteria for parties who both create and suffer from pollution. In the case of the Aurul SA episode, such parties—certainly the polluter at least—may be well defined. In an environment as polluted as Baia Mare, however, where lead levels in the blood exceed safe standards by a factor of six, it will be hard to account for the cascading environmental externalities. In the broader regional geography, where pollution flows across national borders, policymakers and NGOs will be challenged by the difficulty of making upstream polluters truly accountable to their downstream neighbors.

–MICHAEL ASH, UNIVERSITY OF MASSACHUSETTS, AMHERST

References

William J. Baumol and Alan S. Blinder, *Microeconomics: Principles and Policy* (Fort Worth, Tex.: Dryden Press, 1994).

Paul Csagoly, "After the Tisza Disaster," *Bulletin* 9 (2000): 9–11.

Csagoly, "Death of a River," *Bulletin* 9 (2000): 16–23.

John Fitzmaurice, *Damming the Danube: Gabcikovo and Post-Communist Politics in Europe* (Boulder, Colo.: Westview Press, 1996).

Donald Scherer, ed., *Upstream/Downstream: Issues in Environmental Ethics* (Philadelphia: Temple University Press, 1990).

United Nations Environment Programme (UNEP), *Report on the Cyanide Spill at Baia Mare, Romania* (UNEP, 2000).

U.S. WATER POLLUTION

What factors most influenced water-pollution-control legislation by the U.S. Congress in the post–World War II era?

Viewpoint: Congressional legislative policymaking was critical to the creation of water-resource and pollution controls between 1956 and 1972.

Viewpoint: Public-interest advocacy between 1969 and 1972 was central to the debate over water-pollution controls.

American rivers were polluted well before the advent of the Industrial Revolution in the mid nineteenth century. For generations, the Charles River in Boston, like the Hudson River of New York City and the Schuylkill and Delaware Rivers of Philadelphia, had been used as "sinks," places in which to dump effluent, human and otherwise. Whether large or small, most urban river systems served similar functions as sinks, as did the San Antonio River, which a local alderman described as a "natural sewer."

The quantity of sewage only increased with the development of industrial production; because of their tremendous thirst for water as a source of power, as a coolant, and for waste disposal, factories in the United States (and elsewhere) were sited along lakes, rivers, and streams. The amount of waste dumped into these bodies of water was phenomenal. Historian Joel A. Tarr has reported in a contribution to *Out of the Woods: Essays in Environmental History* (1997), for instance, that in 1923 an estimated 38,000,000 tons of ammonia still wastes were discharged into U.S. waterways, much of it in the Ohio River valley. This particular chemical devastated watersheds, but it also had a horrifying impact on drinking supplies; the ammonia reacted badly with chlorine injected into local waterworks to protect human consumers against pathogens, making the water "almost undrinkable."

Local ordinances and state regulation of waste disposal was generally ineffective because of industry resistance to controls placed on its actions. Moreover, given the nature of rivers to cross political boundaries, it was next to impossible to regulate the damaging flow of industrial byproducts. Not until the mid twentieth century did a national debate over the quality and quantity of water supplies erupt. Driven in part by an outraged public that played to and off of an energized environmental movement, this debate was also joined in the halls of Congress; there, senators and representatives sought more-potent remedies for sludge-filled rivers, polluted aquifers, and toxin-laden lakes.

Determining who was more central to the development of one such measure, the omnibus legislative initiative, known as the Clean Water Act of 1972, helps define the source and character of environmental reform. Many historians and political scientists, for example, believe that the post-1945 demand for federal regulation of water in the United States derived from a new environmental ethos that gained strength among educated, middle-class suburbanites. For them, improving the quality and health of their lives—and those like them—prompted their direct participation in the political arena; a green and clean environment was essential to the well-being of the body politic.

Others dispute this argument: instead of championing an environmentalist impulse born of American consumerism, they suggest that congressional action, which depended on different models of conservationism, was largely responsible for the legislative attempt to safeguard water supplies; because those who drafted the relevant legislation advocated the use of new technologies to water treatment, and focused as much on the quantity of water as they did its quality, they represented the continued influence of Progressive Era concerns. Within this debate lies an important reminder of the array of complex ideas and diverse actors who have driven environmental reform in American history.

Viewpoint: Congressional legislative policymaking was critical to the creation of water-resource and pollution controls between 1956 and 1972.

Historians commonly depict the rise of environmental consciousness after World War II as the product of a fundamental reordering of values, derived in turn from a broad set of social, economic, and demographic changes. They focus specifically on the growth of an affluent, educated middle-class population, concentrated in urban or suburban centers, that tended to define "quality of life" with increasing reference to leisure, domesticity, and community. The natural world comprised an integral component of this new standard of living. Access to pristine open spaces provided a regenerative antidote to the pressures and complexities of industrial society. Preventing and controlling the toxic byproducts of an industrial economy also took on a new urgency as modern scientific understanding of health risks accrued. Thus, historians argue, the public demand to protect and preserve environmental amenities distinguished itself from the conservation impulse expressed earlier in the twentieth century, when a narrower network of professionals, scientists, and administrators sought to rationalize the management of material resources in the service of more-efficient economic production. By contrast, postwar environmental initiatives may be properly traced to a broader-based ethos of consumption that underscored the ameliorative effects of nature on human health and well-being.

The preceding framework affords an insightful analysis of a shifting cultural milieu. How accurately, however, does it characterize the substance of public policy that emerged during the postwar era? Did the transition from a production to a consumption-oriented perspective influence the institutional response of the federal government to specific environmental issues, and to what extent did the policymaking process reflect such cultural imperatives?

A closer examination of the evolution of water-pollution-control policy provides a convenient opportunity to address such questions. The progressive application of federal administrative capacity to the nationwide dilemma of deteriorating water quality, particularly in urban-industrial regions occurred in the three decades following World War II. Bringing the power of government to bear on social problems was hardly an unprecedented activity during this era. The fact that Congress (rather than the executive branch) actually set the agenda in the case of water pollution, however, confounds the conventional wisdom on state building. Nevertheless, the legislative branch did exercise the initiative between 1956 and 1972. It is reasonable to expect the most-accessible, representative governing institution to reflect the widest array of public and professional viewpoints during its deliberations; moreover, elected officials, and policy entrepreneurs in particular, tend to be keenly attuned to the shifting moods of their constituencies. Thus, environmental priorities associated with the putative postwar cultural transformation should have had a prominent impact on the process and substance of legislative policymaking. With respect to water pollution, modes of justification based on resource conservation and efficient use would be expected to take a backseat to newer attitudes that linked water quality with "quality of life." To that end, commentators have described how a tangible "ecological" outlook, dedicated to the integrity of biological systems, came to dominate federal approaches to water-pollution control as early as the sixties.

In fact, the history of water-pollution legislation demonstrates how producer-oriented values helped drive environmental policy. Ecological values linked to the aspirations of an expanding urban middle class undoubtedly came to inform the strategies of policymakers over time. Rather than receding in the wake of a shifting zeitgeist, however, the conservation ethos persisted after World War II. State interest in redressing impure streams grew out of a set of priorities apart from those generally associated with broad-based public movements. As a consequence, traditional political agendas, professional discourses, and institutional structures continued to inform, and even enable, "new" legislative initiatives throughout the 1960s and into the early 1970s.

Federal water-pollution-control policy in the postwar era evolved as an adjunct of a far more extensive congressional water-development program. The connection is somewhat ironic. Distributing billions of dollars worth of dam and reclamation projects in the service of regional economic growth befitted the tenets of conservation as well as the organizational idiosyncrasies of the legislative branch; redistributive environmental regulation, however, seemingly ran counter to both. Yet, the same Public Works Committees underwriting this plethora of pork-barrel construction oversaw the fledgling expansion of what would eventually become the largest office of the Environment Protection Agency (EPA).

Such institutional and ideological pedigrees engendered real policy consequences. In the 1950s and 1960s, developmental concerns about water quantity shaped legislative approaches to water quality. Contemporary policymakers viewed water-pollution control through the lens of economic development, rather than environment, per se. From this perspective, pollution was part and parcel of a national water-resource problem: it impeded reuse and exacerbated deficiencies of supply that, experts believed, posed the most ominous threat to regional growth. Quality of life concerns, though increasingly prominent, did not entirely transcend this utilitarian rubric; recreation, for example, was counted among several legitimate functions endangered by dwindling supplies of clean water. The developmental discourse remained a dominant theme in public circles much longer than commonly acknowledged. By the time Congress chose to inaugurate an unprecedented "technology-forcing" regulatory regime during the so-called public interest era of the early 1970s, remnants of the developmental paradigm still managed to influence ecologically oriented statutes such as the Clean Water Act of 1972.

A developmental rationale for pollution control provided the initial impetus for federal action when public environmental awareness was at its lowest ebb. In 1956 John Anton Blatnik (D-Minnesota) of the House Public Works Committee shepherded the first permanent federal water-pollution program through Congress. His success hinged on two factors: the ability to broaden appeal of the issue by casting it in terms of regional economics; and his command of the channels of distributive politics.

Blatnik exhibited a zeal for government-promoted natural-resource development, employment, and economic growth that reflected his political roots in the New Deal order. He understood that a bill with even the most minimally coercive abatement requirements stood little chance of approval without support from constituencies more numerous and influential than the Audubon or Wilderness Societies. Accordingly, he supplemented a politically ineffectual "outdoor" bloc with urban and labor interests. Blatnik pitched his modest regulatory procedures as a means to achieve regional industrial equity: uniform federal enforcement would prevent the flight of northern corporate polluters to solicitous southern states. Unions rallied around this effort to prevent job migration to "right to work" areas. More important, they, together with organizations such as the National Council of Mayors, appreciated the employment opportunities inherent in Blatnik's proposed treatment-plant construction program. The promise of federal grant aid energized municipal interests and helped make the companion regulatory features of the bill palatable to ambivalent legislators. Furthermore, to overcome lingering apathy within Congress, Blatnik used his influence as Rivers and Harbors Subcommittee chairman to, in the words of one of his staffers, "make pollution controllers out of every member who had a channel to dig, a harbor to deepen, a bridge to build, or a post office to name." In short, the quid pro quo of pork-barrel politics facilitated the genesis of a humble regulatory program.

The public-works stamp was visible in other important respects. Blatnik's rhetoric consciously targeted public and professional audiences more attuned to shortage than sewage. The experts he tapped from the Legislative Reference Service (LRS) were engineers who viewed pollution control as "an important and almost inseparable facet of the problem of water resources conservation." Blatnik echoed the conclusions of an LRS report during subcommittee hearings in 1955, when he declared bluntly that "pollution is a waste of water . . . just as effective in reducing a water resource for use as in a period of drought." Given the expanding population and industrial capacity of the nation, the federal government would need multiple strategies to insure the requisite supply of water for all burgeoning future uses. Blatnik concluded that pollution abatement represented an economical supplement to other notoriously expensive conservation outlays, namely construction of storage and transport facilities.

Congress did not merely reflect, but also actively produced knowledge that cast water-pollution control as a central component of resource management. The influential 1960 Senate Select Committee on National Water Resources looked to pollution abatement to sustain developmental politics. Such was not its original intent, however. Members of the Interior and Public Works Committees (a majority of whom were Democrats from Western states) initially hoped to build a rational case against the fiscal frugality of the Eisenhower administration, in order to validate the ongoing "golden age" of water-resource construction. Pleading for "no new starts," President Dwight D. Eisenhower had vetoed rivers-and-harbors legislation repeatedly between 1956 and 1959. Omnibus bills between 1944 and 1954 alone had authorized more than $5 billion in projects; recent legislation pushed for nearly $3 billion more. Eisenhower struggled to stem an unprecedented postwar tide of congressional largesse, which he characterized as the triumph of special-interest politics over impartial administrative stewardship–discrete localities (especially in the West) benefited at the expense of the greater national interest. With the 1960 elections looming on the horizon, Western Democrats sensed an opportunity to redefine water development as an issue of national, not simply regional, import.

Their chosen instrument was a Senate Select Committee charged with determining "the extent to which water resources activities in the United States are related to the national interest." Proponents echoed the assumptions expressed by resource experts in a multitude of executive policy assessments since 1945: water supply represented a critical variable affecting national economic growth, standard of living, and security. Critics cited the plurality of Westerners assigned to the committee–including the undisputed master of distributive politics, Chairman Robert Samuel Kerr (D-Oklahoma)–however, as an indication that its conclusions were preordained.

Yet, Kerr granted his staff free reign to devise their own methodology. Water-resource experts in their own right, they exploited senatorial prestige to assemble an impressive array of engineers and economists from federal agencies, universities, and conservation think tanks such as Resources for the Future. Together they initiated the most-comprehensive study of national water supply and demand ever attempted, and the first "in which the natural variation in water supply ha[d] been systematically related to estimates of population growth, level of economic activity, use of water, and the maintenance of water quality for reasonably homogenous regions." In fact, once the staff set out to devise a sophisticated regional supply-demand model, the central issue they began to ponder became one of water quality. Since water would have to be reused multiple times to accommodate projected usage and sustain economic growth, they concluded, all waterways needed to maintain a higher average level of dissolved oxygen than currently possible. This perspective paved the way for the Public Health Service (PHS), rather than the far more bureaucratically influential U.S. Army Corps of Engineers or Bureau of Reclamation, to shape the assumptions informing conclusions of the Select Committee. The staff turned to the PHS for a series of mathematical simulations to estimate future pollution loads, stream capacities, and methods for achieving target water quality. Limitations in treatment technology meant a significant volume of water would be required to dilute lingering organic and chemical wastes; indeed, adhering to the equations set forth by PHS yielded flow requirements for waste dilution alone that exceeded all other uses by a wide margin.

Consequently, the national water-resources program prescribed by the Senate Select Committee became, "in effect, a program of reservoirs and waste treatment plants." Its final report earmarked $42 billion out of a total of $54 billion in recommended expenditures for waste treatment, with 60 percent of the dam-regulated flow funded by the remaining $12 billion designated to maintain water quality after treatment. The bulk of the money, ironically, was to be spent east of the ninety-sixth meridian, where urban pollution problems were more acute (72 percent of treatment costs, for example, pertained to the East). The emphasis on pollution control annoyed several Westerners on the committee but did not detract from Kerr's grand vision. Indeed, by linking quantity and quality so prominently, the report succeeded brilliantly in framing water resources in a broadly national context. The labors of the committee provided the blueprint for subsequent legislation on water-resources development (Water Resources Research Act of 1964; Water Resources Planning Act of 1965), and insured that studies of water-quality-storage needs at federal impoundments would be included in the Water Pollution Control Act Amendments (1961). In a more general sense, the committee encapsulated the developmental approach to environmental problems and continued to influence policy perceptions well into the next decade.

Historians usually equate environmental policy in the 1960s with the diverse initiatives of the Lyndon B. Johnson administration, collectively dubbed "The New Conservation." Its newness stemmed from a generally more-holistic outlook that placed rhetorical emphasis on aesthetics and ecology. Practitioners such as Interior Secretary Stewart Lee Udall sought to broaden the purview of the federal government beyond remote wilderness to include the "total human environment"; pollution problems undermining quality of life in the urban areas aroused particular concern.

Yet, despite such evolving perspectives, questions of quantity pervaded and shaped the dis-

Water pollution in San Pedro Bay, Long Beach, California

(PR Shirley Richards)

course surrounding the seminal Water Quality Act (1965) of the Senate Public Works Committee. Undoubtedly, congressional approval of Edmund Sixtus Muskie's (D-Maine) system of state-federal water-quality standards suggested a growing appreciation of urban pollution problems. While Muskie sought to strengthen enforcement mechanisms and promote tangible improvement in overall water quality, the rhetoric he most often employed reflected the developmental paradigm. "Pollution of our water courses is merely one complication of an already serious problem–the coming national water shortage," Muskie wrote in *Science and Mechanics* in 1965, "the need for water by cities and industry has been outstripping natural water sources for decades." As governor of Maine in the 1950s, Muskie had promoted "stream improvement" in overtly economic terms, explaining in his 1955 inaugural address how "an abundant supply of clean water has undoubted advantages as an inducement for new industries to locate in this State." The very first witness called before Muskie's Subcommittee on Air and Water Pollution happened to be an economist who served as a consultant for the 1960 Select Committee. Indeed, the most common statistic cited in the media and public forums came from the final committee report: national water demands were expected to increase to 559 billion gallons per day, or 51 percent of total stream flow, by 1980 and 888 bgd (81 percent) by 2000. The necessity of reuse made pollution control an imperative.

The inextricable link between quality and quantity assumed paramount significance in the midst of the most severe Northeastern drought of the twentieth century. This dry spell (1963–1967) had tangible political and policy consequences historians often overlook. By bringing the specter of scarcity home to urban Easterners, it rendered national water-development concerns more credible. Nor did media commentators and politicians fail to note how pollution exacerbated shortages. The plight of New York City proved emblematic: while Upstate reservoirs dwindled, Manhattanites watched helplessly as thirty thousand gallons of Hudson River water flowed to the sea every second, too filthy for use. "While the desecration of one of the nation's scenic resources is bad enough," *Newsweek* opined in 1965, "the destruction of the river as a water resource is criminal." *The New Republic* cited the drought as conclusive evidence that "the Northeast must begin to use its water several times over . . . pollution can no longer be tolerated." Ultimately, ecological and aesthetic factors exerted minimal influence on Congress. "When all is said and done," a congressional aide remarked in 1965, "our best friend on the water pollution bill was the Northeast drought. If anything gives a guy courage to thumb his nose at a lobbyist, it's 400 housewives screaming about watering their lawns."

The drought also inspired institutional and technological innovations, however, that helped shape water-pollution legislation in the public-interest era. Members of the Senate and House Public Works Committees employed the Omnibus Rivers and Harbors Act of 1965 as a vehicle to address the implications of chronic water shortage in the Northeast. The Corps of Engineers, specifically its North Atlantic branch, assumed a central role in coordinating the fruits of this congressional response: the North Atlantic Regional Study (NARS) and the North Eastern Water Supply Study (NEWS). The former comprised a broad "framework" study, the latter a more specific inventory of recommended construction for urban water supply needs, particularly those of the expanding "megalopolis" between Boston and Norfolk.

Both studies employed a new method of planning, first developed by the Harvard Water Program in the late 1950s. Arthur Maass and Maynard Hufschmidt, professors of political science and public administration at the university, had founded the multidisciplinary research and training facility in order to foster new methodologies for designing and evaluating large-scale water-resource projects. NARS and NEWS represented the most systematic application of the Harvard program's most influential innovation, "multiobjective planning." Utilizing the latest techniques in systems analysis and computer modeling of water supply and demand, Corps planners attempted to transcend narrow cost-benefit interpretations of economic efficiency that distinguished past "multi-purpose" planning efforts. They accounted for different social preferences by choosing three broad objectives–national income, regional development, and environmental quality–and then developing alternative land- and water-use policies on the basis of those objectives. The new approach yielded results that departed from conventional Corps studies. The NARS report recommended that investments for waste-treatment facilities and land-management practices take precedence over dams and channel improvements, while NEWS emphasized the tangible link between water supply and waste management. Whether in New York, Newark, Boston, or Washington, D.C., a grossly polluted river invariably represented a potential long-range water-supply source.

Such conclusions buttressed a growing sentiment within the Corps that its active participation in the field of "water quality management" could yield mutual benefits for both the agency and the broader federal pollution-control effort. In the late 1960s the Corps had come under increasing fire for its relentless construction ethic and concomitant environmental insensitivity. The same public interest advocates who derided the Corps, however, simultaneously condemned the limited scope, ambition, and effectiveness of the state-federal pollution-control program. Applying multiobjective regional planning and innovative technology to the water pollution problem, officials reasoned, would enable the developmental expertise of the Corps to accommodate heightened public demands for environmental quality. An influential report authored by the corps' newly established Institute for Water Resources (IWR) in 1970 surmised that the next generation in pollution control would involve the "organization of waste management systems by metropolitan region, with investments rationalized over the long term by river basin and integrated to overall resource development." An agency such as the Corps, "skilled in the management of complex multiple-purpose projects and already involved in other water resource investments," seemed best suited to implement this strategy. "The water supply problem is the water quality problem," the IWR insisted, "and we will not become efficient in the solution of either until the supply agencies see themselves as having equal responsibility for the quality problem."

The Corps subsequently convinced Congress in 1971 to fund five pilot programs in regional wastewater systems planning, located in Cleveland-Akron, Detroit, Boston, Chicago, and San Francisco. The Chief of Engineers, Lieutenant General Frank J. Clarke, described them as the "missing link" in the ability of the Corps to carry out total water-resources planning, as well as an opportunity to develop "comprehensively alternative systems of wastewater management control." These studies aggressively pursued a cutting-edge treatment technology known as land disposal, pioneered at Pennsylvania State University in the mid 1960s and later implemented on a much larger scale in Muskegon County, Michigan. By percolating municipal and industrial sewage through soil, engineers produced an effluent of nearly drinkable quality while recovering pollutants as agricultural nutrients. The so-called living filter epitomized a more-ecological approach to pollution control by handling waste as a "resource out of place" and removing streams from the treatment process. Ironically, Penn State soil experts and geologists had developed the technique in the midst of the great Northeastern drought, as a means to protect and augment the limited water resources of the surrounding community. In order to promote the land-disposal alternative, the Corps hired John Sheaffer, a natural resource expert from the University of Chicago, who had helped design and implement the Muskegon County Wastewater Management System. Sheaffer became the most vocal advocate for the new environmental role of the Corps, both in public and in Congress.

The putative feasibility of the "living filter" helped persuade Muskie's subcommittee to pursue unprecedented legislative objectives for water quality in 1971. Both members and staff heeded the warnings of renowned professional ecologists George M. Woodwell and Gene E. Likens, who served as the official scientific advisers to the Public Works Committee. They cautioned that conventional waste-treatment plants were incapable of filtering the surfeit of organic and toxic materials typically disposed into lakes and streams. These chronic pollutants upset the delicate equilibrium of an aquatic ecosystem's biogeochemical cycles, calibrated over eons of evolutionary time. In order to restore the proper "biological integrity" of natural systems, they suggested, pollution-control legislation needed to mandate a wholesale upgrade in removal technology for both industries and municipalities. At the same time, staff members struggled to come up with solutions for difficult ongoing problems, such as managing nonpoint source pollution (agricultural runoff and urban storm-water overflows) and coordinating the federal grant program for treatment-plant construction to assure maximum regional efficiency.

In this context, the institutional and technological approach Sheaffer endorsed dovetailed perfectly with the subcommittee's practical concerns. The Corps program appealed to staffers such as Thomas C. Jorling (a trained ecologist in his own right), who reminded the senators how land disposal utilized "natural ecological systems to perform treatment roles," returning waste to the soil-based biogeochemical cycles best equipped to handle them. As such, the Corps was offering communities the opportunity to choose an alternative technology grounded in a knowledge base apart from sanitary engineering, a profession that tended to monopolize waste-treatment planning on the local level. In addition, "Muskegon-type" ventures allowed adjoining cities and towns to partake of an integrated, multijurisdictional waste-management system, with an economy of scale sufficient to handle the municipal and industrial effluent of an entire region, as well as the troublesome runoff from urban and rural areas. The precedent of Muskegon and the promise of the five Corps pilot programs facilitated the ambitious technology-forcing effluent controls and strict time tables of the Clean Water Act of 1972–including, ultimately, its "zero-discharge" and "ecological integrity" objectives–and served as the guiding principle for its ambitious "area-wide waste treatment management program." Although the status of the Corps as the primary consulting agency for the latter was qualified in later drafts, the Senate staff nevertheless attempted to do what the 1970 IWR report had recommended: tap the unmatched capacity of the Corps to plan in order to expand the vision and scope of the federal water-pollution-control program.

Undoubtedly, a sea change in social values and cultural perceptions helped create the political landscape that stimulated the remarkable environmental legislation of the late 1960s and early 1970s. The substance of federal water-pollution-control laws, however, cannot be explained solely in those terms. Discourses rooted in a traditional water-development ethos gave rise to the early efforts by Congress to improve stream quality in the years following World War II. Indeed, the legislative branch actively mediated and generated those discourses, adapting them to suit its own designs. Consequently, developmental ideas and institutions continued to inform the process and substance of policy making that culminated with the Clean Water Act. By interpreting modern environmental policy simply as the product of upheaval, or as the outgrowth of a single set of values, one risks overlooking the continuity and diversity of discourses that actually played a part in its evolution.

–PAUL MILAZZO, UNIVERSITY OF VIRGINIA

Viewpoint: Public-interest advocacy between 1969 and 1972 was central to the debate over water-pollution controls.

The most dramatic vote of the 1972 session of the U.S. Congress came on its last day, during the early hours of 18 October. A few minutes before midnight on 17 October, President Richard M. Nixon had vetoed the Federal Water Pollution Control Act Amendments of 1972. The Clean Water Act of 1972, as it also became known, outlined a massive $25 billion program, which to that date was the most comprehensive and expensive environmental legislation ever proposed in U.S. history. Not wanting to appear anticonservation, President Nixon had preferred to pocket veto the bill, but Congress would not adjourn, so the president was forced to act to prevent the legislation from automatically becoming law. In the predawn hours, red-eyed senators, led by Edmund Sixtus Muskie (D-Maine), easily overrode the veto, 52 to 12. The House of Representatives followed the same day, 247 to 33. Not a single representative rose to the president's defense in the House.

In his veto message, President Nixon claimed, not without some validity, that "environmental protection has been one of my highest priorities," but the "staggering, budget-wrecking" scope of the Clean Water Act would not "make our waters cleaner," only "increase the burden" on the taxpayers, the working men and women of America. Nixon was prepared for the possibility of an override by "charge account congressmen lured by the false glitter of public works money for their districts." "I have nailed my colors to the mast on this issue," the president declared, "the political winds can blow where they may."

Nevertheless, there was speculation that the veto was motivated by other than fiscal considerations. For instance, the presidential action came against the advice of Environmental Protection Agency (EPA) administrator William D. Ruckelshaus, who, in a thirty-three-page letter leaked to the press, strongly recommended approval of the measure. It was not the first time Ruckelshaus had irritated the Nixon White House since taking the helm of the brand new environmental agency in December of 1970. In fact, even though he was a lifelong Republican, with his aggressive regulatory efforts at the federal agency Ruckelshaus had earned the opprobrium of the business community–"the best friend of American industry since Karl Marx"–and the distrust of Nixon insiders who considered him a traitorous extremist.

When it came to the water-pollution law, however, most federal legislators and Ruckelshaus were on the winning side–for good reason: the Clean Water Act represented the apotheosis of an explosive reform trend in American polity that pointed to much more than expansive budgets. The new law was revolutionary in every aspect. It far surpassed any previous federal regulatory efforts most commonly identified with the Progressive Movement at the beginning of the twentieth century and the New Deal during the 1930s. By the late 1960s, environmentally aware congressional leaders understood that the landscape of American politics had changed. Environmentalism entered mainstream political discourse full-scale, pushed by a muscular public-interest activism. Citizen environmentalism emerged as the prime countervailing force to business power in American society during the period from 1969 to 1972, replacing labor unions. As the embodiment of the new power of environmentalism, the Clean Water Act symbolized the most-direct and wide-ranging challenge to the political and economic status quo in the history of the United States. One of the most complicated federal laws ever written, running to eighty pages, it stands as a monument to the modern philosophy of government social engineering.

A cursory overview of the regulatory provisions of the 1972 legislation suggests the basis for positing a landmark standing for the federal water law. Like the pioneering Clean Air Act of 1970, the Clean Water Act was speculative lawmaking, a metamorphosis from the earlier incremental laws in which Congress made small policy adjustments in the hidebound pollution-control statutes. The 1972 act was notable for several reasons. First, it was the purest example of "technology forcing" in the federal regulatory code—all polluters were required to conform to the best practicable and best available control technologies by specific dates. Second, it established a pollution-control permit system (known as the National Pollutant Discharge Elimination System) generally under the administrative discretion of the EPA. Under the revised federalism of the period, this policy essentially removed pollution control responsibility from the states and municipalities for the first time. Third, the law provided that citizens could sue to enforce pollution limits in state or federal permits, or to force the EPA to perform regulatory duties. The Clean Water Act and the earlier Clean Air Act were the first federal laws to provide for citizen lawsuits against the government for failing to carry out environmental obligations; from that time they have been increasingly important as EPA action has been hindered by budgetary constraints.

Finally, and most important from an ideological perspective, the act declared the visionary, and improbable, goal of restoring and maintaining "the chemical, physical, and biological integrity of the nation's water." This standard would be accomplished by making all national waters "fishable and swimmable" by 1983 and by "totally eliminating" all pollutant discharges into navigable waters by 1985. This zero-discharge provision had been the source of controversy in the Senate and House versions of the bill as it moved through Congress. The more-conservative members of the House Public Works Committee had removed the Senate "policy" of zero discharge and replaced it with the "goal" of zero discharge. For the leading congressional environmentalist, Senator Muskie, chair of the Subcommittee on Air and Water Pollution, who called the Clean Water law the most complicated legislative endeavor of his career, the difference between "policy" and "goal" meant little. During the House debates, Muskie declared that the 1985 deadline was "not locked in concrete. It is not enforceable. It simply establishes what the [Senate] committee thinks ought to be done on the basis of present knowledge." Muskie's "ought to be done" argument points to the larger meaning underlying the zero-discharge goals of the act. For the first time in federal regulatory law, the Clean Air and Clean Water Acts proposed to manage the quality of all the products of the U.S. industrial system. Earlier federal regulation focused on monopolies or high prices; the new environmental regulation centered on every facility that produced pollution—that is, all citizens and all businesses in every aspect of society. Significantly, the Clean Water Act rejected the long-standing reasonable-use doctrine that had fueled the American economy since early nationhood: pollution was no longer a legitimate use of nature. Despite the absurdly idealistic goals of the law, which, of course, given the size and scope of the U.S. capitalist system, were never met, the Clean Water Act demonstrated that times had changed.

A step back to look at the process and events leading to the 1972 water law helps reveal the revolutionary character of legislation and the significance of environmental activism in the period beginning in 1969. Water-pollution control in the United States after World War II and before 1972 is best defined by the theory of "cooperative pragmatism." As outlined by Terence Kehoe, in *Cleaning Up the Great Lakes: From Cooperation to Confrontation* (1997), and other scholars of the subject, this approach established voluntary cooperation among state regulators, and polluters—businesses and municipalities. A low-cost, flexible, centrist modus operandi found in all the states, the essential idea was to build informal consensus without hurting the prevailing developmentalist view of natural resources—that all water has a best primary use. Pollution was an accepted component of economic growth and social progress. In any case, a major theme in early water-pollution concerns focused on the dominance of a "bacterial paradigm" emphasizing a greater threat of epidemic disease from municipal sewage rather than industrial wastes. By the late 1960s some states, most notably New York under Republican Governor Nelson Aldrich Rockefeller, and also California, Wisconsin, Minnesota, Illinois, and Oregon, were taking action in pollution control. The main thrust of these efforts, however, was to acquire federal money without federal intervention and to ease the increasing fears of the business communities in each state.

The federal government had a limited role in this scheme of "pollution control." Though with the 1956 amendments to the water-pollution-control law, the federal government obtained the discretionary responsibility in implementing regulatory measures for the first time. The so-called enforcement conference mechanism promulgated by the 1956 act allowed federal officials to hold hearings on pollution and potentially file lawsuits against environmental violators. The enforcement-conference procedure, however, proved to be worthless in regard to halting or cleaning up water pollution. As the authors of *Water Wasteland*, a Ralph Nader-sponsored report on federal water-pollution-control policies, asserted in 1971, the word "enforcement" has rarely been so grossly misused. At best, the conferences only served as a focal point for public information and expressions of opinion. The enforcement conference, even after strengthening in subsequent 1961 and 1965 amendments to the federal law, was severely constrained by lack of funding, delays, partisan politics, regulatory discretion, an emphasis on negotiation and compromise, and deference to state's rights and the prevailing socioeconomic conditions. Of the sixty federal water-pollution conferences called between 1957 and 1972, only one actually went to court: a relatively insignificant case involving the city of St. Joseph, Missouri.

Nowhere was the weakness of federal enforcement conferences more obvious than in the story of Lake Erie, perhaps the most prominent water-pollution episode of the 1960s. Public concern for the biological health of Erie surged in 1964 when scientific studies showed that vast areas of the lake bottom were devoid of dissolved oxygen. Eutrophication fostered by more than a century of massive municipal and industrial pollution had turned Erie into a "dead" lake. A public-relations campaign led by a wealthy automobile dealer from Cleveland, David Blaushild, and the local media eventually compelled the Republican governor of Ohio, James A. Rhodes, to ask the federal government to initiate an enforcement conference in 1965. For the next five years, until June 1970, representatives from government, industry, municipalities, and citizens groups from five states met to set abatement plans and timetables for the approximately two hundred municipal and two hundred industrial polluters along the American shore of the lake. By mid 1970, however, the majority of Lake Erie industries and municipalities had failed to meet the "deadlines" set by the conference. Many of those entities that had met the timetables with new facilities were providing inadequate treatment and so required additional capital improvements. Virtually nothing had been accomplished.

Peter Cleary Yeager concludes in his thorough analysis of early water pollution laws in the United States, *The Limits of Law: The Public Regulation of Private Pollution* (1991), that the enforcement-conference procedure did represent increased federal attention to environmental risk. Nevertheless, it "reflected the limited extent to which government was able to challenge this aspect of production relations in the private sector." Thus, "enforcement" was merely symbolic. The political power of business, the predominance of state's rights, and the lack of a strong citizen demand for political action all mitigated against the cleanup of water pollution before the late 1960s.

For many reasons, 1969 marked the watershed year beyond which legislative momentum toward a new clean-water law became unstoppable. The earliest public-opinion polls on environmental issues, first taken in 1965, already indicated growing citizen interest. Broad social trends in the last half of the 1960s, however, pushed environmental concerns, particularly water pollution, into public consciousness with unprecedented speed and urgency: by 1970 environmental protection had become a consensual issue. Historians have decisively shown that modern American environmentalism has roots reaching back to the conservation movement of the late nineteenth century. Still, two developments by 1969 opened the door for a greater effort by the federal government. First, a burgeoning and affluent middle class interested in quality-of-life issues began to balance environmentalism with materialism. Second, more than a decade of civil rights and antiwar activism created a conducive atmosphere for the mobilization of widespread public support for environmental protection. This trend perhaps reached its peak with the celebration of Earth Day on 22 April 1970.

On 28 January 1969 a blowout of an oil-well platform off the coast of Santa Barbara, California, inundated and befouled thirty miles of pristine white beach near the isolated and affluent university community. The oil pollution caused a tremendous general outcry. Historian Hal K. Rothman states, in *The Greening of a Nation?: Environmentalism in the United States Since 1945* (1998), that this oil spill "crystallized pollution problems for the American public" because of the natural beauty of Santa Barbara and because it was a refuge for an elite group willing to speak out, "ironically mak[ing] it an ideal symbol for the antipollution revolution taking place in American society," though Santa Barbara was not the only notorious pollution episode in 1969. Water-pollution controversies irrupted across the United States. A geographic sampling of waters "polluted beyond comprehension" in 1969 would also include the poisonous Texas Houston Ship Canal winding to Galveston Bay, the industry-besotted Calumet region of southern Lake Michigan, and the grotesquely contaminated Raritan Bay at the coastal intersection of New Jersey and New York City.

The Cuyahoga River, flowing through Cleveland, Ohio, and into Lake Erie, certainly was one of the more infamous pollution spots in the United States. Along one four-mile stretch of the Cuyahoga, there were thirty-two distinct industrial discharges, four raw-sewage overflow points, and one hundred storm-water outfalls, as well as the woefully overloaded Cleveland municipal waste plant. As early as 1881, the mayor of Cleveland called the river "an open sewer through the center of the city." Beginning in mid-twentieth century, the Cuyahoga would periodically burst into flames as the chemical and waste-laden river would reach a critical combustion point. When it ignited once again on 22 June 1969, cynical Cleveland residents joked that it was the only body of water in the world that should be declared a fire hazard. When the EPA finally took the steel industry to court for polluting the Cuyahoga in the early 1970s, a Republic Steel executive snapped that Ruckelshaus wanted to turn the river into a "trout stream" and make the air in Cleveland as pure as that of the "Swiss Alps." In 1972, however, when environmentalists asked another Republic Steel spokesman to drink from discharges of his firm into the Cuyahoga, he declined, saying instead that "we put the water back into the river better than we take it out" and that "if it were chlorinated it would probably be drinkable." For Rothman, the recurrent inflammatory plight of the Cuyahoga "seemed a direct challenge to the ethic of progress."

The immediacy and national scope of water-pollution problems in 1969 contrasted with the increasing frustration and despair felt by government officials, congressional leaders, and environmentalists in solving the predicament. Late in the year some activists and federal attorneys in the Chicago region hit upon a novel approach, dusting off an obscure seventy-year-old statute known as the Refuse Act. Actually a section of the Rivers and Harbors Act of 1899, the law prohibited the discharge of any refuse, except municipal wastes, into navigable waters without a permit from the U.S. Army Corps of Engineers. It also provided for criminal fines and prison terms for violators; and a common-law stipulation in the statute allowed for citizens to sue polluters when the government failed to act, and collect half the fines if convictions were obtained. Two U.S. Supreme Court opinions written in 1960 and 1966 by the conservationist Justice William O. Douglas had greatly strengthened the application of the Refuse Act. Congressman Henry Schoellkopf Reuss (D-Wisconsin), chairman of the important Conservation and Natural Resources Subcommittee of the House Government Operations Committee, seized upon the issue early in 1970 as a way to challenge industrial polluters. A hard-nosed environmentalist, Reuss held hearings on the use of the law and issued special Refuse Act information packets ("Reuss Handy Kits") to citizens desiring to file suit against polluters. In a well-publicized instance, Reuss himself even turned over to the Justice Department a list of 270 industrial polluters in his home state for prosecution; and he succeeded in collecting half the conviction fines, which he then gave to Wisconsin authorities to help pay the costs of building expensive, and perpetually underfunded, municipal sewage-treatment plants.

The Nixon administration, responding to public interest and fearful of a grassroots surge of citizen action, began to apply the Refuse Act provisions in mid 1970, most notably using it in mercury-pollution cases and in abating thermal discharges into Biscayne Bay in Florida. In December 1970, the month he established the EPA, President Nixon created a federal program under the Refuse Act, requiring all industrial polluters to acquire permits limiting discharges. This program immediately proved a bureaucratic nightmare, as the new EPA was swamped with twenty thousand permit applications. Furthermore, two subsequent federal court rulings in 1971 and 1972 cast doubt on the entire Refuse Act permit approach. The first ruled that the lengthy environmental-impact statements, mandated under the National Environmental Policy Act of 1969, accompany each permit–a virtual administrative impossibility. The second declared that businesses could not be held criminally responsible for pollution under the Refuse Act. By mid 1972 the once-promising program had come to a standstill.

The entire range of problems associated with the deficiencies in federal water-pollution control and the empowering changes in American environmentalism before 1972 is exemplified by the Reserve Mining case, sometimes called the "longest environmental trial in history." Reserve Mining was a large iron-ore-processing operation situated on the western shore of Lake Superior, about sixty miles north of Duluth, Minnesota. Jointly owned by Republic and Armco Steel, Reserve had beneficiated low grade iron ore–known as taconite–since 1955, supplying 15 percent of the iron requirements of the U.S. steel industry. In the process the mill dumped huge quantities of waste tailings directly into Lake Superior, at times reaching 67,000 tons per day, more than two times the estimated solid waste garbage produced by New York City during the same period. Reserve had acquired permits from the state of Minnesota and the Corps in the late 1940s to discharge this waste. By the late 1960s, however, insurgent environmentalism had altered the political context of water pollution. A U.S. Interior Department investigation in 1968 revealed that the mining operation had massively contaminated Lake

THE SANTA BARBARA DECLARATION OF ENVIRONMENTAL RIGHTS

ALL MEN have the right to an environment capable of sustaining life and promoting happiness. If the accumulated actions of the past become destructive of this right, men now living have the further right to repudiate the past for the benefit of the future. And it is manifest that centuries of careless neglect of the environment have brought mankind to a final crossroads. The quality of our lives is eroded and our very existence threatened by our abuse of the natural world.

MOVED by an environmental disaster in the Santa Barbara Channel to think and act in national and world terms, we submit these charges:

We have littered the land with refuse.

We have encroached upon our heritage of open space and wildland.

We have stripped the forests and the grasses and reduced the soil to fruitless dust.

We have contaminated the air we breathe for life.

We have befouled the lakes and rivers and oceans along with their shorelines.

We have released deadly poisons into earth, air, and water, imperiling all life.

We have exterminated entire species of birds and animals and brought others close to annihilation.

We are overpopulating the earth.

We have made much of the physical world ugly and loud, depriving man of the beauty and quiet that feeds his spirit.

RECOGNIZING that the ultimate remedy for these fundamental problems is found in man's mind, not his machines, we call on societies and their governments to recognize and implement the following principles:

We need an ecological consciousness that recognizes man as member, not master, of the community of living things sharing his environment.

We must extend ethics beyond social relations to govern man's contact with all life forms and with the environment itself.

We need a renewed idea of community which will shape urban environments that serve the full range of human needs.

We must find the courage to take upon ourselves as individuals responsibility for the welfare of the whole environment, treating our own back yards as if they were the world and the world as if it were our own back yard.

We must develop the vision to see that in regard to the natural world private and corporate ownership should be so limited as to preserve the interest of society and the integrity of the environment.

We need greater awareness of our enormous powers, the fragility of the earth, and the consequent responsibility of men and governments for its preservation.

We must redefine "progress" toward an emphasis on long-term quality rather than immediate quantity.

WE THEREFORE, resolve to act. We propose a revolution in conduct toward an environment which is rising in revolt against us. Granted that ideas and institutions long established are not easily changed; yet today is the first day of the rest of our life on this planet. We will begin anew.

Source: *Roderick Nash, ed.,* The American Environment: Readings in the History of Conservation, *second edition (New York: Knopf, 1978), pp. 298–300.*

Superior. This report set off a political struggle lasting into the 1980s that embroiled the federal government, the states of Minnesota, Michigan, and Wisconsin, the steel industry, and the United Steelworkers Union.

The Reserve Mining case is significant for the historical background of the Clean Water Act because it was one of the few federal water-pollution lawsuits filed before the 1972 amendments. Interior Secretary Stewart Lee Udall called an enforcement conference for Lake Superior beginning in May 1969, and the conferees met seven times, until April 1971. Other than the venting of public emotion, the conference accomplished almost nothing, especially when it became obvious that there was a lack of legal power to compel the recalcitrant mining company to cease polluting. By April 1971 the EPA officials chairing the conference had had enough. The federal government abandoned the enforcement conference and proceeded to file suit against Reserve under little-used provisions of the water-pollution-control statutes and the Refuse Act. Symbolically, it was the most important water-pollution case in the country. As Ruckelshaus declared, "the EPA had to be perceived as capable of solving this kind of issue, it was just going on and on." Even so, because it was filed under the archaic pre-1972 statutes, the federal lawsuit against Reserve and its owners lasted until a final settlement in 1982. Under court order, the pollution of Lake Superior with mining wastes had ceased in March of 1980 after Reserve built a gigantic on-land disposal site for its tailings unrivaled in the annals of hard-rock mining, ironically causing environmental problems of almost equal magnitude.

The early years of the Reserve Mining controversy demonstrated how inordinately difficult it was to reach a solution to a complicated water-pollution case on a timely basis before 1972. It also revealed the complete failure of federal pollution laws to achieve their stated aims. As one of the most protracted struggles between economy and environment in the history of environmental law, Reserve Mining suggested that a powerful economic interest could endlessly delay compliance with legal controls, even in the face of overwhelming evidence. As Yeager incisively argues, this case shows that water-pollution laws before 1972 reflected the inequality and structural bias in federal regulation: private production was a primary social value—the pollution laws favored the largest polluters. In the Reserve Mining instance, it meant the steel industry, which was well known for the pervasiveness of its environmental contamination and for obstinately evading environmental cleanup. By 1970 the steel industry had emerged as the leading reactionary force in water-pollution-control debates.

The Reserve Mining issue surfaced throughout the course of the congressional dialogue involving the Clean Water bill during 1971 and 1972. For instance, the Democratic governor of Minnesota, Wendell R. Anderson, was one of the few state executives to testify in favor of the Senate version of the Clean Water amendments during the hearings. Anderson stressed the significance of uniform national pollution standards to prevent business from pitting states against each other in competing for the weakest environmental regulations. Anderson further implied that the Reserve situation, and the incessant shutdown threats of the mining company, led him to this belief. Citing this testimony, Congressman Reuss and a group of environmentalist legislators attempted to amend the law during floor debate to strengthen EPA permit review, removing it from state oversight. In addition, Philip Aloysius Hart (D-Michigan), the conservationist chair of the Environment Subcommittee of the Senate Commerce Committee, in testifying at a congressional hearing, used Reserve Mining as an example of why the federal-enforcement conferences and Refuse Act procedures were bankrupt. Hart asserted that the intransigence of the company demonstrated that citizens must have the right to sue polluters directly to prevent bureaucratic delays and to compel environmental remediation, a provision that became part of the 1972 law.

The influence of Reserve Mining in the Clean Water amendment deliberations was most obvious in the example of John Anton Blatnik (D-Minnesota). Blatnik chaired the powerful House Committee on Public Works, the source of water-pollution-control legislation emanating from that chamber of Congress. Blatnik had authored the 1956 amendments of the Water Pollution Control Act and coauthored all subsequent amendments through 1972. He became known as "the father of water pollution control," often to the dismay of the acolytes of Senator Muskie. Blatnik also represented a district in northern Minnesota that encompassed many iron-mining operations, including Reserve Mining. Throughout his career the congressman was a dedicated promoter of the mining industry.

Blatnik's supposed participation in the Reserve Mining affair—in secretly supporting the mining company—engendered tremendous controversy, especially after *Water Wasteland* roundly condemned him when it appeared in April 1971. For David R. Zwick, editor of the *Harvard Law Review* and one of the authors of *Water Wasteland*, the Reserve case and Blatnik's role in it "was the best illustration of all the reasons why the [federal pollution control] program has failed—weakness in the law, bureaucratic delay, and susceptibility to political pressure." From 1969 until his retirement in 1974, the congressman was under constant attack from environmentalists in his state and nationally in regard to Reserve Mining and his putative hesitancy in supporting strong pollution-control regulations as chair of the House Public Works Committee. The pressure became so intense that Blatnik suffered a heart attack in November 1971, at the peak of the House debates on the water-pollution amendments, effectively removing him from taking part in the final deliberations on the legislation.

Finally, the convergence among the new-style citizen activism, Reserve Mining, and the Clean Water amendments underscores why environmental policymaking had irrevocably changed by 1972 and why the law was so radical in character. Public-interest environmental groups, exemplified in the history of the Clean Water law by the Nader organizations centered in Washington, D.C., had become professionalized and institutionalized. Their approach emphasized technical and legal expertise, legislative initiatives based on a faith in a progressive federal government and citizen power, and a confrontational "sue the bastards" litigious philosophy that placed business on the defensive, shifting the burden of proof to the environmental despoilers. As they had with an earlier study of air pollution, *Vanishing Air* (1970), Nader and his followers redirected the whole water-pollution control congressional debate with the seven-hundred-page *Water Wasteland.* Muskie and Ruckelshaus, among others, acknowledged the importance of the report. Business leaders and political conservatives, on the other hand, hated these new citizen environmentalists. During the public argument over the water-pollution law, the chairman of U.S. Steel Corporation, Edwin Gott, castigated Nader as a "disloyal fraud," a "self-styled savior of society more interested in capitalizing on social, economic, and environmental problems than he is in helping to solve them. We aren't going to allow the environmental issue to be used sometimes falsely and sometimes in a demagogic way to destroy the industrial system that has made this great country." Similarly, in testimony before the House Public Works Committee, Nader's colleague Zwick so incensed the interim chair Representative Robert Emmett Jones Jr. (D-Alabama), who was substituting for a hospitalized Blatnik, with a trenchant and detailed critique of the softened House version of the water bill that Jones's staff aides persuaded him to relinquish the podium until he gained control of his anger.

All the marshaled political influence of business and its supporters in the Nixon administration and Congress, however, could not stop the Clean Water Act from becoming law. In fact, from the passage of the 1969 National Environmental Policy Act on, American industry failed to prevent any major environmental initiative from becoming law in Congress. In this regard, the Clean Water Act was the best example of how business had lost the power to determine environmental policy in the United States. Although they did not achieve all they desired in the 1972 pollution-control legislation, the new public-interest environmentalists had fundamentally transformed the entire lawmaking process. Furthermore, in the recast statute, seemingly intractable water-pollution problems such as Lake Erie, Santa Barbara, the Cuyohoga River, and Reserve Mining all were potentially within the palliative realm of government regulation. The history of implementation, funding, and enforcement of federal water-pollution-control laws after 1972 is a different story that perhaps calls into question some of the maxims of 1970s environmentalism in the United States. Nevertheless, when Congress overrode President Nixon's veto of the Clean Water Act, it established a revolutionary precedent for the future practice of American environmental law, politics, and policy that remains to this day.

–THOMAS R. HUFFMAN, AVON, MINNESOTA

References

Robert F. Blomquist, "What Is Past Is Prologue: Senator Edmund S. Muskie's Environmental Policy Making as Governor of Maine, 1955–58," *University of Maine Law Review,* 51 (1999): 88–128.

Robert Gottlieb, *Forcing The Spring: The Transformation of The American Environmental Movement* (Washington, D.C.: Island Press, 1993).

Samuel P. Hays and Barbara D. Hays, *Beauty, Health, and Permanence: Environmental Politics in The United States, 1955–1985* (Cambridge & New York: Cambridge University Press, 1987).

Hays, "Three Decades of Environmental Politics: The Historical Context," in *Government And Environmental Politics: Essays on Historical Developments Since World War II,* edited by Michael J. Lacy (Baltimore: Johns Hopkins University Press, 1991).

Beatrice Hort Holmes, *History of Federal Water Resources Programs And Policies, 1961–70* (Washington, D.C.: U.S. Department of Agriculture, Economics, Statistics, and Cooperatives Service, 1979).

Terence Kehoe, *Cleaning Up the Great Lakes: From Cooperation to Confrontation* (DeKalb: Northern Illinois University Press, 1997).

Harvey Lieber and Bruce Rosinoff, *Federalism and Clean Waters: The 1972 Water Pollution Control Act* (Lexington, Mass.: Lexington Books, 1975).

Dean E. Mann, "Political Incentives in U.S. Water Policy: Relationships Between Distributive and Regulatory Politics," in *What Government Does,* edited by Matthew Holden Jr. and Dennis L. Dresang (Beverly Hills, Cal.: Sage, 1975), pp. 94–121.

Daniel A. Mazmanian and Jeanne Nienaber, *Can Organizations Change?: Environmental Protection, Citizen Participation, and the Army Corps of Engineers* (Washington, D.C.: Brookings Institution, 1979).

Martin Melosi, "Lyndon Johnson and Environmental Policy," in Robert A. Divine, ed., *The Johnson Years,* volume 2, *Vietnam, the Environment, and Science* (Lawrence: University Press of Kansas, 1987), pp. 113–149.

Martin Reuss, "Coping With Uncertainty: Social Scientists, Engineers, and Federal Water Resources Planning," *Natural Resources Journal,* 32 (Winter 1992): 101–135.

Hal K. Rothman, *The Greening of a Nation?: Environmentalism in the United States Since 1945* (Fort Worth, Tex.: Harcourt Brace College Publishers, 1998).

Joel A. Tarr, "Searching for a 'Sink' for an Industrial Waste," in *Out of the Woods: Essays in Environmental History,* edited by Char Miller and Rothman (Pittsburgh: University of Pittsburgh Press, 1997), pp. 163–193.

David Vogel, *Fluctuating Fortunes: The Political Power of Business in America* (New York: Basic Books, 1989).

Peter Cleary Yeager, *The Limits of Law: The Public Regulation of Private Pollution* (Cambridge & New York: Cambridge University Press, 1991).

David R. Zwick and Marcy Benstock, *Water Wasteland: Ralph Nader's Study Group Report on Water Pollution* (New York: Grossman, 1971).

U.S. WETLANDS

Are wetlands a commons or private property?

Viewpoint: Because they are a commons, it has been essential that the federal government buy up wetlands to maintain their viability.

Viewpoint: Wetlands are both a commons as well as private property, and the legality of taking these lands by means of eminent domain is questionable.

Not surprisingly, wetlands have been at the center of environmental disputes in twentieth-century America. Indeed, during the twentieth century debate over their value and existence is part of a much older pattern of disputation, dating back to the early colonial settlements along the eastern seaboard. Then, as now, the tension revolved around their seemingly odd nature. Inundated during high tides and largely dry during low, wetlands are neither land nor sea, an ecological complexity that has sustained a rich abundance and curious variety of plant and animal life.

As a result they have also generated a raft of legal complications. Generally considered private property, and therefore divisible and salable, their status nonetheless is made uncertain by the tides that regularly wash over them; water, unlike land, is usually considered a commons. In short, determining what wetlands are, and whether or how they can be worked, depends on the vagaries of the moment, a situation that has long been the source of legal challenges and political battles.

Until the mid-nineteenth century these fights were almost exclusively the preserve of local and state governments. But their dynamics were altered with the rise of a conservation movement in the latter half of the nineteenth century, which among other things demanded the preservation of wetlands and marshes. The federal government increasingly entered the fray, brandishing the insights of the emerging science of ecology. It did so in part because scientists trained in the new field had assumed jobs in the national conservation agencies created during the Progressive Era (1890–1915); these scientists, and their agencies, prompted the executive branch of the federal government to begin to articulate the value of wetlands as commons. A sign of this early activism was President Theodore Roosevelt's establishment of the first federally protected refuges.

His set-asides would not be the last. Yet, since that time, government "takings" by eminent domain have become rare. Dating from the 1960s, state and national regulation of wetlands increasingly have been the means by which to protect wetlands. Those who see wetlands as private property, however, believe such regulation is onerous, a costly burden. Those for whom wetlands are a commons assert that governmental regulation is just and essential to the preservation of these landscapes. These differing perspectives fuel the ongoing controversies that swirl around wetlands. In coastal New England states, where some of the first expressions of the new policy were enacted; in Florida, with its magnificent yet greatly threatened Everglades; along lakes and rivers; and up and down the Gulf and Pacific coasts, citizens have fought against what they believe to be an unconstitutional expansion of governmental authority. How simultaneously to resolve these protests and save these critical watery habitats, more than half of which have disappeared in the lower forty-eight states, is a complicated task.

Viewpoint: Because they are a commons, it has been essential that the federal government buy up wetlands to maintain their viability.

At the crux of the debate about how Americans will manage their wetlands lies a paradox that has long made the relationship with wetlands thorny. The word "wetland" reveals a fundamental source of misunderstanding that has plagued swamp and marsh landscapes for centuries. From a modern ecological perspective, wetlands are places where water rests long enough that only plants suited to moist, anaerobic conditions can thrive. Wetlands are wet, but from a legal and social perspective, they have long been considered land—acreage that can be carved up into discrete parcels, farmed, and developed. Traditionally, land has been considered as private property and water as public. Because wetlands are not only land, but also water, regarding them simply as real property has repeatedly presented society with problems.

This paradox was confronted firsthand by an Iowa farmer who fell victim to one of many nineteenth-century Florida swampland hoaxes. When he saw his new property for the first time, the farmer was shocked to find a glistening expanse of watery saw-grass marsh. "I have bought land by the acre, I have bought land by the foot, but, by God," he lamented, "I have never before bought land by the gallon." The farmer's plight typifies the age-old difficulty with understanding wetlands. Though a citizen may purchase a wetland and thereby consider it private property, its inherent wetness means that the land will always have a "commons" component. For example, many wetlands have aqueous connections to rivers and aquifers beyond their land boundaries. Consequently, if someone alters a wetland, there will likely be repercussions elsewhere in the watershed, river basin, or flyway.

This commons aspect of a wetland may involve a public nuisance or a public benefit. Historically, wetlands were a nuisance when they flooded, prevented farming, and harbored malaria. In the twentieth century, however, scientists recognized that wetlands offered many public benefits by purifying water, tempering floodwaters, and providing habitat for fish, wildlife, and waterfowl. Despite all these commons components, Americans have persistently regarded wetlands as private property. The assumption that wetlands can be property like all other land has been an immutable stumbling block for those who have grappled with the problems presented by the wetland commons. In most instances, these problems demanded public attention and eventually government involvement to balance competing private and public interests. One need only look at history to see how the wetland commons have repeatedly challenged private ownership and demanded public action.

One of the earliest problems appeared in the mid-eighteenth century when South Carolina planters began to experiment with rice cultivation in the tidewater zone. Locating their farms just above the extent of saltwater, planters could use the rise and fall of tides to drain and irrigate rice fields with river water. Eventually, slaves cleared swamp forests and built levees around the rice fields along most rivers on the southeastern coast. As planters directed their slaves to alter more swamps, the landscape changed dramatically. Before the plantations, when spring runoff charged downstream, it had overflowed into vast forested swamps and slowly dissipated. With levees already holding water in the rice fields and barricading rivers from remaining swamps, the floodwaters had nowhere to go but downstream, causing property damage and flooding to farms and settlements below. To resolve the uncertain rights and responsibilities of the tidewater swamp farmers, by 1787 both South Carolina and Georgia had passed laws requiring farmers to leave all rice dams empty and open in the spring to prevent dangerous floods. These early state regulations limited what property owners could do with their wetlands in order to avoid the public nuisance of flooding.

More widespread confusion about the private and public aspects of wetlands arose again in the wake of the Swampland Grants of 1849 and 1850 when Congress ceded more than sixty million acres of federally owned swamplands to states for privatization and ultimately cultivation. California was one of the fifteen states to receive a grant. There, enormous seasonal wetlands formed in the Central Valley when Sierra Nevada snowmelt caused the Sacramento River to flood its banks. To turn these flood-created wetlands into croplands, farmers had first to build levees to keep river water out. Only then could the land be ditched and drained. Keeping the river water off its traditional floodplain, however, was a mammoth task. For decades, Californians struggled to reclaim its swamplands, and difficulties usually hinged upon the unrelenting tendency to regard wetlands as private property. When one landowner built a levee to keep the water off his swampland property, the flood simply spilled over onto wetlands across the river; or if several landowners constricted the river with levees on both sides, the resulting faster, larger flow would inundate towns downstream. A spiraling war of fortification between swampland owners and townspeople ensued for decades as floods worsened.

Eventually, in the early 1890s, Californians realized that to successfully control floods and drain wetlands for farming, they needed to adopt a statewide plan to coordinate disparate efforts. Because the state lacked sufficient engineering expertise, state officials asked Congress for help. In response, Congress created a commission of federal engineers that developed a plan. For the first time ever, swampland owners were required to build levees on their property in accordance with government standards. After decades of bitter conflict it was only by recognizing the wetland commons and requiring the cooperation of landowners that California successfully drained its swamplands.

Aside from flooding, swamps and marshes harbored another onerous public nuisance: malaria. At the turn of the twentieth century, scientists finally discovered that malaria was transmitted by parasite-infected mosquitoes, which bred in stagnant water. Armed with new scientific authority, Progressive-era public-health agencies spearheaded drainage efforts to eradicate the disease. In New Jersey, for example, public mosquito-control ditching began in 1902. Eventually, the state required local governments to create their own mosquito-extermination commissions.

While state and local governments sponsored drainage projects in urban and coastal areas, regulation became the primary means to fight malaria in rural areas where public resources were limited. Many officials held landowners responsible. For example, an ordinance in Des Moines, Iowa, deemed it the "duty" of the owner to drain or fill depressions where mosquitoes bred. Although many wetlands were privately owned, because infected insects could fly beyond property boundaries, malaria essentially functioned as a part of the wetland commons. Only by orchestrating public-works projects and requiring landowners to control mosquitoes on their property could governments effectively deal with the nuisance of malaria.

In the cases of flooding, drainage, and malaria, the planning and regulatory roles of government were justified because of the shared problems that resulted when privately owned wetlands failed to provide for use and development like other lands. Government helped to resolve conflicting public and private rights and responsibilities, usually by eliminating nuisances—which often meant destroying wetlands.

As the understanding of wetlands grew over the twentieth century to include the common benefits provided by wetlands, local, state, and federal governments played a similar conciliatory role as they tried to safeguard public values. In these cases the goal was not to eliminate the commons but preserve it. At the turn of the twentieth century, plummeting waterfowl populations called attention to the public benefits of wetlands for the first time. Initially, the decline was attributed solely to overhunting, but biologists soon realized that widespread drainage for agriculture and mosquito control made far-less habitat available. Flying from wetland to wetland along migratory flyway routes, continental waterfowl were another part of the commons. President Theodore Roosevelt tried to assuage the problem at the federal level by designating several national wildlife refuges, but these refuges were too few to sustain waterfowl. As populations continued to drop—especially during the great drought of the 1930s—the federal government took emergency measures and started several projects, including the Duck Stamp program, which raised revenues through hunting-license fees to buy more public waterfowl refuges. Although the government set aside many wetlands for habitat, far greater acreage was converted to farms and developments, especially after World War II. Since then, it became clear that wetlands provided habitat for more than just ducks and geese. The Fish and Wildlife Service estimates that up to 43 percent of all endangered species rely on wetlands for some part of their life cycle.

As scientific understanding grew, other beneficial aspects of wetlands became better known. Studies completed in the late 1950s and early 1960s linked the destruction of coastal wetlands to the decline of ocean fisheries. Marshes and mangrove swamps provided nurseries for juvenile fish and shellfish that later took to the sea. In the Southeast, for example, 96 percent of the commercial harvest depends on coastal wetlands. In states reliant on commercial fishing—principally those on the eastern seaboard—many legislatures passed wetland-protective laws for the first time. Unlike earlier federal refuge policies that depended wholly upon public acquisition to conserve wetlands, most state laws used regulation to limit development in privately owned wetlands to secure the public benefit of their fisheries—essentially another part of the wetland commons.

Plum Island, Parker River Reserve, off the coast of northeastern Massachusetts

(Jonathan Wallen)

Of course, not all states protected their wetlands, so the federal government followed suit with its own regulations, especially after scientists learned more about the hydrological connections between wetlands, aquifers, and rivers in the late 1960s and early 1970s. In particular, studies showed that wetlands acted as giant filters, purifying the water that flowed through them; for example, a thousand-acre marsh could purify the nitrogenous wastes from twenty thousand acres. Concerned about growing water-pollution problems, Congress and the courts interpreted the Clean Water Act of 1972 to protect wetlands from being filled in. By regulating wetlands, federal law sought to help local communities benefit from cleaner water, yet another aspect of the wetland commons.

While state and federal laws sought to safeguard wetlands, new regulations restricted landowners who had planned to fill and develop these areas. By virtue of their inherent nature, wetlands once again defied the conventional concept of property. Because the "wet" part of wetlands offered public benefits, the government had become involved to protect common values; yet, the "land" part had traditionally accorded owners the right to do what they wanted.

Resentment and anger festered among landowners affected by regulations, and for two decades the controversy stewed. With the Clean Water Act up for reauthorization in 1992, the debate picked up new intensity as property-rights advocates rose to spar with wetland conservationists.

According to property-rights proponents, though wetlands furnished public services, they did not generate any gain for landowners; and because of regulations, landowners ended up bearing unfair public costs. In particular, they charged that wetland regulations violated the takings clause of the U.S. Constitution, which specifically precluded the government from taking property without compensation. Their solution, promoted by Representative James Allison Hayes (R-Louisiana), was the Comprehensive Wetlands Management and Conservation Act, a bill that would require the federal government to pay landowners not to develop the most ecologically valuable wetlands. If the government failed to provide compensation within a given time, landowners would be free to develop their lands without restraint.

Several members of Congress raised practical concerns about this compensation provision. If the federal government had to pay people not to fill wetlands, would it have to pay people to follow all laws? The Congressional Budget Office estimated that the law would cost $45 million, and environmentalists warned that more than half of the remaining national wetlands would lose protection.

On the issue of takings, most courts had decided that owners held property with an implied obligation not to use it in ways that harmed the public. If a regulation prevented public injury, then it clearly did not constitute a taking. Wetlands regulations most often did not prevent direct injury to others, however, but rather guarded public goods such as pure drinking water. Courts were less clear about whether destroying public benefits preserved by regulations could be construed as public harm.

During Hayes bill hearings, James Tripp of the Environmental Defense Fund pointedly questioned: "Should Congress care more about the property of the vacation home developer who would turn a wetland into a condominium on the eastern shore of Maryland, or more about the investments of oyster fishermen who have seen their jobs disintegrate at the hands of excess phosphorus that results from wetland loss?" Tripp's eloquent query showed once again that the commons aspects of wetlands made it difficult to consider them simply and solely as private property. In fact, making wetlands fit into the conventional conception of private property was like trying to fit a square peg into a round hole.

Although scientists, beginning in the 1960s, revealed wetlands to be complex ecological systems of land and water, Americans clung to the conventional view of wetlands as property–a way of thinking reinforced by centuries of legal practice. As a result, ongoing private-rights discourse neglected fundamental information offered by scientists and the record of history. When citizens struggled with wetlands commons that were nuisances, they eventually had to modify their vision of private property: rice growers had to abide by open-dam laws; swamp owners had to build uniform levees; and marsh owners had to rid their lands of malaria. Since the 1970s Americans have continually confronted limitations of the private-property concept as they tried to assimilate the knowledge of ecology. To successfully conserve common wetland values, Americans must modify their vision of property: wetland owners will have to abide by certain regulations; taxpayers and wetland users will need to contribute; and there will likely be new ideas as well.

Moving beyond limits of the property concept will be an ongoing process, for one will not end up with dry land to put in the property pigeonhole. To conserve wetlands, Americans need to reach a more-thorough understanding of why these ecosystems are more than just private property. With 54 percent of the wetlands in the conterminous states already converted to farms, shopping plazas, parking lots, airports, and other developments, and with roughly 117,000 acres more lost each year, the need for a new wetland ethic is urgent. Though the gallons described by the Iowa farmer in Florida may seem a far-fetched measure for wetlands, it is clear that acres also fall short in describing this landscape that is part land, part water, part private, part public. To resolve the paradox of the wetland commons, a better way must be found to integrate the important public values of wetlands into prevailing paradigms of land ownership.

–ANN VILEISIS, SOUTHBURY, CONNECTICUT

Viewpoint: Wetlands are both a commons as well as private property, and the legality of taking these lands by means of eminent domain is questionable.

The complexity of the salt-marsh environment is described best by nineteenth-century poet John Greenleaf Whittier, who referred to it as "the low green prairies of the sea," indicating that it has characteristics of both land and sea, yet is neither. For twelve hours of the day it is covered by ocean waters that supply its flora and fauna with important nutrients. Low tide reveals the dynamic nature of the marsh as its biota acclimates to the changes that have occurred during the previous inundation and prepares for the next. Despite its ambiguous and unstable nature, the salt-marsh landscape provided northern New Englanders with grasses to feed livestock for more than three centuries. As a result, farmers regarded this land as private property, which they surveyed, improved, paid taxes on, and transferred from one generation to the next. Any threat to a person's marshland was also a challenge to the survival of the farm family and the constitutional right to own property.

This threat has intensified over time, marking a shift in the relationship between the government and individual salt-marsh owners. From the eighteenth century through the mid-twentieth century, state and local government played the role of protector and promoter of private property rights of marsh owners for their individual benefit. With the development of a national wildlife refuge system, however, the federal government attempted to destroy the rights of marsh owners. Ultimately, the end of subsistence farming, coupled with an increased public knowledge of the importance of salt-marsh ecosystems, persuaded owners to give up their rights to this land.

During the colonial period town officials privatized the salt-marsh landscape by dividing it among town residents as they had done with upland. Generation after generation not only inherited the land but also a sense of stewardship over it. As stewards, colonists improved the marsh landscape by cutting ditches to increase drainage and encourage the spread of certain salt grasses that, when cut, made a more-nutritious fodder for cattle. Ditches, fences, and certain natural features such as rocks and small trees served as property lines for many of the salt-marsh owners. These markers reflect an attempt to prevent other farmers from cutting into an adjacent lot and interlopers from stealing hay. When the system broke down it was usually the result of vague or impermanent property lines and/or high tides lifting the cut hay off the marsh and carrying it away to another farmer's property. Claimants took their disputes to the local court, where a judge usually decided upon the true owner of the hay or sent surveyors out to reexamine the property lines.

The importance of this landscape continued into the mid-nineteenth century, when

WETLANDS PROTECTION

On 26 June 1998 an organization of commercial fishermen from the West Coast presented a statement before a Senate subcommittee looking into wetlands protection.

Fish do not arise from nowhere—they are part of and supported by a complex and fragile ecosystem. The vast majority of commercially valuable species depend for some portion of their biological lifecycle on inland, near shore or estuary wetlands—these are their nursery grounds. Let me give you some examples. Salmon, for instance, are hatched from eggs laid in inland freshwater gravel beds sometimes hundreds of miles from the ocean. The young salmon then make their long immigration downriver to the ocean where they will eventually grow to adulthood and return to spawn, but along the way they depend upon back channel wetlands as a food source, for shelter from predators and (in the case of coho salmon) they need these wetlands to provide "overwintering" habitat to nourish them for up to 18 months. Even then they depend upon salt water wetlands to help them adapt to ocean conditions. Their adaptation from fresh to salt then back to fresh-water fish is one of the most remarkable biological feats in the natural world. However, without salt-water estuaries and salt marsh wetlands within which to make the necessary biological changes, these adaptations would be impossible and they would all die . . .

Without adequate wetlands protection, however, much of the West Coast salmon fishing industry would be doomed. Wetland losses to date have already lost many west coast fishing jobs. According to official federal statistics, Washington state has already lost an estimated 31% of its historic wetlands, Oregon another 38% and California a whopping 91% of all its historic wetlands base. Counting coastal wetlands only, these loss figures would be much greater. In the nine-state region of Arizona, California, Hawaii, Idaho, Nevada, New Mexico, Oregon, Utah and Washington, more than 59% of historic wetlands are now gone. *These wetland losses have already had a dramatic negative impact on salmon and many other fishery resources throughout the west coast, costing tens of thousands of jobs and hundreds of millions of dollars in productive capacity.*

To give another example, nowhere in the nation is the link between wetland habitation and fish production more obvious than in the Gulf states, where National Marine Fisheries Service scientists estimate that *98% of the Gulf commercial harvest comes from inshore, wetlands dependent fish and shellfish.* Louisiana's marshes alone produce an annual commercial fish and shellfish harvest of 1.2 billion pounds worth $244 million in 1991. At this rate of return the Gulf shrimp resources is worth roughly $7.7 billion dollars to the economy of those states. Although by no means alone, Gulf shrimp clearly head the list of the region's wetlands dependent food species. Without strong wetlands protection this extremely valuable commercial fishery would eventually no longer exist in those states. . . .

In fact the war to protection [sic] fishery habitat is being lost. Even under existing law, wetlands losses have not been halted, only the *rate of loss* somewhat reduced. Habitat losses to date have already cost the commercial fishing industry more than $27 billion/year and more than 450,000 jobs. On the other hand, habitat protection and restoration—in particular wetlands protection—would restore that lost productivity and recapture those lost jobs to the economy. This is part of the "economic dividend" to the country of wetlands and other fish habitat protection.

Wetlands protection should not be seen, therefore, as a cost so much as it is an investment in the future of a national commercial and recreational fishing industry that provides $111 billion dollars each year to the nation's economy and 1.5 million family wage jobs.

Source: *"Prepared Statement of the Pacific Coast Federation of Fishermen's Associations,"* Wetlands: Review of Regulatory Changes, Hearing Before the Subcommittee on Clean Air, Wetlands, Private Property and Nuclear Safety of the Committee on Environment and Public Works, United States Senate, *26 June 1997 (Washington, D.C.: U.S. Government Printing Office, 1998), pp. 192–194.*

farmers turned to their salt marshes to solve the problem of infertile uplands. Farmers reclaimed wetlands that had been made fertile by centuries of decaying plant and animal matter. Reclamation required that they build earthen embankments or dikes around the marsh perimeter to halt the flow of saltwater. Once the salt had been leeched from the soil, farmers boasted that they had transformed their morass into fertile farmland capable of producing upland hay, grains, and vegetables. To fund this venture, farmers petitioned the state legislature for the right to incorporate as a diking company. Next, company officials determined the taxes each farmer paid to support construction and repair of the dike based on the amount of salt-marsh acreage each farmer owned. Twenty-five diking companies were formed in northern New England during the nineteenth century.

During the late nineteenth century, scientists developed a greater interest in the marsh environment through their support of reclamation. Under the direction of the U.S. Geological Survey, scientists studied the coastal environment and came to understand that nature maintained an equilibrium between biological and geological forces. Scientist Nathaniel Shaler explained that "as the [marsh] plants changed their conditions over time, so did the biotic community sustained by the new vegetation"; this change, of course, allowed for succession or "the sequential transformation of landscape by vegetation." Shaler and his contemporaries believed that reclamation was the proper way to utilize the salt marshes of New England. Reclamation sped up natural succession and "made the usually wasteful habits of nature more efficient." He speculated that once diked the marshes in Ipswich, Rowley, and Newbury, Massachusetts, would increase in value from $10 an acre to $200 per acre and thus revitalize farming in the area. While Shaler opened the door for further study of the marsh environment, he also promoted the changing of that environment so that it could benefit its individual owners.

Shaler's work attracted additional scientific interest in the natural processes of the salt-marsh environment. In 1913 Charles Wendell Townsend, ornithologist and president of the Massachusetts Audubon Society, captured the complex natural and human history of the Plum Island salt marshes in his book *Sand Dunes and Salt Marshes.* Townsend described the natural processes of the marsh landscape in lay terms. He explained that the destruction of specific biotic elements of this landscape would hinder the development and survival of other components of this wetland world; everything on the marsh, from the smallest creatures to the tallest grasses, has a purpose and interacts with the ocean environment in different ways. Townsend's holistic descriptions of the marsh flora and fauna, and their interactions with the ocean, were prescient. He then challenged the traditional stewards of the marsh, who he thought to be the farmers, to protect this environment to sustain the wildfowl population. Ultimately, members of the Federation of Bird Clubs of New England and the Massachusetts Audubon Society, not the farmers, stepped forward. In 1929 these groups established the Annie Hamilton Brown Wild Life Sanctuary on Plum Island. Six years later the two groups boasted of an increase in the duck population.

The success of the Brown Sanctuary attracted the attention of Ira Gabrielson, director of the Fish & Wildlife Service (FWS). He found the sanctuary and adjacent marshland in Newbury, Rowley, and Ipswich to be an essential part of the Atlantic flyway. He also hoped that incorporation of this land into the federal wildlife-refuge system would end charges that he had done nothing in Massachusetts and New England to fulfill the terms of the Migratory Bird Conservation Act of 1929. Gabrielson initiated condemnation proceedings to acquire the necessary land, which were not uncommon in the development of the national wildlife-refuge system as they allowed the government to purchase small amounts of land inexpensively; in the case of the Parker River Refuge, however, the FWS obtained 8,800 out of 12,368 acres through this process. At first Massachusetts politicians agreed to the proceedings, but they became infuriated when they discovered just how much land the FWS wanted.

The condemnation proceedings promoted public ownership of the marshes under the direction of the federal wildlife-refuge system and challenged centuries of private ownership of the marshland as well as the traditional way of life in northern Essex County. Gabrielson and his colleagues proposed a conservation plan that benefited migratory wildfowl through the creation of freshwater ponds and the colonization of certain species of grasses that ducks used for food and nesting. In the process the usurpation and re-creation of the marsh landscape destroyed access to the grasses and other natural resources that subsistence farmers had depended on for centuries. Some farmers took the small sums of money offered them through the condemnation proceedings, but the majority took their case to a congressional hearing held by the House of Representatives committee on agriculture in 1945.

The hearings reveal the clashing perceptions of the landowners and the FWS. Essex County residents used tradition to defend their right to own marshland. One property owner, for example, testified that he "never could quite understand why they have taken my birthright away from me." Many discovered that they had lost their land only after the fact. One Saturday afternoon Newbury resident Malcolm Fryer received a visit from a U.S. marshal who informed him that "we are taking a lot of the property that you own . . . this now belongs to the Federal Government." He then handed Fryer a twenty-six page document that did more to confuse than explain the proceedings. Farmers claimed that the government had denied them their constitutional right to own land and demanded the "chance to continue living in the normal and accustomed way without Government encroachment or regulations over what they had considered a sacred trust–the privilege of owning land." Some compared their situation to Soviet collectivization. Veterans, such as Francis Fuller, questioned their defense of democracy during World War II and compared the actions of the FWS to that of the Japanese at Pearl Harbor: "I think that the sneak attack on Massachusetts in December 1944 was worse than the one on Pearl Harbor on December 7, 1941. . . . I wanted that [marsh land] in order to make a living in a free world, but I don't think it is a free world any longer. I think I was over there fighting for a free country, and not just to come back here and find I wasn't. . . . If there is going to be a free America I would like to get my land back, so I can make a living."

Fuller and others threatened another Boston Tea Party if the government did not acknowledge their constitutional right to own property and use it in the manner they saw fit. Tragically, the FWS did not understand why the farmers were so passionate about protecting their land because governmental officials did not believe the land held any agricultural value. Gabrielson testified to the committee that FWS took only land considered to be "submarginal . . . or . . . of very low agricultural value" and that "we would never buy one refuge . . . if we had to get the unanimous consent of every landowner involved."

The views of the FWS began to change under the supervision of a new director, Albert Day, who replaced Gabrielson in spring 1946. In the fall of that year Day sent author Rachel Carson as a liaison to muster support and gather information that could be used to help laypeople understand the importance of wildlife conservation. Carson's visit proved fruitful for establishing better relations between the residents and the FWS. In 1947 the government published her report on the Parker River Wildlife Refuge in its *Conservation in Action Series.* Carson acknowledged the importance of the farmers and their marsh activities in the success of the refuge, noting that farmers harvesting the salt hay exposed small creatures that served as bird food. Carson stated that "by a seeming paradox, the refuge has improved hunting even while it has helped conserve the ducks." Instead of staying out to sea after fleeing the sound of the first gunshot, ducks returned to the abundant food supply and nesting areas within the refuge. Carson called for cooperation between the FWS and landowners as key to the conservation of ducks and the marsh landscape.

By the end of the 1940s farmers, too, changed their views regarding the value of salt marshes. Many of the younger stewards realized that they could no longer support their families as subsistence farmers and left farming for the factory. In the process the marshes lost their value and the tradition of salt-hay farming remained only as an important part of the historical consciousness of the region. These changing views by both sides ended the battle in 1948. The FWS agreed to reduce the Parker River Wildlife Refuge to 6,400 acres and permitted a few interested farmers to continue harvesting hay within its boundaries. The FWS also returned the remaining acreage to its original owners. Some farmers never bothered to claim their returned marshland.

During the 1950s a new perception of the marshes emerged from the work of Aldo Leopold, who argued that the "system of conservation based solely on economic self-interest is hopelessly lopsided and that the lack of economic value is sometimes a character not only of species or groups but of entire biotic communities including marshes." His ecological creed, coupled with Carson's ability to explain coastal ecology in laypersons' terms, allowed for the growth of national and state preservation ideals for salt marshes throughout the country. By the mid 1960s federal and state governments enacted the first wetlands protection acts, which, coupled with books and articles that expounded the ecological importance of salt marshes, convinced many Maine residents from Kittery to Scarborough to donate approximately 3,500 acres of marshland and 1,500 acres of upland for the creation of the Rachel Carson National Wildlife Refuge in 1966. As more people became convinced of the importance of tidal wetlands to the health of the planet, they relinquished their property rights for the common good and more salt-marsh acreage became protected within the boundaries of state and national refuges. At the turn of the century Maine had ten refuges, New Hampshire five, and Massachusetts eleven–each serves as a physical legacy of the controversy that swirled around the creation of these protected salt-marsh wetlands, and of the political compromises and scientific insights that shaped the reactions of federal conservationists and local farmers alike.

–KIMBERLY R. SEBOLD, UNIVERSITY OF MAINE AT PRESQUE ISLE

References

Neal W. Allen Jr., ed., *Province and Court Records of Maine, 1692–1711,* volume four (Portland: Maine Historical Society, 1958).

Rachel L. Carson, *Parker River: A National Wildlife Refuge, Conservation in Action #2* (Washington, D.C.: U.S. Fish and Wildlife Service, U.S. Government Printing Office, 1947).

John J. Currier, *History of Newbury, Massachusetts 1635–1902* (Boston, Mass.: Damrell & Upham, 1902).

George Francis Dow, ed., *Records and Files of the Quarterly Courts of Essex County, Massachusetts, 1636–1662,* volume one (Salem, Mass.: Essex Institute, 1911).

Katherine C. Ewel, "Water Quality Improvement by Wetlands," in *Nature's Services: Societal Dependence on Natural Ecosystems,* edited by Gretchen C. Daily (Washington, D.C.: Island Press, 1997), pp. 329–344.

Charles B. Floyd, "The Annie H. Brown Wild Life Sanctuary," *Massachusetts Audubon Bulletin* (October 1929): 5.

John D. Fogg, *Recollections of a Salt Marsh Farmer,* edited by Eric N. Small (Seabrook, N.H.: Historical Society of Seabrook, 1983).

Ira N. Gabrielson, *Wildlife Refuges* (New York: Macmillan, 1943).

Amos Everett Jewett, "Tidal Marshes of Rowley and Vicinity with an Account of the Old-Time Methods of Marshing," *Essex Institute Historical Collections,* 85 (1949): 272–291.

Linda Lear, *Rachel Carson: Witness for Nature* (New York: Holt, 1997).

Benjamin P. Mighill and George B. Blodgette, eds., *The Early Records of the Town of Rowley, Massachusetts, 1639–1672* (Rowley, Mass.: Privately printed, 1894).

Robert E. Moody, ed., *Province and Court Records of Maine, 1680–1692,* volume three (Portland: Maine Historical Society, 1947).

Howard S. Russell, *A Long Deep Furrow: Three Centuries of Farming in New England* (Hanover: University Press of New England, 1976).

Kimberly R. Sebold, "*Low Green Prairies of the Sea:* Economic Usage and Cultural Construction of the Gulf of Maine Salt Marshes," dissertation, University of Maine, 1998.

Nathaniel Southgate Shaler, "Preliminary Report on the Sea-Coast Swamps of the Eastern United States," in *Sixth Annual Report of the U.S. Geological Survey for the Secretary of the Interior, 1884–1885,* edited by John Wesley Powell (Washington, D.C.: Government Printing Office, 1885).

Joseph V. Siry, *Marshes of the Ocean Shore: Development of an Ecological Ethic* (College Station: Texas A&M Press, 1984).

David C. Smith and others, "Salt Marshes as a Factor in the Agriculture of Northeastern North America," *Agricultural History,* 63 (Spring 1989): 270–289.

John and Mildred Teal, *The Life and Death of the Salt Marsh* (Boston: Little, Brown, 1969).

Ralph W. Tiner Jr., *In Search of Swampland: A Wetland Sourcebook and Field Guide* (New Brunswick, N.J.: Rutgers University Press, 1998).

Tiner and others, *Wetlands of the United States: Current Status and Recent Trends* (Washington, D.C.: U.S. Department of the Interior, Fish and Wildlife Service, 1984).

Charles Wendell Townsend, *Sand Dunes and Salt Marshes* (Boston: Estes, 1913).

U.S. Congress, House Committee on Merchant Marine and Fisheries, *Parker River National Wildlife Refuge* (Washington, D.C.: U.S. Government Printing Office, 1946).

Ann Vileisis, *Discovering the Unknown Landscape: A History of America's Wetlands* (Washington, D.C.: Island Press, 1997).

John Greenleaf Whittier, *Snow-Bound: A Winter Idyl* (Boston: Ticknor & Fields, 1865).

Joseph Sutherland Wood, *The New England Village* (Baltimore: Johns Hopkins University Press, 1997).

WATER: COMMODITY

Should water be considered a commodity?

Viewpoint: Urban water supply is an ordinary commodity, but one with important public-good aspects and considerable significance for the debate over privatization.

Viewpoint: Because water is an essential public good of finite quantity, access to it should be on an equitable, rather than commodity, basis so that human and environmental health and functions are maintained.

In classical economic theory, that which is unlimited has no value; components of an ecosystem not put to human use are "non-resources." Water had this status through the late twentieth century. Planners considered the occasional drought to be aberrant and abundance to be normal. The idea that water shortage could be a permanent and limiting condition virtually anywhere in the world began to reach policymakers in the 1980s. Data in the 1900s indicated that thirty-one countries—mostly in the Middle East and Africa—faced water shortage, and that a further seventeen would be added to the list by 2025. Obtaining enough water to sustain life was a problem for millions of people, soon to be billions, to face. As its finite nature was recognized, water moved from a "non-resource" to a "natural resource" with considerable economic value. In 1995 Ismail Serageldin, vice president of the World Bank for Special Programs, declared that water shortages could lead to war. The Global Water Partnership and The World Water Council were formed, which led to the creation of the World Water Commission for the Twenty-first Century to consider management of water resources throughout the world.

A major international debate emerged about whether water was a commodity or a public good. This debate includes a contentious argument about the very nature of economics. While some suggest that current mainstream American economics can, and do, account for "externalities" (such as pollution), others contend that actually there are three distinct economic theoretical perspectives. Patrick Bond, in an article in *Capitalism, Nature, Socialism* #41 (2000), has labeled them orthodox economics, socioecological modernization, and socioenvironmental justice. Orthodox economics is concerned with maximizing gross domestic product and displaces "externalities" (such as pollution) so that the immediate environmental implications are less visible. This approach treats water as an economic good that can be bought and sold with specific pricing mechanisms. Those who can pay the highest cost should have the greatest access—whether the water is wasted, polluted, or otherwise misused.

Socioecological modernization, which underlies the notion of sustainable development, recognizes "externalities" as part of economic activity that should be accounted for in "polluter pays," profit-loss calculations. Regulation or control of environmentally damaging activities is considered to be important because prevention is cheaper than cleanup and restoration. Universal access to water is advocated and positive "multipliers" associated with it are acknowledged: social benefits such as public health, ecological and gender equalization, and economic and geographic social integration.

Socioenvironmental justice economics has a rights-based perspective that poses moral and distributional questions. Water access and pollution are placed within a sociopolitical (and social struggle) context. Whether public or private, water and sanitation are seen as inextricably linked urban services with major public-health, public-order, and equity implications. These services are deeply political, so that the state is always ultimately responsible.

At the turn of the twenty-first century, control of water sources and management of water supplies were seen to be potentially lucrative market opportunities. Privatization programs promoted by international lending agencies guaranteed profits. International corporations experienced with large infrastructure projects such as dams became interested in operating water-supply and management systems. This process was opposed by people around the world who argued that water was a basic human right and that ecosystem function must be preserved. Alternative fora were developed to the World Water Commission, and opposition to the commodification of water became part of the broader antiglobalization struggle.

Viewpoint: Urban water supply is an ordinary commodity, but one with important public-good aspects and considerable significance for the debate over privatization.

In the companion argument to this essay, Gregory Ruiters argues that "water is no ordinary commodity." This notion–that "water is different"–is embedded deeply in the psyche of most water engineers, planners, and managers. After all, the argument goes, water is essential to life. While the same can be said for food, shelter, and clothing, there are few advocates for a "food is different" or "clothing is different" position. Throughout history these essential services have been almost universally commodified and traded in markets, but not water. Over the six millennia separating the development of the first irrigation systems in ancient Babylon from the vast water-supply systems of twenty-first-century megacities, water supply has been the work of government much more often than not. This historical fact seems congruent with our cherished beliefs. Water is, after all, the "enabler and sustainer of civilization." It is said to be the very "source of life" and an "inalienable individual and collective right." One might conclude, therefore, that water is truly "different," and not a market good such as food or shelter. One might also conclude that various modern innovations such as full-cost recovery and privatization are inappropriate or harmful. These conclusions, however, are not correct. They arise from a basic misunderstanding about the subject of the debate. Water supply, especially in the developing world, is distinctly different from the stylized, even mythical, notion of water embodied in the "water is different" arguments.

Urban water supply is an ordinary market good, exhibiting all of the economic characteristics of such a good. The individual and aggregate use of water in an urban area decreases with increasing price, although the price response is relatively small, as expected for a staple commodity (similar to food, housing, and energy). Water use rises with increasing income, also as expected. About the only remarkable economic characteristic is the fact that the provision of urban water is generally a natural monopoly: that is, a single large water-supply agency has inherently lower costs than smaller agencies serving the same area.

This condition, however, is not the expected behavior for something that is essential to life. The observed economic characteristics of urban water supply imply the existence of substitutes and preferences. If water is essential to life, as often stated, there can be no substitutes and, therefore, no preferences. The apparent contradiction is easily resolved. Water is indeed essential to life, but it can be obtained from many sources. Rainfall can be collected in cisterns; wells can be dug or drilled; water can be carried from streams and rivers, contained in food, or purchased from vendors. A water-supply system with either public taps or household connections is but one source, though a particularly desirable one since it requires little time or effort on the part of the user and it has the potential of delivering water that is free of disease-causing organisms. Although users show a strong preference for this system, it is a preference and not a need, so that urban water supply is clearly an economic good.

Individual households prefer urban water-supply systems to other alternatives because they expect to conserve household members' time and effort, to reduce household expenditures, and to avoid disease. Where the alternatives involve carrying water from a distant source, the amount of required time may be substantial, sometimes completely occupying one or more household members. Where water is purchased from vendors, the total cost may range to 40 percent of disposable household income. The cost of water from public systems, by comparison, is

A U.S. water purification facility

often less than 5 percent of household income, even for low-income households in developing countries. Improved health is largely a consequence of better sanitation rather than water quality per se. The availability of adequate quantities of safe water, however, clearly plays a role in reducing morbidity and mortality. All of these factors figure into the household-decision process and contribute to the willingness to pay for urban water supply. If these household effects were the only benefits from public supply, water would be declared a market good and this would be the end of the story–but there is more.

Where an urban water-supply system replaces the carrying of water from distant sources, it does more than simply benefit households. It substantially improves the productivity of the workforce generally, either by adding new members (those formerly occupied with water carrying) or by increasing household production of goods and services (for example, by women and children). This change, which results from the aggregate use of water rather than any individual household use, has the potential to improve income and living standards for the entire community. Benefits accrue to all households, whether or not they have access to the water-supply system. Thus, it is a collective benefit–a public good rather than a market good.

A rather different result may emerge where the former supply was water delivered by vendors. Assuming that there was little household labor involved in the use of water, the main workforce impact will be the reemployment of vendors in new occupations, possibly increasing the production of exportable commodities. A more important result, however, may be the impact of public water supply on low-income households. While all households may realize cost savings from the public system, as compared to vendor costs, these savings will likely be much larger for low-income households. In some cases, discretionary income may be nearly doubled. The overall effect is an improvement in living standards and at least a modest leveling of the distribution of income. As above, this is a collective benefit, a public good.

Finally, even though access to safe water is not the sole determinant of improved health at the household level, it is a matter of some interest at the community level. Even small reductions in the exposure of each household to a communicable disease can have important ramifications for the community. Diseases spread more slowly; fewer people are likely to contract a particular illness; and the general health of the community may increase significantly. Again, this is an aggregate effect, not dependent on any particular household use of water. It is a public good.

The resulting picture of urban water supply is one of a market good with important public-good aspects. Furthermore, the substitutes for public water supply (self-supply, vendors, and so forth) are usually markedly inferior at both the household and community levels. This situation is complicated by the fact that the provision of water supply is almost always a natural monopoly, so that there is no choice among public supply systems, only one between public supply and inferior alternatives. For all of these reasons, societies have generally chosen one of two policies: an urban water supply provided by government or a water supply that is "privatized" (provided by private sector organizations or by public-private combinations of various kinds) and closely regulated by government. In both cases, the active involvement of government is required to protect the public good, and in the latter case to prevent exploitation of monopoly status. This fundamental choice–generally characterized as the "privatization" debate–is the focus of considerable attention in the world. It is also the source of more than a little confusion and misunderstanding.

Much of the rhetoric revolves around the concept of ownership, or property rights. In 1998 an international group of water- and human-rights activists drafted "The Water Manifesto," which states, in part, that no persons "individually or as a group, can be allowed the right to make water private property." While the manifesto takes no position on private-sector involvement in water supply, others have equated privatization of supply with transfer of water ownership. For example, an e-mail message circulated by the Global Resource Action Center for the Environment (GRACE) in March 2000 pleaded with readers to "help stop the global corporate takeover of our common heritage–the very waters of the earth!!!" Without addressing all of the legal or metaphysical implications of this claim, it is sufficient to observe that no such "takeover" has occurred, is threatened, or is even within the realm of possibility. Most legal systems hold that governments manage natural resources, including water, as trustees for the people. Ownership is not the issue. Instead, it is the right to provide water-supply services and to control access to those services.

In most cities throughout the premodern world, residents obtained water in one of two ways: they used their own labor to carry water from a well or stream, or they paid a water vendor to do so. Few would argue that the vendor was not entitled to perform this service, or to be compensated for the time and labor involved. Water vendors still exist in large numbers throughout the developing world, but they have been wholly or partially replaced in most cities by urban water-supply systems. These entities perform the same service as the vendor, but far more effectively and efficiently. In addition, they usually provide treatment services to render the water potable. In most cases, urban water-supply services have been provided by government. The current controversy is whether private firms should have the opportunity to replace governments as the vendors of water.

First of all, it must be noted that there is nothing new or exceptional about this proposal. Private firms have provided water-supply services throughout history and continue to do so. In the United States, about 14 percent of the urban population is served by private water companies, a market share that has remained stable for many decades. This stability has occurred in spite of significant financial discrimination against private utilities in the United States. In 1989 water systems in the United Kingdom were privatized with great fanfare, controversy, and mixed results. The publicity obscured the fact that private-sector water suppliers have existed in England since the nineteenth century (the so-called statutory companies). By the late 1980s there were twenty-nine statutory companies supplying about 22 percent of all piped water in England. Some of the earliest community water systems throughout the world–in places ranging from Jamshedpur, India, to Chicago–were constructed and operated by industrial firms in the interest of the health of their workers. Some of these systems still survive in this form, especially in the developing world. The only possible conclusion one can draw from this history is that private-sector provision of public water is both feasible and sustainable. So the remaining question is whether it is desirable.

The oft-cited concern with a private-sector water supplier is that the firm is driven by profit and thus has no particular incentive to provide for the general welfare of the community, offer universal access, protect low-income users, or minimize the cost of the service to all users. For most commodities delivered by private firms, these problems are not significant. Yet, water supply is characterized by public goods of considerable importance and the private sector supplier is in a position to exploit its monopoly power in various damaging ways. The concerns are real and serious, but they are not unique to water. In our modern, complex world, similar concerns are associated with the provision of electric energy, cooking gas, transportation, and even telecommunications. A reasonable quality of life in an urban environment requires access to all of these items, and their existence provides important benefits to the community as a whole. Further, they are all either natural or potential monopolies, subject to exploitation of monopoly power.

In all of these cases, societies are faced with two choices: either require government to provide the service on terms that are considered socially acceptable, or permit private firms to provide the service subject to government regulation. This regulation is required to protect and enhance the associated public goods, maintain universal access, protect the poor, and minimize exploitation of monopoly power. Assuming that adequate regulation is in place, and that government and private operators have comparable competence, the only remaining basis for choice is relative economic efficiency. Which operator can provide the service at the lowest cost to users? Many have argued for the inherent efficiency of private firms, claiming that the profit motive and fiscal accountability lead to better performance. A closer look reveals, however, that these results depend on the introduction of competition in some form, so that the firm has an incentive to minimize costs as well as maximize profit. Creating a competitive context for operations is a further obligation of government, and there are several ways in which it can be accomplished.

All of these issues seem clear and manageable until the discussion shifts to the developing world. There is considerable and generally well-founded skepticism concerning the ability of governments in medium- and low-income countries to create sufficiently competitive frameworks for private-sector participation in water supply and to provide effective regulation thereafter. Many fear that private operators will not provide universal access, will not offer affordable service to low-income households, will be unconcerned with benefits to society as a whole, and will use their monopoly power to extract excess profits. Critics believe that government will be unwilling or unable to prevent these outcomes. Consider the alternative, however: government provision of water supply. The record of government operation in the developing world is not a good one. Some several billions of people still lack reasonable access to safe water. Even those who are recorded as having access often experience intermittent supply, precluding many of the claimed benefits of public water supply. So-called safe water is often contaminated by the time it reaches the tap. Individual household connections may be limited to upper-income neighborhoods, leaving the poor to share connections or carry water from public taps. Because many systems make little effort to set appropriate tariffs or to collect charges from users, there are no funds to properly operate, maintain, or expand systems, guaranteeing steadily deteriorating service in the future.

After sorting through the rhetoric, the privatization debate can be defined by what it is not about:

> It is not about ownership—there is no question of "owning" the water.
>
> It is not about whether water is or is not a market good—it is clearly a market good.
>
> It is not about whether access to water is essential or important—there are very important public goods associated with universal access to water.
>
> It is not about whether private sector provision of urban water service is feasible or sustainable—there is a long and successful history in industrial countries.

The real debate focuses on developing countries and is concerned with a difficult choice: whether it is better to accept dysfunctional government operation of water-supply systems or to choose more-competent private-sector operation at the probable price of inadequate government regulation. In both cases, individual and social benefits will be sacrificed. One might suggest that countries be helped to improve government operation of these systems. Fifty years of concerted effort in this direction by multilateral and bilateral lending and aid agencies have produced few success stories. Another strategy might be to assist countries in developing effective regulatory institutions, so that private-sector operation can achieve what government could not. This approach gives rise to a fundamental question: is it easier for a typical developing country government to operate a water system effectively and in the public interest, or to regulate a private operator in the public interest? The answer to this question is the solution to the privatization debate—but the answer is still unknown.

—JOHN J. BOLAND, JOHNS HOPKINS UNIVERSITY

Viewpoint: Because water is an essential public good of finite quantity, access to it should be on an equitable, rather than commodity, basis so that human and environmental health and functions are maintained.

Water is part of a nature-society relationship and its production and distribution reveals much about inequality, power, and ethics in a society. More than one billion people (18 percent of the world population) lack potable water; millions die needlessly every year for lack of clean water and, with more urbanization, problems of water pollution and sourcing are increasing. In South Africa water inequality is more extreme than overall inequalities with the poor, who make up 30 percent of the population receiving less than 2 percent of the water of the nation. Widespread punitive water policies in poor towns through disconnecting water of defaulters (including households, bankrupted hospitals, and schools),

BASIC WATER RIGHTS

The following are three of the ten principles established under the "Blue Gold" report, authored by Maude Barlow, Chairman of the International Forum on Globalization (IFG) Committee on the Globalization of Water.

An adequate supply of clean water is a basic human right.

Every person in the world has a right to clean water and healthy sanitation systems no matter where they live. This right is best ensured by keeping water and sewage services in the public sector, regulating the protection of water supplies and promoting the efficient use of water. Adequate supplies of clean water for people in water-scarce regions can only be ensured by promoting conservation and protection of local water resources.

Governments everywhere must implement a "local sources first" policy to protect the basic rights of their citizens to fresh water. Legislation that requires all countries, communities and bioregions to protect local sources of water and seek alternative local sources before looking to other areas will go a long way to halt the environmentally destructive practice of moving water from one watershed basin to another. "Local sources first" must be accompanied by a principle of "local people and farmers first." Local citizens and communities have first rights to local water. Agribusiness and industry, particularly large transnational corporations, must fit into a "local-first" policy or be shut down.

This does not mean that water should be "free" or that everyone can help themselves. However, a policy of water pricing that respects this principle would help conserve water and preserve the rights of all to have access to it. Water pricing and "green taxes" (which raise government revenues while discouraging pollution and resource consumption) should place a heavier burden on agribusiness and industry than on citizens; funds collected from these sources should be used to provide basic water for all.

The best advocates for water are local communities and citizens.

Local stewardship, not private business, expensive technology, or even government, is the best protector of water security. Only local citizens can understand the overall cumulative effect of privatization, pollution and water removal and diversion on the local community. Only local citizens know the effect of job loss or loss of local farms when water sources are taken over by big business or diverted to faraway uses. It must be understood that local citizens and communities are the front-line "keepers" of the rivers, lakes and underground water systems upon which their lives and livelihoods rest.

In order to be affordable, sustainable and equitable, the solutions to water stress and water scarcity must be locally inspired and community-based. Reclamation projects that work are often inspired by environmental organizations and involve all levels of government and sometimes private donations. But if they are not guided by the common sense and lived experience of the local community, they will not be sustained.

In water-scarce regions, traditional local indigenous technologies, such as local water sharing and rain catchment systems that had been abandoned for new technology, are being revisited with some urgency. In some areas, local people have assumed complete responsibility for water distribution facilities and established funds to which water users must contribute. The funds are used to provide water to all in the community.

The public must participate as an equal partner with government to protect water.

A fundamental principle for a water-secure future is that the public must be consulted and engaged as an equal partner with governments in establishing water policy. For too long, governments and international economic institutions such as the World Bank, the OECD and trade bureaucrats have been driven by corporate interests. Even in the rare instances that they are given a seat at the table, non-governmental organizations (NGOs) and environmental groups are typically ignored. Corporations who heavily fund political campaigns are often given sweetheart contracts for water resources. Sometimes, corporate lobby groups actually draft the wording of agreements and treaties that governments then adopt. This practice has created a crisis of legitimacy for governments everywhere.

Processes must be created whereby citizens, workers and environmental representatives are treated as equal partners in the determination of water policy and recognized as the true inheritors and guardians of the above principles.

Source: *"Blue Gold," African Water Page, Internet website.*

along with a cholera epidemic in Kwa-Zulu-Natal, have not only focused the public mind but also led to a swelling political disaffection from the ruling African National Congress (ANC) government. Potable water is no ordinary commodity.

Water conflicts also arise in countries such as Great Britain and France where privatization has led to high prices, poor regulation, profiteering, and scams as extremely powerful transnational utility companies increase their grip on water–even if in absolute terms urban crises are incomparably worse in the Third World. Water poverty, debt, disconnections, and rising social exclusions are national issues in the United Kingdom. Since water systems in the biggest cities in the world are now largely privatized and run by foreign companies, this situation also raises the question of the strategic, national-developmental role of water and sanitation. Internationalization has added a new dimension to the politics of water protests and riots, more common in the Third World.

Should water be regarded as an ordinary commodity for "consumers" or a public service for citizens? In the current water debate, the World Bank and United Nations have set the tone. As part of wider market-driven development orthodoxy and concerns with sustainable development and poverty reduction, it is argued that only by regarding water as a commodity like any other will the true value of water be appreciated. This standard must be applied to the poor as well. The U.N. Panel on Water declared in 1998 that "water should be paid for as a commodity rather than be treated as an essential staple to be provided free of cost." This sentiment was recently echoed by the World Bank, as expressed at the World Water Forum (2000). Water as a product is among the most capital-intensive products, needing large outlays of fixed capital (dams, pipelines, pumps, and distribution networks). Under the sway of the credit system, large loans have to be secured and substantial outlays reserved for maintenance work. Water may fall from the sky, but it circulates both in a subterranean world of pipes and in the world of high finance. As the mayor of a small South African town–where water and sanitation is privatized and hospitals and schools had services cut for several months–put it: "the question of whether access to municipal services was a birthright did not warrant debate as they are commodities like any other merchandise paid for in shops." For the poor the use of prepaid systems has become the norm. For the procommodity view, this system is the final solution to nonpayment of utility bills, as well as the administrative and political burdens of providing services to the poor. Prepaid meters not only discipline consumption, but may also depoliticize service provision through, for example, self-disconnection. The burden is thus squarely thrown onto the "consumer," even if it results in a public health or family crisis. The effects of prepayment on poor women, who by and large have to manage household budgets, and on the family life are not hard to imagine.

Government and political distortions are seen as great obstacles in sound water management with large-scale wastage, an historical emphasis on supply-side solution (more dams, for example), a record of poor investment, and underpriced water supplies. As the new World Commission on Water for the Twenty-First Century argued, "governments should keep out of the water 'business,' except as regulators . . . the private sector should lead." This view reflects a scholarly consensus that "water is no different from any other economic good and obey(s) the normal laws of economics," and the best way to manage water is through the private sector, which has an immediate incentive to reduce water losses.

The above views dovetail with an environmental outlook called eco-modernization, which rejects unqualified economic growth, and puts forward the notion of "development" that should be "sustainable." These are two positive-sounding ideas that both meet objections to blind adherence to growth and are sensitive to the future costs that may be incurred. To be sustainable, industries want input costs such as water to be kept as low as possible. It is argued that tariff increases can reduce water use and help save on costly future capital expenditures (dams and pipelines accessing more-distant supplies). Hence, one meaning of sustainable development is sustainable capital accumulation. Eco-modernization promotes increasing block tariffs, and that tariffs should reflect scarcity value of water.

The needs of the vulnerable and poor (sometimes called the brown agenda) inform a variant of eco-modernization–"socio-eco-modernization." The poor should get a free basic lifeline supply of essential urban services. This approach stresses socioenvironmental sustainability but insists on the idea that in the distribution of essential life-blood products there ought to be social justice. It accepts that public goods are exceptional in market economies: even a smooth market system may fail to invest in certain services. Moreover, it argued that services such as water are best provided through single shared networks to reduce costs. Using tools of cost-benefit analysis, it may be shown mathematically that it is better for society as a whole to provide services as universal entitlements rather than risk epidemics, contamination, interruptions, riots by the marginalized populace, and low productivity. Society should consider positive "multipliers" associated with universal access to water, which translates into many social benefits (public health, ecological, gender equalization, economic, and geographical social integration). Whether public or private, water and sanitation are seen as inextricably linked urban services that have major public health, public order, and equity implications and are deeply political so that the state is always ultimately responsible. Water has had a "civilizational" and democratizing role, for tap water and flush toilets inside homes have long been regarded as essential preconditions for modern, advanced society and effective citizenship. The rationales for a public-goods approach are thus: market failures, natural monopolies, and "neighborhood effects."

Socioecological modernizationists insist that social questions need to be foregrounded. State regulation, a degree of consumption subsidies, and even outright controls on socially and environmentally damaging activity are appropriate within this school of thought. Privatization of nonpublic goods sectors (state-owned steel or oil) is acceptable, but a greater role is accorded the state in providing elementary public services (water, electricity, and garbage collection) and securing citizens' basic socioeconomic rights. This rights-based discourse, included in the South African Bill of Rights in 1996, insists that: "everyone has the right to an environment that is not harmful to their health or well-being . . . everyone has the right to have access to health-care services, including reproductive health care; sufficient food and water; and social security." As the new Minister of Water in South Africa put it, "The Hague vision confused the way we value water as a resource with the way we charge for services. We took a different approach (to the World Bank's "vision") suggesting that we need to manage water in a way that reflects its economic, social and cultural values for all its uses . . . providing access to basic clean water supply is a direct attack on poverty. We must achieve a balance between private and public interests." As the new South African government noted shortly after coming to power, "The history of water in South Africa cannot be separated from the history of the country as a whole and all of the many factors which went to create both one of the darkest and one of the most triumphal chapters of human experience. The history of water is a mirror of the history of housing, migration, land, social engineering and development."

The final approach, socialist ecology, asks much deeper questions, not only about water inequalities and poverty, but in the first instance about the production of water needs and the relationship between need and scarcity. Historically the basic condition for the commodification of water is the separation of the mass of the population from ownership of the means of production–including land and the "free gifts of nature" such as water. In Africa this dispossession was accompanied by centuries of forced labor, forced urbanization, and military conquest, which produced a ravaged landscape with old economies laid waste. Foreign companies wrought ecologically destructive waterscapes as supports for rapid exploitation. As the uneven geography of water development after World War II shows, most major dams, hydroelectric-, irrigation-, and water-supply systems in Africa–often sponsored by the World Bank–served the needs of large foreign-controlled mining companies and local white elites while massively undermining indigenous interests or inadequately meeting their needs.

A second question asked by the deeper approach is that even if one accepts "public goods" notions as progressive, one still needs to know what is the rational basis of cost-benefit calculations (as in the public-goods approach)? The difficulties of economic or monetary and cost-benefit valuations of water, development, and human life itself are legion. Water and sanitation are complex urban services with multiple uses–not disembodied, individual economic units. Focusing on water supply alone may actually worsen sanitation and water-disposal problems. Putting a money valuation on water supply implies an atomistic procedure of removing it from its organic relationships with other aspects of the urban system as a whole. As David Harvey, in *Justice, Nature, and the Geography of Difference* (1996), notes, "To speak in money terms is always to speak in a language which the holders of social power appreciate and understand." Over time and space, money, however, is itself highly unstable as a measure. Are we to measure the value of sustainable water use in dollars, pesos, pulas, or rands? Currencies are only as credible as the power and state that back it. The intense volatility in currency values, interest rates, market prices of fixed assets, and the evidence of periodic crashes in property values make even monetary valuations arbitrary.

Finally, a dual system of basic lifeline supplies for the poor and private water for others is a far cry from universal standards of services and will reinscribe a differentiated social landscape, a kind of neo-apartheid in South Africa. Given the weak capacity of the municipal and legal systems, rapid municipal privatization of water and sanitation could result in the South African landscape becoming a patchwork of different water and sanitation contracts with different firms operating without close scrutiny. This possibility is a dangerous path. Since water privatization has become a global trade and investment issue, the water question in contemporary times raises the wider issue of how to confront global power of money to create and destroy urban place and community. Water provision should not only be decommodified and access assured to vulnerable populations, but the question of the scale of its production and the hedonistic uses of water by a tiny proportion of humanity is also a pressing concern.

–GREGORY RUITERS, UNIVERSITY OF WITWATERSRAND

References

Duane D. Buaman, John J. Boland, and W. Michael Hanemann, *Urban Water Demand Management and Planning* (New York: McGraw-Hill, 1998).

Janice A. Beecher, "Privatization, Monopoly, and Structured Competition in the Water Industry: Is There a Role for Regulation?" *Water Resources Update,* 117 (October 2000): 13–20.

Patrick Bond, "Economic Growth, Ecological Modernization or Environmental Justice?" *Capitalism, Nature, Socialism,* 11 (2000): 33–62.

John Ernst, *Whose Utility?: The Social Impact of Public Utility Privatization and Regulation in Britain* (Buckingham, U.K. & Philadelphia: Open University Press, 1994).

B. Delworth Gardner, "The Efficiency of For-Profit Water Companies versus Public Companies," *Water Resources Update,* 117 (October 2000): 34–39.

David Harvey, *Justice, Nature, and the Geography of Difference* (Cambridge, Mass.: Blackwell, 1996).

Meg Huby and Karen Anthony, "Regional Inequalities in Paying for Water," *Policy Studies,* 18 (1997): 207–217.

Republic of South Africa, *The Constitution of the Republic of South Africa, 1996* (Cape Town, South Africa: The Assembly, 1996).

Paul Seidenstat, "Emerging Competition in Water and Wastewater Industries," *Water Resources Update,* 117 (October 2000): 6–12.

"The Water Manifesto," Committee for the World Water Contract, 1998, Internet website.

APPENDIX

EDITOR'S NOTE:

One of the innovative elements of this volume in the *History in Dispute* series is the inclusion of a set of significant primary documents. In *Arizona* v. *California* (2000), the U.S. Supreme Court weighed in on the long-running battle over rights to the waters of the Colorado River. Although struggles over allocation of the Colorado River's flow date to the 1920s, the first iteration of this particular suit was argued in 1952, as California, Arizona, New Mexico, Nevada, Utah, and five Native American reservations battled over their proportional access to "white gold." The latest suit revolved around the claims of the Quechen tribe for increased water rights based on disputed reservation boundary lands not earlier attributed to tribal ownership. What makes this issue of continuing importance is the crucial role of water in determining life in this arid portion of the country.

The Clean Water Act of 1972 is of similar importance. Indeed, it is a landmark piece of legislation, the goal of which was to "restore and maintain the chemical, biological and physical integrity of the nation's waters." Earlier measures had had the same aspirations, but only this Act, later reinforced in 1977, had what historian John Opie has called "technology forcing" power. Its stipulations that industry reduce its use of water, minimize its discharge of wastes, and recycle, recover, and reuse materials in its production processes, stimulated the creation of new technologies and engineering that aided in the reclamation of badly polluted waterways and groundwater sources.

Global concern for enhanced water quality is also evident in the 1976 Convention for the Protection of the Mediterranean Sea, known as the Barcelona Agreement. Its signatories recognized the special situation of the Mediterranean—this basin, and its many seas and gulfs, then contained some of the most heavily polluted waters in the world. They resolved to prevent and abate effluent flowing into the sea from land-based sources, ship and air transport, and other means; the broader goal was to minimize the threats posed to the "economic, social, health and cultural value" of this unique marine environment.

Two years later, another devastated marine environment received a reprieve. In addition to affirming Canada's and the United States' commitment to cleaning up the Great Lakes, the Great Lakes Water Quality Agreement of 1978 marked an evolution in their resource managers' understanding of the pollution problem they faced. Where the original 1972 document focused on phosphorus reduction, the 1978 Agreement addressed the problem of persistent toxic chemicals and committed the two countries finally to restoring the "chemical, physical and biological integrity" of the Great Lakes.

Water storage, like water quality, has been a central issue in the post–World War II era. Marking a critical rethinking of the use of dams and reservoirs to capture water is the Report of the World Commission on Dams published in late 2000. In contrast to earlier assumptions that the control of rivers through dams was the best, most economical, least disruptive way to secure needed water supplies, the report argues that the environmental and social costs of dam construction almost invariably outweigh the presumed benefits. This document also offers a precise and new set of values by which to determine the goals of future development of water resources.

One of those values—equity—is central to the final document, the Water Manifesto. This citizen initiative is framed by a deepening concern over the impact of rapid population growth and shrinking water supplies. Its authors, who come from around the globe, believe that water is an "inalienable individual and collective right," and thus not a commodity to be sold to the highest bidder. To ensure that all people have a guaranteed right of access to water, they propose the creation of a "World Water Contract" that would include the establishment of a local, national, and international "Parliaments for Water" and an oversight organization, a World Observatory for Water Rights; these and other measures will help advance their conviction that water is "the patrimony" of all humanity.

DOCUMENT 1

ARIZONA V. CALIFORNIA

120 S.Ct. 2304
Supreme Court of the United States
State of ARIZONA, Complainant, v. State of CALIFORNIA, et al.

No. 8 Orig.
Argued April 25, 2000.
Decided June 19, 2000.

State of Arizona brought original action against State of California to determine States' and other parties' rights to waters of Colorado River. United States intervened, seeking water rights on behalf of five Indian reservations. Following determination that United States had reserved water rights for such reservations, 373 U.S. 546, 83 S.Ct. 1468, 10 L.Ed.2d 542, grant of tribes' motions to intervene, 460 U.S. 605, 103 S.Ct. 1382, 75 L.Ed.2d 318, and grant of States' motion to reopen decree, the Supreme Court, Justice Ginsburg, held that: (1) claims of Quechan Tribe for increased rights to water for disputed boundary lands of Fort Yuma Reservation were not precluded by Supreme Court decision finding, inter alia, that United States had reserved water rights for reservations; (2) such claims were not precluded by consent judgment entered in prior Court of Claims proceeding in which Tribe had challenged 1893 Agreement providing for Tribe's cession of such disputed lands; and (3) settlements of claim for additional water for Fort Mojave Reservation and Colorado River Indian Reservation would be approved.

Order accordingly.

Chief Justice Rehnquist concurred in part, dissented in part, and filed opinion in which Justices O'Connor and Thomas joined.

West Headnotes

[1] Judgment

Secretarial Order issued by Department of Interior recognizing Quechan Tribe's beneficial ownership of disputed boundary lands of Fort Yuma Reservation, issued after Department had previously taken the opposite position and after Supreme Court had issued decision determining water rights of States of Arizona and California, United States, and various Indian Tribes, was not "later and then unknown circumstance" that would prevent Tribe's claims for increased water rights from Colorado River from being precluded by such Supreme Court decision, assuming that preclusion principles were otherwise applicable, inasmuch as order did not change underlying facts in dispute, but simply embodied one party's changed view of import of unchanged facts, and Tribe could not have been surprised by Government's shift, given that Tribe had been advocating just such a shift for decades.

[2] Judgment

Claims of Quechan Tribe for increased rights to water from Colorado River for disputed boundary lands of Fort Yuma Reservation were not precluded by 1963 Supreme Court decision determining water rights of States of Arizona and California, United States, and various Indian Tribes, inasmuch as States could have raised preclusion argument in 1979 or 1982, but did not do so until 1989, and supplemental decrees issued in 1979 and 1984 anticipated that disputed boundary issues would be decided not by preclusion but on merits.

[3] Judgment

While the technical rules of preclusion are not strictly applicable in the context of a single ongoing original action, the principles upon which these rules are founded should inform the Supreme Court's decision with respect to a preclusion claim.

[4] Judgment

The principles upon which the technical rules of preclusion are founded rank res judicata an affirmative defense ordinarily lost if not timely raised. Fed.Rules Civ.Proc.Rule 8(c), 28 U.S.C.A.

[5] Judgment

Under preclusion principles, a party may not wake up because a "light finally dawned," years after the first opportunity to raise a defense, and effectively raise it so long as the party was, though no fault of anyone else, in the dark until its late awakening.

[6] Judgment

Supreme Court would not raise sua sponte issue whether claims of Quechan Tribe for increased rights to water from Colorado River for disputed boundary lands of Fort Yuma Reservation were precluded by earlier Supreme Court decision determining water rights of

States of Arizona and California, United States, and various Indian Tribes, inasmuch as Supreme Court plainly had not previously decided the issue presented.

[7] Judgment
If a court is on notice that it has previously decided the issue presented, the court may dismiss the action sua sponte, even though the defense has not been raised; this result is fully consistent with the policies underlying res judicata, in that it is not based solely on the defendant's interest in avoiding the burdens of twice defending a suit, but is also based on the avoidance of unnecessary judicial waste.

[8] Judgment
Where no judicial resources have been spent on the resolution of a question, trial courts must be cautious about raising a preclusion bar sua sponte, thereby eroding the principle of party presentation so basic to our system of adjudication.

[9] Judgment
Claims of Quechan Tribe for increased rights to water from Colorado River for disputed boundary lands of Fort Yuma Reservation were not precluded by consent judgment entered in prior Court of Claims proceeding in which Tribe had challenged 1893 Agreement providing for Tribe's cession of such disputed lands, inasmuch as consent judgment was ambiguous as between mutually exclusive theories of recovery, i.e., taking and trespass, and settlement thus did not necessarily relinquish Tribe's claim to title. U.S.C.A. Const.Amend. 5.

[10] Compromise and Settlement
Settlements ordinarily occasion no issue preclusion, sometimes called collateral estoppel, unless it is clear that the parties intend their agreement to have such an effect.

[11] Judgment
In most circumstances, it is recognized that consent agreements ordinarily are intended to preclude any further litigation on the claim presented but are not intended to preclude further litigation on any of the issues presented; thus consent judgments ordinarily support claim preclusion but not issue preclusion.

[12] Judgment
Generally, issue preclusion attaches only when an issue of fact or law is actually litigated and determined by a valid and final judgment, and the determination is essential to the judgment. Restatement (Second) of Judgments section 27.

[13] Judgment
In the case of a judgment entered by confession, consent, or default, none of the issues is actually litigated, and therefore, the principle of issue preclusion does not apply with respect to any issue in a subsequent action. Restatement (Second) of Judgments section 27.

[14] Compromise and Settlement
Settlement of claim for additional water from Colorado River for Fort Mojave Reservation, arising out of dispute over accuracy of survey, which, inter alia, specified location of disputed boundary and precluded United States and Tribe from claiming additional water rights from River for lands that were subject of disputed survey, would be approved.

[15] Compromise and Settlement
Settlement of claim for additional water from Colorado River for Colorado River Indian Reservation, stemming principally from dispute over location of Reservation's boundary, and providing, inter alia, for award of additional water to Tribe and preclusion of United States or Tribe from seeking additional reserved water rights from River for lands in California, would be approved.

2306 Syllabus [FN]
FN* The syllabus constitutes no part of the opinion of the Court but has been prepared by the Reporter of Decisions for the convenience of the reader. See United States v. Detroit Timber & Lumber Co., 200 U.S. 321, 337, 26 S.Ct. 282, 50 L.Ed. 499.

This litigation began in 1952 when Arizona invoked this Court's original jurisdiction to settle a dispute with California over the extent of each State's right to use water from the Colorado River system. The United States intervened, seeking water rights on behalf of, among others, five Indian reservations, including the Fort Yuma (Quechan) Indian Reservation, the Colorado River Indian Reservation, and the Fort Mojave Indian Reservation. The first round of the litigation culminated in Arizona v. California, 373 U.S. 546, 83 S.Ct. 1468, 10 L.Ed.2d 542 (Arizona I), in which the Court held that the United States had reserved water rights for the five reservations, id., at 565, 599601, 83 S.Ct. 1468; that those rights must be considered present perfected rights and given priority because they were effective as of the time each reservation was created, id., at 600, 83 S.Ct. 1468; and that those rights should be based on the amount of each reservation's practicably irrigable acreage as determined by the Special Master, ibid. In its 1964 decree, the Court specified the quantities and priorities of the water entitlements for the parties and the Tribes, Arizona v. California, 376 U.S. 340, 84 S.Ct. 755, 11 L.Ed.2d 757, but held that the water rights for the Fort Mojave and Colorado River Reservations would be subject to appropriate adjustment by future agreement or decree in the event the *2307 respective reservations' disputed boundaries were finally determined, id., at 345, 84 S.Ct. 755. The Court's 1979 supplemental decree again deferred resolution of reservation boundary disputes and allied water rights claims. Arizona v. California, 439 U.S. 419, 421, 99 S.Ct. 995, 58 L.Ed.2d 627 (per curiam). In Arizona v. California, 460 U.S. 605, 103 S.Ct. 1382, 75 L.Ed.2d 318 (Arizona II), the Court concluded, among other things, that various administrative actions taken by the Secretary of the Interior, including his 1978 order recognizing the entitlement of the Quechan Tribe (Tribe) to the disputed boundary lands of the Fort Yuma Reservation did not constitute final determinations of reservation boundaries for purposes of the 1964 decree. Id., at 636638, 103 S.Ct. 1382. The Court also held in Arizona II that certain lands within undisputed reservation boundaries, for which the United States had not sought water rights in Arizona Ithe socalled "omitted lands"were not entitled to water under res judicata principles. Id., at 626, 103 S.Ct. 1382. The Court's 1984 supplemental decree again declared that water rights for all five reservations would be subject to appropriate adjustments if the reservations' boundaries were finally determined. Arizona v. California, 466 U.S. 144, 145, 104 S.Ct. 1900, 80 L.Ed.2d 194. In 1987, the Ninth Circuit dismissed, on grounds of the United States' sovereign immunity, a suit by California state agencies that could have finally determined the reservations' boundaries. This Court affirmed the Ninth Circuit's judgment by an equally divided vote.

The present phase of the litigation concerns claims by the Tribe and the United States on the Tribe's behalf for increased water rights for the Fort Yuma Reservation. These claims rest on the contention that the Fort Yuma Reservation encompasses some 25,000 acres of disputed boundary lands not attributed to that reservation in earlier stages of the litigation. The land in question was purportedly ceded to the United States under an 1893 Agreement with the Tribe. In 1936, the Department of the Interior's Solicitor Margold issued an opinion stating that, under the 1893 Agreement, the Tribe had unconditionally ceded the lands. The Margold Opinion remained the Federal Government's position for 42 years. In 1946, Congress enacted the Indian Claims Commission Act, establishing a tribunal with power to decide tribes' claims against the Government. The Tribe brought before the Commission an action, which has come to be known as Docket No. 320, challenging the 1893 Agreement on two mutually exclusive grounds: (1) that it was void, in which case the United States owed the Tribe damages essentially for trespass, and (2) that it constituted an uncompensated taking of tribal lands. In 1976, the Commission transferred Docket No. 320 to the Court of Claims. In the meantime, the Tribe asked the Interior Department to reconsider the Margold Opinion. Ultimately, in a 1978 Secretarial Order, the Department changed its position and confirmed the Tribe's entitlement to most of the disputed lands. A few months after this Court decided in Arizona II that the 1978 Secretarial Order did not constitute a final determination of reservation boundaries, the United States and the Tribe entered into a settlement of Docket No. 320, which the Court of Claims approved and entered as its final judgment. Under the settlement, the United States agreed to pay the Tribe $15 million in full satisfaction of the Tribe's Docket No. 320 claims, and the Tribe agreed that it would not further assert those claims against the Government. In 1989, this Court granted the motion of Arizona, California, and two municipal water districts (State parties) to reopen the 1964 decree to determine whether the Fort Yuma, Colorado River, and Fort Mojave Reservations were entitled to claim additional boundary lands and, if so, additional water rights. The State parties assert here that the Fort Yuma claims of the Tribe and the United States are precluded by Arizona I and by the Claims Court consent judgment in *2308 Docket No. 320. The Special Master has prepared a report recommending that the Court reject the first ground for preclusion but accept the second. The State parties have filed exceptions to the Special Master's first recommendation, and the United States and the Tribe have filed exceptions to the second. The Master has also recommended approval of the parties' proposed settlements of claims for additional water for the Fort Mojave and Colorado River Reservations, and has submitted a proposed supplemental decree to effectuate the parties' accords.

Held:

1. In view of the State parties' failure to raise the preclusion argument earlier in the litigation, despite ample opportunity and cause to do so, the claims of the United States and the Tribe to increased water rights for the disputed boundary lands of the Fort Yuma Reservation are not foreclosed by Arizona I. According to the State parties, those claims are precluded by the finality rationale this Court employed in dismissing the "omitted lands" claims in Arizona II, 460 U.S., at 620621, 626627, 103 S.Ct. 1382, because the United States could have raised the Fort Yuma Reservation boundary lands claims in Arizona I, but deliberately decided not to do so. In rejecting this argument, the Special Master pointed out that the Government did not assert such claims in Arizona I because, at

that time, it was bound to follow the Margold Opinion, under which the Tribe had no claim to the boundary lands. The Master concluded that the 1978 Secretarial Order, which overruled the Margold Opinion and recognized the Tribe's beneficial ownership of the boundary lands, was a circumstance not known in 1964, one that warranted an exception to the application of res judicata doctrine. In so concluding, the Special Master relied on an improper ground: The 1978 Secretarial Order does not qualify as a previously unknown circumstance that can overcome otherwise applicable preclusion principles. That order did not change the underlying facts in dispute; it simply embodied one party's changed view of the import of unchanged facts. However, the Court agrees with the United States and the Tribe that the State parties' preclusion defense is inadmissible. The State parties did not raise the defense in 1978 in response to the United States' motion for a supplemental decree granting additional water rights for the Fort Yuma Reservation or in 1982 when Arizona II was briefed and argued. Unaccountably, the State parties first raised their res judicata plea in 1989, when they initiated the current round of proceedings. While preclusion rules are not strictly applicable in the context of a single ongoing original action, the principles upon which they rest should inform the Court's decision. Arizona II, 460 U.S., at 619, 103 S.Ct. 1382. Those principles rank res judicata an affirmative defense ordinarily lost if not timely raised. See Fed. Rule Civ. Proc. 8(c). The Court disapproves the notion that a party may wake up and effectively raise a defense years after the first opportunity to raise it so long as the party was (though no fault of anyone else) in the dark until its late awakening. Nothing in Arizona II supports the State parties' assertion that the Court expressly recognized the possibility that future Fort Yuma boundary lands claims might be precluded. 460 U.S., at 638, 103 S.Ct. 1382, distinguished. Of large significance, this Court's 1979 and 1984 supplemental decrees anticipated that the disputed boundary issues for all five reservations, including Fort Yuma, would be "finally determined" in some forum, not by preclusion but on the merits. The State parties themselves stipulated to the terms of the 1979 supplemental decree and appear to have litigated the Arizona II proceedings on the understanding that the boundary disputes should be resolved on the merits, see, e.g., 460 U.S., at 634, 103 S.Ct. 1382. Finally, the Court rejects the State parties' argument that this Court should now raise the preclusion question sua sponte. The special circumstances in *2309 which such judicial initiative might be appropriate are not present here. See United States v. Sioux Nation, 448 U.S. 371, 432, 100 S.Ct. 2716, 65 L.Ed.2d 844 (REHNQUIST, J., dissenting). Pp. 2314–2318.

2. The claims of the United States and the Tribe to increased water rights for the disputed boundary lands of the Fort Yuma Reservation are not precluded by the consent judgment in Docket No. 320. The Special Master agreed with the State parties' assertion to the contrary. He concluded that, because the settlement extinguished the Tribe's claim to title in the disputed lands, the United States and the Tribe cannot seek additional water rights based on the Tribe's purported beneficial ownership of those lands. Under standard preclusion doctrine, the Master's recommendation cannot be sustained. As between the Tribe and the United States, the settlement indeed had, and was intended to have, claim preclusive effect. But settlements ordinarily lack issue preclusive effect. This differentiation is grounded in basic res judicata doctrine. The general rule is that issue preclusion attaches only when an issue is actually litigated and determined by a valid and final judgment. See United States v. International Building Co., 345 U.S. 502, 505506, 73 S.Ct. 807, 97 L.Ed. 1182. The State parties assert that common law principles of issue preclusion do not apply in the special context of Indian land claims. They maintain that the Indian Claims Commission Act created a special regime of statutory preclusion. This Court need not decide whether some consent judgments in that distinctive context might bar a tribe from asserting title even in discrete litigation against third parties, for the 1983 settlement of Docket No. 320 plainly could not qualify as such a judgment. Not only was the issue of ownership of the disputed boundary lands not actually litigated and decided in Docket No. 320, but, most notably, the Tribe proceeded on alternative and mutually exclusive theories of recovery, taking and trespass. The consent judgment embraced all of the Tribe's claims with no election by the Tribe of one theory over the other. The Court need not accept the United States' invitation to look behind the consent judgment at presettlement stipulations and memoranda purportedly demonstrating that the judgment was grounded on the parties' shared view, after the 1978 Secretarial Order, that the disputed lands belong to the Tribe. Because the settlement

was ambiguous as between mutually exclusive theories of recovery, the consent judgment is too opaque to serve as a foundation for issue preclusion. Pp. 2318–2320.

3. The Court accepts the Special Master's recommendations and approves the parties' proposed settlements of the disputes respecting additional water for the Fort Mojave and Colorado River Reservations. Pp. 2320–2321.

Exception of State parties overruled; Exceptions of United States and Quechan Tribe sustained; Special Master's recommendations to approve parties' proposed settlements respecting Fort Mojave and Colorado River Reservations are adopted, and parties are directed to submit any objections they may have to Special Master's proposed supplemental decree; Outstanding water rights claims associated with disputed Fort Yuma Reservation boundary lands remanded.

GINSBURG, J., delivered the opinion of the Court, in which STEVENS, SCALIA, KENNEDY, SOUTER, and BREYER, J.J., joined. REHNQUIST, C.J., filed an opinion concurring in part and dissenting in part, in which O'CONNOR and THOMAS, J.J., joined.

Jeffrey P. Minear, Washington, DC, for United States.

Mason D. Morisset, Seattle, WA, for Quechan Indian Tribe.

Jerome C. Muys, Washington, DC, for State parties.

*2310 Justice GINSBURG delivered the opinion of the Court.

In the latest chapter of this longlitigated original jurisdiction case, the Quechan Tribe (Tribe) and the United States on the Tribe's behalf assert claims for increased rights to water from the Colorado River. These claims are based on the contention that the Fort Yuma (Quechan) Indian Reservation encompasses some 25,000 acres of disputed boundary lands not attributed to that reservation in earlier stages of the litigation. In this decision, we resolve a threshold question regarding these claims to additional water rights: Are the claims precluded by this Court's prior decision in Arizona v. California, 373 U.S. 546, 83 S.Ct. 1468, 10 L.Ed.2d 542 (1963) (Arizona I), or by a consent judgment entered by the United States Claims Court in 1983? The Special Master has prepared a report recommending that the Court reject the first ground for preclusion but accept the second. We reject both grounds for preclusion and remand the case to the Special Master for consideration of the claims for additional water rights appurtenant to the disputed boundary lands.

I

This litigation began in 1952 when Arizona invoked our original jurisdiction to settle a dispute with California over the extent of each State's right to use water from the Colorado River system. Nevada intervened, seeking a determination of its water rights, and Utah and New Mexico were joined as defendants. The United States intervened and sought water rights on behalf of various federal establishments, including five Indian reservations: the Chemehuevi Indian Reservation, the Cocopah Indian Reservation, the Fort Yuma (Quechan) Indian Reservation, the Colorado River Indian Reservation, and the Fort Mojave Indian Reservation. The Court appointed Simon Rifkind as Special Master.

The first round of the litigation culminated in our opinion in Arizona I. We agreed with Special Master Rifkind that the apportionment of Colorado River water was governed by the Boulder Canyon Project Act of 1928, 43 U.S.C. section 617 et seq., and by contracts entered into by the Secretary of the Interior pursuant to the Act. We further agreed that the United States had reserved water rights for the five reservations under the doctrine of Winters v. United States, 207 U.S. 564, 28 S.Ct. 207, 52 L.Ed. 340 (1908). See Arizona I, 373 U.S., at 565, 599601, 83 S.Ct. 1468. Because the Tribes' water rights were effective as of the time each reservation was created, the rights were considered present perfected rights and given priority under the Act. Id., at 600, 83 S.Ct. 1468. We also agreed with the Master that the reservations' water rights should be based on the amount of practicably irrigable acreage on each reservation and sustained his findings as to the relevant acreage for each reservation. Ibid. Those findings were incorporated in our decree of March 9, 1964, which specified the quantities and priorities of the water entitlements for the States, the United States, and the Tribes. Arizona v. California, 376 U.S. 340, 84 S.Ct. 755, 11 L.Ed.2d 757. The Court rejected as premature, however, Master Rifkind's recommendation to determine the disputed boundaries of the Fort Mojave and Colorado River Indian Reservations; we ordered, instead, that water rights for those two reservations "shall be subject to appropriate adjustment by agreement or decree of this Court in the event that the boundaries of the respective reservations are finally determined." Id., at 345, 84 S.Ct. 755.

In 1978, the United States and the State parties jointly moved this Court to enter a supplemental decree identifying present perfected rights to the use of mainstream water in each

State and their priority dates. The Tribes then filed motions to intervene, and the United States ultimately joined the Tribes in moving for additional water rights for the five reservations. *2311 Again, the Court deferred resolution of reservation boundary disputes and allied water rights claims. The supplemental decree we entered in 1979 set out the water rights and priority dates for the five reservations under the 1964 decree, but added that the rights for all five reservations (including the Fort Yuma Indian Reservation at issue here) "shall continue to be subject to appropriate adjustment by agreement or decree of this Court in the event that the boundaries of the respective reservations are finally determined." Arizona v. California, 439 U.S. 419, 421, 99 S.Ct. 995, 58 L.Ed.2d 627 (per curiam). The Court then appointed Senior Circuit Judge Elbert P. Tuttle as Special Master and referred to him the Tribes' motions to intervene and other pending matters.

Master Tuttle issued a report recommending that the Tribes be permitted to intervene, and concluding that various administrative actions taken by the Secretary of the Interior constituted "final determinations" of reservation boundaries for purposes of allocating water rights under the 1964 decree. (Those administrative actions included a 1978 Secretarial Order, discussed in greater detail infra, at 2313–2314, which recognized the Quechan Tribe's entitlement to the disputed boundary lands of the Fort Yuma Reservation.) Master Tuttle also concluded that certain lands within the undisputed reservation boundaries but for which the United States had not sought water rights in Arizona Ithe socalled "omitted lands" had in fact been practicably irrigable at the time of Arizona I and were thus entitled to water. On these grounds, Master Tuttle recommended that the Court reopen the 1964 decree to award the Tribes additional water rights.

In Arizona v. California, 460 U.S. 605, 103 S.Ct. 1382, 75 L.Ed.2d 318 (1983) (Arizona II), the Court permitted the Tribes to intervene, but otherwise rejected Master Tuttle's recommendations. The Secretary's determinations did not qualify as "final determinations" of reservation boundaries, we ruled, because the States, agencies, and private water users had not had an opportunity to obtain judicial review of those determinations. Id., at 636637, 103 S.Ct. 1382. In that regard, we noted that California state agencies had initiated an action in the United States District Court for the Southern District of California challenging the Secretary's decisions, and that the United States had moved to dismiss that action on various grounds, including sovereign immunity. "There will be time enough," the Court stated, "if any of these grounds for dismissal are sustained and not overturned on appellate review, to determine whether the boundary issues foreclosed by such action are nevertheless open for litigation in this Court." Id., at 638, 103 S.Ct. 1382. The Court also held that the United States was barred from seeking water rights for the lands omitted from presentation in the proceedings leading to Arizona I; "principles of res judicata," we said, "advise against reopening the calculation of the amount of practicably irrigable acreage." 460 U.S., at 626, 103 S.Ct. 1382. In 1984, in another supplemental decree, the Court again declared that water rights for all five reservations "shall be subject to appropriate adjustments by agreement or decree of this Court in the event that the boundaries of the respective reservations are finally determined." Arizona v. California, 466 U.S. 144, 145, 104 S.Ct. 1900, 80 L.Ed.2d 194.

The district court litigation proceeded with the participation of eight parties: the United States, the States of Arizona and California, the Metropolitan Water District of Southern California, the Coachella Valley Water District, and the Quechan, Fort Mojave, and Colorado River Indian Tribes. The District Court rejected the United States' sovereign immunity defense; taking up the Fort Mojave Reservation matter first, the court voided the Secretary's determination of that reservation's boundaries. Metropolitan Water Dist. of S. Cal. v. United States, 628 F.Supp. 1018 *2312 (S.D.Cal.1986). The Court of Appeals for the Ninth Circuit, however, accepted the United States' plea of sovereign immunity, and on that ground reversed and remanded with instructions to dismiss the entire case. Specifically, the Court of Appeals held that the Quiet Title Act, 28 U.S.C. section 2409a, preserved the United States' sovereign immunity from suits challenging the United States' title "to trust or restricted Indian lands," section 2409a(a), and therefore blocked recourse to the District Court by the States and state agencies. Metropolitan Water Dist. of S. Cal. v. United States, 830 F.2d 139 (1987). We granted certiorari and affirmed the Ninth Circuit's judgment by an equally divided Court. California v. United States, 490 U.S. 920, 109 S.Ct. 2273, 104 L.Ed.2d 981 (1989) (per curiam).

The dismissal of the district court action dispelled any expectation that a "final determination" of reservation boundaries would occur in that forum. The State parties then moved to reopen the 1964 decree, asking the Court to determine whether the Fort Yuma Indian Reservation and two other reservations were entitled to claim additional boundary lands and, if so, additional water rights. Neither the United States nor the Tribes objected to the reopening of the decree, and the Court granted the motion.

Arizona v. California, 493 U.S. 886, 110 S.Ct. 227, 107 L.Ed.2d 180 (1989). After the death in 1990 of the third Special Master, Robert McKay, the Court appointed Frank J. McGarr as Special Master. Special Master McGarr has now filed a report and recommendation (McGarr Report), a full understanding of which requires a discussion of issues and events specific to the Fort Yuma Indian Reservation. We now turn to those issues and events.

II

The specific dispute before us has its roots in an 1884 Executive Order signed by President Chester A. Arthur, designating approximately 72 square miles of land along the Colorado River in California as the Fort Yuma Indian Reservation (Reservation) for the benefit of the Quechan Tribe. The Tribe, which had traditionally engaged in farming, offered to cede its rights to a portion of the Reservation to the United States in exchange for allotments of irrigated land to individual Indians. In 1893, the Secretary of the Interior concluded an agreement with the Tribe (1893 Agreement), which Congress ratified in 1894. The 1893 Agreement provided for the Tribe's cession of a 25,000-acre tract of boundary lands on the Reservation. Language in the agreement, however, could be read to condition the cession on the performance by the United States of certain obligations, including construction within three years of an irrigation canal, allotment of irrigated land to individual Indians, sale of certain lands to raise revenues for canal construction, and opening of certain lands to the public domain.

Doubts about the validity and effect of the 1893 Agreement arose as early as 1935. In that year the construction of the All American Canal, which prompted the interstate dispute in Arizona I, see 373 U.S., at 554–555, 83 S.Ct. 1468, also sparked a controversy concerning the Fort Yuma Reservation. When the Department of the Interior's Bureau of Reclamation sought to route the canal through the Reservation, the Department's Indian Office argued that the Bureau had to pay compensation to the Tribe for the rightofway. The Secretary of the Interior submitted the matter to the Department's Solicitor, Nathan Margold. In 1936, Solicitor Margold issued an opinion (Margold Opinion) stating that, under the 1893 Agreement, the Tribe had unconditionally ceded the lands in question to the United States. 1 Dept. of Interior, Opinions of the Solicitor Relating to Indian Affairs 596, 600 (No. M28198, Jan. 8, 1936). The Margold Opinion remained the position of the Federal Government for 42 years.

*2313 In 1946, Congress enacted the Indian Claims Commission Act, 60 Stat. 1049, 25 U.S.C. section 70 et seq. (1976 ed.), establishing an Article I tribunal with power to decide claims of Indian tribes against the United States. [FN1] See generally United States v. Dann, 470 U.S. 39, 105 S.Ct. 1058, 84 L.Ed.2d 28 (1985). The Tribe filed an action before the Commission in 1951, challenging the validity and effect of the 1893 Agreement. In that action, referred to by the parties as Docket No. 320, the Tribe relied principally on two mutually exclusive grounds for relief.

First, the Tribe alleged that the 1893 Agreement was obtained through fraud, coercion, and/or inadequate consideration, rendering it "wholly nugatory." Petition for Loss of Reservation in Docket No. 320 (Ind.Cl.Comm'n.), paragraphs 1516, reprinted in Brief for United States in Support of Exception, pp. 11a27a.

At the very least, contended the Tribe, the United States had failed to perform the obligations enumerated in the 1893 Agreement, rendering the cession void. Id., at paragraph 31. In either event, the Tribe claimed continuing title to the disputed lands and sought damages essentially for trespass. Alternatively, the Tribe alleged that the 1893 Agreement was contractually valid but constituted an uncompensated taking of tribal lands, an appropriation of lands for unconscionable consideration, and/or a violation of standards of fair and honorable dealing, for which Sections 2(3)(5) of the Act authorized recovery. Id., at Paragraphs 19, 22, 25. According to this theory of recovery, the 1893 Agreement had indeed vested in the United States unconditional title to the disputed lands, and the Tribe sought damages as compensation for that taking. During the more than quartercentury of litigation in Docket No. 320, the Tribe vacillated between these two grounds for relief, sometimes emphasizing one and sometimes the other. See Quechan Tribe of Fort Yuma Reservation v. United States, 26 Ind.Cl. Comm'n. 15 (1971), reprinted in Brief for United States in Support of Exception, pp. 29a34a.

FN1. The Act conferred exclusive jurisdiction on the Commission to resolve Indian claims solely by the payment of compensation. Section 2 of the Act gave the Commission jurisdiction over, among other things, claims alleging that agreements between a tribe and the United States were vitiated by fraud, duress, or unconscionable consideration, 25 U.S.C. section 70a(3) (1976 ed.), claims arising from the unlawful taking of Indian lands by the United States, section 70a(4), and claims based upon fair and honorable dealings not recognized by law or equity, section 70a(5). The Commission's "[f]inal determinations," section 70r, were subject to review by the Court of Claims, section 70s(b), and, if upheld, were submitted to Congress for payment, section 70u. Section 15 authorized the Attorney General to represent the United States before the Commission and, "with the approval of the Commission, to compromise any claim presented to the Commission." 25 U.S.C. section 70n (1976 ed.). The Act provided that such compromises "shall be submitted by the Commission to the Congress as a part of its report as provided in section 70t of this title in the same manner as final determinations of the Commission, and shall be subject to the provisions of section 70u of this title." Ibid. Section 22(a) of the Act provided that "[t]he payment of any claim, after its determination in accordance with this chapter, shall be a full discharge of the United States of all claims and demands touching any of the matters involved in the controversy." 25 U.S.C. section 70u(a) (1976 ed.). Pursuant to statute, section 70v, the Commission ceased its operations in 1978 and transferred its remaining cases to the Court of Claims.

The Commission conducted a trial on liability, but stayed further proceedings in 1970 because legislation had been proposed in Congress that would have restored the disputed lands to the Tribe. The legislation was not enacted, and the Commission vacated the stay. In 1976, the Commission transferred the matter to the Court of Claims.

In the meantime, the Tribe had asked the Department of the Interior to reconsider its 1936 Margold Opinion regarding the 1893 Agreement. In 1977, Interior Solicitor Scott Austin concluded, in accord with the 1936 opinion, that the 1893 Agreement was valid and that the cession of the disputed lands had been unconditional. Opinion of the Solicitor, No. M36886 (Jan. *2314 18, 1977), 84 I.D. 1 (1977) (Austin Opinion). It soon became clear both to the Tribe and to interested Members of Congress, however, that the Austin Opinion had provoked controversy within the Department, and, after the election of President Carter, the Department revisited the issue and reversed course. In 1978, without notice to the parties, Solicitor Leo Krulitz issued an opinion concluding that the 1893 Agreement had provided for a conditional cession of the disputed lands, that the conditions had not been met by the United States, and that "[t]itle to the subject property is held by the United States in trust for the Quechan Tribe." Opinion of the Solicitor, No. M36908 (Dec. 20, 1978), 86 I.D. 3, 22 (1979) (Krulitz Opinion). On December 20, 1978, the Secretary of the Interior issued a Secretarial Order adopting the Krulitz Opinion and confirming the Tribe's entitlement to the disputed lands, with the express exception of certain lands that the United States had acquired pursuant to Act of Congress or had conveyed to third parties.

The 1978 Secretarial Order caused the United States to change its position both in Docket No. 320, which was still pending in the Claims Court, and in the present litigation. Because the Secretarial Order amounted to an admission that the 1893 Agreement had been ineffective to transfer title and that the Tribe enjoyed beneficial ownership of the disputed boundary lands, the United States no longer opposed the Tribe's claim for trespass in Docket No. 320. In the present litigation, the Secretarial Order both prompted the United States to file a water rights claim for the affected boundary lands and provided the basis for the Tribe's intervention to assert a similar, albeit larger, water rights claim. See Arizona II, 460 U.S., at 632633, 103 S.Ct. 1382. Those water rights claims are the subject of the current proceedings.

In August 1983, a few months after this Court decided in Arizona II that the 1978 Secretarial Order did not constitute a final determination of reservation boundaries, see supra, at 2311, the United States and the Tribe entered into a settlement of Docket No. 320, which the Court of Claims approved and entered as its final judgment. Under the terms of that settlement, the United States agreed to pay the Tribe $15 million in full satisfaction of "all rights, claims, or demands which plaintiff [i.e., the Tribe] has asserted or could have asserted with respect to the claims in Docket 320." Final Judgment, Docket No. 320 (Aug. 11, 1983). The judgment further provided that "plaintiff shall be barred thereby from asserting any further rights, claims, or demands against the defendant and any future action on the claims encompassed on Docket 320." Ibid. The United States and the Tribe also stipulated that the "final judgment is based on a compromise and settlement and shall not be construed as an admission by either party for the purposes of precedent or argument in any other case." Ibid. Both the Tribe and the United States continue to recognize the Tribe's entitlement to the disputed boundary lands.

III

Master McGarr has issued a series of orders culminating in the report and recommendation now before the Court. He has recommended that the Court reject the claims of the United States and the Tribe seeking additional water rights for the Fort Yuma Indian Reservation. The Master rejected the State parties' contention that this Court's Arizona I decision precludes the United States and the Tribe from seeking water rights for the disputed boundary lands. He concluded, however, that the United States and the Tribe are precluded from pursuing those claims by operation of the 1983 Claims Court consent judgment. The State parties have filed an exception to the first of these preclusion recommendations, and the United States and the Tribe have filed exceptions to the second. In Part IIIA, infra, we consider the exception filed by the State parties, and in Part IIIB we address *2315 the exceptions filed by the United States and the Tribe. The Special Master has also recommended that the Court approve the parties' proposed settlements respecting the Fort Mojave and Colorado River Indian Reservations. No party has filed an exception to those recommendations; we address them in Part III C, infra.

A

The States of Arizona and California, the Coachella Valley Water District, and the Metropolitan Water District of Southern California (State parties) argued before Special Master McGarr, and repeat before this Court, that the water rights claims associated with the disputed boundary lands of the Fort Yuma Reservation are precluded by the finality rationale this Court employed in dismissing the "omitted lands" claims in Arizona II. See supra, at 2311. According to the State parties, the United States could have raised a boundary lands claim for the Fort Yuma Reservation in the Arizona I proceedings based on facts known at that time, just as it did for the Fort Mojave and Colorado River Reservations, but deliberately decided not to do so, just as it did with respect to the "omitted lands." In Arizona II, this Court rejected the United States' claim for water rights for the "omitted lands," emphasizing that "[c]ertainty of rights is particularly important with respect to water rights in the Western United States" and noting "the strong interest in finality in this case." 460 U.S., at 620, 103 S.Ct. 1382. Observing that the 1964 decree determined "the extent of irrigable acreage within the uncontested boundaries of the reservations," id., at 621, n. 12, 103 S.Ct. 1382, the Court refused to reconsider issues "fully and fairly litigated 20 years ago," id., at 621, 103 S.Ct. 1382. The Court concomitantly held that the Tribes were bound by the United States' representation of them in Arizona I. Id., at 626627, 103 S.Ct. 1382.

The Special Master rejected the State parties' preclusion argument. He brought out first the evident reason why the United States did not assert water rights claims for the Fort Yuma Reservation boundary lands in Arizona I. At that point in time, the United States was bound to follow the 1936 Margold Opinion, see supra, at 23122313, which maintained that the Tribe had no claim to those lands. "[I]t is clear," the Master stated, "that the later Secretary of the Interior opinion arbitrarily changing [the Margold] decision was a circumstance not known in 1964, thus constituting an exception to the application of the rule of res adjudicata." Special Master McGarr Memorandum Opinion and Order No. 4, pp. 67 (Sept. 6, 1991). Characterizing the question as "close," the Master went on to conclude that "the Tribe is not precluded from asserting water rights based on boundary land claims on [sic] this proceeding, because although the U.S. on behalf of the Tribe failed to assert such claims in the proceeding leading to the 1964 decree, a later and then unknown circumstance bars the application of the doctrine of res judicata to this issue." Id., at 7.

[1] While the Special Master correctly recognized the relevance of the Margold Opinion to the litigating stance of the United States, he ultimately relied on an improper ground in rejecting the State parties' preclusion argument. The Department of the Interior's 1978 Secretarial Order recognizing the Tribe's beneficial ownership of the boundary lands, see supra, at 23132314, does not qualify as a "later and then unknown circumstance" that can overcome otherwise applicable preclusion principles. The 1978 Order did not change the underlying facts in dispute; it simply embodied one party's changed view of the import of unchanged facts. Moreover, the Tribe can hardly claim to have been surprised by the Government's shift in assessment of the boundary lands ownership question, for the Tribe had *2316 been advocating just such a shift for decades.

[2] The United States and the Tribe, however, urge other grounds on which to reject the State parties' argument regarding the preclusive effect of Arizona I. The United States and the Tribe maintain that the preclusion rationale the Court applied to the "omitted lands" in Arizona II is not equally applicable to the disputed boundary lands, [FN2] and that, in any event, the State parties have forfeited their preclusion defense. We agree that the State parties' preclusion defense is inadmissible at this late date, and therefore we do not reach the merits of that plea. The State parties could have raised the defense in 1979 in response to the United States' motion for a supplemental decree granting additional water rights for the Fort Yuma Reservation. The State parties did not do so then, nor did they raise the objection in 1982 when Arizona II was briefed and argued. [FN3] Unaccountably, they raised the preclusion argument for the first time in 1989, when they initiated the current round of proceedings. See Exception and Brief for the State Parties 16; Motion of the State Parties to Reopen Decree in Arizona v. California, O.T.1989, No. 8 Orig., p. 6, n. 2. The State parties had every opportunity, and every incentive, to press their current preclusion argument at earlier stages in the litigation, yet failed to do so. [FN4]

FN2. The United States and the Tribe point to the holding in Arizona I that Special Master Rifkind had erred in prematurely considering boundary land claims relating to the Fort Mojave and Colorado River Reservations, see 373 U.S., at 601, 83 S.Ct. 1468; they contend that consideration of the Fort Yuma Reservation boundaries would have been equally premature. They further stress that in Arizona II we held the omitted lands claims precluded because we resisted "reopen[ing] an adjudication . . . to reconsider whether initial factual determinations were correctly made," 460 U.S., at 623624, 103 S.Ct. 1382; in contrast, they maintain, the present claims turn on the validity of the 1893 Agreement and the 1978 Secretarial Order, questions of law not addressed in prior proceedings.

FN3. Noting that in Arizona II we "encouraged the parties to assert their legal claims and defenses in another forum," the dissent concludes that the Court probably would have declined to resolve the preclusion issue at that stage of the case even had the State parties raised it then. Post, at 2323. One can only wonder why this should be so. If this Court had held in Arizona II that the United States and the Tribe were precluded from litigating their boundary lands claims, it would have been pointless for the Court to encourage pursuit of those claims "in another forum"; further assertion of the claims in any forum would have been barred. In any event, a party generally forfeits an affirmative defense by failing to raise it even if the relevant proceeding is ultimately resolved on other grounds.

FN4. The dissent's observation that "the only 'pleadings' in this case were filed in the 1950's," post, at 2323, is beside the point. The State parties could have properly raised the preclusion defense as early as February 1979, in their response to the United States' motion for modification of the decree, yet did not do so. See Response of the States of Arizona, California, and Nevada and the Other California Defendants to the Motion of the United States for Modification of Decree, O.T.1978, No. 8 Orig. Alternatively, it was open to the State parties to seek leave to file a supplemental pleading "setting forth . . . occurrences or events which have happened since the date of the pleading sought to be amended." Fed. R. Civ. Proc. 15(d). In such a supplemental pleading, and in compliance with Rule 8(c), the preclusion defense could have been raised. No such supplemental pleading was ever presented, and by 1989 a reasonable time to do so had surely expired. The State parties' tardiness in raising their preclusion defense is hard to account for, while the United States' decision not to assert claims for the disputed boundary lands until 1978 can at least be explained by the continued vitality of the Margold Opinion, see supra, at 23132314. It is puzzling that the dissent should go to such lengths to excuse the former delay while relentlessly condemning the latter.

[3][4][5] "[W]hile the technical rules of preclusion are not strictly applicable [in the context of a single ongoing original action], the principles upon which these rules are founded should inform our decision." Arizona II, 460 U.S., at 619, 103 S.Ct. 1382. Those principles rank res judicata an affirmative defense ordinarily lost if not timely raised. See Fed. Rule Civ. *2317 Proc. 8(c). Counsel for the State parties conceded at oral argument that "no preclusion argument was made with respect to boundary lands" in the proceedings leading up to Arizona II, and that "after this Court's decision in Arizona II and after the Court's later decision in [Nevada v. United States, 463 U.S. 110, 103 S.Ct. 2906, 77 L.Ed.2d 509 (1983)], the light finally dawned on the State parties that there was a valid preclusionor res judicata argument here with respect to Fort Yuma." Tr. of Oral Arg. 4647. We disapprove the notion that a party may wake up because a "light finally dawned," years after the first opportunity to raise a defense, and effectively raise it so long as the party was (through no fault of anyone else) in the dark until its late awakening.

The State parties assert that our prior pronouncements in this case have expressly recognized the possibility that future boundary lands claims for the Fort Yuma Reservation might be precluded. If anything, the contrary is true. Nothing in the Arizona II decision hints that the Court believed the boundary lands issue might ultimately be held precluded. Rather, the Court expressly found it "necessary to decide whether any or all of these boundary disputes have been 'finally determined' within the meaning of Article II(D)(5). . . ." 460 U.S., at 631, 103 S.Ct. 1382 (emphasis added). That Arizona II contains no discussion of preclusion with respect to the disputed lands is hardly surprising, given that the State parties neglected to raise that issue until six years later.

The Court did note in Arizona II that in the district court proceedings the United States had asserted defenses based on "lack of standing, the absence of indispensable parties, sovereign immunity and the applicable statute of limitations," and added that "[t]here will be time enough, if any of these grounds for dismissal are sustained and not overturned on appellate review, to determine whether the boundary issues foreclosed by such [lower court] action are nevertheless open for litigation in this Court." 460 U.S., at 638, 103 S.Ct. 1382 (emphasis added). This passage, however, is most sensibly read to convey that the defenses just mentioned –standing, indispensable parties, sovereign immunity, and the statute of limitations–would not necessarily affect renewed litigation in this Court. The passage contains no acknowledgment, express or implied, of a lurking preclusion issue stemming from our Arizona I disposition.

Moreover, and of large significance, the 1979 and 1984 supplemental decrees anticipated that the disputed boundary issues for all five reservations, including the Fort Yuma Reservation, would be "finally determined" in some forum, not by preclusion but on the merits. See 1984 Supplemental Decree, Art. II(D)(5), Arizona v. California, 466 U.S., at 145, 104 S.Ct. 1900 (Water rights for all five reservations "shall be subject to appropriate adjustments by agreement or decree of this Court in the event that the boundaries of the respective reservations are finally determined."); 1979 Supplemental Decree, Art. II(D)(5), Arizona v. California, 439 U.S., at 421, 99 S.Ct. 995 (same).

The State parties themselves stipulated to the terms of the supplemental decree we entered in 1979. They also appear to have litigated the Arizona II proceedings on the understanding that the boundary disputes should be resolved on the merits. See Arizona II, 460 U.S., at 634, 103 S.Ct. 1382 ("[The State parties] argued . . . that the boundary controversies were ripe for judicial review, and they urged the Special Master to receive evidence, hear legal arguments, and resolve each of the boundary disputes, but only for the limited purpose of establishing additional Indian water rights, if any."); Report of Special Master Tuttle, O.T.1981, No. 8 Orig., p. 57 (describing the State parties' contention "that the boundaries [of all five Reservations] have not been finally determined and that I should make a de novo determination of *2318 the boundaries for recommendation to the Court"). As late as 1988, the State parties asked the Court to appoint a new Special Master and direct him "to conclude his review of the boundary issues as expeditiously as possible and to submit a recommended decision to the Court." Brief for Petitioners in California v. United States, O.T.1987, No. 871165, p. 49.

[6][7][8] Finally, the State parties argue that even if they earlier failed to raise the preclusion defense, this Court should raise it now sua sponte. Judicial initiative of this sort might be appropriate in special circumstances. Most notably, "if a court is on notice that it has previously decided the issue presented, the court may dismiss the action sua sponte, even though the defense has not been raised. This result is fully consistent with the policies underlying res judicata: it is not based solely on the defendant's interest in avoiding the burdens of twice defending a suit, but is also based on the avoidance of unnecessary judicial waste." United States v. Sioux Nation, 448 U.S. 371, 432, 100 S.Ct. 2716, 65 L.Ed.2d 844 (1980) (REHNQUIST, J., dissenting) (citations omitted). That special circumstance is not present here: While the State parties contend that the Fort Yuma boundary dispute could have been decided in Arizona I, this Court plainly has not "previously decided the issue presented." Therefore we do not face the prospect of redoing a matter once decided. Where no judicial resources have been spent on the resolution of a question, trial courts must be cautious about raising a preclusion bar sua sponte, thereby eroding the principle of party presentation so basic to our system of adjudication.

In view of the State parties' failure to raise the preclusion argument earlier in the litigation, despite ample opportunity and cause to do so, we hold that the claims of the United States and the Tribe to increased water rights for the disputed boundary lands of the Fort Yuma Reservation are not foreclosed by our decision in Arizona I.

B

[9] The State parties also assert that the instant water rights claims are precluded by the 1983 consent judgment in the Claims Court proceeding, Docket No. 320. Special Master McGarr agreed, noting the consent judgment's declaration that the Tribe would "be barred thereby from asserting any further rights, claims or demands against the defendant and any future action encompassed on docket no. 320." See Special Master McGarr Memorandum Opinion and Order No. 4, pp. 910 (Sept. 6, 1991). On reconsideration, the Special Master provided a fuller account of his recommendation. The settlement, he concluded, had extinguished the Tribe's claim to title in the disputed boundary lands, vesting that title in the United States against all the world: "The only viable basis for a damage or trespass claim [in Docket No. 320] was that the 1893 taking was illegal and that title therefore remained with the Tribe. When the Tribe accepted money in settlement of this claim, it relinquished its claim to title." Id., No. 7, p. 5 (May 5, 1992). See also id., No. 13, p. 3 (Apr. 13, 1993) ("[T]he relinquishment of all future claims regarding the subject matter of Docket No. 320 in exchange for a sum of money extinguished the Tribe's title in the subject lands. . . ."). Because the settlement extinguished the Tribe's title to the disputed boundary lands, the Master reasoned, the United States and the Tribe cannot now seek additional water rights based on the Tribe's purported beneficial ownership of those lands.

APPENDIX

[10][11][12][13] Under standard preclusion doctrine, the Master's recommendation cannot be sustained. As already noted, the express terms of the consent judgment in Docket No. 320 barred the Tribe and the United States from asserting against each other any claim or defense they raised or could have raised in that action. See supra, at 2314. As between the parties to Docket No. 320, then, the settlement *2319 indeed had, and was intended to have, claim preclusive effect–a matter the United States and the Tribe readily concede. Exception and Brief for the United States 36; Exception and Brief for the Quechan Indian Tribe 20. But settlements ordinarily occasion no issue preclusion (sometimes called collateral estoppel), unless it is clear, as it is not here, that the parties intend their agreement to have such an effect. "In most circumstances, it is recognized that consent agreements ordinarily are intended to preclude any further litigation on the claim presented but are not intended to preclude further litigation on any of the issues presented. Thus consent judgments ordinarily support claim preclusion but not issue preclusion." 18 Charles Alan Wright, Arthur R. Miller, & Edward H. Cooper, Federal Practice and Procedure section 4443, p. 384385 (1981). This differentiation is grounded in basic res judicata doctrine. It is the general rule that issue preclusion attaches only "[w]hen an issue of fact or law is actually litigated and determined by a valid and final judgment, and the determination is essential to the judgment." Restatement (Second) of Judgments section 27, p. 250 (1982). "In the case of a judgment entered by confession, consent, or default, none of the issues is actually litigated. Therefore, the rule of this Section [describing issue preclusion's domain] does not apply with respect to any issue in a subsequent action." Id., comment e, p. 257.

This Court's decision in United States v. International Building Co., 345 U.S. 502, 73 S.Ct. 807, 97 L.Ed. 1182 (1953), is illustrative. In 1942, the Commissioner of Internal Revenue assessed deficiencies against a taxpayer for the taxable years 1933, 1938, and 1939, alleging that the taxpayer had claimed an excessive basis for depreciation. Id., at 503, 73 S.Ct. 807. After the taxpayer filed for bankruptcy, however, the Commissioner and the taxpayer filed stipulations in the pending Tax Court proceedings stating that there was no deficiency for the taxable years in question, and the Tax Court entered a formal decision to that effect. Id., at 503504, 73 S.Ct. 807. In 1948, the Commissioner assessed deficiencies for the years 1943, 1944, and 1945, and the taxpayer defended on the ground that the earlier Tax Court decision was preclusive on the issue of the correct basis for depreciation. We disagreed, holding that the Tax Court decision, entered pursuant to the parties' stipulations, did not accomplish an "estoppel by judgment," i.e., it had no issue-preclusive effect:

"We conclude that the decisions entered by the Tax Court for the years 1933, 1938, and 1939 were only a pro forma acceptance by the Tax Court of an agreement between the parties to settle their controversy for reasonsundisclosed. . . . Perhaps, as the Court of Appeals inferred, the parties did agree on the basis for depreciation. Perhaps the settlement was made for a different reason, for some exigency arising out of the bankruptcy proceeding. As the case reaches us, we are unable to tell whether the agreement of the parties was based on the merits or on some collateral consideration. Certainly the judgments entered are res judicata of the tax claims for the years 1933, 1938, and 1939, whether or not the basis of the agreements on which they rest reached the merits. . . . Estoppel by judgment includes matters in a second proceeding which were actually presented and determined in an earlier suit. A judgment entered with the consent of the parties may involve a determination of questions of fact and law by the court. But unless a showing is made that that was the case, the judgment has no greater dignity, so far as collateral estoppel is concerned, than any judgment entered only as a compromise of the parties." Id., at 505506, 73 S.Ct. 807 (citations omitted).

The State parties, perhaps recognizing the infirmity of their argument as a matter of standard preclusion doctrine, assert that commonlaw principles of issue preclusion *2320 do not apply in the special context of Indian land claims. Instead, they argue, section 22 of the Indian Claims Commission Act created a special regime of "statutory preclusion." [FN5] According to the State parties, the payment of a Commission judgment for claims to aboriginal or trust lands automatically and universally extinguishes title to the Indian lands upon which the claim is based and creates a statutory bar to further assertion of claims against either the United States or third parties based on the extinguished title. The State parties point to several decisions of the Ninth Circuit in support of this contention. See Reply Brief for State Parties 17 (citing United States v. Pend Oreille Pub. Util. Dist. No. 1, 926 F.2d 1502 (C.A.9 1991)); id., at 15 (citing United States v. Dann, 873 F.2d 1189 (C.A.9 1989)); id., at 11 (citing United States v. Gemmill, 535 F.2d 1145 (C.A.9 1976)).

FN5. Section 22 provided:

"(a) When the report of the Commission determining any claimant to be entitled to recover has been filed with Congress, such report shall have the effect of a final judgment of the Court of Claims, and there is authorized to be appropriated such sums as are necessary to pay the final determination of the Commission. "The payment of any claim, after its determination in accordance with this chapter, shall be a full discharge of the United States of all claims and demands touching any of the matters involved in the controversy.

"(b) A final determination against a claimant made and reported in accordance with this chapter shall forever bar any further claim or demand against the United States arising out of the matter involved in the controversy." 25 U.S.C. section 70u (1976 ed.).

We need not decide whether, in the distinctive context of the Indian Claims Commission Act, some consent judgments might bar a tribe from asserting title even in discrete litigation against third parties, for the 1983 settlement of Docket No. 320 plainly could not qualify as such a judgment. Not only was the issue of ownership of the disputed boundary lands not actually litigated and decided in Docket No. 320, but, most notably, the Tribe proceeded on alternative and mutually exclusive theories of recovery. Had the case proceeded to final judgment upon trial, the Tribe might have won damages for a taking, indicating that title was in the United States. Alternatively, however, the Tribe might have obtained damages for trespass, indicating that title remained in the Tribe. The consent judgment embraced all of the Tribe's claims. There was no election by the Tribe of one theory over the other, nor was any such election required to gain approval for the consent judgment. The Special Master's assumption that the settlement necessarily and universally relinquished the Tribe's claim to title was thus unwarranted. Certainly, if the $15 million payment constituted a discharge of the Tribe's trespass claim, it would make scant sense to say that the acceptance of the payment extinguished the Tribe's title. In contrast, the Ninth Circuit cases cited by the State parties (the correctness of which we do not address) all involved Indian Claims Commission Act petitions in which tribes claimed no continuing title, choosing instead to seek compensation from the United States for the taking of their lands. See, e.g., Pend Oreille, 926 F.2d, at 15071508; Dann, 873 F.2d, at 1192, 1194; Gemmill, 535 F.2d, at 1149, and n. 6.

The United States invites us to look behind the consent judgment in Docket No. 320 at presettlement stipulations and memoranda purportedly demonstrating that the judgment was grounded on the parties' shared view, after the 1978 Secretarial Order, that the disputed lands belong to the Tribe. We need not accept the Government's invitation. On the matter of issue preclusion, it suffices to observe that the settlement was ambiguous as between mutually exclusive theories of recovery. Like the Tax Court settlement in International Building Co., then, the consent judgment in the Tribe's Claims Court action is too opaque to serve as a foundation for issue preclusion. Accordingly, we hold *2321 that the claims of the United States and the Tribe to increased water rights for the disputed boundary lands of the Fort Yuma Reservation are not precluded by the consent judgment in Docket No. 320.

C

[14] The Special Master has recommended that the Court approve the parties' proposed settlement of the dispute respecting the Fort Mojave Reservation. The claim to additional water for the Fort Mojave Reservation arises out of a dispute over the accuracy of a survey of the socalled Hay and Wood Reserve portion of the Reservation. See Arizona II, 460 U.S., at 631632, 103 S.Ct. 1382. The parties agreed to resolve the matter through an accord that (1) specifies the location of the disputed boundary; (2) preserves the claims of the parties regarding title to and jurisdiction over the bed of the last natural course of the Colorado River within the agreed upon boundary; (3) awards the Tribe the lesser of an additional 3,022 acre-feet of water or enough water to supply the needs of 468 acres; (4) precludes the United States and the Tribe from claiming additional water rights from the Colorado River for lands within the Hay and Wood Reserve; and (5) disclaims any intent to affect any private claims to title to or jurisdiction over any lands. See McGarr Report 89. We accept the Master's uncontested recommendation and approve the proposed settlement.

[15] The Master has also recommended that the Court approve the parties' proposed settlement of the dispute respecting the Colorado River Indian Reservation. The claim to additional water for that reservation stems principally from a dispute over whether the reservation boundary is the ambulatory west bank of the Colorado River or a fixed line representing a past location of the River. See Arizona II, 460 U.S., at 631, 103 S.Ct. 1382. The parties agreed to resolve the matter through an accord that (1) awards the Tribes the lesser of an additional 2,100 acre-feet of water or enough water to irrigate 315 acres; (2) precludes the United States or the Tribe from seeking additional reserved water rights from the Colorado River for lands in California; (3) embodies the parties' intent not to adjudicate in these proceedings the correct location of the disputed boundary; (4) preserves the competing claims of the parties to title to or jurisdiction over the bed of the Colorado River within the reservation; and (5) provides that the agreement will become effective only if the Master and the Court approve the settlement. See

McGarr Report 910. The Master expressed concern that the settlement does not resolve the location of the disputed boundary, but recognized that it did achieve the ultimate aim of determining water rights associated with the disputed boundary lands. Id., at 1012, 1314. We again accept the Master's recommendation and approve the proposed settlement. [FN6]

FN6. A group called the West Bank Homeowners Association has filed a brief amicus curiae objecting to the proposed settlement of water rights claims respecting the Colorado River Indian Reservation. The Association represents some 650 families who lease property from the United States within the current boundaries of the Reservation. The Court and the Special Master have each denied the Association's request to intervene in these proceedings. See Arizona v. California, 514 U.S. 1081, 115 S.Ct. 1790, 131 L.Ed.2d 720 (1995); Special Master McGarr Memorandum Opinion and Order No. 17 (Mar. 29, 1995). The Master observed that the Association's members do "not own land in the disputed area and [the Association] makes no claim to title or water rights," id., at 2310, thus their interests will "not be impeded or impaired by the outcome of this litigation," id., at 2312. Accordingly, we do not further consider the Association's objections.

DOCUMENT 2

CLEAN WATER ACT, 1972

Federal Water Pollution Control Act Amendments of 1972.

70 Stat. 498: 84 Stat. 91. 33 USC 1151 note.

October 18, 1972 [S. 2770]

Public Law 92-500

AN ACT to amend the Federal Water Pollution Control Act.

Be it enacted by the Senate and House of Representatives of the United States of America in Congress assembled, That this Act may be cited as the "Federal Water Pollution Control Act Amendments of 1972."

Sec. 2. The Federal Water Pollution Control Act is amended to read as follows:

"TITLE 1–RESEARCH AND RELATED PROGRAMS

"DECLARATION OF GOALS AND POLICY

"Sec. 101. (A). The objective of this Act is to restore and maintain the chemical, physical, and biological integrity of the Nation's waters. In order to achieve this objective it is hereby declared that, consistent with the provisions of this Act–

"(1) it is the national goal that the discharge of pollutants into the navigable waters be eliminated by 1985;

"(2) it is the national goal that wherever attainable, an interim goal of water quality which provides for the protection and propagation of fish, shellfish, and wildlife and provides for recreation in and on the water be achieved by July 1, 1983;

"(3) it is the national policy that the discharge of toxic pollutants in toxic amounts be prohibited;

"(4) it is the national policy that Federal financial assistance be provided to construct publicly owned waste treatment works;

"(5) it is the national policy that areawide waste treatment management planning processes be developed and implemented to assure adequate control of sources of pollutants and implemented to assure adequate control of sources of pollutants in each State; and

"(6) it is the national policy that a major research and demonstration effort be made to develop technology necessary to eliminate the discharge of pollutants into the navigable waters, waters of the contiguous zone, and the oceans.

"(b) It is the policy of the Congress to recognize, preserve, and protect the primary responsibilities and rights of States to prevent, reduce, and eliminate pollution, to plan the development and use (including restoration, preservation, and enhancement) of land and water resources, and to consult with the Administrator in the exercise of his authority under this Act. It is further the policy of the Congress to support and aid research relating to the prevention, reduction, and elimination of pollution, and to provide Federal technical services and financial aid to State and interstate agencies and municipalities in connection with the prevention, reduction, and elimination of pollution.

"(c) It is further the policy of Congress that the President, acting through the Secretary of State and such national and international organizations as he determines appropriate, shall take such action as may be necessary to insure that to the fullest extent possible all foreign countries shall take meaningful action for the prevention, reduction, and elimination of pollution in their waters and in international waters and for the achievement of goals regarding the elimination of discharge of pollutants and the improvement of water quality to at least the same extent as the United States does under its laws.

"(d) Except as otherwise expressly provided in this Act, the Administrator of the Environmental Protection Agency (hereinafter in this Act called 'Administrator') shall administer this Act.

"(e) Public participation in the development, revision, and enforcement of any regulation, standard, effluent limitation, plan, or program established by the Administrator or any State under this Act shall be provided for, encouraged, and assisted by the Administrator and the States. The Administrator, in cooperation with the States, shall develop and publish regulations specifying minimum guidelines for public participation in such processes.

"(f) It is the national policy that to the maximum extent possible the procedures utilized for implementing this Act shall encourage the drastic minimization of paperwork and interagency decision procedures, and the best use of available manpower and funds, so as to prevent needless duplication and unnecessary delays at all levels of government.

"COMPREHENSIVE PROGRAMS FOR WATER POLLUTION CONTROL"

"Sec. 102 (a) The Administrator shall, after careful investigation, and in cooperation with other Federal agencies, State water pollution control agencies, interstate agencies, and the municipalities and industries involved, prepare or develop comprehensive programs for preventing, reducing, or eliminating the pollution of the navigable waters and ground waters and improving the sanitary condition of surface and underground waters. In the development of such comprehensive programs due regard shall be given to the improvements which are necessary to conserve such waters for the protection and propagation of fish and aquatic life and wildlife, recreational purposes, and the withdrawal of such waters for public water supply, agricultural, industrial, and other purposes. For the purpose of this section, the Administrator is authorized to make joint investigations with any such agencies of the condition of any waters in any State or States, and of the discharges of any sewage, industrial wastes, or substance which may adversely affect such waters.

"(b) (1) In the survey or planning of any reservoir by the Corps of Engineers, Bureau of Reclamation, or other Federal agency, consideration shall be given to inclusion of storage for regulation of streamflow, except that any such storage and water releases shall not be provided as a substitute for adequate treatment or other methods of controlling waste at the source.

"(2) The need for and the value of storage for regulation of streamflow (other than for water quality) including but not limited to navigation, salt water intrusion, recreation, esthetics, and fish and wildlife, shall be determined by the Corps of Engineers, Bureau of Reclamation, or other Federal Agencies.

"(3) The need for, the value of, and the impact of, storage for water quality control shall be determined by the Administrator, and his views on these matters shall be set forth in any report or presentation to Congress proposing authorization or construction of any reservoir including such storage.

"(4) The value of such storage shall be taken into account in determining the economic value of the entire project of which it is a part, and costs shall be allocated to the purpose of regulation of streamflow in a manner which will insure that all project purposes, share equitably in the benefits of multiple-purpose construction.

"(5) Costs of regulation of streamflow features incorporated in any Federal reservoir or any other impoundment under the provisions of this Act shall be determined and the beneficiaries identified and if the benefits are widespread or national in scope, the costs of such features shall be nonreimbursable.

"(6) No license granted by the Federal Power Commission for a hydroelectric power project shall include storage for regulation of streamflow for the purpose of water quality control unless the Administrator shall recommend its inclusion and such reservoir storage capacity shall not exceed such proportion of the total storage required for the water quality control plan as the drainage area of such reservoir bears to the drainage area of the river basin or basins involved in such water quality control plan.

"(c) (1) The Administrator shall, at the request of the Governor of a State, or a majority of the Governors when more than one State is involved, make a grant to pay not to exceed 50 per centum of the administrative expenses of a planning agency for a period not to exceed three years, which period shall begin after the date of enactment of the Federal Water Pollution Control Act Amendments of 1972, if such agency provides for adequate representation of appropriate State, interstate, local, or (when appropriate) international interests in the basin or portion thereof involved and is capable of developing an effective, comprehensive water quality control plan for a basin or portion thereof.

"(2) Each planning agency receiving a grant under this subsection shall develop a comprehensive pollution control plan for the basin or portion thereof which–

"(A) is consistent with any applicable water quality standards, effluent and other limitations, and thermal discharge regulations established pursuant to current law within the basin;

"(B) recommends such treatment works as will provide the most effective and economical means of collection, storage, treatment, and elimination of pollutants and recommends means to encourage both municipal and industrial use of such works;

"(C) recommends maintenance and improvement of water quality within the basin or portion thereof and recommends methods of adequately financing those facilities as may be necessary to implement the plan; and

"(D) as appropriate, is developed in cooperation with, and is consistent with any comprehensive plan prepared by the Water Resources Council, any areawide waste management plans developed pursuant to section 208 of this Act, and any State plan developed pursuant to section 303(e) of this Act.

"(3) For the purposes of this subsection the term 'basin' includes, but is not limited to, rivers and their tributaries, streams, coastal waters, sounds, estuaries, bays, lakes, and portions thereof, as well as the lands drained thereby. . . .

DOCUMENT 3

CONVENTION FOR THE PROTECTION OF THE MEDITERRANEAN SEA AGAINST POLLUTION, BARCELONA, FEBRUARY 16, 1976

THE CONTRACTING PARTIES,

CONSCIOUS of the economic, social, health and cultural value of the marine environment of the Mediterranean Sea area,

FULLY AWARE of their responsibility to preserve this common heritage for the benefit and enjoyment of present and future generations,

RECOGNIZING the threat posed by pollution to the marine environment, its ecological equilibrium, resources and legitimate uses,

MINDFUL of the special hydrographic and ecological characteristics of the Mediterranean Sea area and its particular vulnerability to pollution,

NOTING that existing international conventions on the subject do not cover, in spite of the progress achieved, all aspects and sources of marine pollution and do not entirely meet the special requirements of the Mediterranean Sea area,

REALIZING fully the need for close cooperation among the States and international organizations concerned in a coordinated and comprehensive regional approach for the protection and enhancement of the marine environment in the Mediterranean Sea area,

HAVE AGREED AS FOLLOWS:

Article 1

Geographical coverage

1. For the purposes of this Convention, the Mediterranean Sea area shall mean the maritime waters of the Mediterranean Sea proper, including its gulfs and seas, bounded to the west by the meridian passing through Cape Spartel lighthouse, at the entrance of the Straits of Gibraltar, and to the east by the southern limits of the Straits of the Dardanelles between the Mehmetcik and Kumkale lighthouses.

2. Except as may be otherwise provided in any Protocol to this Convention, the Mediterranean Sea area shall not include internal waters of the Contracting Parties.

Article 2

Definitions

For the purposes of this Convention:

(a) 'Pollution' means the introduction by man, directly or indirectly, of substances or energy into the marine environment resulting in such deleterious effects as harm to living resources, hazards to human health, hindrance to marine activities including fishing, impairment of quality for use of sea water and reduction of amenities.

(b) 'Organization' means the body designated as responsible for carrying out secretariat functions pursuant to Article 13 of this Convention.

Article 3

General provisions

1. The Contracting Parties may enter into bilateral or multilateral agreements, including regional or sub-regional agreements, for the protection of the marine environment of the Mediterranean Sea against pollution, provided that such agreements are consistent with this Convention and conform to international law. Copies of such agreements between Contracting Parties to this Convention shall be communicated to the Organization.

2. Nothing in this Convention shall prejudice the codification and development of the law of the sea by the United Nations conference on the Law of the Sea convened pursuant to resolution 2750 C (XXV) of the General Assembly of the United Nations, nor the present or future claims and legal views of any State concerning the law of the sea and the nature and extent of coastal and flag State jurisdiction.

Article 4

General undertakings

1. The Contracting Parties shall individually or jointly take all appropriate measures in accordance with the provisions of this Convention and those Protocols in force to which they are party, to prevent, abate and combat pollution of

the Mediterranean Sea area and to protect and enhance the marine environment in that area.

2. The Contracting Parties shall cooperate in the formulation and adoption of Protocols, in addition to the protocols opened for signature at the same time as this Convention, prescribing agreed measures, procedures and standards for the implementation of this Convention.

3. The Contracting Parties further pledge themselves to promote, within the international bodies considered to be competent by the Contracting Parties, measures concerning the protection of the marine environment in the Mediterranean Sea area from all types and sources of pollution.

Article 5

Pollution caused by dumping from ships and aircraft

The Contracting Parties shall take all appropriate measures to prevent and abate pollution of the Mediterranean Sea area caused by dumping from ships and aircraft.

Article 6

Pollution from ships

The Contracting Parties shall take all measures in conformity with international law to prevent, abate and combat pollution of the Mediterranean Sea area caused by discharges from ships and to ensure the effective implementation in that area of the rules which are generally recognized at the international level relating to the control of this type of pollution.

Article 7

Pollution resulting from exploration and exploitation of the continental shelf and the seabed and its subsoil

The Contracting Parties shall take all appropriate measures to prevent, abate and combat pollution of the Mediterranean Sea area resulting from exploration and exploitation of the continental shelf and the seabed and its subsoil.

Article 8

Pollution from land-based sources

The Contracting Parties shall take all appropriate measures to prevent, abate and combat pollution of the Mediterranean Sea area caused by discharges from rivers, coastal establishments or outfalls, or emanating from any other land-based sources within their territories.

Article 9

Cooperation in dealing with pollution emergencies

1. The Contracting Parties shall cooperate in taking the necessary measures for dealing with pollution emergencies in the Mediterranean Sea area, whatever the causes of such emergencies, and reducing or eliminating damage resulting therefrom.

2. Any Contracting Party which becomes aware of any pollution emergency in the Mediterranean Sea area shall without delay notify the Organization and, either through the Organization or directly, any contracting Party likely to be affected by such emergency.

Article 10

Monitoring

1. The Contracting Parties shall endeavour to establish, in close cooperation with the international bodies which they consider competent, complementary or joint programmes, including, as appropriate, programmes at the bilateral or multilateral levels, for pollution monitoring in the Mediterranean Sea area and shall endeavour to establish a pollution monitoring system for that area.

2. For this purpose, the Contracting Parties shall designate the competent authorities responsible for pollution monitoring within areas under their national jurisdiction and shall participate as far as practicable in international arrangements for pollution monitoring in areas beyond national jurisdiction.

3. The Contracting Parties undertake to cooperate in the formulation, adoption and implementation of such Annexes to the Convention as may be required to prescribe common procedures and standards for pollution monitoring.

Article 11

Scientific and technological cooperation

1. The Contracting Parties undertake as far as possible to cooperate directly, or when appropriate, through competent regional or other international organizations, in the fields of science and technology and to exchange data as well as other scientific information for the purpose of this Convention.

2. The Contracting Parties undertake as far as possible to develop and coordinate their national research programmes relating to all types of marine pollution in the Mediterranean Sea area and to cooperate in the establishment and implementation of regional and other international research programmes for the purposes of this Convention.

3. The Contracting Parties undertake to cooperate in the provision of technical and other possible assistance in fields relating to marine pollution, with priority to be given to the special

needs of developing countries in the Mediterranean region.

Article 12

Liability and compensation

The Contracting Parties undertake to cooperate as soon as possible in the formulation and adoption of appropriate procedures for the determination in liability and compensation for damage resulting from the pollution of the marine environment deriving from violations of the provisions of this Convention and applicable Protocols.

Article 13

Institutional arrangements

The Contracting Parties designate the United Nations Environment Programme as responsible for carrying out the following secretariat functions:

(i) to convene and prepare the meetings of Contracting Parties and conferences provided for in Articles 14, 15 and 16;

(ii) to transmit to the Contracting Parties notifications, reports and other information received in accordance with Articles 3, 9 and 20;

(iii) to consider inquiries by, and information from, the Contracting Parties, and to consult with them on questions relating to this Convention and the Protocols and Annexes thereto;

(iv) to perform the functions assigned to it by the Protocols to this Convention;

(v) to perform such other functions as may be assigned to it by the Contracting Parties;

(vi) to ensure the necessary coordination with other international bodies which the Contracting Parties consider competent, and in particular, to enter into such administrative arrangements as may be required for the effective discharge of the secretariat functions.

Article 14

Meetings of the Contracting Parties

1. The Contracting Parties shall hold ordinary meetings once every two years and extraordinary meetings at any other time deemed necessary, upon the request of the Organization or at the request of any Contracting Party, provided that such requests are supported by at least two Contracting Parties.

2. It shall be the function of the meetings of the Contracting Parties to keep under review the implementation of this Convention and the Protocols and, in particular:

(i) to review generally the inventories carried out by Contracting Parties and competent international organizations on the state of marine pollution and its effects in the Mediterranean Sea area;

(ii) to consider reports submitted by the Contracting Parties under Article 20;

(iii) to adopt, review and amend as required the Annexes to this convention and to the Protocols, in accordance with the procedure established in Article 17;

(iv) to make recommendations regarding the adoption of any Additional Protocols or any amendments to this Convention or the Protocols in accordance with provisions of Articles 15 and 16;

(v) to establish working groups as required to consider any matters related to this convention and the Protocols and Annexes;

(vi) to consider and undertake any additional action that may be required for the achievement of the purposes of this Convention and the Protocols.

Article 15

Adoption of Additional Protocols

1. The Contracting Parties, at a diplomatic conference, may adopt Additional Protocols to this Convention pursuant to paragraph 2 of Article 4.

2. A diplomatic conference for the purpose of adopting Additional Protocols shall be convened by the Organization at the request of two-thirds of the Contracting Parties.

3. Pending the entry into force of this Convention the Organization may, after consulting with the signatories to this Convention, convene a diplomatic conference for the purpose of adopting Additional Protocols.

Article 16

Amendment of the Convention or Protocols

1. Any Contracting Party to this Convention may propose amendments to the Convention. Amendments shall be adopted by a diplomatic conference which shall be convened by the Organization at the request of two-thirds of the Contracting Parties.

2. Any Contracting Party to this Convention may propose amendments to any Protocol. Such amendments shall be adopted by a diplomatic conference which shall be convened by the Organization at the request of two thirds of the Contracting Parties to the Protocol concerned.

3. Amendments to this Convention shall be adopted by a three-fourths majority vote of the Contracting Parties to the Convention which are represented at the diplomatic conference and shall be submitted by the Depositary for accep-

tance by all Contracting Parties to the Convention. Amendments to any Protocol shall be adopted by a three-fourths majority vote of the contracting Parties to such Protocol which are represented at the diplomatic conference and shall be submitted by the Depositary for acceptance by all Contracting Parties to such Protocol.

4. Acceptance of amendment shall be notified to the Depositary in writing. Amendments adopted to accordance with paragraph 3 of this Article shall enter into force between Contracting Parties having accepted such amendments on the 30th day following the receipt by the Depositary of notification of their acceptance by at least three-fourths of the Contracting Parties to the Convention or to the Protocol concerned, as the case may be.

5. After the entry into force of an amendment to this Convention or to a Protocol, any new Contracting Party to this Convention or such Protocol shall become a Contracting Party to the instrument as amended.

Article 17

Annexes and amendments to Annexes

1. Annexes to this Convention or to any Protocol shall form an integral part of the Convention or such Protocol, as the case may be.

2. Except as may be otherwise provided in any Protocol, the following procedure shall apply to the adoption and entry into force of any amendments to Annexes to this Convention or to any Protocol, with the exception of amendments to the Annex on Arbitration:

(i) any Contracting Party may propose amendments to the Annexes to this Convention or to any Protocols and the meetings referred to in Article 14;

(ii) such amendments shall be adopted by a three-fourths majority vote of the contracting Parties to the instrument in question;

(iii) the Depositary shall without delay communicate the amendments so adopted to all Contracting Parties;

(iv) any Contracting Party that is unable to approve an amendment to the Annexes to this Convention or to any Protocol shall so notify in writing the Depositary within a period determined by the Contracting Parties concerned when adopting the amendment;

(v) the Depositary shall without delay notify all contracting Parties of any notification received pursuant to the preceding subparagraph;

(vi) on expiry of the period referred to in subparagraph (iv) above, the amendment to the Annex shall become effective for all contracting Parties to this convention or to the Protocol concerned which have not submitted a notification in accordance with the provisions of that subparagraph.

3. The adoption and entry into force of a new Annex to this convention or to any Protocol shall be subject to the same procedure as for the adoption and entry into force of an amendment to an Annex in accordance with the provisions of paragraph 2 of this Article, provided that, if any amendment to the Convention or the Protocol concerned is involved, the new Annex shall not enter into force until such time as the amendment to the Convention or the Protocol concerned enters into force.

4. Amendments to the Annex on Arbitration shall be considered to be considered to be amendments to this Convention and shall be proposed and adopted in accordance with the procedures set out in Article 16 above.

Article 18

Rules of procedure and financial rules

1. The Contracting Parties shall adopt rules of procedure for their meetings and conferences envisaged in Articles 14, 15 and 16 above.

2. The Contracting Parties shall adopt financial rules, prepared in consultation with the Organization, to determine, in particular, their financial participation.

Article 19

Special exercise of voting right

Within the areas of their competence, the European Economic Community and any regional economic grouping referred to in Article 24 of this Convention shall exercise their right to vote with a number of voters equal to the number of their Member States which are Contracting Parties to this Convention and to one or more Protocols; the European Economic Community and any grouping as referred to above shall not exercise their right to vote in cases where the Member States concerned exercise theirs, and conversely.

Article 20

Reports

The Contracting Parties shall transmit to the Organization reports on the measures adopted in the implementation of this Convention and of Protocols to which they are Parties, in such form and at such intervals as the meetings of Contracting Parties may determine.

Article 21

Compliance control

The Contracting Parties undertake to cooperate in the development of procedures enabling them to control the application of this Convention and the Protocols.

Article 22

Settlement of disputes

1. In case of a dispute between Contracting Parties as to the interpretation or application of this Convention or the Protocols, they shall seek a settlement of the dispute through negotiation or any other peaceful means of their own choice.

2. If the Parties concerned cannot settle their dispute through the means mentioned in the preceding paragraph, the dispute shall upon common agreement be submitted to arbitration under the conditions laid down in Annex A to this Convention.

3. Nevertheless, the Contracting Parties may at any time declare that they recognize as compulsory *ipso facto* and without special agreement, in relation to any other Party accepting the same obligation, the application of the arbitration procedure in conformity with the provisions of Annex A. Such declaration shall be notified in writing to the Depositary, who shall communicate it to the other Parties.

Article 23

Relationship between the Convention and Protocols

1. No one may become a Contracting Party to this convention unless it becomes at the same time a Contracting Party to at least one of the Protocols. No one may become a Contracting Party to a Protocol unless it is, or becomes at the same time, a Contracting Party to this Convention.

2. Any Protocol to this Convention shall be binding only on the Contracting Parties to the Protocol in question.

3. Decisions concerning any Protocol pursuant to Articles 14, 16 and 17 of this Convention shall be taken only by the Parties to the Protocol concerned.

Article 24

Signature

This Convention, the Protocol for the prevention of pollution of the Mediterranean Sea by dumping form ships and aircraft and the Protocol concerning cooperation in combating pollution of the Mediterranean Sea by oil and other harmful substances in cases of emergency shall be open for signature in Barcelona on 16 February 1976 and in Madrid from 17 February 1976 to 16 February 1977 by any State invited as a participant in the Conference of Plenipotentiaries of the Coastal States of the Mediterranean Region on the Protection of the Mediterranean Sea, held in Barcelona from 2 to 16 February 1976, and by any State entitled to sign any Protocol in accordance with the provisions of such Protocol. They shall also be open until the same date for signature by the European Economic Community and by any similar regional economic groups at least one member of which is a coastal State of the Mediterranean Sea area and which exercise competences in fields covered by the Convention, as well as by any Protocol affecting them.

Article 25

Ratification, acceptance or approval

This Convention and any Protocol thereto shall be subject to ratification, acceptance, or approval. Instruments of ratification, acceptance or approval shall be deposited with the Government of Spain, which will assume the functions of Depositary.

Article 26

Accession

1. As from 17 February 1977, the present Convention, the Protocol for the prevention of pollution of the Mediterranean Sea by dumping from ships and aircraft, and the Protocol concerning cooperation in combating pollution of the Mediterranean Sea by oil and other harmful substances in cases of emergency shall be open for accession by the States, by the European Economic Community and by any grouping as referred to in Article 24.

2. After the entry into force of the Convention and of any Protocol, any State not referred to in Article 24 may accede to this Convention and to any Protocol, subject to prior approval by three-fourths of the Contracting Parties to the Protocol concerned.

3. Instruments of accession shall be deposited with the Depositary.

Article 27

Entry into force

1. This Convention shall enter into force on the same date as the Protocol first entering into force.

2. The convention shall also enter into force with regard to the States, the European Economic Community and any regional economic grouping referred to in Article 24 if they have complied with formal requirements for becoming Contracting Parties to any other Protocol not yet entered into force.

3. Any Protocol to this Convention, except as otherwise provided in such Protocol, shall enter into force on the 30th day following the date of deposit of at least six instruments of ratification, acceptance, or approval of, or accession

to such Protocol by the Parties referred to in Article 24.

4. Thereafter, this Convention and any Protocol shall enter into force with respect to any State, the European Economic Community and any regional economic grouping referred to in Article 24 on the 30th day following the date of deposit of the instruments of ratification, acceptance, approval or accession.

Article 28

Withdrawal

1. At any time after three years from the date of entry into force of this Convention, any contracting Party may withdraw from this Convention by giving written notification of withdrawal.

2. Except as may be otherwise provided in any Protocol to this Convention, any Contracting Party may, at any time after three years from the date of entry into force of such Protocol, withdraw from such Protocol by giving written notification of withdrawal.

3. Withdrawal shall take effect 90 days after the date on which notification of withdrawal is received by the Depositary.

4. Any Contracting Party which withdraws from this Convention shall be considered as also having withdrawn from any Protocol to which it was a Party.

5. Any Contracting Party which, upon its withdrawal from a Protocol, is no longer a Party to any Protocol to this Convention, shall be considered as also having withdrawn from this Convention.

Article 29

Responsibilities of the Depositary

1. The Depositary shall inform the Contracting Parties, any other Party referred to in Article 24, and the Organization:

(i) of the signature of this Convention and of any Protocol thereto, and of the deposit of instruments of ratification, acceptance, approval or accession in accordance with Articles 24, 25 and 26;

(ii) of the date on which the Convention and any Protocol will come into force in accordance with the provisions of Article 27;

(iii) of notifications of withdrawal made in accordance with Article 28;

(iv) of the amendments adopted with respect to the Convention and to any Protocol, their acceptance by the Contracting Parties and the date of entry into force of those amendments in accordance withe provisions of Article 16;

(v) of the adoption of new Annexes and of the amendment of any Annex in accordance with Article 17;

(vi) of declaration recognizing as compulsory the application of the arbitration procedure mentioned in paragraph 3 of Article 22.

2. The original of this Convention and of any Protocol thereto shall be deposited with the Depositary, the government of Spain, which shall send certified copies thereof to the Contracting Parties, to the Organization, and to the Secretary-General of the United Nations of registration and publication in accordance with Article 102 of the United Nations Charter.

In witness whereof the undersigned, being duly authorized by their respective Governments, have signed this convention.

Done at Barcelona on 16 February 1976 in a single copy in the Arabic, English, French and Spanish languages, the four texts being equally authoritative.

Source: Bernd Rüster, et al., comp. and ed., *International Protection of the Environment: Treaties and Related Documents,* Volume XIX (Dobbs Ferry, N.Y.: Oceana, 1979), pp. 9497–9503.

DOCUMENT 4

GREAT LAKES WATER QUALITY AGREEMENT OF 1978

Revised

Great Lakes Water Quality Agreement of 1978 Agreement, with Annexes and Terms of Reference, between the United States and Canada signed at Ottawa November 22, 1978 and Phosphorus Load Reduction Supplement signed October 16, 1983 as amended by Protocol signed November 18, 1987

Office Consolidation

INTERNATIONAL JOINT COMMISSION UNITED STATES AND CANADA

September, 1989

PROTOCOL AMENDING THE 1978 AGREEMENT BETWEEN THE UNITED STATES OF AMERICA AND CANADA ON GREAT LAKES WATER QUALITY, AS AMENDED ON OCTOBER 16, 1983

The Government of the United States of America and the Government of Canada,

REAFFIRMING their commitment to achieving the purpose and objectives of the 1978 Agreement between the United States of America and Canada on Great Lakes Water Quality, as amended on October 16, 1983;

HAVING developed and implemented cooperative programs and measures to achieve such purpose and objectives;

RECOGNIZING the need for strengthened efforts to address the continuing contamination of the Great Lakes Basin Ecosystem, particularly by persistent toxic substances;

ACKNOWLEDGING that many of these toxic substances enter the Great Lakes System from air, from ground water infiltration, from sediments in the Lakes and from the runoff of non-point sources;

AWARE that further research and program development is now required to enable effective actions to be taken to address the continuing contamination of the Great Lakes;

DETERMINED to improve management processes for achieving Agreement objectives and to demonstrate firm leadership in the implementation of control measures;

Have agreed as follows:

AGREEMENT BETWEEN CANADA AND THE UNITED STATES OF AMERICA ON GREAT LAKES WATER QUALITY, 1978

The Government of Canada and the Government of the United States of America,

HAVING in 1972 and 1978 entered into Agreements on Great Lakes Water Quality;

REAFFIRMING their determination to restore and enhance water quality in the Great Lakes System;

CONTINUING to be concerned about the impairment of water quality on each side of the boundary to an extent that is causing injury to health and property on the other side, as described by the International Joint Commission;

REAFFIRMING their intent to prevent further pollution of the Great Lakes Basin Ecosystem owing to continuing population growth, resource development and increasing use of water;

REAFFIRMING in a spirit of friendship and cooperation the rights and obligations of both countries under the Boundary Waters Treaty, signed on January 11, 1909, and in particular their obligation not to pollute boundary waters;

CONTINUING to recognize that right of each country in the use of the Great Lakes waters;

HAVING decided that the Great Lakes Water Quality Agreements of 1972 and 1978 and subsequent reports of the International Joint Commission provide a sound basis for new and more effective cooperative actions to restore and enhance water quality in the Great Lakes Basin Ecosystem;

RECOGNIZING that restoration and enhancement of the boundary waters cannot be achieved independently of other parts of the Great Lakes Basin Ecosystem with which these waters interact;

CONCLUDING that the best means to preserve the aquatic ecosystem and achieve improved water quality throughout the Great Lakes System is by adopting common objectives, developing and implementing cooperative programs and other measures, and assigning special responsibilities and functions to the International Joint Commission;

Have agreed as follows:

ARTICLE 1 – DEFINITIONS

As used in this Agreement:

(a) "Agreement" means the present Agreement as distinguished from the Great Lakes Water Quality Agreement of April 15, 1972;

(b) "Annex" means any of the Annexes to this Agreement, each of which is attached to and forms and integral part of this Agreement;

(c) "Boundary waters of the Great Lakes System" or "boundary waters" means boundary waters, as defined in the Boundary Waters Treaty, that are within the Great Lakes System;

(d) "Boundary Waters Treaty" means the Treaty between the United States and Great Britain Relating to Boundary Waters, and Questions Arising Between the United States and Canada, signed at Washington on January 11, 1909;

(e) "Compatible regulations" means regulations no less restrictive than the agreed principles set out in this Agreement;

(f) "General Objectives" are broad descriptions of water quality conditions consistent with the protection of the beneficial uses and the level of environmental quality which the Parties desire to secure and which will provide overall water management guidance;

(g) "Great Lakes Basin Ecosystem" means the interacting components of air, land, water and living organisms, including humans, within the drainage basin of the St. Lawrence River at or upstream from the point at which this river becomes the international boundary between Canada and the United States;

(h) "Great Lakes System" means all of the streams river, lakes and other bodies of water that are within the drainage basin on the St. Lawrence River at or upstream from the point at which this river becomes the international boundary between Canada and the United States;

(i) "Harmful quantity" means any quantity of a substance that if discharged into receiving water would be inconsistent with the achievement of the General and Specific Objectives;

(j) "Hazardous polluting substance" means any element or compound identified by the Parties which, if discharged in any quantity into or upon receiving waters or adjoining shorelines, would present an imminent and substantial danger to public health or welfare; for this purpose, "public health or welfare" encompasses all factors affecting the health and welfare of humans including but not limited to human health, and conservation and protection of flora and fauna, public and private property, shorelines and beaches;

(k) "International Joint Commission" or "Commission" means the International Joint Commission established by the Boundary Waters Treaty;

(l) "Monitoring" means a scientifically designed system of continuing standardized measurements and observations and the evaluation thereof;

(m) "Objectives" means the General Objectives adopted pursuant to Article III and the Specific Objectives adopted pursuant to Article IV of this Agreement;

(n) "Parties" means the Government of Canada and the Government of the United States of America;

(o) "Phosphorus" means the element phosphorus present as a constituent of various organic and inorganic complexes and compounds;

(p) "Research" means development, interpretation and demonstration of advanced scientific knowledge for the resolution of issues but does not include monitoring and surveillance of water or air quality;

(q) "Science Advisory Board" means the Great Lakes Science Advisory Board of the International Joint Commission established pursuant to Article VIII of this Agreement;

(r) "Specific Objectives" means the concentration or quantity of a substance or level of effect that the Parties agree, after investigation, to recognize as a maximum or minimum desired limit for a defined body of water or portion thereof, taking into account the beneficial uses or level of environmental quality which the Parties desire to secure and protect;

(s) "State and Provincial Governments" means the Governments of the States of Illinois, Indiana, Michigan, Minnesota, New York, Ohio, Wisconsin, and the Commonwealth of Pennsylvania, and the Government of the Province of Ontario;

(t) "Surveillance" means specific observations and measurements relative to control or management;

(u) "Terms of Reference" means the Terms of Reference for the Joint Institutions and the Great Lakes Regional Office established pursuant to this Agreement, which are attached to and form an integral part of this Agreement;

(v) "Toxic substance" means a substance which can cause death, disease, behavioural abnormalities, cancer, genetic mutations, physiological or reproductive malfunctions or physical deformities in any organism or its offspring, or which can become poisonous after concentration in the food chain or in combination with other substances;

(w) "Tributary waters of the Great Lakes System" or "tributary waters" means all the waters within the Great Lakes System that are not boundary waters;

(x) "Water Quality Board" means the Great Lakes Water Quality Board of the International Joint Commission established pursuant to Article VIII of this Agreement.

ARTICLE II – PURPOSE

The purpose of the Parties is to restore and maintain the chemical, physical, and biological integrity of the waters of the Great Lakes Basin Ecosystem. In order to achieve this purpose, the Parties agree to make a maximum effort to develop programs, practices and technology necessary for a better understanding of the Great Lakes Basin Ecosystem and to eliminate or reduce to the maximum extent practicable the discharge of pollutants into the Great Lakes System.

Consistent with the provisions of this Agreement, it is the policy of the Parties that:

(a) The discharge of toxic substances in toxic amounts be prohibited and the discharge of any or all persistent toxic substances be virtually eliminated;

(b) Financial assistance to construct publicly owned waste treatment works be provided by a combination of local, state, provincial, and federal participation; and

(c) Coordinated planning processes and best management practices be developed and implemented by the respective jurisdictions to ensure adequate control of all sources of pollutants.

ARTICLE III – GENERAL OBJECTIVES

The Parties adopt the following General Objectives for the Great Lakes System. These waters should be:

(a) Free from substances that directly or indirectly enter the waters as a result of human activity and that will settle to form putrescent or otherwise objectionable sludge deposits, or that will adversely affect aquatic life or waterfowl;

(b) Free from floating materials such as debris, oil, scum, and other immiscible substances resulting from human activities in amounts that are unsightly or deleterious;

(c) Free from materials and heat directly or indirectly entering the water as a result of human activity that alone, or in combination with other materials, will produce colour, odour, taste, or other conditions in such a degree as to interfere with beneficial uses;

(d) Free from materials and heat directly or indirectly entering the water as a result of human activity that alone, or in combination with other materials, will produce conditions that are toxic or harmful to human, animal, or aquatic life; and

(e) Free from nutrients directly or indirectly entering the waters as a result of human activity in amounts that create growths of aquatic life that interfere with beneficial uses.

ARTICLE IV – SPECIFIC OBJECTIVES

1. The Parties adopt the Specific Objectives for the boundary waters of the Great Lakes System as set forth in Annex 1, subject to the following:

(a) The Specific Objectives adopted pursuant to this Article represent the minimum levels of water quality desired in the boundary waters of the Great Lakes System and are not intended to preclude the establishment of more stringent requirements.

(b) The determination of the achievement of Specific Objectives shall be based on statistically valid sampling data.

(c) Notwithstanding the adoption of Specific Objectives, all reasonable and practicable measures shall be taken to maintain or improve the existing water quality in those areas of the boundary waters of the Great Lakes System where such water quality is better than that prescribed by the Specific Objectives, and in those areas having outstanding natural resource value.

(d) The responsible regulatory agencies shall not consider flow augmentation as a substitute for adequate treatment to meet the Specific Objectives.

(e) The Parties recognize that in certain areas of inshore waters natural phenomena exist which, despite the best efforts of the Parties, will prevent the achievement of some of the Specific Objectives. As early as possible, these areas should be identified explicitly by the appropriate jurisdictions and reported to the International Joint Commission.

(f) The Parties recognize that there are areas in the boundary waters of the Great Lakes System where, due to human activity, one or more of the General or Specific Objectives of the Agreement are not being met. Pending virtual elimination of the persistent toxic substances in the Great Lakes System, the Parties, in cooperation with the State and Provincial Governments and the Commission, shall identify and work toward the elimination of: (i) Areas of Concern pursuant to Annex 2; (ii) Critical Pollutants pursuant to Annex 2; and (iii) Point Source Impact Zones pursuant to Annex 2.

2. The Specific Objectives for the boundary waters of the Great Lakes System or for particular portions thereof shall be kept under review by the Parties and the International Joint Commission, which shall make appropriate recommendations.

3. The Parties shall consult on:

(a) The establishment of Specific Objectives to protect beneficial uses from the combined effects of pollutants; and

(b) The control of pollutant loading rates for each lake basin to protect the integrity of the ecosystem over the long term.

ARTICLE V – STANDARDS, OTHER REGULATORY REQUIREMENTS, AND RESEARCH

1. Water quality standards and other regulatory requirements of the Parties shall be consistent with the achievement of the General and Specific Objectives. The Parties shall use their best efforts to ensure that water quality standards and other regulatory requirements of the State and Provincial Government shall similarly be consistent with the achievement of these Objectives. Flow augmentation shall not be considered as a substitute for adequate treatment to meet water quality standards or other regulatory requirements.

2. The Parties shall use their best efforts to ensure that:

(a) The principal research funding agencies in both countries orient the research programs of their organizations in response to research priorities identified by the Science Advisory Board and recommended by the Commission;

(b) Mechanisms be developed for appropriate cost-effective international cooperation; and

(c) Research priorities are undertaken in accordance with Annex 17.

ARTICLE VI – PROGRAMS AND OTHER MEASURES

1. The Parties, in cooperation with State and Provincial Governments, shall continue to develop and implement programs and other measures to fulfil the purpose of this Agreement and to meet the General and Specific Objectives. Where present treatment is inadequate to meet

the General and Specific Objectives, additional treatment shall be required. The programs and measures shall include the following:

(a) Pollution from Municipal Sources. Programs for the abatement, control and prevention of municipal discharges and urban drainage into the Great Lakes System. These programs shall be completed and in operation as soon as practicable, and in the case of municipal sewage treatment facilities no later than December 31, 1982. These programs shall include: (i) Construction and operation of waste treatment facilities in all municipalities having sewer systems to provide levels of treatment consistent with the achievement of phosphorus requirements and the General and Specific Objectives, taking into account the effects of waste from other sources; (ii) Provision of financial resources to ensure prompt construction of needed facilities; (iii) Establishment of requirements for construction and operating standards for facilities; (iv) Establishment of pretreatment requirements for all industrial plants discharging waste into publicly owned treatment works where such industrial wastes are not amenable to adequate treatment or removal using conventional municipal treatment processes; (v) Development and implementation of practical programs for reducing pollution from storm, sanitary, and combined sewer discharges; and (vi) Establishment of effective enforcement programs to ensure that the above pollution abatement requirements are fully met;

(b) Pollution from Industrial Sources. Programs for the abatement, control and prevention of pollution from industrial sources entering the Great Lakes System. These programs shall be completed and in operation as soon as practicable and in any case no later than December 31, 1983, and shall include: (i) Establishment of water treatment or control requirements expressed as effluent limitations (concentrations and/or loading limits for specific pollutants where possible) for all industrial plants, including power generating facilities, to provide levels of treatment or reduction or elimination of inputs of substances and effects consistent with the achievement of the General and Specific Objectives and other control requirements, taking into account the effects of waste from other sources; (ii) Requirements for the substantial elimination of discharges into the Great Lakes System of persistent toxic substances; (iii) Requirements for control of thermal discharges; (iv) Measures to control the discharges of radioactive materials into the Great Lakes System; (v) Requirements to minimize adverse environmental impacts of water intakes; (vi) Development and implementation of programs to meet industrial pre-treatment requirements as specified under sub-paragraph (a) (iv) above; and (vii) Establishment of effective enforcement programs to ensure the above pollution abatement requirements are fully met;

(c) Inventory of Pollution Abatement Requirements. Preparation of an inventory of pollution abatement requirements for all municipal and industrial facilities discharging into the Great Lakes System in order to gauge progress toward the earliest practicable completion and operation of the programs listed in sub-paragraphs (a) and (b) above. This inventory, prepared and revised annually, shall include compliance schedules and status of compliance with monitoring and effluent restrictions, and shall be made available to the International Joint Commission and to the public. In the initial preparation of this inventory, priority shall be given to the problem areas previously identified by the Water Quality Board;

(d) Eutrophication. Programs and measures for the reduction and control of inputs of phosphorus and other nutrients, in accordance with the provisions of Annex 3;

(e) Pollution from Agriculture, Forestry, and Other Land Use Activities. Measures for the abatement and control of pollution from agriculture, forestry and other land use activities including: (i) Measures for the control of pest control products used in the Great Lakes Basin to ensure that pest control products likely to have long term deleterious effects on the quality of water or its biota be used only as authorized by the responsible regulatory agencies; that inventories of pest control products used in the Great Lakes Basin be established and maintained by appropriate agencies; and that research and educational programs be strengthened to facilitate integration of cultural, biological and chemical pest control techniques; (ii) Measures for the abatement and control of pollution from animal husbandry operations, including encouragement to appropriate agencies to adopt policies and regulations regarding utilization of animal wastes, and site selection and disposal of liquid and solid wastes, and to strengthen educational and technical assistance programs to enable farmers to establish waste utilization, handling and disposal systems; (iii) Measures governing the hauling and disposal of liquid and solid wastes, including encouragement to appropriate regulatory agencies to ensure proper location, design and regulation governing land disposal, and to ensure sufficient, adequately trained technical and administrative capability to review plans and to supervise and monitor systems for application of wastes on land; (iv) Measures to review and supervise road salting practices and salt storage to ensure optimum use of salt and all-weather protection of salt stores in consideration of long-term environmental impact; (v) Measures to control soil losses from urban and suburban as well as rural areas; (vi) Measures to encourage and facilitate improvements in land use planning and management programs to take account of impacts on Great Lakes water quality; (vii) Other advisory programs and measures to abate and control inputs of nutrients, toxic substances and sediments from agricultural, forestry and other land use activities; (viii) Consideration of future recommendations from the International Joint Commission based on the Pollution from Land Use Activities Reference; and (ix) Conduct further non-point source programs in accordance with Annex 13;

(f) Pollution from Shipping Activities. Measures for the abatement and control of pollution from shipping sources, including: (i) Programs and compatible regulations to prevent discharges of harmful quantities of oil and hazardous polluting substances, in accordance with Annex 4; (ii) Compatible regulations for the control of discharges of vessel wastes, in accordance with Annex 5; (iii) Such compatible regulations to abate and control pollution from shipping sources as may be deemed desirable in the light of continuing reviews and studies to be undertaken in accordance with Annex 6; (iv) Programs and any necessary compatible regulations in accordance with Annexes 4 and 5, for the safe and efficient handling of shipboard generated wastes, including oil, hazardous polluting substances, garbage, waste water and sewage, and for their subsequent disposal, including the type and quantity of reception facilities and, if applicable, treatment standards; and (v) Establishment by the Canadian Coast Guard and the United States Coast Guard of a coordinated system for aerial and surface surveillance for the purpose of enforcement of regulations and the early identification, abatement and clean-up of spills of oil, hazardous polluting substances, or other pollution;

(g) Pollution from Dredging Activities. Measures for the abatement and control of pollution from all dredging activities, including the development of criteria for the identification of polluted sediments and compatible programs for disposal of polluted dredged material, in accordance with Annex 7. Pending the development of compatible criteria and programs, dredging operations shall be conducted in a manner that will minimize adverse effects on the environment;

(h) Pollution from Onshore and Offshore Facilities. Measures for the abatement and control of pollution from onshore and offshore facilities, including programs and compatible regulations for the prevention of discharges of harmful quantities of oil and hazardous polluting substances, in accordance with Annex 8;

(i) Contingency Plan. Maintenance of a joint contingency plan for use in the event of a discharge or the imminent threat of a discharge of oil or hazardous polluting substances, in accordance with Annex 9;

(j) Hazardous Polluting Substances. Implementation of Annex 10 concerning hazardous polluting substances. The Parties shall further consult from time to time for the purpose of revising the list of hazardous polluting substances and of identifying harmful quantities of these substances;

(k) Persistent Toxic Substances. Measures for the control of inputs of persistent toxic substances including control programs for their production, use, distribution and disposal, in accordance with Annex 12;

(l) Airborne Toxic Substances. Programs to identify pollutant sources and relative source contribution, including the more accurate definition of wet and dry deposition rates, for those substances which may have significant adverse effects on environmental quality including the indirect effects of impairment of tributary water quality through atmospheric deposition in drainage basins. In cases where significant contributions to Great Lakes pollution from atmospheric sources are identified, the Parties agree to consult on appropriate remedial programs. The Parties shall conduct such programs in accordance with Annex 15;

(m) Surveillance and Monitoring. Implementation of a coordinated surveillance and monitoring program in the Great Lakes System, in accordance with Annex 11, to assess compliance with pollution control requirements and achievement of the Objectives, to provide information for measuring local and whole lake response to control measures, and to identify emerging problems;

(n) Remedial Action Plans. Measures to ensure the development and implementation of Remedial Action Plans for Areas of Concern pursuant to Annex 2;

(o) Lakewide Management Plans. Measures to ensure the development and implementation of Lakewide Management Plans to address Critical Pollutants pursuant to Annex 2;

(p) Pollution from Contaminated Sediments. Measures for the abatement and control of pollution from all contaminated sediments, including the development of chemical and biological criteria for assessing the significance of the relative contamination arising from the sediments and compatible programs for remedial action for polluted sediments in accordance with Annex 14; and

(q) Pollution from Contaminated Groundwater and Subsurface Sources. Programs for the assessment and control of contaminated groundwater and subsurface sources entering the boundary waters of the Great Lakes System pursuant to Annex 16.

2. The Parties shall develop and implement such additional programs as they jointly decide are necessary and desirable to fulfil the purpose of this Agreement and to meet the General and Specific Objectives. The Parties shall develop and implement such additional programs as they jointly decide are necessary and desirable to fulfil the purpose of this Agreement and to meet the General and Specific Objectives.

ARTICLE VII – POWERS, RESPONSIBILITIES AND FUNCTIONS OF THE INTERNATIONAL JOINT COMMISSION

1. The International Joint Commission shall assist in the implementation of this Agreement. Accordingly, the Commission is hereby given, by a Reference pursuant to Article IX of the Boundary Waters Treaty, the following responsibilities:

(a) Collation, analysis and dissemination of data and information supplied by the Parties and State and Provincial Governments relating to the quality of the boundary waters of the Great Lakes System and to pollution that enters the boundary waters from tributary waters and other sources;

(b) Collection, analysis and dissemination of data and information concerning the General and Specific Objectives and the operation and effectiveness of the programs and other measures established pursuant to this Agreement;

(c) Tendering of advice and recommendations to the Parties and to the State and Provincial Governments on problems of and matters related to the quality of the boundary waters of the Great Lakes System including specific recommendations concerning the General and Specific Objectives, legislation, standards and other regulatory requirements, programs and other measures, and intergovernmental agreements relating to the quality of these waters;

(d) Tendering of advice and recommendations to the Parties in connection with matters covered under the Annexes to this Agreement;

(e) Provision of assistance in the coordination of the joint activities envisaged by this Agreement;

(f) Provision of assistance in and advice on matters related to research in the Great Lakes Basin Ecosystem, including identification of objectives for research activities, tendering of advice and recommendations concerning research to the Parties and to the State and Provincial Governments, and dissemination of information concerning research to interested persons and agencies;

(g) Investigations of such subjects related to the Great Lakes Basin Ecosystem as the Parties may from time to time refer to it.

2. In the discharge of its responsibilities under this Reference, the Commission may exercise all of the powers conferred upon it by the Boundary Waters Treaty and by any legislation passed pursuant thereto including the power to conduct public hearings and to compel the testimony of witnesses and the production of documents.

3. The Commission shall make a full report to the Parties and to the State and Provincial Governments no less frequently than biennially concerning progress toward the achievement of the General and Specific Objectives including, as appropriate, matters related to Annexes to this Agreement. This report shall include an assessment of the effectiveness of the programs and other measures undertaken pursuant to this Agreement, and advice and recommendations. In alternate years, the Commission may submit a summary report. The Commission may at any time make special reports to the Parties, to the State and Provincial Governments and to the public concerning any problem of water quality in the Great Lakes System.

4. The Commission may in its discretion publish any report, statement or other document prepared by it in the discharge of its functions under this Reference.

5. The Commission shall have authority to verify independently the data and other information submitted by the Parties and by the State and Provincial Governments through such tests or other means as appear appropriate to it, consistent with the Boundary Waters Treaty and with applicable legislation.

6. The Commission shall carry out its responsibilities under the Reference utilizing principally the services of the Water Quality Board and the Science Advisory Board established under Article VIII of this Agreement. The Commission shall also ensure liaison and coordination between the institutions established under this Agreement and other institutions which may address concerns relevant to the Great Lakes Basin Ecosystem, including both those within its purview, such as those Boards related to the Great Lakes levels and air pollution matters, and other international bodies as appropriate.

ARTICLE VIII – JOINT INSTITUTIONS AND REGIONAL OFFICE

1. To assist the International Joint Commission in the exercise of the powers and responsi-

bilities assigned to it under this Agreement, there shall be two Boards:

(a) A Great Lakes Water Quality Board which shall be the principal advisor to the Commission. The Board shall be composed of an equal number of members from Canada and the United States, including representatives from the Parties and each of the State and Provincial Governments; and

(b) A Great Lakes Science Advisory Board shall provide advice on research to the Commission and to the Water Quality Board. The Board shall further provide advice on scientific matters referred to it by the Commission, or by the Water Quality Board in consultation with the Commission. The Science Advisory Board shall consist of managers of Great Lakes research programs and recognized experts on Great Lakes water quality problems and related fields.

2. The members of the Water Quality Board and the Science Advisory Board shall be appointed by the Commission after consultation with the appropriate government or governments concerned. The functions of the Boards shall be as specified in the terms of Reference appended to this Agreement.

3. To provide administrative support and technical assistance to the two Boards, and to provide information service for the programs, including public hearings, undertaken by the International Joint Commission and by the Boards, there shall be a Great Lakes Regional Office of the International Joint Commission. Specific duties and organization of the Office shall be as specified in the Terms of Reference appended to this Agreement.

4. The Commission shall submit an annual budget of anticipated expenses to be incurred in carrying out its responsibilities under this Agreement to the Parties for approval. Each Party shall seek funds to pay one-half of the annual budget so approved, but neither Party shall be under an obligation to pay a larger amount than the other toward this budget.

ARTICLE XII – EXISTING RIGHTS AND OBLIGATIONS

Nothing in this Agreement shall be deemed to diminish the rights and obligations of the Parties as set forth in the Boundary Waters Treaty.

ARTICLE XV – SUPERSESSION

This Agreement supersedes the Great Lakes Water Quality Agreement of April 15, 1972, and shall be referred to as the "Great Lakes Water Quality Agreement of 1978."

IN WITNESS WHEREOF the undersigned representatives, duly authorized by their respective Governments, have signed this Agreement.

DONE in duplicate at Ottawa in the English and French languages, both versions being equally authentic, this 22nd day of November 1978.

EN FOI DE QUOI, les représentants soussignées, dûment autorisés par leur Gouvernement respectif, ont signé le présent Accord.

FAIT en double exemplaire à Ottawa en français et en anglais, chaque version faisant également foi, ce 22e jour de novembre 1978.

Source: http://www.on.ec.gc.ca/glwqa/

DOCUMENT 5

THE REPORT OF THE WORLD COMMISSION ON DAMS
AN OVERVIEW–NOVEMBER 16 2000

The Commission

In April 1997, with support from the World Bank and IUCN–The World Conservation Union, representatives of diverse interests met in Gland, Switzerland, in light of a recent World Bank report, to discuss highly controversial issues associated with large dams. The workshop brought together 39 participants from governments, the private sector, international financial institutions, civil society organisations and affected people. One proposal that came out of the meeting was for all parties to work together in establishing the World Commission on Dams (WCD) with a mandate to:

- review the development effectiveness of large dams and assess alternatives for water resources and energy development; and
- develop internationally acceptable criteria, guidelines and standards, where appropriate, for the planning, design, appraisal, construction, operation, monitoring and decommissioning of dams.

The WCD began its work in May 1998 under the Chairmanship of Prof. Kader Asmal, who was then South Africa's Minister of Water Affairs and Forestry; its members were chosen to reflect regional diversity, expertise and stakeholder perspectives.

- The WCD was independent, with each member serving in an individual capacity and none representing an institution or a country
- The Commission conducted the first comprehensive global and independent review of the performance and impacts of large dams, and the options available for water and energy development

• Public consultation and access to the Commission was a key component of the process. The WCD Forum, with 68 members representing a cross-section of interests, views and institutions, was consulted throughout the Commission's work

• The WCD pioneered a new funding model involving all interest groups in the debate: 53 public, private and civil society organisations pledged funds to the WCD process

The final report of the World Commission on Dams, *Dams and Development: A New Framework for Decision-Making*, was released in November 2000.

This overview document provides a highly condensed summary of Dams and Development. We urge readers to refer to the relevant sections in the full report to capture both context and nuances of the findings and recommendations. The full report also includes a detailed list of acknowledgements that could not be reproduced here, as well as a comment note by Medha Patkar.

The WCD Commissioners

Extensive consultation with all interested groups resulted in invitations to eminent persons to serve as members of the World Commission on Dams.

They were selected on the basis of their wide-ranging backgrounds, views, and the expertise they bring to the debate, with the Secretary General appointed an ex-officio member of the Commission.

The Commissioners collectively were responsible for fulfilling the terms of the WCD mandate. The Commissions work was advisory in nature and not investigatory. Unlike a judicial commission, the WCD was not set up to adjudicate on specific disputes.

Chair
Prof. Kader Asmal
Minister of Education
South Africa

Vice Chair
Mr. Lakshmi Chand Jain
Chairperson
Industrial Development Services
India

Mr. Don Blackmore
Chief Executive
Murray-Darling Basin Commission
Australia

Ms. Joji Cariño
Tebtebba Foundation
Philippines

Prof. José Goldemberg
Institute of Electronics and Energy
University of São Paulo
Brazil

Dr. Judy Henderson
Former Chair
Oxfam International
Australia

Mr. Göran Lindahl
President and CEO
ABB Ltd.
Sweden

Ms. Deborah Moore
Senior Advisor
Environmental Defense
United States

Ms. Medha Patkar
Founder
Narmada Bachao Andolan
(Struggle to Save the Narmada River)
India

Prof. Thayer Scudder
Professor of Anthropology
California Institute of Technology
United States

Dr. Jan Veltrop
Honorary President
International Commission on Large Dams
(ICOLD)
United States

Mr. Achim Steiner
WCD Secretary General
(Ex-officio Member of the Commission)
Germany

The WCD Report–In Brief

The WCD report is a milestone in the evolution of dams as a development option. The debate about dams is a debate about the very meaning, purpose and pathways for achieving development. Through its Global Review of the performance of dams, the Commission presents an integrated assessment of when, how and why dams succeed or fail in meeting development objectives. This provides the rationale for a fundamental shift in options assessment and in the planning and project cycles for water and energy resources development.

The Commission's framework for decision-making is based on five core values–equity, sustainability, efficiency, participatory decision-making and accountability. It proposes:

• a rights-and-risks approach as a practical and principled basis for identifying all legitimate stakeholders in negotiating development choices and agreements

• seven strategic priorities and corresponding policy principles for water and energy resources development - gaining public acceptance, comprehensive options assessment, addressing existing dams, sustaining rivers and livelihoods, recognising entitlements and sharing benefits, ensuring compliance, and sharing rivers for peace, development and security; and

• criteria and guidelines for good practice related to the strategic priorities, ranging from life-cycle and environmental flow assessments to impoverishment risk analysis and integrity pacts.

The Commission's rationale and recommendations offer scope for progress that no single perspective can offer on its own. They will ensure that decision-making on water and energy development:

• reflects a comprehensive approach to integrating social, environmental and economic dimensions of development

• creates greater levels of transparency and certainty for all involved; and

• increases levels of confidence in the ability of nations and communities to meet their future water and energy needs

Dams and Development–An Introduction

Dams have been built for thousands of years–dams to manage flood waters, to harness water as hydropower, to supply water to drink or for industry, or to irrigate fields. By 1950, governments, or in some countries the private sector, were building increasing numbers of dams as populations increased and national economies grew. At least 45,000 large dams have been built as a response to meet an energy or water need. Today nearly half of the world's rivers have at least one large dam.

As we start the new century, one-third of the countries in the world rely on hydropower for more than half their electricity supply, and large dams generate 19% of electricity overall. Half the world's large dams were built exclusively or primarily for irrigation, and some 30-40% of the 271 million hectares irrigated world-wide rely on dams. Dams have been promoted as an important means of meeting perceived needs for water and energy services and as long-term, strategic investments with the ability to deliver multiple benefits. Some of these additional benefits are typical of all large public infrastructure projects, while others are unique to dams and specific to particular projects.

Regional development, job creation, and fostering an industry base with export capability are most often cited as additional considerations for building large dams. Other goals include creating income from export earnings, either through direct sales of electricity or by selling cash crops or processed products from electricity-intensive industry such as aluminium refining. Clearly, dams can play an important role in meeting people's needs.

But the last 50 years have also highlighted the performance and the social and environmental impacts of large dams. They have fragmented and transformed the world's rivers, while global estimates suggest that 40-80 million people have been displaced by reservoirs.

As the basis for decision-making has become more open, inclusive and transparent in many countries, the decision to build a large dam has been increasingly contested, to the point where the future of large dam-building in many countries is in question.The enormous investments and widespread impacts of large dams have seen conflicts flare up over the siting and impacts of large dams–both those in place and those on the drawing board, making large dams one of the most hotly contested issues in sustainable development today.

Proponents point to the social and economic development demands that dams are intended to meet, such as irrigation, electricity, flood control and water supply. Opponents point to the adverse impacts of dams, such as debt burden, cost overruns, displacement and impoverishment of people, destruction of important ecosystems and fishery resources, and the inequitable sharing of costs and benefits.

With these conflicts and pressures in mind, the World Commission on Dams began its work in May 1998. One of the Commissioners' first points of agreement was that dams are only a means to an end. What is that end? How central are the challenges that large dams set out to meet? And how well can they meet these challenges?

The WCD concluded that the 'end' that any project achieves must be the sustainable improvement of human welfare. This means a significant advance of human development on a basis that is economically viable, socially equitable and environmentally sustainable. If a large dam is the best way to achieve this goal, it deserves support. Where other options offer better solutions, they should be favoured over large dams. Thus the debate around dams challenges views of how societies develop and manage water resources in the broader context of development choices.

After more than two years of intense study, dialogue with those for and against large dams, and reflection, the Commission believes there can no longer be any justifiable doubt about five key points:

1.) Dams have made an important and significant contribution to human development, and the benefits derived from them have been considerable

2.) In too many cases an unacceptable and often unnecessary price has been paid to secure those benefits, especially in social and environmental terms, by people displaced, by communities downstream, by taxpayers and by the natural environment

3.) Lack of equity in the distribution of benefits has called into question the value of many dams in meeting water and energy development needs when compared with the alternatives

4.) By bringing to the table all those whose rights are involved and who bear the risks associated with different options for water and energy resources development, the conditions for a positive resolution of competing interests and conflicts are created

5.) Negotiating outcomes will greatly improve the development effectiveness of water and energy projects by eliminating unfavourable projects at an early stage, and by offering as a choice only those options that key stakeholders agree represent the best ones to meet the needs in question.

The Changing Context

The Commission's overall conclusions about large dams are grounded in a basic understanding about the relationships between water, dams and development. (See Box 1 for the definition of a large dam.) One of the greatest challenges facing the world in this new century is rethinking the management of freshwater resources. A number of global initiatives and reports have documented the dramatic impact of withdrawals from the world's lakes, rivers and underground aquifers. Total annual freshwater withdrawals today are estimated at 3,800 cubic kilometres–twice as much as 50 years ago.

Box 1. ***What is a large dam?***

According to the International Commission on Large Dams (ICOLD), a large dam is 15 m or more high (from the foundation).

If dams are between 5–15 metres and have a reservoir volume of more than 3 million cubic metres they are also classified as large dams.

Using this definition, there are more than 45,000 large dams around the world.

The imperative to supply growing populations and economies with water when groundwater is depleted, water quality is declining, and there are increasingly severe limits to surface water extraction has brought sustainable water resources management to the top of the global development agenda. These pressures on water contain a wide range of threats, but they also generate the momentum for new opportunities and policy changes.

During the past few decades, societies have moved from seeing water as a free good to viewing it as a limited natural resource and, more recently, as an economic good and a human right. Thus water is recognised as a scarce natural resource, which gives rise to equity considerations in its allocation.

How much water is required for one more person, or one more urban dweller? Water use per capita varies greatly in different regions of the world. Although what constitutes an appropriate level of domestic water consumption is influenced by climate and culture, several international agencies and experts have proposed 50 litres per person per day as enough to cover basic human requirements for drinking, sanitation, bathing and cooking. In 1990, more than a billion people had less than that. At the same time, households in industrial countries and wealthy city-dwellers in developing countries were using 4–14 times as much.

Dams and Development notes the forecasts of leading analysts who foresee growing competition for water to meet demands for agriculture, industry and drinking water.

• Competition will increase among the three largest users in global terms–agriculture (67%), industry (19%) and municipal/residential (9%) uses–and these all will continue to draw from the water needed to sustain natural systems

• A consumption factor that may be significant in dry climates is evaporation from reservoirs, estimated to be close to 5% of total water withdrawals

• A projection prepared for the Vision for Water and Food suggests that irrigation alone may require an increase in water supplies in the range of 15–20% by 2025

• By 2025 there will be a total of 3.5 billion people living in water-stressed countries. Empirical evidence suggests that limited water supplies, combined with current agricultural practices and population growth, are a barrier to meeting the goal of food self-sufficiency in more and more countries, increasing the attention paid to food security and the security of other environmental resources

• Two billion people lack electricity, and electricity demand in developing economies continues to rise

• Freshwater species, especially fish, are increasingly threatened, a significant percentage of wetlands have already been lost, and the capacity of aquatic ecosystems to produce many of the goods and services on which societies depend is rapidly declining, making water for nature an essential consideration

During the last century, much of the world turned to dams to help meet escalating demands for water. Indeed, from the 1930s to the 1970s the construction of large dams became–in the eyes of many–synonymous with development and economic progress. Viewed as symbols of modernisation and humanity's ability to control and use nature's resources, dam construction saw a dramatic increase.

This trend reached a peak in the 1970s, when on average two or three new large dams were commissioned each day somewhere in the world. The decline in dam building since then has been equally dramatic, especially in North America and Europe, where most technically attractive sites are already developed.

The top five dam-building countries account for more than three-quarters of all large dams worldwide, with approximately two-thirds of the world's existing large dams found in developing countries. Hydropower accounts for more than 90% of the total electricity supply in 24 countries, such as Brazil and Norway. Half of the world's large dams are built exclusively for irrigation, and dams are estimated to contribute to 12–16% of world food production. In addition, in at least 75 countries large dams have been built to control floods. For many nations, dams remain the largest single investment project in the country.

These hydropower, irrigation, water supply and flood control services were widely seen as sufficient to justify the significant investments made in dams, and other benefits were often cited as well. These included the impact of economic prosperity on a region due to multiple cropping, rural electrification and the expansion of physical and social infrastructure such as roads and schools. The benefits were seen as self-evident. When balanced with the construction and operational costs–in economic and financial terms–these benefits were seen to justify dams as the most competitive option.

What Is the Debate About?

As noted earlier, the reported returns on the investments made in dams have increasingly been questioned. The notion of costs versus reported benefits emerged as a public concern, given growing experience and knowledge about the performance and consequences of dams. Driven by research and information on the impacts of dams on people, river basins and ecosystems, as well as data on economic performance, opposition began to grow. During the early stages of this process, debate and controversy focused on specific dams and their local impacts. But gradually these locally driven conflicts began to evolve into a more general and ultimately a global debate about dams.

The issues surrounding dams are the same issues that surround water, and how water-related decisions are made, as well as how development effectiveness is assessed. There is little public controversy about the choice between an embankment dam or a gravity dam, or about whether to use earth, concrete or rock-fill. The problems all relate to what the dam will do to river flow and to rights of access to water and river resources; to whether the dam will uproot existing settlements, disrupt the culture and sources of livelihood of local communities, or deplete or degrade environmental resources; and to whether the dam is the best economic investment of public funds and resources.

The debate is partly about what occurred in the past and continues to occur today, and partly about what may unfold in the future if more dams are built. In some countries, it is driven primarily by specific social or environmental concerns; in others, by broader development considerations. In the United States, where the rate of decommissioning is greater than the rate of construction of new large dams, the debate is perhaps as intense as–but qualitatively different from–the debate in India, which along with China is now building the most dams.

The two principal poles in the debate illustrate the range of views on past experience with large dams. One perspective focuses on the gap between the promised benefits of a dam and the actual outcomes. The other view looks at the challenges of water and energy development from a perspective of "nation building" and resource allocation. To proponents, the answer to any questions about past performance is self-evident, as they maintain that dams have generally performed well as an integral part of water and energy resource development strategies in over 140 nations and, with exceptions, have provided an indispensable range of water and energy services.

Opponents contend that better, cheaper, more benign options for meeting water and energy needs exist and have been frequently ignored, from small-scale, decentralised water supply and electricity options to large-scale end-use efficiency and demand-side management options. Dams, it is argued, have often been selected over other options that may meet water or energy goals at lower cost or that may offer development benefits that are more sustainable and more equitable.

Although there may be agreement on such issues as the need to take environmental and social costs of dams more seriously and to consult systematically with affected people, deep fault lines still separate critics and proponents on a number of financial, economic, social and environmental issues. Among the most intractable are:

- the extent to which alternatives to dams are viable for achieving various development goals, and whether alternatives are complementary or mutually exclusive
- the extent to which adverse environmental and social impacts are acceptable
- the degree to which adverse environmental and social impacts can be avoided or mitigated; and
- the extent to which local consent should govern development decisions in the future

The decision to build a large dam today is rarely only a local or national one. The debate has been transformed from a local process of assessing costs and benefits to one in which dams in general are the focus of a global debate about development strategies and choices.

What Did the WCD Global Review of Large Dams Find?

To fulfil its mandate to review the development effectiveness of large dams and assess alternatives for water resources and energy development, the Commission undertook eight detailed case studies of large dams and prepared country reviews for India and China plus a briefing paper on Russia and the Newly Independent States. (See Box 2 for a list of the case study dams.)

A survey of 125 large dams was also developed, along with 17 thematic reviews on social, environmental and economic issues; on alternatives to dams; and on governance and institutional processes. There were also 947 submissions and presentations at four regional consultations. All these inputs formed the core of the WCD Knowledge Base that served to inform the Commission on the main issues surrounding dams and their alternatives.

*Box 2. **WCD Case Study dams***

***Aslantas dam,** Ceyhan River Basin, Turkey*

***Glomma-Lågen Basin,** Norway*

***Grand Coulee dam,** Columbia River, United States/Canada*

***Kariba dam,** Zambezi River, Zambia/Zimbabwe*

***Pak Mun dam,** Mun-Mekong River Basin, Thailand*

***Tarbela dam,** Indus River Basin, Pakistan*

***Tucuruí dam,** Tocantins River, Brazil*

***Gariep and Vanderkloof dams,** Orange River, South Africa (pilot study)*

The Global Review had three components:

- an independent review of the performance and impacts of large dams (looking at technical, financial and economic performance; ecosystem and climate impacts; social impacts; and the distribution of project gains and losses)
- an assessment of the alternatives to dams, the opportunities they provide, and the obstacles they face; and
- an analysis of planning, decision-making and compliance issues that underpin the selection, design, construction, operation and decommissioning of dams

The WCD's evaluation of performance was based on the targets set for large dams by their proponents–the criteria that provided the basis for government approval and financing. The Commission's analysis gave particular attention to understanding why, how and where dams did not achieve their intended outcome, or indeed produced unanticipated outcomes. An integral part of this research involved documenting good practices that have emerged as a response to past shortcomings and difficulties. Presenting this analysis does not overlook the substantial benefits derived from dams, but rather responds to the question of why some dams achieve their goals while others fail.

Technical, Financial and Economic Performance

The degree to which large dams in the WCD Knowledge Base have delivered services and net benefits as planned varied substantially from one project to the next, with a considerable portion falling short of physical and economic targets. In spite of this, the services produced by dams are considerable, as noted earlier. Irrespective of performance against targets, the Knowledge Base also confirmed the longevity of large dams, with many continuing to generate benefits after 30–40 years of operation.

A sectoral review of technical, financial and economic performance of dams in the Knowledge Base in terms of planned versus actual performance suggested the following:

- Large dams designed to deliver irrigation services have typically fallen short of physical targets, did not recover their costs and have been less profitable in economic terms than expected

• Large dams built to deliver hydropower tend to perform close to but still below targets for power generation, generally meet their financial targets but demonstrate variable economic performance relative to targets, and include a number of notable under- and over-performers

• Large dams built for municipal and industrial water supply have generally fallen short of intended targets for timing and delivery of bulk water supply and have exhibited poor financial cost recovery and economic performance

• Large dams with a flood control component have provided important benefits in this regard, but at the same time have led to greater vulnerability to flood hazards due to increased settlement in areas still at risk from floods, and in some cases have worsened flood damages for a number of reasons, including poor operation of dams

• Large dams that serve multiple purposes also under-achieve relative to targets, in some cases exceeding the shortfalls registered by single-purpose projects, demonstrating that the targets established were often over-optimistic

The review of performance suggested two further findings:

• Large dams in the Knowledge Base have a marked tendency towards schedule delays and significant cost overruns

• Growing concern over the cost and effectiveness of large dams and associated structural measures have led to the adoption of integrated flood management that emphasises a mix of policy and non-structural measures to reduce the vulnerability of communities to flooding

The review also examined factors related to the physical sustainability of large dams and their benefits and confirmed that:

• Ensuring the safety of dams will require increasing attention and investment as the stock of dams ages, maintenance costs rise and climate change possibly alters the hydrological regime used as a basis for the design of dam spillways

• Sedimentation and the consequent long-term loss of storage is a serious concern globally, and the effects will be particularly felt by basins with high geological or human-induced erosion rates, dams in the lower reaches of rivers and dams with smaller storage volumes

• Waterlogging and salinity affect one-fifth of irrigated land globally–including land irrigated by large dams–and have severe, long-term and often permanent impacts on land, agriculture and livelihoods where rehabilitation is not undertaken

Using the information on the performance of large dams collected in the WCD Knowledge Base, the Commission's report shows that there is considerable scope for improving the selection of projects and the operation of existing large dams and their associated infrastructure. Considering the enormous capital invested in large dams, it is surprising that substantive evaluations of project performance are few in number, narrow in scope and poorly integrated across impact categories and scales.

Ecosystems and Large Dams

The generic nature of the impacts of large dams on ecosystems, biodiversity and downstream livelihoods is increasingly well known. From the WCD Knowledge Base it is clear that large dams have led to:

• the loss of forests and wildlife habitat, the loss of species populations and the degradation of upstream catchment areas due to inundation of the reservoir area

• the loss of aquatic biodiversity, of upstream and downstream fisheries, and of the services of downstream floodplains, wetlands, and riverine, estuarine and adjacent marine ecosystems; and

• cumulative impacts on water quality, natural flooding and species composition where a number of dams are sited on the same river

On balance, the ecosystem impacts are more negative than positive and they have led, in many cases, to significant and irreversible loss of species and ecosystems. In some cases, however, enhancement of ecosystem values does occur, through the creation of new wetland habitat and the fishing and recreational opportunities provided by new reservoirs.

The Commission found that reservoirs sampled so far by scientists all emit greenhouse gases, as do natural lakes, due to the rotting of vegetation and carbon inflows from the catchment. The scale of such emissions is highly variable. Preliminary data from a Case Study hydropower dam in Brazil show that the gross level of these emissions is significant, relative to emissions from equivalent thermal power plants.

However, in other reservoirs studied (notably those in boreal zones), gross emissions of greenhouse gases are significantly lower than the thermal alternative. A full comparison would require measurements of the emissions from natural pre-impoundment habitats. More research is needed on a case-by-case basis to demonstrate the capacity of hydropower to offset climate change.

Efforts to date to counter the ecosystem impacts of large dams have met with limited success due to the lack of attention to anticipating and avoiding such impacts, the poor quality and uncertainty of predictions, the difficulty of coping with all impacts, and the only partial implementation and success of mitigation measures. More specifically:

• It is not possible to mitigate many of the impacts of reservoir creation on terrestrial ecosystems and biodiversity, and efforts to 'rescue' wildlife have met with little long-term success

• The use of fish passes to mitigate the blockage of migratory fish has had little success, as the technology has often not been tailored to specific sites and species

• Good mitigation results from a good information base; early co-operation between ecologists, the dam design team and affected people; and regular monitoring and feedback on the effectiveness of mitigation measures

• Environmental flow requirements (which include managed flood releases) are increasingly used to reduce the impacts of changed streamflow regimes on aquatic, floodplain and coastal ecosystems downstream

Given the limited success of traditional mitigation measures, increased attention through legislation is now given to avoidance or minimisation of ecological impacts through setting aside particular river segments or basins in their natural state and through the selection of alternative projects, sites or designs. In addition, governments are experimenting with a 'compensatory' approach, offsetting the loss of ecosystems and biodiversity caused by a large dam through investment in conservation and regeneration measures and through protection of other threatened sites of equivalent ecological value.

Finally, in a number of industrialised countries, but particularly in the United States, ecosystem restoration is being implemented as a result of the decommissioning of large and small dams.

People and Large Dams

In terms of the social impacts of dams, the Commission found that the negative effects were frequently neither adequately assessed nor accounted for. The range of these impacts is substantial, including on the lives, livelihoods and health of the affected communities dependent on the riverine environment:

• Some 40–80 million people have been physically displaced by dams worldwide

• Millions of people living downstream from dams–particularly those reliant on natural floodplain function and fisheries–have also suffered serious harm to their livelihoods and the future productivity of their resources has been put at risk

• Many of the displaced were not recognised (or enumerated) as such, and therefore were not resettled or compensated

• Where compensation was provided it was often inadequate, and where the physically displaced were enumerated, many were not included in resettlement programmes

• Those who were resettled rarely had their livelihoods restored, as resettlement programmes have focused on physical relocation rather than the economic and social development of the displaced

• The larger the magnitude of displacement, the less likely it is that even the livelihoods of affected communities can be restored

• Even in the 1990s, impacts on downstream livelihoods were, in many cases, not adequately assessed or addressed in the planning and design of large dams

In sum, the Knowledge Base demonstrated a generalised lack of commitment or lack of capacity to cope with displacement. In addition, large dams in the Knowledge Base have also had significant adverse effects on cultural heritage through the loss of cultural resources of local communities and the submergence and degradation of plant and animal remains, burial sites and archaeological monuments.

The Knowledge Base indicated that the poor, other vulnerable groups and future generations are likely to bear a disproportionate share of the social and environmental costs of large dam projects without gaining a commensurate share of the economic benefits:

• Indigenous and tribal peoples and vulnerable ethnic minorities have suffered disproportionate levels of displacement and negative impacts on livelihood, culture and spiritual existence

• Affected populations living near reservoirs as well as displaced people and downstream communities have often faced adverse health and livelihood outcomes from environmental change and social disruption

• Among affected communities, gender gaps have widened and women have frequently borne a disproportionate share of the social costs and were often discriminated against in the sharing of benefits

Where such inequities exist in the distribution of the costs and benefits, the Global Review emphasises that the 'balance-sheet' approach to adding up the costs and benefits is increasingly seen as unacceptable on equity grounds and as a poor means of choosing the 'best' projects. In any event, the true economic profitability of large dam projects remains elusive, as the environmental and social costs of large dams were poorly accounted for in economic terms.

More to the point, failures to account adequately for these impacts and to fulfil commitments that were made have led to the impoverishment and suffering of millions, giving rise to growing opposition to dams by affected communities worldwide. Innovative examples of processes for making reparations and sharing project benefits are emerging that provide hope that past injustices can be remedied and future ones avoided.

Options for Water and Energy Resources Development

The Global Review examined the options for meeting energy, water and food needs in today's circumstances and the barriers and enabling conditions that determine choice or adoption of particular options. Many options currently exist–including demand-side management (DSM), supply efficiency, and new supply options. These can all improve or expand water and energy services and meet evolving development needs across all segments of society. Viewing these options in an integrated fashion, rather than for individual sectors, suggested the following general findings and lessons:

• Demand-side management options include reduced consumption, recycling and technological and policy options that promote efficiency of water and power at the point of end-use. DSM has significant untapped and universal potential and provides a major opportunity to reduce water stress and power requirements as well as achieve other benefits such as the reduction of greenhouse gas emissions.

• Improving system management can defer the need for new sources of supply by enhancing supply and conveyance efficiency. Needless loss of power and water can be avoided through reductions in water leakages from the system, keeping up with system maintenance and upgrading of control, transmission and distribution technology in the power sector

• Basin and catchment management through vegetative and structural measures offers an opportunity across all sectors to reduce sedimentation of reservoirs and canals and to manage the timing and quantity of peak, seasonal and annual flows, as well as groundwater recharge

• A number of supply options have emerged that are locally and environmentally appropriate, economically viable and acceptable to the public, including recycling, rainwater harvesting and wind power

The ability of various options to meet existing and future needs or to replace conventional supplies depends on the specific context, but in general they offer significant potential, individually and collectively.

Decision-Making, Planning and Compliance

As a development choice, large dams often became a focal point for the interests of politicians, dominant and centralised government agencies, international financing agencies and the dam-building industry. Involvement from civil society varied with the degree of debate and open political discourse in a country. However, dams in the WCD Knowledge Base reveal a generalised failure to recognise affected people as partners in the planning process, with rights, and to empower them to participate in the process.

Foreign assistance has accounted for less than 15% of total funding for dams in developing countries. Still, the funds provided–more than $4 billion per year during the peak of lending in 1975–84–played an important role in promoting and financing large dams in countries building only a few dams. These countries have often been vulnerable to conflicts between the interests of governments, donors and industry involved in foreign assistance programmes, on the one hand, and improved development outcomes for rural people, particularly the poor, on the other hand.

To a lesser extent this assistance has supported larger countries seeking to build many dams (including China, India and Brazil), primarily through the provision of finance for dam-building programmes. In shared river basins, the lack of agreements on water use is an increasing concern and cause for tension, particularly as demands grow and unilateral decisions by one country to build large dams alter water flows within a basin, with significant consequences for other riparian States.

Evaluation of the planning and project cycle for large dams revealed a series of limitations, risks and failures in the manner in which these facilities have been planned, operated and evaluated:

• Participation and transparency in planning processes for large dams frequently was neither inclusive nor open

• Options assessment has been typically limited in scope and confined primarily to technical parameters and the narrow application of economic cost-benefit analyses

• The participation of affected people and the undertaking of environmental and social impact assessment have often occurred late in the process and were limited in scope

• The paucity of monitoring and evaluation activity once a large dam is built has impeded learning from experience

• Many countries have not yet established licensing periods that clarify the responsibilities of the owner towards the end of the dam's effective life

The net effect of these difficulties is that once a proposed dam project has passed preliminary technical and economic feasibility tests and attracted interest from government, external financing agencies or political interests, the momentum behind the project often prevails over further assessments. As a result, many dams were not built based on a comprehensive assessment and evaluation of the technical, financial and economic criteria applicable at the time, much less the social and environmental criteria that apply in today's context. That many such projects have not met standards applicable in either context is therefore not surprising, but nonetheless cause for concern.

Conflicts over dams stem also from the failure of dam proponents and financing agencies to fulfil commitments made, observe statutory regulations and abide by internal guidelines. In some cases, the opportunity for corruption provided by dams as large-scale infrastructure projects further distorted decision-making, planning and implementation. Whereas substantial improvements in policies, legal requirements and assessment guidelines have occurred, particularly in the 1990s, it appears that business is often conducted as usual when it comes to actual planning and decision-making. Moreover, where substantial differences arise between proponents and those potentially affected, efforts to modify plans and decisions often must resort to legal or other action outside the normal planning process. Regional Consultations held by the Commission underscored that past conflicts remain largely unresolved for a number of reasons, including poor experience with appeals, dispute resolution and recourse mechanisms.

Throughout the Global Review recent examples and illustrations of good practice are presented that form the basis of the Commission's optimism that these barriers are surmountable, and that these difficulties are not inevitable. As a means of reducing negative impacts and conflicts, these experiences indicate that there are opportunities, and indeed a responsibility, to:

- increase the efficiency of existing assets;
- avoid and minimise ecosystem impacts;
- engage in participatory, multi-criteria analysis of development needs and options;
- ensure that displaced and project-affected peoples' livelihoods are improved;
- resolve past inequities and injustices, and transform project-affected people into beneficiaries;
- conduct regular monitoring and periodic review; and
- develop, apply and enforce incentives, sanctions and recourse mechanisms–especially in the area of environmental and social performance.

The Commission's recommendations deliver a way forward that can improve planning, decision-making and compliance, and thereby capitalise on the options available–whether technological, policy or institutional in nature–and provide economically efficient, socially equitable and environmentally sustainable solutions to meet future water and energy needs.

How Can We Achieve Better Outcomes?

The debate about dams is a debate about the very meaning, purpose and pathways for achieving development. Along with all development choices, decisions on dams and their alternatives must respond to a wide range of needs, expectations, objectives and constraints. They are a function of public choice and public policy. To resolve underlying conflicts about the effectiveness of dams and their alternatives, a broad consensus is needed on the norms that guide development choices and the criteria that should define the process of negotiation and decision-making.

To improve development outcomes in the future we need to look at proposed water and energy development projects in a much wider setting–a setting that reflects full knowledge and understanding of the benefits and impacts of large dam projects and alternative options for all parties. It means that we have to bring new voices, perspectives and criteria into decision-making, and we need to develop an approach that will build consensus around the decisions reached. This will result in fundamental changes in the way decisions are made.

Such a process must start with a clear understanding of the shared values, objectives and goals of development. The Commission grouped the core values informing its understanding of these issues under five main headings:

1.) equity,

2.) efficiency,

3.) participatory decision-making,

4.) sustainability, and

5.) accountability

These five values run through the entire report and are the foci of concerns raised by the evidence presented in the Global Review. They are also aligned with the international framework of norms articulated in the UN Declaration of Human Rights that the Commission cites as a powerful framework of internationally accepted standards.

Considerable support exists for rights, particularly basic human rights, to be considered as a fundamental reference point in any debate on dams - starting with the adoption of the Universal Declaration of Human Rights in 1948 and the related covenants adopted thereafter, through to the Declaration on the Right to Development adopted by the General Assembly in 1986 and the Rio Principles agreed to at the UN Conference on Environment and Development in 1992.

Given the significance of rights-related issues as well as the nature and magnitude of potential risks for all parties concerned, the Commission proposes that an approach based on 'recognition of rights' and 'assessment of risks' (particularly rights at risk) be developed as a tool for guiding future planning and decision-making. This will also provide a more effective framework for integrating the economic, social and environmental dimensions for options assessment and the planning and project cycles.

Clarifying the rights context for a proposed project is an essential step in identifying those legitimate claims and entitlements that might be affected by the proposed project - or indeed, its alternatives. It is also the basis for effective identification of stakeholder groups that are entitled to a formal role in the consultative process, and eventually in negotiating project-specific agreements relating, for example, to benefit sharing, resettlement or compensation.

The notion of risk adds an important dimension to understanding how, and to what extent, a project may have an impact on such rights. Traditional practice is to restrict the definition of risk to the risk of the developer or corporate investor in terms of capital invested and expected returns. These voluntary risk-takers have the capacity to define the level and type of risk they wish to take and explicitly to define its boundaries and acceptability. In contrast, as the Global Review showed, a far larger group often has risks imposed on them involuntarily and managed by others. Typically, these involuntary risk-bearers have little or no say in overall water and energy policy, in the choice of specific projects or in project design and implementation. The risks they face directly affect individual well-being, livelihoods, quality of life, even their spiritual world view and very survival.

Dealing with risks cannot be reduced to consulting actuarial tables or applying a mathematical formula. In the end, as in the case of rights and entitlements, they must be identified, articulated and addressed explicitly. This will require the acknowledgement of risk to be extended to a wider group than governments or developers in order to include both those affected by a project and the environment as a public good.

A rights-and-risks approach to options assessment and to the planning and project cycles presents an effective framework to determine who has a legitimate place at the negotiation table and what issues need to be on the agenda. It empowers decision-making processes based on the pursuit of negotiated outcomes, conducted in an open and transparent manner and inclusive of all legitimate actors involved in the issue, thereby helping to resolve the many and complex issues surrounding water, dams and development. While presenting greater demands at early stages of options assessment and project design, it leads to greater clarity and legitimacy for subsequent steps in decision-making and implementation.

Having laid the groundwork of five core values and a rights-and-risks approach, the Commission developed a constructive and innovative way forward for decision-making in the form of seven strategic priorities and corresponding policy principles. These are written in terms of the outcomes to be achieved. They are supported by a practical set of principles and guidelines designed for adoption, adaptation and use by all those involved in the dams debate. These move from a traditional top-down, technology-focused approach to advocate significant innovations in assessing options, managing existing dams, gaining public acceptance and negotiating and sharing benefits.

Strategic Priorities for Decision-Making

Gaining Public Acceptance

Public acceptance of key decisions is essential for equitable and sustainable water and energy resources development. Acceptance emerges from recognising rights, addressing risks, and safeguarding the entitlements of all groups of affected people, particularly indigenous and tribal peoples, women and other vulnerable groups.

Decision-making processes and mechanisms are used that enable informed participation by all groups of people, and result in the demonstrable acceptance of key decisions. Where projects affect indigenous and tribal peoples, such processes are guided by their free, prior and informed consent.

- Recognition of rights and assessment of risks is the basis for the identification and inclusion of stakeholders in decision-making on energy and water resources development
- Access to information, legal and other support is available to all stakeholders, particularly indigenous and tribal peoples, women and other vulnerable groups, to enable their informed participation in decision-making processes
- Demonstrable public acceptance of all key decisions is achieved through agreements negotiated in an open and transparent process conducted in good faith and with the informed participation of all stakeholders

• Decisions on projects affecting indigenous and tribal peoples are guided by their free, prior and informed consent, achieved through formal and informal representative bodies.

Comprehensive Options Assessment

Alternatives to dams often do exist. To explore these alternatives, needs for water, food and energy are assessed and objectives clearly defined. The appropriate development response is identified from a range of possible options. The selection is based on a comprehensive and participatory assessment of the full range of policy, institutional and technical options.

In the assessment process, social and environmental aspects have the same significance as economic and financial factors. The options assessment process continues through all stages of planning, project development and operations.

• Development needs and objectives are clearly formulated through an open and participatory process before the identification and assessment of options for water and energy resource development

• Planning approaches that take into account the full range of development objectives are used to assess all policy, institutional, management and technical options before the decision to proceed with any programme or project

• Social and environmental aspects are given the same significance as technical, economic and financial factors in assessing options

• Increasing the effectiveness and sustainability of existing water, irrigation and energy systems is given priority in the options assessment process.

• If a dam is selected through such a comprehensive options assessment, social and environmental principles are applied in the review and selection of options throughout the detailed planning, design, construction and operation phases.

Addressing Existing Dams

Opportunities exist to optimise benefits from many existing dams, address outstanding social issues and strengthen environmental mitigation and restoration measures.

Dams and the context in which they operate are not seen as static over time. Benefits and impacts may be transformed by changes in water use priorities, physical and land use changes in the river basin, technological developments, and changes in public policy expressed in environment, safety, economic and technical regulations.

Management and operation practices must adapt continuously to changing circumstances over the project's life and must address outstanding social issues.

• A comprehensive post-project monitoring and evaluation process and a system of longer-term periodic reviews of the performance, benefits and impacts for all existing large dams are introduced

• Programmes to restore, improve and optimise benefits from existing large dams are identified and implemented. Options to consider include: rehabilitate, modernise and upgrade equipment and facilities; optimise reservoir operations; and introduce non-structural measures to improve the efficiency of delivery and use of services

• Outstanding social issues associated with existing large dams are identified and assessed; processes and mechanisms are developed with affected communities to remedy them

• The effectiveness of existing environmental mitigation measures is assessed and unanticipated impacts are identified; opportunities for mitigation, restoration and enhancement are recognised, identified and acted on

• All large dams have formalised operating agreements with time-bound license periods; where re-planning or relicensing processes indicate that major physical changes to facilities, or decommissioning, may be advantageous, a full feasibility study and environmental and social impact assessment is undertaken

Sustaining Rivers and Livelihoods

Rivers, watersheds and aquatic ecosystems are the biological engines of the planet. They are the basis for life and the livelihoods of local communities. Dams transform landscapes and create risks of irreversible impacts. Understanding, protecting and restoring ecosystems at river basin level is essential to foster equitable human development and the welfare of all species.

Options assessment and decision-making around river development prioritises the avoidance of impacts, followed by the minimisation and mitigation of harm to the health and integrity of the river system. Avoiding impacts through good site selection and project design is a priority. Releasing tailor-made environmental flows can help maintain downstream ecosystems and the communities that depend on them.

• A basin-wide understanding of the ecosystem's functions, values and requirements, and how community livelihoods depend on and influence them, is required before decisions on development options are made

• Decisions value ecosystem, social and health issues as an integral part of project and river basin development, and avoidance of impacts is given priority, in accordance with a precautionary approach

• A national policy is developed for maintaining selected rivers with high ecosystem functions and values in their natural state. When reviewing alternative locations for dams on undeveloped rivers, priority is given to locations on tributaries

• Project options are selected that avoid significant impacts on threatened and endangered species. When impacts cannot be avoided, viable compensation measures are put in place that will result in a net gain for the species within the region

• Large dams provide for releasing environmental flows to help maintain downstream ecosystem integrity and community livelihoods and are designed, modified and operated accordingly

Recognising Entitlements and Sharing Benefits

Joint negotiations with adversely affected people result in mutually agreed and legally enforceable mitigation and development provisions. These provisions recognise entitlements that improve livelihoods and quality of life, and affected people are beneficiaries of the project.

Successful mitigation, resettlement and development are fundamental commitments and responsibilities of the State and the developer. They bear the onus to satisfy all affected people that moving from their current context and resources will improve their livelihoods. Accountability of responsible parties to agreed mitigation, resettlement and development provisions is ensured through legal means, such as contracts, and through accessible legal recourse at national and international levels.

• Recognition of rights and assessment of risks is the basis for identification and inclusion of adversely affected stakeholders in joint negotiations on mitigation, resettlement and development-related decision-making.

• Impact assessment includes all people in the reservoir, upstream, downstream and catchment areas whose properties, livelihoods and non-material resources are affected. It also includes those affected by dam-related infrastructure such as canals, transmission lines and resettlement developments

• All recognised adversely affected people negotiate mutually agreed, formal and legally enforceable mitigation, resettlement and development entitlements

• Adversely affected people are recognised as first among the beneficiaries of the project. Mutually agreed and legally protected benefit-sharing mechanisms are negotiated to ensure implementation

Ensuring Compliance

Ensuring public trust and confidence requires that governments, developers, regulators and operators meet all commitments made for the planning, implementation and operation of dams. Compliance with applicable regulations, with criteria and guidelines, and with project-specific negotiated agreements is secured at all critical stages in project planning and implementation.

A set of mutually reinforcing incentives and mechanisms is required for social, environmental and technical measures. These should involve an appropriate mix of regulatory and non-regulatory measures, incorporating incentives and sanctions. Regulatory and compliance frameworks use incentives and sanctions to ensure effectiveness where flexibility is needed to accommodate changing circumstances.

• A clear, consistent and common set of criteria and guidelines to ensure compliance is adopted by sponsoring, contracting and financing institutions, and compliance is subject to independent and transparent review

• A Compliance Plan is prepared for each project prior to commencement, spelling out how compliance will be achieved with relevant criteria and guidelines and specifying binding arrangements for project-specific technical, social and environmental commitments

• Incentives that reward project proponents for abiding by criteria and guidelines are developed by public and private financial institutions

• Costs for establishing compliance mechanisms and related institutional capacity, and their effective application, are built into the project budget

• Corrupt practices are avoided through enforcement of legislation, voluntary integrity pacts, debarment and other instruments

Sharing Rivers for Peace, Development and Security

Storage and diversion of water on transboundary rivers has been a source of considerable tension between countries and within countries. As specific interventions for diverting water, dams require constructive co-operation. Consequently, the use and management of resources increasingly becomes the subject of agreement between States to promote mutual self-interest for regional co-operation and peaceful collaboration. This leads to a shift in focus from the narrow approach of allocating a finite resource to the sharing of rivers and their associated benefits in which States are innovative in defining the scope of issues for discussion. External financing agencies support the principles of good faith negotiations between riparian States.

• National water policies make specific provision for basin agreements in shared river basins. Agreements are negotiated on the basis of good faith among riparian States. They are based on principles of equitable and reasonable utilisation, no significant harm, prior information and the Commission's strategic priorities

• Riparian States go beyond looking at water as a finite commodity to be divided and embrace an approach that equitably allocates not the water, but the benefits that can be derived from it. Where appropriate, negotiations include benefits outside the river basin and other aspects of mutual interest.

• Dams on shared rivers are not built in cases where riparian States raise an objection that is upheld by an independent panel. Intractable disputes between countries are resolved through various means of dispute resolution including, in the last instance, the International Court of Justice

• For the development of projects on rivers shared between political units within countries, the necessary legislative provision is made at national and sub-national levels to embody the Commission's strategic priorities of 'gaining public acceptance', 'recognising entitlements' and 'sustaining rivers and livelihoods'

• Where a government agency plans or facilitates the construction of a dam on a shared river in contravention of the principle of good faith negotiations between riparians, external financing bodies withdraw their support for projects and programmes promoted by that agency

A New Focus for Planning and Decision-Making

The strategic priorities recommended by the Commission lie within a broad framework of existing and emerging policy and regulation at local, national and international levels. Turning these priorities and their underlying principles into reality requires a new focus for planning and management in the water and energy sectors.

This can best be achieved by focusing on the key stages in decision-making that influence final outcomes and where compliance with regulatory requirements can be verified. The Commission has identified five critical decision points when water and energy options are considered. The first two relate to planning, leading to decisions on a preferred development plan:

1.) Needs assessment–validating the needs for water and energy services

2.) Selecting alternatives–identifying the preferred development plan from among the full range of options

Where a dam emerges from this process as a preferred development alternative, three further critical decision points occur:

3.) Project preparation–verifying that agreements are in place before tender of the construction contract

4.) Project implementation–confirming compliance before commissioning

5.) Project operation–adapting to changing contexts

Each of the five decision points represents a commitment to actions that govern the course of future conduct and the allocation of resources. They are points where ministries and government agencies need to test compliance with preceding processes before giving the green light to proceed to the next stage. They are not exhaustive, and within each stage many other decisions have to be taken and agreements reached. The five stages and associated decision points need to be interpreted within the overall planning contexts of individual countries. The Commission also noted that even when these decision points have been passed, there are certain steps that should be taken to improve outcomes (See Box 3).

Box 3. ***Dams in the pipeline***

There are many dam projects today at various stages of planning and development. It is never too late to improve the outcomes of projects–even ones this large in scale and scope. Dams and Development calls for an open and participatory review of all ongoing and planned projects to see whether changes are needed to bring them into line with the WCD strategic priorities and policy principles. In general, regulators, developers and, where appropriate, financing agencies should ensure that such a review:

uses a stakeholder analysis based on recognising rights and assessing risks, in order to identify a stakeholder forum that is consulted on all issues affecting them

enables vulnerable and disadvantaged stakeholder groups to participate in an informed manner

includes a distribution analysis to see who shares the costs and benefits of the project

develops agreed mitigation and resettlement measures to promote development opportunities and benefit sharing for displaced and adversely affected people

avoids, through modified design, any severe and irreversible ecosystem impacts

provides for an environmental flow requirement, and mitigates or compensates any unavoidable ecosystem impacts; and

designs and implements recourse and compliance mechanisms

This process of review implies added investigations or commitments, the re-negotiation of contracts and the incorporation of a Compliance Plan. But additional financial costs will be recouped in lower overall costs to the operator, to government and to society in general as a consequence of avoiding negative outcomes and conflicts.

Social, environmental, governance and compliance aspects have been undervalued in decision-making in the past. In light of this, the Commission developed criteria and 26 guidelines to complement the body of knowledge on good practices and to add value to current national and international guidelines, including those on technical, economic and financial aspects. Seen in conjunction with existing decision-support instruments, the Commission's criteria and guidelines provide a new direction for appropriate and sustainable development.

Bringing about this change will require:

- planners to identify stakeholders through a process that recognises rights and assesses risks
- States to invest more at an earlier stage to screen out inappropriate projects and facilitate integration across sectors within the context of the river basin
- consultants and agencies to ensure outcomes from feasibility studies are socially and environmentally acceptable
- all players to promote open and meaningful participation during planning and implementation, leading to negotiated outcomes
- developers to accept accountability through contractual commitments, for effectively mitigating social and environmental impacts
- independent reviewers to improve compliance; and
- dam owners to apply lessons learned from past experiences through regular monitoring and adapting to changing needs and contexts

The Commission offers its criteria and guidelines to help States, developers and owners, as well as affected communities and civil society in general, meet emerging societal expectations when faced with the complex issues associated with dam projects. This will foster informed and appropriate decisions, thereby raising the level of public acceptance and improving development outcomes.

What's Next?

Dams and Development distills more than two years of intense study, dialogue and reflection by the World Commission on Dams and the WCD Stakeholders' Forum and literally hundreds of individual experts on every facet of the dams debate. It contains all the significant findings that result from this work and expresses everything that the Commissioners feel is important to communicate to governments, the private sector, civil society, international organisations and affected peoples–in short, to the entire spectrum of participants in the dams debate.

The directions are clear. It is one thing, however, to see this. It is another to actively break through traditional boundaries of thinking–to look at familiar issues from a different perspective. This is what the Commission had to do, and found was indeed possible. Similar constructive processes are at work among many of the constituencies that participated so actively in the WCD process.

It is time to bring the debate home. The controversy over dams has appropriately been raised to the international stage. A dissipation of that controversy, however, should allow decisions about fundamental water and energy development choices to be made at the most appropriate level–one where the voices of powerful international players and interests do not drown out the many voices of those with a direct stake in the decisions. For this to work, all the actors have to make a commitment to step out of their familiar frames of reference. The Commission recommends that the report be used as the starting point for discussions, debates, internal reviews and reassessments of what may be established procedures and for an assessment of how they can evolve to address a changed reality.

Dams and Development proposes a number of entry points to help organisations identify steps they can take right away in response to the report. In general, the Commission hopes that all interested parties will:

- review carefully and actively disseminate the report
- issue public statements of support for the approach taken
- review dams currently under development with the WCD criteria and guidelines in mind; and
- support investments in building capacity, particularly in developing countries, for options assessment and improved decision-making

Specific proposals are included for national governments and line ministries, civil society groups, the private sector, bilateral aid agencies, multilateral development banks, export credit agencies, international organisations, and academic and research bodies. (See Box 4.) Engaging through these entry points would initiate permanent changes to advance the principles, criteria and guidelines in the report.

Box 4. ***Selected recommendations for key stakeholders in the dams debate***

National governments *can:*

• *require a review of existing procedures and regulations concerning large dam projects*

• *adopt the practice of time-bound licences for all dams, whether public or privately owned*

• *establish an independent, multi-stakeholder committee to address the unresolved legacy of past dams*

Civil society groups *can:*

• *monitor compliance with agreements and assist any aggrieved party to seek resolution of outstanding disagreements or to seek recourse*

• *actively assist in identifying the relevant stakeholders for dam projects, using the rights-and-risks approach*

Affected peoples' organisations *can:*

• *identify unresolved social and environmental impacts and convince the relevant authorities to take effective steps to address them*

• *develop support networks and partnerships to strengthen the technical and legal capacity for needs and options assessment processes*

Professional associations *can:*

• *develop processes for certifying compliance with WCD guidelines*

• *extend national and international databases, such as the ICOLD World Register of Dams, to include social and environmental parameters*

The ***private sector*** *can:*

• *develop and adopt voluntary codes of conduct, management systems and certification procedures for best ensuring and demonstrating compliance with the Commission's guidelines, including, for example, through the ISO 14001 management system standard*

• *abide by the provisions of the anti-bribery convention of the Organisation for Economic Co-operation and Development*

• *adopt integrity pacts for all contracts and procurement*

Bilateral aid agencies *and* ***multilateral development banks*** *can:*

• *ensure that any dam options for which financing is approved emerge from an agreed process of ranking of alternatives and respect WCD guidelines*

• *accelerate the shift from project- to sector-based finance, especially through increasing financial and technical support for effective, transparent, and participatory needs and options assessment, and the financing of non-structural alternatives*

• *review the portfolio of projects to identify any past ones that may have under-performed or present unresolved issues*

The trust required to enable different sectors and players to work together must still be consolidated. Early and resolute action to address some of the issues arising from the past will go a long way towards building that trust in the future. So, too, would an assurance to countries still at an early stage of economic development that the dams option will not be foreclosed before they have had a chance to examine their water and energy development choices within the context of their own development process.

The experience of the Commission demonstrates that common ground can be found without compromising individual values or losing a sense of purpose. But it also demonstrates that all concerned parties must enter into the process in good faith if we are to resolve the issues surrounding water and energy resources development. It is a process with multiple heirs and no clear arbiter. We must move forward together or we will fail.

There will, of course, be further disagreement on these issues. Dynamic debate leads frequently to better outcomes. The Commission believes, however, that business as usual is not a viable strategy. The report closes with a call to action and a challenge to all readers:

We have conducted the first comprehensive and global review of the performance of dams and their contribution to development. We have done this through an inclusive process that has brought all significant players into the debate. And we believe we have shifted the centre of gravity in the dams debate to one focused on options assessment and participatory decision-making. The rights-and-risks approach we propose will raise the importance of social and environmental dimensions of dams to a level once reserved for the economic dimension.

We have told our story. What happens next is up to you.

Source: The World Commission on Dams, http://www.dams.org

DOCUMENT 6

THE WATER MANIFESTO

The right to life

We come from Africa, Latin America, North America, Asia and Europe. We gathered together in 1998 with no other legitimacy or representativeness than that of being citizens concerned by the fact that 1.4 billion of the planet's 5.8 billion inhabitants do not have access to drinking water, the fundamental source of life. This fact is intolerable. Now, the risk is great that in the year 2020 when the world population reaches around 8 billion human beings, the number of people without access to drinking water will increase to more than 3 billion. This is unacceptable. We can and must prevent the unacceptable becoming possible. How?

We think that we can do this by applying the principles and rules outlined below.

1.) Water "the source of life" belongs to all the inhabitants of the Earth in common

As the fundamental and irreplaceable "source of life" for the eco-system, water is a vital good, which belongs to all the inhabitants of the Earth in common. None of them, individually or as a group, can be allowed the right to make it private property. **Water is the patrimony of mankind.** Individual and collective health depends upon it. Agriculture, industry and domestic life are intimately linked to it. Its "unsubstituable" character means that the whole human community–and each of its members–must have the right of access to water, and in particular, drinking water, in the necessary quantity and quality indispensable to life and economic activity. There is no production of wealth without access to water. Water is not like any other resource: it is not an exchangeable, marketable commodity.

2.) The right to water is an inalienable individual and collective right

Water belongs more to the economy of common goods and wealth sharing than to the economy of private and individual accumulation and other's wealth expropriation. While the sharing of water has often been a major source of social inequality in the past, today's civilisations recognise that access to water is a fundamental, inalienable individual and collective right. **The right to water is a part of the basic ethics of a "good" society and a "good" economy.** It is up to society as a whole and at the different levels of social organisation to guarantee the right of access, according to the double principle of co-responsibility and subsidiarity, without discrimination of race, sex, religion, income or social class.

3.) Water has to contribute to the strengthening of solidarity among people, communities, countries, genders, generations

Fresh water resources are unequally distributed on the Earth. Income also. This does not mean that there also must be **inequality of access to water between people and communities and regions.** Moreover, the inequality in the distribution of water and financial wealth does not mean that the people rich in water and rich in revenue can make use of it as they please, indeed sell it (or buy it) "abroad" to derive the maximum profit (or pleasure). In many regions of the world water remains a source of inequalities **between men and women** the latters bearing all the burden of homework dependent on water. These inequalities must be removed. There are still **too many water-related wars** ongoing on our Planet because most States continue to use water as an instrument in support of their geo-economic strategic interests as regions' "hegemonic" power. It is necessary and possible to make water free from the influence of a hegemony-oriented State. Water is a "res publica."

4.) Water is the citizens' business

Creating the conditions necessary to ensure the most effective and sustainable access to water is everybody's concern.. It is also an inter-generational issue so that it is up to present generations to use, valorise, protect and conserve water resources in such a way that future generations can enjoy the same freedom of action and choice that we wish for ourselves today. **The citizen must be at the centre of decision-making.** The integrated and sustainable management of water belongs to the sphere of democracy. It goes beyond the skills and to the know-how of technicians, engineers and bankers. The users have a key role to play by their choices and practices to ensure environmental, economic and societal sustainability.

5.) Water policy implies a high degree of democracy at the local, national, continental and world level

By definition, water calls for decentralised management and transparency. The existing institutions of representative democracy must be strengthened. When necessary, new forms of democratic government have to be created. **Participatory democracy is unavoidable.** This is possible, with or without the new information and communication technologies, at the level of local communities, cities, basins, regions. New coherent **regulatory frameworks at international and global level** must be designed and implemented, enhancing the visibility of a sustainable water policy at global level by the global community. **Parliaments** are the natural loci and players in this respect. This is why we also believe that it is urgent and essential to (re)valorise **local and traditional water harvesting practices.** An important heritage of knowledge, skills and community based practices, highly efficient and sustainable, has been dilapidated and run down. It runs the risk of being destroyed still further in the years to come.

6.) Access to water necessarily takes place through partnership. It is time to go beyond

the logic of "warlords" and economic conflicts for the domination and conquest of markets

Citizenship and democracy are founded on co-operation and mutual respect. They exist by and through partnership. "Partnerships for water" is the inspiring principle behind all the plans (such as "the river agreements") that have permitted the efficient resolution of conflicts which in certain regions of the world have traditionally poisoned relationships between riverside communities who shared the same hydrographic basin. Indeed, we support a real local/national/world and real public/private partnership. A sustainable water management in the general interest cannot but be founded on the respect for cultural diversity and socio-economic pluralism. A partnership predominantly subject, as at present, to the logic and interests of private actors in relentless competition against each other for market conquest could only do harm to the objectives of access to water for all and global integrated sustainability.

7.) **We believe that the financial responsibility for water must be at once collective and individual according to the principles of responsibility and utility**

Ensuring access to water for the vital and fundamental needs of every person and every human community is an obligation for society as a whole. It is society which must collectively assume all of the costs related to the collection, production, storage, distribution, use, conservation and recycling of water in view of supplying and guaranteeing access to water in the quantities and qualities considered as being the indispensable minimum. The costs (including the negative externalities which are not taken into account by market prices) are common social costs to be borne by the collective as a whole. This principle is even more relevant and significant at the level of a country, a continent and the world society. The financing must be ensured by collective redistribution. The mechanisms of individual price-fixing, according to progressive pricing must start from a level of water usage that goes beyond the vital and indispensable minimum. Beyond the vital minimum, progressive pricing must be a function of the quantity used. Finally, at a third layer, all abuses and excesses of usage must be considered illegal.

Proposals

In order that the rules become a living reality in the course of the next 20 to 25 years, when two billion human beings will be added to the present population, we propose that the following measures be taken and implemented in a kind of "World Water Contract" alongside two main axes :

the creation of a "Network of Parliaments for Water"

the promotion of information campaign, awareness raising and mobilisation on "Water for All".

We also propose the establishment of a World Observatory for Water Rights.

The Creation of a Network of Parliaments for Water

It is in Parliaments, the principal organs of political representation in "westernised" societies, and in comparable institutions, in other civilisational contexts, that the responsibility falls, to modify the existing legislation by applying the principles and rules outlined above. Defining a new legal framework at local and national levels but also at the international and world level is a major task for Parliaments to fill up the void that exists in this domain at the world level.. The priority is to establish a **"World Water Treaty"** legalising water as a vital patrimonial good, common to all humanity. This "treaty", for example, should exclude water from all international commercial conventions (such as those existing within the framework of the World Trade Organisation), as is already the case for the cultural domain.

Promotion of information campaigns, awareness-raising and mobilisation concerning

1.) the development (or modernisation) of the systems of **water distribution and sanitation for the 600 cities** in Russia, African, Asian, Latin American and European countries which will have more than a million inhabitants by the year 2020 and whose water system is even today obsolete, inadequate, indeed, non-existent.

2.) **The fight against new sources of water pollution in the cities** of North America, Western Europe and Japan where contamination of the soil and both surface and deep ground water, is becoming more and more troubling, serious and in certain cases, irreversible.

These actions would respond to the objective of **"3 billion taps" by 2020.**

NGO's, trade unions and scientists have in this respect an essential and determining role to play.

To these purposes, **priority should be given to**

- **The structural reform of irrigation systems in highly intensive industrial agriculture**

The solutions exist already such as, for example, "drip irrigation".

Existing "modern" agriculture is the principal consumer of the planet's freshwater resources (accounting for 70% of total world extraction, of which the largest part is for irrigation). Yet, 40% of irrigation water is lost en route from source to sink). Furthermore, industrial agriculture is source of major damages and threats to the environment (soil salinity and hydromorphism in particular)

• **A 10 to 15 year-moratorium in the construction of new large dams** which have so far created considerable short- and long-term problems for the environment, local populations and the possibility of integrated, sustainable water management.

The establishment of a World Observatory for Water Rights.

The main goal of this observatory will be to collect, produce, distribute and disseminate the most rigorous and reliable information possible on water access from the point of view of individual and collective rights, water production, its use, its conservation/ protection and democratic sustainable development. The Observatory must become one of the world reference points for information on water rights, in support of the most effective forms of water partnership and solidarity.

Members of the Committee for the World Water Contract

Mario **Soares,** former President of the Republic of Portugal

Mario **Albornoz,** Professor at the University of Quilmès, Argentina

Raoul **Alfonsin,** former President of the Republic of Argentina

Driss **Ben Sari,** Professor at Rabat University, Morocco

Rafaeil **Blasco Castany,** Presidencia de la Generalitat Valenciana

Rinaldo **Bontempi,** Member of the European Parliament, Italy

Larbi **Bouguerra,** President of the Group of Lausanne, Tunisia

David **Brubaker,** Global Resource Action for the Environment, USA

João **Caraça,** Director at the Gulbenkian Foundation, Portugal

Susan **George,** Assistant-director of the Transnational Institute, USA/France

Antonio **Gonçalves Henriques,** Vice-President of the Institute of Water, Portugal

Pierre-Marc **Johnson,** Heenan Blaikie Consultancy, McGill University, Canada

S.A.R. **Le Prince Laurent,** President of the Royal Institute for the Sustainable Management of Natural Resources, Belgium

Candido **Mendes,** Senator, President of the Candido Mendes University

Hasna **Moudud,** President, The National Association for Resources Improvement, Bangladesh

Sunita **Narain,** Assistant-director for the Science and Environment Centre, India

José Antonio **Pinto Monteiro,** Minister of the Environment, Cape Verde

Frédéric **Ténière-Buchot,** Mission for Water, United Nations Environment Programme, France

Abou **Thiam,** Professor at the University of Dakar, Senegal

Lars **Ulmgrend,** general Secretary of the Stockholm International Water Institute, Sweden

Anders **Wijkman,** Director at the Ministry of Foreign Affairs, Sweden

Riccardo **Petrella,** Secretary of the Committee, President of the Group of Lisbon, Italy

Last update: 19 August 1999

Source: The Global Water Contract. A Citizen Initiative.

http://www.users.skynet.be/green/english/water_manifesto.htm

GLOSSARY

Albedo: The reflective characteristics of the surfaces of the earth, especially of water, which are dependent upon the solar sun angle; a concept used in the identification of conditions of drought or desertification.

Aquaculture: The process of raising aquatic species (for example, fish), often in human-created environments such as reservoirs created by dams or in wetland ecosystems such as mangrove swamps; the breeding of fish or crustaceans (for example, shrimp) under controlled conditions.

Aquifer: A geological formation that contains groundwater.

Assured Safe Yield: A long-term sustainable quantity of water that can be obtained from a source such as a dam or aquifer on an annual basis.

Basin: An area drained by a river or stream (for example, a catchment basin).

Biodiversity (Biological Diversity): The richness of the variety and number of genes, species, or organisms in an area.

Borehole: A hole drilled vertically or at an angle into the ground to tap into water-bearing rock or sediments; boreholes usually are fitted with a mechanical or wind-driven pump to draw water from beneath the ground to the surface.

Catchment: The area within which rainfall-derived water flows into a river.

Compensation: The restitution of all losses sustained by individuals, households, communities, groups, and villages as a result of the construction of a project. Compensation is done either in case or in kind (for example, land for land, fodder for loss of grazing resources). According to world standards, compensation is aimed not only at restoring livelihoods but also enhancing the standards of living of affected persons.

Dam: A structure, usually made of earth, rock, or concrete, or a combination of materials, that is constructed across a river, stream, or valley in order to hold water and create a storage system for agricultural, drinking, hydropower, fishery, industrial, or recreational use.

Demand Management: The managing of the amount of water that people use through pricing, regulation, and enhanced environmental awareness.

Desert: An area with low and highly variable rainfall inputs, often with little and sometimes no vegetation.

Desertification: The process of land degradation caused by a combination of human and natural (including climatic) factors in the arid, semiarid, and subhumid areas of the world in which vegetation cover is reduced or transformed and soil erosion occurs, with an overall loss of biological productivity, which lead to the land taking on the characteristics of a desert.

Dessication: The process of longer-term reductions in moisture availability resulting from a dry period often lasting for decades.

Development: Process whereby a nation or agency attempts to raise the living standards of its citizens or members and to enhance their well-being; Sustainable Development is development that can support people at one period and over the long term, benefiting future generations–development that does not require continuous inputs from outside to sustain itself.

Disaster: A process or event involving a combination of a potentially destructive agent(s) from the natural and/or social environment that results in damage, loss, or destruction; an actual historical event that results in problems for a society, community, or individual.

Drought: A deficiency of precipitation that results in water shortage for some activity (for example, plant growth) or for some group (such as farmers); a rainfall-induced shortage of economic good (for example, grazing for livestock) brought about by inadequate or badly timed rainfall.

Easement: A legal agreement or negotiated arrangement that provides for common access to a resource, facility, commodity, service, or area that is claimed to belong to more than one party.

El Niño Southern Oscillation (Enso); El Niño ("The Christ Child"): The name given to the warming of the Pacific Ocean that occurs periodically, usually in December, resulting in changes in weather patterns (for example, droughts in some areas, heavy rainfall and floods in others) and shifts in ocean currents, causing changes in the distribution of faunal and floral species; El Niño is thought to affect southern African rainfall and thus agricultural and livestock productivity.

Environmental Impact Assessment: The evaluation of the effects on the environment of a specific project or development activity; a management tool used to predict and then mitigate impacts of a project.

Estuary: A portion of a river where it meets the sea or another large body of water, often containing a mixture of fresh and salt water.

Famine: A severe shortage or inaccessibility of appropriate food (including water) along with related threats to survival, affecting major parts of a population; severe food shortages caused by decline in food production or supply in successive years.

Freshwater: Surface water, usually derived from rainfall or snowmelt, that is a natural resource crucial to the survival of humans, animals, plants, and other species; freshwater represents approximately 2.5 percent of the total volume of water on earth; two-thirds of this water is locked in glaciers and polar ice caps; freshwater can be divided into renewable and nonrenewable (for example, fossil) water; only that water flowing through the hydrological cycle is renewable.

Green Revolution: The application of high-yielding varieties (HYVs) of plant seeds along with fertilizers and other inputs (such as herbicides) in order to increase crop yields; this approach to agricultural development was responsible for increasing net agricultural yields, but it also had significant social, economic, and environmental impacts.

Helsinki Rules: A set of guidelines drawn up by the International Law Association in 1966 that deal with the nonnavigational use of water in river basins that is shared by different countries; provides guidance for the sharing and equitable allocation of water from international rivers that allow for maximum benefit to the states involved.

Homestead: A unit that comprises one or more families, with one or more heads, who live together in the same residence.

Household: A group of kin-related and/or socioeconomically linked persons who see themselves as a unit, which shares or cooperates in the exchange of goods, resources, and services and has mutual rights, obligations, and responsibilities.

Impoundment: A body of water formed behind a weir or dam wall.

Infiltration: The process whereby water soaks or infiltrates into deeper layers of soil.

Infrastructure: Structural foundations of a society such as roads, water systems, and electricity supply (physical), as well as schools, clinics, and community centers (social); those facilities that form the basis for social and economic performance of a society.

Integrated Catchment Management: Management of a river catchment or basin that integrates the views and demands of all the affected parties and that seeks the most effective long-term use of the water resources of that catchment.

Irrigation: The process of supplying water, usually to crops, through such methods as flooding land by damming rivers or digging canals to channel water from a source to places where it is used.

"Liebig's Law of the Minimum": The idea, proposed in 1840 by German agricultural chemist Justus Liebig, that an organism is no stronger than the weakest link in its ecological chain; the essential environmental factors necessary in minimal quantity during the most critical period of the year or years of a climatic cycle.

Lifeline Volume: The minimum amount of water that is required to sustain life, and which is provided at a subsidized charge or free to low-income (poverty-stricken) groups.

Limiting Factors: Those factors that are required in order for an organism to sustain itself; ecological events such as growth or reproduction are often regulated by the availability of one or more factors or requisites in short supply.

Linear Oasis: A river that flows through a desert; in essence, a line of water and its associated vegetation and soils in a desert environment.

Mobility Strategies: Movement patterns of human groups; organizational responses to the structure and dynamics of the environments in which human groups shift residences (Residential Mobility) so as to take advantage of resource concentrations; alternatively, they send out task groups (Logistical Mobility) to obtain resources and bring them back to a base location (Home Base); frequently, these home bases are near water sources such as rivers or lakes.

Moisture Deficit: The difference between the amount of rain that falls in an area and the amount of water that can evaporate from it. Arid (very dry) climates have a high moisture deficit (for example, in the Namib Desert, evaporation exceeds rainfall inputs by eight to ten times).

Nonconsumptive Use: Use of water that returns it to the system or source after it is utilized.

Optimum Use: Use (for example, of water) that gives the greatest benefits and is the most favorable to all concerned.

Perennial River: A river that flows through all seasons of the year, as opposed to a seasonal river, one that flows during the wet season, or one that flows periodically, usually just after rains (an ephemeral river).

Pollution: The poisoning of water or land with materials or factors that reduces its ability to support life (for example, by toxins).

Potential Evaporation: The maximum amount of water that can evaporate.

Precipitation: Water that falls to the ground in the form of rain, hail, snow, or fog.

Ramsar Convention: Convention on Wetlands of International Importance Especially as Waterfowl Habitat; also known as "the wetland treaty," it is an international agreement named after the city in Iran where it was drawn up and agreed upon in 1971.

Recharge: The process by which an aquifer is filled or resupplied with water; the replacement of groundwater that is lost through abstraction, evaporation, or transpiration.

Refugee: A person who, owing to well-founded fear of being persecuted for reasons of race, religion, nationality, or membership in a particular social group or political opinion, is outside the country of his or her nationality; "environmental refugees" are people who fled their homes because of environmental stress (drought, disasters); "oustees" or "development refugees" are people who have been forced from their homes because of a development project such as a dam, road, or agricultural project.

Resettlement and Relocation: The involuntary removal of households and individuals to another location because of the implementation of a development, conservation, infrastructure, or water project.

Resilience: The ability of a system to recover from or adjust easily to change; the ability to assure persistence in the face of fluctuations; sometimes defined as adaptability.

Riparian Ecosystems: Those ecosystems associated with rivers that include the vegetation, animals, and microorganisms adapted to life on the riverbanks, the beds of ephemeral rivers, and areas adjacent to rivers.

River Basin: Land area occupied by a river and all its tributaries, from the highlands or mountains where the main river and its tributaries arise, to its lowest point where it enters the sea or drains into an internal depression.

Runoff: Water that does not filter into the soil but instead flows over the surface, eventually going into a river; the flow of rainwater over the surface of the ground, or, alternatively, the amount of water that passes a certain point in a river (often calculated as Mean Annual Runoff).

Salinization: The process whereby water and/or soils become salty; the accumulation of salts that affects the productivity of crops or other resources.

Savanna: A grassland ecosystem characterized by a pronounced wet-dry cycle; these ecosystems are a transitional between deserts and forests and are found in tropical, subtropical, and temperate areas; fire-managed ecosystems that are dominated by grasses.

Sedentism (Sedentarization): the process whereby a group settles down and remains residentially stationary year-round; the process of mobility reduction.

Sedimentation: The process by which sediments (fine sand or soil particles) are deposited, usually in the bed of a river or in a delta.

Silt: Particles of soil that are carried in water and that are deposited as the water slows down.

Species Diversity: The ratio between the number of species and individuals in an area; high-diversity systems are those composed of a variety of different elements.

Subsistence: A situation in which people supply all or the majority of their own needs, often through the exploitation of wild natural resources (animals, plants, fish, and marine mammals) rather than earning wages to pay for goods and services.

Stability: The tendency for a system to stay the same or resist change; property of a system that causes it, when disturbed from a condition of equilibrium or steady motion, to restore itself to the original condition; self-regulating (homoeostatic) mechanisms are ones that bring about a return to a constant state.

Storage: The safekeeping of goods in a depository; setting aside goods as a means of getting through those periods when resources are not available in the habitat.

Surface Runoff: Water that does not filter into the soil but instead flows over the surface and joins a river or another body of water.

Swamp: A marsh or waterlogged, well-vegetated wetland.

Symbiosis: Interaction between organisms or populations in which each is dependent upon the other; the living together in more or less intimate association of two dissimilar organisms in a mutually beneficial or cooperative relationship (mutualism).

Territory: An area that is used exclusively by an organism or population; that is defended by an organism; or supplies the resources necessary to sustain a population during the course of a year or, in some cases, several years.

Total Dissolved Solids (TDS): The total amount of chemicals, such as calcium or sodium, that are dissolved in water.

Tragedy of the Commons: The concept developed by Garrett Hardin that refers to the degradation or loss of resources because of communal (common property) access (as opposed to private property); a highly formalized model of human behavior that assumes that all individuals attempt to maximize their own returns at the expense of others and the natural environment.

Tributary: A river or stream that flows into a larger river.

Turbidity: A measure of the visible impurities in water, which are a result of such factors as clay, silt, or algae (either organic or inorganic particles or both).

Water Cycle (Hydrological Cycle): A natural or continuous process in which water changes from one state to another and redistributes itself, and, in so doing, purifies itself; processes that include a combination of evaporation, cloud formation, rainfall, runoff, and recharge.

Water Table: A level in the soil below which all or most spaces between soil particles are saturated with water.

Watershed: High ground that divides one river basin from another.

Wetland: An area that contains or holds water, even if it is dry much of the time, and that often contains vegetation adapted to periodic floods or to water inputs; also an area that is either wet continually or affected by water for substantial periods; an area of marsh, peat land, or water, whether natural or artificial, temporary or permanent, static or flowing.

–ROBERT K. HITCHCOCK, UNIVERSITY OF NEBRASKA-LINCOLN

REFERENCES

1. General

Daily, Gretchen C., ed. *Nature's Services: Societal Dependence on Natural Ecosystems.* Washington, D.C.: Island Press, 1997.

Hagen, Joel B. *An Entangled Bank: The Origins of Ecosystem Ecology.* New Brunswick, N.J.: Rutgers University Press, 1992.

Hardin, Garrett. "The Tragedy of the Commons," *Science,* 162 (1968): 1243–1248.

Harvey, David. *Justice, Nature, and the Geography of Difference.* Cambridge, Mass.: Blackwell, 1996.

Lacy, Michael J., ed. *Government and Environmental Politics: Essays on Historical Developments Since World War II.* Baltimore: Johns Hopkins University Press, 1991.

Lash, Scott and John Urry. *Economies of Signs and Space.* London & Thousand Oaks, Cal.: Sage, 1994.

Miller, Char and Hal K. Rothman, eds. *Out of the Woods: Essays in Environmental History.* Pittsburgh: University of Pittsburgh Press, 1997.

Payer, Cheryl. *The World Bank: A Critical Analysis.* New York: Monthly Review, 1982.

Scherer, Donald, ed. *Upstream/Downstream: Issues in Environmental Ethics.* Philadelphia: Temple University Press, 1990.

Siry, Joseph V. *Marshes of the Ocean Shore: Development of an Ecological Ethic.* College Station: Texas A&M Press, 1984.

Tarr, Joel A. *The Search for the Ultimate Sink: Urban Pollution in Historical Perspective.* Akron: University of Akron Press, 1996.

Teal, John and Mildred. *The Life and Death of the Salt Marsh.* Boston: Little, Brown, 1969.

Tiner, Ralph W. *In Search of Swampland: A Wetland Sourcebook and Field Guide.* New Brunswick, N.J.: Rutgers University Press, 1998.

White, Richard. *The Organic Machine.* New York: Hill & Wang, 1995.

Wilson, Edward O. *Biophilia.* Cambridge, Mass.: Harvard University Press, 1984.

Winner, Langdon. *The Whale and the Reactor: A Search for Limits in an Age of High Technology.* Chicago: University of Chicago Press, 1986.

Yeager, Peter Cleary. *The Limits of Law: The Public Regulation of Private Pollution.* Cambridge & New York: Cambridge University Press, 1991.

2. Africa

Adams, W. M. *Wasting the Rain: Rivers, People, and Planning in Africa.* Minneapolis: University of Minnesota Press, 1992.

Bond, Patrick. *Uneven Zimbabwe: A Study of Finance, Development and Underdevelopment.* Trenton, N.J.: Africa World Press, 1998.

Botswana, Government of. *National Policy on Agricultural Development.* Gaborone, Botswana: Government Printer, 1991.

Chenje, Munyaradzi and Phyllis Johnson, eds. *Water in Southern Africa: A Report by SADC–Southern African Development Community, IUCN–the World Conservation Union, and SARDC–Southern African Research & Documentation Centre.* Maseru, Lesotho: SADC, Environment and Land Management Sector Coordination Unit; Harare, Zimbabwe: IUCN, Regional Office for Southern Africa, SARDC, 1996.

DHV. *Countrywide Animal and Range Assessment Project.* Seven volumes. Gaborone: Republic of Botswana, Ministry of Commerce and Industry, Department of Wildlife, National Parks, and Tourism, 1979–.

Egner, E. B. and A. L. Klausen. *Poverty in Botswana.* Gaborone: University College of Botswana, 1980.

Ferguson, James. *The Anti-Politics Machine: "Development," Depoliticization and Bureaucratic Power in Lesotho.* Cambridge & New York: Cambridge University Press, 1990.

Khosa, Meshack, ed. *Empowerment through Service Delivery.* Pretoria, South Africa: Human Sciences Research Council, 2000.

Pearson, D. S. and W. L. Taylor. *Break-Up: Some Economic Consequences for the Rhodesias and Nyasaland.* Salisbury, South Rhodesia: Phoenix Group, 1963.

Pickford, John, ed. *Water and Sanitation for All: Partnerships and Innovations: Selected Papers of the 23rd WEDC Conference, Durban, South Africa, 1997.* London: Intermediate Technology Publications, 1998.

Windrich, Elaine. *Britain and the Politics of Rhodesian Independence.* London: Croom Helm, 1978; New York: Africana, 1978.

3. Asia

Agarwal, Anil and Sunita Narain, eds. *Dying Wisdom: Rise, Fall and Potential of India's Traditional Water Harvesting Systems.* New Delhi: Centre for Science and Environment, 1997.

Arundhati, Roy. *Greater Common Good.* Bombay: India Book, 1999.

Large Dams and Their Alternatives: South Asia Consultation from SANDRP, South Asia Network on Dams, Rivers and People. New Delhi, India, 1999.

Postel, Sandra. *Pillar of Sand: Can the Irrigation Miracle Last?* New York: Norton, 1999.

Ramaswamy, Iyer, and others. *Large Dams: India's Experience: A Report for the World Commission on Dams.* Cape Town: World Commission on Dams, 2000.

Singh, Satyajit. *Taming the Waters: The Political Economy of Large Dams in India.* Delhi: Oxford University Press, 1997.

4. Europe

Barber, Margaret and Grainne Ryder, eds. *Damming the Three Gorges: What Dam Builders Don't Want You to Know: A Critique of the Three Gorges Water Control Project Feasibility Study.* London: Earthscam, 1993.

Barnes, Samuel H. and János Simon, eds. *The Postcommunist Citizen.* Budapest: Erasmus Foundation, 1988.

Berrisch, G. *Construction and Operation of Variant C of the Gabcikovo-Nagymaros Project under International Law.* Brussels: WWF, 1992.

Bravard, Jean-Paul. *The French Upper Rhône: Historical Geography and Management of a River.* Denver: Bureau of Reclamation, 1988.

DeBardeleben, Joan, ed. *To Breathe Free: Eastern Europe's Environmental Crisis.* Washington, D.C.: Woodrow Wilson Center Press / Baltimore: Johns Hopkins University Press, 1991.

Dominick, Raymond H., III. *The Environmental Movement in Germany: Prophets and Pioneers, 1871–1971.* Bloomington: Indiana University Press, 1992.

Ernst, John. *Whose Utility?: The Social Impact of Public Utility Privatization and Regulation in Britain.* Buckingham, U.K. & Philadelphia: Open University Press, 1994.

Feshbach, Murray and Alfred Friendly, Jr. *Ecocide in the USSR: Health and Nature under Siege.* New York: BasicBooks, 1992.

Fitzmaurice, John. *Damming the Danube: Gabcikovo and Post-Communist Politics in Europe.* Boulder, Colo.: Westview Press, 1996.

Froehlich-Schmitt, Barbara. *Salmon 2000.* Translated by Karin Wehner. Translation revised by the European Translation Centre. Koblenz, Germany: International Commission for the Protection of the Rhine, 1994.

Frost, Robert L. *Alternating Currents: Nationalized Power in France, 1946–1970.* Ithaca, N.Y.: Cornell University Press, 1991.

Grenon, Michel and Michel Batisse, eds. *Futures for the Mediterranean Basin: The Blue Plan.* Oxford & New York: Oxford University Press, 1989.

Haas, Peter M. *Saving the Mediterranean: The Politics of International Environmental Protection.* New York: Columbia University Press, 1990.

Hallanaro, Eeva-Liisa. *The Environment in Finland: Current Status and Measures to Protect It.* Helsinki, Finland: Ministry of the Environment, 1999.

Hicks, Barbara. *Environmental Politics in Poland: A Social Movement Between Regime and Opposition.* New York: Columbia University Press, 1996.

International Commission for the Protection of the Rhine. *The Rhine: An Ecological Revival.* Koblenz, Germany: Internationale Kommission zum Schutze des Rheins, 1993.

Katko, Tapio S. *Water!: Evolution of Water Supply and Sanitation in Finland from the Mid-1800s to 2000.* Helsinki: Finnish Water and Waste Water Works Association, 1997.

Kraats, J. A. van de, ed., *Rehabilitation of the River Rhine: Proceedings of the International Conference on Rehabilitation of the River Rhine, 15–19 March 1993, Arnhem, The Netherlands.* Oxford, U.K. & Tarrytown, N.Y.: Pergamon, 1994.

Kuisel, Richard F. *Capitalism and the State in Modern France: Renovation and Economic Management in the Twentieth Century.* Cambridge & New York: Cambridge University Press, 1981.

Margalef, Ramón, ed. *Western Mediterranean.* Oxford & New York: Pergamon, 1985.

McNeill, J. R. *The Mountains of the Mediterranean: An Environmental History.* New York: Cambridge University Press, 1992.

Mellor, Roy E. H. *The Rhine: A Study in the Geography of Water Transport.* Aberdeen: University of Aberdeen, 1979.

Özhan, Erdal, ed. *MEDCOAST 93: Proceedings of the First International Conference on the Mediterranean Coastal Environment, November 2–5, 1993, Antalya, Turkey.* Ankara: MEDCOAST Permanent Secretariat, 1993.

Petts, G. E., H. Möller, and A. L. Roux, eds. *Historical Change of Large Alluvial Rivers: Western Europe.* Chichester & New York: Wiley, 1989.

Pryde, Phillip R., ed. *Environmental Resources and Constraints in the Former Soviet Republics.* Boulder, Colo.: Westview Press, 1995.

Raftopoulos, Evangelos. *The Barcelona Convention and Its Protocols: The Mediterranean Action Plan Regime.* London: Simmonds & Hill, 1993.

Raun, Toivo U. *Estonia and the Estonians.* Stanford, Cal.: Hoover Institution Press, Stanford University, 1987.

Rees, Goronwy. *The Rhine.* New York: Putnam, 1967.

Roose, Antti. *Põlevkivist Ehitatud Eesti.* Translated by Erika Puusemp, as *Estonia Built on Oil Shale.* Rakvere, Estonia: Virumaa Foundation, 1991.

Royal Institute of International Affairs. *Regional Management of the Rhine.* London: Chatham House, 1975.

Stanners, David and Philippe Bourdeau. *Europe's Environment: The Dobris Assessment.* Copenhagen: European Environment Agency, 1995.

Tana, Jukka and Karl-Johan Lehtinen. *The Aquatic Environmental Impact of Pulping and Bleaching Operations–An Overview.* Helsinki: Finnish Environment Institute, 1996.

United Nations Environment Programme (UNEP). *Report of the Ninth Ordinary Meeting of the Contracting Parties to the Convention for the Protection of the Mediterranean Sea Against Pollution and Its Protocols.* Athens, Greece: UNEP, 1995.

United Nations Environment Programme (UNEP). *The State of the Marine and Coastal Environment in the Mediterranean Region.* Athens, Greece: UNEP, 1996.

Walle, F. B. de, M. Nikopoloulou-Tamvakli, and W. J. Heinen, eds. *Environmental Conditions of the Mediterranean Sea: European Community Countries.* Dordrecht & London: Kluwer Academic Publishers, 1993.

Whitton, B. A. ed., *Ecology of European Rivers.* Oxford & Boston: Blackwell Scientific Publishers, 1984.

5. Fish and Fishing Industry

Allison, Charlene J., Sue-Ellen Jacobs, and Mary A. Porter, eds. *Winds of Change: Women in Northwest Commercial Fishing.* Seattle: University of Washington Press, 1989.

Brown, Bruce. *Mountain in the Clouds: A Search for the Wild Salmon.* New York: Simon & Schuster, 1982.

Committee on Protection and Management of Pacific Northwest Anadromous Salmonids, Board on Environmental Studies and Toxicology, Commission on Life Sciences. *Upstream: Salmon and Society in the*

Pacific Northwest. Washington, D.C.: National Academy Press, 1996.

Cone, Joseph. *A Common Fate: Endangered Salmon and the People of the Pacific Northwest.* New York: Holt, 1995.

Cone and Sandy Ridlington, eds. *The Northwest Salmon Crisis: A Documentary History.* Corvallis: Oregon State University Press, 1996.

Cowx, Ian G. and Robin L. Welcomme, eds. *Rehabilitation of Rivers for Fish: A Study Undertaken by the European Inland Fisheries Advisory Commission of FAO.* Oxford & Malden, Mass.: Fishing News Books, 1998.

Friday, Chris. *Organizing Asian American Labor: The Pacific Coast Canned-Salmon Industry, 1870–1942.* Philadelphia: Temple University Press, 1994.

Groot, C. and L. Margolis, eds. *Pacific Salmon Life Histories.* Vancouver: University of British Columbia Press, 1991.

Independent Scientific Group. *Return to the River: Restoration of Salmonid Fishes in the Columbia River Ecosystem: Development of an Alternative Conceptual Foundation and Review and Synthesis of Science Underlying the Columbia River Basin Fish and Wildlife Program of the Northwest Power Planning Council.* Portland, Ore.: Northwest Power Planning Council, 1996.

Lichatowich, Jim. *Salmon Without Rivers: A History of the Pacific Salmon Crisis.* Washington, D.C.: Island Press, 1999.

McEvoy, Arthur F. *The Fisherman's Problem: Ecology and Law in the California Fisheries, 1850–1980.* Cambridge & New York: Cambridge University Press, 1986.

Martin, Irene. *Legacy and Testament: The Story of Columbia River Gillnetters.* Pullman: Washington State University Press, 1994.

Newell, Diane, ed. *The Development of the Pacific Salmon Canning Industry: A Grown Man's Game.* Kingston, Ontario: McGill-Queen's University Press, 1989.

Rinne, John N. and W. L. Minckley. *Native Fishes of Arid Lands: A Dwindling Resource of the Desert Southwest.* Fort Collins, Colo.: U.S. Department of Agriculture, Forest Service, Rocky Mountain Forest and Range Experiment Station, 1991.

Save Our Wild Salmon Coalition. *River of Red Ink: A Common Sense Guide to Saving Taxpayers Money and Restoring Northwest Salmon.* Washington, D.C.: Taxpayers for Common Sense, 1996.

Save Our Wild Salmon Coalition. *Wild Salmon Forever: A Citizens' Strategy to Restore Northwest Salmon and Watersheds.* Seattle: Save Our Wild Salmon Coalition, 1994.

Taylor, Joseph E. III. *Making Salmon: An Environmental History of the Northwest Fisheries Crisis.* Seattle: University of Washington Press, 1999.

6. Middle East

Allan, J. A. and Chibli Mallat, eds. *Water in the Middle East: Legal, Political, and Commercial Implications.* London & New York: Tauris, 1995.

Biswas, Asit K., ed. *International Waters of the Middle East: From Euphrates-Tigris to Nile.* Bombay & New York: Oxford University Press, 1994.

Bulloch, John and Adel Darwish. *Water Wars: Coming Conflicts in the Middle East.* London: Gollancz, 1993.

Kazemi, Farhad and John Waterbury, eds. *Peasants and Politics in the Modern Middle East.* Miami: Florida International University Press, 1991.

Naff, Thomas and Ruth C. Matson. *Water in the Middle East: Conflict or Cooperation?* Boulder, Colo.: Westview Press, 1984.

Rogers, Peter and Peter Lydon, eds. *Water in the Arab World: Perspectives and Prognoses.* Cambridge, Mass.: Harvard University, 1994.

Shapland, Greg. *Rivers of Discord: International Water Disputes in the Middle East.* New York: St. Martin's Press, 1997.

Spagnola, John, ed. *Problems of the Modern Middle East in Historical Perspective: Essays in Honour of Albert Hourani.* Reading, U.K.: Ithaca Press, 1992.

Starr, Joyce. *Covenant over Middle Eastern Waters: Key to World Survival.* New York: Holt, 1995.

Starr and Daniel C. Stoll, eds. *Politics of Scarcity: Water in the Middle East.* Boulder, Colo.: Westview Press, 1988.

Water Issues Between Turkey, Syria and Iraq. Ankara, Turkey: Ministry of Foreign Affairs, 1995.

7. Native Americans

Barber, Katrine. "After Celilo Falls: The Dalles Dam, Indian Fishing Rights, and Federal Energy Policy on the Mid-Columbia River." Dissertation, Washington State University, 1999.

Boxberger, Daniel. *To Fish in Common: The Ethnohistory of Lummi Indian Salmon Fishing.* Revised edition. Seattle: University of Washington Press, 1999.

Burton, Lloyd. *American Indian Water Rights and the Limits of Law.* Lawrence: University Press of Kansas, 1991.

Checchio, Elizabeth and Bonnie G. Colby. *Indian Water Rights: Negotiating the Future.* Tucson: Water Resources Research Center, University of Arizona, College of Agriculture, 1993.

Landeen, Dan and Allen Pinkham. *Salmon and His People: Fish and Fishing in Nez Perce Culture.* Lewiston, Idaho: Confluence Press, 1999.

Lawson, Michael L. *Dammed Indians: The Pick-Sloan Plan and the Missouri River Sioux, 1944–1980.* Norman: University of Oklahoma Press, 1982.

McCool, Daniel. *Command of the Waters: Iron Triangles, Federal Water Development, and Indian Water.* Berkeley: University of California Press, 1987.

McGuire, Thomas R., William B. Lord, and Mary G. Wallace, eds. *Indian Water in the New West.* Tucson: University of Arizona Press, 1993.

Shurts, John. *Indian Reserved Water Rights: The Winters Doctrine in its Social and Legal Context, 1880s–1930s.* Norman: University of Oklahoma Press, 2000.

Sly, Peter W. *Reserved Water Rights Settlement Manual.* Washington, D.C.: Island Press, 1988.

Ulrich, Roberta. *Empty Nets: Indians, Dams, and the Columbia River.* Corvallis: Oregon State University Press, 1999.

Woody, Elizabeth. *Seven Hands, Seven Hearts.* Portland, Ore.: Eighth Mountain Press, 1994.

8. Nuclear Power and the Environment

Aron, Joan. *Licensed to Kill?: The Nuclear Regulatory Commission and the Shoreham Power Plant.* Pittsburgh: University of Pittsburgh Press, 1997.

Balogh, Brian. *Chain Reaction: Expert Debate and Public Participation in American Commercial Nuclear Power, 1945–1975.* Cambridge & New York: Cambridge University Press, 1991.

Bedford, Henry F. *Seabrook Station: Citizen Politics and Nuclear Power.* Amherst: University of Massachusetts Press, 1990.

Dawson, Jane I. *Eco-Nationalism: Anti-Nuclear Activism and National Identity in Russia, Lithuania, and*

Ukraine. Durham, N.C.: Duke University Press, 1996.

Hecht, Gabrielle. *The Radiance of France: Nuclear Power and National Identity in France After World War II.* Cambridge, Mass.: MIT Press, 1998.

Walker, J. Samuel. *Containing the Atom: Nuclear Regulation in a Changing Environment, 1963–1971.* Berkeley: University of California Press, 1992.

Wellock, Thomas Raymond. *Critical Masses: Opposition to Nuclear Power in California, 1958–1978.* Madison: University of Wisconsin Press, 1998.

9. U.S. Environment

Abbott, Carl. *The Metropolitan Frontier: Cities in the Modern American West.* Tucson: University of Arizona Press, 1993.

Divine, Robert A., ed. *The Johnson Years.* Volume 2. *Vietnam, The Environment, And Science.* Lawrence: University Press of Kansas, 1987.

Executive Office of the President, Council on Environmental Quality. *Environmental Quality: The Twenty-fourth Annual Report of the Council on Environmental Quality (1993).* Washington, D.C.: U.S. Government Printing Office, 1994.

Findlay, John M. *Magic Lands: Western Cityscapes and American Culture after 1940.* Berkeley: University of California Press, 1992.

Gottlieb, Robert. *Forcing The Spring: The Transformation of The American Environmental Movement.* Washington, D.C.: Island Press, 1993.

Harvey, Mark W. T. *A Symbol of Wilderness: Echo Park and the American Conservation Movement.* Albuquerque: University of New Mexico Press, 1994.

Hays, Samuel P., with Barbara D. Hays. *Beauty, Health, and Permanence: Environmental Politics in the United States, 1955–1985.* Cambridge & New York: Cambridge University Press, 1987.

Hurley, Andrew. *Environmental Inequalities: Class, Race, and Industrial Pollution in Gary, Indiana, 1945–1980.* Chapel Hill: University of North Carolina Press, 1995.

Hurley, ed. *Common Fields: An Environmental History of St. Louis.* St. Louis: Missouri State Historical Society, 1997.

Jackson, Kenneth T. *Crabgrass Frontier: The Suburbanization of the United States.* New York: Oxford University Press, 1985.

Landy, Marc K., Marc J. Roberts, and Stephen R. Thomas. *The Environmental Protection Agency: Asking the Wrong Questions from Nixon to Clinton.* New York: Oxford University Press, 1994.

Lear, Linda. *Rachel Carson: Witness for Nature.* New York: Holt, 1997.

Logan, Michael F. *Fighting Sprawl and City Hall: Resistance to Urban Growth in the Southwest.* Tucson: University of Arizona Press, 1995.

Mazmanian, Daniel A. and Jeanne Nienaber. *Can Organizations Change?: Environmental Protection, Citizen Participation, and the Army Corps of Engineers.* Washington, D.C.: Brookings Institution, 1979.

Melosi, Martin V. *Coping with Abundance: Energy and Environment in Industrial America.* Philadelphia: Temple University Press, 1985.

Melosi. *The Sanitary City: Urban Infrastructure in America from Colonial Times to the Present.* Baltimore: Johns Hopkins University Press, 2000.

Parker, Kittie F. *An Illustrated Guide to Arizona Weeds.* Tucson: University of Arizona Press, 1972.

Rome, Adam Ward. "Prairie Creek Hills Estates: An Environmental History of American Homebuilding, 1945-1970." Dissertation, University of Kansas, 1996.

Schwantes, Carlos A. *The Pacific Northwest: An Interpretive History.* Revised edition. Lincoln: University of Nebraska Press, 1996.

Sebold, Kimberly R. "*Low Green Prairies of the Sea:* Economic Usage and Cultural Construction of the Gulf of Maine Salt Marshes." Dissertation, University of Maine, 1998.

Stephenson, R. Bruce. *Visions of Eden: Environmentalism, Urban Planning, and City Building in St. Petersburg, Florida, 1900–1995.* Columbus: Ohio State University Press, 1997.

Tiner, Ralph W., Jr. and others. *Wetlands of the United States: Current Status and Recent Trends.* Washington, D.C.: U.S. Department of the Interior, Fish and Wildlife Service, 1984.

Vileisis, Ann. *Discovering the Unknown Landscape: A History of America's Wetlands.* Washington, D.C.: Island Press, 1997.

U.S. Department of the Interior. Bureau of Reclamation. *Investing in the Future: Fiscal Year 1998 Annual Report.* Washington, D.C.: U.S. Government Printing Office, 1999.

Warne, William E. *The Bureau of Reclamation.* New York: Praeger, 1973.

White, Richard. *"It's your misfortune and none of my own": A History of the American West.* Norman: University of Oklahoma Press, 1991.

10. Water and Dam Policy, General

Baumann, Duane D., John J. Boland, and W. Michael Hanemann. *Urban Water Demand Management and Planning.* New York: McGraw-Hill, 1998.

Brandon, Thomas W., ed. *Groundwater: Occurrence, Development and Protection.* London: Institute of Water Engineers and Scientists, 1986.

Brooks, L. Anathea and Stacy D. VanDeveer, eds. *Saving the Seas: Values, Science and International Governance.* College Park: Maryland Sea Grant College, 1997.

Clark, Lewis. *The Field Guide to Water Wells and Boreholes.* Milton Keynes, U.K.: Open University Press / New York: Halsted Press, 1988.

Donahue, John M. and Barbara Rose Johnson, eds. *Water, Culture and Power: Local Struggles in a Global Context.* Washington, D.C.: Island Press, 1998.

Driscoll, Fletcher G. *Groundwater and Wells.* St. Paul, Minn.: Johnson Division, 1986.

Fraenkel, Peter. *Water Pumping Devices: A Handbook for Users and Choosers.* London: Intermediate Technology Publications, 1986.

Harper, David M. and Alastair J. D. Ferguson, eds. *The Ecological Basis for River Management.* Chichester & New York: Wiley, 1995.

Hofkes, E. H., ed. *Small Community Water Supplies: Technology of Small Water Supply Systems in Developing Countries.* The Hague: International Reference Center, 1981.

Kerr, Charles. *Community Water Development.* London: Intermediate Technology Publications, 1989.

McCully, Patrick. *Silenced Rivers: The Ecology and Politics of Large Dams.* London & Atlantic Highlands, N.J.: Zed Books, 1996.

More Water for Arid Lands: Promising Technologies and Research Opportunities: Report of an Ad Hoc Panel of the Advisory Committee on Technology Innovation, Board on Science and Technology for International Development, Commission on International Relations. Washington, D.C.: National Academy of Sciences, 1974.

Moss, Brian. *Ecology of Fresh Waters: Man and Medium.* Oxford & Boston: Blackwell Scientific Publications, 1988.

Murphy, Earl Finbar. *Water Quality: A Study in Legal Control of Natural Resources.* Madison: University of Wisconsin Press, 1961.

Pacey, Arnold and Adrian Cullis. *Rainwater Harvesting: The Collection of Rainfall and Run-off in Rural Areas.* London: Intermediate Technology Publications, 1986.

Pickford, John, ed. *Integrated Development for Water Supply and Sanitation.* Loughborough, U.K.: Water, Engineering and Development Centre, 1999.

Price, Michael. *Introducing Groundwater.* London & Boston: Allen & Unwin, 1985.

Raghunath, H. M. *Ground Water: Hydrogeology, Ground Water Survey and Pumping Tests, Rural Water Supply and Irrigation Systems.* New Delhi: Wiley Eastern, 1982.

Smith, Norman. *Man and Water: A History of Hydro- Technology.* New York: Scribners, 1975.

11. Water and Dam Policy, United States

Carothers, Stephen W. and Bryan T. Brown. *The Colorado River Through Grand Canyon: Natural History and Human Change.* Tucson: University of Arizona Press, 1991.

Colborn, Theodora E. and others. *Great Lakes, Great Legacy?* Washington, D.C.: Conservation Foundation, 1990; Ottawa, Ontario: Institute for Research on Public Policy, 1990.

DeBuys, William and Joan Meyers. *Salt Dreams: Land and Water in Low-Down California.* Albuquerque: University of New Mexico Press, 1999.

Dietrich, William. *Northwest Passage: The Great Columbia River.* New York: Simon & Schuster, 1995.

Edmondson, W. T. *The Uses of Ecology: Lake Washington and Beyond.* Seattle: University of Washington Press, 1991.

Elkind, Sarah S. *Bay Cities and Water Politics: The Battle for Resources in Boston and Oakland.* Lawrence: University Press of Kansas, 1998.

Fiege, Mark. *Irrigated Eden: The Making of an Agricultural Landscape in the American West.* Seattle: University of Washington Press, 1999.

Fradkin, Philip L. *A River No More: The Colorado River and the West.* Revised edition. Berkeley: University of California Press, 1996.

Green, Donald E. *Land of the Underground Rain: Irrigation on the Texas High Plains, 1910–1970.* Austin: University of Texas Press, 1973.

Harden, Blaine. *A River Lost: The Life and Death of the Columbia.* New York: Norton, 1996.

Holmes, Beatrice Hort. *A History of Federal Water Resources Programs, 1800–1960.* Washington, D.C.: U.S. Department of Agriculture, Economic Research Service, 1972.

Holmes. *History of Federal Water Resources Programs, 1961–1970.* Washington, D.C.: U.S. Department of Agriculture, Economics, Statistics, and Cooperatives Service, 1979.

Hundley, Norris, Jr. *Dividing the Waters: A Century of Controversy between the United States and Mexico.* Berkeley: University of California Press, 1966.

Jackson, Donald C. *Building the Ultimate Dam: John S. Eastwood and the Control of Water in the West.* Lawrence: University Press of Kansas, 1995.

Kehoe, Terence. *Cleaning Up the Great Lakes: From Cooperation to Confrontation.* DeKalb: Northern Illinois University Press, 1997.

Lang, William L. and Robert C. Carriker, eds. *Great River of the West: Essays on the Columbia River.* Seattle: University of Washington Press, 1999.

Lieber, Harvey and Bruce Rosinoff. *Federalism and Clean Waters: The 1972 Water Pollution Control Act.* Lexington, Mass.: Lexington Books, 1975.

MacDonnell, Lawrence J. *From Reclamation to Sustainability: Water, Agriculture, and the Environment in the American West.* Niwot: University of Colorado Press, 1999.

Miller, Char, ed. *Fluid Arguments: Five Centuries of Western Water Conflict.* Tucson: University of Arizona Press, 2001.

Miller, ed. *On the Border: An Environmental History of San Antonio.* Pittsburgh: University of Pittsburgh Press, 2001.

Miller, ed. *Water in the West: A High Country News Reader.* Corvallis: Oregon State University Press, 2000.

Opie, John. *Ogallala: Water for a Dry Land.* 2nd edition. Lincoln: University of Nebraska Press, 2000.

Palmer, Tim. *The Columbia: Sustaining a Modern Resource.* Seattle: The Mountaineers, 1997.

Petersen, Keith C. *River of Life, Channel of Death: Fish and Dams on the Lower Snake.* Lewiston, Idaho: Confluence Press, 1995.

Proceedings of the National Conference on Water Pollution in Washington, D.C., December 12–14, 1960. Washington, D.C.: U.S. Department of Health, Education, and Welfare, Public Health Service, 1961.

Reisner, Marc. *Cadillac Desert: The American West and Its Disappearing Water.* New York: Viking, 1986.

Robinson, Michael C. *Water for the West: The Bureau of Reclamation, 1902–1977.* Chicago: Public Works Historical Society, 1979.

Rothman, Hal K. *The Greening of a Nation?: Environmentalism in the United States Since 1945.* Fort Worth, Tex.: Harcourt Brace College Publishers, 1998.

Schneiders, Robert Kelley. *Unruly River: Two Centuries of Change Along the Missouri.* Lawrence: University Press of Kansas, 1999.

Sherow, James Earl. *Watering the Valley: Development along the High Plains Arkansas River, 1870–1950.* Lawrence: University Press of Kansas, 1990.

Stine, Jeffrey K. *Mixing the Waters: Environment, Politics, and the Building of the Tennessee-Tombigbee Waterway.* Akron: University of Akron Press, 1993.

U. S. Department of the Interior. *The Hoover Dam Documents.* Prepared by Ray Lyman Wilbur and Northcut Ely. Washington, D.C.: U. S. Government Printing Office, 1948.

U.S. Western Water Policy Review Advisory Commission. *Water in the West: The Challenge for the Next Century: Report of the U.S. Western Water Policy Review Advisory Commission.* Arlington, Va.: The Commission, 1998.

Wheeler, William Bruce and Michael J. McDonald. *TVA and the Tellico Dam, 1936–1979: A Bureaucratic Crisis in Post-Industrial America.* Knoxville: University of Tennessee Press, 1986.

Wilkinson, Charles F. *Crossing the Next Meridian: Land, Water, and the Future of the West.* Washington, D.C.: Island Press, 1992.

Willingham, William F. *Army Engineers and the Development of Oregon: A History of the Portland District, U.S. Army Corps of Engineers.* Washington, D.C.: U.S. Government Printing Office, 1983.

Worster, Donald. *Dust Bowl: The Southern Plains in the 1930s.* New York: Oxford University Press, 1979.

Zwick, David and Marcy Benstock, *Water Wasteland: Ralph Nader's Study Group Report on Water Pollution* (New York: Grossman, 1971).

REFERENCES

NOTES ON CONTRIBUTORS

ALLEN, Cain: Historian at the Center for Columbia River History; previously the assistant editor of the *Oregon Historical Quarterly*; teaches courses on Columbia River history at Portland State University.

ASH, Michael: Assistant professor of economics and public policy at the University of Massachusetts–Amherst; research focuses on issues of environmental justice in the United States and Europe.

BIHARI, Gábor: Doctoral candidate at the Mantra College of Natural Sciences in Budapest; project coordinator for the Citizens Advice and Information Services Project in Budapest, Hungary.

BOLAND, John J.: Teaches environmental economics and policy at Johns Hopkins University; has studied water-supply issues in more than twenty countries; consultant for the United Nations, World Bank, Inter-American Development Bank, United States Agency for International Development (USAID), and other agencies.

BOND, Patrick: Teaches political economy at the University of the Witwatersrand, Johannesburg; research associate of the Alternative Information and Development Centre; author of policy documents for the African National Congress government, as well as a half dozen books on southern African development and environment problems; author of *Uneven Zimbabwe: A Study of Finance, Development and Underdevelopment* (1998).

BOOKER, Matthew S.: Doctoral candidate in American history at Stanford University; his dissertation is an environmental history of tidal wetlands along the Pacific Coast of the United States.

CHEW, Matthew: Statewide Natural Resources Planner and State Natural Areas Program Coordinator for Arizona State Parks; served on the Board of the Arizona Riparian Council since 1994 and worked on various local, state, and interagency riparian projects in the West since 1986; earned B.S. and M.S. degrees from Colorado State University.

CIOC, Mark: Professor of German and Austrian history at the University of California, Santa Cruz; author of *The Rhine: An Eco-Biography, 1815–2000* (forthcoming).

COLTEN, Craig E.: Associate professor of geography at Louisiana State University; editor of *Transforming New Orleans and Its Environs: Centuries of Change* (2000); coauthor, with Peter N. Skinner, of *The Road to Love Canal: Managing Industrial Waste before EPA* (1996).

DONAHUE, John M.: Professor of anthropology at Trinity University; co-editor with Barbara Rose Johnston, *Water, Culture, and Power: Local Struggles in a Global Context* (1998); author of "Sitting Down at the Table: Mediation and Resolution of Water Conflicts" in *San Antonio: An Environmental History*, edited by Char Miller (forthcoming).

FROST, Robert L.: Visiting associate professor in the School of Information at the University of Michigan, Ann Arbor; author of *Alternating Currents: Nationalized Power in France, 1946–1970* (1991); current research focuses on Fordism in France and the emergence of technological and social standards since 1800.

GREEFF, Liane: Program Manager of the Water Security Program of the Environmental Monitoring Group, a nongovernmental organization, which focuses on environmental justice issues in South and Southern Africa.

GRIPNE, Stephanie L.: Doctoral student in forestry at the University of Montana; Boone and Crockett Wildlife Conservation Program Fellow; research member of the Bitterroot Ecosystem Management Research Project Team; author of *Evaluation of Factors Influencing Fish Assemblages in the Minnesota River* (1999).

HARPER, Krista: Postdoctoral Fellow at the Political Economy Research Institute in the Department of Anthropology at the University of Massachusetts–Amherst; research focuses on Hungarian environmental activism.

HARVEY, Mark: Associate professor of history at North Dakota State University; author of *A Symbol of Wilderness: Echo Park and the American Conservation Movement* (1994); writing a biography of Howard Zahniser, a former executive director of the Wilderness Society.

HITCHCOCK, Robert K.: Associate professor of anthropology, Director of International Studies, and coordinator of African Studies at the University of Nebraska at Lincoln; has been working on southern African development and environmental issues for the past twenty-five years; member of the

Panel of Environmental Experts (POE) of the Lesotho Highlands Water Project (LHWP).

HUFFMAN, Thomas R.: Ph.D. in history from the University of Wisconsin-Madison; author of "Legislatures and the Environment," in *Encyclopedia of the American Legislature System,* volume 3, edited by Joel H. Silbey (1994); author of *Protectors of the Land and Water: Environmentalism in Wisconsin, 1961–1968* (1994).

HUSSEY, Stephen: Coordinator of a local NGO in Zimbabwe that works with groups of rural people, mainly women, to develop small-scale sustainable water supplies. He has spent more than thirty years in Zimbabwe in water- and rural-development programs, working at all aspects and levels of technology and social intervention, and is presently researching and documenting small-scale interventions for a Ph.D. in order to publicize the alternate method of sand-abstraction.

IYER, Ramaswamy R.: Former secretary, Water Resources, India; Visiting Professor (formerly Research Professor) at the Centre for Policy Research, New Delhi; consultant to the World Bank in a review of water-sector strategy; consultant to the World Commission on Dams for a study of India's experience with large dams; member of India's National Commission on Integrated Water Resource Planning; Member of the "Vision 2020 Committee" of India's Planning Commission.

KEHOE, Terry: Research associate with Morgan, Angel & Associates, a public-policy consulting firm; author of *Cleaning Up the Great Lakes: From Cooperation to Confrontation* (1997).

KEINER, Christine: Author of "W. K. Brooks and the Oyster Question: Science, Politics, and Resource Management in Maryland, 1880–1930," *Journal of the History of Biology* (1998); currently working on a book that explores the transition from economic to ecological management of the Chesapeake Bay between 1880 and 2000.

KLINGLE, Matthew W.: Doctoral candidate in history at the University of Washington; finishing dissertation on the environmental and social history of Seattle; author of "Plying Atomic Waters: Lauren R. Donaldson and the 'Fern Lake Concept' of Fisheries Management," *Journal of the History of Biology* (Spring 1998).

KONTTINEN, Esa: Senior lecturer in the Department of Social Sciences and Philosophy at the University of Jyväskylä; research focuses on the Finnish environmental movement; co-author of *All Shades of Green* (1999).

KORTELAINEN, Jarmo: Assistant professor in the Department of Geography at the University of Joensuu; research focuses on environmental conflicts and water questions in the Finnish forest industry; author of "The River as an Actor-network: The Finnish Forest Industry Utilization of Lake and River Systems," *Geoforum* (1999).

LEES, Susan H.: Hunter College, City University of New York; author of *The Political Ecology of the Water Crisis in Israel* (1998); co-editor, with Moshe Schwartz and Gordon M. Kressel, of *Rural Cooperatives in Socialist Utopia: Thirty Years of Moshav Development in Israel* (1995).

LOXSOM, Frederick Meers: Professor of physics at Trinity University in San Antonio, Texas; teaches a course in environmental physics, participates in local environmental activities, interested in Mexican environmental issues, and conducts research in regional air pollution; author, with Silvia Eidels-Dubovoi and Eugenio González-Avalos, of "Measured and Modeled Spectral Irradiance and Actinic Flux in Mexico City during Spring 2000," Poster Session, AGU Fall Meeting, San Francisco, December 2000.

MAYO KIELY, Ann: Graduate student in recreation resources management at the University of Montana; George E. Bright Fellow; member of the Isle Royale National Park Wilderness Management Team.

MAZLUM, Ibrahim: Research assistant and doctoral candidate of Political Science and International Relations at Marmara University, Turkey.

MCCOOL, Daniel: Professor of political science and director of the American West Center, University of Utah; author of *Command of the Waters: Iron Triangles, Federal Water Development, and Indian Water* (1994); co-author of *Staking Out the Terrain: Power Differentials Among Natural Resource Management Agencies* (1996); editor of *The Waters of Zion: The Law, Policy and Politics of Water in Utah* (1995); co-editor of *Contested Landscape: The Politics of Wilderness in Utah and the West* (1999).

MCNEILL, J. R.: Professor of history at Georgetown University; author of *The Mountains of the Mediterranean World: An Environmental History* (1992) and *Something New Under the Sun: An Environmental History of the 20th-Century World* (2000).

MILAZZO, Paul: Scholar from the University of Virginia; dissertation entitled "Legislating the Solution to Pollution: Congress and the Development of Water Pollution Control Policy, 1945–1975" (2001).

MILLER, Char: Professor and chairman of the history department at Trinity University; editor of *Water in the West: A High Country News Reader* (2000) and *Fluid Arguments: Five Centuries of Water Conflicts* (2001).

MORGAN, Daniel: Environmental specialist and independent scholar from Los Angeles.

OPIE, John: Distinguished Professor, Emeritus, New Jersey Institute of Technology; author of *Nature's Nation: An Environmental History of the United States* (1998) and *Ogallala: Water for a Dry Land* (1993).

OSBORN, Alan J.: Adjunct associate professor of anthropology at the University of Nebraska at Lincoln; has been working on human ecology issues for the past thirty years in South and North America and, recently, in Africa, .

PALMER, Tim: Author of *The Columbia: Sustaining a Modern Resource* (1997), *The Heart of America: Our Landscape, Our Future* (1999), *Lifelines: The Case for River Conservation* (1994), and other books about rivers and the environment.

PEARSON, Byron E.: Assistant professor of history, West Texas A&M University.

PERKINS, Jeremy: Range ecologist whose Ph.D. is from the University of Sheffield; has extensive experience in range evaluation in the Sahel, eastern Africa, south Australia, and Tajikistan.

PRITCHARD, Sara B.: Doctoral candidate in history at Stanford University; dissertation, "Recreating the Rhône: Nature and Technology in France After World War II"; research interests include environmental history and the history of technology.

READ, Jennifer: Research associate in environmental policy and history, Great Lakes Institute for Environmental Research, University of Windsor, associated with the Great Lakes Commission; author of "Youth, Science and Indignation: The Emergence of the Canadian Environmental Movement," in *Canada, Confederation to Present* (forthcoming) and, with G. D. Haffner and P. Murray, "Mercury and PCB Contamination of the Detroit River," in *Honouring Our River, Caring for Our Home,* edited by John Hartig (forthcoming).

RUITERS, Gregory: Lecturer in political studies at the University of Witwatersrand, Johannesburg, South Africa; codirector of the Municipal Services Project.

SCHLICHER, L. S.: Ph.D. in Oriental Studies from Oxford University; fellow of the Grunebaum Center for Near Eastern Studies at the University of California, Los Angeles; former president of the Syrian Studies Association.

SCHNEIDER, Reinhold: Holds a degree in Forest Science from the University of Munich and currently works as a freelance consultant to forest owners and development aid agencies; lives in Regensburg, Germany, where he frequently lectures on topics of forest management and environmental landscaping.

SEBOLD, Kimberly R.: Assistant professor of history at the University of Maine–Presque Isle; Ph.D. in Environmental History from the University of Maine (1988).

SHEROW, James Earl: Associate professor of history at Kansas State University; his publications and research interests include water studies and environmental histories of the American West; author of *Watering the Valley: Development along the High Plains Arkansas River, 1870–1950* (1990).

SHOWERS, Kate B.: Research fellow at the African Studies Center at Boston University; coordinator of the African Urban Water Project (BU African Studies Center/MIT Department of Urban Studies and Planning, 1999–2000); a soil scientist interested in the interactions between societies, water, and landscapes; for the last twenty-two years her research has concentrated on southern Africa, where she lived and worked for more than six years.

SIMONDS, William Joe: Historian/Cultural Resources Management Specialist in the Office of Policy at the Bureau of Reclamation, Denver, Colorado.

SLY, Peter: Attorney in Oakland, California, who specializes in federal water rights; graduate of Stanford University and Yale Law School; director of the Conference of Western Attorneys General from 1985–1988; author of the *Reserved Water Rights Settlement Manual* (1988).

SMURR, Robert W.: Doctoral candidate in the History Department at the University of Washington, Seattle; currently completing his dissertation, titled "Perceptions of Nature, Expressions of Nation: An Environmental History of Estonia."

SNAJDR, Edward: Adjunct professor in anthropology and a visiting researcher in the School of Criminology and Criminal Justice at Florida State University; conducted fieldwork on the environmental movement in Slovakia from 1994–1995.

THAKKAR, Himanshu: Coordinator of the South Asia Network on Dams, Rivers, and People (SANDRP); engineer from the Indian Institute of Technology; activist with *Narmada Bachao Andolan* (Save Narmada Movement); author of the India Irrigation Options study for the World Commission on Dams.

THOMAS, Jack Ward: Director of the Boone and Crockett Wildlife Conservation Program at the University of Montana; former chief of the U.S. Forest Service; member of the Interagency Scientific Committee; led the Federal Interagency Forest Ecosystem Management and Assessment Team; editor of *Wildlife Habitats in Managed Forests: The Blue Mountains of Oregon and Washington* (1979); editor, with Dale E. Toweill, of *Elk of North America: Ecology and Management* (1982).

THOMPSON, Bruce: Lecturer in history at the University of California at Santa Cruz; editor of "Critical History," a special issue of the *Stanford Humanity Review* (2000).

VANDEVEER, Stacy D.: Assistant professor of political science at the University of New Hampshire; co-editor, with L. Anathea Brooks, of *Saving the Seas: Values, Scientists and International Governance* (1997) and, with Geoffrey D. Dabelko, *Protecting Regional Seas: Developing Capacity and Fostering Environmental Governance in Europe* (2000).

VILEISIS, Ann: Independent scholar; author of the award-winning book *Discovering the Unknown Landscape: A History of America's Wetlands* (1997).

WALKER, J. Samuel: Historian of the U.S. Nuclear Regulatory Commission; author of *Containing the Atom: Nuclear Regulation in a Changing Environment, 1963–1971* (1992) and *Permissible Dose: A History of Radiation Protection in the Twentieth Century* (2000).

WARD, Evan R.: Instructor at the University of Georgia; recently received Ph.D. in history from the University of Georgia; his dissertation, "The Irrigated Oasis: Transformation of the Colorado River Delta, 1940–1975," examines the role of water use in the regional development; author of "The Twentieth-Century Ghosts of William Walker: Conquest of Land and Water as Central Themes in the History of the Colorado River Delta," *Pacific Historical Review* (forthcoming) and "Geo-Environmental Disconnection and the Colorado River Delta: Technology, Culture, and the Political Ecology of Paradise," *Environment and History* (forthcoming).

WEBER, Ken: Ph.D. in cultural anthropology from the University of Oregon; M.B.A. from the University of Colorado at Boulder; chief of Outdoor Recreation Management and Social Science Research Branch, Science Center, Grand Canyon National Park.

WELLOCK, Thomas Raymond: Ph.D. in history from the University of California, Berkeley; assistant professor at Central Washington University; author of *Critical Masses: Opposition to Nuclear Power in California, 1958–1978* (1998).

INDEX

B

C

D

INDEX

E

F

G

INDEX

H

INDEX

J

K

L

M

Q

R

S

T

U

V

W

X

Y

Z